THE EVOLUTIONARY NEUROETHOLOGY OF PAUL MACLEAN

Recent Titles in
Human Evolution, Behavior, and Intelligence

THE EVOLUTIONARY NEUROETHOLOGY OF PAUL MACLEAN

CONVERGENCES AND FRONTIERS

Edited by Gerald A. Cory, Jr. and
Russell Gardner, Jr.

Foreword by Jaak Panksepp

Human Evolution, Behavior, and Intelligence
Seymour W. Itzkoff, Series Editor

Westport, Connecticut
London

Library of Congress Cataloging-in-Publication Data

The evolutionary neuroethology of Paul MacLean : convergences and frontiers / edited
by Gerald A. Cory, Jr. and Russell Gardner, Jr. ; foreword by Jaak Panksepp.
    p. cm.—(Human evolution, behavior, and intelligence, ISSN 1063–2158)
  Includes bibliographical references and index.
  ISBN 0–275–97219–4 (alk. paper)
    1. Brain—Evolution. 2. Animal behavior. 3. Neuropsychology. 4. MacLean, Paul D. I.
Cory, Gerald A. II. Gardner, Russell, 1938– III. Series.
QP376.E875 2002
612.8—dc21   2002021588

British Library Cataloguing in Publication Data is available.

Library of Congress Catalog Card Number: 2002021588
ISBN: 0–275–97219–4
ISSN: 1063–2158

First published in 2002

Praeger Publishers, 88 Post Road West, Westport, CT 06881
An imprint of Greenwood Publishing Group, Inc.
www.praeger.com

Printed in the United States of America

The paper used in this book complies with the
Permanent Paper Standard issued by the National
Information Standards Organization (Z39.48–1984).

10 9 8 7 6 5 4 3 2 1

CONTENTS

PART VI: SOCIAL PSYCHOLOGY AND SOCIAL THEORY

FOREWORD: THE MACLEAN LEGACY AND SOME MODERN TRENDS IN EMOTION RESEARCH

Jaak Panksepp

I offer this foreword to validate and extend Paul MacLean's strategic conjectures concerning the evolved bases for emotions and related neuromental processes. Neuroevolutionary perspectives such as those advocated by MacLean are essential to explore the fundamental nature of the human mind. It remains a pity that some neuroscientists currently marginalize the approach to brain/mind organization that the MacLean legacy constitutes. I do not believe these investigators provide credible theoretical alternatives. It is true that some emotion researchers who have criticized or ignored MacLean's contributions (*e.g.*, Joseph LeDoux and Edmund Rolls, respectively) have made important contributions to relatively circumscribed areas, but MacLean sought to elucidate the overall mind-brain puzzle as a functioning whole. Surely the path to substantive progress must be paved by a synthesis of molecular and molar perspectives. Those who pursue proximal fine-grained research ought not to pretend they offer more robust interpretations than does MacLean (and others who hew to more conceptually integrative points of view). Indeed, the larger evolutionary considerations must frame molecular analyses—not *vice versa*.

I do not here reiterate critical points raised in the many fine chapters in this volume (note especially the one by Jerry Cory to whose points I will add). I certainly affirm, however, that some critics unfairly treat MacLean's legacy; they sweep his sagacious and broad perspective away as if it were detritus of a pre-scientific past. MacLean's "limbic system" concept (didactically sound though it is) and his enunciation of general patterns in the evolution of brain and emotions (sound though they are as well) have too commonly been the focus of recent attacks by those who seem to consistently ignore MacLean's abundant empirical contributions. Some senselessly gratuitous attacks reflect inadequate historical or conceptual perspectives while misrepresenting MacLean's position, perhaps with opportunistic intent.

The breadth of MacLean's work continues to influence individuals who are truly interested in understanding the evolved nature of emotions in human and animal brains. Investigators who focus on conditioning reflexive emotional behaviors ought not pretend their work relates to the deep nature of emotionality in the evolved brain. They would more fittingly acknowledge that they work to clarify a modest corner of a much vaster mystery.

Work that attempts to draw broad conceptual outlines rather than to harvest small empirical peppercorns is an ever-easy target for attack. Perhaps this is why much of modern neuroscience is scornful of theory, calling it mere *speculation*. As a result there is currently little thought—much less discussion—of how coherent functional brain systems evolved, notably the ancient phylogenetically derived emotional systems of the mammalo-human mind and brain. By contrast, MacLean offers a vision of human neuromental organization that broadly achieves such a summary perspective. Moreover, his is not mere speculation but in fact a superb theoretical structure, with abundant predictions, built upon a solid foundational body of data from an extensive study of the functional neural systems of our brethren species.

Beyond the popular molecular science approaches permitted by modern technologies, there are other more reasonable paradigmatic perspectives—for example, distributed network models—from which to think about our emotional nature. It's partly a matter of scale. Emotions are global *state* processes of the brain that cannot yet be epistemologically incorporated into a fine-grained focus on issues of neuronal microstructure and function, although they are ontologically quite compatible.

Thus, this compendium should be valuable to all who would understand how minds are created by the brain's evolved networks. I should pointedly add that this is an especially good book for neuroscientists as many among them have much to learn at the important evolutionary interface of mind and brain issues. Unfortunately, many prominent emotion researchers—especially neo-behaviorists who now inundate neuroscience—continue to cultivate remarkably restricted paradigms from which they claim to have achieved substantive understanding of the nature of emotions. They fail to acknowledge or perhaps appreciate that such systems cannot be adequately conceptualized at a level where single cells of the brain learn about environmental contingencies. While fine-grained neurobehaviorism has advanced important insights into how learning can guide emotional tendencies, such microanalyses cast only scattered dim light upon the mammalian brain's integrative psychobehavioral systems that generate global state/action processes comprising the basic emotions.

Investigators who pursue such microanalyses often deny that the *experience* of emotion, especially in animal subjects, possesses relevance for their science. Yet abundant reason allows us to conclude that many of the emotional states humans experience with affective urgency are experienced similarly by other creatures. Therefore, the continued unwillingness of behavioral neuroscientists to address such questions openly retards understanding of how affective mental states arise from brain dynamics. Without a more coherent elucidation of the evolved state-processes of the brain, there is little hope neuroscience can clarify fundamental neuropsychological issues or otherwise provide a coherent foundation for biological psychiatry.

For MacLean, one of the keys to understanding emotions hinges on how the human brain/mind actually creates affective *experiences*. This bears even more fundamentally on understanding emotions than on how other behavioral tendencies emerge from brain activities. MacLean blazes a trail along the most effective path in his provisional acceptance that behavioral and psychological phenotypes arise on a continuum in nature and, consequently, that many other species also have homologous affective experiences.

We in the neuroscience research community should willingly assume that most species we study in behavioral neuroscience laboratories do, in fact, experience internal feelings; that is, various positive and negative affects. Indeed, if internalized neurobiologically based experiences do characterize them, then without considering such neurodynamics little hope exists that we will understand their brains, much less our own. Even in this era of PET and fMRI mind/brain mapping, no unambiguous ways have yet been laid out for imaging the neural details of affective states except perhaps by understanding the brain systems for the *natural* emotional actions and related behavioral choices of other animals. I suspect precisely this inferential aspect of MacLean's work still disturbs the sensibilities of the abundant behaviorists and cognitivists who have only lately recast themselves as neuroscientists.

Even though no one has devised a *mindscope* to measure emotional states, other than through various indirect behavioral and physiological indices, we should not marginalize neuromental constructs simply because they operate through large-scale neurodynamics that cannot be monitored unambiguously at the present time. To do so tacitly serves the agenda of a positivistic-behavioristic tradition that has consistently denied the scientific existence of human and animal mental processes—particularly those derived from phylogeny—throughout the 20th century. Those who deny to other animals essential neuromental abilities, such as affective experiences to guide long-term behavioral strategies, reinforce an arrogant neo-dualistic cortical creationism that severely constrains modern neuroscience from coming to terms with the evolved mental apparatus of human beings. This does not deny that the cortico-cognitive abilities of humans have brought with them an impressive rational(izing) "higher" mind. But we must also consider that the formation of such a mind could only have built upon a more ancient evolved apparatus of basic emotional urges and motivational values.

Behavioristically oriented investigators rarely care to infer what our animal brethren may feel. Hence they sustain a dismal ontological position—that mindless Cartesian zombies largely occupy animate life. Because they cannot directly measure neurodynamic affective states of the animals they study, they claim that such functions of animal brain/mind remain nothing more than statements of faith. They appear to have conveniently *chosen* to forget that science thrives on predictions, probabilities and the weight of evidence, not certainties. By extension they ignore the power of theoretically cogent empirical predictions that can be made about human feelings from animal behavioral neurochemical studies.

Mind evolution must necessarily be inferred from living brain functions, not fossilized tissues. None can parse such issues with the precision all would desire, but this should not prevent continuing inquiry into such important topics. Here I note that MacLean pursued these matters with a unique devotion, one adventurous, scientific and humanistic. Regrettably, modern molecular neuroscience does not adequately admire his intuitive sensibility. Rather, the guiding principle once again holds that *if you can't measure it concretely and unambiguously, it would be best to be silent.* Many have forgotten or never recognized Immanuel Kant's famous dictum from *The Critique of Pure Reason*: "Concepts without factual content are empty; sense-data without concepts are blind. The senses cannot think, the understanding cannot see. By their union only can knowledge be produced."

The most productive avenue to understanding the evolved emotional systems of the brain would specify how coordinated systems of neuronal activities generate global behavioral and psychological "existential" states in sentient organisms. Ethological study of natural behavior in animals best delineates global functions of the brain and mind. A minute analysis of isolated elements can lead instead to an ontological myopia that focuses on molecular analyses for their own sake rather than conceptualizing and perceiving actual neuromental operating systems. In other words, reductionism with no clear vision of *what* needs to be reduced litters the grove of science with leaves in need of raking and composting.

We see similar premature reductionism in biological psychiatry. A psychiatry that only pays attention to molecules, and not to evolutionary issues of how brain emotional systems are organized represents an extreme case of scientific short-sightedness. It often misses the functional forests (e.g., networks) because it details the neuronal-molecular undergrowth. Paul MacLean recognized the necessity of viewing both the broad sweep of the canopies and the underlying details: he charted a path by which we might study both levels. This volume shares his broad vision, without dismissing the essential details to which all scientists must attend.

Now all reasonable scholars, unlike the behaviorists of the 20th century, accept that we need neuronal concepts to understand how behavior and the mind work. But few recognize the important corollary: without certain basic psychological concepts—ones best represented by the instinctual affective urges of animals—we cannot understand the brain. When we understand such intrinsic mind/brain processes, we can more ably develop an evolutionary psychiatry that sees the ancient affective personality-creating forces of the brain/mind as novel targets for both chemotherapy and psychotherapies. This level of analysis will also inform us how these ancient phylogenetic progressions of brain/mind development still affect the subjective complexities of human lives.

The specific mental contents of individual lives—thoughts and memories that make us fully human—are brought to us abundantly by various informationally encapsulated "channel-functions" of the brain. Yet the affective foundations for mental being stem from more ancient and deeply organic network "state-functions" of the brain. These underlying organic processes generate massive analog states of mind that we experience as primary process feelings. They do this through the cooperation of many widely ramifying neuronal operating circuits and systems. Although much neuronal functioning happens unconsciously, the massively interacting neuronal networks do produce an emergent affective consciousness. This phylogenetic emotional "intelligence", genetically-coded to a substantial degree, permits the experiential intersubjectivity essential for individual social learning. There could be no emotionally resonant infant-mother "psychic-dance"—perhaps an essential ingredient for healthy childhood development—without the ingrained affective potentials of the brain (Stern 1985, 1999; Panksepp 2001; Trevarthen 2001).

Such experiential capacities have causal consequences for what organisms do in order to survive and multiply. If we envision such ancient evolved value/ action systems, interacting dynamically with the myriad individual experience-dependent channel-control functions, we may be less tempted to pursue the scientific reduction of individual experience and culture to molecular neurobiology. Instead, we would seek substantive *supervenient* relationships between levels of analysis. Paul MacLean's views pointed us in that direction.

A dilemma of modern neuroscience hinges on the fact that the "neuron doctrine" that captivated neuroscientists of the 20th century does not effectively identify the evolved global functions of the brain/mind. It simply does not do justice to large ensembles of neurons working together in a mode that can be transmitted via the heuristics of Darwinian evolution. For this we desperately need a new "network doctrine."

Through impressive mental gymnastics and a profound mind-blindness, MacLean's critics presume holistic approaches offer little; yet their approaches typically fail to envision how different levels of organization actually exist in nature. Ultra-positivistic approaches commonly overlook the productive philosophical concept of *supervenience*. This accepts that there are true levels of organization in nature, and that the higher levels of organization do not simply reduce to lower levels. Recognition of relationships between levels of organization should encourage search for coherent linkages between levels of analysis, rather than focus on ever more molecular levels that marginalize analyses on more global levels or that pretend that complete reductionism between levels can really work. An adequate recognition of this concept can allow scientists to live more peacefully and supportively with other investigators who work at different levels of analysis. Through supervenient approaches that aspire to supplement and conceptually guide work at different levels—rather than destroy each other—a coherent, scientifically credible appreciation of the whole may gradually emerge. That would allow us to understand eventually how emotional systems and affective feelings really operate.

The concept of the evolved *limbic system* encapsulates the most globally integrative and productive image of emotions we presently possess. This brain territory, as MacLean advocated, needs to be searched for the details whereby neuronal networks construct emotional processes. Some recently have claimed MacLean's limbic-emotional brain concept misleads and is therefore of no use to modern neuroscience. Such a conclusion speaks more loudly about human arrogance than thoughtful neuroscience. Were such critics to construct a composite brain map of emotional processing from modern brain-imaging studies, they would need to admit that MacLean's original concept, in fact, pointed us in the right direction. They would also be wise to reconsider MacLean's empirical contributions that brilliantly document how the ancient recesses of the brain help elaborate specific emotional impulses.

In summarizing these general conceptual issues, let me again emphasize that evolved emotional operating systems cannot be identified simply by studies of single neuron activities, even though the latter can provide important correlates between behavior and brain activities. Coherently operating brain systems must also be identified through the neuroethological analyses of basic emotional behavior patterns that animals exhibit spontaneously with little need for social learning. A "network-doctrine" is essential to make sense of such global state variables. While MacLean and various other investigators have sought to capture those broader, system-wide emergent dynamics, most behavioristically oriented neuroscientists focus their attentions on the fine neuronal details, especially single unit activities related to learning experiences under stimulus control.

Unfortunately, these neurophysiological *correlates* provide little insight into the overall dynamics of emotional systems in action. Understandably, modern scientists are always drawn to look where the light and funding is brightest, especially as new technologies become available. However, in doing so they commonly study more manageable proximal problems rather than the larger concerns that must also frame insightful inquiries. With such shifts of emphasis and amid competitive funding, they often succumb to the temptation to denigrate the rigorous work of those still engaged with the global and holistic issues of concern to the educated public at large.

While examining for meaningful neuromental correlates to psychological and behavioral responses, we must accept that certain natural phenomena do exist as complex emergent manifestations of distinct levels of organization. From this point of view, molecular neuroscientists commonly lack tools to attack the hardest mind-brain problems, such as the psychological consequences of many interacting brain systems. This does not mean effective tools are unavailable, but rather that the utilization of such tools must, by necessity, link to *theoretical inferences.* Neuroscientists unfortunately are often loathe to consider these. I think this lies at the heart of the dilemma that MacLean's theorizing poses for many who simply detest the concept of "the limbic system" as the epicenter of the emotional brain. They harvest data more comfortably than make predictions from theoretical premises.

This present volume goes a long way to rectify errors of interpretation and to reaffirm how heuristic MacLean's ideas have actually been. His lasting contributions to date relate to having spurred many disciplines to think more coherently about important issues. MacLean's thinking finally brought brain issues to bear upon important topics where there had been no coherent neuroscientific thought at all. MacLean always encouraged additional development and refinement with remarkably little personal egoism. A sad day will dawn for our pedagogy and science should the superficial views of the neo-behaviorist critics prevail indefinitely. In my estimation, intellectual travesties ensue without a holistic view of emotions that aspires to clarify the neuronal-network foundations upon which such large-scale mind/brain processes subsist. The molecular analyzes of some critics have usefully worked out details of limited problems, but shed little light on how brain matters eventually generate coherent emotional states and affective experiences.

Thus far I have spoken generally. Now let me be more concrete and frank in extending Jerry Cory's rebuttal of selected MacLean critics; his chapter principally considers those who reviewed MacLean's 1990 opus. Since he doesn't refer specifically to the views of Joseph LeDoux, I will bring these into focus. Widely hailed as "the leading expert on the emotional brain" (Gazzaniga, et al. 1998, *Textbook of Cognitive Neuroscience,* p. 516), LeDoux's empirical work in fact represents the apotheosis of a learning-centered, neo-behaviorist neuroscience that hasn't yet come to grips with the evolved nature of emotionality. He has been most dismissive of MacLean's integrative views, and he has been the most sustained opponent of the limbic system concept within "the emotional brain" community. In articulating and pushing forward his own agenda, LeDoux (1996, 2000) has explicitly misrepresented MacLean's perspectives. To all appearances he has done so intentionally—unless he has either misunderstood or not carefully read what MacLean actually wrote in *The Triune Brain in Evolution.*

A malaise in modern brain-emotion research emerges from neuroscientists ignoring affective states of consciousness. By applying some bitter medicine, I hope to make some critical points that are hard to achieve using more sugar-coated (i.e., unforthright) intellectual maneuvers. Although I may not change the minds or hearts of those who need it most, a new generation of scholars may learn through the mistakes and miscommunications of present and preceding eras.

LeDoux selected what he perceives to be the weakest link in the armor of the competition (i.e., Paul MacLean's "limbic system" concept as an *anatomical* entity) for launching a subtle attack on those who accept emotional feelings as an important topic for neuroscientific inquiry. Indeed, LeDoux has falsely claimed that MacLean employed the "limbic system" as an *explanation* of a monolithic emotion process—a simply incorrect statement. MacLean applies the concept only to circumscribe approximate neuronal territories as appropriate targets for inquiry. LeDoux's claim is especially arbitrary since he cites no chapter or verse from MacLean's *magnum opus* (indeed, the book is not even cited in most of his recent reviews, with preference given to MacLean's earlier and less timely materials).

Although LeDoux's group has done excellent empirical work in the area of fear learning, he ignores whole swaths of relevant data collected under conceptual approaches other than his own. Along the way he has selected subsidiary issues (e.g., the "limbic system" concept of MacLean's work, and my own ontological position that certain other animals probably experience emotional feelings) as reasons to disregard our empirical work and to avoid our epistemological strategies. With marginalization of this magnitude on a topic of mutual interest, one must suspect that factors other than scientific ones guide strategic choices. The approach resembles a Madison Avenue type of "public relations" campaign: namely, if one caricatures or disregards other substantive ideas and data, the more one's own ideational progeny may thrive. In part, competition fuels this—for difficult-to-obtain research grants. One needs to win "Zeitgeist-compliant," molecularly-oriented, grantsmanship competitions that often leave little room for theoretically innovative research. Parenthetically, MacLean's work probably could not readily have been conducted anywhere else than the safe-haven of a financially protected NIH lab.

Being one of the few behavioral neuroscientists (except for MacLean, of course), who took evolutionarily ingrained emotional systems and animal feelings seriously in the 1970s, I was delighted when young investigators like LeDoux exhibited some revolutionary fervor for pursuing emotional topics of first-rate importance, as opposed to pursuing simply the obligatory domains of learning, memory and certain well-accepted motivational processes (e.g., feeding, drinking, sleeping and sexing). Practically no one in the USA obtained extramural funding for basic brain-emotion research at the time LeDoux entered the field—unless they complied with traditional behavioristic methodology and atheoretical positivistic assumptions. This has continued to the present day in behavioral neuroscience.

LeDoux learned his lesson about the power of behaviorism—then and still—when he applied for initial funding to study the classical conditioning of fear (a mainstay topic of behavioral analysis for the better part of the 20th century). As he poignantly related in public (i.e., at a Society for Neuroscience Symposium in the 90s), his first request for federal support in the 1980s provided him a powerful, that is "emotional," lesson in modern grantsmanship. The study section indicated that nothing in his proposal to study the brain substrates of classical conditioning of fear required the concept of emotion. All could be done under the concepts of learning and memory.

He chose to revise his grant as recommended. As publicly related, he merely changed every usage of the word "emotion" to memory-related terms. Promptly rewarded for this accommodating (duplicitous?) maneuver, he continued to receive substantially more funding than anyone else in the animal brain-"emotion" field ever since.

When LeDoux initiated his modern neuroscience research program, everyone in the field had known for years that the amygdala was the optimal place for working out the details of fear learning. His group has now made first-rate contributions to clarifying the nature of that phenomenon, but not to the bigger and more urgent question—the nature of the evolved brain operating systems that mediate emotionality. He has made no major contribution to our under-standing of animals' diverse emotional repertoires, nor has he *helped* us understand the possible experiential-existential states these systems help create in humans. Indeed, he has simply chosen to ignore the weight of evidence that points to the importance of such issues as well as strategic ways to approach their solution.

As the years have passed, LeDoux's investigation of amygdaloid partici-pation in perceptual fear learning emerged as examples of how modern neuro-science tools can effectively take up difficult problems in learning and memory. It generally simulates Nobel Laureate Eric Kandel's research in the study of electric-shock mediated classical conditioning in Aplysia. However, the success should not foster any illusion that the work has focused either on the evolutionary or integrative nature of emotionality. His work resembles the activity of the proverbial gentleman looking for his keys under the street lamp. Curiously, in "looking well" at restricted problems, he has convinced too many scholars that his research revealed the core processes of emotions.

By conceptualizing the amygdala as the heart of emotional processing in the brain and by relegating subcortical meso-diencephalic core functions to simple motor outputs, he captivated the imaginations of psychologists traditionally little interested in brain functions. Gradually, the amygdala assumed the role of some master integrator of many emotions. This new "insight" has been blown vastly out of proportion in the popular press, though informed workers and clinicians know it represents only a small part of the emotion story. This reification represents a more simple-minded and incorrect formulation than does MacLean's broad concept of the limbic system, and until recently, LeDoux has done little to dissuade simplifiers from that tack. However the clinical evidence already shows that people with bilateral amygdaloid lesions exhibit an emotional naivete and fail to demonstrate some forms of fear conditioning, but also they demonstrate no global disorder of emotions. Their feelings related to social attachments remain intact, and they fully feel internally generated emotional turmoil (Damasio 1999).

In any event, LeDoux vigorously implemented the new armamentarium of tools created by neuroscientists in the 1970s and 1980s, even as MacLean's career increasingly approached the "retirement phase." LeDoux's laboratory applied these tools with impressive skill and they made a vast number of worthy contributions. We now feel confident that the conditioning of fear to auditory cues stems from specific amygdaloid subareas. This helps us appreciate that amygdala, astride the diencephalic and midbrain systems that instantiate coherent emotional responses, plays a major role in mediating ubiquitous interactions between emotion and cognition.

Unfortunately fear conditioning tells little about how the potential for affective experience arises from human or animal brains and minds. It contri-butes only to our understanding of where and how neutral stimuli gain access into a single brain emotional system. Why LeDoux has failed to emphasize the evolutionary antecedents of fear learning (i.e., fear *states*) remains unanswered, but this may hinge on the fact that deep evolutionary views don't have popular-ity in either behavioral or cognitive neuroscience. Moreover, such attention would entail explicit recognition of an ancient and coherently operating FEAR system, proposed by others, that courses between the central amygdala to the periaqueductal gray (Panksepp 1990, 1998). LeDoux, a prominent opinion-leader in the field, does not willingly acknowledge such manifest facts. Had he done so, contemporary neuroscience and cognitive science might already have forthrightly contextualized fear among the manifold emotional operating systems of the brain, and made meaningful distinctions between the system for FEAR and others that mediate different kinds of anxiety such as social separation distress/PANIC. Although LeDoux claims to accept an evolutionary point of view, he ignores the varieties of brain emotional phylogenies that MacLean recognized first amongst neuroscientists.

While LeDoux criticizes MacLean's general limbic system concept, he commends his own approach which recognizes that *"since different emotions are involved with different survival functions—defending against danger, finding food and mates, caring for offspring, and so on—each may well involve different brain systems that evolved for different reasons. As a result, there may be not one emotional system in the brain but many"* (in Gazzaniga et al. 1998: 516). In response I recommend reading *The Triune Brain in Evolution*, because MacLean's approach to the brain and mind distinguishes all these issues with sophistication and completeness.

LeDoux's contributions to emotional learning have enough importance that he need not avoid or misrepresent the contributions of others. Yet while he claims to espouse evolutionary views, he consistently avoids detailing the work of those who have pursued Darwinian neuroethology more systematically. Further, while MacLean confronted a central problem of emotion research—the nature of affective experience—LeDoux makes clear he does not consider emotional feelings a workable puzzle for brain research, but demeans it as mere "icing" on the "cake" (LeDoux 1996: 302). Rather, the reflexive response patterns of unfeeling Cartesian zombies is deemed to be the central problem. That he has convinced so much of the attentive general readership that he actually works on understanding the full gamut of emotions, as commonly understood, represents one of the marketing successes of modern neuroscience.

Investigators of brain and mental function know they face an enormous challenge in linking psychobehavioral with biological concepts. Anyone courageous enough to accept this challenge realizes that only successive approximations of affective phenomenological "reality" can be obtained. How unfortunate that investigators who aspire to deal forthrightly with such integrative problems find their work ignored by colleagues unwilling to sail beyond the safe harbor of positivistic molecular and neuronal science.

Few have noticed that LeDoux characterizes feelings, the experience of emotion, as a trivial side-show of consciousness not a main theme neuroscientists should try to illuminate. While those interested in consciousness increasingly accept the importance of emotional feelings as a way for the brain to assign value to world objects and behavioral strategies, LeDoux claims these issues are epistemologically unworkable and hence ancillary to his own research into one reflexive, and perhaps largely unconscious, emotional response. Meanwhile, LeDoux's implicit theory of consciousness is unsophisticated, relying as it does on a concept of "higher" working memory too little involved with the Extended Reticulo-Thalamic Activating Systems (ERTAS). The ERTAS essentially underpins all working memory in a manner much more widely distributed than the dorsolateral pre-frontal cortex. Likewise, he has ignored the importance of Damasio's (1999) basic insight that body mapping (and by implication, particularly the mapping of the *needs* of the body in the environment of evolutionary adaptation) represents a foundation for integrative neuroscience in general and consciousness studies in particular. Most theories of attentional functions (prerequisite to working memory) assume that working memory distills what attentional functions capture in conscious workspace. They thereby emphasize the importance of a host of subcortical, midline thalamic and reticular structures structurally very close to the affective core of the brain and probably inexorably intertwined with such systems.

MacLean put these *epistemic* concerns at the forefront of his agenda of brain research; for this reason, many humanists have admired his work. Rather than conceptualize the fuller complexity of brain substrates of emotionality, LeDoux chose to "escape from the shackles of subjectivity" (2000: 156). However, in pursuing the "easily" doable, he employs a series of subtle "sleight of mind" marketing-type tricks which help many believe he has actually been studying and encouraging the study of *basic* emotional processes in the brain, something rather far from the truth. In his most recent book, LeDoux (2001) lists the various traditional memory-learning information-processing "tricks" he uses to study "emotions." Although his traditional memory research program is solid, he offers no credible *new* solution to "the emotion problem." To sustain such Janus-faced posturing, different and more substantive ideas of others must be ignored and/or suppressed. His studied inattention to actual neuroethological research implicitly emphasizes such work as irrelevant to emotional processes. Instead of dealing with substantive empirical and theoretical issues while criticizing MacLean, LeDoux chooses shallow criticism of subsidiary or surface issues remarkably easy to caricature. Of course, the same could easily be done for amygdalar research (Panksepp 2000a: 139–140).

The way MacLean posits the *limbic-system* little resembles the way LeDoux abuses the concept. Surely there have been many others who have employed MacLean's ideas in oversimplified ways, but MacLean used the concept as biologists might use taxonomic concepts such as genera, kingdoms, etc.—to partition the complexity of nature. Most evolutionists recognize that such concepts have no ontological reality—rather they represent "practical kinds" that conceptualize inquiry more effectively than the positivistic harvesting of data without guiding *theories.*

The main practical question about the limbic system concept concerns whether it pointed effectively toward the main brain areas essential for emotionality. Overwhelming evidence shows the concept is robustly affirmed, as through meta-analysis of PET and fMRI imaging of brain arousals during felt-emotions. Did the limbic concept give us a definitive mechanistic explanation of how emotions emerge from detailed operations of enormous numbers of neural systems that course through the limbic system? No, it did not. However, it identified a set of neuronal correlates that must always precede causal studies. Many investigators who take the expanded limbic neuro-geography seriously have made enormous advances in characterizing those causes. In this context, it is worth noting that the most comprehensive PET study of internally experienced emotions by Damasio et al. (2000) showed that the amygdala exhibited no significant arousal except, quite surprisingly, during happiness! In fact, those brain areas that are aroused during deep human affective experiences are the ones strongly implicated as causal in neuroethological analyses of spontaneous animal emotionality (MacLean 1990; Panksepp 1998).

LeDoux has not come to grips with affective experiences and the spontaneous emotionality of animals because he studies primarily sensory-perceptual events that instigate one simple set of unconsciously triggered emotional reflexes. To convince others that this work has much to do with the brain's intrinsic evolved capacity for fear, amygdalophilic fear researchers envision amygdala efferents as mere unconscious response systems—outputs with few implications for experiential hermeneutics of fearfulness (not to mention other primary emotions, uniformly ignored). This "mere output" assumption consistently omits consideration of evidence that indicates how these so-called "outputs" (which, in fact, are integrative systems) are essential for emotional feelings.

For LeDoux, progress on the mental aspects of brain functions must await solution of "the mind-body problem" (2000: 156). This represents a *problem* (indeed, a neo-dualistic *speculation*) only if one does not accept emergent psychological properties arising from complex neural network dynamics. MacLean's position consistently affirmed the need of neuroscientists to come to terms with the emergent subjective aspects of many brain functions. He begins his *magnum opus* with a discussion of *epistemics*, the subjective experiences that can arise from the evolutionary potentials of the brain. MacLean believes this problem solvable, but most behaviorists and many information-processing cognitivists consider it either a non-problem or unsolvable. Their nihilism stifles needed discussion and also, because of the continued hegemony of the *neurobehaviorist counterrevolution*, co-opts funding needed for the necessary inquiries. Remarkably, certain investigators who eschew such issues in their own work have been able simultaneously to convince the world they in fact immerse themselves in them.

This, I believe is the crux of the matter: MacLean gives provisional solutions to a problem most behavioral neuroscientists would rather not address, so they have marginalized his work. In this battle over paradigmatic issues, I encourage young investigators to side with those who argue that the role of neuromental experience in behavioral control represents a substantial part of what the animal brain does for adaptation to complex physical and social worlds where unconscious reflexes do not suffice. In fact, the weight of evidence shows emotionalities represent evolutionarily stable solutions through which values encoded as global experiential states substantially arise from neural matrices guiding adaptive instinctive behaviors. Perhaps the most poignant examples show up in drug addiction.

Most investigators recognize drugs of abuse commandeer natural reward and punishment functions of the brain organized similarly in mice and humans (Hill & Newlin 2002). We might well ask *would drug addiction exist if drugs did not change our internal feelings*? Clearly the answer is no—and not only for members of our own species. At this point, the neo-behaviorists (including LeDoux 2001), commonly trot out the study of Lamb et al. (1991) to highlight that unconscious reinforcement processes mediate addictive behaviors. Yet this study did not involve reinforcement. In this cognitively-mediated, fixed–ratio 3000 task a substantial number of subjects felt they were getting some morphine at the lowest doses, but certainly not enough to get high. This supposedly unconscious reinforcement process in fact represents nothing more than a cognitively mediated demand characteristic; because the infusions were so dilute, Lamb's subjects probably deliberately sought something affectively unattainable. But the experimenters did *not* ask simple and sensible questions about the subjects' motivation! For a more complete analysis, see Panksepp et al. (2002).

Animals avidly consume these same agents because they probably also experience brain changes in many distinctly positive ways. These changes yield to evaluation, to some extent, by state-dependent conditioning paradigms, and also other measures such as emotional vocalizations (Knutson, Burgdorf & Panksepp 2002; Panksepp, Knutson & Burgdorf 2002a). This does not imply nonexistence of vast and unconscious neural properties to support the brain functions that create feelings. Such unconscious components for emotions exist in greater abundance than the pieces of an internal combustion engine, and just as in an automobile, many components must operate together for effective motility to emerge in the one case and affective urgency in the other. When many unconscious components work together in the brain to yield system states, a glimmer of mind begins to *emerge*. Many reasons point to the ideas that the first such glimmers in the emergence of consciousness were affective feelings (Panksepp 2000b, 2002a). Therefore, to marginalize feelings as do the neo-behaviorists represents a disservice to science as well as to a deep and realistic respect for animate life. MacLean always conveyed a sincere respect for those mysteries. He was also most eager to promote research to work out the essential details. The work of none of MacLean's critics represents that tradition, even though some "speak" forcefully for a unified mind science (e.g., LeDoux 1999).

MacLean would surely have been more influential on my own research program had we not been essentially tackling similar issues at the very same time. Both of us have been intrigued by the nature of separation distress and playfulness, (me, early in my career and he, toward the end of his laboratory activities). However, I have always felt his a kindred spirit particularly in his commitment to deal with the fuller complexity of the many emotional processes of the brain that the rest of neuroscience was neglecting. Within my intellectual home of behavioral neuroscience, practically no support existed for research of that type, a state of affairs, that regrettably persists.

The heart of the paradigmatic battle is: are emotional feelings an important neuroscientific topic? Those who say yes, as I do, find MacLean a sure and guiding star. We take the position emotional feelings are thoroughly neurobiological in a deep evolutionary sense. Those who are waiting for *definitions* of such processes before they begin research, should recognize that they can't be adequately defined before our inquiries have borne substantive fruit, and that simply can't happen without adequate theories to get well-targeted empirical inquiries initiated. Those who find no favor with such concerns turn away from emotive evolution with revulsion, as if the topic were both impolite and irrelevant (e.g., Blumberg & Sokoloff 2001, and see comments by Panksepp 2002b).

I suspect the animal-rights movement's remarkable success in quelling research in the United States resulted partly because so many reasonable lay-people cannot agree with investigators who assert still, as did Descartes, that nonhuman animals are largely unconscious, unfeeling creatures. Our prolonged agony with this problem reflects, in part, the continuing tragedy of the behaviorist tradition that has been *unwilling* to conceptualize mind and emotional feelings in neurobiological terms (have the practitioners been *unable* to do that because of some alexithymia among scientists? See Panksepp 2000c). Every neo-behaviorist needs to repeat: *Affective experience is a completely natural emergent product of neurobiological complexity within the mammalian brain, and at the present stage of our intellectual development it must be scientifically studied indirectly through testable neurotheoretical inferences.*

Overwhelming evidence shows that animal brains elaborate many states of affective consciousness. Some scholars feel that animal data cannot guide predictions in humans and claim this ontological position is scientifically unworkable. If homologous neuromechanisms exist in our brains, those scholars must be wrong. When we, the brain/mind scientists, fail to take such emotional perspectives seriously, we support fundamentally narrow-minded and unethical practices and perspectives. Rather we should continue our behavioral brain research on other animals with a more coherent and respectful vision of what we are doing (e.g., see my *Affective Neuroscience,* pp. 6–7). If our recent findings hold true, that a primordial form of joyous laughter may be emanating from the brains of playing and tickled rats, then we may have to rethink many mind issues (Panksepp & Burgdorf 1999).

So, do other animals experience emotional states? Of course there is no ultimate "proof" in science, merely the weight of evidence. To me it remains a mystery that certain scientists can ignore the mass of relevant evidence from: (i) behavioral reinforcement studies, (ii) place preference-aversion studies, (iii) manifest and ubiquitous emotional vocalizations, (iv) neuroethological studies evoking emotional behaviors and states from the same human/animal brain homologs and (v) the coherent translations between human and animal psychopharmacological work. With evidence like that, the issue of animal feelings represents more than a mere ontological ambiguity. Rather it approaches epistemological certainty.

Perhaps I have only caricatured the position of the neo-behaviorists who populate modern neuroscience, but my own experience tells me otherwise. The remarkably deep rift in our shared scientific culture humiliates our self-conception as guardians of the truth in a world where belief and persuasion generally matter more than evidence. So what do we do with the mountain of data, both direct and indirect, that animals have affective experiences as a birth right of the types of brains they and we have inherited? Do we continue to ignore the weight of evidence, and sustain our uniquely human arrogance about our place in nature?

LeDoux states (in Gazzaniga et al. 1998: 516): "*Many emotions . . . involve phylogenetically old brain systems that evolved to control the body behaviorally and physiologically in response to environmental challenges. These systems take care of things like defense against danger, sexual behavior, maternal behavior, eating, and other things like this. These are the kinds of emotional systems we can study in the animal brain.*" He skillfully avoids addressing the issue of affect in enunciating this view. In any event, these are the types of systems MacLean and investigators following in his tradition have long studied using all the care of standard science. For some of us interested in human emotions, such studies entail the reasonable corollary that a study of the neural substrates of the objective natural emotional behaviors of animals can guide us to an understanding of the ancestral neural sources of *human* feelings.

A half century ago the field of emotion research needed a preliminary surveyor to plot the organizational framework for understanding emotions. MacLean provided a most credible plot, as long as one is willing to absorb it *all* with an open mind and appreciate that some needed "corrections" and elaborations are inevitable (Panksepp 1998). This type of work and thinking can interface with an understanding of psychiatric issues more readily than any other pre-clinical strategy that is available. Emotional *states* probably have phenomenological meaning for all mammals.

In sum, evolved functions of the brain, such as the various emotional systems, cannot be adequately conceptualized in *channel-function* information-processing terms. Additionally needed are concepts that recognize hundreds of thousands of neurons working spontaneously together to generate organic pressures for action and feeling within the visceral neural core of animate existence. In 1949 and 1952 MacLean offered the "limbic system" concept as the most suitable piece of neuroevolutionary territory wherein we could *begin* to investigate emotional systems in earnest. During the ensuing forty years, he followed his own advice well, and the weight of evidence still affirms he had surveyed the functional terrain of the brain remarkably accurately.

Let me now re-emphasize a key distinction I have used throughout this foreword—one all investigators need to consider if interested in the intimate relations between brain functions and mind. Emotional feelings are not simply informationally encapsulated "channel functions" of the brain (as Marcel Mesulam used the term in his *Behavioral Neurology*). Rather, evolved emotional systems represent global "state-functions" reliant on complex organic organization of broadly operating brain systems. Single unit electrophysiological approaches ideally suited for studying channel functions cannot inform on the state functions emerging from large ensembles of neurons and supportive organic processes operating dynamically together to weave the "whole cloth" of the basic psychobehavioral processes of the brain. To understand neuromental "organ systems" requires experimental strategies other than single cell recordings from one brain location; classical *stimulus-control* paradigms may not optimally capture the patterned activities of such evolved brain/mind systems. What is needed are multiple, simultaneous recordings from many brain sites during spontaneous emotional behaviors, and an integration of those data with neurogenetic, neurochemical and neuroethological perspectives.

Concurrent electrophysiological and neurochemical studies may provide great insights using *many* probes positioned at just the right points *within* specific emotional systems (starting in higher regions of the amygdala and working down to the periaqueductal gray). Increasingly sophisticated EEG and MEG algorithms may usher in new and insightful neurodynamic measures that may monitor emotional feelings more directly (e.g., as Walter Freeman's EEG measurement of chaotic neurodynamics highlighted perceptual processes; see *How the Brain Makes Up Its Mind*). The broad anatomies of emotional systems will expand (like the "limbic system" expanded) as our knowledge ripens from harvesting the right kinds of facts. No single center for emotions in the brain exists, contrary to the implications of certain amygdalophiles. The "limbic system," as originally proposed, simply recognized the major brain territory in which our empirical confrontation with the diverse circuits for the various emotional miseries and joys might be most successfully consummated. MacLean's insight has proven fundamentally correct.

The information-processing metaphor holds more importance for analyzing the many "channel functions" of the brain that control sensory processes rather than for understanding the more organic and holistic emotional processes. Clearly the cognitive revolution oversold "information-processing," at least for understanding the deeper sources of our emotions and motivations, and perhaps even the foundations of certain cognitive processes. This unfortunately draws many young investigators to the comparatively idle pursuit of computing mind before they gain clear understanding of the global neural underpinnings of organic action systems that evolution built into the lower reaches of the neuro-mental apparatus shared with so many other creatures.

Despite heavy investment in behavioristic models of fear-learning and the associated information processing of conditioned stimuli, investigators should open their minds to larger evolutionary issues entailed by neuro-ethological and psycho-ethological *state-systems* approaches. Traditional *perception-to-action* models, with response systems deemed totally unconscious, do not suffice. As we come to understand the evolved emotional operating systems of the brain, *action-to-perception* processes may end up as more important for understanding the foundations of consciousness than the now dubious promise of cognitive computationalism (Jerry Fodor 2000, *The Mind Does Not Work That Way*). In sum, the evolved "instinctual" action systems that control emotional states of the brain represent essential targets for study if we wish to understand how emotional feelings arise within the brain.

MacLean sought to tackle such important issues, and we would have a much healthier climate for research on the neural basis of emotions if all relevant approaches could work in some type of consilience rather than the present competitively fearsome "conformity enforcement." At least animal investigators now agree emotional *behaviors* are in the objective realm of traditional science, while many investigators of human psychology have taken the next step and also agree that affective experiences should be included among the neuroscientific attributes that need to be clarified. Such aspects of mind should no longer be deemed unworkable problems, even in other animals (Panksepp et al. 2002a,b). Indeed, the discovery of apparently homologous neurochemical codes for many emotional and motivational processes in all mammals, allows us to go from studies of animal emotional behaviors to a study of human affective experience (Panksepp 1998, 1999).

Paul MacLean's great contribution was his establishment of a general paradigm that is more realistic and experimentally more effective than any that had gone before. As Gardner in this volume emphasizes, this lastingly contributed to our continuing and realistic desire to dock mind-brain functions in meaningful ways. We will solve the semantically created mind-body problem gradually by confronting key issues, not by avoiding them.

No, there is no *mindscope* yet that we can apply to either animals or humans. Only their behavior is testament to what is happening inside their brains. Because of that, we have only two options: (1) to deny experiential aspects of the mind, explicitly or implicitly, to all the other animals (as have all too many scientists for the past 400 years since Descartes bequeathed us the endless mischief of mind-body dualism), or (2) to study those neurobiological processes indirectly in ways theoretically well-guided—quite as particle physicists have probed inside the atom.

Currently, the most substantive understanding of those emotional processes has emerged from the type of evolutionarily informed neuroethological work epitomized in Paul MacLean's approach. He, like all great scientists, fully understands Descartes' third law of science; that *the world is a complex place, and we cannot make progress unless we simplify, and gradually and through successive approximations, aspire toward a more comprehensive knowledge.* MacLean also recognizes that to solve the emotion puzzle, work must conceptually derive from the inside of the system, where core "active organism" principles are created by evolved state-control systems of the brain/mind. The puzzle simply will not yield to study of learned surface features (i.e., mere information-processing). The brain does much more than that.

The chapters of this volume converge from many different perspectives to demonstrate, with many different strengths, the intellectual force of Paul MacLean's neuroevolutionary psychobiology. This is an important testimonial for a neuroscientific paradigm that attempts to deal forthrightly with the full grandeur and mystery of the neuromental assemblages that makes us the types of spectacularly complex and difficult creatures that we are. Clearly, the fundamental nature of affect is a topic of critical importance for understanding our animal nature.

This volume of essays amplifies the evolutionary interconnected layering of mind so compellingly envisioned in Paul MacLean's concept of *The Triune Brain in Evolution.* The various phylogenetic regressions that can transpire in the human mental apparatus continue to inform biological psychiatry, evolutionary psychology, and the philosophy of science. The "natural" blackjack set of contributions in this volume summarize diverse points of view of a rich fabric of thought and data. Although chapters vary in depth and other qualities, none trivializes the core processes that underpin our extremely rich cognitive apparatus. For those interested in the archeology of mind, and the tethers that bind us still to the evolutionary adaptations that emerged in "deep time," this volume will be treasured. We will not understand the emergence of new mind/brain functions, such as trends for semantically-mediated sociality, mild-mannered deception as well as scientific Machiavellianism and the underpinnings of cultural ritual unless we pay our full respects to the older adaptations upon which our higher mental faculties are grounded.

NOTE

I wish to acknowledge useful comments on earlier versions of this foreword by Russell Gardner, Anesa Miller, David Pincus, Doug Watt, and Daniel Wilson.

REFERENCES

Blumberg, M.S., & Sokoloff, G. (2001). Do infant rats cry? *Psychological Review*, 108, 83–95.

Damasio, A.R. (1999). *The Feeling of What Happens, Body and Emotion in the Making of Consciousness.* New York: Harcourt Brace.

Damasio, A.R., Grabowski, T.J., Bechara, A., Damasio, H., Ponto, L.L.B., Parvizi, J. & Hichwa, R.D. (2000). Subcortical and cortical brain activity during the feeling of self-generated emotions. *Nature Neuroscience,* 3, 1049–1056.

Fodor, J. (2000) *The Mind Doesn't Work That Way: The Scope and Limits of Computational Psychology.* The MIT Press: Cambridge UK.

Freeman, W.J. (1999). *How Brains Make up Their Minds.* London, Weidenfeld & Nicolson.

Gainotti, G. (2001). Hemisphere asymmetries for autonomic functions, Evidence from normal subjects and brain-damaged patients. In A. Kazniak (ed.) *Emotions, Qualia and Consciousness.* (Pp. 235–246), London, World Scientific.

Gazzaniga, M.S., Ivry, R.B. & Mangun, G.R. (1998). *Cognitive Neuroscience: The Biology of Mind.* New York: W.W. Norton.

Hill, E.M., & Newlin, D.B. (eds.) (2002). Special Issue: Evolutionary Psychobiological Approaches to Addiction. *Addiction,* 97, 375–474.

Knutson, B., Burgdorf, J. & Panksepp, J. (2002). Ultrasonic vocalizations as indices of affective states in rats. *Psychological Bulletin,* In press.

Lamb R. J.; Preston K. L.; Schindler C. W.; Meisch R. A.; Davis F.; Katz J. L.; Henningfield J. E.; & Goldberg S. R. (1991). The reinforcing and subjective effects of morphine in post-addicts: a dose-response study. *The Journal of Pharmacology and Experimental Therapeutics*, 259, 1165–1173.

LeDoux, J.E. (1996). *The Emotional Brain.* New York, Simon & Schuster.

LeDoux, J.E. (1999). Psychoanalytic theory, Clues from the brain. *NeuroPsychoanalysis*, 1, 44–49.

LeDoux, J.E. (2000). Emotion circuits in the brain. *Annual Review of Neuroscience,* 23, 155–184.

LeDoux, J.E. (2001). *The Synaptic Self.* New York: Viking.

MacLean, P.D. (1990). *The Triune Brain in Evolution, Role in Paleocerebral Functions.* New York: Plenum Press.

Mesulam, M.M. (2000). *Principles of Behavioral and Cognitive Neurology, 2ⁿᵈ edition*, New York: Oxford University Press.

Panksepp, J. (1982). Toward a general psychobiological theory of emotions. *The Behavioral and Brain Sciences*, 5, 407–467.

Panksepp, J. (1990). The psychoneurology of fear: Evolutionary perspectives and the role of animal models in understanding human anxiety. In *Handbook of Anxiety*. (pp. 3–58), Amsterdam: Elsevier/North-Holland Biomedical Press.

Panksepp, J. (1998). *Affective Neuroscience, The foundations of human and animal emotions.* New York: Oxford University Press.

Panksepp, J. (1999a). Emotions as viewed by psychoanalysis and neuroscience, An exercise in consilience, *NeuroPsychoanalysis*, 1, 15–38.

Panksepp, J. (1999b). Drives, id energies, and the neuroscience of emotions: Response to the commentaries. *NeuroPsychoanalysis, 1*, 69–89.

Panksepp, J. (2000a). Emotions as natural kinds within the mammalian brain. In: M. Lewis and J. Haviland (eds.) *The Handbook of Emotions*, 2ⁿᵈ edition, pp. 137–156. New York: Guilford.

Panksepp, J. (2000b). The neuro-evolutionary cusp between emotions and cognitions, implications for understand consciousness and the emergence of a unified mind science. *Consciousness & Emotion*, 1, 17–56.

Panksepp, J. (2000c). On preventing another century of misunderstanding, Toward a psychoethology of human experience and a psychoneurology of affect. *Neuro-Psychoanalysis*, 2, 240–255.

Panksepp, J. (2001). The long-term psychobiological consequences of infant emotions: Prescriptions for the twenty-first century. *Infant Mental Health Journal*, 22, 132–173.

Panksepp, J. (2002a). At the interface of affective, behavioral and cognitive neurosciences. Decoding the emotional feelings of the brain. *Brain and Cognition*, In press.

Panksepp, J. (2002b). Can anthropomorphic analyses of "separation cries" in other animals inform us about the emotional nature of social loss in humans? *Psychological Review* (in press).

Panksepp, J. & Burgdorf, J. (1999) Laughing rats? Playful tickling arouses high frequency ultrasonic chirping in young rodents. In , S. Hameroff, C. Chalmers, and A. Kazniak,(eds). *Toward a science of consciousness III* (pp. 231–244) Cambridge, MA: MIT Press.

Panksepp, J., Knuston, B. & Burgdorf, J. (2002a). The role of emotional brain systems in addictions: A neuro-evolutionary perspective. *Addiction*, 97, 459–469.

Panksepp, J., Nocjar, C., Burgdorf, J., Panksepp, J.B., & Huber, R. (2002b). The role of emotional systems in addiction: A neuroethological perspective. In R. Bevins & M. Bardo (eds). *50ᵗʰ Nebraska Symposium on Motivation: Motivational Factors in the Etiology of Drug Abuse*, (in press) Lincoln, Nebraska: Univ. of Nebraska Press.

Stern, D.N. (1985). *The Interpersonal World of the Infant: A view from psychoanalysis and developmental psychology.* New York: Basic Books.

Stern, D.N. (1999). Vitality contours: The temporal contour of feelings as a basic unit for constructing the infant's social experience. In P. Rochat (Ed.), *Early Social Cognition: Understanding other in the first months of life.* (pp. 67–80). Mahwah, NJ: Erlbaum.

Trevarthen, C. (2001). Intrinsic motives for companionship in understanding: Their origin, development, and significance for infant mental health. *Infant Mental Health Journal*, 22: 95–131.

ACKNOWLEDGMENTS

The editors wish to thank Seymour Itzkoff, series editor, Dr. James Sabin, Director of Academic and Research Development, Catherine A. Lyons, production supervisor, Megan Peckman and Terri M. Jennings, production editors, Greenwood Publishing Group for their support and guidance in the production of this book. We are grateful for a grant from Pfizer Corporation in support of the symposium on the work of Paul MacLean sponsored by the Across Species Comparisons and Psychopathology Society (ASCAP) held in Boston, Massachussetts, July 16–17, 1999, the essential proceedings of which are reported in this volume. We also wish to acknowledge the valuable support of Suzi Gardner in organizing and producing the Boston symposium. The production of this book was further supported by a grant from the Center for Behavioral Ecology, San Jose, California. Tony Tidwell, Alex Bayne, Nicole Bayne, Abby Bayne and other staff members of the Center were of great support in the research and preparation of the manuscript.

PERMISSIONS

Valerius Geist generously granted permission to use the quote contained on page 322.

The editors wish to thank the following publishers for permissions as indicated:

Elsevier Science for permission to use Tables 10.1 (pp. 172–173), 10.2 (175–177), and 10.3 (178–180) from Pontius, A.A. 1997. "Homicide linked to moderate repetitive stresses kindling limbic seizures in 14 cases of Limbic Psychotic Trigger Reaction." *Aggression & Violent Behavior,* 2: 125–141.

Lippincott, Williams, and Wilkins for permission to reprint Figure 12.2, page 219 (spike and wave EEG seizure discharges) from Mirsky AF, Tecce, JJ:

The analysis of visual evoked potentials during spike-and wave EEG activity. *Epilepsia* 1968; 9: 211–220.

Little Brown Time Warner Books for permission to reprint Figure 12.3 page 220 (diagram of centrencephalic system) from Jasper, W. and Penfield, H.H. *Epilepsy and the Functional Anatomy of the Human Brain*, 1954.

The American Physiological Society for permission to reprint Figure 12.4, page 221 (the ascending reticular activating system) from Lindsley DB: Attention, consciousness, sleep and wakefulness. In Field J, Magoun HW, Hall VE (Eds): *Handbook of Physiology, Section 1: Neurophysiology, Volume III.* Washington, DC: American Physiological Society, 1960, pp. 1553–1593.

Academic Press for permission to use Figure 12.5, page 222 (effect of electrical stimulation of the brain on visually controlled behavior in the *Macaca mulatta*) from Bakay Pragay E, Mirsky AF, Fullerton BC, Oshima HI, Arnold SW: Effect of electrical stimulation of the brain on visually controlled (attentive) behavior in the *Macaca mulatta. Experimental Neurology* 1975; 49: 203–220.

Kluwer Academic for permission to use Figure 12.6, page 223 (frequency histograms of task-related neuronal activity in single cells in the monkey) from Mirsky AF, Duncan CC: Behavioral and electrophysiological studies of absence epilepsy. In Avoli N, Gloor P, Kostopoulos G, Naquet R (Eds): *Generalized Epilepsy: Neurobiological Approaches.* New York: Plenum, 1990, pp. 254–269.

Kluwer Academic for permission to use Figure 12.7, page 224 (semi-schematic representation of attention system of human brain) from Mirsky AF, Anthony BJ, Duncan CC, Ahearn MB, Kellam SG: Analysis of the elements of attention: A neuropsychological approach. *Neuropsychology Review* 1991; 2: 109–145.

INTRODUCTION

Paul MacLean, a trailblazer in evolutionary brain science, profoundly influenced medical neuroscience over the last half of the twentieth century. His concepts of the limbic system and the triune brain, deriving from an evolutionary perspective, helped biological psychiatry emerge and provided a framework and impetus for linking brain science with social theory and moral consciousness. In mainstream academic neuroscience, however, his work has been largely overlooked or ignored. Amazingly, his seminal work has not even been acknowledged in the newly popular primarily anthropological approach of evolutionary psychology. Major works in mainstream evolutionary psychology contain no references whatsoever to MacLean's work. Yet, MacLean is surely among the most eminent and original thinkers in evolutionary neuroscience, so this omission by researchers in evolutionary psychology is indeed glaring and unfortunate for the health and progress of this subset of the discipline. Panksepp and Panksepp (2000) have recently discussed in detail several of the problems resulting from evolutionary psychology's failure to consider long-established research findings from cross-species research in brain science.

Antonio Damasio, in his book *The Feeling of What Happens* (1999: 38–42) calls attention to the root problem. Accompanying the curious scientific neglect of emotion (in favor of cognition) in mainstream neuroscience, he cites a parallel neglect of three other important aspects that should be central to the study of neuroscience: (1) neglect of an evolutionary perspective, (2) neglect of the concept of homeostasis, and (3) neglect of the concept of the organism as a whole. Paul MacLean's work, among others, notably integrates all the lacking elements cited by Damasio. Damasio recognizes this.

Working to correct this neglect by mainstream neuroscience and evolutionary psychology, this book reports selected papers from the proceedings of a symposium held July 16–17, 1999, in Boston, Massachussetts, to assess the convergences and frontiers, motivated by MacLean and others' related research and theory, across a multidisciplinary spectrum ranging from molecular neurobiology, clinical psychotherapy, cognitive neuroscience, through emerging linkages in social and economic theory.

The first chapter by Karl Pribram, an early colleague of MacLean, helps to set a historical perspective and suggests some of the controversies that have shaped in part the discussions within neuroscience for the most recent five decades. The two pioneers had a dialectical collaboration characterized by alternating periods of conflict and convergence. As Pribram notes, their interlocking history provides a window on the scientific process, where differences in perspective, style, and technical focus make a difference in how problems are approached and how results are interpreted. Three essential differences seem to stand out between the two men. (1) Reductionism versus integration. This is the issue of the organism as a whole cited by Damasio. MacLean moves between reductive, fine-grained research and an ambitious level of integration in interpretation of results, whereas Pribram remains largely at a more focused, fine-grained reductive approach. (2) Evolutionary approach versus the structural/functional perspective (that parallels a deficit cited by Damasio). MacLean clearly prefers an evolutionary approach; Pribram, seemingly a functional anatomical one. (3) MacLean contemplates subjective experience and emotion, whereas Pribram more usually inclines toward a cognitive and objective position. The differences in perspective of the two men, in a manner, anticipated (and perhaps contributed to) the divergences characterizing the neuroscience community for the succeeding five decades. Some of these legitimate differences, reflecting alternative perspectives requiring future convergence, later became distorted by others through unreflective and unexamined repetition.

Such distorted divergences occupy the chapter by Gerald Cory. Cory appraises MacLean's triune brain concept in response to a rather inept and unfortunate review of MacLean's landmark opus, *The Triune Brain in Evolution: Role in Paleocerebral Functions* (1990). This review appeared in *Science* (Oct 12, 1990) and inaccurately reported and somewhat caricatured MacLean's work. This red flag review unjustifiably inhibited the use of MacLean's important contributions by other scholars and contributed to the further neglect of an evolutionary perspective as well as the study of emotion. The inhibiting effect of this review article, and others that uncritically followed it, especially impacted scholars in cognitive studies, evolutionary psychology, and the other social sciences, who were unable to independently evaluate the controversy. As a notable example, cognitive scientist Steven Pinker in his *How the Mind Works* (1997) rejects and in the process presents an extraordinary caricature of MacLean's position based on a single reference to the defective review in *Science*. If he had consulted MacLean's work closely, Pinker may have found it solidly underpinning his own evolving thought. Following a detailed rebuttal of the *Science* review, Cory's chapter concludes that MacLean's work is soundly grounded in evolutionary neuroscience and provides the best foundation in neuroscience yet articulated for application to the essential issues of cognitive science and evolutionary psychology as well as other social sciences.

The chapter by C.U.M. Smith deals with the new findings in developmental evolutionary biology and molecular genetics. These new fields provide insights into the evolutionary process, which is characterized by a remarkable mix of conservation and divergence in brain evolution as well as body plans and other features. Smith relates these exciting new discoveries to the evolutionary perspective of MacLean, which emphasized the conservation of ancient brain structures as well as the variation emanating therefrom in the phylogenetic history of change, leading toward the full evolution of the human brain. Smith emphasizes especially the continuities in the development of the visual system.

The chapter by Neil Greenberg, who early worked with MacLean on the striatal system in lizards, updates that earlier work with new findings that extend our understanding of this portion of our neural architecture, already prominent in reptiles ancestral to present-day mammals and, indeed, humans. In keeping with MacLean's earlier insights, the striatal complex (MacLean's protoreptilian complex) demonstrably affects and organizes not only motor behavior, but the sequencing of complex behavior, including language and cognition. This is also emphasized by Philip Lieberman in *Human Language and Our Reptilian Brain* (2000).

Russell Gardner, Jr.'s chapter appropriately provides the foundation for a two-part focus on clinical theory and applications. Gardner draws upon the new findings discussed in the previous chapters to address the current lack of a satisfactory framework for psychiatry and the related helping sciences. Gardner sees MacLean's emphasis on social behaviors that stemmed from adaptations originating in deep time as a impetus for a revival of MacLean's influence. Results from data generated by the genome project, as well as other genetic and brain research, combine with the need of psychiatry and related disciplines to connect brain actions with normal human communicative behavior. This convergence leads Gardner to the idea that psychiatry's basic science should be designated sociophysiology. He concludes that the social brain concept allows psychiatry and its allied clinical disciplines to utilize pathogenesis in a manner parallel to practice in other specialties.

The next three chapters apply triune theory to the theoretical and applied study of clinical depression. John Price applies the triune model to early vertebrate escalation and de-escalation (fight/submission) strategies. The paleomammalian, or limbic emotional centers add intense emotional tone to these strategies including the anger, exhilaration, and rage of the escalation strategy and the fear, depression, shame, and guilt of de-escalation. The neomammalian or higher cortical structures bring conscious, rational decision to fight or to submit. Depressive illness may result from conflict between the newer and older centers.

Leon Sloman discusses the social competition model of depression to clarify the evolutionary and communicative function of subordinate mechanisms that contribute to psychological and biological features of depression. Within a context inclusive of other models, such as attachment theory, discrete emotion theory, and cognitive behavior therapy, variations in self-esteem and mood fluctuations reflect the operation of genetically programmed mechanisms with an important adaptive function. Daniel Wilson's paper reconciles manic-depression with triunian neuroethology via a review and analysis of both manic-depression and the triune brain theory with respect to (1) relevant evolutionary epidemiology, and (2) consilience with game theoretic models.

The next three chapters take different clinical directions. James Harris discusses the development of the essential human quality of empathy and its failure to emerge in the disorder of autism. Harris accounts for both empathy and autism in terms of integration of the triune brain. In autistic disorder, failure of the development of limbic structures (amygdala, hippocampus) and cerebellum may cause a failure in empathy. Anneliese Pontius' chapter focuses on a specific neurophysiological dysfunction, which she proposes to call limbic psychotic trigger reaction. Seizures associated with this reaction have been triggers to apparently motiveless homicides. She discusses how MacLean's evolutionary model of brain organization led to the insights that identified this previously unexplained clinical phenomenon.

Glenn Weisfeld's chapter in several respects ties together the clinical picture for an evolutionary psychiatry. He begins by acknowledging that the study of comparative neuroanatomy makes clear that motivated behaviors evolved earlier than complex cognitive capacities. As MacLean has repeatedly emphasized, the brain stem, basal ganglia, and limbic system predated the neocortical expansion. He then outlines the role of the prefrontal lobes in pride and shame as well as in the mediating of complex social behavior.

The chapter by Allan Mirsky and Connie Duncan shifts from depression, dysfunction, and emotion to the important complementary issue of attention. Modern concepts have moved from the earlier notions of attention as a single monolithic function to conceiving of it as a group of behaviors, each defined separately with a specifically articulated function for the organism. Some theorists have posited that each specific function depends on the integrity of a distinct brain region, even though in the intact brain, the regions form an integrated system. Mirsky and Duncan propose a heuristic model of attention, derived in large part from neuropsychological data from patients with seizures or other neurospsychiatric disorders. They hold that MacLean's triune concept provides a remarkable armature upon which to build a concept of the organization and development of attentional functions from the evolutionary point of view.

The next three chapters offer differing perspectives. James Brody thoughtfully integrates Stuart Kauffman's triadic concepts in statistical physics with MacLean's triune evolutionary model. Brody derives interesting parallels suggesting that physical constraints promote binary and tertiary models. He also links concepts from physics and evolutionary theory to clarify clinical diagnostic theory and practice. Seymour Itzkoff argues for a perspective on vertebrate, and especially mammalian brain evolution, led not by lower brain regions but by the shaping effect of emerging neocortical centers. In this, he reverses the traditional perspective that focuses on the selective prominence of the striatal and limbic complexes. Itzkoff's analysis reminds us that the evidence can also be interpreted in a top-down fashion or at least in a more interactive manner. The chapter by Roger Masters, like that of Pontius provides a very specific, although different focus. Applying findings of evolutionary neuroscience to social theory and policy, he reports new information on how environmental pollution by heavy metals affects evolved neural architecture of the human central nervous system. Introduction of these heavy elements into the environment by modern industrialized and technological civilization factors importantly in causing behavioral abnormalities, including violence and learning deficits. Since these important social effects can only be properly understood by a full appreciation of the advances in evolutionary neuroscience, Masters concludes by calling for an end to academic isolation between the natural and the social sciences.

Following this challenge by Masters, albeit at a different level of integration, the next four chapters also move to a convergence between neural architecture and social interactions. Steven Peterson's chapter opens this section with a discussion of the connection between ancient brain structures and the socially and politically significant phenomena of reification and hegemony. He shows how MacLean's research provides valuable insight for understanding the biological roots of these human social tendencies. Kent Bailey's paper represents his most current application of phylogenetic regression-progression theory. Building on MacLean's three levels of the brain (neocortical, paleo-mammalian, and reptilian), Bailey's theory postulates that human experience, at any given moment, is the product of the dynamic interplay of newer progressive (neocortical) tendencies with older and often more urgent regressive ones. The theory postulates that regression is inherently pleasurable, easily stimulated, and reflects a loss or diminution of higher cortical controls linked to inhibition by social enculturation. Bailey applies his model to explicating the recent school tragedy at Littleton, Colorado.

Gerald Cory's chapter uses the dynamic interaction of MacLean's three-level concept to develop reciprocal algorithms of behavior, based upon the tug and pull of ego and empathy, neocortical representations of early vertebrate self-preservational programming, and later evolved mammalian affectional program-ming. Cory argues for the shaping effect of this neural architecture upon social exchange, economics, and political institutions. The chapter by Daniel Levine and Nilendu Jani applies contributions from the perspective of neural and cognitive modeling to triunian theory. They construct and report preliminary testing of a neural network model that simulates the dynamic interaction of the ego-empathy reciprocal algorithm. Inclusively, the three chapters show potential for convergence toward a multidimensional model of individual and social interaction.

The concluding chapter sums up the several convergences indicated by the previous chapters, assesses the current state of MacLean's contribution, and focuses appropriate questions toward the frontiers of research and theory.

REFERENCES

Damasio, A. (1999) *The Feeling of What Happens.* NY: Harcourt, Inc.

Lieberman, P. (2000). *Human Language and Our Reptilian Brain*. Cambridge, MA: Harvard University Press.

MacLean, P. D. (1990) *The Triune Brain in Evolution: Role in Paleocerebral Functions*. NY: Plenum.

Panksepp, Jaak and Jules B. Panksepp. (2000). "The Seven Sins of Evolutionary Psychology." Pp. 108–131 in *Evolution and Cognition*. Vol 6, No 2.

Science. 1990. *Review* of MacLean's *The Triune Brain in Evolution* V. 250 (Oct 12), 303–305.

PART I

PERSPECTIVES

1

PRIBRAM AND MACLEAN
IN PERSPECTIVE

Karl H. Pribram

Shortly after accepting a position at Yale University in 1948 in John Fulton's department of physiology as director of a "lobotomy project" sponsored by the Veteran's Administration, I was for the first time introduced to the politics of academe. Politics at Yale were serious. Yale is a prestigious university and therefore attracts ambitious individuals—that included me. But I was totally unprepared for what I had to deal with. At one time I wrote Karl Lashley for advice. His reply was simple: "You need to decide whether you want to do politics or do science." I chose to do science.

The politics arose from my initial success in relating frontal lobe anatomy, physiology, and behavior to the limbic forebrain (Fulton, Pribram, Stevenson & Wall 1949; Kaada, Pribram & Epstein 1949; Pribram, Lennox & Dunsmore 1950; Lennox, Dunsmore, Epstein & Pribram 1950, reviewed by Pribram 1954, 1961). As a result, pressure was put on me and on John Fulton by the Veterans Administration to add personnel to the project. As a result, among those who joined the project was Paul MacLean, who had obtained his M.D. and was taking a postdoctoral year at the Massachusetts General Hospital. He had asked to come to Yale because we were doing just the kind of work he was interested in.

My colleagues warned me that the newcomers would take over and that they would usurp our carefully initiated research. They predicted that MacLean would be known for the anatomical and physiological research on the limbic forebrain, and that the psychologists would assert their territorial prerogative on the neurobehavioral studies of the frontal and temporal lobes. I heeded Lashley's advice and concentrated on the research, but this was not easy. I informed Fulton when he returned from Europe of what I had been told and that I felt that we should go ahead with the new appointments despite these dire predictions. Trained psychologists would certainly be a great help in enlisting the advice and cooperation of the excellent people in the psychology department and Paul

MacLean's interests and mine were so compatible that I was sure it would be a joy to have him collaborate.

MacLean and I did a series of experiments together. He was a delightful companion, and it was a joyous experience all around. We continued the chemical stimulation studies begun by Warren McCulloch, Gerhardt Bonin and Percival Bailey, concentrating on the medial and basal cortex which they had not been able to reach (MacLean & Pribram 1953; Pribram & MacLean 1953). We worked with monkeys, with acallosal opossums (they really smelled awful), and found the cortical region (orbitofrontal and perirhinal) excited by electrical stimulation of the vagus nerve. But then, when it came to writing up our results, we encountered great difficulty. MacLean's gift for naming, though often useful in promoting ideas, seemed to me to be applied rather rashly: The term "limbic" used by Paul Broca (his Grande Lobe Limbique) was at that time restricted to the cortex of the cingulate gyrus. My friend and mentor Jerzy Rose was dead set against extending the term to the entire mediobasal rim of the hemisphere. MacLean's persuasion won the day, and I happily supported his enterprise since I had shown a commonality of physiological effects from electrical stimulation of the entire region and a commonality of effects on behavior from resections of the variety of anatomical structures that comprised the Grande Lobe (Pribram 1954; Pribram 1958a; Pribram & Bagshaw 1953; Pribram & Fulton 1954; Pribram & Kruger 1954).

Another term that MacLean coined was the "schizophysiology" of cortical processing. This term was based on the finding we obtained using strychnine neuronography: Although much of the neocortex had an input to the hippocampus, there was apparently no direct output from the hippocampus to the neocortex. This was an important finding, which I have used recently in trying to model the functions in learning of the hippocampus. The term schizophysiology never attained the recognition it deserved, partly because chemical stimulation of the cortex, that is, strychnine neuronography, went out of fashion.

But all did not go so smoothly with the term "visceral brain." On the basis of the work that Livingston, Ward, Kaada, Epstein and I had done to show that electrical excitation of the mediobasal cortex produced changes in respiratory and heart rate, in blood pressure (and later in gastrointestinal activity), MacLean coined the term the "visceral" brain to apply to the limbic forebrain. This resonated with established views.

James Papez had pronounced his famous (limbic) circuit to be responsible for emotions. William James had popularized the James-Lange theory that emotions were due to feedback to the brain from the viscera when they were engaged by a stimulating event. Walter Cannon and P. Bard had critiqued James' theory and replaced it with a thalamic theory. Lashley had critiqued the Cannon-Bard theory as similarly flawed. Papez and MacLean came to the rescue: The limbic system, not the thalamus nor the viscera per se, was responsible for our emotions—though both (hypo)thalamus and viscera are critically involved because of their connections to the limbic brain.

But I had reservations. These stemmed from a patient I had described who had localized seizures of sweating (a viscero-autonomic response) induced by a localized tumor in the classical precentral motor cortex (Bucy & Pribram 1943).

I had enlisted Patrick Wall to use the same stimulation technique I had used to map the mediobasal (limbic) motor cortex to map viscero-autonomic responses from the lateral cortex. We aimed to discern whether the lateral and mediobasal responses could be distinguished as to which were more para-sympathetic and which were more sympathetic. We were unable to make such a distinction, but the experiments did demonstrate that the mediobasal motor cortex is not the exclusive cortical regulator of the viscero-autonomic system (Wall & Pribram 1950). In fact, our data supported Papez's view that emotions were attitudes that involved the entire body, including the somatic as well as the visceral musculature.

The lack of exclusivity of viscero-autonomic control by the mediobasal cortex made it inappropriate to call the limbic forebrain a visceral brain. Nor could I go along with the uncritical acceptance of the James-Lange viscerally based theory of emotions. MacLean and I agreed to seriously disagree on this point and did so publicly on several occasions.

Some years later, my experiments discovered the importance of the amygdala to the habituation of the orienting response. My colleague Muriel Bagshaw and I used visceral and autonomic indicators and showed that when viscero-autonomic activity failed to be involved in generalized orienting, the response failed to become habituated (Bagshaw, Kimble & Pribram 1965; Kimble, Bagshaw & Pribram 1965; Pribram, Reitz, McNeil & Spevack 1979). Orienting to novelty was, as the experiments of Eugene Sokolov had shown, due to a mismatch between an established representation of the familiar, a neuronal model, and the current sensory input. (Sokolov and Luria had visited my new laboratories at Stanford University when I received an appointment there in 1959.) MacLean's intuition was not so far off after all. However, viscero-autonomic processing had more to do with the familiarization and valuation of episodes of experience based on familiarity, a kind of memory process, than it has to do with emotional feeling per se.

By the end of the 1970s, I endorsed Nina Bull's attitude theory of emotions to which Lashley had alerted me. I found out her theory was also supported by James Papez in a chapter of her book (Bull 1951/1968). The attitude theory's biological base included not only visceral manifestations but also endocrine and, importantly, somatic muscular responses to social and other environmental situations, and therefore practically the entire brain (Pribram 1970, 1980).

Another and perhaps the most widely known "name" that MacLean proposed is that of the triune brain. The idea for a division of the brain into a core, a limbic, and a neo- set of systems came about after World War II. Before that time the techniques available divided the central nervous system horizontally: spinal, brain stem, isolated forebrain and decorticated preparations were ordinarily studied. By contrast, during the 1940s and 1950s, three groups of investigators began to study the brain "from the inside out." Magoun and Lindsley, first at Northwestern University in Chicago and then at the University of California in Los Angeles, dropped electrodes into the reticular formation of the brain stem and stimulated as well as lesioned this core system. The concept of a reticular activating system as distinct from a "shell" of sensory-motor relays emerged and became the focus of a number of popular explanations of mind-brain relationships.

At the Montreal Neurological Institute, Wilder Penfield and Herbert Jasper studied "recruiting" of rhythmic bursts of forebrain electrical activity by stimulation of the midline and intralaminar nuclei of the diencephalon. The results led them to propose a "centrencephalic locus" for management of mental functioning.

Finally, at Yale I developed surgical techniques to expose the medial and basal surfaces of the forebrain so that we could (1) electrically and (2) chemically stimulate these limbic formations to (3) record electrically from them and to (4) resect them to study the effects of such resections on the behavior of nonhuman primates. MacLean joined me in the chemical stimulation experiments which, as noted, provided basic insights into the relationship between the convexal and frontal cortex with limbic formations. I reviewed these studies in 1960 in the *Annual Review of Psychology* (Pribram 1960). MacLean added to the conceptualizations derived from these studies by bringing to bear phylogenetic considerations. In this he was in tune with the earlier pre-war theorizing with an added emphasis on the structures of the limbic forebrain.

It is with respect to the naming of the three parts of the "triune brain" that I could not agree: Reptilian (later called the R complex), Mammalian and Primate capture what MacLean meant it to—phylogenetic "growth spurts" in brain development. At the same time, however, the names hide two important aspects of brain phylogenetic development: innovative origin and current endpoint. Major innovations occurred in amphibians as they adapted to life on land. It is these innovations that subsequently make up the R complex. C. Judson Herrick in his book on *The Brain of the Tiger Salamander* chronicles these innovations.

The origins of limbic structures, both archi- and paleo-structures, actually antedate some of those in the R complex—e.g., elasmobranch fishes (sharks) already possess rudimentary hippocampal tissues. As to current development, each of the parts of the triune brain have neo-accretions. The outermost parts of the basal ganglia—those giving rise to the cellular migrations that form adjacent areas of cortex have been implicated in behavioral processes similar to those of the overlying cortex; e.g., trial unique tasks for anterior frontal cortex and the head of the caudate nucleus; visual discrimination tasks for the inferotemporal cortex and the underlying putamen (see review in Pribram 1991, Lectures 7 & 10).

Each of the structures of the limbic forebrain also has neo-accretions with regard to their involvement in behavior. Anatomically these paralimbic neocortical accretions make up the juxallocortex. I reviewed these anatomical, physiological and behavioral data in several publications during the 1950s (Pribram 1958a; Pribram 1958b; Pribram 1961; Pribram & Kruger 1954).

In summary, there is good reason to partition the brain from inside out. However, when it comes to the relationship of core, mid, and outer parts to behavior, the segmentation is more appropriate to a division between extero-ceptive, somatic and hedonic with all of the parts partaking of each division. The further out from the core, the more refined (discriminable) the processes that are involved.

The MacLean-Pribram collaborations, both agreements and divergences, provide an excellent window on the scientific process. Differences in aptitude, style, and technical facility make for differences in how problems are approach-ed and how results are interpreted. Historically the Pasteur-Koch confrontations and those of Freud and Jung have been well documented. What I believe has been different in the MacLean-Pribram adventures is that Paul, through his charm and graciousness, has made it possible for us to remain friends despite what have often been painful differences. Over a lifetime we have been proved pretty much even in who's "right" and who's "wrong." In closing, it appears from MacLean's recent writings (the past decade) endorsing ideas such as quantum neurodynamics (MacLean 1990, 1997) and mine (Pribram 1971, 1991, 1999) that we have reached the same way of thinking about what has concerned us most—how brain processes contribute to our conscious experience.

REFERENCES

Bagshaw, M. H., Kimble, D. P. & Pribram, K. H. (1965) The GSR of monkeys during orienting and habituation after ablation of the amygdala, hippocampus and inferotemporal cortex. *Neuropsychologia*, 11, pp. 111–119.

Bucy, P. C. & Pribram, K. H. (1943) Localized sweating as part of a localized convulsive seizure. *Archives of Neurology & Psychiatry*, 50, pp. 456–461.

Bull, N. (1951/1968) *The Attitude Theory of Emotion. Nervous and Mental Disease Monographs Series*, No. 81. NY: Johnson Reprint Corporation.

Fulton, J. F., Pribram, K. H., Stevenson, J. A. F., & Wall, P. (1949) Interrelations between orbital gyrus, insula, temporal tip and anterior cingulate gyrus. *Transactions of the American Neurological Association*, pp. 175–179.

Kaada, B. R., Pribram, K. H. & Epstein, J. A. (1949) Respiratory and vascular responses in monkeys from temporal pole, insula, orbital surface and consulate gyrus. *Journal of. Neurophysiology*, 12, pp. 347–356.

Kimble, D. P., Bagshaw, M. H. & Pribram, K. H. (1965) The GSR of monkeys during orienting and habituation after selective partial ablations of cingulate and frontal cortex. *Neuropsychologia*, 3, pp. 121–128.

Lennox, M. A., Dunsmore, R. H., Epstein, K. A., & Pribram, K. H. (1950) Electrocor-ticographic effects of stimulation of posterior orbital, temporal, and cingulate areas of Macaca Mulatta. *Journal of Neurophysiology*, 13, pp. 383–388.

MacLean, P. D. (1990) *The Triune Brain in Evolution: Role in Paleocerebral Functions.* New York: Plenum.

MacLean, P. D. (1997) The brain and subjective experience: Question of multilevel role of resonance. *The Journal of Mind and Behavior,* Vol. 18, Nos. 2 & 3, pp. 247 [145] 268 [166].

MacLean, P. D. & Pribram, K. H. (1953) Neuronographic analysis of medial and basal cerebral cortex. I. Cat. *Journal of Neurophysiology*, 16, pp. 312–323.

Pribram, K. H. (1954) Concerning three rhinencephalic systems. *Electroencephalo-graphy & Clinical Neurophysiology*, 6, pp. 708–709.

Pribram, K. H. (1958a) Comparative neurology and the evolution of behavior. In A. Roe & G. G. Simpson (Eds.), *Behavior and Evolution*. New Haven: Yale University Press, pp. 140–164.

Pribram, K. H. (1958b) Neocortical function in behavior. In H. F. Harlow & C. N. Woolsey (Eds.), *Biological and biochemical bases of behavior*. Madison: University of Wisconsin Press, 1953, pp. 151–172.

Pribram, K. H. (1960) A review of theory in physiological psychology. *Annual Review of Psychology*, 11, pp.1–40.

Pribram, K. H. (1961) Limbic System. In D. E. Sheer (Ed.), *Electrical Stimulation of the Brain*. Austin: University of Texas Press, pp. 311–320.

Pribram, K. H. (1970) Feelings as monitors. In M. B. Arnold (Ed.), *Feelings and Emotions*. NY: Academic Press, pp. 41–53.

Pribram, K. H. (1980) The biology of emotions and other feelings. In R. Plutchik & H. Kellerman (Eds.), *Emotion: Theory, Research & Experience, Vol. 1: Theories of Emotion*. NY: Academic Press, pp. 245–269.

Pribram, K. H. (1971) *Languages of the Brain: Experimental Paradoxes and Principles in Neuropsychology*. Englewood Cliffs, NJ: Prentice-Hall; Monterey, CA: Brooks/Cole, 1977; NY: Brandon House, 1982.

Pribram, K. H. (1991) *Brain and Perception: Holonomy and Structure in Figural Processing*. Mahwah, NJ: Lawrence Erlbaum Associates.

Pribram, K. H. & Bagshaw, M. (1953) Further analysis of the temporal lobe syndrome utilizing front-temporal ablations. *Journal of Comparative Neurology*, 99, pp. 347–375.

Pribram, K. H. & Fulton, J. F. (1954) An experimental critique of the effects of anterior cingulate ablations in monkey. *Brain*, 77, pp. 34–44.

Pribram, K. H. & Kruger, L. (1954) Function of the "olfactory" brain. *Annals of the New York Academy of Science*, 54, pp. 109–138.

Pribram, K. H., Lennox, M. A., & Dunsmore, R. H. (1950) Some connections of the orbito-fronto-temporal limbic and hippocampal areas of Macaca mulatta. *Journal of Neurophysiology*, 13, pp. 127–135.

Pribram, K. H. & MacLean, P. D. (1953) Neuronographic analysis of Medial and basal cerebral cortex. II. Monkey. *Journal of Neurophysiology*, 16, pp. 324–340.

Pribram, K. H., Reitz, S., McNeil, M. & Spevack, A. A. (1979) The effect of amygdalectomy on orienting and classical conditioning. *Pavlovian Journal of Biological Science*, 14, pp. 203–217.

Wall, P. D. & Pribram, K. H. (1950) Trigeminal neurotomy and blood pressure responses from stimulation of lateral central cortex of Macaca Mulatta. *Journal of Neurophysiology*, 13, pp. 409–412.

2

REAPPRAISING MACLEAN'S TRIUNE BRAIN CONCEPT

Gerald A. Cory, Jr.

INTRODUCTION

Paul D. MacLean is a scientific thinker well ahead of his time. Following his deeply held interest in the larger questions of human life, he started out studying philosophy. Being unable to find satisfactory answers to questions such as the origin and meaning of life—why humans in spite of their unrivaled intelligence often behaved in seemingly irrational ways threatening their individual as well as species survival—he turned to medicine and the study of the human brain. He anticipated the brain, as the biological substrate of these behaviors, held the key to better understanding of these fundamental questions as well as hopefully their answers.

MacLean was, for many years, chief of the Laboratory of Brain Evolution and Behavior of the National Institute of Mental Health. In 1952, drawing upon the nineteenth century French scientist Paul Broca's designation of the great limbic node that surrounded the brain stem of mammals, he introduced the conceptual term "limbic system" into the neuroscientific literature. In 1968 he introduced the concept of the triune brain, which became widely popularized after the publication of Carl Sagan's rather overly dramatic and simplified discussion of it in *The Dragons of Eden* (1977). MacLean, further developing the triune brain concept, which aroused great interest in psychiatry, education, and the lay public, produced his detailed and highly documented volume, *The Triune Brain in Evolution: Role in Paleocerebral Functions* in 1990.

THE TRIUNE BRAIN CONCEPT AND ITS CRITICS

MacLean's triune brain concept has been acknowledged the single most influential idea in neuroscience since World War II (e.g., Durant in Harrington 1992: 268). Nevertheless, following the publication of his 1990 opus, MacLean received highly critical reviews in two prominent science periodicals, *Science* (October 12, 1990: 303–305) and *American Scientist* (September–October 1992: 497–498). Both reviews were written by neurobiologists who claimed that MacLean's triune brain concept has had limited acceptance or been largely ignored by professional neurobiologists.[1]

Anton Reiner, at that time a recent graduate, wrote the *Science* review, the more extensive of the two. After initially recognizing MacLean as a trailblazer of neuroscience, whose triune brain concept has been well-received outside the field of brain research, as the centerpiece of Sagan's popular, *The Dragons of Eden*, and frequently as the only discussion of brain evolution in psychiatry and psychology textbooks, Reiner makes several points critical of the triune brain concept.

He notes firstly that since MacLean introduced the concept, there has been tremendous growth in neuroscientific research that has greatly extended our knowledge of brain function and evolution. This statement carries the general implication, which Reiner later makes explicit, that the concept is out of date.

Second, in initiating a criticism of MacLean's concept of the limbic system, Reiner writes: "MacLean's presentation of the role of the hippocampus in limbic functions is not well reconciled with the current evidence that the hippocampus plays a role in memory" (1990: 304).

Third, Reiner contends that current research indicates that MacLean's reptilian complex is not a reptilian invention but seems to be present in vertebrates all the way back to jawless fishes.

Fourth, Reiner asserts that MacLean overreaches the evidence when he claims that the basal ganglia are the neural seat for the control of species-typical types of behaviors.

Fifth, Reiner states that the limbic system, a widely used term MacLean authored as a pioneer neuroresearcher, is not properly represented by MacLean. Contrary to MacLean, as Reiner would have it, the limbic system did not appear first in early mammals. Amphibians, reptiles, and birds also have limbic features such as the septum, amygdala, a different-looking hippocampal complex, and maybe even a cingulate cortex.

Sixth, Reiner maintains that MacLean assigns the functions of parental behavior, which Reiner claims that MacLean regards as uniquely mammalian, to the mammalian cingulate cortex, ignoring the fact that some reptiles (crocodiles), all birds, and possibly even some extinct reptiles (dinosaurs) also engaged in parental behavior.

Seventh, Reiner makes a couple of other criticisms of MacLean concerning (a) his preference for correspondence over the more evolutionarily appropriate concept of homology and (b) his apparently uncritical acceptance of Haeckel's idea that ontogeny recapitulates phylogeny.

Finally, although Reiner praises MacLean's motives and acknowledges the appeal of the triune brain concept for dealing with "big" behaviors that we are all interested in, such as: "How does our animal heritage affect our behavior? Why do we do the things we do? Why can we not live together more harmoniously?," he feels that there are some telling shortcomings, as recited above, in MacLean's scholarship. He concludes that "neuroscience research *can* (emphasis mine) shed light" on these important human questions, "though *perhaps* (emphasis mine) not in as global and simple a way as MacLean has sought"(1990: 305).

CRITIQUING THE *SCIENCE* CRITIQUE

Book reviews because of their very nature are usually overly brief and usually cannot deal in depth with the points they take issue with. Reviewers, then, are often themselves guilty of the same kinds of oversimplifications and misinterpretations that they seek to expose in their reviews. When Reiner states "I strongly believe the triune-brain idea to be wrong," he is caught up in the same oversimplifying tendency that he claims unjustifiably to find troublesome in MacLean.

The triune brain concept may be wrong in some of its particulars, right in others, but still be very useful and valid in its more general features. After all, at this stage of our knowledge of the brain, although it is quite advanced over the 1960s and 1970s, there are not a great number of things we can say with absolute confidence—very few generalizations that are without arguable interpretations of more detailed research data. Further, Reiner takes apart but does not offer a replacement generalization. His analysis is destructive, not constructive. This type of analysis is the easy part of the job. Almost anybody can do it.

However in his apparent eagerness to discredit and take apart MacLean's useful generalization, Reiner also fails to study his subject closely and therefore engages in some very careless scholarship. He makes significant omissions, outright errors, and substantial misrepresentations of MacLean's work. Let's look at the points Reiner raises one by one.

1. Reiner blatantly misstates the facts when he claims that the triune brain concept as well as MacLean's book are outdated and lack up-to-date documentation. Reiner's first point (i.e., that there has been a great growth in knowledge about the brain since MacLean first announced his triune brain concept in the 1960s and 1970s) implies that MacLean has left the concept untouched and undocumented since that time and has therefore not considered any of the more recent findings. The implications of this statement are belied by the currency of research cited by MacLean and included in his discussions. To back up his case for the alleged outdated ideas and data in the book, Reiner baldly states "only a handful of papers from the '80s' are cited" (Reiner 1990: 305). This categorically false statement is easily contradicted by a count of bibliographic items. The bibliography of this work contains over 180 entries (a big handful indeed!) that date from 1980 to at least 1988 and over 220 entries that date between 1975

and 1979. This amounts to at least 400 entries of rather recent documentation—keeping in mind that the publication date of MacLean's book and Reiner's review was for both 1990.

2. Reiner misstates or ignores the facts when he says, "MacLean's present-ation of the role of the hippocampus in limbic functions is not well reconciled with the current evidence that the hippocampus plays a role in memory." The phrasing of this statement implies that MacLean is unaware of or fails to report on the extensive research indicating the role of the hippocampus in memory. Such an implication is totally unwarranted. MacLean devotes fully two chapters to reporting and discussing such research. These chapters even have "memory" in their titles. Chapter 26 is titled *Microelectric Study of Limbic Inputs Relevant to Ontology and* *Memory* (emphasis mine). Chapter 27 is titled *Question of Limbic Mechanisms Linking a Sense of Individuality to* *Memory* (emphasis mine) *of Ongoing Experience.* These chapters deal at length with the role of the hippocampus in memory and propose an integrative role for the hippocampus in tying learning to affect or emotion (For a summary of MacLean's discussion on these matters, consult 1990: 514–516).

3. Claiming that the reptilian complex is not a reptilian invention, Reiner misrepresents MacLean's position. On this third point, Reiner contends that current research indicates that MacLean's reptilian complex is not a reptilian invention but seems to be present in vertebrates all the way back to jawless fishes. This is largely a taxonomic question. At what point do we declare something to be a fish, an amphibian, an amniote, a reptile, or a mammal? And do we view mammals as branching off from the amniote tree before we have distinct reptiles in the line of descent? Or do we prefer the more likely probab-ility that mammals descended in a line from the ancient mammal-like reptiles of the predinosaur Permian-Triassic periods called therapsids, who represent a branching of the ancient reptile line (cotylosaurs). Therapsids appeared approxi-mately 230 millions years ago, and approximately 50 million years before the emergence of the great dinosaurs of the Jurassic and Cretaceous periods.

MacLean knows these facts and clearly acknowledges them, while support-ing a lineage for mammals that traces back to the therapsids, of the synapsida subclass that branched off from the diapsida line that eventually produced the great dinosaurs many years later. This is the standard position in evolutionary theory today. One might wish to compare the phylogenetic tree in MacLean (1990: 34) with Butler and Hodos (1996: 72), Strickberger (1996: 396), and Hickman et al. (1984: Fig. 27.1). And it is the accepted position of standard zoology texts (e.g., Miller & Harley 1992; Hickman et al. 1984, 1990). Mam-mals, and ultimately us humans, then, did not evolve from dinosaurs but from a parallel lineage that split much further back in geologic time.

If the term reptilian brain or reptilian complex causes confusion with modern reptiles, and because the reviewers don't wish to read MacLean's work closely, the reptilian complex could be thought of, and perhaps redesignated, as the ancient amniote complex or even the early vertebrate complex. And, of course, as MacLean acknowledges thoroughly, this early brain complex is *not* the reptilian brain of modern reptiles but it is also not the same as that of the early vertebrates, amniotes, or therapsids. At several points in his book, MacLean makes this unequivocally clear by his reference to stem reptiles (cotylosaurs) (MacLean 1990: 33, 82), those early reptiles from which both the diapsid and synapsid lines branched off. To ensure the proper evolutionary context, MacLean also uses the term "protoreptilian" in his initial definition and adds the clarifying comment that he refers to the reptilian complex (or R-complex) only for brevity's sake (see MacLean 1990: 15–16, 244, 519). This protoreptilian, or stem reptile brain has been altered by modifications that include those produced by differentiation and elaboration of earlier structures (e.g., see MacLean 1990: 243). These modifications, to include differentiations and elaborations, provide, in addition to their previous maintenance and behavioral functions, neural circuitry in support of the enhanced limbic structures of mammals. These enhanced mammalian limbic structures necessarily engage and enhance prior circuitry in the brain stem. And together these enhanced limbic and brain stem circuits provide support for the greatly enhanced neocortex (or isocortex) which eventually got modifications sufficient to permit language and the development of complex technological societies.[2]

4. Reiner misrepresents MacLean's position on the basal ganglia. Reiner says he knows of no one other than MacLean who believes the basal ganglia to be the neural seat for the control of species-typical types of behaviors (1990: 305). This statement is a misrepresentation of MacLean's position as well as an admission of ignorance on the part of Reiner. In the first place, MacLean never uses the inclusive term "neural seat." Further, MacLean is not talking about all species-typical behavior but only some. He specifically excludes from this discussion such mammalian class/species-typical behavior as maternal nursing and play, which are attributed primarily to other brain parts and treated in other chapters of the book.

In Part II on the *Striatal Complex with Respect to Species-Typical Behavior*, MacLean repeatedly emphasizes that the traditional view that the striatal complex is primarily involved in motor functions represents an oversimplification. He writes that the purpose of the present investigation is to test the hypothesis that the striatal complex plays an "essential" role in certain species typical behaviors as well as certain basic forms of behavior common to both reptiles and mammals (MacLean 1990: 243). At one point after reciting the evidence, MacLean says that the results "suggest that the medial globus pallidus (a structure of the basal ganglia) is a site of convergence of neural systems involved in the species-typical mirror display of gothic-type squirrel monkeys" (MacLean 1990: 189). Also, a little further on, MacLean tells us that "findings indicate that in animals as diverse as lizards and monkeys, the R-complex is *basically involved* (emphasis mine) in the organized expression of species typical, prosematic communication of a ritualistic nature" (1990: 189).

Additional research, some predating others postdating Reiner's review and of which Reiner is apparently ignorant, adds further support to MacLean's hypothesis. For example, J. Wayne Aldridge and colleagues from the University of Michigan in a research report titled "Neuronal Coding of Serial Order: Syntax of Grooming in the Neostriatum,"(1993) conclude that there is "direct evidence that the neostriatum *coordinates the control* (emphasis mine) of rule-governed behavioral sequences." This study builds upon a series of earlier studies of species-typical grooming behavior of the rat (e.g., Berridge & Fentress 1988; Berridge & Whishaw 1992; Cromwell & Berridge 1990). These earlier and more recent studies certainly support MacLean's hypothesis that the striatal complex plays an essential role in some species typical behaviors of a ritualistic nature.

And, of course, there is the growing body of clinical evidence, going well back into the 1970s and 1980s, that neurological disorders in humans (such as Parkinson's, Huntington's, and Tourette syndromes) that involve damage to the neostriatum produce specific deficits in the sequential order of movement, language, and cognitive function (e.g., Holthoff-Detto et al. 1997; Cummings 1993; Benecke et al. 1987; Marsden 1982, 1984; Oberg & Divac 1979). Such serial order patterns in behavior are phylogenetically old as well as pervasive and often constitute the basis of identifying so-called species-typical behaviors. Greenberg, this volume, who did early work with MacLean, provides a comprehensive update of the research on the striatum.

5. Reiner misrepresents the facts when he claims that MacLean says the limbic system first appeared in mammals. MacLean does not claim that the limbic system first appeared in early mammals. He acknowledges that limbic features appear in fishes, reptiles, and birds, but are rudimentary and poorly developed when compared with those of mammals (MacLean 1990: 247, 287). According to MacLean's view, then, it is not the presence or absence of limbic features themselves in ancestral amniote or reptilian vertebrates, but rather the significant and prominent development of limbic features in mammals that is appropriately of interest in understanding the evolution of characteristically and uniquely mammalian behavior. Further, care must be exercised in making comparisons across existing modern species. We can only infer that the structures and undeveloped and/or rudimentary homologues of such structures in modern species were also present in ancestral lines. Brains do not fossilize, so the point cannot be made conclusively. The currently accepted inferential position in neuroscience is that there are homologues of limbic structures going well back into vertebrate history, although these homologues in modern species are often difficult to establish and sometimes downright dubious (Striedter 1997; Veenman et al. 1997).[3]

6. Reiner displays careless scholarship and misrepresents the facts of neuroscience, evolution, and animal behavior as well as MacLean's position on parental behavior and the cingulate cortex. He claims that MacLean assigns the functions of parental behavior to the cingulate cortex and that MacLean regards parental behavior as uniquely mammalian. According to Reiner, MacLean's alleged position "ignores the fact that some reptiles, such as crocodiles, and all birds engage in parental behavior, not to mention the possibility suggested by paleontological data that some extinct reptiles, namely dinosaurs, also engaged in parental behavior"(Reiner 1990: 305).

Such a blanket claim makes one wonder if Reiner felt it worth his while to even consult the book he is reporting on. First, MacLean does not "assign" parental behavior to the cingulate cortex. Instead he reports the recent (at that time) research on maternal mechanisms in the septal or medial preoptic area (MacLean 1990: 351–353) and indicates that this area may have provided the initial potentiality for full scale mammalian maternal behavior (MacLean 1990: 354), that would include play and the development of empathy. The very title of his Chapter 21 is *Participation* (emphasis mine) *of Thalamocingulate Division in Family-Related Behavior*. Participation is participation not unilateral and unequivocal assignment. And MacLean uses the systemic term "thalamocing- ulate" to indicate intra-limbic nuclei and cortical connections, not simply cingulate cortex as Reiner states. MacLean cites good evidence for thalamo- cingulate participation in "nursing, conjoined with maternal care"(MacLean 1990: 380). After all, lesions in certain portions of the cingulate cortex interfere with nursing and other maternal behavior (Stamm 1955, Slotnick 1967), not with blanket parental care as Reiner asserts.

Perhaps it may be too early or simply erroneous in neuroscience to assign anything specifically and finally to any exclusive part of the limbic area. More likely there is some localization of minor function, but for most behaviors of any scale there seems to be fairly wide-ranging neural circuitry that may be inter- rupted by lesions at many different points. For example, recent research on maternal behavior (nursing, retrieval, nestbuilding) in rats has focused on the medial preoptic area with its connections to other limbic structures and the brain stem (Numan 1990). Alison Fleming and her colleagues (1996), summarize what we know about the neural control of maternal behavior. Not only the medial preoptic area with its brain stem projections, but also other limbic sites are involved, including the amygdala (Numan et al. 1993; Fleming et al. 1980), hippocampus (Terlecki & Sainsbury 1978; Kimble et al. 1967), septum (Fleischer & Slotnik 1978), and cingulate cortex (Slotnik 1967, Stamm 1955).

Most emotions, emotional behaviors, and emotional memories seem to be distributed, involving multiple pathways. Specific behaviors and categories of behaviors can be interrupted by lesions at varying points in these multiple pathways. More recent research has again confirmed that the cingulate cortex is involved in emotion and motivation (Stern & Passingham 1996). In a recent research report John Freeman and colleagues conclude that the neural circuitry formed by interconnected cingulate cortical, limbic thalamic, and hippocampal neurons has fundamentally similar functions in the affective behaviors of approach and avoidance (Freeman et al. 1996).

Like any good scientist with an open mind, MacLean, at the close of his chapter on participation of the thalamocingulate division in family-related behavior, calls for more neurobehavioral research to explore the extent of this participation (MacLean 1990: 410). It is also noteworthy that MacLean is one of the few thinkers in neuroscience who shows concern for the neural substrate of such family-based behavior, characteristic of mammals, as play and the underpinning but illusive quality of empathy. Although such characteristics have been reported on behaviorally (e.g., for play, see Burghardt 1988, 1984; Fagen 1981), they have largely been ignored in the search for neural substrates, not because they are unimportant, but because of the extreme difficulty in defining and objectifying them. But the evidence clearly points to neocortical as well as limbic cortical and subcortical representation (e.g., see Fuster 1997: esp. 169; Frith 1997: 98; Frith 1989: 154–155). Recent reports by Damasio (1999), Panksepp (1998) and Carter et al. (1997) provide hope that mainstream neuro-science will direct more serious research toward a better understanding of these difficult and ignored questions which are so critical to a full understanding and appreciation of humanity.

Reiner also indiscriminately uses the blanket term "parental behavior" coupled with attributing that same blanket usage to MacLean. In this usage, Reiner shows a remarkable deficit of scholarship, naivete, or both. MacLean is not discussing all parental behavior. He is discussing those nurturing behaviors that are the most distinguishing characteristic of mammals and a fundamental part of their taxonomic classification and differentiation from birds and reptiles. These behaviors must be found in either new structures or modifications to existing structures. As Butler and Hodos point out, new structures may be added to organ systems, but modification of existing structures appears to be more common (1996: 86). The jury is still out on the neurophysiology of these defining mammalian behavioral features. What is more, with the emphasis on cognition in neuroscience, until very recently surprisingly little attention has been paid to the extensive work on the neural and hormonal basis of the motivational and emotional aspects of maternal care. This is openly acknow-ledged by leading scholars in the brain science field (e.g., Rosenblatt & Snowden 1996; LeDoux 1997: 68; Kandel, Schwartz & Jessell 1995). The previously cited works by Panksepp (1998) and Carter et al. (1997) represent a step in the right direction.

The blanket term "parental care" as used by Reiner in his criticism of MacLean amounts to condemnation by indiscriminate generalization. Parental care has been defined by a leading authority as "any kind of parental behavior that appears likely to increase the fitness of the parent's offspring" (Clutton-Brock 1991: 8). This very broad and inclusive term includes even nest and burrow preparation. The very production of eggs is included. This kind of "parental care" is found in the earliest vertebrates with very primitive brains indeed. If the all-inclusive definition of parental care can be stretched to include the production of eggs and digging a hole to place them in, perhaps it could conceivably be stretched to include even the sharing of cellular .membranes during asexual reproduction by single-celled organisms.

But specifically, what about parental care in modern reptiles? Contrary to Reiner's claim, MacLean reports on parental care in crocodiles (MacLean 1990: 136–137) and also in some species of skink lizards (MacLean 1990: 136, 248–249). A recent review article on parental care among reptiles by Carl Gans of the Department of Biology, University of Michigan, brings us up to date. Gans claims that the most spectacular example of reptilian parental care takes place among crocodiles. Both parents respond to the call of hatchlings who vocalize underground while emerging from the eggs. The adults dig them up and transport them to water in their large buccal pouch (Pooley 1977). The young are then washed and stay shortly in association with the adults. After a relatively brief period, however, the juveniles' response to the adults reverses. The juveniles disperse suddenly into small, nearby channels where they may dig themselves tunnels. Gans notes: "In view of the fact that crocodylians may be *cannibalistic* (emphasis mine), there seems to be both an inhibition of cannibalism in the parents and an inhibition of a possible adult avoidance reaction in the neonates" (1996: 153).

This kind of short-lived parental care during which the cannibalism of parents is inhibited may be impressive in reptiles, but it is a far, far cry from the highly developed family-related behavior in mammals; behavior that is so further developed in the human species that it extends often throughout an entire lifetime and becomes the basis for a vastly extended social life. The *equating* of parental care in reptiles with parental care in mammals is simply ludicrous. It is this mammalian family behavior that concerns MacLean, and the neural substrate is appropriately sought in the brain modifications that became prominent with the appearance of mammals.

7. Reiner's further inaccuracies: recapitulation, homology, and correspondence, and so on. Near the end of his review Reiner makes the following isolated statement: "MacLean also errs in his apparent sweeping acceptance of Haeckel's idea that ontogeny recapitulates phylogeny" (1990: 305). Again, Reiner distorts and misrepresents. From a close review of the book it is by no means clear that MacLean "sweepingly" accepts Haeckel's concept. In fact he only refers to it once (MacLean 1990: 46), while at the same time noting the well-known exceptions. Haeckel's concept has been largely superceded in neuroscience today by the principles of von Baerian recapitulation. The von Baerian version holds that while ontogeny does not recapitulate phylogeny in the thoroughgoing Haeckelian sense, it does recapitulate the features of an organism in terms of the organism's general to more specific classification. In other words, the von Baerian principles state that the more general features of an organism develop before the more specific features do (Butler & Hodos 1996: 51–52). The issue, however, is still not so clearly settled. The emergent discipline of evolutionary developmental biology is looking more closely into such questions (Hall 1992; Thomson 1988). For instance, evolutionary biologist Wallace Arthur, in summarizing the main themes of this emerging discipline, writes: "No single comparative embryological pattern is universally found or can be described as a 'law'. Von Baerian divergence, its antithesis (convergence) and a broadly Haeckelian (quasi-recapitulatory) pattern can all be found, depending on the comparison made"(1997: 292).

On the additional point that MacLean prefers to think in terms of correspondence rather than homology probably reflects his functional-behavioral orientation. In fact it is specifically in discussing the issue of the relationship between structure and behavior that (MacLean 1990: 37) makes this comment. Later, he returns to a more standard use of homology (MacLean 1990: 228). There is, in fact, presently no sure-fire way of demonstrating that homologues have the same one-to-one functions or produce the same one-to-one behaviors across species. In reporting that MacLean, at one point, expresses preference for the term "correspondence" because of the confusion in the definition of homology, Reiner shows what can only be considered a misplaced and sophomoric "gotcha" exuberance. He writes that MacLean's comment "should leave Stephen J. Gould, not to mention all other students of evolution, aghast," adding that such a comment constitutes a "very critical misjudgment to make in a work on evolution."(Reiner 1990: 305).

This is truly a naive, if not preposterous statement by Reiner. Could it be that Reiner is not aware of the long history of the pervasive problems associated with the definition of homology? For example, Leigh Van Valen, of the biology department of the University of Chicago, in the first sentence of his frequently referenced article on homology and its causes, writes: "Homology is the central concept of anatomy, yet it is an elusive concept" (1982: 305). Further on, in view of the persistent definitional ambiguities, Van Valen practically equates the two terms "homologue" and "correspondence" when he writes: "In fact, homology can be defined, in a quite general way, as *correspondence* (emphasis mine) caused by a continuity of information," although in a footnote Van Valen admits that correspondence itself needs further definition beyond the scope of his paper (305: fn. 1; cf. Roth 1994). Although there has been some sharpening of the concept of homology, with emphasis on phyletic continuity, the ambiguities have by no means been adequately resolved (Gehring 1998; Trevarrow 1998; Striedter 1998; Arthur 1997: 171–177; Hall 1994, 1996). The study of molecular biology and the genome is adding further insights into the conservation of homologues from very early life forms indeed (e.g., see Gehring 1988; C.U.M. Smith, this volume).

And there remains the haunting question that is still wide open for research and investigation: Do most homologous behaviors share a homologous structural basis or can homologous behaviors be rooted in nonhomologous structures? (see Hall 1996: 29: fn. 23). The recent report by William Blessing on the lower brain stem emphasizes the question of multiple neural representations of body parts and behavior, in that behavior originally represented and controlled in the brain stem of an earlier vertebrate may maintain its brain stem representation, but be controlled by an added representation in the frontal cortex of a more highly developed mammal. Such multiple representations at different levels as the brain became more complex would certainly confuse the issue of a straightforward homologous match of structure and function (1997: 1–18; see also, Brown 1977).

Research on very limited aspects of function is often suggestive but far from conclusive even on such limited function. Establishing homologues of the prefrontal cortex can be particularly vexing. A recent research article by Gagliardo and colleagues, "Behavioural effects of ablations of the *presumed* (emphasis mine) 'prefrontal cortex' or the corticoid in pigeons" (Gagliardo et al. 1996), indicates, not only in its discussion and conclusions, but in the very title itself, the uncertainty, ambiguity, and cautions that currently characterize such research efforts (see also Fuster 1997: 7–11).

An awful lot of assuming goes on in some quarters of neuroscience on this issue, which simply cannot be settled at this time based on the empirical evidence. This is one of the problems and cautions that must be acknowledged when generalizing across species, say from rats to humans. In maternal behavior, for example, can we say factually that the medial preoptic area plays the same part in the maternal behavior of humans that it does it the rat brain? No, we cannot. At least not yet. But neuroscientists, after first hedging themselves, and following homologous logic, seem inclined to think so. Nevertheless, it is entirely within the realm of possibility that we may find that it does so only in part or not at all. As neuroresearcher Joseph LeDoux notes: "Some *innate* (emphasis mine) behavioral patterns are known to involve hierarchically organized response components" (1996: 120). And further on he adds: "Species differences can involve any brain region or pathway, due to particular brain specializations required for certain species-specific adaptations or to random changes"(1996: 123). And neurologist Richard Restak points out that in the case of animals, multiple limbic areas may increase, modify or inhibit aggression. He notes further that even the same area may increase or inhibit responses under different experimental conditions and depending on the animal selected for experiment. As an example, he points out that the destruction of the cingulate gyrus (a limbic component) increases aggressive behavior in cats and dogs, whereas, on the contrary, such an operation has a calming effect in monkeys and humans (1994: 149).

Or perhaps, as Blessing notes, there are multiple representations. Then we might have to go to correspondence rather than homology (even homoplasy might not apply, since homoplasy, or parallel evolution, would probably not apply in such closely related species) to account for the behavioral circuitry. In other words, the corresponding neural circuitry—that circuitry controlling maternal behavior—may be found in the same, slightly differing, multiple, or perhaps (though highly unlikely) even totally different structural homologues or modifications.

In fact, if homology is correct and functionally, to include behaviorally, uniform—that is, the same structures account for the same functions and behaviors across classes, orders, and species—this finding would support the triune brain concept as set out by MacLean, which says generally that the protoreptilian complex common to both reptiles and mammals functions largely the same in both classes. This finding would also support MacLean's position that the expanded circuitry areas of the mammalian complex bear characteristically mammalian functions and are the circuitry for characteristically mammalian behaviors, such as nursing; a defining taxonomic feature of mammals (which, in part distinguishes them from reptiles and birds).

In a final series of somewhat gratuitously negative comments, Reiner writes about some of MacLean's legitimate speculations. For example, Reiner states "and mathematical skill (he thinks the cerebellum could be involved)"(Reiner 1990: 305).

And why not? See MacLean's discussion on the subject (MacLean 1990: 548–552). Recent research indicates that the cerebellum is not just a motor mechanism, but is also likely involved in higher cognitive and perhaps even language function. Especially relevant is the rather well-supported hypothesis that indicates a cerebellar mechanism involved in all tasks that require precise temporal computations. This could well suggest an involvement in mathematical processes. True, the evidence is insufficient to permit firm conclusions as to the cerebellar role in higher cognitive processes, but it is a research direction that needs further refinement and is currently pursued by a number of neurobiologists (Daum & Ackermann 1995; Dimitrov et al. 1996; Altman & Bayer 1997: esp. 749–751).

Overall, given the outright errors, careless scholarship, misrepresentations, and sophomoric, prejudicial tone of Reiner's review, it probably should never have been allowed to appear in a publication of the stature and influence of *Science.* Such reviewing should perhaps raise questions of standards in the academic-scientific community.

REVIEW BY CAMPBELL IN AMERICAN SCIENTIST

The review by Campbell in *American Scientist* (1992) is a much shorter review than that of Reiner. It brings up some of the same points, but is less prejudicial in its tone. Since it is less detailed it expresses primarily the preferences and value judgements of the reviewer. Campbell repeats Reiner's erroneous charge about outdatedness. He writes: "that except for a very few papers, most of the references were published prior to 1980" (1992: 498). I have already noted that this "handful" of items amounts to more than 180 citations. One suspects that Campbell proceeded from his preconceptions and found what he expected to find. Campbell ends his review with the statement: "Unfortunately, the data presented are, *to some degree* (emphasis mine), outdated, and the evolutionary reasoning is unsophisticated" (1992: 498). The use of the term "unsophisticated" by the reviewer is totally unwarranted. For anyone who has closely read MacLean's detailed and thoughtful work, the evolutionary reasoning is, on the contrary, quite thoughtful, well-presented, and sophisticated. Such blanket judgments tell us more about the sociology of neuroscience and neuroscientists that they do about the subject matter of the discipline itself.

COMMENTS OF BUTLER AND HODOS

In their recent comprehensive and overall admirable work on comparative vertebrate anatomy, Butler and Hodos attempt to formalize the assignment of MacLean's work to the relics of history. Their comments reflect the standard oversimplified criticisms, misrepresentations, and errors that have become popular to repeat ever more unreflectively. Butler and Hodos assign the triune brain concept, inaccurately and indiscriminately, to a category they call "theories of addition." And without any detailed discussion or analysis of the very significant, indisputable points of accuracy in MacLean's concept, they write that the past three decades of work in comparative neurobiology "unequivocally" contradicts MacLean's theory (1996: 86).

How incredible that two such qualified authors should accept the same flagrant misrepresentations, inaccuracies, and oversimplifications of MacLean's work that have become commonplace in some sectors of neurobiology over the past decade. They seemingly merely parroted the errors and misrepresentations of Reiner and others rather than reading MacLean's 1990 work closely and open-mindedly. There is no point in repeating the responses given earlier to Reiner's review. The same points hold for Butler and Hodos' comments. The rebuttal points are clearly made and easily accessible to verification by anyone who chooses to make the effort. The categorical statement by Butler and Hodos that the extensive body of work in comparative neurobiology over the past three decades unequivocably contradicts MacLean's theory, which they apparently have not read, constitutes on that point poor, if not irresponsible, scholarship.

MACLEAN'S TRIUNE BRAIN CONCEPT: UTILITY AND VALIDITY

The triune brain concept may have its limitations. But its shortcomings have been patently misrepresented in some cases and grossly exaggerated in others. Whatever its faults may ultimately prove to be, the triune brain concept gets at a fundamental evolutionary pattern. The mammalian modifications, differentiations, and elaborations to the early vertebrate and ancestral amniote brains had the effect of introducing endothermy (warm-bloodedness), maternal nursing, enhanced mechanisms of skin contact and comfort, as well as enhanced visual, vocal, and other cues to bond parents to offspring and serve as the underpinning for the extended and complex family life of humankind. The mammalian modifications, therefore, added greatly enhanced affectional, other-interested behavior to the primarily (although not exclusively) self-preservational, self-interested behaviors of ancestral amniotes and early vertebrates (not necessarily their modern representatives).

The simplistic representation and attempted demolition of MacLean's triune brain concept is not good science. Reiner's review, where it has any validity at all, is like discovering a termite or two in the bathroom wall, and then proceeding to pronounce a full alarm that the house is full of termites, only to find that it is necessary to treat a few boards in the subflooring. Further, in his deconstructive, analytic fervor, Reiner has offered no alternative higher level generalization. The review represents a dysfunction common to a lot of scientific practice, that of an analytical approach that takes apart but can't put back together. Perhaps we should call it analytic myopia. Uninterested in the bigger questions of humanity that we so desperately need help on, and lacking an interest in therapy, these analytic myopics continue their fine-grained focus. Fine-grained focus is fine, laudable, and very much needed. It becomes analytically myopic, however, when it fails to place in context what it finds and defines, when it employs sloppy scholarship, and when it attempts prejudicially to destroy or deconstruct that which it lacks the imagination and courage to put together.

On the other hand, the theories of brain evolution that Butler and Hodos review favorably and the synthesis that they present at the end of their book focus on the immunohistological, hormonal, and morphological mechanics

(1996: 463–473). They say, in fact, almost nothing at all about behavior or the significance for behavioral evolution of the various mechanisms of evolution they identify. And they make no attempt whatsoever to confront the larger behavioral questions of humanity where we need help and guidance from neuroscience in defining the neurobiological basis of human nature in order to establish links up the scale of generalization with the social sciences. The theories they present are only of interest to the technical aspects of neuroscience. They are not, however, incompatible, but tend to support MacLean's concepts when these concepts are accurately and thoughtfully considered.

The key point in comparing these theories with that of MacLean's is that they are comparable, at best, only in part. They ask and respond to different questions. MacLean tries to address the larger questions of human nature and behavior. The others show no interest in such questions but address the fine-grained technical questions of anatomical and functional evolution. At the level where they meet, they do not contradict each other but are largely compatible. At the point where they diverge, they primarily address different questions. This is, I think, the root of the tension between the two. MacLean's concept facing up the scale of integration is useful and has been appropriately well received in the therapeutic sciences, and is also very useful for the social sciences. On the other hand, it has not been, but may yet become, more useful and better received in other quarters of neuroscience, especially when subjective experience is eventually given its due in the study of consciousness. There are, in fact, recent signs that the importance of subjective experience, which is of great interest to MacLean, is gaining fuller recognition in the newer studies of consciousness (Damasio 1994, 1999; Smith 1996: 471–474; Searle 1997; Edelman & Tononi 2000, Cory 2000a,b).

The triune brain concept may need modification, then, as the body of neuroscience grows—but certainly not outright rejection. With appropriate clarifications, it is still by far the best concept we have for linking neuroscience with the larger, more highly integrated concepts of the social sciences. This is true even if its level of integration has limited utility for some neuroscience researchers who are doing ever more fine-grained research into neural architecture and function.

The transitions from early vertebrate to amniote to synapsid reptile to mammal were in behavioral effect transitions from nearly exclusively self-preserving organisms with relatively little or less complex social life to, at least in part, a nurturing, "other-maintaining," "other-supporting," or "other-interested" organism. And that makes all the difference in the world for human evolution. Our other-maintaining mechanisms combined with our self-preserving ones provide the biological glue as well as the dynamic for our remarkable behavioral evolution, our social life, and ultimately the crucial social and political factor of our moral consciousness.

The qualitative differences between the familial and social behaviors of even the most caring of reptiles (say, modern crocodiles), birds or social insects and the mammal we call human are overwhelmingly evident. Humans with their social, cognitive, and language skills, for better or for worse, dominate the planet and no other species comes close. Any neurobiologist who cannot see or appreciate the difference suffers from analytic myopia or some form of misplaced species egalitarianism (cf. Butler & Hodos 1996: 3–4). The proper study of humans is humans and to some extent their lineal ancestors. The triune brain concept integrates some fundamental patterns out of much that is yet unknown and uncertain in neuroscience. And this generalization, when properly understood, appreciated, and applied, is the most useful bridging link, thus far articulated, between neuroscience and the larger and pressingly critical questions of humanity's survival, as well as the hoped for transformation of humanity into a truly life-supporting, planet-preserving and enhancing custodial species.

When other neuroscience researchers reach the conceptual point in their grasp of the discipline that they feel an increasing obligation to take a more integrative view and proceed to move up the scale of generalization in order to confront the larger questions of human life, they will likely produce concepts closely resembling the triune brain. Homology and behavioral evolution will almost inevitably take them in that direction. Frankly, despite its current lack of popularity in some quarters of neurobiology, I think that the triune brain concept will continue to be influential, and with appropriate modifications as research progresses, provide an important underpinning for interdisciplinary communication and bridging. The chapters constituting this volume amply demonstrate its heuristic value and it integrative utility.

NOTES

1. A highly favorable review of MacLean's 1990 book was written by Emre Kokmen, M.D., of the Mayo Clinic, Rochester, Minnesota, in *Journal of Neurosurgery*. V. 75, Dec, 1991, p. 998. In this chapter I focus on the reviews in *Science* and *American Scientist* because they have reached a wider audience and have become red flag reviews unjustifiably inhibiting the thoughtful application of the triune brain concept in related fields as well as in the psychological and social sciences.

2. The use of the term "additions" is deliberately avoided here because it has been the source of some confusion (see Butler & Hodos 1996: 86). New brain structures do not spring de novo out of nowhere but rather evolve from the differentiation of previously existing structures. When differentiations become sufficiently established, they are often referred to loosely as "additions." This does not deny that seemingly new additions may possibly and occasionally arise, but the intent here is to emphasize the phylogenetic continuity that underpins the concept of homology.

3. The accuracy and utility of the concept and term "limbic system" has itself been a separate topic of some disagreement in recent years. Some authors state that it does not represent a truly functional system and that the term should be discarded. Others defend its use. Most texts continue to find the term useful and because of its longtime usage it will probably remain in the literature. Some recent and prominent scholars illustrate the controversy well. Pierre Gloor of the Montreal Neurological Institute, McGill University, in his thoroughgoing work *The Temporal Lobe and Limbic System*, by the very use of the term in the title indicates his position. Further on in the text, while acknowledging the controversy he writes that this system in mammals exhibits an organization that is

sufficiently different from that characterizing other areas of the cerebral hemisphere to merit such a designation (Gloor 1997: 106).

And well-known neurologist Richard Restak tells us that based upon a large body of experimental work, it is appropriate to conclude that, "depending on the areas stimulated, the limbic system serves as a generator of agreeable-pleasurable or disagreeable-aversive affects" (1994: 143). Nevertheless, there is little agreement among neuroscientists concerning the contributions of the different components, and their mutual influence on each other (1994: 149).

On the other hand William Blessing, a neuroscientist at Flinders University, in his study of the lower brain stem, feels that emphasis on the limbic system has detracted from the study of brain stem mechanism, that it has been "plagued by its anatomical and physiological vagueness and by the lack of precision with which the term is used" (Blessing 1997: 15). Further, he thinks the term should be dropped from the literature (Blessing 1997: 16).

A third recent author, neuroscientist Joseph LeDoux (1996: Ch. 4) argues that because the limbic system is not solely dedicated to the single global function of emotion, a claim that MacLean fully recognizes in his chapters on memory (1990: Chs: 26 & 27), that the concept should be abandoned. LeDoux apparently prefers a single functional criterion for the definition of a system, whereas MacLean seems to prefer a combination of functional and anatomical criteria. Le Doux concludes his argument by stating: "As a result, there may not be one emotional system in the brain but many" (1996: 103). Compare this with the concluding line of the definitional description by Kandel et al., authors of the most widely used textbook on neuroscience and behavior: "The limbic system contains neurons that form complex circuits that play an important role in learning, memory, and emotion"(1995: 708).

The use and value of the conceptual term "limbic system," then, seems to depend on one's research focus and how one chooses to define a system. It might be added that the definition of what constitutes a system is controversial in all disciplines, not just in neuroscience.

REFERENCES

Aldridge, J., Berridge, K., Herman, M., and Zimmer, L. 1993. "Neuronal Coding of Serial Order: Syntax of Grooming in the Neostriatum." *Psychological Science*. V. 4, N. 6 (Nov): 391–395.

Altman, J. and Bayer, S. 1997. *Development of the Cerebellar System: In Relation to its Evolution, Structure, and Functions*. NY: CRC Press.

Arthur, Wallace. 1997. *The Origin of Animal Body Plans: A Study in Evolutionary Developmental Biology*. Cambridge: Cambridge University Press.

Benecke, R., Rothwell, J., Dick, J., Day, B., and Marsden, C. 1987. "Disturbance of Sequential Movements in Patients with Parkinson's Desease." *Brain*. V. 110: 361–380.

Berridge, K. C. and Fentress, J.C. 1988. "Disruption of Natural Grooming Chains after Striatopallidal Lesions." *Psychobiology*. V. 15: 336–342.

Berridge, K. C. and Whishaw, I.Q. 1992. "Cortex, Striatum, and Cerebellum: Control of Serial Order in a Grooming Sequence." *Experimental Brain Research*. V. 90: 275–290.

Blessing, William W. 1997. *The Lower Brainstem and Bodily Homeostasis*. Oxford: Oxford University Press.

Brown, Jason. 1977. *Mind, Brain, and Consciousness*. NY: Academic Press.

Burghardt, G. 1988. "Precocity, Play and the Ectotherm–Endotherm Transition." Pp. 107–148 in *Handbook of Behavioral Neurobiology.* V. 9. Ed. by E. Bass. NY: Plenum.

Burghardt, G. 1984. "On the Origins of Play." Pp. 5–41 in *Play in Animals and Humans.* Ed. by P Smith. NY: Basil Blackwell.

Butler, Ann B. and Hodos, William. 1996. *Comparative Vertebrate Neuroanatomy: Evolution and Adaptation.* NY: Wiley-Liss.

Campbell, C. B. G. 1992. "Book Review (MacLean: The Triune Brain in Evolution)." *American Scientist.* V. 80 (Sept-Oct 19): 497–498.

Carter, C. S. Lederhendler, I., and Kirkpatrick, B. (Eds.). 1997. *The Integrative Neurobiology of Affiliation.* NY: Annals of the New York Academy of Sciences. V. 807.

Clutton-Brock, T. H. 1991. *The Evolution of Parental Care.* Princeton, NJ: Princeton University Press.

Cory, Gerald A., Jr. 2000a. "From MacLean's Triune Brain Concept to the Conflict Systems Neurobehavioral Model: The Subjective Basis of Moral and Spiritual Consciousness." *Zygon Journal of Religion and Science.* V. 35. N.2.: 385–414.

Cory, Gerald A., Jr. 2000b. *Toward Consilience: The Bioneurological Basis of Behavior, Thought, Experience, and Language.* NY: Kluwer Academic/ Plenum.

Cory, Gerald A., Jr. 1999. *The Reciprocal Modular Brain in Economics and Politics: Shaping the Rational and Moral Basis of Organization, Exchange, and Choice.* NY: Kluwer Academic/Plenum.

Cory, Gerald A., Jr. 1997. "The Conflict Systems Behavioral Model and Politics: A Synthesis of Maslow's Hierarchy and MacLean's Triune Brain Concept with Implications for New Political Institutions for a New Century." *Annals of the American Political Science Association.*

Cromwell, H. C. and Berridge, K. C. 1990. "Anterior Lesions of the Corpus Striatum Produce a Disruption of Stereotyped Grooming Sequences in the Rat." *Society for Neuroscience Abstracts.* V. 16: 233.

Cummings, Jeffrey L. 1993. "Frontal-Subcortical Circuits and Human Behavior." in *Archives of Neurology* V. 50 (Aug): 873–880.

Damasio, A. 1999. *The Feeling of What Happens.* NY: Harcourt, Inc.

Damasio, A. 1994. *Descarte's Error: Emotion, Reason, and The Human Brain.* NY: Grosset/Putnam.

Daum, Irene and Ackermann Hermann. 1995. "Cerebellar contributions to cognition." in *Behavioural Brain Research.* 67: 202–210.

Dimitrov, M.; Grafman, J.; Kosseff, P.; Wachs, J.; Alway, D.; Higgins, J.; Litvan, I.; Lou, J.; and Hallett, M. 1996. "Preserved cognitive processes in cerebellar degeneration." *Behavioural Brain Research.* 79: 131–135.

Edelman, G. and Tononi, G. 2000. *A Universe of Consciousness.* NY: Basic Books.

Fagen, R. 1981. *Animal Play Behavior.* NY: Oxford University Press.

Fleischer, S. and Slotnik, B.M. 1978. "Disruption of maternal behavior in rats with lesions of the septal area." *Physiological Behavior.* 21: 189–200.

Fleming, A.; Morgan, H.; and Walsh, C. 1996. "Experiential Factors in Postpartum Regulation of Maternal Care." Pp. 295–332 in *Parental Care: Evolution, Mechanisms, and Adaptive Intelligence.* Ed. by J. Rosenblatt and C. Snowden. NY: Academic Press.

Fleming, A.; Vaccarino, F.; and Leubke, C. 1980. "Amygdaloid inhibition of maternal behavior in the nulliparous female rat." *Physiological Behavior.* 25: 731–743.

Freeman, J.; Cuppernell, C.; Flannery, K.; Gabriel, M. 1996. "Limbic thalamic, cingulate cortical and hippocampal neuronal correlates of discriminative approach learning in rabbits." *Behavioural Brain Research.* 80: 123–136.

Frith, Uta. (1993) 1997. "Autism." Pp. 92–98 in *Scientific American: Mysteries of the Mind*. Special Issue V. 7, N.1.

Firth, Uta. 1989. *Autism: Explaining the Enigma*. Cambridge, MA: Basil Blackwell.

Fuster, J. 1997. *The Prefrontal Cortex: Anatomy, Physiology, and Neuropsychology of the Frontal Lobe*. Third Edition. NY: Lippincott-Raven.

Gagliardo, A.; Bonadonna, and F.; Divac, I. 1996. "Behavioural effects of ablations of the presumed 'prefrontal cortex' or the corticoid in pigeons." *Behavioural Brain Research*. 78: 155–162.

Gans, Carl. 1996. "An Overview of Parental Care among the Reptilia." Pp. 145–157 in *Parental Care: Evolution, Mechanisms, and Adaptive Intelligence*. Ed. by J. Rosenblatt and C.Snowden. NY: Academic Press.

Gehring, Walter J. 1998. *Master Control Genes in Development and Evolution: The Homeobox Story*. New Haven: Yale University Press.

Gloor, Pierre. 1997. *The Temporal Lobe and the Limbic System*. Oxford: Oxford University Press.

Hall, B.K. 1996. "Homology and Embryonic Development." Pp. 1–37 in *Evolutionary Biology*. V. 28. Ed. by M. Hecht, R. MacIntyre, and M. Clegg. NY: Plenum Press.

Hall, B.K., (Ed.) 1994. *Homology: The Hierarchical Basis of Comparative Biology*. San Diego: Academic Press.

Hall, B.K. 1992. *Evolutionary Developmental Biology*. London: Chapman & Hall.

Harrington, Anne. (Ed.) 1992. *So Human a Brain*. Boston: Birkhauser.

Hickman, C.; Roberts, L.; and Hickman, F. 1990. *Biology of Animals*. Fifth edition. Boston: Times Mirror/Mosby College Publishing.

Hickman, C., Roberts, L., and Hickman, F. 1984. *Integrated Principles of Zoology*. Seventh edition. St. Louis: Times Mirror/Mosby College Publishing.

Holthoff-Detto, V.; Kessler, J.; Herholz, K.; Bonner, H.; Pietrzyk, U.; Wurker, M.; Ghaemi, M.; Wienhard, K.; Wagner, R.; Heiss, W. 1997. "Functional Effects of Striatal Dysfunction in Parkinson Desease." *Archives of Neurology*. V. 54(Feb): 145–150.

Kalin, Ned H. 1997. "The Neurobiology of Fear." Pp. 76–83 in *Scientific American Mysteries of the Mind*. Special Issue V. 7, N.1.

Kandel, E R.; Schwartz, J.; and Jessell, T. 1995. *Essentials of Neural Science and Behavior*. Norwalk, CT: Appleton & Lange.

Kimble, D.; Rogers, L.; and Hendrickson, C. 1967. "Hippocampal lesions disrupt maternal, not sexual behavior in the albino rat." *Journal of Comparative Physiological Psychology*. 63: 401–405.

Kokmen, Emre 1991. "Book Review (The Truine Brain in Evolution)." *Journal of Neurosurgery*. Vol. 75 (December): 998.

Krasnegor, N A. and Bridges, R. (Eds.). 1990. *Mammalian Parenting: Biochemical, Neurobiological, and Behavioral Determinants*. Oxford: Oxford University Press.

LeDoux, J. 1997. "Emotion, Memory, and the Brain." Pp. 68–75 in *Scientific American Mysteries of the Mind*. Special Issue. V. 7, N.1.

LeDoux, J. 1996. *The Emotional Brain*. NY: Simon & Schuster.

Leon, M.; Coopersmith, R.; Beasley, L.; and Sullivan, R. 1990. "Thermal Aspects of Parenting." Pp. 400–415 in *Mammalian Parenting: Biochemical, Neurobiological, and Behavioral Determinants*. Ed. by N. Krasnegor and R. Bridges. Oxford: Oxford University Press.

MacLean, Paul D. 1990. *The Triune Brain in Evolution: Role in Paleocerebral Functions*. NY: Plenum.

Marsden, C.D. 1984. "Which Motor Disorder in Parkinson's Desease Indicates the True Motor Function of the Basal Ganglia?" Pp. 225–241 in *Functions of the Basal Ganglia* (Ciba Foundation Symposium 107). London: Pitman.

Marsden, C.D. 1982. "The Mysterious Motor Function of the Basal Ganglia: The Robert Wartenberg Lecture." *Neurology*. V. 32: 514–539.

Miller, S. and Harley, J. 1992. *Zoology*. Duberque, IA: Wm. C. Brown Publishers.

Numan, M.; Numan, M.J.; and English, J.B. 1993. "Excito-toxic amino acid injections into the medial amygdala facilitate maternal behavior in virgin female rats." *Hormones and Behavior*. 27: 56–81.

Numan, M. 1990. "Neural Control of Maternal Behavior," Pp. 231–259 in *Mammalian Parenting: Biochemical, Neurobiological, and Behavioral Determinants*. Ed. by N. Krasnegor and R. Bridges. Oxford: Oxford University Press.

Oberg, R.G.E. and Divac, I. 1979. "'Cognitive' functions of the Neostriatum." Pp. 291–313 in *The Neostriatum*. Ed. by I. Divac and R.G.E. Oberg. Oxford: Pergamon Press.

Panksepp, J. 1998. *Affective Neuroscience*. NY: Oxford University Press.

Ploog, Detlev W. 1992. "Neuroethological Perspectives on the Human Brain: from the Expression of Emotions to Intentional Signaling." Pp. 3–13 in *So Human a Brain*. Ed. by A. Harrington. Boston: Birkhauser.

Pooley, A.C. 1977. "Nest opening response of the Nile crocodile." *Journal of Zoology*. (London). 182: 17–26.

Rosenblatt, J. and Snowden, C. 1996. *Parental Care: Evolution, Mechanisms, and Adaptive Intelligence*. NY: Academic Press.

Reiner, Anton. 1990. "An Explanation of Behavior" (review of MacLean's The Triune Brain in Evolution). *Science*. V. 250 (Oct 12): 303–305.

Restak, Richard M. 1994. *The Modular Brain*. . NY: Charles Scribner's Sons.

Sagan, Carl. 1977. *The Dragons of Eden*. NY: Random House.

Searle, J. 1997. *The Mystery of Consciousness*. NY: NY Times Review of Books.

Slotnik, B. M. 1967. "Disturbances of maternal behavior in the rat following lesions of the cingulate cortex." *Behavior*. 29: 204–236.

Smith, C. U. M. 1996. *Elements of Neurobiology*. 2nd Edition. NY: Wiley.

Stamm, J. S. 1955. "The function of the medial cerebral cortex in maternal behavior in rats."*Journal of Comparative Physiological Psychology*. 48: 347–356.

Stern, C. and Passingham, R. 1996. "The nucleus accumbens in monkeys (Macaca fascicularis): II. Emotion and motivation." *Behavioral Brain Research*. 75: 179–193.

Strickberger, M W. 1996. *Evolution*. Sudbury, MA: Jones and Bartlett Publishers.

Striedter, G. F. 1998. "Stepping into the Same River Twice: Homologues as Recurring Attractors in Epigenetic Landscapes." *Brain, Behavior, and Evolution*. 52: 218–231.

Striedter, G. F. 1997. "The Telencephalon of Tetrapods in Evolution." *Brain, Behavior, and Evolution*. 49: 179–213.

Terlecki, L.J. and Sainsbury, R.S. 1978. "Effects of fimbria lesions on maternal behavior of the rat."*Physiological Behavior*. 21: 89–97.

Thomson, K. S. 1988. *Morphogenesis and Evolution*. Oxford: Oxford University Press.

Trevarrow, Bill. 1998. "Developmental Homologues: Lineages and Analysis." *Brain, Behavior and Evolution*. 52: 243–253.

Van Valen, Leigh M. 1982. "Homology and Causes." *Morphology*. 173: 305–312.

Veenman, C.; Medina, L.; and Reiner, A. 1997. "Avian Homologues of Mammalian Intralaminar, Mediodorsal and Midline Thalamic Nuclei: Immuno-histochemical and Hodological Evidence." *Brain, Behavior, and Evolution*. 49: 78–98.

PART II

MOLECULES, BODY PLANS, AND THE STRIATUM

3

DEEP TIME AND THE BRAIN: THE MESSAGE OF THE MOLECULES

C.U.M. Smith

INTRODUCTION

The hallmark of Paul MacLean's neuroscience is its evolutionary perspective. He was not, of course, the first to recognise that the human brain has a vast evolutionary ancestry. That priority should probably be accorded Herbert Spencer. When he was composing his pioneering *Principles of Psychology* (1855) he wrote to his father that what he was doing was quite new and "alien to preceding psychologists."[1] Much to his chagrin the first edition of the *Principles* fell almost stillborn from the press; the second edition, however, published in 1870/1872, had one very influential reader: John Hughlings Jackson. Jackson became a disciple. He never tired of admitting his debt to Spencer.[2] But neither Spencer nor Jackson left, in the one case the philosopher's study and in the other the neurological ward, to research the behaviour of infrahuman animals in the field. Paul MacLean did. In consequence, he may with justice be regarded as pioneering an approach to understanding the human brain through what might be called evolutionary neuroethology.

MacLean's extensive studies of reptilian ethology helped to provide evidence for his well-known concept of the triune brain. His vision of the mature human brain grows, like that of Herbert Spencer, from a conviction that it has a vast evolutionary history. MacLean has also been touched by the molecular revolution of our times; a revolution that, we may imagine, would have also received the enthusiastic attention of Herbert Spencer and John Hughlings Jackson. MacLean writes of how this revolution has shown us how the cells of our remote ancestors "must have worked" and that "in all animals there are molecular commonalities . . . that carry over into complex molecular assemblies."[3] His clinical understanding is rooted in this evolutionary understanding. Biologists cannot but find this approach appealing. For, as Theodosius Dobzhansky famously said, "nothing in biology makes sense without evolution."

TIME SCALES

I have titled this chapter *Deep Time and the Brain* because the time scales of molecular evolution are far greater than even the 200 million years which MacLean considers in his "palaeopsychology." Indeed, one must increase that vast number by more than an order of magnitude. For the first biological molecules appeared on the surface of the planet well over three thousand million years ago (Figure 3.1). The earliest vestiges of living organisms can be detected in South African and Australian rocks dating back 3.5 billion years BP. It is humbling to realise that the world of bacteria has held tenure on the earth throughout the vast period of time from that day to this. *Homo sapiens* has been around for at most 0.001% of that duration. It took, however, an immense length of time for the next significant development to occur: the origin of the eukaryocytes. No doubt there were many false starts, many unsuccessful ventures, but the earliest eukaryote microfossils date back little further than 1.5 billion years ago.[4] Then evolution accelerates. After the elapse of only about another 0.75 billion years we begin to find the traces of multicellular forms. These take the form of worm tracks and the occasional simple platyhelminth-like worm itself. Then in the Burgess shales of 525 million years ago, and the slightly older Ediacaran outcrops in Australia, we find preserved a remarkable array of metazoan forms. These have been brilliantly described by Stephen Gould in his best-seller, *Wonderful Life*, and by Conway Morris in his equally fascinating book, *The Crucible of Creation*.

MOLECULAR PALAEONTOLOGY

One of the most fascinating developments of recent years stems from the coming together of the centuries-old subject of palaeontology and the up-to-the-minute, laboratory-bound, highly fashionable and highly technical study of molecular biology. For it turns out that the molecules, and not only the molecules but also the molecular systems and cascades on which our bodies depend have locked up in their structure messages from times past. For eyes that can read them they speak of our ancestry and of the vicissitudes of our ancestors. Not all biological molecules, of course. The smaller molecules and even the sometimes quite large lipids and carbohydrates do not bear the imprint of the past. But the molecules that have been called the "informational macromolecules," the proteins and nucleic acids, by that very token, do.

As mutations alter the sequence of nucleotides over geological time so the sequence of amino acids in the proteins for which they code also alter. The situation is not (it never is!) straightforward. Homologous genes within different taxa evolve at different rates; different genes within the same taxa evolve at different rates; different sites within a given nucleotide sequence mutate at different rates: all these (and many other subtleties) make molecular phylogeny, at present, an inexact and controversial science. There is no space here to review these different problems (see reference[5]). Often differential mutation rates have clear functional significance: fibrinopeptides, for instance, evolve comparatively rapidly, histones comparatively slowly; sequences which code for important active sites change only slowly, if at all; sequences which code for functionally unimportant parts of a protein, or for nothing at all, change comparatively rapidly. Neutral mutations play an important role and have, as Kimura and others have shown, to be taken into account.[6]

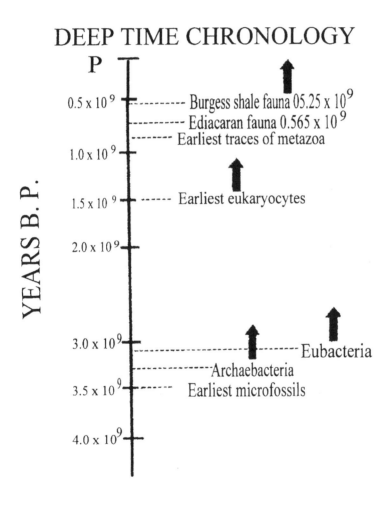

Figure 3.1. Deep Time Chronology of Life

In addition to evolutionary change of nucleotide sequences in the genome, other forces for change are also at work. Again there is no space to discuss them in detail. Suffice it to say that these include exon shuffling, the insertion and deletion of transposons, differential posttranscriptional splicing, RNA-editing, post-translational processing, and so on.[7] A significant neurobiological example is provided by the opioid and opioid-related proteins: alpha, beta and gamma MSH (melanocyte stimulating hormone), ACTH (adrenocorticotropic hormone), beta-endorphin, met- and leu-enkephalin, dynorphin, CLIP (corticotrophin-like intermediate lobe protein), beta-LPH (lipotropic hormone), and so on.[8] All these important neuroactive peptides are derived from three large precursor proteins: pro-opiomelanocortin (POMC) (265 amino acid residues), pre-proenkephalin A (263 amino acid residues) and preproenkephalin B (256 amino acid residues) by posttranslational processes which cut the amino-acid chain at different points. The fact that the precursor proteins are so nearly the same size suggests that they are derived from evolutionarily related genes by differential splicing of mRNA chains after post-transcriptional excision of introns. It turns out that the human pre-proenkephalin A gene is located on chromosome 12 while the POMC gene is found on chromosome 2. It may be that this indicates an episode of transposon shuffling in the evolutionary past. This short example gives a taste of some of the hidden complexity of molecular evolution.

It would be wrong to finish this section without emphasising one very important evolutionary mechanism: gene duplication and deletion. This can occur when homologous chromosomes align themselves imprecisely at meiosis. If a chiasmata forms between the chromatids at this point of misalignment, one of the daughter chromosomes may contain two copies of a given gene and the other will lack that gene altogether. If the gene codes for an important protein, it is unlikely that the daughter cell lacking the gene will survive. The daughter cell containing the duplicated gene will, however, be fully viable. But the selective pressure on one of the two genes in this daughter cell will be reduced. Whilst its twin continues programming a perhaps vital protein it can mutate comparatively freely. Many instances of this are known in molecular biology and, as we shall see, in molecular neurobiology. Indeed there is evidence to suggest that two episodes of large-scale gene duplication, probably duplications of the entire genome, occurred early in vertebrate evolution, one before the divergence of Gnathostomata and the Agnatha, and the other before the divergence of the fish and the tetrapod land fauna.[9]

WHEN DID BRAINS BEGIN?

When did brains begin? The answer to this question depends on what is meant by the term "brain." One is tempted to say as soon as bilaterality evolved. The radial symmetry of the Cnidaria and Ctenophora induces little more than a nerve net. But the so-called "urbilateralia" of 800 million years ago, like all bilateral forms, naturally entered new environments one end pointing forwards. Over time an antero-posterior axis would become established. At some point in the vast Precambrian period, the assembly of morphopoietic genes known as the *Hox* complex developed.[10] This complex then, as now, is responsible for morphological differentiation along the antero-posterior axis. Each segment in our worm-like ancestor came to have a separate identity. Well before the times when the Ediacaran and Burgess deposits were laid down the so-called "zootype," a heterotrophic, bilateral, anteroposteriorly differentiated, form had evolved.

Once the antero-posterior axis had been established sensory cells—chemo-receptors, mechanoreceptors, even photoreceptors—would tend to concentrate on the anterior extremity where new environments were first encountered. The process, which Ariens Kappers termed neurobiotaxis,[11] would then take over. Nerve complexes concerned with the analysis of input from the sensory surfaces would develop in close association with these surfaces. In this process we can see the origin of a major anteriorly placed ganglion, or "brain." Similarly neuro-biotaxis would have ensured that ganglia and their connectives would develop in a longitudinal strip close to the ventral surface, next to the substratum, where tactile and other stimuli would predominate.

It is thus of considerable interest to find that several genes controlling the early development of the neurectoderm of invertebrates (*Drosophila*) show sequence homology with several of those controlling the early development of the neurectoderm in vertebrates (*Xenopus*). Evidently these genetic systems predate the evolutionary schism between the protostomata and the deutero-stomata: an event which occurred at least 750 million years ago. But yet more interestingly it has been shown that these homologous genes control develop-ment of the *ventral* surface in invertebrates (*Drosophila*) and the *dorsal* surface in vertebrates (*Xenopus*).[12] It looks as though the old idea that one of the early events in chordate evolution was a 180° twist so that the nerve cord faces upwards has received confirmation from modern molecular embryology. The twist, presumably, is to be associated with the adoption of a free-swimming life-style in the surface waters of ancient oceans by our chordate ancestors. In this position the major sensory input, light and the shadows of predators and prey, would come from above rather than below.

After these preliminaries let us turn to some particular instances of mole-cular evolution in the brain. I shall start with the ubiquitous "serpentine" 7TM proteins, then look briefly at the molecular designs of voltage—and ligand-gated ion channels, and end with a brief account of the remarkable homogeneity of the molecular processes at work in the early phases of neuroembryology. I hope to leave you with an impression of the depth of the interrelationships between all animal brains, an impression of the huge antiquity of the molecular mechanisms at work, with, in short, the impression which the young Charles Darwin expressed in 1837 in one of his post-*Beagle* notebooks: "animals our fellow brethren in pain, disease, death and suffering . . . we may all be netted together."[13] And this, I feel sure, is also the vision that energised Paul MacLean's thinking in developing his theory of the triune brain.

THE 7TM "SERPENTINE" MOLECULES

This is one of the most ubiquitous of all conformational motifs (see Figure 3.2).

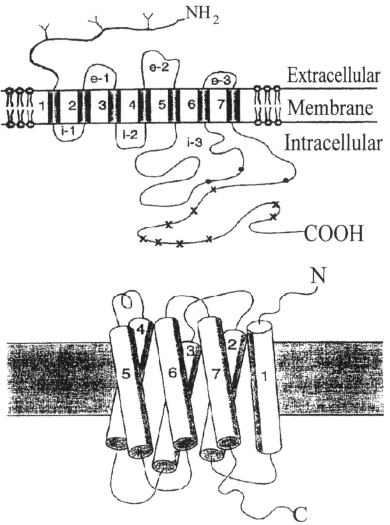

Figure 3.2. Conformation of 7TM "Serpentine" Molecules. In the upper part, the cylinders represent alpha-helical stretches of the molecule. The lower part represents the "barrel of staves" conformation.

In essence the protein contains seven alpha-helical segments. These alpha-helical segments, moreover, consist predominantly of hydrophobic amino acids. They are consequently believed to span the membrane. The upper part shows a plan view. *In vivo* (the lower part) the conformation also makes use of the third dimension to give the so-called "barrel-of-staves" structure.

The most ancient 7TM proteins are found in the halophilic (salt-loving) bacteria. This group of bacteria is classified with the Archaebacteria, which, in being able to survive extreme temperatures, salt concentrations, pH, and so on, is thought to number amongst its members representatives of the earliest life forms on the planet's surface. The membrane of *Halobacterium halobium* can be separated into three fractions: yellow, red, and purple. The purple fraction can be formed into crystalline sheets that can be examined in the electron microscope. In addition to lipids it contains a 26 kDa protein, bacterio-rhodopsin, which because of the crystalline nature of the purple membrane can be subjected to X-ray diffraction. The seven closely packed alpha-helices extending through the membrane can thus be examined in atomic detail.[14] As with other rhodopsins, the opsin apoprotein of bacteriorhodopsin is loosely bound to a retinal chromophore which lies across the tunnel in the centre of the "barrel of staves." It can, perhaps, be seen as a trapped agonist. On receipt of a photon of appropriate wavelength the retinal transforms from an all trans to a 13-cis configuration and transfers a proton from the cytoplasmic to the extracellular side. In contrast to the rhodopsins of vertebrate retinae the retinal does not detach and migrate from its opsin apoprotein to regenerate, nor does it function as a photosensor. In the bacterial membrane it acts as a proton pump.

In the animal kingdom 7TM proteins seem to have evolved in association with second-messenger (especially G-protein) signaling systems. G-proteins are again, exceedingly ancient. They are well known in the prokaryocytes as well as in the eukaryocytes. They constitute a large superfamily whose members all have the ability to dephosphorylate GTP.[15] This enables them to act as molecular time switches. In consequence, G-proteins linked to 7TM membrane receptors are found in many parts of the animal body, not only in many sensory systems but also in the subsynaptic membranes of metabotropic synapses. They are at work, for instance, in alpha and beta adrenergic synapses, muscarinic cholinergic synapses, dopaminergic synapses, the many subtypes of serotinergic (5HT) synapses, in metabotropic glutamate synapses, in many peptidergic synapses, and so on. The neurotransmitter activates a 7TM receptor, which then activates the G-protein system and this, in turn, activates a membrane effector, often adenylyl cyclase, to generate a second messenger, which diffuses away into the cytosol. Some 2 to 3% of the mammalian genome is believed to be devoted to coding different variants of the 7TM conformation. They form a huge evolutionarily related family.[16]

7TM proteins and G-protein signaling systems also constitute the molecular bases of many sensory systems. These include photoreceptor cells, the rods and cones (where the G-proteins are known as transducins), olfactory cells, some, but not all, gustatory cells, and, possibly, some thermoreceptors.[17] We have already touched on bacteriorhodopsin. Let us now look briefly at the rhodopsins of the animal kingdom.

Although rhodopsins form the basis for photoreception throughout the Animalia, invertebrate and vertebrate rhodopsins differ in several ways. For instance, in the vertebrates the chromophore, retinal, on receipt of an appropriate photon, detaches from opsin in order to regenerate the all-trans form. In the invertebrates, in contrast, there is no such detachment. Transformation to the all-trans form takes place *in situ*. There are several other differences in detail to which it would be inappropriate to devote space in this context. Not all animal eyes are, of course, sensitive to the same wavelengths of light. Some can see far into the ultraviolet, others into the infrared. The wavelength to which a visual pigment is maximally sensitive, λ_{max}, is determined by the precise amino-acid make-up of the opsin tunnel surrounding the retinal chromophore.[18,19] The dominant mechanism appears to be interaction of the retinal chromophore with dipolar amino acid side chains in the surrounding helices of the barrel of staves.[20]

Sequence analysis suggests that vertebrate and insect opsins shared a common ancestor over 750 million years ago. Colour vision based on variation in amino acid sequence in the vicinity of retinal has evolved separately in the two lineages. Conway Morris, in his great book on Precambrian palaeontology, *The Crucible of Creation*,[21] suggests that only certain "morphospaces" are available for evolution to exploit. So far as photopigments are concerned, rhodopsin seems to represent the colonisation of one very significant morphospace. Furthermore, variation in amino acid composition, independently hit upon by opsins in the vertebrate and arthropod lines, represents the autonomous discovery and occupation of available subdivisions of the rhodopsin morphospace.

VOLTAGE AND LIGAND-GATED ION CHANNELS

Let us turn from the great superfamily of 7TM, G-protein coupled channels to the equally ubiquitous, equally important, directly operated ion channels. There are two cases: Those that respond to voltage changes across the membrane and those which respond to various ligands; such as Acetylcholine, Glycine, and GABA. The former respond very rapidly (c. 0.5 msec) to changes in voltage across the membrane in which they are situated. These are responsible for all the electrical activity upon which the nervous system depends. The latter, which are equally important, open (though rather more slowly) to allow the passage of ions in response to various chemical ligands.

It has been suggested that the great assemblage of ion channels all originated from the stretch-sensitive channels of prokaryocytes (see Figure 3.3). The latter channels are ubiquitous. All prokaryocytes need some means of sensing and responding to osmotic stress (caused, perhaps, by rain downpours). They also need some means of sensing cell volume in order to trigger cell division. Two such channels have been analysed in molecular detail in *E.coli*: the MscL (mechanosensitive large) channel is unselective; the MscS (mechanosensitive small) channel is anion selective. Stretch-sensitive channels are also well known in the metazoa, though not (yet) at the molecular level.

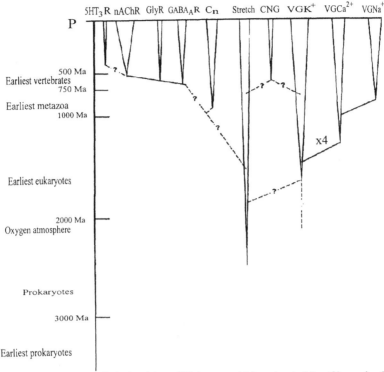

Figure 3.3. Evolutionary Relationships of Voltage and Ligand-gated Ion Channels. Cn = connexin channel; CNG = cyclic nucleotide gated channel; GABA$_A$R = gamma-amino-butyric acid type A receptor; GlyR = glycine receptor; 5HT$_3$R = 5-hydroxytryptamine type 3 receptor; nAChR = nicotinic acetylcholine receptor; VGCa^{2+} = voltage gated Ca^{2+} channel; VGK$^+$ = voltage gated K$^+$ channel; VGNa$^+$ = voltage gated Na$^+$ channel.

The voltage-gated ion channels (VGICs) of metazoan animals form a family of related proteins. The earliest VGICs are the K$^+$-channels succeeded later by Ca^{2+}-channels. Both these channels are found among the protista. The K$^+$ channel is the oldest. The best known type has a 6TM structure with, interposed between the 5th and 6th TM segments, a "hairpin" conformation which is thought to determine the ion-selectivity of the channel. The fully formed K$^+$-channel consists of a group of four of these 6TM units arranged around a pore. The hairpin conformation of each of the four subunits forms the lining of the canal.

Because K$^+$-channels consist of four independently programmed subunits, they show great biochemical and hence biophysical diversity. Different combinations of the variant subunits ensure that more than 20 physiologically different K$^+$-channels are developed. If the small nematode worm *C.elegans* genome is anything to go by many more will be found when the human genome project is complete. Differing populations of these variant K^+-channels go far to ensure that each neuron in the brain is physiologically unique: each has its own "personality."

Figure 3.3 shows that voltage-gated Ca^{2+} and Na^+ channels are thought to be derived from the voltage-gated K^+-channel by two gene duplications. They consist of a single huge protein (over 1800 amino acid residues) made up of four homologous domains each of which resembles a single K^+-subunit. The voltage-gated Na^+-channel has not so far been found in the protista. It appears to have been invented by stem metazoa for long distance signaling (i.e. nerve impulses). It is interesting to note that whilst it is found in the Cnidaria (jelly fish) it is absent from the nervous system of the tiny nematode *C.elegans*.

Figure 3.3 summarises the evolutionary relationships amongst these ion channels as they are presently understood. The expanding triangles of the figure indicate the increasing diversity of each receptor over evolutionary time. This increasing diversity over time was also, of course, a feature of the metabotrobic receptors discussed in the previous section. At least twelve different types of G-protein coupled 5HT receptor are known. The structural and hence biophysical diversity of metabotropic receptors is increased yet further by the heterogeneity of G-protein subunits and second messengers. It is also worth noting in Figure 3.3 that ligands did not gain control over ion channels until quite late in evolutionary history and have subsequently undergone rather rapid and rather huge diversification: 60 subtypes of nACh-R; 40 subtypes of $GABA_A$-R, and so on. When one speaks of "the" nACh-R, for instance, or of "the" 5HT-R, one is not referring to a unique molecular structure such as, for instance, glucose or phenylalanine, but of a whole family of similar molecules. The brain is heterogeneous all the way down.

MOLECULAR EMBRYOLOGY

Molecular embryology is a vast and extremely rapidly developing subject. The early control of the development of dorsoventrality in vertebrates and invertebrates was mentioned in a previous section. It is impossible to do more than merely point to one or two further relevant examples in a chapter such as this. In this section, therefore, I shall merely outline a couple of cases that show, at the molecular level, that animals retain hidden potentialities which can be uncovered in appropriate circumstances. Can we see this as a molecular parallel to Gardner's "psalics"[22] or of MacLean's ideas on the uncovering of what he calls "palaeomentation" in neuropathology? I'd like to mention two cases: the work by Kollar and Fisher[23] on hens' teeth and the recent work on *Pax-6* and eye development.[24, 25]

Kollar and Fisher note that embryonic induction can normally be got to work between tissues of different origin, suggesting that the molecular mechanisms lie latent and conserved. They point out, first, that undifferentiated chick corneal epithelium responds to mouse dermis by producing feathers. Differentiation, in other words, proceeds in a way determined by the genetic repertoire of the responding tissue. But, more interestingly, they provide evidence to show that if mouse dental papilla are combined with chick epithelium, the latter is induced to secrete dentine and enamel and the beginnings of teeth: Something not seen in the avian line since the time of *Archaeopteryx*, more than a hundred million years ago. It seems that the genetic information necessary for producing teeth lies dormant in the chick, awaiting an appropriate trigger. It has not been lost during a hundred million and more years of evolution.

In the last few years molecular genetics has begun to give us other fascinating hints of molecular commonalities. Some of the most interesting work has concerned the ancestry of eyes. The question has often been asked, when reviewing the vast variety of complex eyes developed in the animal kingdom: did all these different designs arise independently, or do they share a common ancestry? The answer may well be provided by study of the molecular biology of early development: it is beginning to look as if a common ancestor can be traced back to before the proterostome/deuterostome divergence some 670 million years ago. The evidence for this remarkable conclusion comes from study of a gene known as *Pax-6*.

Pax-6 is one of a number of genes involved in the early development of eyes. As its suffix number indicates it is a member of a large family of genes which regulate the transcription of other genes. The family plays an important role early in early embryology when its members control the transcription of cascades of other developmental genes. The nomenclature, *Pax*, refers to the fact that these genes all possess a 384 base-pair (bp) sequence which encodes a 128 amino-acid sequence that binds to DNA. This 384 bp sequence is known as the "*pa*ired bo*x*" (hence *Pax*) motif since it was first found in the pair rule genes that determine the early segmentation of *Drosophila* embryos. In addition to the paired domain, all members of the *Pax* family share a highly conserved homeodomain.

Pax-6 has been found in many different species of animal, from humans through insects and molluscs to round worms (nematodes) and ribbon worms (nemertines). In the early vertebrate embryo *Pax-6* expression is at first widely distributed in the central nervous system and it can still be detected in the adult brain, especially in some of the nuclei of the forebrain, the substantia nigra of the midbrain and the granule cell layer of the cerebellum. So far as the forebrain is concerned, its expression becomes largely confined to the regions destined to develop into olfactory (olfactory epithelium, olfactory bulb) and optic (lens, cornea and optic vesicle) structures.

Mutations of *Pax-6* have disastrous effects. In the mouse they cause a condition known as small eye (*Sey*). In the heterozygous condition *Sey* mice eyes have significantly smaller lenses and optic cups. Homozygous *Sey* is lethal. Early mice embryos (9.5 days) show no lens placode and the neural layers of the retina are highly abnormal. The olfactory placode, similarly, fails to develop, and the embryo shows no sign of nasal pits nor an olfactory bulb. Clearly, *Pax-6* plays a crucial role in the early development of eye and nose. Humans, heterozygous for *Sey* suffer from a condition known as *aniridia*. In this condition there is a complete or partial failure of the iris to develop along with other defects including cataract, corneal opacity, glaucoma and so on. The incidence lies between 1/64 000 and 1/96 000. In addition, mutations of *Pax-6* can lead to defects in the anterior chamber of the eye, including opacity of the central cornea, known as Peter's anomaly. In fact, differences in the degree of inactivation of *Pax-6* lead to a large number of ocular defects affecting numerous parts of the eye, especially the anterior chamber.

As indicated above, *Pax-6* is found throughout the animal kingdom. *Drosophila* geneticists have shown that it is possible to transplant the gene into other parts of the embryo insect's anatomy where it will induce "ectopic" eyes. Eyes can be induced in legs, antennae, wings, and so on. The insect can be covered with eyes! These eyes, moreover, are no mere approximations to the real thing. They consist of a full complement of different cells and structures: primary, secondary and tertiary pigment cells, cornea, cone and pseudocone cells, retinula cells with fully developed rhabdomeres, and so on. The cells are organised to form ommatidia and are electrically active. It is not yet known, however, whether the optic nerve fibres project to the correct regions of the insect's brain. Here, then, is a striking instance of latent morphopoietic mechanisms waiting to be triggered or "uncovered" in insect cells.

Further work has shown that *Pax-6* extracted from embryo mice will also induce ectopic eyes (not, of course, mouse eyes!) in *Drosophila*. Finally, it has been found that *Pax-6* from squid, normally essential in the early development of cephalopod's highly evolved eye, can also induce ectopic eyes in *Drosophila*. These eyes, again, are anatomically almost normal. Both squid and mouse eyes are vesicular eyes bearing no obvious resemblance to the compound eyes of arthropods.

All of these findings appear to point in one direction. They suggest that very early in the evolution of the animal kingdom, perhaps at the stage represented by the urbilateralia, a genetic system evolved to program the development of complex eyes. This system has remained, essentially unchanged, at the basis of all the huge variety of different complex animal eyes. Instead of a polyphyletic origin it may be that all eyes, above the level of simple eyes (eyespots), or ocelli, have a unitary origin. At the time of writing the jury is still out. But, taken together with the other evidence from molecular biology discussed above, the story of the *Pax-6* gene reinforces the gathering vision of a remarkable unity in diversity throughout the animal kingdom. We look down through more than half a billion years and recognise ourselves.

CONCLUSION

In this chapter, I have briefly reviewed a few salient examples of the molecular evolution of the brain. With the huge torrent of data deluging from the laboratories of molecular biology, our understanding of the evolutionary past of the human brain is bound to increase dramatically in the twenty-first century. It is not only the human genome project that is nearing completion, but we shall soon have complete data on the mouse, *Mus*, the fruit fly, *Drosophila*, the Zebrafish, *Danio*, and so on. The total genome (10, 099 genes; 97 Mbp) of the nematode, *Caenorhabditis elegans*, was published in 1998.[26] It appears that over 30% of the genome codes for the nervous system. Neurotransmitter receptors, synthesis and release systems, all show remarkable molecular similarity to those found in *Homo sapiens* and other mammals. The genome contains genes for over 80 VGK^+ channels, 9 $VGCa^{2+}$ channels and some 90 neurotransmitter-gated channels (LGICs).[27]

Locked up in the deluge of data from the molecular biology and molecular neurobiology labs will be many messages detailing the evolutionary history of the brain. Messages which will make those described in the foregoing pages pale into insignificance. Nevertheless, even our present understanding reminds us, at the molecular level, of MacLean's theory. The molecular mechanisms at work in our brains, the synaptic receptors and ion channels upon which that neurophysiology is built, reach back deep into time, to origins in the precambrian. Their molecular sequences speak to us of the relatedness of all living forms. Locked up in within them are messages which hint at dramatic events in the remote past: such as the genome duplications mentioned earlier. Molecular embryology, furthermore, reveals that ancient systems persist, often overlaid by more recent strata, but still waiting for, and capable of, being triggered or uncovered by appropriate stimuli. Does this not remind us, at the molecular level, of Paul MacLean's evolutionary neurobiology and evolutionary neuro-psychiatry? We are thus, I believe, fully justified in concluding that the message of the molecules is entirely consistent with his vision. The human brain is conditioned by, and bears the mark of, the "vast backward and abysm" of evolutionary time.

NOTES

1. Spencer, Herbert, 1855, *The Principles of Psychology,* London: Longman, Brown, Green and Longmans; see also C.U.M. Smith, 1982, "Evolution and the Problem of Mind, Part 1: Herbert Spencer," *Journal of the History of Biology,* 15, 55–88.

2. See Smith, C.U.M., 1982, "Evolution and the Problem of Mind, Part 2: John Hughlings Jackson," *Journal of the History of Biology,* 15, 241–262.

3. MacLean, P.D., 1990, *The Triune Brain in Evolution: Role in Paleocerebral Functions.* New York: Plenum, p.13.

4. Maynard Smith, J. and E. Szathmary, 1995, *The Major Transitions in Evolution,* *Oxford:* Freeman.

5. Lake, J. and J. Moore, 1998. "Phylogenetic analysis and comparative genomics," *Trends in Bioinformatics,* pp.22–24, Cambridge: Elsevier; see also H. Philippe and J. Laurent, 1998, "How good are deep phylogenetic trees?" *Current Opinion in Genetics and Development,* 8, 616–623.

6. Kimura, M., 1994, *Population Genetics, Molecular Evolution and the Neutral Theory,* ed. N. Takahata, Chicago: University of Chicago Press.

7. See C.U.M. Smith, 2002, *Elements of Molecular Neurobiology* (3rd edition), Chichester: Wiley.

8. Douglass, J., O. Clivelli and E. Herbert, 1984, "Polyprotein gene expression," *Annual Review of Biochemistry,* 53, 665–715.

9. Sidow, A., 1996, "Gen(om)e duplications in the evolution of early vertebrates," *Current Opinion in Genetics and Development,* 6, 715–722.

10. Morata, G. and E. Sanchez-Herrero, 1999, "Patterning mechanisms of the body trunk and appendages in Drosophila," *Development,* 126, 2823–2828.

11. Ariens Kappers, C., 1919, "Phenomena of neurobiotaxis as demonstrated by the position of motor nuclei of the oblongata," *Journal of Nervous and Mental Disorders, 50,* 1–16. A modern discussion of neurobiotaxis may be found in Nieuwenhhuys, R., H., J. Ten Donkelar and C. Nicholson, 1998, *The Central Nervous System of Vertebrates,* Berlin: Springer Verlag.

12. E. de Robertis and Y. Sasai, 1996, "A common plan for dorsoventral patterning in bilaterali," *Nature,* 380, 37–40.

13. Darwin, C.R., 1837, B Transmutation Notebook: p. 232 in P. H. Barrett, 1980, *Metaphysics, Materialism and the Evolution of Mind: Early Writings of Charles Darwin,* Chicago: University of Chicago Press.

14. Henderson, R., et al., 1989, "Model for the structure of bacteriorhodopsin based on high resolution electron cryo-microscopy," *Journal of Molecular Biology,* 213, 899–929.

15. Smith, C.U.M., 1995, "Membrane signaling systems," in Anthony Lee, ed., *Biomembranes, vol. 1: General Principles,* Greenwich, Ct: JAI Press, pp.245–270.

16. Fryxell, K. J and E. M. Meyerowitz, 1991, "The Evolution of rhodopsins and neurotransmitter receptors," *Journal of Molecular Evolution,* 33, 367–378.

17. Smith, C.U.M., 2000, *The Biology of Sensory Systems,* Chichester: Wiley.

18. Nathans, J., D. Thomas and D. Hogness, 1986, "Molecular genetics of human colour vision: the genes encoding blue, green and red pigments," *Science,* 232, 193–202.

19. Yokoyama, S., 1995, "Amino acid replacements and wavelength absorption of visual pigments in vertebrates," *Molecular Biology and Evolution,* 12, 53–61.

20. Kocheudoerfer. G. G., et al., 1999, "How color visual pigments are tuned," *Trends in Biochemical Sciences,* 24, 300–305.

21. Gardner, R., 1988, "Psychiatric syndromes as infrastructure for intraspecific communication" in M.R.A.Chance, Ed., *Social Fabrics of the Mind,* Hove and London: Lawrence Erlbaum.

22. Morris, S.C., 1998, *The Crucible of Creation,* Oxford: Oxford University Press.

23. Kollar, E. and C. Fisher, 1980, "Tooth inductions in chick epithelium: expression of quiescent genes for enamel synthesis," *Science,* 207, 993–995.

24. Callaerts, P., G. Halder and W. J. Gehring, 1997, "*Pax-6* in development and evolution," *Annual Review of Neuroscience,* 20, 483–532.

25. Tomarev, S. I; P. Callaerts; L. Kos; R. Zinovieva; G. Halder; W. Gehring and J. Platigorsky, 1997, "Squid *Pax-6* and eye development," *Proceedings of the National Academy of Science,* 94, 2421–2426.

26. The *C.elegans* sequencing consortium, 1998, "Genome sequence of the Nematode *C.elegans*: A Platform for Investigating Biology," *Science,* 282, 2012–2018.

27. Bargmann, C.I., 1998, "Neurobiology of the *Caenorhabditis elegans* Genome," *Science,* 282, 2028–2033.

4

ADAPTIVE FUNCTIONS OF THE CORPUS STRIATUM: THE PAST AND FUTURE OF THE R-COMPLEX

Neil Greenberg

INTRODUCTION

As Paul MacLean indicated the basal ganglia is emerging from the shadow cast by the most conspicuous clinical expression of its dysfunction: motor disorders. What is revealed is the nexus of a widely distributed system which functions in integrating action with cognition, motivation, and affect. Prominent among non-motor functions are striatal involvement in building up of sequences of behavior into meaningful, goal-directed patterns and repertoires and the selection of appropriate learned or innate sequences in concert with their possible predictive control. Further, the striatum seems involved in declarative and strategic memory (involving intentional recollection and the management of retrieved memories, respectively). Findings from reptile experiments indicate striatal control over specific assemblies of innate units of behavior that involve autonomic modulation. Its involvement in the appropriate expression of species-typical action patterns in reptiles and primates provides an interesting vantage point from which to interpret its involvement in the assembly of units of behavior into specific adaptive behavioral patterns.

THE BASAL FOREBRAIN AND STRIATAL COMPLEX ANATOMY AND CONNECTIONS

"Basal ganglia" is the term most favored by clinicians for the striatal complex—an array of structures collectively called the R-complex by Paul D. MacLean ("R" for "reptilian)." It includes the corpus striatum (caudate and putamen). The putamen is so intermeshed with an afferent projection (the globus pallidus) that the two structures are occasionally regarded together as the lenticular nucleus. The nucleus accumbens—once regarded as part of the septum or olfactory system—is, along with the olfactory tubercle, sometimes called the "olfactostriatum" in higher primates, and it is now viewed as a medial extension of the caudate-putamen in mammals. The caudate, putamen, and globus pallidus are sometimes referred to collectively as "neostriatum" while nucleus accumbens, olfactory tubercle, and ventral pallidum are called "paleostriatum." These terms suggest relative phylogenetic antiquity that Butler and Hodos (1996) find unwarranted, and so they term these aggregates dorsal and ventral "striato-pallidal complex," respectively, in their recent textbook of comparative vertebrate neuroanatomy. The collection of structures includes adjacent gray matter termed substantia innominata which encompasses nucleus basalis (the basal nucleus of Meynert) which is well interdigitated with the overlying lenticular nucleus.

Although often included in the basal ganglia because of topology, MacLean did not include the amygdala and claustrum. The amygdala has multiple connections with the hypothalamus and is regarded as part of the limbic system although it may well function as the major mediator of interactions between limbic and striatal functions. The claustrum has no known major connections with core striatal structures. Neither did MacLean define substantia nigra as part of the striatal complex but he discussed its outputs in concert with those of the striatum because of the similarities of its pars reticulata to globus pallidus. Andre Parent (1986) proposed as core structures, the dorsal striatum (caudate nucleus, putamen), ventral striatum (nucleus accumbens and part of the olfactory tubercle), and the pallidum. As associated structures, he identified the substantia nigra, ventral tegmental area, and subthalamic nucleus (see Table 4.1). The core structures, striatum and pallidum, which originate in the lateral and medial parts of the developing telencephalon along with the associated structures, are now often regarded as a basal ganglia system. The structural plan is very conservative and manifest from amphibians through reptiles, birds, and mammals (Marin, Smeets & Gonzalez 1998). In the dorsal striatum, chemospecific stains reveal that two classes of chemically (and probably functionally) specific cells are present. Strands of cells called "striosomes" are embedded in a larger "matrix" and appear to possess reciprocal connections with the dopaminergic cells of the substantia nigra. They thus have the potential to regulate dopaminergic activity, and indeed, stimulation in or near a striosome is more likely to evoke self-stimulation by an animal that can control its own electrode. The matrix consists of neurons that participate in paths between cortical areas and lower centers.

Parent and Hazrati (for example, 1995a, 1995b) incorporate striatum, pallidum, and substantia nigra, along with the subthalamic nucleus as basal ganglia. While the first three are regarded as main axis, the subthalamic nucleus, along with the pars compacta of substantia nigra, the centromedian/ parafascicular thalamic complex, dorsal raphe and pedunculopontine tegmental nucleus are regarded as control structures that provide various neurochemical modulation (Parent and Hazrati 1995b). They reviewed the anatomical details of corticostriatal projections, the intrinsic organization of the striatum, the striatofugal system, and the output structures of the striatum, positing a cortico-basal ganglia-thalamocortical loop. The unexpected complexity of intrinsic organization and the orderliness of its highly structured repetitive units make it ideal for selective control of psychomotor functions.

Table 4.1. Structures of the Mammalian Basal Ganglia[*]

CORE STRUCTURES

    Striatum
        caudate and putamen (sometimes "dorsal" or "non-limbic striatum"),
        ventral striatum (sometimes, "limbic striatum"), n accumbens and part of
        olfactory tubercle; = olfactostriatum

    Pallidum (globus pallidus)
        external segment
        internal segment (entopeduncular n in nonprimates)
        ventral pallidum (comprising part of the substantia innominata)

ASSOCIATED STRUCTURES

    Substantia Nigra (reciprocal connections with caudate and putamen)
    Ventral Tegmental Area (reciprocal connections with ventral striatum)
    Subthalamic Nucleus (reciprocal connections with pallidum)

Note: *Adapted from Parent (1986).

To clarify the basal ganglia's potential for information processing, Parent and Hazrati (1995a) analyzed the anatomy (as above) and considered the evidence they provide for two views of information processing: the "parallel processing" and the "information funneling" hypotheses. As Parent and Hazrati characterize these, parallel processing involves processing different kinds of cortical information through well-segregated cortico-basal-ganglia-thalamo-cortical loops. Information funneling, on the other hand, is informed by the fact that striatal axons from distinct functional areas are received by widely arborizing dendrites of pallidum and substantia nigra. Parent and colleagues (references in Parent & Hazrati 1995a) have used new and highly sensitive anterograde tract-tracing to determine that there is extensive dendritic arborization of pallidal and nigral neurons that could in principle lead to convergent "funneling." But such an apparent convergence does not mean that functional specificity is thereby lost—they acknowledge that they have yet to ascertain if specificity is retained in the loops from cortex to basal ganglia to thalamus to cortex.

STRIATAL CONNECTIONS WITH THE
CEREBRAL CORTEX AND THEIR POSSIBILITIES

The rich connections the striatum receives from the cortex feed forward into other parts of the basal ganglia such as the internal and external pallidum, and from the internal pallidum to the thalamus and thence back to the cortex. This one-way traffic involving inhibitory as well as excitatory synapses consists of a fairly well-separated parallel pattern. In Edelman's view, this pattern is ideally suited to effect independent neural routines. But further, because of the way these isolated parallel loops are connected to the thalamocortical system with its dynamic reciprocities, these routines would remain, in Edelman and Tononi's (2000) view, unconscious for cognitive routines much like those of motor programs. These routines within the basal ganglia or between the basal ganglia and cortex might then compete for representation in the cortex in a way that maintains the seeming "unity of behavior and thought," and explains why we tend to have or implement one conscious activity at a time (Edelman & Tononi 2000: 186).

The basal ganglia seem as important as the prefrontal cortex in the analysis of serial order in which events or perceptions are detected and the control of behavior based on such information. Beiser and Houk (1998) noted that frontal lobe patients and those with Huntington's or Parkinson's disease can manifest strikingly similar deficits. This led them to propose a model to gain insight into the ways the prefrontal cortex and basal ganglia work to transform sequences of input into patterns of neural activity. The model involves an encoding process whereby the serial order of stimuli is represented as a spatial pattern of neural activity, utilizing topographically specific circuits that loop from prefrontal cortex through basal ganglia and thalamus and then back. Recurrent cortico-striatal projections and collateral inhibition between striatal spiny units were able, then, to sustain representations of contextual events in working memory. A decoding process would then transform spatial patterns of neural activity to sequences of actions.

The Interface: Nucleus Accumbens

The nucleus accumbens, a dominant part of the ventral striatum, is the leading candidate for the interface between sites that integrate affective, motiva-tional, and cognitive functions with action. As MacLean (1990) points out, as the recipient of limbic (hippocampal and amygdalar) inputs, and by virtue of its projections to ventral pallidum and substantia nigra, the accumbens is often regarded as the key limbic-motor interface (for example, Mogenson et al. 1980). "An important link between the motivational-emotional parts of the brain and certain effector regions," as Groenewegen et al. (1996: 510), put it. Graybiel (1997) goes further in speculating that "this limbic basal ganglia system has a key function in translating action plans related to drive states and homeostatic control into action repertoires" (p. 460) or stereotyped responses (such as "fixed action patterns") in general.

For example, the accumbens has been linked to the highly stereotyped behavior of laughing, whether in response to a joke or contagious laughter, by means of MRI (Shibata et al. 2000). Different causes of laughter were interpreted at other sites (ventromedial frontal lobe for "getting it" or anterior supplemental motor area for contagious laughter), but all scans also showed activity in the nucleus accumbens.

While the accumbens is also often associated with appetitive motivation (for example, Paradiso et al. 1999) and reward (Wise & Bozarth 1984; other references in Paradiso et al. 1999), various stressful situations evoke dopamine release in accumbens (Salamone 1994; but not the nigrostriatal system; Herve et al. 1982; Thierry et al. 1976, in: Bowers et al. 1987).

Accumbens is also prominently associated with negative emotional valence in adult humans shown pictures designed to evoke affect. Subjects whose brains were being scanned by positron emission tomography (PET) while being shown neutral, negative, or positive affect-evoking pictures manifested different patterns of activity depending on the stimulus. Negative valence would reasonably dominate an aversive or avoidance situation while positive valence implies a pleasant or approach situation. When compared to the effects of a neutral stimulus, viewing unpleasant pictures stimulated increased blood flow primarily in limbic striatum, including nucleus accumbens. Pleasant pictures, on the other hand, evoked increased activity in the phylogenetically newer cortical limbic areas including prefrontal cortex (Paradiso et al. 1999). The authors suggest that detection and rapid stereotyped response to avoidance situations is reasonably coordinated with older, conserved mechanisms, but the basal ganglia may in Graybiel's (1995) view also be a critical part of a distributed forebrain system that helps assemble and express learned as well as innate sequences of behavior. Indeed, Graybiel feels evidence is accumulating that basal ganglia may participate significantly in planning and cognition (1997).

Neurochemistry, Neuroendocrinology

The known and growing understanding of basal ganglia connections is converging with findings about regional histochemistry. As Graybiel has pointed out, basal ganglia contains "a remarkable diversity of neuroactive substances organized into functional subsystems that have unique developmental histories and vulnerabilities in neurodegenerative diseases" (1990: 254). Although the neurotransmitter dopamine (DA) is prominently associated with the basal ganglia because of the famous clinical manifestations of an insufficiency or excess, the neurotransmitter of most striatal neurons is gamma aminobutyric acid (GABA). GABA is present in striatum (as in hypothalamus) in relatively high concentration as are the opiate-like endorphins, receptors for which were found in high concentration in the corpus striatum. In fact, as MacLean (1990) emphasizes, endorphin concentrations are several times higher in the external segment of the globus pallidus than in other cerebral structures. Substance P, a vasodilating agent described in the 1930s, was found about 20 years later to exist in high concentrations in the medial segment of the globus pallidus, as well as caudate nucleus and hypothalamus.

Dopamine (DA) is the neurotransmitter most prominently associated with the basal ganglia, and indeed, across taxa, it is one of its most conservative traits (see Marin, Smeets & Gonzalez 1998). In mammals, different subclasses of dopaminergic receptors, D1 and D2 are associated with the so-called direct and indirect basal ganglia subsystems, respectively. These pathways represent the conceptual if not anatomical basis for understanding of motor control and their disorders. These systems are recently viewed in terms of an "opponent parallel pathway hypothesis" in which direct and indirect systems compete with each other to cause net inhibition or excitation of activity, respectively. This is similar to Mink's (1996) "focused selection and inhibition hypothesis," in which a specific motor program is activated while competing programs are broadly inhibited. In either event, motor activity is perceived as the outcome of a balance in activity of these pathways maintained in part by activation of D1 and D2 dopamine receptors. Thus, if the direct pathway predominated, motor activity might be excessive (as in Huntington's disease) and if the indirect pathway was relatively more active, Parkinsonian poverty of movement might be seen (Graybiel 2000). Interestingly, D1 and D2 receptors can be seen in a laminar pattern in lizards (Clark et al. 2000, see below).

In the mammalian brain, DA is found principally in the substantia nigra, from whence it is projected to caudate/putamen (dorsal striatum), and in the ventral tegmental area, the mesolimbic projection of which supplies forebrain sites (including nucleus accumbens, olfactory tubercle, amygdala, septal area, and the prefrontal cortex). There is also a dopaminergic projection from the hypothalamus to the median eminence (where it modulates reticular formation output), in a system around the fourth ventricle, and in local circuits intrinsic to the retina, olfactory bulb, and the optic tectum.

The functional specificity of alternative projections was underscored by the finding that a single gene (in the mutant mouse, weaver) could differentially cause severe dopamine depletion in the mesolimbic and nigrostriatal systems affecting the "nonlimbic" dorsal (caudate/putamen) but not the "limbic" ventral (including n. accumbens) striatum (Roffler-Tarlov & Graybiel 1984). While diseases of the basal ganglia can impair learning of sensorimotor skills, the effects, according to Gabrieli (1998), are not uniform. Repetitive tasks appear basal ganglia-dependent while tasks requiring new associations apparently depend on the cerebellum. Alternatively, Gabrieli suggests that open-loop skill learning (depends on planning and delayed feedback about errors) is cerebellar, while closed-loop skill learning (continuous feedback about errors) is striatal.

Striatal Functions and Dysfunctions

The R-Complex is the basal "reptilian" structure in Paul MacLean's well-known heuristic model, the triune brain, reflecting the predominant behavioral functions believed to have been first integrated in its constituent neural structures in evolutionary time (MacLean 1990).

Of course, neural structures and systems continue to evolve after the initial innovation that provided an advantage in its initializing environment of evolutionary adaptiveness, and other structures can come to coordinate comparable behavioral patterns. The idea of the triune brain remains controversial, in part because of its vulnerability to oversimplification, but the basic idea of a nested hierarchy of structures is attractive. Point-to-point continuity, however, cannot be expected. For example, as MacLean points out, the newest (thalamo-cingulate) part of the limbic system has no representation in reptiles (1990: 247).

The basal ganglia are prominently associated with motor control, probably because of the dramatic, often devastating effects of dysfunction on movement (see below). Although an array of corollary functions such as motor learning and automatization were long suspected, only recently are these structures coming to be understood as indispensably involved in many functions (and dysfunctions) beyond those traditionally ascribed to it (cf. Tables 4.1 & 4.2). Ann Graybiel's observations that the basal ganglia have learning and memory functions driven by cortically-derived information, identifies them as likely key components in an assortment of behavioral disorders not commonly associated with striatal dysfunctions (for example, 1997, 2000).

The comparative approach has brought forth some of the best insights when unlikely constraints on behavior or an unexpected expression of an organism's potential are manifested. A sense of the evolutionary process is evoked when specific traits in various taxa are compared. When they are seen to be related through a possible common ancestor, we can posit a homology between them and explore the ways in which the function of a putative ancestral trait can be adapted by circumstances to the needs of the organism. When comparable functions are performed by fundamentally dissimilar structures, we suspect they are analogous and can speculate on the capacity of organisms to cope in different ways to similar selection pressures. There is a long history of looking to ethology to provide possible models for understanding dysfunctional behavior (White 1974; McGuire & Fairbanks 1974).

Another powerful way of envisioning the possibilities and constraints of neural structures is through dysfunction, and the basal ganglia are significant participants in several disorders that provide interesting clues. The study of basal ganglia functions presents a wonderful exemplar of the "logic of the lamppost." Employing this seductive mode of reasoning, traditionally treated by analogy with looking for lost keys in a dark parking lot where we can search only under the illumination of a solitary lamppost, we tend to forget that the keys may yet be discovered some place in the darkness. Our illumination until recently has been the more easily discerned evidence of motor dysfunction as a consequence of striatal damage.

Table 4.2. Putative Functions of the Basal Ganglia*

Motor Functions
>•initiates motor patterns of cognitive or motivational significance (Heimer et al. 1982)
>•motor sequence planning, coordination (Graybiel 1995)
>•inhibition of competing motor programs (Mink 1996)

Sensory Functions
>•somatosensory motor control (Schneider & Lidsky 1981; other refs in Brown et al. 1997)
>•somatosensory discrimination; pain (see Brown et al. 1997)
>•visual discrimination (Pribram 1977) including facial expression and
>•hallucinations (Middleton & Strick 1996, other refs in Brown et al. 1997)
>•auditory (see Brown et al. 1997)

Cognitive Functions
>•cognitive sequence planning ("acquisition, retention, and expression of
>•cognitive patterns" Graybiel 1997)
>•expectations, prediction (ventral striatum, Schultz et al. 1992; Schultz 1998)
>•attention (Schneider 1984; Parent 1986: 247; Brown and Marsden 1998; Hayes et al. 1998)
>•categorizing (tactile stimuli, Merchant et al. 1997)
>•learning (Jueptner et al. 1997); procedural memory (for habits and skills: Jog et al. 1999); habit learning & acquisition of nonmotor dispositions and tendencies (Knowlton et al. 1996)
>•classify spatial patterns and serial ordering of sensory events (Beiser & Houk 1998)
>•executive function ("focused and sustained attention in concert with flexibility of thought . . . planning and regulation of adaptive and goal directed behavior . . . [utilizing] working memory" (Peigneux 2000; and see Brown et al. 1997)
>•creativity (ventral striatum becomes activated when predictions are violated by stimuli that appear in an unexpected context: references in Cotterill 2001).

*Note. Adapted from Brown et al. (1997), Parent (1986), and MacLean (1990) and others. These are exemplars of research reports and reviews that demonstrate or suggest the diversity of functions in which the basal ganglia (see Table 4.1) integrates or participates; no attempt has been made to be exhaustive.

Motor Functions

Deficits in motor behavior correlated with basal ganglia damage or insufficiency have dominated perceptions of its function for generations, but among the symptoms of the "shaking palsy" described early in 1817 by James Parkinson was also an impairment of intellectual and cognitive processes ("bradyphrenia") with an associated depression sometimes preceding the more overt neurological symptoms. MacLean (1990) pointed out that despite a century of prominent textbooks of neurology expressing great caution, if not reserve, about regarding the basal ganglia as an organ of motor control, popular textbooks continued to make the point. Autonomic dysfunctions are also present and physical or psychological stress can alter the clinical profile in one of two ways: "freezing," an exacerbation or precipitation of neurological deficits, or "paradoxical kinesia," a sudden transient remission of bradykinesia when confronted with a life-threatening emergency (Zigmond, Stricker & Berger, 1987). The extraordinary expression of motor effectiveness in otherwise dyskinetic Parkinson patients under conditions in which compelling stimuli are suddenly presented (see Brown & Marsden 1998, above), suggests the neurological components of the emergency stress response may be involved (see Greenberg 2001).

Another intriguing dimension of Parkinsonism is an apparently faulty internal model of movement: when an unimpaired person is following the trajectory of a moving target, he can extrapolate to fill in a brief gap in visual feedback, while the Parkinson's patient cannot, and seems to lose track. This seems related to the fact that while initiation and execution of motor patterns are affected in Parkinson's, accuracy is largely unimpaired as long as there is feedback from other senses. Indeed, other senses can seemingly ameliorate the disorder (see Stein 1986). Mink (1996) views motor dysfunctions less as a failure to generate the proper signals than as the result of a failure to successfully inhibit one of several possible competing motor programs that originated with the cerebral cortex or cerebellum.

Stereotyped Behavior: Fixed Action Patterns, Stereotypies, and Obsessive-compulsive Behavior

Another significant class of motor-related basal ganglia functions are stereotypies and stereotyped "fixed action patterns," which likely share more than mere etymology. Stereotyped behavior involves fixity of form. Social displays are among the most prominent of these and are excellent exemplars of the evolutionary process of ritualization—the progressive fixity in form that develops over evolutionary time (Morris 1956; Huxley 1966). The stereotypy of a display functions to reduce its ambiguity as a communicative signal and enhance the precision of stimulus control. These displays are often cobbled together from fragments of motor patterns and autonomic reflexes and can confer clear adaptive advantages. Unlike most learned or automatized motor patterns, they are presumed to be heavily influenced by genetics but subject to specific shaping during early development (Hailman 1969).

Highly aroused, energized individuals may repeat stereotyped patterns frequently; but such displays also resemble clinical stereotypies, typically expressed at levels of repetition that are clearly inappropriate or dysfunctional. While most dysfunctional stereotypies are manifest in abnormal contexts such as zoos or laboratories or as a result of trauma or extreme stress (discussed below), the stereotyped nature of adaptive expressions of behavior is observed to be spontaneously expressed in natural habitats. The form of such ethological stereotypies, often termed "fixed action patterns" by early ethologists (Heymer 1977; Tinbergen 1951) might involve complex motor sequences and were presumed to be under genetic control. Once triggered by an appropriate stimulus (a "sign stimulus" or "releaser"), the sequence was invariably completed.

Among the most interesting of fixed action patterns are those that serve communications. Most displays have evolved from motor patterns or autonomic reflexes with externally detectable expression; they have evolved under a selection pressure to be unambiguous (Morris 1956) and are often used by animals to discriminate members of their own species. Such species-typical behavioral patterns, particularly social displays, have provided much robust data to illuminate neural corollaries of complex behavioral functions. MacLean (1978) demonstrated that lesions of the globus pallidus in the area where fibers converge to form the ansa lenticularis, or of the ansa itself, impaired a species-typical "greeting" display in the squirrel monkey, probably by interrupting the pallidal projection to the tegmental area.

The head-bobbing display of the green anole (described below) is such a stereotyped "greeting" display. Imposed upon the stereotyped bobbing pattern are slight variations such as number of bobs, forelimb contribution to the bobbing movement, erection of a slight nuchal crest, or erection of a hyoid bone that extends a conspicuous dewlap, that can modify the message to indicate aggressive or reproductive motivation. The expression of these and related units of behavior is presumed to have become progressively more precise and stereotyped because of an advantage that precision confers, such as the correct identification of the species or gender doing the display. For example, the anole's "signature" display, while precisely executed, is evoked by a broad spectrum of situations but units of behavior are added or deleted to modify the core display and send different messages (Jenssen 1978, 1979).

In a sense, stereotypies can be viewed as efforts to reduce stress or discharge high arousal levels channeled by circumstance. Inappropriate motor patterns or their expression in a dysfunctional context characterize dysfunctional stereo-typies, and their possible function in reducing stress or arousal levels recalls Freud's famous idea that a neurosis is an attempt at self-therapy. Indeed, in addition to stereotypies, behavioral patterns such as eating, aggression, and sexual behavior in response to mild stress have been characterized as "chemotherapy without drugs" (Antelman & Caggiula 1980). Their expression may be significantly affected by progressive sensitization of underlying neural mechanisms attributable to positive feedback from the expression of the behavioral pattern. This possibility has informed the Jacksonian view that stereotypies are expressed when higher nervous functions fail to control motor patterns organized at a lower level (Dantzer 1986).

Dysfunctional stereotypies in humans are associated with schizophrenia and early autism where they appear in apparent independence of the environment, and in captive animals or those impaired by brain damage or dopamine-affecting drugs, where they appear more context dependent. Repetitive patterns as rocking movements, grooming patterns, vocalizations, and pacing, although apparently rooted in adaptive behavioral patterns, can rapidly become dysfunctional. Clinicians associate them with frustration such as that when a selection cannot be made between incompatible alternatives. A stressfully barren stimulus environment or restrictive confinement and unavoidable stress are also prominently associated with the expression of stereotypies (see Mason 1991 for a critical review).

Motor stereotypies were found by Canales and Graybiel (2000) to be related to an apparent imbalance of activation between the two neurochemically distinct elements of the striatum, striosomes and the extrastriosomal matrix, in which they are embedded. When they induced different levels of stereotypy in rats by applying psychomotor stimulants in concert with dopamine receptor agonists, the degree of imbalance between activity of striosomes and the matrix predicated the degree of motor stereotypy.

Motor stereotypies (and possible comparable cognitive phenomena) are often fragments of more complex ensembles. The "chunking" of action repertoires within the striatum was proposed by Graybiel (1998) as a counterpart of the older idea of information chunking. As an adaptive mechanism, the assembly, adjustment, and reassembly of a relatively small number of behavioral patterns is much more efficient than the mastery of a huge collection of alternative programmed sequences. For example, the striatal coding of action sequences is apparently reorganized as the learning of new habits proceeds (Jog et al. 1999).

Tom Insel (1988) correctly cautioned that the repetitive motor performance of obsessive-compulsive disorder may not be homologous, but their common underlying neural circuitry in normal and inappropriate expression may yield important clues about potential sites for therapeutic intervention. Further clues may be expected from considering the selective modulation of circuits by specific elements of the stress response or other neurochemically distinctive mechanisms for maintaining balance between competing, opposing, or complementary systems. It is interesting that stereotyped motor patterns are seen in different but related contexts. Highly adaptive forms such as species-typical displays and clearly dysfunctional forms such as clinical stereotypies are related not only by the fixity of expression but by stress-evoking context. Indeed, attempts at stress reduction have been implicated in the etiology of pathological expressions of repetitive motor patterns (Cooper & Nicol 1991).

Stereotypies beg comparison with obsessive-compulsive (OCD) behavior, which has been associated with basal ganglia since at least the mid 1980s (Cummings & Frankel 1985). For example, OCD was specifically associated with lesions of the lenticular nuclei, especially the pallidum by Laplane (1994).

Ranjit C. Chachko and colleagues observed five cases in which the symptoms presented by patients, associated with depression, could be mistaken for a delusional disorder, but more likely involved an impaired cortex-basal ganglia-thalamus-cortex circuit (Chachko et al. 2000). In Baxter's (et al. 2000) review, activity of the caudate was significantly correlated with that of orbital cortex and thalamus in untreated patients who subsequently responded well to treatment. In a smaller population who did not respond well, the correlation of activity in these brain regions was weaker.

Attention-deficit hyperactivity disorder (ADHD) is, along with Tourette's Syndrome and OCD (with which it is often comorbid—Sheppard et al 1999), often regarded as a dopamine-based frontostriatal neurodevelopmental disorder (e.g., Bradshaw & Sheppard 2000). When striatal activity was determined by tomographic assessment of regional blood flow in children with ADHD, it was found to be low (Lou et al. 1989). This may be attributable to functional abnormalities of the putamen, as determined by a new type of fMRI used by Anderson and colleagues (2000) to look at steady-state rather than dynamic brain activity. Interestingly, students suffering from ADHD appear to have reduced sympatho-adreno-medullary responses to cognitive challenge (Anderson et al. 2000).

Schizophrenia can also be regarded as a frontostriatal disorder. The dopaminergic systems have long been implicated in the etiology of psychosis and the success of dopamine-blocking neuroleptic drugs was a major impetus to the so-called dopamine hypothesis of schizophrenia. Projections from the ventral tegmental area to the ventral striatum (nucleus accumbens) were especially implicated. Haber and Fudge (1997) reviewed the dopamine system with particular attention to its amygdalar connections and hypothesized that overstimulated amygdalar projections to the substantia nigra stimulates excessive midbrain dopaminergic activity. In a review of the few studies that examined pathology of the basal ganglia associated with schizophrenia, Heckers (1997) found little support for neuropathies involving regional brain volume or cell density. Neuromodulation, on the other hand, remains an important potential variable. Graybiel (1997) suspected that the basal ganglia's potential function as a cognitive pattern generator that parallels its function as an organizer of motor patterns made it a candidate for a role in schizophrenia. Shortly thereafter, Holt (et al. 1999) hypothesized that cholinergic interneurons of the striatum might be responsible for impaired output and tested the idea by measuring densities of neurons marked by their immunoreactivity to choline acetyltransferase. A patchy decrease in cell densities was identified in the ventral striatum (ventral caudate and nucleus accumbens) of schizophrenic versus control brains. Holt's tentative conclusion is that the reduced function of striatal interneurons disrupted the pathways from ventral striatum that end in the prefrontal cortex.

Stress

It is significant that the physiological stress response is so intimately involved with the expression or exacerbation of behavioral disorders. The stress response is one of the organism's most ancient adaptive mechanisms. While typically defined as a response to challenges to the maintenance of homeostasis (e.g., Moberg 1999), it also deals with many real or perceived challenges to the capacity of the organism to meet any of a variety of needs (reviewed in Greenberg 2002). McEwen's definition of a stressor is particularly useful because it implicitly acknowledges that homeostasis is only the most urgent of many possible needs: "Stress may be defined as a threat, real or implied, to the psychological or physiological integrity of an individual" (McEwen 1999). The literature on the effects of stress on stereotyped behavior and stereotypies implicates the basal ganglia. For example, Scott et al. (1996) bred 5 generations of rats that differed markedly in their susceptibility to showing decreased struggling activity in a swim test after being exposed to an uncontrollable stressor. Compared to susceptible rats, those that displayed no decrease in struggling after shock manifested an array of symptoms, including more home-cage activity, larger shock-induced depletions of norepinephrine (NE) and 3-methoxy-4-hydroxy-phenylglycol (MHPG) in the locus coeruleus and much higher concentrations of dopamine (DA) and dihydroxyphenylacetic acid (DOPAC) in striatum and nucleus accumbens than susceptible rats.

Perceptions of circumstances and their potential challenges to welfare are also important—the phrase "real or perceived" emphasizes the fact that among the most potent stressors are expectations. Organisms apparently invoke responses that are most likely to be adaptive, even under adverse circumstances. A mirror image of the ecological concept of "maximizing" the effectiveness of a strategy relative to cost, the organism's anticipatory stress response can be viewed as "minimizing" the future adverse impact of a prospective challenge to meeting its needs. This is directly related to an animal's perception of the "controllability" of the stressful situation, the attribute of a stressor at the heart of the "learned helplessness" paradigm postulated by Martin Seligman and colleagues (e.g., Seligman 1975; Seligman et al. 1975).

Interestingly, the effects of stressful experience on the basal ganglia system's mesoaccumbens dopaminergic system is highly dependent on an animal's perceived controllability of the stressor (Cabib & Puglisi-Allegra 1996) and the basal ganglia are demonstrably able to couple expectations to sensory input in support of developing new habits (Schultz et al. 1992; Kawagoe et al. 1998).

Attention

Teuber (1976) was convinced that, along with motor difficulties, the impairment of striatal structures resulted in characteristic perceptual and cognitive deficits (see Parent 1986 on nucleus basalis). The idea that attentional competition involves ventral striatum in a manner parallel to dorsal striatum's apparent involvement in competition between actions was found very attractive to Dayan et al. (2000). They speculated that stimulus reliabilities could be stored in corticostriatal connections while stimulus predictability could be stored in the basolateral nuclei of the amygdala.

Attention has often been associated with human striatal dysfunctions because of the striking phenomenon of paradoxical kinesia. The phenomenon of transient release from akinesia inspired Brown and Marsden (1998) to hypothesize that the basal ganglia are integral to nonconscious attention (see below). They envisioned that basal ganglia damage altered the flow of information from sensory input to motor output. In paradoxical kinesia, if heightened attention is demanded by a specific situation, the impairment may be overridden, often dramatically. For example, an akinetic Parkinson's patient might successfully avoid some sudden emergency such as an oncoming car. Brown and Marsden hypothesized that the basal ganglia facilitate the synchronization of distributed and perhaps competing neural responses related to action and bring them to focus on a specific motor act or thought sequence, that is, bring them to attention.

The basal ganglia may serve to sort and recombine information about current circumstances and predictions about future possibilities to serve adaptive ends. This view informs Graybiel's (2000) hypothesis that a dysfunction of excess (of activation) might lead to repetitive actions or thoughts while one of deficit would lead to a diminished competence of action or thought. Graybiel and colleagues (1994) related estimates of future possibilities ("predictive control") to relatively rare but distinctive dopamine-dependent striatal cells that are tonically active and which are recruited and change responsiveness when exposed to stimuli predictive of reward and then diminish during extinction. An organism's expectations are apparently reflected in the activity of ventral striatum (Schultz et al. 1992) as a result of error-signal detection by dopaminergic neurons (Schultz, Dayan & Montague 1997). Schultz (1998) has observed that the activity of dopamine neurons in the ventral striatum, once evoked by a rewarding stimulus, come to be controlled by reward-predicting stimuli over time. Considering the critical importance of an organism's capacity for making predictions to create associations between stimuli and responses and to help discriminate most favorable responses, ventral striatal neurons are apparently involved in the information processing that underlies motivation (as reviewed by Schultz 1998).

In Divac's (1977) attempt to reconcile conflicting views of neostriatal function, he found that even though there was topographic evidence for independent functional units of neostriatal areas receiving specific neocortical afferents, the uniformity of neostriatal cytoarchitecture indicates that these units conducted neural processing of information in comparable ways. This view, in concert with the position of the neostriatum in the chain of neocortical control of motor mechanisms, converged on the idea that the neostriatum intermediates between cognition and action. Divac and Oberg (1979), impressed by the fact that behavioral deficits subsequent to lesions of the striatum and their cortical projection targets were comparable, suggested that striatum was directly involved in cognition. In this regard it is interesting that Cools and van den Bercken (1977) regarded the neostriatum as the substrate of high-order information processing needed to link two or more behavioral acts to form an integrated behavioral program (Cools 1985).

The nucleus basalis varies greatly between taxa and is most distinctively differentiated in cetaceans and primates. Functional differences between its neurons and those of other basal ganglia (Parent 1986) and its significant projections to limbic and widespread neocortical sites (MacLean 1990: 57) suggest it is likely involved in cognitive functions such as learning and attention, at least in primates (Parent 1986: 247).

Among the diversity of significant problems that attend damage to basal ganglia, some resemble specific symptoms of schizophrenia. For example, damage to the substantia nigra in the area where the loop involving TE is likely to synapse (medial pars reticulata) can evoke hallucinations, probably by altering the normal balance of inhibitory and excitatory influences in a way that results in abnormal excitation of Area TE, known to be able to stimulate hallucinations. Middleton and Strick (1996) pointed out that the visual anomalies attributable to interfering with the TE-striatal loop are much like those sometimes seen as a side effect of dopaminergic therapy for Parkinsonism, "Might this mechanism also underlie the hallucinations of schizophrenia?" they ask. There is supporting data, they note, indicative of significant changes in activation of areas that participate in the proposed loop during hallucinations of schizophrenics. A detailed and closely reasoned argument for the involvement of basal ganglia in the etiology of schizophrenia was advanced by Graybiel (1997).

The major output structures of the basal ganglia, GPi and SNr, report back to the ventral anterior and lateral thalamic nuclei, which then project back to the cerebral cortex. Parent and Hazrati (1995a) regard this as a source of redundancy, which can make the same information available to different brain centers. Their analysis includes other targets of the GPi and SNr, such as the centromedian thalamic nucleus (which receives information from cortical motor and sensory cortices as well as brain stem reticular information), the habenula (a major limbic relay that may constitute a functional limbic interface with basal ganglia), and the pedunculopontine tegmental nucleus (which may be a functional interface between cerebellum and basal ganglia). Other targets are functionally associated with memory, rewarded motor behavior, and various ways of combining cortical information at the striatal level.

Selective neurochemistry is the key to our fullest understanding of function. For example, there is a growing sense that the reward functions of dopamine are less significant than—and may even be explained by—its role in underscoring the significance of stimuli that predict reward. This in part helps explain why nonrewarding behavior may be manifest if it is associated with a dopamine surge, as is often the case in addiction to cigarette smoking or cocaine use (see brief review by Wickelgren 1998 and references therein). Another unexpected way dopamine affects behavior was shown by Hayes (et al. 1998) on Parkinson's patients asked to shift attentional set (the conditions that regulate responding, executive process) from (for example) the color of a stimulus to its shape as a cue for a response. These patients were significantly slower than control subjects and had difficulty filtering a competing but irrelevant set. When the deficit in switching was correlated with the amelioration of motor symptoms attributable to an l-dopa-based medication, it became apparent that deficit is based on dopamine insufficiency.

Memory and its Disorders

Participation of the corpus striatum in long-term memory systems, classically known from studies of patients with brain lesions, has been more recently complemented by functional neuroimaging techniques. This information was reviewed recently by Gabrieli (1998), who observed that basal ganglia are significantly involved, particularly in declarative memory (involving conscious or intentional recollection) and strategic memory (involving the evaluation, manipulation, and transformation of retrieved declarative memories). The pattern of memory impairment and reasoning in diseases of the basal ganglia such as Parkinson's or Huntington's led Gabrieli to hypothesize that strategic memory impairment is a result of limited reasoning ability attributable to reduced capacity for working memory. A decline in working memory, reasoning, and strategic memory seems to correspond to normal 5-10% per decade reduction in dopaminergic function across the lifespan, however Gabrieli is careful to point out that the extent to which these functions are causally related rather than merely correlative has not yet been determined (1998).

Basal ganglia are associated with human amnesia indirectly because that dysfunction is a core symptom of Alzheimer's disease, which also involves (among other things) a loss of cholinergic cells in the basal ganglia. Hemorrhage-induced basal forebrain damage can also impair memory. But the role of the basal ganglia is generally regarded as uncertain because there is generally related damage to medial temporal (much more often associated with amnesia) or frontal lobes. This situation is reviewed briefly by Goldenberg (et al. 1999), who observed a patient with amnesia who suffered damage limited largely to the nucleus accumbens. By excluding the roles of structures that suffered collateral damage and because the n. accumbens is positioned to "integrate inputs from multiple cortical and subcortical areas including the hippocampus and the amygdalae, and to exert modulatory influences on widespread cortical function," the authors conclude the n. accumbens is an important candidate for direct involvement in memory processes (and see an editorial commentary by Mayes 1999).

Confabulation may be a related disorder of episodic memory generally in concert with faulty executive functions. Although associated with forebrain dysfunction, it has presented itself after focal basal forebrain damage in a way suggesting that both circuits from striatum to both medial temporal and frontal lobes must be simultaneously impaired (Fisher et al. 1995; Hashimoto et al.

2000). When lesions were limited to the basal forebrain, a more transient expression of confabulation may result (Fischer et al. 1995).

Cognition

The sensory and multimodal cortices of the forebrain receive information about the world, analyze it, and share it with the prefrontal association cortex where it may be incorporated into complex, often skilled, adaptive actions implemented by means of the premotor and motor cortices. Many theorists assume the function of cognition is to model reality by selective simplification of received information. In this, shared properties of stimuli are important in the economy of cognitive functions, and it is often assumed that the simplest generality possible that is not contradicted by experience is utilized. But modeling also involves potential responsive actions and, in this, the extrapyramidal and cerebellar control systems may provide essential support. The selection or execution of actions are then more or less energized by the perceived relevance of the situation, necessarily involving motivational and affective variables.

Nieuwenhuys (1996) reviewed the "greater limbic system" and its constituent "emotional motor system," which probably executes emotional and motivated behavioral patterns by means of fibers from the central nucleus of the amygdala, the bed nucleus of the stria terminalis, and the lateral hypothalamic area. The striatum is barely mentioned: Ventral striatum is identified as a participant in a loop involved initiating locomotor activity (p: 575). The large association area of the frontal lobe, however, manifests a pattern of linkages in its outflow in which cascades of short association fibers connect successive structures, suggesting their participation in the planning and sequencing of complex motor tasks (Nieuwenhuys 1996, citing Fuster 1991).

Ann Graybiel (1995) gave important impetus to the view that the "basal ganglia . . . are critically involved in building up sequences of behavior into meaningful, goal-directed repertoires." Her review indicates, as she put it,

that the basal ganglia act as part of a distributed forebrain system that helps to encode such repertoires through behavioral learning, and that is engaged in the expression of such repertoires once they have been internalized. The basal ganglia also may be critical to the expression of innate behavioral routines. Experimental findings on reward-based learning suggest that neural activity in the striatum and substantia nigra, pars compacta changes during behavioral learning. New evidence also suggests extreme specificity in the neural connections interrelating the basal ganglia, cerebral cortex, and thalamus. Adaptive control of behavior may centrally depend on these circuits and the evaluator-reinforcement circuits that modulate them.

Graybiel (1997) came to call the sequences "cognitive pattern generators" and she suggested that by analogy with the central pattern generators of the motor system "these pattern generators operate to organize neural activity underlying aspects of action-oriented cognition. It is further proposed that the basal ganglia are involved in the control of cognitive as well as motor pattern generators. Disorders of the basal ganglia may thereby contribute to neural circuit dysfunctions that are expressed as positive and negative symptoms of schizophrenia." Further, they are likely important in initiating volitional activity (Graybiel 1990).

Cotterill (2001) echoes Mink's (1996) idea that basal ganglia control activity mainly by the inhibition of competing motor programs (above) but goes further in his belief that modulation of sensory cerebrum signals to motor areas by the basal ganglia and cerebellum can lead to cognition and consciousness. Assuming the primacy of output over sensation for adaptive behavior, Cotterill considers that consciousness serves mainly to review probable outcomes of likely motor patterns in a given situation and hold those that have potentially adverse outcomes at a subthreshold level—thought but not actions.

Connections and loops between basal ganglia and other sites associated with cognitive function further underscore the adaptive potential of these structures. The cerebral frontal, parietal, and temporal cortices provide input to the basal ganglia, while only the frontal lobe was believed to be a major target of the striatum. The inferotemporal cerebral site known as Area TE is one of two specific visual areas associated with visual discrimination and recognition, and has recently been determined to also receive from, as well as project to, the basal ganglia. Using retrograde transneuronal tracers, Middleton and Strick (1996) observed that the pars reticulata of the substantia nigra, a major striatal output nucleus, projects back to TE by means of the thalamus. In the authors' view, if a portion of these connections forms a closed loop, as seems likely, striatal structures could influence high-order visual processing, which could explain some perceptual anomalies as well as movement disorders.

A strict segregation of striatal output pathways, however, is less certain in light of findings by Parent and others (briefly reviewed in Parent et al. 2000) of striatal efferents with highly collateralized axons, most of which reach two or three target structures. "It is now apparent," Parent et al. write, "that the basal ganglia system is a complex and widely distributed neuronal network" (2000: S23).

Creativity

Creative behavior, despite its obvious significance in behavior is "one of psychology's orphans" (Sternberg & Lubart 1999). Its neuropsychological causes and consequences are rarely approached by researchers, largely due to traditions of scholarship and academic parochialism. When carefully defined in terms of biological adaptation however, creativity is accessible to the scrutiny of neuroethology. The capacity to generate innovative responses represents a behavioral trait of the highest importance, particularly when an organism confronts unique internal or environmental challenges to its capacity to meet its needs. Indeed, the stresses evoked by environmental change can affect organisms in ways that require novel ways of coping, which can change selection pressures in ways that feed back to affect their subsequent evolution (see, e.g., Jablonski & Bottjer 1990; Hoffmann & Hercus 2000). Adaptive behavior is the outcome of the assimilation of a continuing stream of experience into the structure and coordination of the brain. Coping with challenges to meet adaptive needs almost constitutes a working definition of stress, and in light of recent ideas about the effects of coping on selective activation of specific pathways (for example, Huether 1996; Greenberg 2001), specific neurophysiological components of the stress response may well be central to the expression of creativity as well as its continuing adaptive function. But deviation from the norm is a hazardous business, and thus creativity and dysfunction are hazardously close, linked often, at least, in popular culture.

Among the hallmarks of creative behavior is the recombination of information from different sources in novel and potentially useful ways. The striatum may well be capable of combining information from different cortical areas as their respective terminal fields converge (see Parent & Hazrati 1995a). Adaptive and dysfunctional creativity both depend upon the selective expression of neural events that ultimately result in the creation and/or expression of novel neural constructs, typically known by their influence on behavior. These may represent familiar things seen in new ways, new things seen unhindered by their evocation of stereotypes, and various combinations of clarity of discrimination or categorizing. Cotterill (2001) reviews the idea that stimuli detected out of expected context likely activate the ventral striatum, as it monitors the reliability of predictions made in the prefrontal cortex. Expectations may be cognitive as well as motor and the fact that chemical signals of the stress response are evoked by even mild dissonance (Hadley 1996), such as discrepancies between perceptions and expectations (Goldstein 1987), it is reasonable that the basal ganglia, known to be sensitive to stress (Zigmond, Stricker & Berger 1987; Salamone 1994) are deeply involved.

NEUROETHOLOGY OF STRIATAL FUNCTIONS IN A REPRESENTATIVE REPTILE: REPTILES AND REPTILE NEUROETHOLOGY

Can we penetrate appearances, misconceptions, and tangled nomenclature to the underlying common features that could link the rich mammalian literature with findings in reptiles? In their analysis of the paleostriatal system (PS) of Caiman and their comparison of this reptilian PS with both avian PS and mammalian basal ganglia, Brauth and Kitt (1980) concluded that overall design and possibly function are comparable in these three taxa and indicate a common function in spatial orientation and attention. (Paleostriatum is also termed ventral striatum by many authors while the overlying dorsal ventricular ridge (DVR) is also termed, dorsal striatum; the reptilian nucleus accumbens just medial to the PS is probably homologous with that of mammals (Parent 1986)). Unlike mammals which have comparably rich ascending and descending pathways from the basal ganglia, the corresponding structures in reptiles influence motor patterns only by descending pathways (Parent 1986). The dorsal ventricular ridge (DVR) has long been suspected to be related to the prominence of species-typical motor patterns in the life of reptiles (Bellairs 1970: 336).

When Marin, Smeets and Gonzalez (1998) integrated their work with the amphibian basal ganglia into a phylogenetic overview, they discerned dorsal and ventral striatopallidal systems in all tetrapods. Inputs from the thalamus and cortex ("pallium" in lower vertebrates) are always through the striatum and provide access to several classes of information. The cortex of mammals has excellent representation in the striatum, whereas the reptilian basal ganglia receives most of its projects from the dorsal ventricular ridge. This large distinctive subventricular structure is apparently derived from the pallium and often compared to isocortex of mammals. Further, the proposition that well-organized projections of modulatory dopaminergic neurons from a substantia nigra/ventral tegmental complex to dorsal and ventral striatum in all tetrapods can be defended by new findings in amphibians. They concluded that although many functions of the basal ganglia system are unique to mammals, the conservatism of the system is remarkable. There is, however, an interesting difference detailed by Clark & Baxter (2000). They used a radio-tagged marker (^{125}I-DOI) that preferentially binds to specific classes of serotonergic receptors. While such staining highlights a patchy striosomal pattern in mammals, the lizard, *Anolis carolinensis* shows no such pattern.

The major connections of the basal ganglia in the lizard, *Varanus* are illustrated in Figure 4.1.

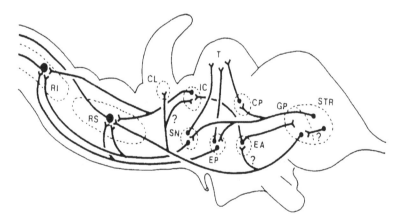

Figure 4.1. Basal Ganglia Connections in a Lizard. Major connections of the basal ganglia in the lizard, *Varanus*. CL = lateral cerebellar nucleus, CP = nucleus of the posterior commissure, EA = anterior entopeduncular nucleus, EP = posterior entopeduncular nucleus, GP = globus pallidus, IC = intercollicular nucleus, RI = nucleus reticularis inferior, SN = substantia nigra, STR = striatum, T = optic tectum (after Parent 1986 and Ten Donkelaar and De Boer-Van Huizen 1981).

The successes of the ethological method are grounded in close observation of behavioral patterns spontaneously performed in nature or in response to naturalistic stimuli. The heuristic power of a coordinated concern for the questions and methods of developmental biology, ecology, evolutionary biology, and physiology has informed ethological understanding ever since Tinbergen (1951) identified these perspectives. The ignorance of critical life history variables and the arbitrariness of stimuli for which organisms are unprepared had become progressively misleading to students of behavior even as they began to appreciate in principle the comparative method. Complementary detail from neurology, the growing clarity of neurotransmitter specificity and distribution, and even the promise of functional radiology, are converging on a newly invigorated understanding of adaptive constraints and possibilities as individuals as well as species endeavor to cope with a dynamic environment.

Species-typical Behavior of the Green Anole

Research on the function of the reptilian corpus striatum is based on a detailed ethological study of social behavior of a lizard, the green anole, *Anolis carolinensis* (Greenberg 1977) in conjunction with an atlas of the forebrain (Greenberg 1982). The fine-grained resolution of such ethological studies are important to a fuller understanding of behavior which is very likely amalgams of several units of behavior, each with their own respective evolutionary and developmental histories. Such ensembles of units of behavior often acquire communicative significance and their continuing evolution to become more precisely evoked and effective as a signal is termed "ritualization." In evolutionary terms, brains are conservative: Most internal change is driven by environmental changes and stresses they place on the organism. As the stimulus control of units of behavior and their orchestration shifts, proximate neural causation is affected, and to the extent the change is adaptive, becomes a new selection pressure for evolutionary change in the brain.

When reproductively active male green anoles in a laboratory vivarium are confronted with an intruder, they respond with a characteristic sequence of displays. A typical first response is the "assertion" display. It is the definitive species-typical "signature" of many lizards, *Anolis carolinensis* included. In most lizards it is performed by highly alert animals, possibly patrolling their territories. It is often seen in the absence of any apparent specific stimuli or when an intruder of either sex becomes apparent to the focal animal. It is also commonly seen when a lizard is apparently startled by, for example, a sudden move by another lizard of another species or even by an insect too large to be regarded as prey. In other words, it is an indication of elevated nonspecific arousal rather than a response to any specific evocative stimulus.

The "signature" display of a green anole also serves as an "advertisement." If a sexually responsive female conspecific intrudes into a displaying male's territory and observes his display, she may provide feedback indicative of status as a potential mating partner. Most commonly this is by responding to the assertion display with a species-typical head-nodding behavior. This response generally elicits a switch in the male's behavior to courtship: a series of rapid nods performed while approaching with a unique "strutting gait." If an intruder is a male, on the other hand, and reacts with his own sequence of headnods coordinated with push-ups and extension of the dewlap, the resident will rapidly escalate its display into "challenge" (see Figure 4.2D).

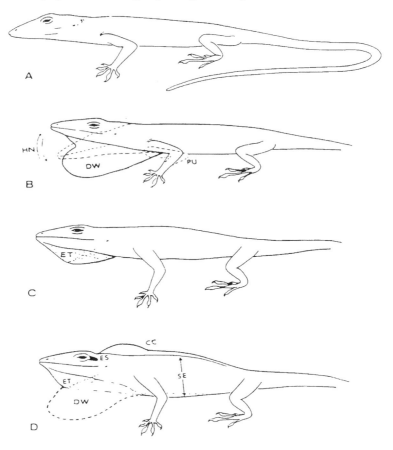

Figure 4.2. Posture and Display of the Lizard, *Anolis Carolinensis*. A, anole at rest. B, ethological units of behavior that are coordinated in the "bobbing" display: HN = headnods, PU = pushups, and DW = dewlap extension. C, expression of modifier. ET = extended throat, expressed when the animal is in the presence of a potential adversary. D, when a conspecific adversary is identified, modifiers denoting conspec- ific aggression appear and are often imposed upon the basic bobbing display, CC = nuchal and dorsal crest, DW = dewlap extension, ES = darkly pigmented "eyespot" appears, ET = extended throat, and SE = sagittal expansion, enlargement of the profile of the body in the sagittal plane (adapted from Greenberg 1977).

By virtue of the display, with its species-typical sequence of headbobs and pushups, the resident apparently "recognizes" the intruder as a member of the same species. In this context, the display is complemented by postural changes: the animal expands the sagittal profile of his body and displays to the intruder in a manner that maximizes its apparent size. As aggressive encounters escalate, the male's behavior is accompanied by autonomic responses: After about 30 seconds, an erectile crest will appear along its neck and back and body color darkens. A black "eyespot" appears just behind the eye. The intruder responds in kind as they stalk each other with slow, deliberate, apparently tense movements. In both lizards, the episode is often accompanied by changes between green and brown body color as the animals appear to assess their position relative to each other. In *Anolis carolinensis*, body color is dependent upon the flux and changing ratios of epinephrine and norepinephrine and relative autonomic tone may be important: the male that first manifests the eyespot invariably wins the contest (Summers & Greenberg 1994).

Forebrain Control of Species-typical Behavior in a Lizard

Studies in which the brain was explored by electrical stimulation failed to reveal sites of influence on stereotyped responses in the brain of *Iguana iguana* (Distel 1978). Locomotion was occasionally elicited by stimulation, but tongue-flicking behavior was reliably elicited in the lateral striatal area, although the stimulation of more medial sites resulted in the greatest number of such responses of any site investigated, possibly due to the proximity to olfactory structures. Work by Sugerman and Demski (1978) on another iguanid lizard species, *Crotaphytus collaris*, did elicit stereotyped agonistic behavior in response to electrical stimulation at several sites that roughly formed a column from the telencephalon to the rhombencephalon, but striatal sites were not tested. Tarr (1982) specifically stimulated striatal sites in the fence lizard, *Sceloporus occidentalis*, and observed stereotyped assertion displays at or near the tip of the lateral ventricle, nucleus accumbens. Points eliciting the more complex challenge displays were just anterior and dorsal to the nucleus sphericus in the posterior area of the dorsal ventricular ridge. Interpretation of stimulation experiments is always complicated, as Distel (1978) has indicated, by the difficulty in discriminating direct motor stimulation, sensory excitation, motivational changes, or general arousal. Much the same problems plague interpretation of lesion experiments. But still the techniques, in concert with further knowledge of striatal anatomy, will help point the way to progressively more specific hypotheses that can significantly inform future investigations of function.

Forebrain Lesions

Many of the aforementioned attempts to identify a brain region with aggressiveness or stereotyped behavior were difficult to interpret because of the diversity and nonspecificity of effects caused by the treatment. In a series of experiments devised in the MacLean lab, we hoped these difficulties could in part be circumvented by taking advantage of the natural split-brain preparation that lizards provide. The absence of a corpus callosum in this taxon allows us to experiment with unilateral lesions, which provides the advantage of each individual being his own progressive control. Responses of animals tested when visual input went to the lesioned hemisphere had as progressive, perfectly matched controls, tests with visual input directed to the intact side (Greenberg et al.1979). Lizards were anaesthetized in crushed ice and small electrolytic lesions placed at specific coordinates determined with the aid of a stereotaxic atlas devised for the purpose (Greenberg 1982; animal care and research protocols in Greenberg 1992).

The behavior of lizards after surgery gave no evidence of any impairment of behavior until they were confronted with intruding conspecifics. Only then was it clear that lesions of the paleostriatum of male anoles profoundly alter their social dynamics. Where vigorous territorial combat might be expected when an individual views an intruding conspecific (Greenberg 1977), the brain-lesioned resident, while responsive to the presence of the intruder, is unresponsive to the species-typical releasers of territorial aggression it provides (Greenberg et al. 1979).

This inability to recognize appropriate stimulus input might be characterized as "social agnosia." Interestingly, a striatal role in visual discrimination was already indicated by a lesion study of the forebrain of the turtle, *Chrysemys* (Reiner & Powers 1980). In other experiments, lizards with comparable lesions courted females quite normally (Greenberg et al. 1984).

An analysis of the forebrain activity of green anoles was undertaken by Baxter (1999; Baxter & Ackerman 1997) who used the eye-patch technique to limit visual input to one hemisphere or the other and then used a radio-tagged glucose (2-deoxyglucose, 2-DG) to indicate areas that were metabolically active. After injecting 2-DG, they placed animals in habitats with a mirror that effectively evoked displays from isolated, dominant or subordinate males. Using this technique they determined that the hemisphere which received visual input was significantly more active than the contralateral, "eye-patched" hemisphere. The dorsolateral basal ganglia (DL-BG) was particularly active, and the number of aggressive pushup displays performed correlated with the activation in the "seeing" dorsolateral basal ganglia's activation.

Subsequent analyses were performed on individuals who had established a dominance relationship and then isolated in a vivarium with a mirror. They each responded to their image with their "status-typical" display, and demonstrated that not only was activity increased in the "seeing" DL-BG of animals performing aggressive displays, but decreased in the "seeing" ventromedial basal ganglia (VM-BG). Further, the subjects that were submissive in the presence of the social dominant showed 2DG diminution in DL-BG and increased VM-BG activity. Interestingly, activity of a lateral segment of the overlying anterior DVR was correlated with DL-BG activation while a medial portion of the aDVR showed 2-DG accumulation when VM-BG showed activity.

Social Dominance

If intact animals, fresh from the field and known to be reproductively active, are allowed to cohabit a vivarium after a territorial confrontation, the winner typically goes about his business, alert to the cohabiting loser, but generally unperturbed as long as the loser responds with appropriate indications of deference when subjected to an occasional challenge display. A classic social dominance relationship has been established. The winner monopolizes the best sites to watch for predators, prey, or mating opportunities, while the loser, no less active in foraging or feeding, acts with apparent indifference to the trappings of power. Observed for as long a month in this condition, such subordinate males were found to have elevated levels of the chronic stress hormone corticosterone (Greenberg et al. 1984) and roughly half the normal circulating levels of the hormone testosterone (Greenberg & Crews 1990), indicating that the change in behavior subsequent to losing a fight is more likely a consequence of an altered hormone-mediated motivational state than a conditioned response to a more powerful cagemate.

The significance of the famous bobbing display and its variations awaits the clarifying resolution of ethological analysis to more fully appreciate the significance of their control by the basal forebrain. It seems relevant, however, that the ability to express the species-typical action pattern is unaffected, but the capacity to recognize a conspecific and manifest the appropriate response to an intruding male's species typical display is profoundly impaired. This is not a mere motor impairment. If the consequences of basal ganglia lesions can be construed as social agnosia, a defect of cognitive processing, is the process impaired in this lizard? In mammals, one of the several cerebral cortical inputs to basal ganglia is area TE in the inferotemporal area. This is interesting because this area, apparently essential to visual recognition and discrimination, also receives input from substantia nigra pars reticulata via the thalamus, creating a circuit that allows basal ganglia to influence higher order aspects of visual processing (Middleton & Strick 1996). Possibly related is the finding that rats which work for stimulation of their nucleus accumbens will reduce their responding under uncontrollable (but not controllable) stress in a way that indicated a loss or reduction of the reinforcing value associated with the stimulation (Bowers et al. 1987), recalling the social agnosia of paleostriatal lesioned lizards mentioned earlier.

Neurotransmitters in the Behavior of Anoles

When territorial lizards confront each other in an experimental vivarium in which they likely perceive each other as intruders, as observed in tests described above, losers of territorial fights invariably became socially subordinate, displayed darker color, selected lower perch sites, and maintained lower body posture than the winners. The subordination was unambiguous. When midbrain and hindbrain were analyzed for indolamines, catecholamines, and their metabolites by coulochem electrode array high-pressure liquid chromatography, Summers and I learned that central serotonin production and turnover is more rapidly activated in losers of fights (destined to behave in a subordinate way) than in winners (Summers & Greenberg 1995).

A closer analysis revealed that serotonergic activity in dominants and subordinates had a distinctive time course as well as regional distribution in the brain (Summers et al. 1998). Brain slices of dominant and subordinate males were micropunched to isolate specific areas and analyzed by high pressure liquid chromatography (HPLC). We found the greatest serotonergic changes in the telencephalon of subordinate males. One hour after a fight, the hippocampal cortex and nucleus accumbens showed increased ratios of 5-hydroxyindoleacetic acid/serotonin. Just as in earlier studies of the brain stems of these animals (Summers & Greenberg 1995), the ratio gradually decreased as the animal's social status became consolidated, and within one month, ratios had returned to normal. Measured in the brains of lizards sacrificed at an hour, day, week, and month following a fight, changes were seen to be more rapid in dominant males. The patterns of serotonergic activation are so similar in hippocampus, nucleus accumbens, and brain stem that a coordinated response may be involved in mediating short-term social stress and aggression. Similarly, medial and lateral amygdala exhibit corresponding, but delayed patterns in subordinate males, suggesting a coordinated response in these regions mediating longer-term stress responses (Summers et al. 1998).

Interestingly, low serotonin levels in the brains of a primate model have been associated with impulsiveness. Recent work by Baxter (1999) has shown in the *Anolis* lizard model, that beyond a sharp increase in forebrain serotonin during dominant displays and a decrease during subordinate displays, there was an activation of dorsolateral basal ganglia and deactivation of the ventromedial area. Clark and colleagues went further to analyze the subtypes of serotonin receptors and their distribution in *Anolis carolinensis*, confirming important commonalities with other taxa (Clark & Baxter 2000). In a series of analyses on dopamine receptors, the occurrence, distribution, and pharmacological specificity of dopamine D1 and D2 receptor sub-types were also seen to be similar to those of mammals. One interesting difference, however, is that neural tissue in the parts of basal ganglia outside the ventral striatum (see Table 4.1) characterized by D1 and D2 receptor subtypes is largely separated, rather than commingled as in mammalian basal ganglia (Clark et al. 2000).

Subsequent work on free-ranging lizards, *Sceloporus jarrovi*, provided consilient results: tissue samples from their telencephala and diencephala that were analyzed for monoamines, their precursors and metabolites, revealed significant differences according to social status. There was more serotonin activity and turnover in subordinates (satellite males without territories) compared to territorial males (Matter et al. 1998). Such findings also agree with findings in fish (Winberg et al.1992) and mammals (Yodyingyua et al. 1985, in primates), suggesting a phylogenetically conserved mechanism of monoamine behavioral modulation.

Aggression is stressful in the short run whatever one's status and whatever the outcome, but the experience of that stressful episode apparently evokes different long-term consequences for winners and losers. Wins or losses, real or perceived, likely lead to significantly different endocrine tone. Serotonin elevation is associated with acute stress in all animals studied (e.g., Winberg et al. 1992 among others) but only in losers of encounters does serotonin elevation persist.

Other data supportive of the idea of the relative resilience in dominants is apparent in color change data. In *Anolis carolinensis*, the circulating epinephrine-dependent eyespot appears earlier during an aggressive exchange in the future-dominant, and fades more quickly (Summers & Greenberg 1994).

The basal ganglia, the integrity of which is essential to an expression of a green anole's aggressive display, also mediates displays that characterize social status. Baxter and colleagues measured both activation of forebrain sites and changes in function in lizards displaying the pushup and profile change that characterize aggressive dominants and those that characterize subordinates. In dominant animals but not subordinates, increased 5-HT correlated well with dorsolateral basal ganglia activation. The complete decussation of optic tracts in anoles was exploited by Baxter in much the same manner as Greenberg, to direct visual stimuli to a hemisphere that can then be compared to the contralateral hemisphere for an effect. The glucose mimic, 2-DG (^{14}C-2-deoxyglucose) accumulates preferentially in more active cells. When eye-patched lizards were housed together, dominants and subordinates came to express their respective social displays repeatedly to mirrors, and accumulations of 2-DG were seen in the basal ganglia only of dominants and only in the hemisphere opposite the unpatched eye (Baxter et al. 2000).

Connections

As mentioned earlier striatal structures in reptiles differ from those of mammals in that descending pathways predominate (Parent 1986). An alternative attempt to clarify the connections and role of paleostriatum involved the use of a neurotoxin that will selectively destroy dopaminergic cells. The meperidine analog, MPTP (methylphenyltetrahydropyridine), was believed to be toxic to dopaminergic cells by its being selectively incorporated into neurons through their re-uptake systems. The procedure became popular because the symptoms produced can be similar to idiopathic Parkinson's disease (Marsden & Jenner 1987), presumably by means of toxic effects on the dopaminergic substantia nigra pars compacta, although some studies also report effects in locus caeruleus and the ventral tegmental area (reviewed by Langston & Irwin 1986). While the primary site of cell death is the pars compacta of the substantia nigra (SN), the adjacent ventral tegmental area and other sites are also often affected. The selectivity appears sensitive to both the age of the animal (less selective in older subjects, Marsden & Jenner 1987) and the amount of MPTP administered. In fact, at low levels, many SN cells may survive while conspicuous mesostriatal axonopathies appear and tyrosine hydroxylase immuno-reactivity in the striatum decreases (Kitt et. al. 1987).

MPTP Experiment

To help us confirm and extend our understanding of dopaminergic pathways and their possible influences on behavior, several *Anolis carolinensis* were injected intraperitoneally with varying doses of MPTP. At high doses (100 mg/kg) the lizards showed postural rigidity, convulsions, stereotyped head and neck movements, and died within 24 hrs of injection. Lower doses resulted in a transient behavioral syndrome consisting of hypokinesia and signs of adrenal activation. Acute behavioral changes in MPTP-treated animals included indications of a physiological stress response and, in particular, color changes, including the formation of a post-orbital darkening (the "eye spot"), and nuchal crest erection, both indications of adrenal activation (see Greenberg & Crews 1983). These effects and a pronounced hypokinesia remitted in all but 8 individuals who received in excess of 50mg/kg of the drug and subsequently died. These individuals also developed akinesia, postural rigidity, episodic convulsions, and occasionally manifested stereotyped head and neck movements. Most individuals, however, survived and showed no further symptoms of physiological stress (Font, Switzer & Greenberg 1988; Font et al. 1988). This survival is consistent with the idea of functional recovery of involved neural tissue; the individuals that did not survive may have suffered a crisis of adaptation due to massive and persevering adrenal activation (Barbeau et al. 1985). Most subjects that received smaller doses, while showing clear indications of neurological damage, displayed no significant behavioral deficits; several, however, showed episodic rigidity and diminished spontaneous behavior. In tests of species-typical aggressive behavior, such subjects performed appropriate stereotyped behavior, albeit at low intensities (Greenberg et al. unpublished data).

After behavioral observations, cytopathological effects were assessed using the cupric silver method of method of de Olmos et al. (1981). Degenerating axons were observed ascending in the lateral forebrain bundle from the midbrain tegmentum (substantia nigra and ventral tegmental area) to targets in the anterior dorsal ventricular ridge, ventral striatum, nucleus accumbens, anterior and posterior entopeduncular nuclei, dorsal nucleus of the posterior commissure, and tectum mesencephali. Two types of argyrophilic perikarya were observed: degenerative and reactive. Cytopathological changes were apparent at several loci ranging from the forebrain to the cervical cord. Degenerative changes were also seen in striatal terminals in areas that also show catecholamine histofluore-scence and AChE reactivity (Greenberg, Font & Switzer 1988), supporting the putative homology of the reptilian striatal afferents and the mammalian meso-striatal pathway.

The projections revealed by the MPTP treatment confirm and extend our knowledge of ascending midbrain projections in lizards. Parts of this projection system are similar to the mesostriatal dopaminergic pathway of mammals; however, the distribution of argyrophilic perikarya found in lizards markedly differs from reports of cell damage in MPTP treated mammals. Difficulty in interpretation is attributable to species variability (Langston & Irwin 1986; Kopin & Markey 1988) and the possibility that non-catecholaminergic neurons may be affected by MPTP (Switzer & Campbell 1987 with C57 mice).

When aggressive pairs of rats set up social dominance relationships, both are stressed, but subordination involves additional burdens. Such males manifest behavior much like chronic depression. They appear defensive, voluntary alco-hol consumption increases, and lifespans are shortened. Corticosterone is eleva-ted and testosterone is reduced in rats much as in lizards (above) and most vertebrates. Most relevant to understanding the neurochemistry of stress and stress-related dysfunction, subordinates also manifest changes in serotonin systems indicative of increased 5-HIAA/5-HT ratios in various brain areas and altered 5-HT(1A) receptor binding at some sites (Blanchard et al. 1993).

ENVOI AND NEED FOR FUTURE STUDY

The diverse assortment of phenomena in which the basal ganglia participate vividly conveys a sense of the nested priorities of organisms. The unique qualities of the basal ganglia from its most ancient expression in vertebrates through humankind are consistently involved with the allocation of resources and the attempt to respond to environmental stimuli with the optimal balance of responses. These responses include those firmly embedded in an organism's behavioral repertoire as well as more recent and innovative behavioral patterns.

Specialists approach the problems of structure and function from their respective perspectives. Clinicians are appropriately preoccupied with expres-sions of pathology, most often negative symptoms such as, functional deficits or losses, rather than positive signs such as excesses. And comparative neurologists are acutely sensitive to the fundamental promise of the more recently evolved structures to shape and control more "primitive" behavioral patterns organized at lower levels. Ethology, having been guided as an emerging field more by zoology than psychology, emphasizes the differences between organisms more than the commonalities. It is alert to the boundary conditions that reflect the limits of possibility. Neuroethology sought the best of both worlds: the necessarily evolutionary conservative nervous system and the incredible diversity of behavior manifest in diverse environments. As evolution cobbles together fragments of the organism's rich potential into new ways of coping with various selection pressures, only our broad experience of possibilities can prepare us to make the most of what natural or laboratory experiments show us. Striatal-lesioned lizards, for example, may appear unimpaired unless provided with an appropriate venue for expression—an expression one might never look for or find if ignorant of the details of their natural history.

In recent decades, research is becoming more collaborative. The isolation that results from great disciplinary depth is being overcome by interdisciplinary research teams. But even in such an environment, ideas are born in a single mind and then shared, and often the visionary idea is the next generation's dogma. In an echo of the evolutionary process, ideas that lead to insights that successfully solve problems are retained and when the problems are solved they become available for some other use or are even allowed to disappear. Insights about the basal ganglia, which began as gross estimates based on major trauma or disease, have become replaced by progressively more subtle understanding as more detail becomes available and particularly as the diversity of precisely described behavioral patterns associated with their function in a diversity of taxa and contexts is examined.

This is the essence of the ethological method, in which an appreciation of the expressions of comparable behavioral patterns in diverse taxa and in their natural environments instills a sense of the awesome richness of possibilities that nature fosters. An appreciation of this breadth of application by supreme masters of their fields such as Paul D. MacLean will continue to enrich us by virtue of their model of wide-ranging imagination grounded in deep disciplinary understanding.

REFERENCES

Anderson, Carl M., Ann Polcari, Carol A. Glod, Luis C. Maas, Perry F. Renshaw, and, Martin H. Teicher. 2000. "Functional deficits in basal ganglia of children with attention-deficit/hyperactivity disorder shown with functional magnetic resonance imaging relaxometry." *Nature Medicine.* 6 (4):470–473.

Anderson G. M., M. A. Dover, B. P. Yang, J. M. Holahan, E. S. Shaywitz, K. E. Marchione, L. M. Hall, J. M. Fletcher, and B. A. Shaywitz. 2000. "Adreno-medullary function during cognitive testing in attention-deficit/hyperactivity disorder." *Journal of the American Academy of Child Adolescent Psychiatry.* 39(5): 635–643.

Antelman, Seymour M. and Anthony R. Caggiula. 1980. "Stress-induced behavior: Chemotherapy without drugs." In: *The Psychobiology of Consciousness*, J.M. Davidson and R. J. Davidson (editors). Plenum Press, New York. Pp. 65–104.

Austin, James H. 1998. *Zen and the Brain.* MIT Press, Cambridge, MA.

Barbeau, A., L. Dallaire, N. Buu, J. Poirier, and E. Rucinska. 1985. "Comparative behavioral, biochemical and pigmentary effects of MPTP, MPP+ and paraquat in Rana pipiens," *Life Science.* 37: 1529–1538.

Baxter Lewis R. 1999. "Serotonin and brain circuitry mediating ritualistic territorial displays in anmiotes, from reptiles to humans." In: *Workshop on studies stemming from the life work of Dr. Paul MacLean, T. Insel and M. George, chairs, Social Biology and Psychiatry Annual Meeting*, Washington, DC, May 15, 1999.

Baxter Lewis R. and R. F. Ackermann. 1997. "Specific brain circuit activation and 5-HT function during ritualistic territorial display vs. non-display in the anole lizard, Anolis carolinensis." *Proceedings of the Society of Neuroscience Annual Meeting,* p. 744 (abstract).

Baxter, Lewis R. jr., E. C. Clark, M. Iqbal, and R. F. Ackerman. 2000. *Cortical-subcortical systems in the mediation of obsessive-compulsive disorder.* (In Press).

Beiser, David G. and James C. Houk. 1998. "Model of cortical-basal ganglionic processing: encoding the serial order of sensory events." *Journal of Neurophysiology.* 79: 3168–3188.

Bellairs, Angus. 1970. *The Life of Reptiles.* Vol. 2. Universe Books, New York.

Blanchard D. C.; R. R. Sakai, B. McEwen, S. M. Weiss, and R. J. Blanchard. 1993. "Subordination stress: behavioral, brain, and neuroendocrine correlates." *Behavioral Brain Research.* 58(1–2): 113–121.

Boden, Margaret. 1990. *The Creative Mind .* Basic Books, New York.

Bosch, Alexander P. M. van den. 1996. "The dopamine theory of Parkinson's disease." at: *http://tcw2.ppsw.rug.nl/~vdbosch/pd.html,* November 22, 1996. Rijksuniversiteit, Groningen.

Bowers, Wayne J., R. M. Zacharko, and H. Anisman. 1987. "Evaluation of stressor effects on intracranial self-stimulation from the nucleus accumbens and the substantia nigra in a current intensity paradigm." *Behavioral BrainResearch.* 23: 85–93.

Bradshaw, J., D. Sheppard. 2000. "The neurodevelopmental fronto-striatal disorders: evolutionary adaptiveness and anomalous lateralization." *Brain and Language.* 73(2): 297–320.

Brauth, S. E. and C. A. Kitt. 1980. "The paleostriatal system of Caiman crocodilus." *Journal of Comparative Neurology.* 189: 437–465.

Brown, Lucy L., Jay S. Schneider, and Theodore I. Lidsky. 1997. "Sensory and cognitive functions of the basal ganglia." *Current Opinion in Neurobiology.* 7: 157–163.

Brown, P. and C. D. Marsden. 1998. "What do the basal ganglia do?" *The Lancet.* 51 (9118): 1801–1804.

Butler, Ann B. and William Hodos. 1996. *Comparative Vertebrate Neuroanatomy: Evolution and Adaptation.* Wiley, New York.

Cabib S. and S. Puglisi-Allegra. 1996. "Stress, depression and the mesolimbic dopamine system." *Psychopharmacology (Berl).* 128 (4): 331–342.

Canales, J. J. and A. M. Graybiel. 2000. "A measure of striatal function predicts motor stereotypy." *Nature Neuroscience.* 3(4): 377–383.

Chachko, R.C., M. A. Corbin, and R. G. Harper. 2000 "Acquired obsessive-compulsive disorder associated with basal ganglia lesions." *Journal of Neuropsychiatry and Clinical Neuroscience.* 12: 269–272.

Clark, Edward C. and Lewis R. Baxter, Jr. 2000. "Mammal-Like Striatal Functions in *Anolis* I. Distribution of Serotonin Receptor Subtypes, and Absence of Striosome and Matrix Organization." *Brain, Behavior, and Evolution* 56 (5): 235–248.

Clark, Edward C., Lewis R. Baxter, Jr., Leon S. Dure, Robert F. Ackermann, George F. Kemp, and Susan E. Bachus. 2000. "Mammal-Like Striatal Functions in Anolis II. Distribution of Dopamine D1 and D2 Receptors, and a LaminarPattern of Basal Ganglia Sub-Systems." *Brain, Behavior, and Evolution.* 56 (5): 249–258.

Cools, A. R. 1985. "Brain and behavior: hierarchy of feedback systems and control of input." In: *Perspectives in Ethology*, P. P. G. Bateson, P. H. Klopfer (editors). 6: 109–168. Plenum Press, New York.

Cools, A. R. and J. H. L. van den Bercken. 1977. "Cerebral organization /of behaviour and the neostriatal function." In: *Psychobiology of the Striatum.* Cools, Lohman, Van Den Bercken (editors). Elsevier, NY. Pp. 119–140.

Cooper, Jonathan J. and Christine J. Nicol. 1991. "Stereotypic behavior affects environmental preference in bank voles, *Clethrionomys glareolus*." *Animal Behavior* 41: 971–977.

Cooper, W. E. Jr. and N. Greenberg. 1992. "Reptilian coloration and behavior."In: *Hormones, Brain, and Behavior*, Vol. 18 of *Biology of the Reptilia.* C. Gans and D. Crews (editors). University of Chicago Press. Pp 298–422.

Cotterill, Rodney M. J. 2001. "Cooperation of the basal ganglia, cerebellum, sensory cerebrum, and hippocampus: possible implications for cognition, consciousness, intelligence, and creativity." *Progress in Neurobiology.* 64: 1–33.

Cummings, J. L. and M. Frankel. 1985. "Gilles de la Tourette's syndrome and the neurological basis of obsessions and compulsions." *Biological Psychiatry.* 20: 1117–1126.

Dantzer, Robert. 1986. "Behavioral, physiological and functional aspects of stereotyped behavior: a review and re-interpretation." *Journal of Animal Science.* 62: 1776–1786.

Dayan, Peter, Sham Kakade and P. Read Montague. 2000. "Learning and selective attention." *Nature Neuroscience.* 3: 1218–1223.

de Olmos, J. S., S. O. E. Ebbesson, and L. Heimer. 1981. "Silver methods for impregnation of degenerating axons." In *Neuroanatomical Tract-Tracing Methods.* L. Heimer and T. Robards, (editors) Plenum Press, New York. Pp 117–170.

Distel, H. 1978. "Behavioral responses to the electrical stimulation of the brain in the green iguana." In: *Behavior and Neurology of Lizards.* N. Greenberg and P. D. MacLean (editors). National Institute of Mental Health, Rockville, MD, DHEW No. (ADM) 77-491. Pp. 135–147.

Divac, I. 1977. "Does the neostriatum operate as a functional entity?" In: *Psychobiology of the striatum*, A. Cools, Lohman, Van Den Bercken(editors). Elsevier, New York. Pp. 21–30.

Divac, I. and R. G. E. Oberg. 1979. "Current conceptions of neostriatal functions." In *The Neostriatum.* I. Divac and R.G.E. Oberg (editors). Pergamon, Oxford. Pp. 215–230.

Edelman, Gerald M. and Giulio Tononi. 2000. *A Universe of Consciousness: How Matter Becomes Imagination.* Basic Books, New York.

Fischer, R. S., M. P. Alexander, and M. D'Esposito, R. Otto. 1995. "Neuropsychological and neuroanatomical correlates of confabulation." *Journal of Clinical and Experimental Neuropsychology.* 17(1): 20–28.

Font, E., R. C. Switzer III, and N. Greenberg. 1988. "MPTP-induced neuropathology and behavior in the lizard *Anolis carolinensis*." unpublished data.

Fuster, J.M. 1991. "The prefrontal cortex and its relation to behavior." *Progress in Brain Research.* 87: 201–211.

Gabrieli, J.D.E. 1998. "Cognitive neuroscience of human memory." *Annual Review of Psychology.* 1998. 49: 87–115.

Goldenberg, G., U. Schuri, O. Gromminger, and U. Arnold. 1999. "Basal forebrain amnesia: does the nucleus accumbens contribute to human memory?" *Journal of Neurology, Neurosurgery, and Psychiatry.* 67: 163–168.

Goldstein, D. S. 1987. "Stress-induced activation of the sympathetic nervous system." *Baillieres Clin Endocrinol Metab.* 2: 253–278.

Graybiel, Ann M. 1990. "Neurotransmitters and neuromodulators in the basal ganglia." *Trends in Neuroscience.* 13 (7): 244–254.

Graybiel, Ann M. 1995. "Building action repertoires: Memory and learning functions of the basal ganglia." *Current Opinion in Neurobiology.* 5: 733–741.

Graybiel, Ann M. 1997. "The basal ganglia and cognitive pattern generators." *Schizophrenia Bulletin.* 1997 23: 3459–3469.

Graybiel, Ann M. 1998. "The basal ganglia and chunking of action repertoires." *Neurobiology, Learning, and Memory.* 70 (1–2: 119–136).

Graybiel, Ann M. 2000. "The basal ganglia." *Current Biology.* 10: R509–R511.

Graybiel, Ann M., Toshihiko Aosaki, Alice W. Flaherty, and Minoru Kimura. "The basal ganglia and adaptive motor control." *Science.* 265: 1826–1831.

Greenberg, Neil. 1977. "A neuroethological investigation of display behavior in the lizard, *Anolis carolinensis,* (Lacertilia, Iguanidae)." *American Zoologist.* 17(1): 191–201.

Greenberg, Neil. 1978. "Ethological considerations in the experimental study of lizard behavior." In: *Behavior and Neurology of Lizards,* Neil Greenberg and Paul D. MacLean (editors). National Institute of Mental Health, Rockville, Md., DHEW No. (ADM) 77-491. Pp. 204–224.

Greenberg, Neil. 1982. "A forebrain atlas and stereotaxic technique for the lizard Anolis carolinensis." *Journal of Morphology.* 174(2): 217–236.

Greenberg, Neil. 1983. "Central and autonomic aspects of aggression and dominance in reptiles." In: *Advances in Vertebrate Neuroethology.* J. P. Ewert, R. R. Capranica, D. J. Ingle (editors). Plenum Press, New York. Pp.1135–1144.

Greenberg, Neil. 1990. "The behavioral endocrinology of physiological stress in a lizard." *Journal of Experimental Zoology.* Supplement 4: 170–173.

Greenberg, Neil. 1992. "The saurian psyche revisited: Lizards in research." In: *The Care and Use of Amphibians, Reptiles, and Fish in Research.* D. O. Schaeffer, K. M. Kleinow, and L. Krulish (editors). Scientists Center for Animal Welfare, Bethesda, MD. Pp. 75–91.

Greenberg, Neil. 2002. "Behavioral causes and consequences of the stress response in reptiles." *Journal of Integrative and Comparative Biology.* (formerly American Zoologist). in press.

Greenberg, Neil and David Crews. 1990. "Endocrine and behavioral responses to aggression and social dominance in the green anole lizard, Anolis carolinensis." *General Comparative Endocrinology.* 77: 1–10.

Greenberg, Neil and David Crews. 1983. "Physiological ethology of aggression in amphibians and reptiles." In: *Hormones and Aggressive Behavior.* B. Svare, (editor). Plenum Press, New York. Pp. 469–506.

Greenberg, Neil and John Wingfield. 1987. "Stress and reproduction: Reciprocal relationships." In: *Reproductive Endocrinology of Fish, Amphibians, and Reptiles.* D. O. Norris and R. E. Jones (editors). Plenum Press, New York. Pp. 461–503.

Greenberg, Neil, E. Font, and R. Switzer. 1988. "The reptilian striatum revisited." In: *The Forebrain in Reptiles: Current Concepts of Structure and Function.* W. K. Schwerdtfeger and W. J. Smeets (editors). Karger-verlag, Basel. Pp 162–177.

Greenberg, Neil, M. Scott, and D. Crews. 1984. "Role of the amygdala in the aggressive and reproductive behavior of the lizard, *Anolis carolinensis.*" *Physiology & Behavior.* 32(1): 147–151.

Greenberg, Neil, Thomas Chen, and David Crews. 1984. "Social status, gonadal state, and the adrenal stress response in the lizard, *Anolis carolinensis.*" *Hormones and Behavior.* 18: 1–11.

Greenberg, Neil, G. Burghardt, D. Crews, E. Font, R. Jones, and G. Vaughan. "Reptile models for biomedical research." In: *Animal Models in Biomedical Research.* Avril D. Woodhead (editor). CRC Press, N. Y. Pp. 289–308.

Greenberg, Neil, P. D. MacLean, and L. F. Ferguson. 1979. "Role of the Paleostriatum in species-typical display of the lizard, *Anolis carolinensis.*" *Brain Research.* 172: 229–241.

Greenberg, Neil and P. D. MacLean, Editors. 1978. *Behavior and Neurology of Lizards.* National Institute of Mental Health, Rockville, MD, DHEW No. (ADM) 77–491. 352.

Groenewegen, Henk J., Christopher I. Wright, and A V. J. Beijer. 1996. "The nucleus accumbens: gateway for limbic structures to reach the motor system." *Progress in Brain Research.* 107: 485–511.

Hadley, Mac E. 1996. *Endocrinology.* (fourth edition) Prentice Hall, Upper Saddle River, N.J.

Haber, S. N. and J. L. Fudge. 1997. "The interface between dopamine neurons and the amygdala: implications for schizophrenia." *Schizophrenia Bulletin.* 23 (3): 471–482.

Hailman, J. 1969. "How an Instinct Is Learned." *Scientific American.* 221: 98–106.

Hashimoto R., Y. Tanaka, and I. Nakano. 2000. "Amnesic confabulatory syndrome after focal basal forebrain damage." *Neurology.* 54(4): 978–980.

Hayes, Amy E., Matthew C. Davidson, Steven W. Keele, and Robert D. Rafal. 1998 "Toward a functional analysis of the basal ganglia." *Journal of Cognitive Neuroscience.* 10: 178–198.

Heckers, Stephan. 1997. "Neuropathology of schizophrenia: cortex, thalamus, basal ganglia, and neurotransmitter-specific projection systems."*Schizophrenia Bulletin.* 23(3): 403–421.

Heimer, L., R. C. Switzer III, and G. W. Van Hoesen. 1982. "Ventral striatum and ventral pallidum. Components of the motor systems?" *Trends in Neuroscience.* 5: 83–87.

Herve, D., G. Blanc, J. Glowinski, and J. P. Tassin. 1982. "Reduction of dopamine utilization in the prefrontal cortex but not in the nucleus accumbens after selective destruction of noradrenergic fibers innervating the ventral tegmental area in the rat." *Brain Research.* 237: 510–516.

Heymer, Armin. 1977. *Ethological Dictionary.* Verlag Paul Parey, Berlin.

Hoffmann, A. A. and M. J. Hercus. 2000. "Environmental stress as an evolutionary force." *Bioscience.* 50(3): 217–226.

Holt, D. J., M. M. Herman, T. M. Hyde, J. E. Kleinman, C. M. Sinton, D. C. German, L. B. Hersh, A. M. Graybiel, and C. Saper. 1999. "Evidence for a deficit in cholinergic interneurons in the striatum in schizophrenia." *Neuroscience.* 94(1): 21–31

Huether G. 1996. "The central adaptation syndrome: psychosocial stress as a trigger for adaptive modifications of brain structure and brain function." *Progress in Neurobiology.* 48(6): 569–612.

Huxley, J. 1966. "A discussion on ritualization of behavior in animals and man.*" Philosophical Transactions of the Royal Society, London, Series B. Biological Sciences.* 772 (251): 247–526.

Insel, Thomas R. 1988. "Obsessive-compulsive disorder: new models." *Psychopharmacology Bulletin.* 24(3): 365–369.

Jablonski, D. and D. J. Bottjer. 1990. "The ecology of evolutionary innovation: The fossil record." In M. H. Nitecki (ed.), *Evolutionary Adaptations.* Pp. 253–288. University of Chicago Press, Chicago.

Jenssen, Thomas A. 1978. "Display diversity in anoline lizards and problems of interpretation." In *Behavior and Neurology of Lizards.* Neil Greenberg and Paul D. MacLean (editors). National Institute of Mental Health, DHEW Publication (ADM) 77–491. Rockville, Maryland. Pp. 269–286.

Jenssen, Thomas A. 1979. "Display modifiers of Anolis opalinus (Sauria, Iguanidae)." *Herpetologica.* 35: 21–30.

Jenssen, Thomas A., Neil Greenberg, and K. A. Hovde. 1995. "Behavioral profile of free-ranging lizards, *Anolis carolinensis*, across breeding and post-breeding seasons." *Herpetology Monographs.* 9: 41–62.

Jog, Mandar S., Yasuo Kubota, Christopher I. Connolly, Viveka Hillegaart, and Ann M. Graybiel. 1999. "Building neural representations of habits." *Science.* 286: 1745–1749.

Jueptner, M., C. D. Frith, D. J. Brooks, R. S. J. Frackowiak, and R. E. Passingham. 1997. "Anatomy of motor learning. II. Subcortical structures and learning by trial and error." *Journal of Neurophysiology.* 77: 1325–1337.

Kawagoe, Reiko, Y. Takakawa, and O. Hirosaka. 1998. "Expectation of Reward Modulates Cognitive Signals in the Basal Ganglia." *Nature Neuroscience.* 1(5): 411–416.

Kitt, C. A., L. C. Cork, E. Eidelberg, E. T. H. Tong, and D. L. Price. 1987. "Injury of cate-cholaminergic neurons after acute exposure to MPTP." *Annals of NY Academy of Science.* 495: 730–731.

Knowlton, Barbara J., Jennifer A. Mangels, and Larry R. Squire 1996. "A neostriatal habit learning system in humans." *Science.* 273: 1399–1402.

Kopin,, I. K. and S. P. Markey. 1988. "MPTP Toxicity: Implications for research in Parkinsons desease." *Annual Review of Neuroscience.* 11: 81–96.

Langston, J. W. and I. Irwin.. 1986. "MPTP: current concepts and controversies." *Clinical Neuropharmacology.* 9: 485–507.

Laplane, D. 1994. "Obsessions et compulsions par lesions des noyaux gris centraux." *Revue Neurologie.* (Paris) 150 (8-9): 594–598 (by abstract).

Lou, H., L. Henriksen, P. Bruhn, H. Borner, & J. Nielsen. 1989. "Striatal dysfunction in attention deficit and hyperkinetic disorder." *Archives of Neurology.* 46: 48–52.

MacLean, P. D. 1978. "Effects of lesions of globus pallidus on species-typical display behavior of squirrel monkeys." *Brain Research.* 149: 175–196.

MacLean, P. D. 1990. *The Triune Brain in Evolution.* Plenum, New York.

Marin, O., W. J. Smeets, and A. Gonzalez. 1998. "Evolution of the basal ganglia in tetrapods: A new perspective based on recent studies in amphibians." *Trends in Neuroscience.* 21(11): 487–494.

Marsden, C. D. and P. G. Jenner. 1987. "The significance of 1-methyl-4phenyl-1,2,3,6-tetrahydropyridine, in Selective Neuronal Death," *CIBA Symposium*, 126: 239.

Mason, G. J. 1991. "Stereotypies: a critical review." *Animal Behavior.* 41: 1015–1037.

Matter, John M., Patrick J. Ronan, and Cliff H. Summers. 1998. "Central monoamines in free-ranging lizards: Differences associated with social roles and territoriality." *Brain Behavior, and Evolution.* 51: 23–32.

Mayes, A. R. 1999. "What basal forebrain lesions cause amnesia?" *Journal of Neurology, Neurosurgery, and Psychiatry.* 67: 140.

Merchant, Hugo, Antonio Zainos, Adrian Hernandez, Emilio Salinas, and Ranulfo Romo. 1997. "Functional properties of primate putamen neurons during the categorization of tactile stimuli." *Journal of Neurophysiology.* 77: 1132–1154.

McEwen, Bruce S. 1999 "Stress." *The MIT Encyclopedia of the Cognitive Sciences.* Robert A. Wilson and Franz Keil, (general editors). MIT Press, A Bradford Book.

McGuire, Michael T. and Lynn A. Fairbanks. 1974. *Ethological Psychiatry: Psychopathology in the context of evolutionary biology.* Grune & Stratton, New York.

Middleton, Frank A. and Peter L. Strick. 1996. "The temporal lobe is a target of output from the basal ganglia." *Proceeding of the National Academy of Science.* 93(16): 8683–8687.

Mink, J W. 1996. "The basal ganglia: focused selection and inhibition of competing motor programs." *Progress in Neurobiology.* 50(4): 381–425.

Moberg, Gary P. 1999. "When does stress become distress?" *Lab Animal.* 28(4): 22–26.

Mogenson, G. J., D. L. Jones, C. Y. Kim. 1980 "From Motivation to Action: functional interface between the limbic system and the motor system." *Progress in Neurobiology.* 14 (2–3): 69–97.

Morris, D. 1956. "The feather postures of birds and the problem of the origin of social signals." *Behaviour.* 75–113.

Nieuwenhuys, Rudolf. 1996. "The greater limbic system, the emotional motor system and the brain." *Progress in Brain Research.* 107 (G. Holstege, R. Bandler, and C. B. Saper, editors). Pp. 551–580.

Paradiso, S., D. L. Johnson, N. C. Andreasen, and D. S. O'Leary. 1999. "Cerebral blood flow changes associated with attribution of emotional valence to pleasant, unpleasant, and neutral visual stimuli in a PET study of normal subjects." *American Journal of Psychiatry.* 156(10): 1618–1629.

Parent, A, 1986. *Comparative Neurobiology of the Basal Ganglia.* Wiley, NY.

Parent, A., and L-N. Hazrati. 1995a. "Functional anatomy of the basal ganglia I. The cortico-basal ganglia-thalamo-cortical loop." *Brain Research Review.* 20(1): 91–127.

Parent , A., and L-N. Hazrati. 1995b. "Functional anatomy of the basal ganglia. II. The place of subthalamic nucleus and external pallidum in basal ganglia circuitry." *Brain Research Review.* 20(1): 128–154.

Parent, A. F. Sato, Y. Wu, J. Gauthier, M. Levesque, and M. Parent. 2000. "Organization of the basal ganglia: The importance of axonal collateralization." *Trends in Neuro-science.* 23(10), suppl. Basal ganglia, Parkinson's disease and levodopa therapy): S20–S27.

Peigneux P, P. Maquet, T. Meulemans, A. Destrebecqz, S. Laureys, C. Degueldre, G. Delfiore, J. Aerts, A. Luxen, G. Franck, M. Van der Linden, and A. Cleeremans. 2000. "Striatum forever, despite sequence learning variability: a random effect analysis of PET data." *Human Brain Mapping.* 10(4): 179–194.

Pribram, K. 1977. "New dimensions in the functions of the basal ganglia." *In Psycho-pathology and Brain Dysfunction.* C. Shagass, S. Gershon, and I. Friedhoff, editors. Raven Press, New York. Pp. 77–94.

Reiner, A.and A. S. Powers. 1980. "The effects of extensive forebrain lesions on visual discriminative performance in turtles (Chrysemys picta picta)."*Brain Research.* 192: 327–337.

Roffler-Tarlov S. and A.M. Graybiel. 1984. "Weaver mutation has differential effects on the dopamine-containing innervation of the limbic and nonlimbic striatum." *Nature.* 307 (5946): 62–66.

Salamone, J. D. 1994. "The involvement of nucleus accumbens dopamine in appetitive and aversive motivation." *Behavioral Brain Research.* 61: 117–133.

Saper, C. B. 1996. "Role of the Cerebral Cortex and Striatum in Emotional Motor Responses." *Progress in Brain Research.* 107: 537–550.

Schneider, J. S. and T. I. Lidsky. 1981. "Processing of somatosensory information in striatum of behaving cats." *Journal of Neurophysiology.* 45: 841–851.

Schultz, Wolfram. 1998. "Predictive Reward Signal of Dopamine Neurons." *Journal of Neurophysiology.* 80(1): 1–27

Schultz W., P. Dayan, and P. R. Montague. 1997. "A neural substrate of prediction and reward." *Science.* 275: 1593–1599.

Schultz W., P. Apicella, E. Scarnati, and T. Ljungberg. 1992. "Neuronal activity in monkey ventral striatum related to the expectation of reward." *Journal of Neuroscience.* 12(12): 4595–4610.

Scott P. A., M. A. Cierpial, C. D. Kilts, and J. M. Weiss. 1996. "Susceptibility and resistance of rats to stress-induced decreases in swim-test activity: a selective breeding study." *Brain Research.* 725(2): 217–230.

Seligman, M., R. Rosellini, and M. Kozak. 1975. "Learned helplessness in the rat." *Journal of Comparative Physiological Psychology.* 88: 542–547.

Seligman, M. 1975. *Helplessness.* Freeman & Co., San Francisco.

Sheppard, D. M., J. L. Bradshaw, R. Purcell, and C. Pantelis. 1999. "Tourette's and comorbid syndromes: obsessive compulsive and attention deficit hyperactivity disorder. A common etiology?" *Clinical Psychology Review.* 19(5): 531–552.

Shibata, Dean K., Jianhui Zhong, Edmund Kwok, David A. Shrier, Yuji Numaguchi, and Henry Z. Wang. 2000. Reported at the 86th annual meeting of the Radiological Society of North America, Chicago.

Stein, J. F. 1986. "The control of movement." In: *Functions of the Brain.* Clive Coen (editor). Clarendon Press, Oxford. Pp. 67–97.

Sternberg, Robert J. and Todd I. Lubart. 1999. "The concept of creativity: Prospects and paradigms." In: *Handbook of Creativity.* Robert J. Sternberg (editor). Cambridge University Press, New York. Pp. 3–15.

Sugerman, R. A. and L. S. Demski. 1978. "Agonistic behavior elicited by electrical stimula-tion of the brain in western collared lizards, Crotaphytus collaris." *Brain, Behavior, and Evolution.* 15: 446–469.

Summers, Cliff H. and Neil Greenberg. 1994. "Somatic correlates of adrenergic activity during aggression in the lizard, Anolis carolinensis." *Hormones and Behavior.* 28: 29–40.

Summers, Cliff H. and Neil Greenberg. 1995. "Activation of central biogenic amines following aggressive interactions in male lizards, Anolis carolinensis." *Brain, Behavior, and Evolution.* 45: 339–349.

Summers, Cliff H., Earl T. Larson, Tangi R. Summers, Kenneth J. Renner, and Neil Greenberg. 1998. "Regional and temporal separation of serotonergic activity mediating social stress." *Neuroscience.* 87(2): 489–496.

Tarr, R. S. 1982. "Species typical display behavior following stimulation of the reptilian striatum." *Physiology and Behavior.* 29: 615–620.

Teuber, H. L. 1976. "Complex functions of basal ganglia." In *The Basal Ganglia.* P. Yahr (editor). Raven Press, New York. Pp.151–168.

Thierry, A. M., J. P. Tassin, G. Blanc, and J. Glowinski. 1976. "Selective activation of the mesocortical DA system by stress." *Nature.* 263: 242–244.

Tinbergen, N. 1951. *The Study of Instinct.* Clarendon Press, Oxford.

Wickelgren, Ingrid. 1998. "Getting the brain's attention." *Science.* 278: 35–37.

White, Norman F. 1974. "Ethology and psychiatry." In: *Ethology and Psychiatry.* N. F. White (editor). University of Ontario Press. Pp. 1–25.

Winberg, S., G. E. Nilsson, and K. H. Olsen. 1992. "Changes in brain serotonergic activity during hierarchic behavior in Arctic charr (Salvelinus alpinus L.) are socially induced." *Journal of Comparative Physiology.* A, 170: 93–99.

Wise, R. A. and M. A. Bozarth. 1984. "Brain reward circuitry: four circuit elements 'wired' in apparent series." *Brain Research Bulletin.* 12: 203–208.

Yodyingyuad, U., C. de la Riva, J. H. Abbott, and E. B. Keverne. 1985. "Relationship between dominance hierarchy, cerebrospinal fluid levels of amine transmitter metabolites (5-hydroxyindoleacetic acid and homovanillic acid) and plasma cortisol in monkeys." *Neuroscience.* 16: 851–858.

Zigmond, M. J., E. M. Stricker, and T. W. Berger. 1987. "Parkinsonism: insights from animal models utilizing neurotoxic agents." Pp. 1–38 in *Animal Models of Dementia.* Ed. by J. T Coyle. Alan R. Liss, New York.

PART III

THE SOCIAL BRAIN: CLINICAL THEORY AND APPLICATIONS— DEPRESSION AND MANIA

5

MacLean's Paradigm and Its Relevance for Psychiatry's Basic Science

Russell Gardner, Jr.

The decision to move from "theory" to "reality" is one we make in the absence of formal rules. (Malcolm Macmillan, 2000)[1]

INTRODUCTION

MacLean's neuroethology flared in popularity in the third quarter of the twentieth century,[2] but then undeservedly suffered reduced reputation at the century's end. As the new one begins, however, his emphases take on added importance; his focus, that is, upon social behaviors that stemmed from adaptations originating in deep time. This conclusion results from supporting data generated by the genome project as well as other genetic and brain research, on the one hand, and the need for psychiatry (and its allied clinical human service disciplines) to connect brain actions with normal human communicative behavior, on the other hand. Ability to do this helps both the assessment and treatment of those needing care. Caretaking of any kind, a social behavior, usually involves conspecifics (fellow members of a same species), an outcome of the expanded human brain: These facts combined with the largely social or communicative nature of psychiatric symptoms fostered the idea that psychiatry's basic science should be designated sociophysiology.[3,4] Such a basic science characterizes the ills of this medical specialty as variations in the social and communicational functions of the body mediated in the brain. MacLean underlined ancient roots of communicative behavior in a way now unfortunately ignored by leading neuroscientists. Practical and research implications follow from dividing psychopathology, its treatments and normal related social communications into those evolved early versus late, roughly speaking, components that humans share with other animals and those uniquely human.

Paul MacLean began this process; those of us doing clinical and correlated research work need to continue it to render our efforts more rational and more effective. MacLean's influence should foster our clinical enterprises becoming ever more relationship-based, nonexploitative benefits of the enlarged human brain.

PARADIGM GAINED

Among his contributions MacLean testified to the importance of communicational mechanisms evolved in deep time that hold great present significance in daily human lives. For each person other people possess great meaning. "'To be' is to be related."[5] Human relating has the ancient roots of mating and territoriality seen throughout the animal kingdom with its modern expansions in human language and storytelling. Recognition of and interaction with conspecifics probably date back to the initial uses of sexual reproduction in freely moving ancestral animals that countered predation on them by microparasites.[6] Besides mating, many other things that people do together had precursors in the conspecifics of our remote ancestors, some behaviors seen in animals that only remotely resemble humans, such as lizards and other reptiles. Others, group-living animals who share space with the group-living people, seem more familiar, especially dogs and cats.[7] In many ways popular esteem continues to regard positively MacLean's implicit focus on communication. But his work also found disfavor among neuroscientists as the fashion of science turned away. Yet the direction of his theory takes on substantiation from the various genome projects that testify to origins more dramatically ancient than even the depths he plumbed. Thus, he went no further back than reptiles, though a third century ago such "relatives" represented a heroic distance back into deep time. The new data take relevant history back much further still, as they show that we share many genes with invertebrates, such as DNA elements—the homeobox—that organize the body plan.[8]

The first issues of MacLean's career entailed the temporal lobes that deal with feelings and motivation. Clinical patterns stem from damage to the medial temporal region; for instance, some people display partial complex seizures as well as personality changes between seizures, including, for instance, "interpersonal stickiness"—an inability to disconnect from another person when in conversation. With an unusually comprehensive perspective, MacLean imaginatively reconstructed the onset of the mammalian family in connection with core structures that must have operated to allow conspecific attachments to happen. He knew that basic plans for behavior resembled in their ancientness—yet persistence—structural ones, such as four limbs and the vertebrate endoskeleton. He also knew conspecifics of all kinds communicate extensively and richly, using shared neuronal mechanisms that stemmed from genomic basic plans. And such cellular and other structural encodings determine organism behavior. When Mayr refined the meaning of "species," he hinged it on the behavior of reproducing.[9]

So, parallel to structure, old behaviors fulfilling their core functions persist in various modified forms. Natural selection involved mating, territoriality and social rank hierarchy as early and continuing devices that serve organism function, well-being, and survival. The basic plans giving rise to proteins and structures result in traces that remain preserved in the fossil record in contrast to the movements that always remain inferential, never observable in the long-dead animals that exhibited them once. Yet inferred or not, we presume from observations of present-day species that they must have occurred.

Deviations from these fundamental DNA and protein brain structures produce present-day pathology in psychiatry and abnormal psychology. These "disorders" appear as maladaptive communications and social functions, for example, on direct inspection, mania represents the patient as in a state that dictates the person take over, even when doing that gives the individual (and those close to him or her) problems.[10] The person does not represent a resource for others as would be the case if functionally taking over leadership of, say, a needy group. For MacLean subcortical structures that evolved as foundations to cortex required more emphatic investigational attention than did the cortical structures and functions themselves (he in fact worked little with cortical mechanisms despite their great volume and structural homogeneity). Thus, he fruitfully examined contemporary lizards, readily available reptiles whose common ancestor with humans extended to more remotely deep time than any mammal. In reptiles, MacLean (often with Neil Greenberg, who contributed a chapter to the present volume) described not only courtship and territoriality with which we are all familiar in ourselves and in fellow humans, but an added host of behaviors that surface in an out-of-context manner after people experience frontal lobe trauma or are impacted by damage to the subcortical connections with the frontal lobes, especially basal ganglia.

Thus, in psychiatric clinical evaluations, I have noted the behaviors of patients with deficient frontal lobes. Characteristic signs and symptoms of such damage include perseveration (repetition of the same behavior), echopraxia (imitating the examiner's behavior in an obligatory manner), and echolalia (although reptiles do not speak, their tendency to imitate extends to this sphere in brain-damaged humans). One easily concludes that for most of us most of the time, cortical structures that evolved during mammalian stages of development, suppress, modulate and/or alternatively express such tendencies. We normally exhibit more subtle repetitions, echopraxia and echolalia in our communicational repertoires; compared to someone with deficient frontal cortex, intact brains allow a person to integrate these functions smoothly and subtly. For instance, normal conversation features postural echoing of the participants to each other; doing so often means each signals reassurance and good feeling. A speaker's words earn the compliment of repetition by the listener which indicates an appreciation of the speaker's point while urging continuation of the interaction. Such smooth useful integration represents some of the benefits of these late-developing brain parts. Old tendencies and modern talents merge in the ebbs and flows of meaningful conversation that we take for granted.

MacLean anticipated the genomic revolution of recent times when he stated:

It is now recognized that in all animals there are molecular commonalities with respect to genetic coding, enzymatic reactions, and so on, that carry over into complex cellular assemblies. Nowhere is the uniformity of complex cellular assemblies more striking than in the cerebral evolution of vertebrates . . . the human forebrain has evolved and expanded to its great size, while retaining commonalities of three neural assemblies that reflect an ancestral relationship to reptiles, early mammals, and late mammals.

Genetic coding for language seems to have evolved recently, concomitantly with the expanded neocortex three times the weight in humans compared to chimpanzees. Yet Lieberman, influenced by MacLean, notes that language clearly features numerous subcortical components, fostered in a manner similar to the way that echoing postures and movements take on the functions of facilitating communication as I illustrated above.[11] David Baltimore in the February 15, 2001, issue of *Nature* that featured the genome project,[12] asserts:

[W]e do not gain our undoubted complexity over worms and plants by using many more genes . . .[indeed], Where do our genes come from? Mostly from the distant evolutionary past. In fact, only 94 of 1,278 protein families in our genome appear to be specific to vertebrates. The most elementary of cellular functions . . . evolved just once and stayed pretty fixed since the evolution of single-celled yeast and bacteria. The biggest difference between humans and worms or flies is the complexity of our proteins . . . The history is one of new architectures being built from old pieces.

In his research, MacLean made ethological observations similar to those made standard by the 1973 Nobel Prize winning European ethologists, such as the already mentioned reptilian behaviors. Also he worked on the neurophysiology of subcortical areas in monkeys using conventional techniques of the time, deploying implanted electrodes for recording and stimulation purposes, examined neuroanatomy by using brain sections and appropriate tissue staining. But in his speaking he, unconventionally for a neuroscientist, worked to make sense of brain-related things for their moral and other human implications. He quoted Cajal that everything that goes on in our perceived universe reflects the structure of the brain.[13] He urged study of "epistemics," that is, learning about the subjective *via* examination of the brain. For him the value of ancient behavior patterns and communications does not diminish because they happened to have originated in reptiles or before. His writing especially resounds with the importance of the mammalian family, generated in part one gathers from his own family highly valued by him.

Part of MacLean's popularity stemmed from the wide scope of his observations, including lizards, rats, and squirrel monkeys with information sought on many purposive animal communicational behaviors, some territorial and social rank hierarchical, and others sexual, for example, determining the brain sites that when stimulated caused erections in male monkeys. He resurrected Broca's 19th century term, "grande lobe limbique." Broca called it that for its rim-like (limbus) location, but eschewed speculation about function although he knew the structure was not limited to subserving smell as previously thought, because he found it well developed in the dolphin, an animal without olfactory nerves.[14] MacLean, however, expanded on Papez's early description of the core circuitry for emotion and proposed that neurons in the limbic structures possessed critical meaning for the distinctively mammalian family which he concluded probably originated in an early mammal seemingly transitional from reptilians. Candidate transitional animals, the therapsids, left great numbers of fossils behind in South Africa, a fact that MacLean felt represented opportunity for future investigations.

I recall MacLean's speaking to a completely filled auditorium at the 1982 annual meeting of the American Psychiatric Association (APA). Among many findings, he told the audience that lizards sometimes die after losing status in a social rank struggle. This note, significant for psychiatrists involved daily with suicidal patients, paralleled developments from other writers, who, similar to him and acknowledging his pioneering observations, saw affective states as deeply inherited parts of ancient body plans that provided the neuronal framework for individuals to communicate with their conspecifics. Thus, Price[15] and Gardner[10] especially highlighted the social rank hierarchical nature of what have been traditionally labeled "affective" disorders. Subsequently, Jaak Panksepp, who investigates emotions in mammals, paid tribute to the pioneering efforts of MacLean in the forward of his own impressive work entitled *Affective Neuroscience.*[16] Panksepp studied with John Paul Scott, a MacLean contemporary, who wrote on the evolution of culture in 1989.[17] Panksepp demonstrated that emotions prominently associate with conspecific social life.

MacLean's neuroethology paved the way for the sociophysiology framework.[3, 4] This holds that the physiology of social processes essentially provides the foundation for the medical specialty as well as for its related clinical human sciences. The postulation promises to align psychiatry with its sister specialties in explaining its pathologies in light of normal brain operations fashioned over evolutionary time. McKinney and Tucker in their editorial introduction[18] to a special issue of *Seminars in Clinical Neuropsychiatry* suggest that psychiatry should redevelop as a "relationship focused enterprise grounded in sociophysiology to encompass complex behaviors, especially communication, ancient reaction patterns, brain functions, cellular actions and genomic mechanisms."

In summary, MacLean emphasized evolutionary happenings in deep time, especially conspecific communication mediated in the brain's subcortical structures (emphasizing the cortical mantle less). He underlined the approximate origins of family life, which he asserts the evolution of the limbic system likely made possible. He pioneered methodology focusing on across-species comparisons and contrasts. These ideas and research should have importantly configured a basic science for psychiatry utilized to frame clinical procedures and guide research efforts for the medical specialty and its related clinical human sciences. But as yet this does not represent common knowledge. The advent of sociophysiology is recent, still considered provocative rather than obvious. MacLean's work and the paradigm that he framed out represent template-forming precursors for our subsequent work; yet his reputation seems to have nose-dived, not even outlasting his active career. This requires examination.

PARADIGM LOST

In Cory's discussion of the decline in MacLean's reputation (see Chapter 2 this volume), he attributed it largely to inadequate reviews that did not reflect legitimate, data-backed contentions. A negative *Science* review of MacLean's 1990 book signaled, Cory concluded, that MacLean was not to be taken seriously by the broader scientific community, who in turn cued the general public. I agree with Cory's conclusions but also suspect that trivializing senti-ments had spread widely well before the reviews. I suspect that these attitudes were held though not directly or publicly articulated by senior and influential figures in the neuroscience community. Rather, they felt this among themselves over many years and exerted influence on their younger colleagues. The *Science* review probably represented a late-appearing capstone to this sentiment, written by a then junior figure who felt little need to check the facts assiduously (see Cory for details) because, I presume, that he knew he was on the "right side" of correct senior opinion. In fact, in a 1999 volume that included MacLean's and other neuroscientists' autobiographies, the editorial inclusion on his fame strangely referred only to his early work, mentioning the limbic system, "visceral brain," and psychosomatic disease.[19] The editor notably failed to men-tion the triune brain or the neurobiology of family life. I sense that MacLean's emphasis on communication and social science somehow approached a taboo subject that during his heyday could not be countered directly, given his stature and influence.

For indirect evidence on this conclusion, I relate a medical school exper-ience. During a first-year neurophysiology laboratory class at the University of Chicago in 1959, I recall the professor becoming not just angry but enraged and plethoric when a student asked casually about the possible neurobiology of creativity. I recall his strong feelings though not the reasons he articulated for them. I do recall that he claimed to represent a general position. The teacher had seemed knowledgeable and bright so his feelings communicated powerful messages to me and my fellow students. The incident taught us that such issues constituted off-limits questions deliberately not considered by serious scientists. To my mind, however, the question had seemed not only unprovocative, but highly interesting as such matters had preoccupied me since my humanities-oriented college instruction. This made MacLean's work—when I discovered it three years later—all the more enticing, enhanced by his own gentlemanly demeanor. He seemed above such concerns as he ably spoke his mind. Indeed, he seemed to feel obligated to provide the public the benefit of his thinking given his authoritative position and grasp of truth along with his moral convictions. I suspect that MacLean's open and articulate interest in things beyond strict neuroanatomy and neurophysiology—stemming in part perhaps from his being a conscientious minister's son—caused his reputation to float away from neuroscience recognition, though hopefully not permanently.

More evidence for this includes the fact that other authorities summarized or mentioned MacLean's work with condescending attitudes towards what I had felt were his most important and ultimately enduring contributions. In common they highlight arguable details of his argument, rejecting them, and then suggest that for such reasons that the corpus of his work can be dismissed. Pierre Gloor, for instance, contended that MacLean was wrong in alluding to age of brain components using prefixes such as "archi-" and "neo-."[20] Six-layered or isocortex had existed from the beginning, he asserted, though to lesser extents, that is, "mammalian neocortex has phylogenetic roots just as ancient as the hippocampal and piriform allocortex." He summarized briefly the triune brain but dismissed this major MacLean contribution with his contention about age of the cortices. I take his point about isocortex being a better term than neocortex, but of course use of time-related terms has not been limited to MacLean. Neocortex, not isocortex, whether right or not represents a term generally used in neuroscience literature, as seen indeed in the title and content of a *Nature* review[21] co-authored nine years later by Anton Reiner, the 1990 *Science* reviewer who gave proximate cause for the plummeting of MacLean's reputation. Adding to the ephemeral nature of this objection, MacLean exhibited least interest in this volumetrically elaborated part of the neuraxis.

But another trend de-emphasizing his work included a popular line of thinking that shifted scientific attention away from across-species comparisons to across-species contrasts. The work of Sperry and his co-workers involved surgical hemisphere separation in severe seizure patients, for example, Gazzaniga gained further reputation through subsequent work on the resulting hemisphere disconnection syndromes.[22] This focused attention on the later developed mushroomed cerebral cortices that dominate the human brain in their appearance and in their availability for study, as with neuroimaging studies and away from the relatively smaller deep structures that MacLean especially examined.

Provocatively, Panksepp and Panksepp demonstrate that this may have produced an overvaluation of the prehuman-human transition as a time of principal change in the thinking of evolutionary psychologists.[23] They emphasize that structures well in place before the cortical mushrooming persist in guiding roles, dominating the programmed behavior of animals in the form of emotions, for instance. Activation of these structures focuses the individual's attention regardless of the more complex analyses that the neocortex might foster. Psychiatrist Frank Koerselman suggestively notes that the cortex does fundamentally "trivial" things; the contrasting and never trivial emotions determine what the cortex analyzes despite the classic and misleading division between intellect and emotions; those with a "passion for the truth" accomplish worthwhile things for others.[24] Brain structures for emotions establish values and then matter-of-factly enlist the cortical calculations required for the important actions. The Panksepps noted that evolutionary psychologists overly based their thinking on the seemingly revolutionary changes in the transition from precursor primate to human that presumably enlisted new genes to underlie new behaviors. In the best sense of falsifying Popperian science.[25] Baltimore's above citation refutes this. Nearly all of human biology (and behavior) stems from precursor species, not arisen *de novo*!

LeDoux, Gazzaniga's student, wrote a widely read and reviewed book on emotions[26] which suggested that MacLean overly emphasized how they all stem from the limbic system as though acting singly; rather, LeDoux emphasized his impression that each emotion had an independently acting system. Again, his prevailing critique attacked the overall work via criticizing such details while seeming to miss the signal contribution that connected the evolution of such organism attributes to ancient structures stemming from deep time, on the one hand, and the organism's need to communicate with its conspecifics on the other hand. LeDoux's book strikingly omits reference to animals more primitive than mammals. He may also be wrong on some items. For example, LeDoux asserted MacLean was wrong to include the hippocampus in the emotion system, saying this because the explicit memory function of this brain part has come clear in recent decades. Yet in this era of understanding how brain parts interact, who can say that it departed from the emotion system? Memory connects strongly to emotional charge of an experience. LeDoux thus joins in the problematic overemphasis on cortex, a tendency shared by linguists such as Pinker, who working in the shadow of Chomsky, prefers to think of language as a localized cortical function.[27] As already mentioned, Lieberman, another linguist, more recently argued for increased emphasis on subcortical systems. In contrast to LeDoux, Panksepp credits MacLean for recognizing the import of ancient evolutionarily derived systems while delineating seven emotion systems in the rat subcortex.[16]

A quarter century ago, E.O. Wilson's sociobiology sustained attacks for being politically (not factually) incorrect.[28] This may have also influenced attitudes about MacLean's work. Segerstrale reviewed the controversies about sociobiology,[29] and concluded that Wilson's application of population biology to the affairs of many animals, even human, was a more correct track than that of the critics (despite her initial bias in the other direction). Why had they been so critical? What fears dictate the preventive actions of countering such research work? A partial factor stems from an unfortunate public infatuation with eugenics that occurred in many countries in the early 20th century, especially after it became conflated with the horrible and unethical research conducted by the Nazi regime in World War II.[30] Additionally, we now know that application of eugenics to combat mental illness, mental retardation and various inherited illnesses does not work, as inheritance mechanisms are multiplex and often weak. The full horror of the era seems to have taken some decades to sink in.[31] Thus, the current neglect of the work of Paul MacLean may additionally stem from its post-World War II timing. Much of his work preceded the 1975 opus of Wilson and bore more directly on the brain than did that of Wilson, an entomologist. Certainly, neither Wilson's nor MacLean's thinking and research endorsed eugenic or Nazi horrors. Rather MacLean with confidence integrated neuroscience, family and other behaviors with evolutionary neuroscience. He could not have been more prosocial.

Another factor may relate his interest in cultural and social factors to the pendulum swings reflected in the *Sturm und Drang* over psychoanalysis. The medical micro-culture of our times often eschewed psychoanalysis and its offshoots as unscientific and even harmful, whereas cells, molecules, drugs and the like seemed comfortably reliable. Research on them has long represented a comfortable source of added information that took on more exaggerated qualities when a revolution overtook psychiatry in the last third of the twentieth century. A once dominant clinical paradigm in academic psychiatry, psycho-analysis gave way in academe several decades ago to descriptive psychiatry that stated an aim of returning to the practices of "normal" medicine. Curiously, however, because psychoanalysis postulated many pathogenetic theories on the psychological level alone, the new theoreticians eschewed pathogenesis. This of course contrasts dramatically to the rest of medicine. But for psychiatry over a quarter century, the baby of pathogenesis floated away with the bathwater of unproven therapies and their rationale. Though MacLean's persuasive capability helped him during his active career, such factors with the conservative attitudes of neuroscientists seems to have pervasively reduced his impact during the last decade of the twentieth century. Of course, knowledgable psychoanalysts, crea-tive artists, and some in the social sciences remain interested and involved in his findings and theories. Curiously, however, the research prompted by the critic-isms of the psychoanalytic movement has prompted appropriately control-led research that shows both efficacy and effectiveness of psychotherapy.[32]

Kandel and Squire's extensive review of last century's neuroscience failed to mention MacLean in their list of notable figures.[33] Part of the explanation stems from their limiting behavior-experience-mental (BME) variables to cognition and memory only, completely omitting social and emotional factors from their considerations. This is doubly curious because Kandel, a 2000 Nobel Prize winner, started as a psychiatrist to become an extraordinarily accomplished neuroscientist later by focusing attention on simple organisms such as the sea snail, *Aplysia*. Despite his strategy of going after ever more finely grained details as neurotransmitters, synaptic interactions and critical circuits, Kandel remained interested in psychiatry and has regularly presented at the APA and published in the *American Journal of Psychiatry*, effectively arguing to his clinician audiences that measures such as psychotherapy do indeed have brain effects.[34] Indeed, only when neuroimaging showed changes in the oxygen utilization in brain parts did this become recognized fully. The Cartesian mind/brain split maintained itself in the minds of many people until then and only when Kandel with his enormous prestige amplified the message did the practicing public realize this fully. At the same time, he disavows interest in changing psychiatry.[35] "I am just a shoemaker—my specialty is the neurobiol-ogy of learning and memory."

So in summary, why then did the sophisticated Kandel and Squire omit MacLean? Superficially, perhaps, because Squire reigns as an expert selectively on memory and Kandel in his experiments on *Aplysia* showed disinterest in the animal's social context, instead using withdrawal of the animal's siphon when electrically stimulated as the model for "fear" or "anxiety." Additionally, they expressed enthusiasm towards the discoveries in the molecular-cellular-organic (MCO) realms of analysis rather than issues in the BME realms. Thus, they excitedly focused on discoveries involving the ancient sources of neuronal mechanisms and propounded that this would accelerate the continued work with BME issues. This has tremendous importance for the sociophysiological framework for psychiatry and related clinical activities. But what they do not seem to have tumbled to, or have actively avoided, are the social and communicational facets of neuronal process. The sociophysiological perspective argues, on the other hand, that the analyses should represent a BME-MCO docking with two-way travel of information and discoveries.

In the meantime, mainstream psychiatry in the wake of post-psychoanalytic thinking gained respectability for its work guided by firm operational criteria for its disorders even though considerations no longer take center stage of mechanisms for how disorders come about. Effective drugs make treatments briefer and seemingly more scientific, because their actions are anchored in brain chemistry. Yet debate ensues about whether the overall quality of life has increased and interminable discussions of drug side effects preoccupy many psychiatrists and their patients during the brief "med-check" sessions, the only ones available with present funding practices. A curious avoidance continues of discussion on the brain's involvement with cultural, psychological, societal and humanitarian concerns.

In my opinion, as a need for this gains power with increased public demand for explanations, MacLean's reputation will grow again. It stems from a confluence of factors that I sense possesses importance for clinicians and researchers. Partly this hinges on the framework of descriptive-pharmaceutical psychiatry combined with medical economic strictures. Influences that foster the "twisted molecule" model of illness envision ever more precise drugs to do their remedies by untwisting the knots (similar to the way that psychoanalysts once aimed at untwisting developmental knots). Sensitive observers have suggested that drug companies and managed care together work towards the "the goal of relationshipless psychiatry." Least contact with greatest impersonality represents an ideal powered by managed care's need to restrict costs combined with drug companies wishing to emphasize their products. These extraordinarily powerful economic forces frame much of a present day clinician's work with patients. This argument does not deny drug benefits; they exist and some people benefit greatly, but patients regret the loss of personal relationship with the psychiatrist—of all specialties one might expect interpersonal expertise in this realm of medicine, but this seems to be fading fast.

Dramatic evidence reveals the approach's downside. At this time, only about 500 of 15,000 U.S. medical school graduates go into psychiatry, compared to 12% of my 1962 graduating class at the University of Chicago. I conjecture that the new trend resulted in part from the lack of a satisfying intellectual framework for the field, as well as medical school curricula trending away from psychiatry in order to encourage students to go into primary care specialties (if they do not, they lose funding based on state and national strictures). In the meantime, psychoanalytic and other psychotherapeutic clinicians provide the time for the details of their patient's experience; they work outside managed care. From informal contacts, I conclude that they are in demand by people willing to pay for skill and confidentiality.

Despite these trends and facts, I believe that the time will come when not only psychiatry, but also the humanities and other disciplines will view brain studies as integral to their traditions in the realms of thought products and other results of human endeavors. Daniel X. Freedman, another MacLean student and psychiatrist leader, suggested that the term "biological psychiatry" represented a redundancy. All psychiatry must be biological just as phenomena on the BME level of analysis must stem from brain actions. In like vein, there can be no unbiological social science. In *Three Seductive Ideas,* Kagan suggests[36] that clinical and social-psychological sciences must be integrated with the rest of biology, stating specifically, "At present the fragile threads that comprise concepts in the social sciences are far too separate." He also noted, "One must know the history of . . . animals to predict their current behavior." Isaac Marks in surveying anxiety disorders concluded that highly functional propensity states underlie fear that become malfunctional in the relatively benign present human existence.[37] A recent quote from biologist Deric Bownds[38] suggests in a MacLean-like crescendo: "Newer structures of the brain encapsulate older ones. Their feedback to lower levels of the brain can modulate the way in which more ancient structures regulate homeostasis, emotions, and movement."

PARADIGM EXTENDED

Thus Freedman, Kagan, Marks, and Bownds with many others testify to the importance of a docking between BME and MCO levels of analysis. MacLean's neuroethology explicitly pioneered this. His research program exemplified the first clear view of the paradigm of sociophysiology. The biology of social processes requires additional exploration. The highly similar concepts of neuroethology and sociophysiology differ only in that the latter term more closely coheres to the model furnished by the rest of medicine (cardiovascular, gastrointestinal or renal physiology) and therefore more fittingly entitles a basic science of psychiatry. Sociophysiology focuses on normal behaviors of special relevance to psychiatry and related clinical disciplines on the one hand. Thus, all the disturbances that bring patients or clients to caregivers entail disruptions in social and communicational attributes; ranging from panics that are aided by someone nearby, to certainty of harm stemming from out-group enemies (persecutory delusions), to limitations in memory functions that then disrupt normal social life. On the other hand, physiology refers to body-workings—much in the brain of course—that mediate this sociality as well as its disturbing and distressing components that bring people to the helping professional. These can range from family quarrels and accompanying violence, to school-related problems such as attention deficit hyperactivity disorder, to persecutory delusions, to fear and anxiety. Of course, the over-intrusiveness of the manic patient and the under-intrusiveness of the depressed person represent familiar patterns to anyone. I now turn to a more intensive discussion of evolutionary processes.

William Calvin showed that the "descent by modification" of Darwin could be generalized to the products of brain action,[39] contemporaneously with Gerald Edelman who coined the term "neural darwinism" to describe the process by which very complex brains derive from just a few thousand genes[40] (most recent estimates, about 30,000).[12] Edelman had pioneered use of Darwin's natural selection to body processes, namely, the immune system, for which he gained the 1972 Nobel Prize. Calvin's Darwin machine uses six steps: (1) a pattern exists; (2) that can be copied; (3) variations on the pattern co-occur; (4) competition for a workspace exists; (5) the environment biases the competition for which pattern version will win (selection); and (6) the process reiterates with closed repeating loops for copying, variation. and selection steps.

Calvin showed that this process applies to many mental phenomena, such as words for a story. Many word variants compete for selection according to an environment that includes strongly the storyteller's idea of the audience for the communication. The brain, perhaps especially the human brain, speeds up the processes via which Darwin machine processes work. But if this mechanism holds and is currently operative, it also does so on a stable background. Basic plans of ancient origination and little fundamental change persist in nearly all living creatures.

Basic plan persistence gained controversial recognition in the early nineteenth century. Thus, Geoffery St. Hilaire observed the lobster's anatomy finding himself struck by how its body resembled that of vertebrates.[41] He subsequently argued that the two phyla possess a body plan in common. Cuvier, the authority of the time, however, authoritatively stated that no evidence existed for this conception and carried the day in a famous 1830 debate. St. Hilaire's vindication came one and a half centuries later with the discovery of the homeobox. Walter Gehring discovered these distinctive genes in 1984 and they have been extensively studied; many mammalian—including human—genes turn out to be shared by drosophila, nematodes, even yeast.[8] Fortey suggests they existed already in the long extinct trilobites.[42] Martindale and Kourakis observe that the body plan (or common anatomic organization) determines in what phylum a metazoan resides.[43]

[T]he body plans of almost all living animals appeared in a very short time, over half a billion years ago, and have remained essentially unchanged ever since. The evolutionary information from most genes . . . is lost by random mutation over this evolutionary timescale. It would be ideal to examine evolution of the developmental regulatory genes that are involved in generating metazoan body plans. These genes should . . . have paralleled the stasis of the body plans they helped to create . . . The Hox genes encode transcription factors, and they have been found in all metazoans examined.

In summary, both the invertebrate and vertebrate body plans lay deeply buried within their genomes. The age of common insect-vertebrate ancestor is over 500 million years before the present. Both express central organizational functions that have retained much in common in presently living animals. Thus, Hom genes in drosophila homologous to Hox genes in vertebrates are both oriented in the same direction. Knocking out anterior genes "allows" the usually more posterior ones to actuate in the more anterior position. The mouse Hox-6 gene put in the fly produces the same developmental controls as does the fly's original gene.[8] Discovery of these "master control genes" signaled that basic body plan extended further back in deep time than had been anticipated. Evolution uses old architecture in its new projects.

Behavior, though it leaves no manifest traces in fossils, does dictate physical structure. Form follows function. A highly respected neuroanatomist in the tradition of Cajal during the first half of the twentieth century, C. Judson Herrick, summarized this thesis in his posthumously published *The Evolution of Human Nature*.[44] "In all animals that have a nervous system, it controls the adaptation of the species to its environment. When its behavior is adequate the species survives; the more complex the behavior, the more elaborate is the structure of the nervous system." Conspecifics needed to recognize one another, including their sexual identity and mating potential. Might such recognitions stem from ancient gene constellations not yet discovered? Fly genes expressed in developing mouse brain include orthodenticle that produces a protein almost identical to that of drosophila. Exploring genes that clearly underlie behavior, the drosophila gene *per* determines circadian cyclicity. The fly *fruitless* gene less clearly determines sex, but its disruption alters the ability of fruitflies to carry through the sequence of mating.[41] Though expressed in mammals, we do not know yet how it might represent a component of the brain base for vertebrate mating. Yet we know already at this early stage of investigation that this must exemplify something too important to lapse (so that natural selection has not reinvented it). This would represent behavior as reflecting homology rather than convergent evolution, a core tenet for the key sociophysiological proposition that psychiatric behaviors stem from ancient origins, though poorly timed and aimed. Curiously, Darwin's *Expression of the Emotions in Man and Animals* made a similarly conservative argument.[45]

Price[15] and I[10] suggested several decades ago that the ancient biology of social rank hierarchy likely underpins affective illness. In fact these represent "communicational states." Manic behavior indeed resembles out-of-context leadership communication. With the concept of propensity states antedating language in communication (psalic), sociophysiology proposes that communication and sociality represent important ancient brain states.[46] Signaling the "planful" attributes of living matter emphasized by Ernst Mayr,[47] psalic also refers to programmed spacings and linkages in conspecifics, fundamental aims of communication. Particular psalics take definition from the three legs of existing in (1) normal humans, (2) psychiatrically disturbed humans, and (3) animals. Two psalics alluded to here include alpha psalic (seen in mania, normal leadership, and animal dominance) and audience psalic (state of receptivity to conspecifics as in cult membership, normal audiences, and animal subordination). Other psalics include those labeled mating, nurturant, nurturance-eliciting, in-group omega, and out-group omega.

Psychiatry's famous *DSM-III* and its successors can be viewed as a series of ethological descriptions that recognize the "naturalness" of psychiatric disorders that occur with high prevalences. Daniel Wilson suggests with his concept of "evolutionary epidemiology" that such high frequency testifies to their having adaptive features; disorders may not be adaptive for the individual but their high prevalence shows them to possess features that served adaptations, perhaps expressed in other forms.[48] The designers of the nosology manuals labored towards empiricism so that they did not examine the communicational meaningfulness of the behaviors that constitute the disorders, for example, depression communicates low profile attitudes with no threat communicated to other people. If they had examined such observable features, insights to psychiatric pathogenesis might have emerged. Studying psychiatric pathogenesis should entail examination of the purposefulness of communications and communicational states along with the adaptive consequences of an individual remaining in the same state over time (mania may resemble leadership, for instance, but the person displaying the communications typifying the state does so at the wrong times or to the wrong audiences, yet patients remain stubbornly in the state until treated or the episode otherwise ends). Full analysis will require MCO levels, aided by the pharmacology of the syndrome in question, for instance, taking into consideration differences from the normal counterpart state, or through analysis of animal versions of the state or via neuroimaging of people in these states.

Dissection of such provides tasks for the next decades. For instance, each psalic needs descriptive and analytic work. Some doubtless will bear up more adequately than others, for instance, some may meet fates similar to Kagan's critiques of fear as an abstraction, one of his "three seductive ideas."[36] He holds that fear is not a unitary phenomenon and that the following probably involve different brain circuits (and therefore involve different brain states): a sudden unexpected noise, a grizzly bear lunging at your throat, seeing a light that has been associated experimentally with electric shock, and a worry about losing job while walking in a quiet meadow. Yet all represent fear as a unitary process. So we think of it in a first approximation carried into our sociophysiologic and psychiatric nomenclature to be modified with research and other new information. I expect parallel developments with the evolution of scientific investigation of the psalics.

Investigations of psalics may be helped by Panksepp's concept of emotion systems.[16] Following MacLean, he noted that "many of the ancient evolutionarily derived brain systems all mammals share still serve as the foundations for the deeply experienced affective proclivities of the human mind. Such ancient brain functions evolved long before the emergence of the human neocortex with its vast cognitive skills." Panksepp labeled (1) an appetitive, motivational SEEKING system that fosters energetic search and goal-directed behaviors, (2) a RAGE system that aroused by thwarting experiences correlates with frustration, (3) a FEAR system that minimizes bodily destruction, (4) a PANIC apparatus with separation distress that enhances bonding, (5) a LUST system that fosters mating and reproduction, (6) a maternal CARE system that nurtures infants, and (7) a roughhousing PLAY system that provides youngsters with skill-honing opportunities.

Genome deletion syndromes represent natural experiments for future BME-MCO interactional analyses. Examples include Fragile X Syndrome, Prader-Willi (PWS) and Angelman Syndromes (AS). The latter two feature a deletion in chromosome 15q11-13, and differ from each other in that PWS lacks chromosome material from the father and AS parallel material from the mother. This phenomenon represents parental or genomic imprinting. The two syndromes differ markedly phenotypically with a hypothalamic deficiency in PWS and in AS the cortex affected; these patients show more severe retardation; they never learn to speak but laugh incessantly. This has permitted the speculation that through parental imprinting mechanisms, cortex normally results from action of the mother's genes and hypothalamic structures from the father's counterpart genes. PWS patients show infantile flaccidity, overeating from ages 2-6 on, they remain sexually underdeveloped even with sexual hormone treatments, but in striking contrast to AS patients show only mild to moderate retardation. They demonstrate typical personalities. In work that I conducted at Texas Children's Hospital, 125 patients were investigated using questionnaire survey of parents and other significant others. All showed tempestuous demanding behavior with low threshold to frustration regardless of age. They showed tantrums and never-ending "terrible twos." On the other hand, an anecdotal case of a patient showed overeating but not the frustration-aggression pattern had been labeled with "acquired PWS" because he sustained hypothalamic damage from surgery for a brain tumor in the hypothalamus; he did not in fact have PWS at all.

Frustration-aggression needs examination. The behaviorally interactive pattern also shows up in other retarded patients. In normal development any parent is well aware of the problem. Normally this modulates over time, though as any parent also knows, he or she—even though adult and supposedly mature—remains also vulnerable to it as when a child becomes aggravating. Frustration-aggression links to low levels of serotonin in the brain. How hypothalamus connections to the orbital frontal lobe foster modulation or exacerbation of such reactions in connections to variously intact nervous systems represents necessary future work, part of a future MacLean-inspired research program. We need to learn how the behavior constellation is encoded in the genome and how it is modulated over normal development. What circuits in the brain are activated, what circumstances with other people typically affect it, and how are its cell assembly characteristics parallel to R-complex cell assembly? Where is it triggered and how is it modulated?

SOCIOPHYSIOLOGY SUMMARIZED

This chapter suggests that sociophysiology fittingly represents a framework to underpin psychiatry and other helping professions. This schema, building on MacLean's neuroethology, labels more precisely the clinical world for which it exhibits relevance. In connection with this, the present author began a decade and a half ago the publication of a monthly *Across-Species Comparisons and Psychopathology (ASCAP) Newsletter* that became a quarterly bulletin in 2000. Multiple contributors wrote material then distributed internationally. This in turn fostered The ASCAP Society in 1991 that meets annually or more often. In 1999, the group called a two-day meeting to discuss the work and implications of Paul D. MacLean's work. Moreover, John Price, when chairman of the Section on Psychotherapy of the World Psychiatric Association (WPA), arranged that the Newsletter/Bulletin become the official news distributing organ of the section—an action approved by the WPA. A number of papers in refereed journals stemmed from discussions in the pages of the newsletter. Notably, a paper in 1994 by Price et al. entitled, "The social competition hypothesis of depression" was carried in the *British Journal of Psychiatry* and subsequently anthologized by Simon Baron-Cohen in an edited book.[49] A volume entitled *Genes on the Couch* edited by Paul Gilbert and Kent Bailey has also resulted.[50]

Sociophysiology concerns paleopsychology[51] and paleobiology, interpersonal and group relations, and psychopathology. The mission statement of the Across-Species Comparisons and Psychopathology Society has read as follows since its origination in 1991:

The ASCAP Society represents a group of people who view forms of psychopathology in the context of evolutionary biology and who wish to mobilize members and resources of various disciplines so as to enhance the further investigation and study of the conceptual and research questions involved. This scientific society is concerned with the basic plans of behavior that have evolved over millions of years and that have resulted in psychopathologically related states. We are interested in the integration of various methods of study ranging from cellular processes to individuals in groups.

The research committee of the Group for the Advancement of Psychiatry (GAP), a specialty think-tank group agreed on the following[52] during its Spring, 2000, meeting:

Members of the Research Committee of the Group for Advancement of Psychiatry (GAP), a specialty think-tank, has addressed psychiatry's need for a unifying scientific foundation. Such a foundation would consider the disorders commonly treated by psychiatrists in terms of the physiological baseline from which they depart, much as heart disease is understood as deviation from normal cardiac function. The relevant physiological focus for psychiatry is the social brain.

The social brain concept focuses on the interaction between brain physiology and the individual's environment. The brain is the organ most influenced on the cellular level by social factors across development; in turn, the expression of brain function determines and structures an individual's personal and social experience. The social brain framework may have greater direct impact on the understanding of some psychiatric disorders than others. However, it helps organize and explain all psychopathology. A single gene-based disorder like Huntington disease is expressed to a large extent as social dysfunction. Conversely, traumatic stress has structural impact on the brain as does the socially interactive process of psychotherapy.

Brains, including human brains, derive from ancient adaptations to diverse environments and are themselves repositories of phylogenetic adaptations. In addition, individual experiences shape the brain through epigenesis, i.e., the expression of genes is shaped by environmental influences. Thus, the social brain is also a repository of individual development. On an ongoing basis, the brain is further refined through social interactions; plastic changes continue through life with both physiological and anatomical modifications.

In contrast to the conventional biopsychosocial model, the social brain formulation emphasizes that all psychological and social factors are biological. Conversation, feeling, and thinking can happen only from brain-actions in the involved individuals. Non-biological and non-social psychiatry cannot exist. Molecular and cellular sciences offer fresh and exciting contributions to such a framework but provide limited explanations for the social facets of individual function.

The social brain formulation is consistent with current research and clinical data. Moreover, it ultimately must:

* *unify the biological, psychological and social factors in psychiatric illness,*

* *dissect components of illness into meaningful functional subsets that deviate in definable ways from normal physiology,*

* *improve diagnostic validity by generating testable clinical formulations from brain-based social processes,*

* *guide psychiatric research and treatment,*

* *provide an improved language for treating patients as well as educating trainees, patients, their families and the public, and*

* *account for the role of interpersonal relationships for brain function and health.*

In conclusion, the concept of the brain as an organ that manages social life provides significant power for psychiatry's basic science. Burgeoning developments in neural and genetic areas put added demands on the conceptual structures of psychiatry. Findings from such incoming work must be juxtaposed and correlated with the behavioral and experiential facets of psychiatry to give it a complete and rational basis. Psychiatry's full and unified entry into the realm of theory-driven and data-based medical science has arrived. The social brain concept allows psychiatry to utilize pathogenesis in a manner parallel to practice in other specialties.

Contrasts and comparisons of humans and nonhuman animals provide ways to approach the impact of evolutionary history on our brains and behavior relevant to clinical work. While nearly all of the human genome has constancy with that of the chimpanzee, the human burgeoning brain size is three times larger than that of chimps or gorillas. Yet, we also know that it works under the guidance of older systems heralded as important by MacLean. What does the bigger brain accomplish? Social facilitation, communicational subtlety via both verbal and nonverbal means, and storytelling. Jerome Kagan notes that awareness that we behaved in a particular way in a particular place at a particular time in the past is a state unique to humans, suggesting that "ability of humans to generate ideas of events that might occur years in the future might explain why we are the only species to have populated so much of the world." [36] Gerald A. Cory has been working hard to reveal neuronal algorithms that guide our behaviors and would do so better if acknowledged directly for the power that they possess.[53,54]

In summary, constellations of core communicative behaviors need to be conceptually integrated with genomics (wherein individual people are identical to one another), genetics (individuals differ), and brain systems that separately evolve in each person yet result in remarkably similar behaviors. What pathogenetic linkages do patients also share in common? Finally, how will Paul D. MacLean prove to have been prophetic in his insistence on examining the most primitive brain parts and brain states as fundamental? How will his communicational paradigm be utilized in the future to benefit psychiatry, other patients of any doctor or treating professional, and people who need more information to guide their lives most effectively?

NOTES

1. Macmillan, Malcolm: *An Odd Kind of Fame: Stories of Phineas Gage.* Cambridge, MA: The MIT Press, 2000, p. 9.

2. MacLean PD: *The Triune Brain in Evolution: Role in Paleocerebral Functions.* New York, NY: Plenum, 1990.

3. Gardner R: Psychiatry needs a basic science titled sociophysiology. *Biological Psychiatry* 1996; 39: 833–834.

4. Gardner R: Sociophysiology as the basic science of psychiatry. *Theoretical Medicine.* 18: 335–356, 1997.

5. Bohm D: On dialogue. In *Unfolding Meaning*. Ojal, CA: David Bohm Seminars, 1990, pp. 1–41 (32).

6. Lively CM: Evidence from a New Zealand snail for the maintenance of sex by parasitism. *Nature*. 1987; 328: 519–521.

7. Thomas, Elizabeth Marshall: *The Social Life of Dogs: The Grace of Canine Company*. NY: Simon and Schuster, 2000.

8. Gehring, Walter J: *Master Control Genes in Development and Evolution: The Homeobox Story*. New Haven, CT: Yale University Press, 1998.

9. Gee, Henry: *In Search of Deep Time: Beyond the Fossil Record to a New History of Life*. NY: The Free Press, 1999.

10. Gardner, R: Mechanisms in manic-depressive disorder: an evolutionary model. *Archives of General Psychiatry*. 1982; 39: 1436–1441..

11. Lieberman, P: *Human Language and Our Reptilian Brain: The Subcortical Bases of Speech, Syntax, and Thought*. Cambridge, MA: Harvard University Press, 2000.

12. Baltimore, D: Our genome unveiled. *Nature*. 2001: 409: 814–816. MacLean, 1999.

13. MacLean, PD: Paul D. MacLean autobiography. In Larry R Squire (Ed). *In The History of Neuroscience in Autobiography*. San Diego, CA: Academic Press, Volume 2, 1999, pp. 245–275.

14. Schiller, F: *Paul Broca: Explorer of the Brain*. NY: Oxford U Press, 1992.

15. Price, JS: Hypothesis: the dominance hierarchy and the evolution of mental illness. *Lancet*. 1967; 2: 243–246.

16. Panksepp, J: *Affective Neuroscience: The Foundations of Human and Animal Emotions*. NY: Oxford University Press. 1998.

18. Scott, JP: *The Evolution of Social Systems*. NY: Gordon and Breach Science Publishers, 1989.

17. McKinney, WT, Tucker GJ: Introduction. *Seminars in Clinical Neuropsychiatry* 2001; 6: 102.

19. Squire, L: Introduction to Paul D. MacLean autobiography. In Larry R Squire (Ed). *In The History of Neuroscience in Autobiography*. San Diego, CA: Academic Press, Volume 2., 1999, pp. 243–244.

20. Gloor, Pierre: *The Temporal Lobe and Limbic System*. NY: Oxford University Press, 1997, p. 27.

21. Kaas, JH, Reiner A: Evolutionary neurobiology: the neocortex comes together. *Nature* 1999; 399: 418–419.

22. Gazzaniga, MS: *The Bisected Brain*. NY: Appleton-Century-Crofts, 1970.

23. Panksepp J, Panksepp JB: The seven sins of evolutionary psychology. *Evolution and Cognition* 2000; 6: 108–131.

24. Koerselman, F: Psychiatry and Biological Psychotherapy. Presentation at Annual Meeting of the American Psychiatric Association, New Orleans, LA, May 8, 2001.

25. Pratt, JR: Strong inference. *Science*. 1964;146: 347–353.

26. LeDoux, Joseph: *The Emotional Brain: The Mysterious Underpinnings of Emotional Life*. NY: Simon & Schuster, 1996.

27. Pinker, S: *The Language Instinct: How the Mind Creates Language*. NY: William Morrow and Company, 1994.

28. Wilson, EO: *Sociobiology: The New Synthesis*. Cambridge, MA: Harvard University Press, 1975.

29. Segerstrale, Ullica: *Defenders of the Truth: The Battle for Science in the Sociobiology Debate and Beyond*. NY: Oxford University Press, 2000.

30. Walker, M: German eugenics. Review of book by S.F. Weiss: *Race Hygiene and National Efficiency*. Berkeley: University of California Press, 1988. *Science* 1988; 240: 1053.

31. Paul, DB: A history of the eugenics movement and its multiple effects on public policy. Review of book by Daniel J. Kevles: *In the Name of Eugenics: Genetics and the Use of Human Heredity*. Alfred A. Knopf. *Scientific American*, January, 1986, pp 27–31.

32. Gabbard, GO: Editorial: Empirical evidence and psychotherapy: a growing scientific base. *American Journal of Psychiatry*. 2001;158: 1–3.

33. Kandel, ER, Squires, LR: Neuroscience: breaking down scientific barriers to the study of the brain and mind. *Science*. 2000; 290: 1113–1120.

34. Kandel, Eric: A new intellectual framework for psychiatry. *American Journal of Psychiatry*. 1998; 155: 457–469.

35. Rosack, J: Nobel-Prize winner to speak at annual meeting. *Psychiatric News*. May 4, 2001, pp. 16–17.

36. Kagan, Jerome: *Three Seductive Ideas*. Cambridge, MA: Harvard University Press, 1998.

37. Marks, IM: *Fears, Phobias, and Rituals: Panic, Anxiety, and Their Disorders*. NY: Oxford University Press, 1987.

38. Bownds, Deric: *Biology of Mind: Origins and Structures of Mind, Brain, and Consciousness*. Bethesda, MD: Fitzgerald Science Press, 1999.

39. Calvin, WH: *The Ascent of Mind: Ice Age Climates and the Evolution of Intelligence*. NY: Bantam Books, 1990.

40. Edelman, GM: *Neural Darwinism: The Theory of Neuronal Group Selection*. NY: Basic Books, 1987.

41. Weiner, J: *Time, Love, Memory: A Great Biologist and His Quest for the Origins of Behavior*, 1999.

42. Fortey, Richard: *Trilobite: Eyewitness to Evolution*. NY: Alfred A. Knopf, 2000.

43. Martindale, MQ, Kourakis, MJ: Hox clusters: size doesn't matter. *Nature*. 1999; 399: 730–731.

44. Bartelmez, GW: Charles Judson Herrick October 6, 1868–January 29, 1960. National Academy of Sciences: *Biographical Memoirs Volume XLIII*. Washington, D.C.: National Academy Press, 1973, pp. 77–108.

45. Darwin, C: *The Expression of the Emotions in Man and Animals*. London: John Murray, 1872.

46. Gardner, R: The brain and communication are basic for clinical human sciences. *British Journal of Medical Psychology*. 1998; 71: 493–508.

47. Mayr, E: *The Growth of Biological Thought: Diversity, Evolution, and Inheritance*. Cambridge, MA: Harvard University Press, 1982.

48. Wilson, DR: Evolutionary epidemiology: Darwinian theory in the service of medicine and psychiatry. *Acta Biotheoretica*. 1993; 41: 205–218.

49. Price, J, Sloman, L, Gardner, R Jr., Gilbert, P, Rohde, P. (1994) The social competition hypothesis of depression. *British J. Psychiatry*. 164: 309–315. Reprinted in Baron-Cohen, S. (Ed.) (1997) *The Maladapted Mind: Classic Readings in Evolutionary Psychopathology*. Hove, East Sussex, UK: Psychology Press.

50. Gilbert, Paul, Bailey, Kent G. (editors): *Genes on the Couch*. Philadelphia, PA: Taylor & Francis, 2000.

51. Bailey, Kent: *Human Paleopsychology: Applications to Aggression and Pathological Processes*. Hillsdale, NJ: Lawrence Erlbaum Associates, 1987.

52. Bakker, C, Gardner, R, Koliatsos, V, Kerbeshian, J, Looney, JG, Sutton, B, Swann, A, Verhulst, J, Wagner, KD, Wamboldt, F, Wilson, DR (listed alphabetically)

(November, 2000*): The Social Brain: A Unifying Foundation for Psychiatry.* A manuscript submitted for publication composed by the Research Committee of GAP.

53. Cory, Gerald A, Jr.: *The Reciprocal Modular Brain in Economics and Politics: Shaping the Rational and Moral Basis of Organization, Exchange, and Choice.* NY: Kluwer Academic/Plenum Publishers, 1999.

54. Cory, Gerald A, Jr.: *Toward Consilience: The Bioneurological Basis of Behavior, Thought, Experience, and Language.* NY: Kluwer Academic/Plenum Publishers, 2000.

6

THE TRIUNE BRAIN, ESCALATION DE-ESCALATION STRATEGIES, AND MOOD DISORDERS

John S. Price

INTRODUCTION

Paul MacLean described three "central processing assemblies" in the neomammalian, paleomammalian, and reptilian brains that make decisions about responses to environmental social events relatively independently. In this chapter, I apply this model to explaining the two alternative strategies of escalation (fight) and de-escalation (escape or submission). At the neomammalian level there is a conscious, rational decision either to fight or give in. At the paleomammalian level which relates to emotions and the limbic system, there is deployment of either the escalatory emotions of anger, exhilaration, and so on, or of the de-escalation emotions of fear, depression, shame, etc. I suggest that at the reptilian level of the forebrain, the escalating strategy consists of elevated mood and the de-escalating strategy consists of depressed mood, which is unfocused or self-focused. In some cases the responses of the levels may be incompatible. The implications for mood disorders and their treatment are examined.

BACKGROUND

The message I got from the work of Paul MacLean entailed the following: the mammalian forebrain has evolved into three "central processing assemblies" for coordination of information and decision-making about how to respond to changes in the environment.[1] These three assemblies coordinate their actions but make somewhat independent decisions. For ease of communication I talk about the rational brain situated roughly in the neocortex (MacLean's neomammalian brain), an emotional brain in the limbic system (MacLean's paleomammalian brain), and an instinctive brain situated in the corpus striatum (MacLean's reptilian brain or R-complex). The rational brain uses all the information that we normally consider conscious, and its decisions have the character of voluntariness with full awareness. The emotional brain has restricted access to the information of consciousness; its decisions have both voluntary and involuntary components, with only partial awareness of its decisions; the information used in emotional brain decision-making includes elements unavailable to the rational brain, as Pascal noted in his famous aphorism "Le coeur a ses raisons que la raison ne connait pas" (The heart has its reasons which are not known to Reason). The instinctive brain has different sources of information that have not been much studied yet; its decisions are involuntary with no awareness of any ensuing course of action until that action takes place.

This new conception of the forebrain replaced my previous idea, that of homogeneous brain expansion since the time of the common human and reptilian ancestor some 250 million years ago, and included the general principle that higher centres control the lower ones, largely through inhibition.

The numerous theories of unconscious processes attest to psychiatry's inevitable concern with brain or mind levels.[2] When treating patients with depression and anxiety, the clinician finds it obvious that higher centres do not control the lower ones. No patient with his rational brain can command his emotional brain to feel less depressed or anxious. From the time of Coue and Samuel Smiles to the more recent efforts of psychological healers, people have stood before their mirrors and repeated to themselves such phrases as, "Every day, in every way, I am getting better and better." But these techniques do not work. In fact, they make patients worse, because they arouse expectations of improvement that remain unfulfilled, therefore resulting in disappointment and a sense of failure. An outstanding feature of psychiatric practice hinges on the fact that the rational brain of homo sapiens, the acme of the evolutionary process, has no more control over the lower brain centres than does the rider over a runaway horse.

Rational control over the lower brains could easily have evolved. The fact that it has not should tell us something—namely, that painful and incapacitating processes such as depression which emerge so much against our conscious will are, in fact, performing one or more functions of adaptive value. It appears that the rider does not always know best. There is survival value in having a horse that sometimes makes the decisions.

WHAT NORMAL BEHAVIOR UNDERLIES MOOD CHANGE?

In an evolutionary analysis of psychopathology, we must determine what kind of behaviour is being affected. A depression may or may not be adaptive, but it likely, at least, exaggerates or distorts some piece of adaptive behaviour. In the case of mood disorders, no general agreement exists on what this normal adaptive behaviour might be; except, perhaps, that it involves some form of social behaviour. The extreme incapacity of depression can only be maladaptive for nonsocial events. Generally, we agree that when depression has a cause, it involves some form of loss or failure. But if, for example, in a group of our hunter/gatherer ancestors, hunting had gone badly, it would not be adaptive for the hunters to become so depressed that they were unable to gather effectively. As with foraging decisions, so with predator avoidance, there is little place for depressed mood. Only in the case of dealing with climatic adversity do we get a suggestion that depression might perform some function analogous to hibernation during the winter, and keep us out of harm's way until spring comes along. But, in spite of the attention devoted recently to seasonal affective disorder (SAD), psychiatry is not a seasonal matter, and there is no suggestion that we might close our consulting rooms during the summer and take jobs as water-ski instructors.

Social theories of the adaptive value of depression take the form of cries for help, changes of social niche, relinquishing of unattainable social goals, and adjustment to loss. At the time I first became engaged with this field, it was thought that depression served some function in relation to loss, separation or bereavement. This reasoning never convinced me. Although it was clear that a social or romantic bond of many years' duration could not be broken without some grief, it never seemed likely that a depressive episode of several months' duration could be adaptive following the loss of a good ally or partner. Depression is incapacitating, and if you lose a partner, there is the work of the partner to do in addition to your own, so that an increase in capacity would be more advantageous than depression.

SOCIAL COMPETITION

More likely has been the possibility that elevation and depression of mood serve a function in relation to social competition. The reasons for this are as follows:

> Depressed patients feel like failures and losers.[3]
> Manic patients feel successful and like winners.[4]
> The basic strategy set of social competition contains the two alternative strategies of escalation (fight) and de-escalation (flight or submission), which have similarities to elevated and depressed mood, respectively.[5]
> Competing animals can switch rapidly from escalation to de-escalation in the way that a manic-depressive patient can switch from mania to depression.
> Monkeys who have failed in social competition and thus are low ranking may behave in a restricted and dysphoric manner similar to that of depressed patients.[6]

However, there are problems with this line of thinking:

> Some high-ranking people are depressed.
> Some low-ranking people are perfectly happy.

> Some depressed patients are very powerful—they may be stubborn, demanding
> and manipulative. Aaron Beck warned, "Beware of locking horns with a
> depressed patient, or you may be pushed clean out of the consulting room!"
> Depressed patients do not act in a submissive way or show deference to more
> powerful people.

In our discussions of these matters, we played with ideas of there being two
different types of submission, voluntary and involuntary, and that depression
reflected only involuntary submission—so that an alternative to depression
could be those forms of voluntary submission that go under the terms of
humility, reasonableness, and willingness to compromise. But the water was
murky, and we could not see the way ahead clearly.

THE TRIUNE MIND/BRAIN

Then came triune brain theory. Although it would be too much to say that all
then was light, it did clarify our ideas greatly. One could say that we passed the
white light of escalation/de-escalation theory through the prism of triune brain
theory and saw the resolution of clearly identifiable patterns of behaviour at
each level of the triune brain (see Table 6.1 next page).

In response to social adversity, or ranking stress as we called it, each level of
the triune brain seemed to make a decision between escalation and de-escalation.
Sometimes the decisions agreed. Then there was likely to be a quick resolution
of the conflict through either defeat, acceptance of defeat, and reconciliation on
the one hand, or success, acceptance of the other's submission, and reconciliation on the other. At other times the decisions did not agree, and then trouble
ensued, leading to psychopathology.

We have been concerned at the amount of criticism MacLean has received
from his fellow neuroanatomists, but we note that these criticisms have been
over details, and have not challenged the essential concept of three relatively
independent central processing assemblies; in fact, in their authoritative mono-
graph on the evolution of the vertebrate nervous system, Butler and Hodos
state: "Longitudinal transmission of information within the nervous system and
the presence of rostrocaudally localised areas of integration and control are
keystones of the chordate nervous system."[7, p 465]

The most efficient way to bring about conflict resolution operates at the
rational level. One of two competitors should be able to say, "The other guy is
more powerful, so I will give in." The lower agonistic strategy sets can be left
alone and this could be called functional agonism. But, unfortunately, the human
animal often prefers to not give in. On the way to my present location, I passed a
T-shirt with the caption, "Never surrender," and this sums up a slogan which has
been reiterated over the centuries ever since the Titans were thrown out of
Heaven.

Table 6.1. The Social Competition Strategy Set at Three Levels of the Triune Brain/Mind

	Escalation	De-escalation
Rational/ Neocortical	Formation of goals Proclamation of goals Overcoming of opposition Social participation Self-assertion Decision to fight on	Giving up of personal goals Adoption of others' goals Submission Acceptance Resignation Self-effacement
Emotional/ limbic	Joy, rapture Enthusiasm Oceanic feeling Anger Indignation	Boredom Apathy Shame Guilt Depressed emotion
Instinctive/ Reptilian	Increase of RHP/SAHP Increase of resource value Increase of "ownership" value Increase of energy Elevated mood (IDS)	Loss of RHP/ SAHP Loss of resource value Loss of "ownership value" Loss of energy Depressed mood(ISS)

Another form of functional agonism works as follows: The rational brain decides to fight, but the emotional and/or instinctive brains decide to de-escalate. These de-escalations affect the thinking of the rational brain, moving it in a more pessimistic direction. To put it technically, there is a loss of resource-holding potential (RHP), resource value and "ownership," so that the individual feels less confident of winning, sees the prize as less valuable, and feels less entitled to the ownership of the prize.[8] Due to this more pessimistic thinking, the rational level switches its strategy from escalation to de-escalation, there is graceful losing, with the way paved for reconciliation. In this process, the lower brain controlled the upper brain. And this seems to be its function. The upper brain seems designed for escalation, to win at all costs, and not to jeopardise its fighting efficiency by any thought of possible damage or defeat. This moni-toring of possible defeat has been relegated to, or retained by, the lower brain. In some way the lower brain seems to keep a tally of punishment received, and when this gets too great it exerts its authority telling the upper brain to de-escalate. The upper brain, which was in any case having a fairly difficult encounter, now has the added handicap of depressive incapacity. So, if it does not capitulate gracefully at this stage, the individual likely gets carried out of the arena on a stretcher.

We have identified depression with instinctive de-escalation, and the com-monest cause of prolonged instinctive de-escalation appears to be continued inappropriate rational escalation, or, to put it another way, blocked rational de-escalation. There are many causes for this, and I will defer discussion of them to a later section.

Prolonged instinctive de-escalation may also stem from inappropriate emotional escalation. An example entails the parents whose child has been killed by a drunken hit-and-run driver. The parents know there is nothing they can do at the rational level, but there is often sustained anger that cannot be satisfied or usefully discharged. The continued "punishment" and hurt accesses the instinctive agonistic strategy set and if de-escalation is selected, chronic depression ensues that cannot be resolved because continued emotional escalation persists.

The third clinical variety is emotional de-escalation associated with rational escalation. This describes, characteristically, wives consulting for marriage guidance.[8] They experience emotional distress, weep, and otherwise de-escalate emotionally. But at the rational level they have escalated in that they are determined to change their husbands' behaviour; to make him less spendthrift, or less unfaithful, or just to pay them more attention. Their failure to achieve this change for the better in the husbands took them to marriage guidance. But the husbands typically sit in the session stony-faced, turned away from their weeping wives, apparently unmoved by their distress. They do not want to change, but they feel confused by their wives' behaviour, escalated at one level and de-escalated at the other.

In a fourth clinical variety the patient de-escalates at all levels, but the submission is not being accepted by the important other person. This occurs sometimes from ignorance, sometimes from cruelty. The fifth and final example of dysfunctional agonism is seen when the instinctive strategy set is too easily accessed, and de-escalation occurs inappropriately to the situation. These patients are oversensitive, too easily moved to tears. Sloman's chapter in this volume deals with them extensively.

TREATMENT

The treatment that arises from our model can be listed in four stages with the injunction: Try the first stage first, and if that doesn't work, try the second stage, and so on.

1. Find a rational solution. There is nothing wonderful about the operation of the lower levels, and their mobilisation of emotional distress and depressed mood suggest failsafe mechanisms because the higher-level has failed to solve the problem.

The therapist's task involves:

(a) identifying the conflict.

(b) estimating the chances of winning, or of leaving the arena, or of submitting the conflict to arbitration; and if any of these seem possible, helping the patient achieve them.

(c) if the problem is one of blocked voluntary yielding (inappropriate rational-level escalation), devising a means for the patient to give in (or give up) without loss of face. This best happens before the administration of antidepressant drugs, because the "giving-up" component of the depressive cognitions may help. In fact, when this situation arises, this giving-up depressive cognition typically has not been strong enough to achieve the necessary yielding. It needs the depression plus the therapist to complete the job.

(d) if a third party is causative, dealing with the problem. Such a third party may be demanding obedience that conflicts with obedience to another, therefore preventing the patient from making a desired submission. This occurs commonly in patients caught between the demands of a dominant parent and a dominant spouse. They cannot submit to both at the same time, because the demands are incompatible. Or the third party may not accept the submission, perhaps because he or she fails to recognise what is going on.

(e) if the patient's instinctive agonistic strategy set is too easily accessed, perhaps due to "kindling" by physical or emotional abuse in childhood, setting in motion appropriate measures. These may range from long-term individual psychotherapy to a self-assertion class. (See Sloman, this volume.)

(f) if the patient has had to give up some unattainable goal or much-loved incentive, considering the need for "bereavement counselling" of some sort. Rosen[9] discusses this well.

2. Reframing the situation. If the situation that gave rise to the depression seems insoluble, consider how it may seem differently to the patient. Here the rational brain tries to control the informational input to the emotional brain. Since it cannot influence the emotional brain directly, this represents the closest approximation to influencing the decision-making function at the emotional level. The best reframing process in the Western world is Christianity. Reframed pain and suffering take on Christ-like qualities: the more one suffers, the more one shares the experience of the Saviour. Gurdjieff reframed suffering to his disciples as opportunities to work on the self and so improve the "true self" which, given enough opportunity and enough work, might become immortal.[10] The classical reframing, quoted by Watzlawick,[11] is Tom Sawyer's punishment of having to paint a fence. This prevented him from going fishing with his friends, so Tom reframed it as a marvellous opportunity to have fun with paint. This reframing gained such success that his friends forgot all about fishing and begged him to let them do the job themselves. For the parent of a child killed by a hit-and-run driver, it may help to see the driver as someone sick rather than bad, perhaps as someone in the throes of epilepsy or a heart attack.

3. Substitute group conflict for individual conflict. We have suggested that the tendency to depressive illness evolved as part of the yielding component of ritual agonistic behaviour. Essentially this stems from a dyadic interaction. The same considerations do not apply to conflict between groups because group conflict lacks the primitive ritual quality of dyadic encounters. In other words, when groups lose a conflict, the members may become demoralised, but they do not become depressed in the way that individual losers do. Therefore, if the patient can join other people engaged in the same conflict, the whole operation may switch from individual agonistic behaviour to an intergroup process. The parents who lost their child to the hit-and-run driver can join other parents and express their grief and rage in a group fashion, and hopefully thereby direct their energies into such positive action as campaigning for more severe laws on drunk driving.

4. Last, provide salves and ointments to the symptoms themselves. This should represent very much a last-ditch action. One hopes that in most cases one of the preceding three methods would have worked. If not, the symptoms may be addressed directly. I am indebted to Leon Sloman for the vignette of the alpine climber who has a panic attack on the side of a snow-covered mountain. He heard a rumble and feared an avalanche. His breathing accelerated by anxiety caused him to blow off too much carbon dioxide, his blood became alkaline, and his muscles went into tetany. In this case, encouraging him to breathe more slowly results in restoration of the acid-base balance of his blood to normal so his legs move again and he can walk to safety. Of course, even here, common sense must be used. The therapist chose the breathing. He would have had less success if he had applied ointment to the tetanic muscles.

In this case, we accept that higher level solutions were not available. The therapist might have done better to produce a cell phone and summon up a helicopter to take the patient off the mountain to safety. Or reframing the situation, he could have pointed out that they were not in fact on a real mountain at all—they were actors taking part in an alpine movie, and the rumbling he had heard was the movement of a mock Mont Blanc on its castors to take up a new location. However, we accept that the deus ex machina of a helicopter is seldom to be summoned, even with a cell phone, and that most climbers who panic at the thought of an avalanche are on real mountains and not taking part in films. But this direct attack on symptoms represents a last resort, unlike some cognitive behaviour therapists who spend time trying to argue patients out of their depressive delusions.

RESEARCH

Like other evolutionary interpretations, the foregoing represents speculation in the last resort untestable. But definitive implications for treatment result. These might have been deduced from another theory, but they have not. Treatment either works or it does not; and this can be tested in a controlled trial. The following plan would constitute such a test: (1) recruiting a center already conducting manualized psychotherapy of depression, e.g., interpersonal therapy or IPT;[12] (2) inserting into their research design additional or replacement interventions based on the evolutionary theory as delineated above. We predict that the results would show quicker and greater power.

THE TRIUNE MIND

For centuries, thinkers have expressed intimations that the mind functions in a way dictated by the triune nature of the brain. Plato, in a chapter entitled "The three parts of the soul" describes various functions and asks: "Are we using the same part of ourselves in all these three experiences, or a different part in each? Do we gain knowledge with one part, feel anger with another, and with yet a third desire the pleasures of food, sex, and so on? Or is the whole soul at work in every impulse and in all these forms of behaviour?" [13, p. 132]

Eastern philosophy, brought to the West after World War I by Gurdjieff,[10] used the metaphor of the horse and cart to describe the mind. It talked of a driver, a horse and a cart, and of the connections between the three elements. The driver represents the rational mind, the horse the emotional mind, and the cart the instinctive mind. This philosophy aimed to create a fourth element, the "true self" representing a "master," who controlled the driver, and told him where to go. Gurdjieff established a teaching centre near Paris; its prospectus proclaimed:

a modern man represents three different men in a single individual—the first of whom thinks in complete isolation from the other parts, the second merely feels, and the third acts only automatically, according to established or accidental reflexes of his organic functions . . . they not only never help each other, but are, on the contrary, automatically compelled to frustrate the plans and intentions of each other; moreover, each of them, by dominating the other in moments of intensive action, appears to be the master of the situation, in this way falsely assuming the responsibility of the real "I." [14, p. 138]

CONCLUSION

In summary, the concept of the triune mind has been part of human folk knowledge for over two millennia. Paul MacLean's description more recently provided a neuroanatomical basis for this knowledge, offering an enormous boost to the heuristic value of the triune model. In this chapter and elsewhere[15] I attempted to demonstrate some applications to psychiatric practice; and in the future I would anticipate that it will have a profound influence on the fields of individual and social psychology.

It is, of course, just a theory, that should be compared with other theories dealing with the same material. Birtchnell, for example, has put forward a two level theory [16,17] that may have advantages in certain circumstances; sometimes it is useful to contrast the rational brain with the remainder of the brain.[18] However, the three-level theory has the advantage of dealing with the emotions separately. For instance, it clarifies the relation between depressed emotion and depressed mood (the former focused on an object rapidly responds to changes in the object's situation, in contrast to depressed mood that remains unfocused or self-focused, and unresponsive to circumstances present). The present theory challenges previous theories of emotion, which, for instance, combine anger and depressed emotion in the same category of negative emotion in contrast to the positive emotions of joy and happiness. According to triune mind/brain theory, anger joins with joy as an escalating emotion, in contrast to depressed emotion seen as a component of a de-escalating strategy. Empirical research will decide which theory most usefully conceptualizes the data.

NOTES

1. MacLean PD: *The Triune Brain in Evolution*. New York: Plenum Press, 1990.

2. Ellenberger HF: *The Discovery of the Unconscious: The History and Evolution of Dynamic Psychiatry*. New York: Basic Books, 1970.

3. Beck AT: The development of depression. In D Freedman & H Kaplan (Eds.) *Comprehensive Textbook of Psychiatry*. Philadelphia, PA: Williams and Wilkins, 1974. Pp. 3–27.

4. Gardner R: The brain and communication are basic for clinical human sciences. *British Journal of Medical Psychology.* 1998, 71: 493–508.

5. Huntingford F & Turner A: *Animal Conflict*. London: Chapman & Hall, 1987.

6. Price JS: The effect of social stress on the behaviour and physiology of monkeys. In K Davison & A Keff (Eds.) *Contemporary Themes in Psychiatry*. London: Gaskell, 1989, pp. 459–466.

7. Butler AB & Hodos W: *Comparative Vertebrate Neuroanatomy*. New York: Wiley Liss, 1996.

8. Gardner R, Jr. & Price JS: Sociophysiology and depression. In: T Joiner & JC Coyne (Eds.) *The Interactional Nature of Depression: Advances in Interpersonal Approaches*, Washington, DC: APA Books, 1999, pp. 247–268.

9. Rosen DH: *Transforming Depression: Egocide, Symbolic Death, and New Life*. NewYork: Putnam, 1993.

10. Ouspensky PD: *In Search of the Miraculous: Fragments of an Unknown Teaching*. London:Routledge & Kegan Paul, 1950.

11. Watzlawick P, Beavin JH, Jackson DD: *The Pragmatics of Human Communication: A Study of Interactional Patterns, Pathologies and Paradoxes*. New York: W.W. Norton, 1950.

12. Weissman NM & Markowitz JC: (1994) Interpersonal psychotherapy: current status. *Archives of General Psychiatry,* 1994; 51: 599–606.

13. Cornford FM: *The Republic of Plato*. Translated with introduction and notes. London: Oxford University Press, 1992.

14. Bennett JG: *Gurdjieff. Making a New World*. London: Turnstone Books, 1976.

15. Price JS: The adaptive function of mood change. *British Journal of Medical Psychology* 1998; 71: 465–477.

16. Birtchnell J: The inner brain and the outer brain. *The ASCAP Newsletter*, 1999, 12 (01), 11–17.

17. Birtchnell J: *Relating in Psychotherapy: The Application of a New Theory.* Westport CT: Praeger, 1999.

18. Price J: A case of hedonic emotional/limbic escalation. *ASCAP Newsletter* 1999; 12 (No.5), 10–12.

7

INVOLUNTARY DEFEAT STRATEGY AS BACKDROP FOR DEPRESSION

Leon Sloman

INTRODUCTION

The extensive history of conspecific conflict in humans makes it hard to believe that humans can be endowed with strategies designed to prevent and terminate fighting. However, these conflicts would have been even more severe, if it had not been for the Involuntary Defeat Strategy (IDS), which has played a key role in the avoidance and rapid termination of conflict. I will discuss the IDS and show how it can, at times, have a more pathological outcome by contributing to certain forms of depression. I plan to examine factors associated with a negative outcome and propose that a crucial issue features whether or not the IDS functions effectively. I will distinguish between effective and ineffective funct-ioning of the IDS, and consider factors that render it more and less effective and demonstrate how an ineffective functioning of the IDS contributes to depressive disorders and other forms of psychopathology. I will also discuss the link between dominance and mania and present the "see-saw" model of bipolar disorder. Finally, I will describe clinical interventions designed to promote the IDS's more effective functioning.

BACKGROUND

Price (1967) drew on Zuckermann's (1932) observations of long-tailed macaques to note the similarity between depressed patients and animals who lose in hierarchical encounters and are pressed into a subordinate social role. He proposed that "states of depression, anxiety, and irritability are the emotional concomitants of behavior patterns which are necessary for the maintenance of dominance hierarchies in social groups" and claimed (1969:1107) that depression, anxiety, and feelings of inferiority evolved as the "yielding component of ritual agonistic behaviors."

According to Price (1967: 243), "factors which increase or reduce dominance behavior will have malignant or beneficial effects on mental illness." Price et al. (1994) renamed the "yielding subroutine" the "Involuntary Subordinate Strategy" (ISS) and postulated that "the depressive state evolved in relation to social competition as an unconscious ISS, enabling the individual to accept defeat in a ritual agonistic encounter and to accommodate to what would otherwise be unacceptably low social rank." Price and Sloman (1987) proposed that human beings share with other vertebrates an older, more primitive mechanism for yielding that evolved as a component of ritual agonistic in the common ancestor of present-day birds and mammals and that the "hardware" for this mechanism is situated in the "reptilian brain." MacLean (1985a) deleted elements of ritual agonistic behavior by ablation studies of the "reptilian" brain. Recently, Sloman and Gilbert (2000) introduced the term "Involuntary Defeat Strategy" (IDS) for greater specificity.

The IDS is a genetically preprogrammed strategy triggered by an individual's recognition that defeat in social competition is inevitable. The strategy reduces the risk of injury or death to both combatants by convincing the loser of the futility of further struggle and triggering either flight or submission and promoting subjective acceptance of the new status quo. In addition, it conveys to the winner that his opponent no longer threatens because the battle is more or less over. This may convince him to accept his opponent's submission and end the struggle. The IDS is "involuntary" because it is triggered automatically by the recognition that he has lost the competitive encounter or that defeat is inevitable. The term "defeat" refers to the fact that the IDS is triggered by defeat and also to its role in promoting accommodation to subordinate status. The term "strategy" reflects its genetic preprogramming to fulfill an adaptive function (Sloman 2000).

I now explore the differences between an effective and an ineffective IDS.

THE EFFECTIVE IDS

The effective IDS reduces motivation to continue the struggle, adjusts aspirations, and increases readiness to flee or submit, while engaged or considering engaging in a confrontation. While a mild IDS may be characterized as "disappointment," a more powerful IDS may be associated with feelings of depression.

Flexible responsiveness to a changed situation and a strong "sense of self" represent hallmarks of an effective IDS. A more self-confident person finds it easier to change his stance and admit he was wrong. The behavior of the winner may have a substantial impact on the loser's IDS. For example, the winner may show magnanimity and perhaps share the spoils of the fight or, in other species, accept grooming from the defeated rival. This friendliness and positive acknowledgment of the loser's prowess makes it easier to accept defeat.

The effective functioning of the IDS brings a recognition that further struggle would be futile, which ends the conflict and leads to the acceptance of the new status quo, which switches off of the IDS. When the conflict is over, the IDS no longer serves any useful function, except in an attenuated form by discouraging the individual who has lost from attacking the victor who has demonstrated superior prowess. The effective IDS leading to acceptance of defeat thus frees the individual to resume more productive activities, resume an affiliative relationship with the opponent, or run away to safety. Effective functioning of the IDS causes loss of motivation to struggle any more, which prompts the decision that it would be useless to continue. This is followed by adjustment to the new situation, namely, acceptance of the subordinate role which, in turn, leads to a termination of the IDS. The outcome of such encounters may leave people with a more realistic appraisal of their own and others' strengths and abilities and also leave them free to move on to face new challenges. However, in the instance of escape, the IDS may be terminated without acceptance, since the individual may be generating resources for renewed attack.

To summarize, when the IDS functions effectively, it helps avoid unnecessary conflict or brings conflict to an end. Termination of the conflict leads to escape, or submission and/or acceptance. When the submission has been accepted and the need to submit subsides, the IDS switches off. Similarly, if one escapes and feels free, the IDS is no longer required. However, if the IDS does not bring them to relinquish their unattainable goals, individuals may become depressed, abusive to others, or locked into unproductive power struggles that lead to dysfunctional interactions in both family and other social domains (Sloman 1981).

SOCIAL COMPETITION AND ATTACHMENT

Because attachment theory and social competition theory evolved independently, the close interrelationship between the two models (Sloman & Atkinson 2000; Sloman, Atkinson, Milligan, & Liotti, in press) is often overlooked. A secure attachment contributes towards effective functioning of the IDS. For example, support from someone with whom one is affiliated can give one the confidence to challenge a competitor and, if one loses the agonistic encounter, the presence of someone to whom one is securely attached can lower one's level of arousal, thus enabling one to accept defeat and move on to more productive activities. Similarly, if one has just lost an agonistic encounter with someone to whom one is securely attached, one's trust in the other may cause one's resentment to fade. This promotes acceptance of defeat which brings the struggle to an end, thus turning off the IDS.

According to Hilburn-Cobb (1998), subordination mechanisms like the IDS can be used in the services of attachment. For example, Dorothy to be described below, would burst into tears at times of potential confrontation. These tears were designed to head off the opponent's expected wrath. Some clients, when faced with a challenge, turn to those closest to them for support. Therefore, attachment mechanisms can maintain a subordinate stance (Sloman & Atkinson 2000).

Gilbert (1997) concluded that competition by attraction has largely replaced competition by intimidation and is the main form of competition seen in primitive tribes by anthropologists. We compete to be seen as worthy, able, and attractive. Those with insecure preoccupied attachments require constant signals that they are attractive, desired and wanted, and fear not being able to call on others for support. Also, they more likely see attachment as something that must be earned in competition. Their inner models of attachment organize around dimensions of power, control, and competitiveness. When these individuals lose out in competition by attraction, their IDS is triggered, which makes them feel more inadequate and therefore more unlovable, resulting in a still more insecure attachment. This may make them more competitive while further undermining their chances of success.

THE INEFFECTIVE IDS

Effective functioning of the IDS reduces the likelihood of certain forms of psychopathology, while ineffective functioning can lead to depression or other forms of psychopathology. An effective IDS leads to submission and/or acceptance. However, anger associated with a need to win may force a continuation of the struggle, even though there is no prospect of winning.

There are three possible outcomes. First, the increased effort causes the tide to turn in one's favor, thereby switching off the IDS; second, continued failure convinces the individual that further struggle is hopeless so that he flees, or accepts defeat, submits, and brings the struggle to an end; third a more negative outcome occurs in that though the IDS has been triggered, one cannot give up the struggle because of strong feelings of resentment, or because the opponent refuses to accept the submission. This can cause cognitions associated with the IDS to intensify, because of the apparent futility of one's efforts. Accordingly, one feels increasingly disempowered and becomes more and more depressed. In these situations, the IDS continues to operate and the features that are geared to bring the struggle to an end (i.e., to de-escalate) have failed to achieve their purpose and, instead, caused an intensification at the intrapsychic level and possibly at the interpsychic level. At the intrapsychic level, feelings of helplessness and hopelessness, with the function of triggering submission or flight, are no longer effective. Because these feelings are designed to terminate conflict, the fact that the conflict continues causes them to intensify, and they then manifest as depressive disorder. At the interpsychic level, the intensification may manifest as power struggles (Sloman 1981), put-downs or "double-bind" communications (Bateson et al. 1956). The presence of the persistent IDS may prevent the individual from engaging in open conflict, but the conflict may continue covertly.

The presence of a persistent IDS can be attributed to neuronal "kindling" (Post & Weiss 1998; Segal, Williams, Teasdale & Gemar 1996). Kindling accounts for how, when the IDS has been overstimulated at an earlier point in time, a smaller amount of stimulation is subsequently required to produce the same strength of reaction. The notion of kindling purports to explain why the first depressive illness may be precipitated by a major loss, while subsequent relapses are triggered by much smaller losses.

When accepting subordinate status functions better than persisting in a self-defeating strategy, why are we not programmed to show acceptance more readily? One answer involves fighting strategies. To win, we must maintain our belief that victory will come our way. If we react to every minor setback, we might betray this information to our adversary. This would give him more heart and thus bring about our own defeat. It seems likely that one reason why the IDS evolved was to counteract this implacable resolve to win at all costs. Social life would not be possible with a Titan mentality (Price, personal communication).

GAME THEORY

Maynard Smith (1982), using game theory, showed how assessor strategy allows the contestant to evaluate whether the opponent or potential opponent is stronger or weaker and then respond appropriately. If the animal correctly evaluates that it would lose if it came to a fight, it might be in that animal's interest to take flight relatively uninjured. On the other hand, if the animal correctly evaluates that it would win, its best interest may be served by fighting and benefiting from the spoils of victory. These spoils might comprise a rise in status with better access to food, territory, and mating partners. Thus, that the animal makes an accurate judgment of comparative strength holds great importance. If the assessor strategy is off the mark, the IDS might be prematurely triggered or may fail to be triggered at the appropriate times. Both of these can have negative consequences for the individual.

FACTORS AFFECTING EFFECTIVENESS OF THE IDS

The individual's ability to give up the struggle to achieve an unattainable goal may be influenced by a number of factors. One is the value the individual attaches to the resource that is the object of the struggle. In many conflicts of interest, the practical consequences of defeat are minor, which makes it easier to accept that status. However, at times, submission to the opponent entails giving up a great deal. As a result, the options of submitting or continuing the struggle are both unacceptable so that one feels there is no way out. Richard II, as portrayed by Shakespeare, majestically exemplifies this.

> Or I'll be buried in the King's highway,
> Some way of common trade, where subjects' feet
> May hourly trample on their sovereign's head;
> For on my heart they tread now whilst I live,
> And buried once, why not upon my head?

The king's pain of having his "subjects tramping hourly on his heart" may not appear like the IDS, because it can take the form of incapacity, such as illness, old age, possession by the devil, or some other condition unrelated to the contest at issue. However, for the king this helps him submit. Is it not more reassuring to see your opponent old and sick than stepping down in full possession of his faculties, still able to make a speech which rings our heart with sympathy, and oratorical ability but which could have been turned alternatively to speeches requesting allies to support him in a come-back? For the king to become reconciled and step down gracefully may not have been a viable option (Price, personal communication). Those of less exalted status, who experience a major defeat may find other arenas where they can experience success so that their setback is only temporary.

The relationship between the competitors may make it painful for the loser to submit and for the winner to accept the submission. For example, if the contestants feel too much bitterness, triggering of the loser's IDS may fail to stimulate acceptance by either party. If the adversary refuses to accept submission and continues to behave agonistically by using put-downs, for instance, this is likely to generate more anger and resentment. There may also be pressure from other members of the same group who want the struggle to continue.

Support from other members of the group can also make it easier to accept defeat. This may take the form of solicitude, or praise for the loser's efforts.

SUBMISSIVE BEHAVIOR AND VULNERABILITY TO PSYCHOPATHOLOGY

Physical and sexual abuse as well as neglect and insecure attachment in childhood are likely to frequently and/or powerfully trigger the IDS. This may, in fact, help the young child adapt, but in later years foster frequent, premature, and unneeded triggering of the IDS. Overly submissive behavior may result. Submissiveness, or low assertiveness relates to depression and social anxiety (Gilbert & Allan 1994). Some forms of submissive behavior, particularly those associated with passive/withdrawal and inhibition, associate with a wide variety of psychological problems, especially depression (Gilbert 2000; Allan & Gilbert 1997). These findings support the proposed link between the IDS and depression.

THE BIOLOGY OF THE NORMAL IDS

During an intense competitive encounter, the human or nonhuman primate experiences increased arousal with an adaptive rise in plasma cortisol levels, which mobilizes metabolic, cognitive, and behavioral resources. If the individual clearly foresees that the encounter will be lost and that further arousal will be counterproductive, the IDS is triggered. If effective, this serves to de-escalate behavior and HPA (hypothalamus-pituitary-adrenal)-axis functioning. A successful escape/submission results in acceptance of the loss and new social status, and the IDS then terminates. At this point, the HPA-axis returns to its baseline point and reestablishes homeostasis.

At a neuroanatomical level, the IDS can be thought of as a preprogammed neural circuit linking the limbic system, prefrontal cortex, and striatum, which mediate, respectively, the emotional, cognitive, and behavioral components of the IDS. In response to an agonistic threat, the limbic system activates first with a concomitant increase in arousal and HPA-axis functioning. Once agonistic loss becomes inevitable, the prefrontal cortex, responsible for higher order cognitive functions including anticipation and planning, activates and triggers cognitions related to anticipation of defeat. Shortly thereafter, the striatum would be activated to trigger the behavioral/motor sequence needed to produce adaptive gesturing and, if necessary, rapid flight from the encounter. Effective functioning of the IDS might incorporate adaptive motor behaviors mediated by the striatum, a new cognitive set of acceptance mediated at the prefrontal cortex, and decreased arousal concomitant with both decreased activation of the limbic system and HPA-axis which establishes a successful return to steady state.

RELATION BETWEEN BIOLOGICAL CHANGES IN SUBORDINATES AND DEPRESSION

If the IDS links to depression, biological changes should be associated with defeat and with depression. Animal studies have found a significant relationship between the biological changes in animals experiencing defeat in hierarchical contests and those associated with human depression (Gilbert 2000; Levitan, Hasey & Sloman 2000; and McGuire et al. 2000).

How does one explain this apparent relationship between the biological changes in defeat and depression? The IDS normally functions to de-escalate conflict so that, when the IDS is ineffective, de-escalation does not occur and the physiological activation that is normally adaptive in conflict persists. The physiological changes in the subordinate baboon (Sapolsky, Alberts & Altmann 1997) remain because it remains primed for combat. The changes observed in human depression may similarly be attributed to a failure of demobilization; the clinically depressed individual remains primed for combat, though he recognizes that he cannot win (Levitan, Hasey & Sloman 2000).

DEFEAT AND ENTRAPMENT

Schjelderup-Ebbe (1935) coined the term "pecking order" as he described the consequences of losing dominance in barnyard fowl, where escape to a new territory was not possible. Following defeat, the bird's "behavior becomes entirely changed. Deeply depressed in spirit, humble with dropping wings and head in the dust it is—at any rate directly upon being vanquished—overcome with paralysis, though one cannot detect any physical injury. The bird's resistance now seems broken, and in some cases the effects of the psychological condition are so strong that the bird will sooner or later come to grief." These birds' severe reaction to agonistic loss can be attributed to their inability to flee the scene because of being in captivity.

Gilbert (2000) and Gilbert and Allan (1998) argue that having to stay in the arena following defeat is much more problematic than being able to escape. They suggest that, when there is a strong motive to take flight, depression and "entrapment" may be a preferable construct to "learned helplessness" (Seligman 1975).

MacLean (1985b & 1990) also noted that reptiles who lose rank often lose their bright colors and may die soon afterwards, and Von Holst (1986) found that defeated tree shrews could suffer the same fate. Defeat and entrapment can, therefore, have severe untoward effects.

DOMINANCE, MANIA AND BIPOLAR DISORDER

Gardner (1982) found that alpha individuals on the dominance hierarchy and manic patients responded to questionnaires in a similar fashion, and his proposal of a relationship between dominant behavior and manic illness represents a seminal contribution. He deduced that inborn strategies that had an adaptive function by helping alpha individuals attain and maintain their dominant status could also become maladaptive by contributing to manic illness. Gardner's model of manic illness complements Price's (1969) model of depression. According to Price, increasing intensity of the Involuntary Defeat Strategy associated with continued agonistic loss can culminate in depressive illness. Similarly, deduced from Gardner's formulations, an increasingly intense out-of-control Involuntary Dominant Strategy culminates in mania.

One unanswered question is whether mania is more closely related to one particular form of dominant behavior. For example, is it related to the immediate reaction to winning, which is associated with feelings of elation, high self-confidence, and ritualistic behavior like throwing one's arms up in the air or doing a victory dance? Or, is it related to the more long-term pattern associated with being at the top of the hierarchy? After the feelings of triumph associated with winning have faded, a residuum often manifests as increased self-confidence. A third pattern that can be called "pseudo-dominance," is characterized by a bullying or controlling attitude towards those perceived as weaker than oneself and hierarchically lower. This behavior could be considered to be a defense against inner feelings of inadequacy or insecurity. Bullying additionally involves constant put-downs of other people, unproductive power struggles and "double-bind" (Bateson et al. 1956) interactions. Though a bullying person works hard to avoid defeat, he cannot truly assert himself or try to win.

Paul Gilbert (2000) lists various types of submissive behavior: escape/flight strategies, ambivalent defensive strategies and arrested flight, blocked escape strategies, loss of control strategies, social defeat strategies, enclosed avoidance strategies, submissive display strategies, infantile and illness strategies. He differentiates between friendly and hostile submission. One can also subcategorize dominant behaviors too, by distinguishing between friendly and hostile dominance, for example. Greater specificity about the manic's kind of dominant strategy would help define a postulated relationship between manic illness and the dominant strategy.

Gilbert (1992:195) speaks of a recent shift from exerting social control via threat/aggression towards the need to present oneself as attractive to others. Today, in Western culture, display of strength is emphasized less than "invest in me and I will be useful to you" (Buss 1988). Gilbert coined the term "social attention-holding power" (SAHP), that depends on abilities to control others' attention favorably. One can distinguish certain leaders who derive their strength from the use of threat/aggression (e.g., Saddam Hussein) and others, who rely more on the use of attractiveness (e.g., Bill Clinton). Oddly enough, both of these individuals have created trouble for others by going overboard in their use of the techniques that got them into power. If any psychopathology does develop, the pattern of dominance might well influence the nature of psychopathology. For example, Gilbert (1992: 557-558) compares the biological and symptom differences in depression in individuals with autocratic and achievement-focused personalities who are highly up-rank motivated and those who are more affiliative and less autocratic? He concludes "Personality studies have found that endogenous depressives and bipolar patients are more ambitious and competitive than neurotics."

Adversarial escalation initially triggers the flight response which, in turn, becomes regulated by the winner and loser's reaction to the results of the agonistic encounter. One can conceptualize the dominant (winning) and defeat strategies as existing at opposite ends of a biological see-saw. The see-saw model is used to illustrate the close interrelation between reactions to winning and losing. For example, when the subordinate strategy functions normally, the dominant strategy switches off and vice versa. The relation between the two ends of the see-saw reminds one of a thermostat where a shift in temperature might result in switching off the heating or air conditioning; one does not expect the air conditioning and heating system to operate simultaneously. When a previously successful individual falls in the hierarchy, the higher end of the individual's see-saw falls to the ground. The close connection between winning and defeat strategies is further emphasized by the fact that, while engaged in agonistic encounters, we are primed, depending on the outcome, to respond either dominantly or subordinately at very short notice. One would expect that both responses would be primed until one or the other has been triggered. The close interrelationship between winning and losing is also shown by the fact that the greatest triumph may be to "pluck victory from the jaws of defeat." Gardner (1982: 143–148) commented that both mania and depression are obviously primitive in that they are separated from social reality. This enables one to argue, in these conditions, the likely reptilian origins of agonistic behavior.

Early learning plays an important role in the priming of the biological see-saw. When conditions are optimal, the child learns when to challenge and when to submit. The abused or severely repressed child tends to be overly primed to respond in a subordinate fashion. In later years this child's subordinate response may be prematurely triggered by any minor or imagined slight, exhibiting an unbalanced see-saw.

In some cases, because genetic and experiential factors interplay, forceful and frequent moves of the see-saw lead to an oscillation between overactivation (depression) at one end of the see-saw and overactivation (mania) at the other end. Sharp transitions from depression to mania and vice versa may exemplify this, as observed in bipolar disorder. This oscillation may also occur with a lesser force in cyclothymic personality. Overactivation refers to the escal-ation of a normally adaptive mechanism to the point that it becomes largely maladaptive as when the IDS manifests as clinical depression, the dominant strategy manifests as mania, or when fear, anxiety vomiting, and diarrhea, all of which have important adaptive functions, intensify too much.

SOCIAL COMPETITION THEORY AND COGNITIVE BEHAVIORAL THERAPY

Swallow (2000), a cognitive behavior therapist, points out that self-denigrat-ing cognitions may be part of a submissive defensive response to terminate the motive to keep trying in no-win situations and that the overarching goal of this system is self-protection. It therefore makes sense, he says, for cognitive theorists to conceptualize depressive thinking patterns in terms of their prev-iously evolved functional significance as well as in terms of their content or structure. Swallow argues that such a conceptualization—the IDS perspective— might have important implications for the way cognitive therapists address negative thinking in depression. Because the IDS perspective suggests that the individual may be motivated to see herself as no good in order to avoid some putative threat such as being cut down to size by another person, the person may be quite resistant to giving up this self-denigrating belief. Therapeutically this motivation can be clarified by asking patients to consider what protection they obtain from the belief that they are no good. Or what concerns would emerge for them if they did not think that way about themselves.

CLINICAL EXAMPLES

Case of Dorothy

Dorothy, a 32-year-old married woman, suffered from mild depression. Her father exhibited violent fits of rage during her childhood. Her older and younger sisters had been openly rebellious, but she was compliant and had always tried to mediate when her father berated her mother. Her inability to be assertive manifested as chronic low self-esteem and her problem in being assertive was compounded by her tendency to use her subordinate strategy in the service of her attachment needs. That is to say, displaying weakness and helplessness was her way of eliciting support and reassurance. I had tried to help her avoid triggering her subordinate strategy in situations where she had the capacity to hold her own. She had already made good progress in terms of improved self-assertion. Towards the end of a particular psychotherapy session she said that whereas she normally felt better at the end of a session, that today she felt as flat as when she first came to treatment. When I asked her how she had perceived our relationship during the session, she said that, at one point, she had perceived me as being judgmental of her. When I inquired whether this would have been something she could have mentioned spontaneously, she said "no." I then suggested that she must have felt angry with me and avoided expressing this by adopting a subordinate role (the IDS). She acknowledged this had happened; and then added she now felt less tired and more energetic. We discussed progress she had made in eliminating the ghosts of the past—particularly the ghost of her father—but also the work remaining to be done in this area.

Case of Leila

Leila was a 42-year-old married woman I saw in couples therapy. She had been abused by her previous husband and we had been working on how she could give up playing a victim role. In a dream a few days after the previous session, Leila found herself in an anxiety-producing situation and felt that she could react in an angry or frustrated way. She suddenly realized that she didn't have to react in either way and felt an incredible sense of calm. She became aware that she had been reacting as if she had a great need for power and was reminded of the biblical injunction "The meek shall inherit the earth." She had been trying to make sense of why she needed to take a subordinate position. When she could give up her need for power, she became less involved in agonistic conflicts. This, in turn, relieved her of having to take a "one-down" position.

These cases illustrate two sides of the same coin. Dorothy illustrates the value of freeing up people to express themselves without triggering the subordinate strategy. Leila illustrates the merits of avoiding getting into agonistic conflict with opponents who are clearly more powerful than oneself. These two approaches are interdependent as people often compensate for feelings of inferiority associated with their own subordinate reactions by developing an inordinate need for power. Similarly, those with an inordinate need for power more likely find themselves engaged in agonistic conflicts with others more powerful than themselves, which triggers their subordinate strategies and results in a self-defeating vicious cycle. The therapist's task involves breaking up this vicious cycle by whatever means deemed most appropriate, including psychotherapy, medication, and physical education.

SUMMING UP

A variety of treatment approaches, with seemingly disparate mechanisms of action, effectively treat depression. One explanation holds that these various treatments intervene at different levels of the same final common pathway. Considering first biological treatments, the two most established modalities are antidepressant medications and electro-convulsive therapy. Serotonergic medications might work at several levels to render the IDS more effective. As described above, increased serotonin activity decreases impulsive behavior and hostility, while enhancing social affiliation and status in primates (Raleigh et al. 1991; Fuller et al. 1996). Recent work suggests that serotonergic drugs may also enhance affiliative behavior in humans (Knutson et al. 1998), while improving the symptoms of social anxiety (Stein et al. 1998). Taken as a whole, these various lines of research suggest that serotonergic drugs may directly affect brain mechanisms important in mediating primate affiliative behavior, so important in promoting the normal unfolding of the IDS de-escalation strategy.

Regarding psychosocial treatments, various interventions including crisis interventions and psychotherapeutic approaches likely have significant effects on levels of perceived and actual stress, helping to decrease hypothalamic-pituitary-adrenal (HPA) axis activity and arousal. Especially, this may be true in the earlier stages of depression before the HPA-axis loses its regulatory input, or in the partially recovered or remitted patient who might otherwise relapse in response to stress.

How specifically might particular psychological interventions normalize the IDS? Interpersonal therapy could enhance the effectiveness of the IDS through several mechanisms, including augmenting affiliative relationships, acceptance of new roles, and promotion of normal grieving. Cognitive therapy might work by eliminating negative cognitions that inappropriately exaggerate defeat behavior and/or by promoting greater acceptance in response to perceived failures. Each of the varied approaches promotes effective functioning of the IDS by aiding de-escalation when the conflict is clearly lost. This may explain the common therapeutic effects of otherwise distinct treatments for depression.

REFERENCES

Allan, S., and Gilbert, P. (1997). Submissive behavior and psychopathology. *British Journal of Clinical Psychology.* 36, 467–488.

Bateson, G., Jackson, D. D., Haley, J., Weakland, J. (1956). Toward a theory of schizophrenia. *Behavioral Science.* 1, 251–264.

Buss, A.H. (1988). *Personality; Evolutionary Heritage and Human Distinctiveness.* Hillsdale, N.J. Lawrence Erlbaum Associates Inc.

Fuller, R. W. (1996). The influence of fluoxetine on aggressive behavior. *Neuropsychopharmacology.* 14, 77–81.

Gardner, R. (1982). Mechanisms in manic-depressive disorder; an evolutionary model. *Archives of General Psychiatry* 39, 1436–1441.

Gilbert, P. (1992). *Depression; The Evolution of Powerlessness,* Guilford Press, NY.

Gilbert, P. and Allan, S., (1994). Assertiveness, submissive behavior and social comparison. *British Journal of Clinical Psychology.* 33, 295–306.

Gilbert, P. (1997) The evolution of social attractiveness and its role in shame, humiliation, guilt and therapy. *British Journal of Medical Psychology,* 70, 113–147.

Gilbert, P., and Allan, S., (1998). The role of defeat and entrapment (arrested flight) in depression; an exploration of an evolutionary view. *Psychological Medicine,* 28, 1–14.

Gilbert, P. (2000) Varieties of Submissive Behavior as Forms of Social Defense; Evolution and Psychopathology. In L. Sloman & P. Gilbert, (Eds.*) Subordination and Defeat; An Evolutionary Approach to Mood Disorders and Their Therapy.* Mah Wah, NJ: Lawrence Erlbaum Associates Inc.

Hilburn-Cobb, C. (1998, Oct 2–3) Adolescent disorganization of attachment and its relation to psychopathlogy Presented at *Attachment and Psychopathology; Second International Conference,* Toronto.

Klein, D.F. (1971) Approaches to measuring the efficacy of treatment of personality disorders; analysis and program, In *Principles and Problems in Establishing the Efficacy of Psychotropic Agents.* US Department of HEW, Public Health Service No 2138, Washington D.C.

Knutson, B.; Wolkowitz, O. M.; Cole, S. W.; Chan, T.; Moore, E. A.; Johnson, R.C.; Terpstra, A.; Turner, R. A. & Res, V. I. (1998). Selective alterations of personality and social behavior by serotonergic intervention. *American Journal of Psychiatry.* 155, 373–379.

Kohut, H., and Wolfe, E. (1978) The disorders of the self and their treatment; an outline. *International Journal of Psycho Analysis.* 59, 413–425.

Levitan, R., Hasey, G. & Sloman, L. (2000) Major Depression and the Involuntary Defeat Strategy; Biological Correlates. In L. Sloman & P. Gilbert, (Eds.) *Subordination and Defeat; An Evolutionary Approach to Mood Disorders and Their Therapy.* Mah Wah, NJ: Lawrence Erlbaum.

MacLean, P. D. (1995a). Evolutionary psychiatry and the triune brain. *Psychological Medicine.* 15, 219–221.

MacLean, P. D. (1985b). Brain evolution relating to family, play, and the separation call. *Archives of General Psychiatry.* 42, 405–417.

Maclean, P. D. (1990) *The Triune Brain in Evolution: Role in Paleocerebral Functions.* NY: Plenum.

Post, R.M., & Weiss, S. R. B. (1998). Sensitization and kindling phenomena mood, anxiety and obsessive-compulsive disorders; The role of serotonergic mechanisms in illness progression. *Biological Psychiatry.* 44; 193–206.

Maynard Smith, J. (1982) *Evolution and the Theory of Games.* Cambridge University Press, Cambridge.

McGuire, M.; Fawzy, J.; Spar, J & Troisi, A. (2000). Dysthymic disorder, regulation dysregulation theory, CNS blood Flow and CNS metabolism. In L. Sloman and P. Gilbert (Eds.), *Subordination and Defeat; An Evolutionary Approach to Mood Disorders and Their Therapy.* Mah Wah, NJ: Lawrence Erlbaum Associates Inc.

Price, J. S. (1967) Hypothesis: the dominance hierarchy and the evolution of mental illness. *Lancet.* H; 243–246.

Price, J. S., (1969) The ritualization of agonistic behavior as a determinant of variation along the neuroticism stability dimension of personality. *Proceedings of the Royal Society of Medicine.* 62, 1107–1110.

Price, J.S. & Sloman, L. (1987) Depression as yielding behavior; an animal model based on Schjelderup-Ebbe's pecking order. *Ethology and Sociobiology.* 85S–98S.

Price, J. S., Sloman, L., Gardner, R., Gilbert, P. and Rohde, P. (1994). The social competition hypothesis of depression. *British Journal of Psychiatry.* 164, 309–315.

Raleigh, M. J.; McGuire, M. T.; Brammer, G. I.; Pollack, D. B & Yuwiler, A. (1991). Serotonergic mechanisms promote dominance behavior in adult male vervet monkeys. *Brain Research.* 559, 181–190.

Sapolsky, R. M., Alberts, S. C., Altmann, J. (1997). Hypercortisolism associated with social subordinance or social isolation among wild baboons. *Archives of General Psychiatry.* 54, 1137–1143.

Schjelderupp-Ebbe, T., (1935). Social behavior of birds. In *Handbook of Social Psychology*, C. Murchison (ed.) Worcester MA: Clark University Press, pp. 947–972.

Seligman, M. E. P., (1975). *Helplessness; on Depression, Development, and Death,* San Francisco, Freeman.

Segal, Z. V.; Williams, J. M.; Teasdale, J. D.; and Gemar, M. A (1996) Cognitive science perspective on kindling and episode sensitization in recurrent affective disorder. *Psychological Medicine.* 26, 371–380

Sloman, L., (1981). Intrafamilial struggles for power; an ethological perspective. *International Journal of Family Therapy.* 2, 13–33.

Sloman, L. (2000). How the Involuntary Defeat Strategy contributes to depression. In L.Sloman and P. Gilbert (Eds.), *Subordination and Defeat; An Evolutionary Approach to Mood Disorders and Their Therapy.* Mah Wah, NJ: Lawrence Erlbaum Associates Inc.

Sloman, L. & Atkinson, L. (2000). Socal competition and attachment. In L. Sloman and P. Gilbert (Eds.), *Subordination and Defeat; An Evolutionary Approach to Mood Disorders and Their Therapy.* Mah Wah, NJ: Lawrence Erlbaum Associates Inc.

Sloman, L.; Atkinson, L.; Milligan, K. & Liotti, G. (in press). Attachment, social rank, and affect regulation; speculations on an ethological approach to family interaction, *Family Process.*

Stein, M. B.; Liebowitz, M. R.; Lydiard, R. B.; Pitts, C. D.; Bushnell, W. & Gergel, I (1998). Paroxetine treatment of generalized school phobia; a randomized controlled trial. *J.A.M.A.* 280, 708–713.

Swallow, S. (2000). A cognitive behavioral perspective of the Involuntary Defeat Strategy. In L. Sloman and P. Gilbert (Eds.) *Subordination and Defeat; An Evolutionary Approach to Mood Disorders and Their Therapy.* Mah Wah, NJ: Lawrence Erlbaum Associates Inc.

Von Holst, D. (1986). Vegetative and somatic components of tree shrews' behaviour. *Journal of the Autonomic Nervous System.* (suppl), 657–670.

Zuckermann, S. (1932). *The Social Life of Monkeys and Apes.* London: Kegan Paul.

8

THE EVOLVED BASIS OF MOOD AND THOUGHT DISORDERS: NEUROETHOLOGIC, GAME MATHEMATIC, AND EVOLUTIONARY EPIDEMIOLOGIC ANALYSES

Daniel R. Wilson

INTRODUCTION

MacLean (1949, 1985, 1990), elaborating on the earlier ideas of Flourens (1824), Broca (1878), and Papez (1937), has given us the classic account of reptilian behavior. In *The Triune Brain in Evolution*, somber reptilian ritualized antagonistic behavior and resource holding algorithms are noted to yet reside amid more cozy mammalian complexes such as thermoregulation, motherhood, parentalism, pair bonding, kin selection, play, and eusocial affiliation (MacLean 1985, 1990). Vertebrate brains have an analogue of self-esteem, with neuro-mentalities raised or lowered by signals from conspecifics (Eibl-Eibesfeldt 1975). Such signals entail reliance on an apparatus that is phylogenetically quite old and deeply rooted in those genomic elements that organize behavior. While this apparatus has greatly elaborated in subsequent mammalian and primate evolution (Bucy & Kluver 1955), changes have often come to overlay but not wholly replace earlier features (Spencer 1855; Hughlings Jackson 1881; Brown & Schafer 1888; Sherrington 1906; Kluver & Bucy 1937; Pribram 1958; Brady 1958; Harlow 1965).

Hence, conceptualizations of human neuromental phenomena must account not only for reptilian origins but also ongoing retentions. Retentions were modified in the course of integration with newer primatomammalian neuro-mentalities (e.g., the later limbic, cortical, neo-cortical tissues, and related neuroendocrine innovations). However, phylogenetically old adaptations can be operationally released in certain, often pathological, circumstances, as when functional tensions arise between R-complex and upper cortical operations—usefully termed *phylogenetic regression* (Bailey 1987)—to induce pathopheno-typies such as mania, depression, and thought disorder. It is, however, especially revealing to explore the convergence of MacLean's concepts with another potent model in behavioral evolution: game theoretic Darwinism. Here competition stratifies populations in terms of reproductive fitness in each generation within each species. Game theory models two alternatives in social competition: *escalation*, Hawk, or *de-escalation*; Dove evolutionary stabilized strategies; or "ESS" (Maynard Smith 1982). Variations on these strategies appear to be part of what defines either an entire species genome or a polymorphism therein (Krebs & Davies 1981). The Hawk-Dove ESS exemplifies deeply canalized, successive and genetically polymorphic triune neuromentalities entirely compatible with both the basic and clinical science germane to manic-depression (Price 1998). This chapter attempts to reconcile mania and depression with triunian neuro-ethological research in support of the larger project of evolutionary medicine. This is done via a brief review of both mania and depression and the triune brain with respect to (1) relevant historical considerations, (2) evolutionary epidemi-ology, and (3) consilience with game theoretic models. A basic familiarity with triune brain concepts is assumed and redundancies are avoided with material detailed in other chapters.

HISTORICAL OVERVIEW

The triune concept of brain, though now principally associated with the work of Paul MacLean, is actually quite a staple of medical history. The Smith Papy-rus, ca 1750 BCE, is the earliest extant written reference to "brain" (Garrison 1929). However, despite their otherwise advanced attention to matters of body and mind, even as the body itself was ritualistically embalmed for mummifi-cation and all other major organs were venerated in cenoptic jars, the Egyptians paid so little regard to the neuromental substance that it was routinely disgorged from the brain case and discarded. The Egyptian civilization, which was advan-ced in so many aspects, did not contribute much to neuroscience theory or practice.

Nevertheless, the Greeks as early as Plato established sophisticated con-cepts of brain science (although Aristotle held to the less accurate belief that the heart was the seat of the soul). This Platonic neuroscience is noteworthy in many respects, not the least by its close resemblance to MacLean's tripartite arrange-ment. The "*Epithimetikon*" constituted the basic appetitive level over which operated the "*Thimoeides*" apparatus of affect and the "*Logistikon.*" a more rarefied level of rationality. These clearly correspond to basal midbrain, limbic and cerebral components identified in contemporary neurology.

Thereafter, Galen of Pergamum, among his many accomplishments, likewise propounded a triunian concept of neuromentality. Not only was he prescient in fixing "the seat of the soul" in the frontal lobes, he further noted this lay above mere vegetative and animal levels of the brain. St. Augustine of Hippo, too, had a tripartite system. This took shape in his masterful weaving of Neo-Platonism into the fabric of Christianity. His works such as *Confessiones* or *De civitate Dei*, and especially *De Trinitate*, constructed a triunian foundation upon which much of the apparatus of Western culture was subsequently raised. Thus, via the extended vitality of Galenic ideas in medicine and Augustinian ideas in theology, triunian concepts secured primacy for well more than a millennium of early neuroscience.

Hence, any triune conceptual system has considerable resonance with essential characteristics of Western culture as well as subtle but inescapably religious overtones. Other examples abound. More recently, Freud put forth a highly influential triune schema with *id, ego,* and *superego* having obvious correlates in MacLean's neuroethological discoveries (MacLean 1990).

So, old though it is, the triune model entered the 20th century with remarkable vigor and soon came to explicitly influence contemporary neuroscience. But other crucial discoveries accrued between the waning days of medieval scholasticism and the extraordinary efflorescence of neuroscience in the late 20th century. These can concisely be recapped with reference to a series of classic events that relate intimately to the theme of this chapter and this book overall.

In 1664, Thomas Willis published the first meaningful dissection and assessment of the functional anatomy of distinct subcortical structures including the basal ganglia, or corpus striatum (Parent 1986). Its central position and wide range of vivid cortical and brain stem tracts led Willis to believe it was perhaps the "*sensorium communale*" of Aristotle, a structure which was at the time thought to originate all motor efferents and receive all sensory afferents.

However, neurology soon turned its attentions toward exciting histological studies of the cortex, and efforts to localize higher mental functions as cortical research reigned in the 18th and 19th centuries. A few scholars sustained research on the basal ganglia and discovered that functions long ascribed to it were actually properties of adjacent corticospinal paths and, so, the striatum "seemed to fall from its high estate and depreciate in physiological significance" (Wilson 1914: 428). Yet experimental research pertaining to the striatum advanced rapidly via lesion-induced disorders of motor functions (Wilson 1914; Cajal 1928).

The corpus striatum re-emerged as a major element of the "extrapyramidal motor system," which grouped it with brain stem nuclei as a complete and independent motor unit (Carpenter 1981; Parent 1986). The term "basal ganglia" generally refers to these major anatomical telencephalic subcortical nuclei at the base of the forebrain, formally the corpus striatum (striatum and globus pallidus), with the substantia nigra and subthalamic nucleus. This work, both in methods and findings, was of a piece with the subsequent experiments of neuroethologists in general, and MacLean in particular.

Meanwhile, in 1878, Broca published his crucial hypothesis concerning "*le grande lobe limbique*" which helped to begin to break loose a variety of popular quasi- and pseudoscientific formulations (The author, who once taught medicine and anthropology at the University of Cincinnati, is especially appreciative of the "System of Medical Anthropology," which his predecessor, Professor Buchanan, taught at the university in 1847 as something of a phrenology of the body whole; as it happens, "the region of moral insanity" is depicted from the mid-thigh to the navel of a Rubenesque lady). As for Professor Broca, his great achievements and their connections with 20th century neuroethology are detailed elsewhere in this and other volumes. Here it is necessary only to note how Broca also was of a piece with the neuroethology soon to follow.

In 1921, the German-born American physiologist Otto Loewi identified the *vagusstoff*, which is to say the first neurotransmitter has been known for less than a century. From this, a plethora in structure and function of types, subtypes and variations upon neurotransmitters continue to be identified as neuroethology was greatly enriched by continuing research. Then in 1937, Papez extended Broca's hypothesis toward a more complete description of the mechanisms of emotion that MacLean subsequently elaborated in remarkable detail.

This brief sketch of the general historical context in which triunian neuro-ethology arose is further enriched by diverse, yet keenly relevant parallel findings, as from evolutionary neurobiology, neurotransmitter research, and game mathematics. These findings are discussed next as prelude to a preliminary effort to delineate how such compatible findings from diverse fields form a coherent picture of the Darwinian origins of mental and brain pathophenotypies, emphasizing manic-depression as an example. Therefore, we turn to a brief review of neuromental evolution before examining all this in connection to disorders of mood and thought processes as typified in and by mania and depression.

NEUROMENTAL PHYLOGENY AND ONTOGENY: A BILLION YEARS AND BILLIONS OF BRAINS IN BRIEF

Though neurons are distinct from general somatic cells, the pattern of their evolutionary derivation from less specialized cells is obvious. Essentially, in the course of physiologic operations living cells inevitably induce micro-electrical potentials across the membrane. This sets the stage in which phylogenetic refinements of transmembrane conduction evolved from depolarization phenomena. Disturbance of primitive cell membranes alters electrical potentials only locally. Yet, rather basic refinements in the spatial and chemical aspects of cells gave rise to processes of propagative depolarization that, coupled with synapsitic complexes, provide the principal means of interneuronal communication.

From such beginnings developed dispersed neural systems, as is evident in Medusa (jellyfish). Here there is coordinated neural action to maintain the swimming sweep but nothing anatomically identifiable as a nervous system in a centralized sense. The helminths are the earliest taxa with an overt central neural apparatus. That is, worms have a brain from and to which a neural cord entrains the rest of the soma. This arrangement is highly canaled in the HOX (homeobox) gene cluster with imago anatomical referents in all subsequent species (Vernier et al. 1995). Still, though a central brain of sorts is evident in helminths, much somatic intellect is retained at this phylogenetic level; decapitated worms can breed, feed, dig, locomote, and inure to mazes.

With insects comes a more advanced neural apparatus by which a compart-mentalized brain coordinates end-organ activity via giant fiber tracts, i.e., as in rapid nerve conduction of motor efferents for wing muscle movement. Insect brain has three differentiated assemblages—protocerebrum, deutocerebrum, and tritocerebrum. Moreover, insects have a larger sensory organ domain than any other taxonomic level including vertebrates (odors, sound, luminescence texture, pressure, humidity, temperature and chemognosis). The concentration of these complex sense organs in the capitum of insects is yet another layer of bio-engineering efficiency as the depolarization circuits are all the shorter and more alacritous. These features together account for the uncanny "intellect" all too often on display by insect neural apparatus which is, no doubt, intimately related to their status as the most numerous of Earthly multicellulates.

Yet vertebrates further refine the neural assemblage with a calcific armor through which ascending and descending tracts govern more advanced activities. With vertebrates, the central nervous system emerged as a series of three anterior spinal cord enlargements constituting the hindbrain, midbrain and fore-brain (analogous to the insectival anatomy and mediated via HOX genes). Late reptiles and early mammals retained the basic vertebrate structure but further accreted at the forebrain a paleocortical "limbic system" and then a range of domain-specific neocortical centers as well. The efflorescence, plasticity and self-awareness of these later structures are especially remarkable among social mammals, notably primates.

Thus, the brain evolved in a series of three assemblages above the merely vegetative level, quite in keeping with MacLean's synthesis (1990). At the outset, from a most primitive dispersed neural network was centralized an amalgamated hierarchy of brain upon neural tube, all of which was later encased in vertebrate osseous tissue. In this growth, this brain set down neuromental substrates for the ritualized antagonistic behavior of classic reptiles at what is now termed the midbrain or basal ganglia. Thereafter followed greater encephal-ization with progressively increased neuronal and synaptic density, plasticity, and diversity in the forebrain areas. This enhancement of the range of neural operations fostered brain and behavioral self-regulation of experience by which novel perceptuomotor abilities, memory, and learning emerged.

An overarching theme of neuromental phylogeny is the accretion of successively higher and more pluralistic mechanisms for executive action built upon complex integration. Thus behavior is the business of channeling percep-tions in relation to environmental cues. Moreover, while such cues are directed to a wide spectrum of complex proximal biosocial ends, these are ultimately engaged in the maximization of reproductive success. Such success is contingent upon both acute and sustained realization—via neuromental representation and summated behavior—of environmental referents. In the most reduced sense, and apart from predator avoidance, such realizations must negotiate access to nutritional and fertility needs. Even bacteria "sense" environmental realities as with chemotaxis. However, among advanced mammals, as the biosocial environment became more complex so too did the neuromental means by which this complexity was represented, analyzed, and behaviorally engaged.

Such a phylogenetic perspective perhaps presumes a rather determined neuromentalistic apparatus. However, selectionistic explanations only carry the phenotype so far, particularly with respect to complex behavior. It is certainly true that things are often quite tightly "wired up" (Gilbert 1989).

But it is already well established that the complexities of advanced nervous systems exceed the semiotic encoding capacities of their associated genomes. The human neocortex has some one thousand million million synapses while the total human genome has only 3.5 billion (3.5×10^9) nucleotide base pairs. Thus, the genome lacks capacity by which the details of neural connectivity could be wholly encoded via genetic specificity.

Hence, normative neural development is contingent upon phenotypic adjustments between the genomic heritage and individual experience. Quite remarkably, much of this phenotypic adjustment appears to be mediated by de-selection of neurons within individual development. Ongoing, severe synaptic pruning rapidly follows the fetal blossoming of neurons via phenotypic experience (Charney et al. 1999). More precisely, much of this pruning is expectant reaction to experience as is evident in autopsy sampling:

Increased synaptic density plus expansion of total cortical volume leave no doubt the postnatal period is one of very rapid synaptogenesis in human frontal cortex. By age 2 years, synaptic density is at its maximum; at about the same time when other components of cerebral cortex also cease growing and when total brain weight approaches that of the adult. Synaptic density declines subsequently, reaching an adult value that is only about 60% of the maximum (Huttenlocher 1990).

This accounts for much of the plasticity of behavioral phenotypes in higher social animals. Normal neuromental development is governed by selective *loss* of synaptic connectivity. Thus, it not surprising that the adult brain is subject to increased (though not complete) constraints on learning and behavior as well as "cortical blindness" in the wake of insufficient expectant-experiential cues from the environment of ontogeny of which visual acuity is perhaps the best known example. Consequently, the brains of advanced social animals are the product not just of elaborate basic plans (as with the HOX genes). Rather, these robust templates are modified by developmental experience. Moreover, as one moves along the phylogenetic line, the degree to which phenotypy is simultaneously organized by template AND environment increases.

EVOLUTIONARY EPIDEMIOLOGY OF NEUROTRANSMISSION

Neurotransmitter biology has advanced rapidly in the past generation. Yet, it is impossible to discuss the evolution of neurotransmission in detail. After all, this encompasses 1,000 million years of phylogeny. Moreover, in the human brain this entails 1,000 million neurons. Each neuron may engage up to 10,000 synapses each, or in excess of 10 trillion per brain. Likewise, to catalog the dozens of neurotransmitter systems, their molecular biology and functional biochemical neuroanatomy would, in itself be a Herculean effort requiring volume upon volume. Thus, our scope at this juncture is to relate key aspects of human neurotransmitter evolution with triune neuroethology and thereby expand Price's (1996) game mathematic model of manic-depression.

Though the extraordinarily ancient nature of the major classes of neurotransmitters has been established, neuroscience has thus far done little to consider the implications of such ancient origins. Likewise, the degree to which the nervous system has evolved via gene duplication or "autologous cloning" is remarkable (Wilson 1993). But so too are woefully overlooked the implications of this crucial mode of polymorphic diversification in the course of neurotransmitter evolution. That is to say, for a given neurotransmitter there exist a variety of types and subtypes of receptors originated within truly ancient multigenic families. These families derive from terminal modifications of genes duplicated in phylogeny. Such modifications render advantageous otherwise merely neutral redundancies (Vernier et al. 1995). Thus a brief recap of the venerable origins and unusual mechanisms in the phylogeny of neurotransmission is worthwhile in itself but, further, introduces a new avenue for neurethological and evolution-ary psychological research.

The biogenic amines are indeed old and have preserved basic functions as intracellular signals even as they acquired later capacities for intercellular communication and hormonal action. They are found in many protozoans and nearly all metazoans. The cognate enzyme, monoamine oxidase, is found even in prokaryotes. Moreover, the biogenic amines have a conserved secondary structure but diverged in the course of the evolution of complex neural systems. Hence a phylogenetic hierarchy of multiple G-protein linked catecholamine receptor subtypes accrued largely via gene duplication and subsequent modification.

Gamma Amino Butyric Acid (GABA), identified in all flatworms, is some 1,000 million years old. One of the first events was the evocation of catecholamine receptors from primordial muscarinic acetylcholine receptors. This occurred prior to the divergence of arthropod and chordate lineages. The first to so arise was likely a form of dopamine as it is found in all chordates. Thus, the earliest catechols are common to vertebrates and appeared at least late in the classic era of the cephalochordates some 700 million years ago.

Thereafter, second-messenger pathways arose homologously in both muscarinic and catecholamine receptor populations. This occurred after the chordate-arthropod split but before the separation of avians and mammalians from the common reptilian line, as norepinephrine is common to all vertebrates. Moreover, adrenergic and dopaminergic second-messenger pathways did not arise independently. Rather, the original receptor population was repeatedly duplicated and modified in subsequent evolution to organize epinephrine, norepinephrine, dopamine, and octopamine receptor systems (Fryxell 1995).

Serotonin which may have originated in chordate gut tissue is well developed in cyclostome (lamprey) brain tissue and other primitive vertebrates. The sculpting of fetal neural development was among its first functions. Thus serotonin arose at the chordate-vertebrate interface (Peroutka & Howell 1994).

Manifestly, these neural systems were recruited to modulate increasing information-processing demands, psychomotor activity, attentional systems and emotional drives. There is consensus on the early origin of prototypical neuro-transmitter classes but only a dawning realization that the subsequent evolution-ary diversification of these moieties—via autologous cloning and modification of redundant gene templates—follows a hierarchical pattern. Moreover, this hierarchy is quite compatible with MacLean's triune brain schematic in that subcortical neurotransmission varieties are quite modal across species, whereas far more phyletic divergence is noted in comparisons of limbic microanatomy and remarkably more when diverse species' cortical tissues are contrasted. Indeed, most tantalizing for neuroethology may be evidence of spectacular evolutionary refinement of receptor subtypes in the past 100 million years of evolution in the primate line (Peroutka & Howell, 1994). With this it is useful to consider serotonin and dopamine in more detail.

Dopamine and serotonin long have been of special relevance to mood disorders, but novel molecular analytic techniques have been needed to more fully appreciate the physiological and genetic complexity of these neurotrans-mitter systems (Owens & Risch 1995). Generally, they have reciprocal physio-logical effects: Dopamine is an essentially stimulating neurotransmitter and serotonin being inhibitory. This is evident in pharmacological experimentation: Compounds active in serotonin circuits have antidepressant effects whereas dopamine agonists serve as antipsychotic (antimanic) agents. Finally, and of particular interest to neuroethology, serotonin and dopamine subsystems have quite clearly coevolved in the course of mammaloprimatoid brain and social evolution.

Dopamine was long thought to exist in only two types. More recently at least five variant loci have been identified, some with considerable point polymor-phism (Owens & Risch 1995). A similarly more complex picture has been obtained with respect to serotonin (Hen 1993). There are even more detailed racemes in each of these neurotransmitter families, both of which can be further grouped into at least two clusters of similar function and distribution.

With respect to dopamine, five receptors have sprouted in the respective lineages of either the original D^1 or D^2 typology. These aggregations reflect similarities in anatomy, physiology, and evolution. In the present discussion, the D^2 cluster is of special interest. Its D^2, D^3, D^4 subtypes appeared in later phylogeny in clear response to requirements for more subtle facilitation of higher level cognitive-affective expressions evolved in response to mammalian evolutionary pressures. Notably among these pressures was the need to mediate conspecific social interactions. The D^1 cluster arose in the face of more primitive selective pressures that shaped classical reptilian neuromental assemblages now deeply canalized in evolution. The D cluster is therefore manifestly more primi-tive as it subserves both extrapyramidal tract and midbrain functional demands.

Neuronal receptor networks in brain are identified by the distribution unique, protein-typical mRNA (Chio et al. 1990). Assays of mRNA bear out differen-tial distribution across the subtypes. For example, densities of the D^2 cluster localize to the hypothalamic, limbic, and frontocortical areas far more discriminately than do those of the D^1 cluster. Such differential distribution explains the relative efficacy and limited toxicity of antipsychotic drugs that operate on mammaloid D^2 —opposed to more primitive reptilo-vertebrate circuits (Owens & Risch 1995).

These very distinctive anatomical and functional dopamine receptor subtypes indubitably derive from a phylogenetically common ancestral form. Each subtypic modification of the template branched off as an innovative resolution of specific selective pressures extant at different times in the environment of phylogenetic adaptation (MacLean 1990). In mammaloprimatoid brain, such innovations were necessary to modulate social behavior in increasingly sophisticated ways.

Again, the complexity of serotonin is akin to that of dopamine (Owens & Risch 1995). However, serotonin is even more widely distributed in the brain (and thus may have less specific subdistribution than dopamine). Serotonin clusters within four types with a total of more than a dozen subtypes. As it happens, the rapid pace of discoveries in serotonergic microneuronanatomy makes a detailed account of current knowledge not only difficult but all too ephemeral and is, in any event, well beyond the range of present discussion.

Crucially, assays of serotonin receptor mRNA densities vary considerably across brain regions but, taken together, these assays indicate serotonin mediation of widely diverse cognitive and behavioral activities; notably, the projections of the dorsal raphe-striatum. These are phylogenetically earlier features largely fixed in the course of reptilian brain evolution in a mode similar to D^1. The serotonin projections of medial raphe-hippocampal system originated later in evolution and address different phylogenetic demands. Given such robust microanatomical and functional links to limbic structures and functions, these later serotonin innovations modulate affective-cognitive demands unique to mammalian social evolution (MacLean 1990).

In aggregate, these rapidly accruing researches concerning neurotransmitter subtypology call for a revised dopamine hypothesis in which normal thought and mood are contingent upon orchestrated actions of diverse modulators— perhaps especially dopamine and serotonin—as well as other quasi-transmitter agents such as neurohormones and endogenous opioids. As for the classic neurotransmitters, dopamine and serotonin appear to mediate normative moods and thoughts whereas derangements in dopamine/serotonergic physiology induce disease such as psychosis, abulia, mood and extrapyramidal effects.

Psychotic and mood symptoms arise when prefrontal cortex and/or meso-limbic systems are significantly altered with respect to dopaminergic and/or serotonergic function (Janssen et al. 1988; Davis et al. 1991; Meltzer 1992). Serotonin depletion typically aggravates symptoms via initial escalation of mood and activity, soon followed by irritability and thought disorder. Such irritability is frequently accentuated by reduction of serotonergic circuits, particularly when these are also affected by sleep deprivation (Keck, *pc* 1997). Moreover, compounds with high (S_{rhl} /D_2) ratios of raphe-hippocampal-limbic circuit serotonin (S_{rhl}) to dopamine of the limbic type (D_2) may be especially efficacious in the treatment of psychotic and mood disorders, including severe manic-depression (Meltzer 1992).

Serotonin inhibits dopamine striatal efferents while serotonin re-uptake inhibitors rouse mood but inhibits dopaminergic limbic structures, notably the nucleus accumbens, and can induce extrapyramidal effects. Moreover, lesions of serotonergic dorsal raphe tracts reduce neuroleptic-induced catalepsy. Serotonin effects on dopamine are modulated by receptors of the 1_A, 2 and 3 serotonin subtypes. The highly unique profile of clozapine microphysiology, both *in vitro* and *in vivo*, is revealing in that it has increased affinity for limbic D_4 receptors and antagonizes 5-HT_2 moieties. These moieties elicit dopamine release "downstream" in the striatum and, so, limit extrapyramidal symptoms induced by dopamine antagonists elsewhere in the brain.

Hence, abnormalities of thought and mood (the largely mammalian capacities of positive and negative symptoms) can be ameliorated without significant effect of lower reptilian circuits evident in involuntary motor symptoms. Thus, novel antipsychotics such as risperidone improve both psychotic disorders of thought and derangements of mood with few motor effects as an effect of 5-HT_2 antagonism in tandem with D_4 (Janssen et al. 1988).

A significant calculus of social rank hierarchy and particulars of serotonin-dopamine neurotransmission functions as an expression of these neuromodulators. Moreover, such a calculus is further embedded in algorithms of animal behavioral escalation and de-escalation (Gawin & Ellenwood 1988; Wyatt et al. 1988; Kosten 1993). For example, cocaine is mimetic of both manic and depressive symptoms: Acute administration increases synaptic dopamine—via the inhibition of pre-synaptic dopamine re-uptake—which escalates mood and activity. Yet chronic overstimulation of D_2 receptors eventually induces down-regulated physical dependence. Likewise, abrupt cessation of cocaine depletes dopamine and induces acute agitated depression but a chronic syndrome of anhedonia, dysphoria, lethargy, somnolence, and apathy can extend for up to a year.

Serotonergics reduce both pre-dependent appetites for dopaminergics and dopamimetics as well as the post-dependent withdrawal syndromes. Dopaminergics similarly affect modal activity in serotonin circuits. Thus, patterns of dopamine physiology in humans constitute a model of manic-depressive neuromentation (a discussion to be taken up anew in the context of hawk-dove escalation/de-escalation-evolved stable strategies).

THE SOCIAL COMPETITION HYPOTHESIS

In the new field of evolutionary psychiatry there have been developments that parallel the triumph of kinship genetics and neuroscientific progress. Among these parallel developments is the specification of the social competition hypothesis of mood disorders in which has been marshaled a great deal of evidence concerning the evolved basis of moral and social behavior in humans (Price et al. 1994).

At this juncture it is useful to summarize the essential elements of the social competition hypothesis before relating it to kinship genetics or neuroscience. There is general agreement that mood disorders constitute some contemporary phenotypic expression of a phylogenetically healthy behavioral repertory (Lewis 1934; Hill 1968; Beck 1987; Glantz & Pearce 1989; Gilbert 1992; Wilson 1993). Clearly, some variant phenotypes of current mood disorders performed adaptive functions among ancestral hominids. Thus, beyond the constraints of clinical theory and practice, the phylogenetic precursors of what are now diagnosed as mood disorders can be better appreciated as having performed some function in connection to social competition (Price 1967; Sloman 1976; Gardner 1982; Gilbert 1992; Wilson 1993).

The essential result of social competition in any taxon is that winners behave differently than losers (Price et al. 1994). Yet phylogeny appears to have modulated competitive drives as a key step in the emergence of sociality. Indeed, recent trends in studies of behavioral ecology posit that most social mammals cooperate or compete in one of two basic social modes (Chance 1988). In clinical terms these two modes, the agonic and hedonic respectively, relate closely to syndromes of depression and mania. Clinical depression is readily identified in evolutionary psychological terms as a strategy of de-escalation or loss while mania is a strategy of winning via engagement and assertion (Price et al. 1994).

A further definition of the hypothesis is that humans retain, among other possibilities, a phylogenetically structured capacity to yield (become depressed) or assert (become expansive) in the face of socially competitive situations. A logical—though not explicit—extension of the hypothesis is that severe or persistent derangements of the sociophysiological mechanisms of rank hierarchy may induce formal disorder of thought; that is, psychosis (arising perhaps particularly as mediated by stress hormones).

The hypothesis specifies social competition algorithms at several neuromental levels, which link the etiology of mood disorders to pathologies of social competition expressed in hierarchical fashion. The hierarchy subsumes sexual selection, social stratification, ritual antagonistic behavior, resource-holding potential, social attention-holding potential, among other domains. These are skillfully detailed elsewhere (Gilbert 1992; Price et al. 1994).

In the most fundamental sense, mood disorders appear to have emerged (1) in taxonomic terms at the reptilian-mammalian interface, (2) in neurobiological terms at the subcortical-limbic interface, and (3) in psychological terms at the egoic/superegoic interface.

Yet such interfaces are not, in themselves, the defining aspects of mammalo-primatoid psychology. Instead, the attainment of social dominance via social appeal and prestige rather than hierarchical threat has come to characterize behavior in the hominoid line (Barkow 1989; Gilbert 1992). Put differently, influence rather than raw intimidation is more commonly successful as a means to social dominance among primates. This has been confirmed in both ethological and socioanthropological field studies (Paglia 1994). Moreover, an ethological consensus accrues however much a culturogenic-socioconstructivist view has been favored by "academes" (Paglia 1994).

Nonetheless, sociocultural factors most certainly do shape phenotypic expression of human mood states and disorders. In humans, social competition may induce either yielding or assertion. Such yielding or assertion may cause emotional dysregulation, especially where there is a crescendo of interpersonal affects. Such escalations or de-escalations may have been quite salubrious in the environment of evolutionary adaptation. However, any further dysregulations may, in the context of contemporary culture, constitute syndromes of clinical depression or mania. Consequently, the neurotransmitter genetics and physiology of mood disorders are relevant in that these molecules subserve crucial variations in the phenotypic expression of behavior.

Depression and mania, as is now more widely agreed, are diseases having a fundamentally neurobiological and genetical foundation as population polymorphisms (Wilson 1998). It is, therefore, useful to attempt some connection between the social competition hypothesis and recent trends in neuroscientific research.

MANIC ESCALATION AND DEPRESSIVE DE-ESCALATION AS HAWK-DOVE NEUROMENTAL STATES

In most mammals, reproductive success depends on success in various social roles. One key role is in besting others who are pursing the same resources (Barash 1977; Gilbert 1989; Krebs & Davies 1993; Trivers 1971).

As noted earlier, primate social hierarchy is a key factor in reproductive and social success. Those higher up have more breeding opportunities and often make more attractive allies than those lower down. Thus, navigating hierarchical relationships wherein some individuals are more powerful than others has been a selective pressure for millions of years.

Social neuromentalities evolved in the context of conspecific behaviors of either competition or cooperation. Further, these evolved neuromentalities propitiate the adoption of predictable, context-dependent roles and behaviors that modulate both competition and cooperation (Nesse 1990). In some respects, social neuromentalities are synonymous with the everyday term "state of mind" to the extent that each embodies algorithms of social roles. Gradations in states of mind are to be expected between individuals across the social hierarchy. That is, the state of mind of a dominant differs from those of hierarchical subordinates. Being neuromentalities, these differences in state of mind have proved to be measurable psychobiological variables. The consequences can be profound.

Most remarkably, in some fishes such inhibition can cause change of sex (significantly, the subordinate's genes can thus be maintained by mating with dominants; Keenleyside 1979). Likewise, dominant naked mole rats and New World monkeys have been observed to directly suppress sexual reproductive physiology in subordinates (Abbott et al. 1989). Studies have also documented major biological distinctions between dominant and subordinate baboons, notably stress hormones which have been linked to the pathophysiology of affective and anxiety disorders (Sapolsky 1989, 1990a,b; Ray & Sapolsky 1992). Biological profiles of subordinates differ from those of more dominant animals in other species (Henry 1982; Henry & Stephens 1977).

Pharmacological probes are also revealing. Drug effects can vary between dominant and subordinate animals, sometimes quite markedly. For example, the social rank of rhesus monkeys given amphetamine determines key aspects of response. Dominants showed increased threat, chase, and attack behaviors whereas subordinates showed increased submissive behavior, for example, fear grimaces and turning away (Harbour et al. 1981).

Harbour and Barters (1984) reported a case in which amphetamine was given to a female rhesus monkey that moved between two groups. In the first group, she was highly subordinate, isolate, and fearful with quite limited affiliation. Amphetamine accentuated all of these submissive behavioral patterns quite dramatically. However, when moved to a new group, the alpha male conspicuously favored her. Her behavior changed markedly with this increased rank. When administered amphetamine as the dominant female in this novel social milieu her threats increased dramatically. She did not evidence submissive behavior as previously, but instead increased her social approach.

Several empirical studies have confirmed that social competition psychobiologically modulates mood states in primates. A recent review of neuroendocrine correlates of social rank confirms that endocrine states are highly sensitive to social feedback (Sapolsky 1993). Hormone levels in both dominant and subordinate animals vary as a function of group stability. However, instability of the social rank hierarchy affects individuals differently both with respect to directional trends in rank (going up vs. down) as well as basic temperament (Sapolsky 1994). In this sense dominance-subordination is largely controlled by sociophysiological feedback in the environment.

Perhaps the most significant evidence to date is the correlation of the primate social rank spectrum with serotonin parameters that mirror human mood swings. Physiological changes can be both the cause and the consequence of rank changes (Raleigh et al. 1984; Hartmann 1992). Blood levels of serotonin are significantly higher in dominant male vervet monkeys as compared to their subordinates (Raleigh et al. 1984).

Sham deposition of the alpha male was followed by a sharp fall in his serotonin blood level but a sharp rise in that of the subordinate male who was raised to dominant status. Restoration some weeks later of the formerly dominant male was marked by a reversal of these serotonin findings as well as his renewed tenure as the group alpha. Significantly, this restoration led to a fall in both social rank and serotonin level of the new dominant below that of his original beta baseline. Social ascendance with subsequent fall in rank produced sociophysiological changes, which rendered the subordinate in a lessened biosocial status than had no change occurred.

Sex hormones similarly reflect such social contexts. Androgen levels in humans, both male and female, vary at baseline depending both upon the degree of social competition or cooperation and also vary directly with success in competitive games (Kemper 1990). These rises can include even nonphysical contests such as chess (Mazure et al. 1992). Thus neurotransmitter and endocrine parameters not only reflect general features of social status, affect, and mood but directly link to reproductive biology itself.

Major subtypes of neurotransmitter receptors, particularly dopamine and serotonin, have unique anatomical distributions and functional consequences. These consequences are quite germane to, among other concerns, the resolution of stress engendered by social competition. This resolution is most often accomplished via innovative capacities for cognitive-affective assessment and behavior. These capacities successively typified the brains and psychology of reptiles, then social mammals and, most distinctively primates (Dunbar 1988; Mithen 1996).

EXPANDING THE SOCIAL COMPETITION HYPOTHESIS: INTEGRATING NEUROTRANSMITTER BIOLOGY AND HAWK-DOVE GAME MATHEMATICS

Thus we come full circle. The functional anatomy of neurotransmitters as sketched here is intended to link, in a plausible but only preliminary manner, to the pathological sociophysiology of manic-depressive neuromentality. Such etiopathophysiology arises as triunian brain phylogenies encounter hierarchies of current ontogenic demands. For example, manic-depression expresses an enduring population polymorphism of the human genome increasingly mismatched in the contemporary environment as the human genome reacts to novel situations far removed from archetypic modes of tribal life.

Indeed it is timely to consider beneficial aspects that both inhere to and help explain this manic-depressive polymorphism. Major subtypes of dopamine and serotonin neurotransmitter receptors each has anatomical distributions and functional consequences quite germane to, among other concerns, the behavioral resolution of social competition via innovative cognition and affective assessment capacities that increasingly typified the brains and psychology of social mammals.

With this in mind, it is useful to return to the social competition hypothesis of mood disorders to begin integrating neurotransmitter evolution and game mathematics within this model. In tabular form it is more readily apparent how the Platonic hierarchy closely converges on MacLean's triarchic model and, further, how such a system gives order to a wide range of evolutionary, neurobiological, game theoretical, neurotransmitter genetics and psychiatric nosology (see Table 8.1).

Table 8.1. Triune Hierarchies

EVOLUTIONARY NEUROMENTALITIES, GAME MATHEMATICS &
NEUROTRANSMISSION

	"HAWK"	"DOVE"
NEOMAMMALIAN		
"Logistikon"		
CORTEX SAHP*	ATTRACTIVE	AVOIDANT
Sociotropic-cognitive/ SAHP	Optimistic, charming	Pessimistic, ashamed
Cognition > affect	Manic/sociopathy	Depressed/ obsessed
$S2 > S1 \sim D3,4 > D1$	S2, D3,4 & NE *High*	S2 *Low* D3,4 & NE?
*(social attention holding potential)		
PALEOMAMMALIAN		
"Thimoeides"		
LIMBIC RHP*	DOMINANT	SUBMISSIVE
Acquisitive - emotive/ RHP	Roused mood,	Low mood
	likely to win	likely to lose
Affect > cognition	Aggressive/sadistic	Morbid/
		Masochistic
$S1 > S2 \ D2,3,4 > D1 \ +EPS$	S1, D3,4 & NE *High*	S1, D3,4 & NE
*(resource holding potential)		*Low*
REPTILIAN		
"Epithimetikon"		
MIDBRAIN RAB*	FIGHTING	FLEEING
Territorial - instinctive/ RAB	Strident, strong	Cowering, weak
Instinct > affect > cognition	Violent, solipsistic	Fright, abulia
$S1 >> S2 \ << D1 >> D2,3,4$	D1 & NE *High* S?	D1 & NE *Low* S?
*RAB (ritualized antagonistic behavior)		

SUMMARY

The neuromental advancements that characterize behavioral evolution, particularly as mediated among mammals by the limbic apparatus and neocortex, have served to inhibit both the structures and functions of the underlying reptilian residue. This evolution was spurred by inclusive fitness strategies increasingly consequential to parallel growth of mammalian social capacities; e.g., live birth, kindred bands.

Nevertheless, functional tensions can arise between the R-complex and the operations mediated by upper neuromental strata. Typically, intellective capacities can modulate more primitive reptilian drives; however, the R-complex can prevail either adaptively or, more often, maladaptively. The latter maladaptive release of reptilian repertoires is usefully termed "phylogenetic regression" (Bailey 1987).

A major inhibition on social dynamics which might otherwise tend toward robustly Nietzschean "will to power" among individuals—kin or not—is the mother-offspring unit itself. Many lower species, especially those of an r-selected nature—depend on extravagant numbers of little cared-for offspring rather than extravagant nurturance of few offspring; indeed, some parents, not recognizing their young, cannibalize them (Pianka 1970).

However, this emphasis on quality of reproductive effort shifts toward quality as species become more K-selected. These trends are utmost in eusocial mammals such as the primates. As kinship becomes better recognized, inclusive survival is promoted via more perspicacious nurturant investments such as nursing, teaching, and so on. MacLean (1985) outlines the behavioral patterns evolved in consequence to in the evolution of mother-offspring bonds. Caring dependency fosters greater exploration of the environment as well as enhanced play with peers, and so, social skills and insight are acquired.

Such skills art the cement of eusociality and are, in turn, subserved by the magnificent efflorescence of neurotransmitter subtypologies whose evolutionary origins and functions have been sketched here in a preliminary manner as a spur to improved current and, especially future, understanding via novel programs of synthetic research.

REFERENCES

Abbott, D.H.; Barrette, J.; Faulkes, C.G.; George, A. (1989) Social contraception in naked moles rats and marmoset monkeys. *Journal of Zoology London.* 219:703–710.

Bailey, K. (1987) *Human Paleopsychology: Applications to Aggression and Pathological Process.* Hillsdale, NJ: Lawrence Erlbaum.

Barash, D.P. (1977) *Sociobiology and Behavior.* London: Heinemann.

Barkow, J. (1989) *Darwin, Sex and Status: Biological approaches to mind and culture.* Toronto: University of Toronto Press.

Beck, A.T. (1967) *Depression: Clinical, Experimental and Theoretical Aspects.* NY: Hoeber.

Brady, J. (1958). The Paleocortex and Behavioral Motivation. In *Biological and Biochemical Bases of Behavior* (H. Harlow and C. Woolsey, Eds.). Madison: University of Wisconsin Press. Pp. 193–235.

Broca, Paul. (1878). Anatomie comparee des circonvolutions cerebrales. La Grand Lobe Limbique et la scissure limbique dans la serie des mammiferes. *Revue Anthropologie.* 1. Ser. 2, 385–498.

Brown, S. and Shafer, E. (1888). An Investigation into the Functions of the Occipital and Temporal Lobes of the Monkey Brain. *Philosophical Transactions Royal Society, London.* Ser. B. 179: 303–327.

Bucy, P. C. and Kluver, H. (1955). An Anatomical Investigation of the Temporal Lobe in the Monkey (*Macaca mulata*). *Journal of Comparative Neurology.* 103: 151–252.

Cajal, S. R (1928*) Studies on the Degeneration and Regeneration of the Nervous System.* 2 Vols. Oxford: Oxford University Press.

Carpenter, M. (1981) Anatomy of Corpus Striatum and Brain Stem Integrating Systems. *American Physiology Handbook of "Motor Control."* Ed. by V. Brooks. Williams and Wilkens, Baltimore, pp. 947–995.

Chance, M. (Ed.) (1988) *Social Fabrics of the Mind.* London: Lawrence Erlbaum.

Charney, D. S.; Nestler, E. J.; Bunney, B. S. (1999) *Neurobiology of Mental Illness.* Oxford: Oxford University Press.

Chio, C. L.; Hess, G. F.; Graham, R S. (1990) A Second Molecular Form of D2 Dopamine Receptor Found in Rat and Bovine Caudate Nucleus. *Nature.* 343: 266–269.

Davis K. L.; Kahn, R. S.; Ko, G.; Davidson, M. (1991) Dopamine in schizophrenia: a review and reconceptualization. *American Journal of Psychiatry.* 148:1474–1486.

Dunbar, R. I. M. (1988) *Primate Social Systems.* London: Croom Helm.

Eibl-Eibsfedlt, I. (1970). *Ethology: The Biology of Behavior.* NY: Holt, Winston, & Rinehart.

Flourens, M-J-P. (1824). *Recherches expérimentales sur les propriétés et les fonctions du système nerveux, dans les animaux vertébrés.* Paris: Crevot.

Fryxell, K. J. (1995) The evolutionary divergence of neurotransmitter receptors and second messenger pathways. *Journal of Molecular Evolution.* 41(1): 85–97.

Gardner, R.J. (1982) Mechanisms in Major Depressive Disorder: an evolutionary model. *Archives of General Psychiatry.* 39: 1436–1441.

Garrison, F.H. (1929) *History of Medicine.* London: W.B. Saunders.

Gawin, F.A.; Ellenwood, E.H. (1988) Cocaine and other stimulants. *NEJM* 318: 1173–1182.

Gilbert, P. (1989) *Human Nature and Suffering.* London: Lawrence Erlbaum.

Gilbert, P. (1992) *Depression: the evolution of powerlessness.* NY: Guilford.

Glantz, K. and Pearce, J. (1989) *Exiles from Eden: Psychotherapy from an Evolutionary Perspective.* NY: Norton.

Hamilton, W.D. (1963) The evolution of altruistic behavior. *American Naturalist.* 97: 354–356.

Harlow, H. and Harlow, M. (1965). The Affectional Systems." *Behavior of Non-Human Primates.* Ed. by A. Schrier, H. Harlow, F. Stollnitz. NY: Academic Press.

Hartmann, L. (1992) Presidential address: Reflections on humane values and biopsychosocial integration. *American Journal of Psychiatry.* 149: 1135–1147.

Hen, R. (1993) Structural and functional conservation of serotonin receptors throughout evolution. *EXS.* 63: 266–278.

Henry, J.P. (1982) The relation of social to biological processes in disease. *Social Science Medicine.* 16: 369–380.

Henry, J. P.; Stephens, P. M. (1977) *Stress, Health and the Social Environment: A Sociobiological Approach to Medicine.* New York: Springer Verlag.

Hill, D. (1968) Depression: disease, reaction or posture? *American Journal of Psychiatry.* 125: 445–456.

Huttenlocher, P. R. (1990) Morphometric study of human cerebral cortex development. *Neuropsychologia.* 28(6): 517–527.

Jackson, J.H. (1932) *Selected Writings of John Hughlings Jackson* (2 Vols.). Edited by J. Taylor. London: Hodder and Stoughton (Jackson's *Croonian Lectures on Evolution and Dissolution of the Nervous System,* appeared in series 1881–1887).

Janssen, P. A.; Niemegeers, C.J.; Awouters, F. (1988) Pharmacology of risperidone (R64 766), a new antipsychotic with serotonin-S2 and dopamine-D2 antagonist properties. *J. Pharm Exper Therap.* 244: 685–693.

Keck, P. (1997) *Personal Communication.*

Keenleyside, M.H.A. (1979) *Diversity and Adaptation in Fish Behavior.* Berlin: Springer.

Kemper, T. D. (1984) Power, status and emotions: A sociobiological contribution to a psychological domain. In K Scherer; P Ekman (Eds.) *Approaches to Emotion.* Hillsdale, NJ: Lawrence Erlbaum.

Kluver, H. and Bucy, P. (1937). "Psychic-Blindness and other Symptoms following Bilateral Temporal Lobectomy in Rhesus Monkeys. *American Journal of Physiology.* 119: 352–353.

Kosten T.R. (1993) Pharmacotherapies for cocaine abuse: neurobiological abnormalities reversed with drug intervention. *Psychiatric Times.* 10: 25.

Krebs, J. R.; Davies, N. B. (1981) *An Introduction to Behavioural Ecology.* Oxford: Blackwell.

Lewis, A. J. (1934) Melancholia: a clinical survey of depressive states. *Journal of Mental Science,* 80: 277–378.

MacLean, P. D. (1949). Psychosomatic Desease and the "Viceral Brain." Recent Developments Bearing on the Papez Theory of Emotion. *Psychosomatic Medicine.* 11: 338–353.

MacLean, P. D. (1985). Evolutionary Psychiatry and the Triune Brain. *Psychological Medicine.* 15. 219–221.

MacLean, P. D. (1990) *The Triune Brain in Evolution.* NY: Plenum.

Maynard Smith, J. (1982). "The Evolution of Social Behavior: a Classification of Models." *Current Problems is Sociobiology.* Ed. by King's College Sociobiology Group. Cambridge University Press, pp. 28–44.

Mazure, A., Booth, A., Dabbs, J.M. (1992) Testosterone and chess competition. *Social Psychology Quarterly,* 55: 70–77.

Meltzer, H. (1992) The importance of serotonin-dopamine interactions in the action of clozapine. *British Journal of Psychiatry.* 160 (suppl 170): 22–29.

Mithen, S. (1996) *Prehistory of the Mind.* London: Thames and Hudson.

Nesse, R. M. (1990) Evolutionary explanations of emotions. *Human Nature.* 1: 261–289.

Nestler, E.; Hyman, S. (1993) *Foundations of Molecular Psychiatry.* Washington, APA.

Owens, M .J.; Risch, S. C. (1995) Atypical Antipsychotics, in *Psychopharmacology,* Schatzberg, A.; Nemeroff, C., (eds). Washington: APA Press.

Paglia, C. (1994) *Vamps and Tramps.* New York: Vintage.

Papez, J. W. (1937). A Proposed Mechanism of Emotion. *Archives of Neurology and Psychiatry.* 38: 725–743.

Parent, A. (1986) *Comparative Neurobiology of Basal Ganglia.* NY: Wiley.

Peroutka, S. J. & Howell, T. A. (1994) The molecular evolution of G-protein coupled receptors: focus on 5-hydrosytryptamine receptors. *Neuropharmacology,* 33: 319–324.

Pianka, E. R. (1970) On R- and K-selection. *American Naturalist.* 104: 592–597.

Powles, W. E. (1992) *Human Development and Homeostasis: the Science of Psychiatry.* Madison, CT: International Universities Press.

Pribram, K. H. (1958) Neocortical function in behavior. In H. F. Harlow & C. N. Woolsey (Eds.), *Biological and Biochemical Bases of Behavior.* Madison: University of Wisconsin Press, pp. 151–172.

Price, J. (1967) Hypothesis: the dominance hierarchy and the evolution of mental illness. *Lancet.* ii, 243–246.

Price J. (1998) The adaptive function of mood change. *British Journal of Medical Psychology.* 71: 465–477.

Price, J.; Sloman, L.; Gardner, R.; Gilbert, P.; Rhode, P. (1994) The social competition hypothesis of depression. *British Journal of Psychiatry.* 164: 309–315.

Raleigh, M.; McGuire, M.; Brammer, G.; Yuwiler, A. (1984) Social status and whole blood serotonin in vervets. *Archives of General Psychiatry.* 41: 405–410.

Raleigh, M.; McGuire, M.; Brammer, G.; Yuwiler, A. (1991) Serotonergic mechanisms promote dominance acquisition in adult male vervet monkeys. *Brain Research.* 181–190.

Ray, J., Sapolsky, R. (1992) Styles of social behavior and their endocrine correlates among high-ranking wild baboons. *American Journal of Primatology.* 28: 231–250.

Richards, R. (1987) *Darwin and the Emergence of Evolutionary Theories of Mind and Behavior.* Chicago: University of Chicago Press.

Ruse, M. (1986) *Taking Darwin Seriously.* Oxford: Basil Blackwell.

Sapolsky, R. (1989) Hypercortisolism among socially subordinate wild baboons originates at the CNS level. *Archives of General Psychiatry.* 46: 1047–1051.

Sapolsky, R. (1990a) Adrenocortial function, social rank and personality among wild baboons. *Biological Psychiatry.* 28: 862–878.

Sapolsky, R. (1990b) Stress in the Wild. *Scientific American.* 1: 106–113.

Sapolsky, R. (1993) Endocrine alfresco: Psychoendocrine studies of wild baboons. *Recent Progress in Hormone Research.* 48: 437–468.

Sapolsky, R. (1994) Individual differences in the stress response. *Seminars in the Neurosciences.* 6: 261–269.

Sherrington, C. (1906/1947). *The Integrative Action of the Nervous System.* Second Edition. New Haven: Yale University Press.

Sloman, L. (1976) The Role of Neurosis in Phylogenetic Adaptation with Particular Reference to Early Man. *American Journal of Psychiatry.* 133: 543–547.

Spencer, H. (1855). *The Principles of Psychology.* London: Longman, Brown, Green.

Trivers, R. L. (1971) The evolution of reciprocal altruism. *Quarterly Review of Biology.* 46: 35–57.

Vernier, P.; Cardinaud, B.; Valdenaire, O.; Philippe, H.; Vincent, J.D. (1995) An evolutionary view of drug-receptor interaction: the bioamine receptor family. *Trends Pharmacol Sci.* 16(11): 375–381.

Wilson, D. R. (1993) Evolutionary Epidemiology: Darwinian theory in the service of medicine and psychiatry. *Acta Biotheoretica.* 41: 205–218.

Wilson, D. R. (1994) Autologous clones. *Acta Biotheoretica,* 42.

Wilson, D. R. (1998) Evolutionary epidemiology and manic depression. *British Journal of Medical Psychology.* 71: 375–395.

Wilson, S. A. K. (1914) An Experimental Research into the Anatomy and Physiology of the Corpus Striatum. *Brain.* 36: 427–492.

Wyatt, R. J.; Karoum, F.; Suddath, R.; Hitri, A. (1988) The role of cocaine in dopamine use and abuse. *Psychiatr Ann,* 18: 531–534.

PART IV

THE SOCIAL BRAIN: CLINICAL THEORY AND APPLICATIONS— AUTISM, FORENSICS, AND ATTENTION

9

Empathy, Autism, and the Integration of the Triune Brain

James C. Harris

The brain provides foresight in planning for ourselves and others. There is also evidence that it functions to help us gain insight into the feelings of others . . . in the complex organization of the old and new structures, we have presumably a neural ladder, a visionary ladder, for ascending from the most primitive sexual feelings to the highest level of altruistic sentiments . . . If through education, we could only apply what the brain already knows, the year 2000 might see the beginning of a truly golden age. (MacLean, P. D., 1968)

INTRODUCTION

Paul MacLean has long emphasized the importance of the integration of the triune brain and spoken of our capacity to act altruistically toward others. He brings to neuroscience and cognitive neuroscience an approach that is uniquely an evolutionary perspective on the integration of the brain functions and behavior as illustrated in this opening quotation.

I propose to focus on the evolution of sociability as the outcome of the integration of the triune brain. In doing so I will review the contributions of Adolph Meyer, Charles Darwin, Kropotkin and the Russian evolutionists, Antonio Damasio, and Frans De Waal. I will discuss recent investigations in autistic disorder to illustrate the impact of the failure of brain development on socialization. In taking this theme I draw upon three of MacLean's key points:

(1) The integration of the brain results in empathetic responses. Vision is a cold sense that must be linked to feeling to allow one to look with feeling; that is, to have empathy. This linking emerges from the connections of the prefrontal cortex with the limbic cingulate cortex (in MacLean's terms the parental cortex and its connections). The prefrontal cortex is associated with the executive functions of self-regulation, planning, anticipation, but also with emotion regulation and potentially with empathetic and altruistic feelings.

(2) We should study the neurobiology of kindness. When interviewed in the New York Times about the role of the amygdala in fearful responding and the startle response, MacLean was quoted asking why are we not studying the neurobiology of kindness and other prosocial emotions as well.

(3) We should demonstrate our knowledge of such integrated functioning when dealing with others.

SELFISH GENES AND/OR EVOLUTIONARY CONTINUITY

I begin with the proposal that the evolutionary process proceeds toward greater sociability and that brain integration is aided by mutual interpersonal support. Still there are competing viewpoints about the value of studying the brain to appreciate the origins of sociability. On the one hand, Richard Dawkins, the author of *The Selfish Gene* (1976), writes "Be warned that if you wish, as I do, to build a society in which individuals cooperate generously and unselfishly toward the common good, you can expect little help from biological nature. Let us try to teach generosity and altruism, because we are born selfish" (Dawkins 1981).

But Stephen Jay Gould counters with this statement: "Why should our nastiness be the baggage of an apish past and our kindness uniquely human? Why should we not seek continuity with other animals for our noble traits as well?" De Waal (1996) provides evidence for the view expressed by Gould (1980, 1988). In his *Good Natured: The Origins of Right and Wrong in Humans and Other Animals*, he provides the example of the Japanese macaque, Mozu, who at age 18 had survived as a member of her troop and raised five offspring despite having no hands and feet. From paleontology there are examples from the fossil record of survival into adulthood of Neanderthal and other early humans afflicted with dwarfism, paralysis of limbs, and inability to chew. The survival of the handicapped who are a burden to the group may be the earliest example of compassion in evolution. Although others have suggested that such evidence may merely indicate tolerance, De Waal provides evidence from ecological studies of macaques, chimpanzees, and bonobos where examples of animal empathy and social intelligence have been observed. This includes observations of responses to the distress of another, self-awareness, transmission of information, and the manipulation of social relationships. He provides examples from the primate literature of coalition formation where help from a friend is obtained in a confrontation, of friendly reunions following aggressive encounters, and of social support provided to the loser by others who were not involved.

Such interest in the evolutionary origins of culture are continuing as discussed in the June 25, 1999 issue of *Science*. Two reviews, "Chimps in the Wild Show Stirrings of Culture" (Vogel 1999) and "Are Our Primate Cousins Conscious" provide summaries of recent research.

Consistent with the findings of De Waal, van Schaik and his colleagues (Pennisi 1999), when comparing five chimpanzee field studies, noted that those with the higher social tolerance (e.g., meat sharing, female-female grooming) had the highest tool use. This suggests the importance of social tolerance in development. The authors ask: Is there a rudimentary consciousness in chimpanzees, even the prerequisites for morality? We are a long way from chimpanzees in evolutionary terms, but there were many evolutionary links to humans, with selective forces acting from *Australopithecus africanus* (4.5 million years ago) to *Homo erectus* (1.8 million years ago) to *Cro-Magnon to Homo sapiens.* The capacity to overcome instinctive behavior is an evolutionary advance marked by the emergence of increasing social intelligence. According to Kramer (1999) and de Waal (1989) this may involve the ability to categorize social stimuli (including vocal and nonvocal communication); recognize kin and non-kin; understand dominance hierarchies; courtship and mating behavior; form alliances; resolve conflicts; cooperate in predator vigilance and defense; cooperate in foraging and hunting; engage in deception; and participate in social learning.

The advances are associated with being aware of one's self and others' (and knowing the difference), and understanding that others also have mental states, a critical aspect of recent "theory of mind research." We have moved in our understanding of animal behavior from David Premack's query, "Do chimps have a theory of mind?" to Marc Hauser's "Wild Minds" and Frans de Waal's: *Good Natured: the Origins of Right and Wrong in Humans and other Animals.*

HISTORICAL BACKGROUND

Charles Darwin, Kropotkin, and the Russian evolutionists offered theoretical approaches to understanding brain evolution and behavior. Although Charles Darwin spoke of both sociability and survival of the fittest, his followers, notably Herbert Spencer, placed the emphasis on the survival of the fittest, a position that became known as Social Darwinism. And Thomas Henry Huxley in his *Evolution and Ethics* (1889) portrayed morality as the sword forged by *homo sapiens* to slay the dragon of its animal past. He proposed combat with our animal nature, apparently suggesting that morality is the antithesis of this nature. This interpretation has led to evolutionary justifications for the naturalness of aggressive behavior. Yet the complementarity of aggression and subsequent social reunion is more commonly observed.

Dan Todes (1989), a historian in the Department of the History of Medicine at Johns Hopkins reminds us of another school of evolutionary thought, that of the Russian Evolutionists. In his book, *Darwin without Malthus: The Struggle for Existence in Russian Evolutionary Thought,* he discusses Kropotkin and other Russian evolutionists who emphasized mutual aid as the primary motive force in evolution. In Kropotkin's classic book, *Mutual Aid* (1989), the reader is reminded of the importance of psychosocial aspects of survival and the need for group support.

Todes points out that Darwin described natural behavior in tropical settings that were rich in resources, where organisms were packed tightly, wedgelike, into every available space, where a small advantage could bring prosperity to one form at the expense of another. Yet he reminds us that in Russia the natural setting was a great, sparsely populated plain. "Where were Darwin's wedges in this environment?" In Russia the populations were most obviously checked by physical circumstances. These circumstances were often so severe that one form's slight advantage over another could easily seem insignificant. He notes that "a sudden blizzard or an intense drought might obliterate entire populations of insects, birds, and cattle without regard for difference among them." Thus the Russian evolutionists proposed "mutual aid" as the driving force in evolution that allowed survival to continue. They pointed out that those species with the most highly evolved brains have the greatest brain weight, show the greatest social cooperation, and are the most sociable (Todes 1989). This view proposes that brain evolution may be moving toward greater sociability. The work of de Waal (1996) that was previously mentioned provides modern support for the mutual aid hypothesis. De Waal points to the work of Trivers (1972) on the evolution of reciprocal altruism and to the more controversial topic of group selection for altruistic behavior (Wilson & Sober 1994).

Further support of the role of the brain in sociability and evidence for the grounding of morality in neurobiology comes from case reports of changes in human behavior following brain damage. The most famous case may be that of Phineas Gage, a 25-year-old railroad foreman, whose brain damage was sustained when a iron tamping rod was forced through his ventromedial frontal cortex. Remarkably he survived with his elementary mental functions intact. His speech was reported to be normal as was his memory, however, his personality changed. Previously pleasant and reliable, he became irresponsible and lost respect for social conventions. Damasio's *Descarte's Error* (1994) provides other examples of similar antisocial personality change following brain tumors and other damage to this brain region. Damasio continues with the theme of the importance of the "body in the mind" in *The Feeling of What Happens: Body and Emotion in the Making of Consciousness* (1999). Dolan (1999) follows up on these findings in his "On the Neurology of Morals."

PAUL MACLEAN AND THE INTEGRATION OF THE TRIUNE BRAIN

The work of Paul MacLean has considered the brain's evolutionary underpinnings for social behavioral deficits and altruism. MacLean's work on the integrated function of the triune brain is in keeping with the Russian evolutionists' emphasis in evolutionary theory. Such evolutionary steps toward sociability have been investigated by MacLean in his studies of the effects of brain lesions on behavior in lizards, rodents, and squirrel monkeys.

He discusses an increase in sociability and social responsiveness that emerges with particular evolutionary advances in brain development as we move up the evolutionary ladder from reptiles to primates. Most striking are those evolutionary changes that lead to cooperation in family life. Indeed, based on MacLean's work, it has been proposed that consciousness may have its rudimentary beginnings with affective arousal directed toward the feeding of the young

(Harris 1998). Advances in sociability emerge as the mother develops the capacity to attend to the infant's cry, nurse her infant, and provide a safe environment for mastery play. Among primates chimpanzees display eye-to-eye contact with the young and the capacity to grieve the loss of conspecifics. In human evolution, not only grief, but also expressive gestures of comfort toward the bereaved make their clearest appearance. Yet in some neurodevelopmental disorders such as autism, there is a failure in the development of these basic mechanism leading to sociability.

The steps in the establishment of social life linked to the separation cry, maternal care, and play (MacLean 1985b) have received increased support in the work of the ethologists, neuroethologists, psychologists, and psychiatrists. Social support is being investigated through studies of attachment, hierarchies of relationships, affective modulation, working models of relationships, and response to novelty. The child development literature is beginning to trace the emergence of mother-infant attunement and attachment, the physiology of the separation response, and to address the biology of play. The role of the REM sleep in adaptive responses that lead to psychological individuality has been considered by Jouvet (1999).

THE CONTRIBUTIONS OF ADOLPH MEYER

An approach that emphasizes brain integration and adaptive behavior is consistent with the proposal of Adolph Meyer that we define mental health in terms of disciplined spontaneously responsible acts. In 1933, he wrote that "one hears frequent inquiries about distinguishing between what one is born with and what one acquires during life and through living, a distinction between nature and nurture . . . the far more accessible and far more important question is what a person does when he is pushed to act . . . what one uses out of himself and on his own." Meyer drew attention to disciplined spontaneously effective acts, in contrast to unreflected impulsive ones, as indicative of mental health. He asked what occurs before the "here and now," when we are confronted, that prepares us to act. We occupy ourselves in psychiatry with the emergent person, with the range of the individual's spontaneity. By spontaneity, Meyer meant to know what can we expect of a person at any moment, and in the course of time to understand his or her own response, and the initiative leading to that response, when challenged to perform an integrated action. For Meyer what the person may be expected to rise to, and rise with "sua sponte," in responding to others is to be observed. For example, is a response adaptive and responsible or dictated by a disturbance in mood such as depression or a deviation in thought such as a delusion. He developed a classification of the "person in action" and used the term *ergasia* (from the *Greek ergazomai,* to be active) rather than the term conduct or behavior to describe the person in action. In his Maudsley lecture he said he preferred to use this term "ergasia" to refer to the performance of a person. In his classification of ergasias, for example, he used the designation thymergasia (from *thymos,* mood) to describe a pattern of individual performance influenced by affective state rather than the term we use today, depressive disorder.

Meyer spoke of integrated mental functioning and MacLean uses the metaphor of the integration of the triune brain. Such formulations may be helpful in monitoring the outcome of psychotherapy as the therapist looks for examples of spontaneous acts of prosocial behavior as evidence of integrated functioning. An integrated performance by the individual that is responsible and that is ethically correct is a goal to work toward in psychotherapy. One literary example of a disciplined spontaneous gesture is in Herman Hesse's *The Glass Bead Game,* when Joseph Knecht, knowing the risk to his life, dives to save a drowning child. Although he drowns himself in the act of saving the child's life, his act of self-sacrifice has enduring effects on the behavior of others.

What are the evolutionary origins of responsible behavior and self-sacrifice for the benefit of others? Is it, perhaps, based in parenting behavior? Did parental behaviors evolve only to maintain the gene pool or do they also provide, in acts of courage or in empathetic responses, models to establish a culture of generosity? Meyer focused on a "disciplined spontaneity" as indicative of integrated performance of the "person in action;" responsible, effective, and adaptive.

PSYCHOTHERAPY

One issue that becomes apparent as we study brain evolution and behavior is that evolutionary approaches can inform psychotherapy. A goal of psychotherapy is to reduce self-deception in relationships with others and, in so doing, to become empathetic and demonstrate compassion towards others. This linking of affect and cognition is basic to psychotherapy. Psychotherapy is an interpersonally attuned approach to the person that deals with the minute particularities of moments of therapeutic contact between therapist and patient. Such an interpersonal encounter provides an opportunity for empathetic understanding and, as a result, for changes in behavior. MacLean's emphasis on epistemics, the study of subjective understanding, is particularly important for psychotherapy where an understanding of one's own self-deception and the recognition of deceptive behavior towards others is most pertinent. Indeed it may be that the goal of psychotherapy is to realize, confront, and confirm the effects of self-deception on oneself and others and to change one's subsequent behavior. The metaphor of the integration of the triune brain may be considered a basis for psychotherapy as the therapist looks for spontaneous acts of prosocial behavior as outcome variables and as evidence of integrated functioning.

FAILURE OF INTEGRATED BRAIN FUNCTIONING IN AUTISTIC DISORDER

If there is an evolutionary trend toward the integration of the triune brain, what we can learn about this integration from the study of neurodevelopment in those developmental disorders where there is abnormal brain development?

Autistic disorder is a neurodevelopmental disorder where hypotheses about the failure of integrated functioning of the triune brain can be investigated. In this disorder social understanding is lacking, particularly in regard to the recognition of social deception and social betrayal by others. In autistic disorder there is a lack of social referencing, a failure in affective attunement, and a failure in the establishment of a sense of "We-ness," the subjective sense that we are doing something together. Severely autistic children do not demonstrate imaginative play that is reflective of an inner language. The failure of integrated social functioning and the lack of appropriate use of social gestures is characteristic of an autistic disorder. It leads the evolutionary oriented psychiatrist (MacLean 1985) to consider how we can profitably study those brain mechanisms in autistic disorder that might be involved in interpersonal relationships, for example; the linkage of executive function with emotion regulation, emotional memory consolidation, and mastery play in children and adults. Such an approach may help to clarify and to develop a model for the integration of the triune brain.

Paul MacLean has expressed concern about relying only on neuroimaging techniques in our study of brain and behavior. Therefore, I will begin with the autopsy reports of brains from autistic persons by Bauman and Kemper (1985, 1994, 1995; Kemper & Bauman 1993, 1998) before discussing the proper role of neuroimaging studies. Abnormal development of particular brain regions may result in failure in the development of social understanding and of empathy reported in this disorder (Gillberg 1992; Bacon et al. 1998). As Sigmund (1998) notes, there are stable deficits in joint attention, representational play, and responsiveness to the emotions of others in autistic persons. To follow up on neuroanatomical findings, neuroimaging studies may be used to document dysfunction *in vivo,* and hopefully, also, to monitor therapeutic change over time.

NEUROPATHOLOGY OF AUTISM

Kemper and Bauman (1998), in summarizing their neuroanatomic studies of autism, report failure of the appropriate development of limbic structures (e.g., amygdala, hippocampus) and cerebellum. These authors have carried out systematic surveys of the whole brain and completed serial sections of the brains of nine autistic individuals and comparable controls. They found selective abnormalities in the forebrain limbic system and the related inferior olivary nucleus in the brain stem and evidence for a pathological process that extends from the period of fetal development into adulthood.

In the study of the brains of autistic individuals, brain weight was measured in 19 cases. An age difference was noted; 8 of 11 brains from persons younger than 12 years of age showed a significant increase in brain weight compared to the control group. However, 6 of 8 brains of those over age 18 had weights that were lower than expected, although not statistically significantly reduced. In the neocortex no abnormality in external configuration of the cortex was identified. However, on microscopic examination, 8 of the 9 brains had unusually small and more closely packed neurons and less distinct laminar architecture in the anterior cingulate gyrus; in one brain there was a minor malformation in the orbitofrontal cortex in one hemisphere. The remainder of the cerebral cortex appeared unremarkable.

In the allocortex and subcortical forebrain area no abnormalities were found in the striatum, pallidum, thalamus, hypothalamus, basal forebrain, bed nucleus of the stria terminalis, or in myelination. In all 9 brains the forebrain abnormalities were confined to the limbic system. The neurons in the hippocampal fields, CA 1-4, subiculum, entorhinal cortex, mammillary bodies, amygdala, and medial septal nucleus were abnormally small and more densely distributed than in age- and sex-matched controls. When Golgi methods were used to demonstrate neuronal processes, the neurons in hippocampal CA 1 and CA 4 regions showed reduced complexity and in the extent of their dendritic arbors.

In the amygdala, small neuronal size and increased cell packing density were most pronounced in the cortical, medial and central nuclei, whereas the lateral nuclei appeared to be comparable to controls in 8 of 9 brains. The significant exception to this pattern was in a 12-year-old boy with normal intelligence and significant behavioral problems. In this brain the entire amygdala was diffusely abnormal. These findings are of considerable interest because the human amygdala is required for accurate social judgments (Bechara et al. 1995; Adolphs & Damasio 1998). Bilateral damage to the amygdala impairs processing fearful facial expressions (Adolphs & Damasio 1998).

Abnormalities in the cerebellum and brain stem included: (1) curtailment of normal development of neurons in the forebrain limbic system; (2) apparent congenital decrease in the number of Purkinje cells; and (3) age related changes in cell size and number of neurons in the nucleus of the diagonal band of Broca, in the cerebellar nuclei, and in the inferior olive. Kemper and Bauman (1998) conclude that, although their report is descriptive, their neuropathological findings are consistent with the origins of infantile autism being in the prenatal development of the brain with ongoing pathological processes that persist into adult life. They note that the best correlations with clinical features of autism are the consistent findings in the limbic forebrain. The findings in the anterior cingulate, hippocampus, subiculum, entorhinal cortex, and mammillary body are aspects of an interrelated forebrain circuit that is linked to the septum and amygdala. Experimental lesions in these areas have produced deficits in memory, emotion, and other behaviors like those described in autistic persons. These abnormalities in the development of the cingulate and limbic brain are consistent with MacLean's lesions revealing effects on parenting and play when these regions are lesioned in intact animals (Murphy, MacLean & Hamilton

1981). These findings are also consistent with the work of Murray and Mishkin (1985), who reported that bilateral ablations of the amygdala result in severe impairment in crossmodal associative memory in monkeys. These authors propose that the amygdala may be important for the integration and generalization of modality-specific information by multiple sensory systems in the brain, a problem that is a characteristic feature in autism. Malkova et al. (1997) found that socioemotional deficits that followed bilateral ablation of the amydala and hippocampus in neonatal monkeys increased with age and persisted into adulthood; however, comparable lesions placed in adult monkeys resulted in relatively mild behavioral deficits. Animal models such as these are consistent with the neurodevelopmental deficit proposed in autism because there is evidence that representational memory in humans is normally acquired after birth. Therefore, it is possible that a developmental abnormality in the limbic memory circuit may become clinically evident after birth, consistent with a deterioration in social, language, and cognitive ability that is commonly reported in the first two years of life in autism.

NEUROIMAGING

Neuroimaging studies may be utilized to evaluate brain structure and functioning. Such studies may be used to confirm structural changes in the brains of autistic persons that are based on a small number of autopsied cases. Moreover, neuroimaging studies can test functional hypotheses based on abnormalities in brain circuits based on the same anatomical evidence. Imaging studies may also be used to evaluate theoretical models of autism. These include, metarepresentational models (theory of mind), affective models (lack of eye contact, abnormal response to danger, and abnormal response in fearful situations), and intersubjectivity (integrating cortex and limbic brain).

Fletcher et al. (1995) carried out a functional imaging study to evaluate mentalizing or "theory of mind" in normal subjects. Story comprehension was used to identify brain regions involved in mentalizing (theory of mind), i.e. in the understanding of the beliefs and desires of others and having the capacity to attribute independent mental states to others in order to explain or predict their behavior. This imaging study in normal volunteers assessed brain activity through story comprehension tasks necessitating the attribution of mental states. Brain activity was compared with that measured in two control physical tasks that did not require mental attribution. One was unlinked sentences, the other was a physical story that did not require mental attribution. Both story conditions, when compared to unlinked sentences, showed significant increases in regional blood flow in the temporal poles bilaterally, the left supratemporal gyrus, and posterior cingulate cortex. Only the theory-of-mind story when compared with the physical story produced activation in the medial frontal gyrus on the left suggesting its selective activation in theory-of-mind tasks. Subsequently, Happe et al. (1996) used the same paradigm in a PET study involving five patients with Asperger syndrome, a variant of autism, who had normal intellectual functioning. As predicted no task related activity was found in the left medial prefrontal cortex but activity was found in the immediately adjacent areas again pointing to this region as involved in understanding a brain system involved in understanding other minds. Gallagher et al. (2000) have demonstrated that both the story task (verbal) and a cartoon task (nonverbal) showed overlap in activating the medial prefrontal area. In a structural MRI study in 15 high-functioning individuals with autistic disorder, Abell et al. (1999) identified grey-matter differences in an amygdala based system when compared to 15 age matched and IQ matched control subjects. These findings of differences in amygdala structure are consistent with the autopsy findings in autism regarding the amygdala. These studies also have implications for the neural basis of autism.

Future imaging studies in autism may focus on neuroimaging of amygdala activation in response to emotional stimuli. Such studies have been conducted in normal volunteers. Whalen et al. (1998) report that masked presentations of emotional facial expression modulate amygdala activation without explicit knowledge (i.e., in the absence of knowledge that such stimuli were being presented). Morris, Ohman, and Dolan (1999) report a subcortical pathway to the right amygdala mediating "unseen fear."

The treatment of autistic disorder requires an understanding of the autistic nervous system and a recognition of the failure of integration of the triune brain in this disorder. Because this is a neurodevelopmental disorder there is the possibility of neurodevelopmental interventions to treat the behavior abnormality. Our goal in treatment is to facilitate better integrated brain function and establish the normalization of autistic persons in society. Thus, the model of the integration of the triune brain may serve not only as a metaphor in our future treatments but lead to specific early interventions.

REFERENCES

Abell, F.; Krams, M.; Ashbumer, J.; Passingman, R.; and Friston, K. (1999). The neuro-anatomy of autism: a voxel-based whole brain analysis of structural scans. *Neuroreport.* 10: 1647–1651.

Adolphs, R. and Damasio, A. (1998) The Human Amygdala in Social Judgment. *Nature.* 393: 470–474.

Bacon, A. L.; Fein, D.; Morris, R.; Waterhouse, L.; and Allen, D. (1998) The responses of autistic children to the distress of others. *Journal of Autism and Developmental Disabilities.* 28: 129–142.

Bauman, M. L. and Kemper, T .L.(1985) Histoanatomical observations of the brain in early infantile autism. *Neurology.* 35: 866–874.

Bauman, M. L. and Kemper, T. L. (1994) Neuroanatomical observations of the brain in autism. In Bauman, M. and Kemper, T. (eds.) *The Neurobiology of Autism.* Baltimore: Johns Hopkins University Press, pp. 119–145.

Bechara, A.; Tranel, D.; Damasio, H.; Adolphs, R.; Rockland, C.; and Damasio, A. (1995). A Double Dissociation of Conditioning and Declarative Knowledge Relative to the Amygdala and Hippocampus in Humans. *Science.* 269: 1115–1118.

Damasio, A. (1994). *Descartes' Error: Emotion, Reason, and the Human Brain.* NY: G.P. Putnam.

Damasio, A. (1999). *The Feeling of What Happens. Body and Emotion in the Making of Consciousness.* NY: Harcourt Brace & Company.

Dawkins, R. (1981) In defense of selfish genes. *Philosophy.* 56: 556–573.

Dawkins, R. (1976) *The Selfish Gene.* Oxford: Oxford University Press.

de Waal, F. (1989) *Peacemaking among Primates.* Cambridge, MA: Harvard University Press.

de Waal, F. (1996) *Good Natured: the origins of good and evil in primates.* Cambridge, MA: Harvard University Press.

Dolan, R.J. (1999) On the Neurology of Morals. *Nature Neuroscience.* 2: 927–929.

Fletcher, P. C.; Happe, F.; Frith, U.; Baker, S. C.; and Dolan, R. J. (1995) Other minds in the brain: a functional imaging study of "theory of mind" in story comprehension. *Cognition.* 57: 109–128.

Gallagher, H. L.; Happe, F.; Brunswick, N.; Fletcher, P. C.; Frith, U.; and Frith, C. D. (2000) Reading the mind in cartoons and stories: an fMRI study of "theory of mind" in verbal and nonverbal tasks. *Neuropsychologia.* 381: 1–21.

Gillberg, C.L. (1992) Autism and autistic-like conditions: subclasses among disorders of empathy. *Journal of Child Psychology and Psychiatry.* 33: 813–843.

Gould, S. J. (1980) So cleverly an animal. In *Ever since Darwin.* Harmondsworth, Penguin. pp. 260–267.

Gould S. J. (1988) Kropotkin was no crackpot. *Natural History.* 97: 12–21.

Greenberg, N. (1977) A neuroethological study of display behavior in the Lizard Anolis Carolinensis. *American Zoologist.* 191–201.

Happe, F.; Ehlers, S.; Fletcher, P.; Frith, U.; and Johansson, M. (1996) "Theory of Mind" in the brain. Evidence from a PET scan study of Asperger's syndrome. *Neuroreport.* 8: 197–201.

Harris, J. and Newman, J. (1987) Mediation of Separation Distress by Alpha-2 Adrenergic Mechanisms in a Nonhuman Primate. *Brain Research.* 410: 353–356.

Harris, J. and Newman, J. (1988) Primate Models for the Management of Separation Anxiety. In: *Psychological Control of Mammalian Vocalization.* Newman, J. (Ed.), NY: Plenum Press.

Harris, J. and Newman, J. (1988) Enhancement of Vocalizations in Adult Squirrel Monkeys by Combined Opiate and Alpha-2 Adrenergic Receptor Blockade. *Pharmacology, Biochemistry, and Behavior.* 31: 223–226.

Harris, J.C. (1998) *Developmental Neuropsychiatry: Fundamentals.* Volume 1. Oxford University Press: New York. p. 159.

Huxley, T. H. (1888) Struggle for existence and its bearing upon man. *Nineteenth Century.* Feb.

Huxley, T. H. (1989)[1894] *Evolution and Ethics.* Princeton: Princeton University Press.

Jouvet, M. (1999) (trans. by L. Garey) Is paradoxical sleep the guardian of individuality in *The paradox of sleep: the story of dreaming.* NU press, pp. 135–157.

Kanner, L. (1943). Autistic disturbances of affective contact. *The Nervous Child.* 2: 217–250.

Kemper T. L. and Bauman, M. L. (1993) The contibution of neuropathological studies to the understanding of autism. *Behavioral Neurology.* 11: 175–187.

Kemper T. L. and Bauman, M. L. (1998) Neuropathology of Infantile Autism. *Journal of Neuropathology and Experimental Neurology.* 57: 645–652.

Kramer, D. A. (1999) The evolutionary biology of family psychotherapy. Paper presented at the annual meeting of the American Academy of Child and Adolescent Psychiatry, Chicago, October.

Kropotkin, P.I. (1989) *Mutual aid: A factor in evolution.* Black Rose: Montreal.

Malkova, L.; Mishkin, M.; Suomi, S. J.; and Bachevalier, J. (1997) *Annals of the New York Academy of Sciences* 807: 538–540.

MacLean, P. D. (1968) Alternative neural pathways to violence in Ng, L. (ed) *Alternatives to Violence.* pp. 24–34.

MacLean, P. D. (1978) Effects of lesions of globus pallidus on species-typical display behavior of squirrel monkeys *Brain Research.* 149: 175–196.

MacLean, P. D. (1985) Evolutionary psychiatry and the triune brain. *Psychological Medicine.* 15: 219–221.

MacLean, P. D. (1985) Brain evolution relating to family, play, and the separation call. *Archives of General Psychiatry.* 42: 404–417.

MacLean, P. D. (1990) *The Triune Brain in Evolution: Role in Paleocerebral Functions.* NY: Plenum Press.

Meyer, A. (1957) On Spontaneity in *Psychobiology: A Science of Man.* Springfield, Ill.: Charles C. Thomas.

Morris, J. S.; Ohman, A.; and Dolan, R. J. (1999) A subcortical pathway to the right amygdala mediating "unseen fear." *Proceedings of the National Academy of Science,* USA. 16: 1680–1685.

Murray, E. A. and Mishkin, M. (1985) Amygdaloidectomy impairs crossmodal association in monkeys. *Science.* 228: 604-606.

Murphy, M. R.; Maclean, P. D.; and Hamilton, S. C. (1981) Species-typical behavior of hamsters deprived from birth of the neocortex. *Science.* 213: 459–461.

Newman, J. D. and MacLean, P. D. (1982) Effects of tegmental lesions on the isolation call of squirrel monkeys. *Brain Research.* 232: 317–329.

Pennisi, E. (1999) Are Our Primate Cousins 'Conscious'? *Science.* 284 (5423): 2073–2076.

Sigmund, M. (1998) Change and Continuity in the Development of Children with Autism. *Journal of Child Psychol. Psychiatry.* 39: 817–827.

Todes, D.P. (1989) *Darwin without Malthus: The struggle for existence in Russian evolutionary thought.* Oxford: Oxford University Press.

Trivers, R. (1971) The evolution of reciprocal altruism. *Quarterly Review of Biology.* 46: 35–57.

Van Schaik, C.P.; Deaner, R.O.; and Merrill, M.Y. (1999) The Conditions for Tool Use in Primates: Implications for the Evolution of Material Culture. *Journal of Human Evolution.* 36(6): 719–741.

Vogel, G. (1999) Chimps in the Wild Show Stirrings of Culture. *Science.* 284(5423): 2070–2073.

Whalen, P. J.; Rauch, S. L.; Etcoff, N. L.; McInerney, S. C.; Lee, M. B.; and Jenike, M. A. (1998) Masked presentations of emotional facial expressions modulate amygdala activity without explicit knowledge. *Journal of Neuroscience.* 18: 411–418.

Wilson, D. S. and Sober, E. (1994) Reintroducing group selection to the human behavioral sciences. *Behavioral and Brain Sciences.* 17: 585–654.

10

NEUROETHOLOGY, EXEMPLIFIED BY LIMBIC SEIZURES WITH MOTIVELESS HOMICIDE IN "LIMBIC PSYCHOTIC TRIGGER REACTION"

Anneliese A. Pontius

INTRODUCTION

Paul MacLean's evolutionary hierarchical model of the organization of the human brain has paved the way toward insights into otherwise unexplainable clinical phenomena. His model provides a basis for conceptualizing sudden, brief atavistically regressive acts during partial nonconvulsive seizures starting in the evolutionarily old limbic system. Secondarily, such seizures appear to upset briefly the normal fronto-limbic balance. Thus, the reciprocally related, evolutionarily young frontal lobe system becomes transiently dysfunctional. Over two decades of clinical forensic studies, MacLean's model enabled me to propose a transient "Limbic Psychotic Trigger Reaction" (LPTR) consisting of 13 specifically interrelated symptoms and signs. These implicate the neurophysiological mechanism of limbic seizure kindling.

The symptomatology has been delineated in the following: atavistically regressive acts accompanied by autonomic arousal and a brief *de novo* psychosis. Such apparent behavioral seizures are associated with out-of-character motiveless, unplanned acts of sudden onset and cessation, committed with flat affect, typically against a stranger who happened to provide an individualized stimulus that revived a memory of past intermittent mild to moderate stresses (a setting characteristic of limbic seizure kindling). The symptomatology reflects three seizure-related phases (aura, ictus, post-ictus) with preserved consciousness and memory of the puzzling acts of homicide (17 cases), destruction by fire (3 cases), and primitive, acquisitional bank robbery (1 case). Eleven of the 21 cases of LPTR had a known history of closed head injury and 14 had some positive finding on a brain test in their lifetimes. LPTR remains to be ruled out by further research on nonfelonious similarly emotionless sudden acts.

HISTORICAL SURVEY OF THE LIMBIC SYSTEM CONCEPT

Great concepts do not suddenly emerge like Aphrodite out of foam but have an evolving history. Thus, in 1952 Paul MacLean, who for the first time coined the term "limbic system" (a central part of his "three brain" or "triune brain" concept) belongs to a lineage of great creative researchers (Mega et al. 1997). To trace the essential steps, this lineage started with Paul Broca's (1878) "grand lobe limbique," which focused on olfactory processing. James Papez (1937) combined anatomical findings with clinical reports of emotional disturbances with lesions to the cingulate and other medial structures. He proposed a mechanism of emotions, processed within a two-way circuit, known as the "Papez circuit," leading to internal or external expression of emotion. Next, in 1948, Paul Yakovlev distinguished three phylogenetic functional zones of brain development, as reflected by myelogenetic stages: These zones comprised the oldest inner zone, the visceral system or entopallium; the middle zone or the mesopallium which includes Broca's grand limbic lobe—as well as orbitofrontal and insular cortex; and the most recently developed neocortical outer zone. Yakovlev's conception stemmed from physiological and cytoarchitectonic findings.

Finally, Paul MacLean's (1952) limbic system concept links Papez' medial circuit with Yakovlev's basal lateral structures of the "middle zone." As pointed out in a recent survey by Mega et al. (1997: 5), MacLean's concept of the limbic system has survived—with refinement typical in science—as "consistent anatomic-clinical correlations have been found."

Thus, recently investigators increasingly focus on a potential role of limbic system structures in neuropsychiatric disorders, including schizophrenia (Arnold 1997); depression (Mayberg 1997): drug abuse and the reward system (Koob & Nestler 1997). Further research addresses the spontaneously occurring auras of partial seizures. Such auras are frequently analogous to experiential phenomena elicited through electrical stimulation of limbic structures (Fried 1997a).

Herein such anatomico-physiological findings are supplemented by clinical correlation that utilizes frequently neglected contributions of clinician scientists (Geschwind 1984). As MacLean (1998: 274) warned: "the marvelous technique of brain imaging has led to the wrongful impression that it will replace classical methods," including patients' case histories. Further, Reich et al. report findings on information coding suggesting that simple averaging of neuronal firing as used in imaging techniques significantly underestimates the information-processing that is occurring.

HALLMARK OF CREATIVE CONCEPTUALIZING

Paul MacLean, one of those rare creative conceptualizers, has dared attempting an integration of results from animal experiments with uniquely human insights and experiences. His background in the classics and in philosophy greatly enhanced his integrative power.

In this chapter, I shall exemplify the stimulating influence of Paul MacLean's work in two respects: The content of his work influenced my proposed new subtype of a partial seizure, "Limbic Psychotic Trigger Reaction" (LPTR) (Pontius 1981–1999). Further, MacLean's integrative work over the years employed not only the straight-line logico-deductive reasoning of the experimenter, but he also dared to use formal thought processes of "retroductive reasoning" ("abduction") for the detection of new patterns (Hanson 1965; Hayek 1964; Pontius 1995).

Retroductive (Abductive) Reasoning

The process of pattern detection, largely based on retroductive reasoning, is "not for the faint-hearted," as Kuhn (1971) emphasizes. Retroductive pattern detection contrasts with statistics, which, according to Hayek (a nobelist in economics), simplifies its task by "substituting a single attribute for the unascertainable individual attributes in the collective." (Hayek 1964). Such a statement achieves congruence with similar ones by Hanson (1965), a theoretical physicist at Yale.

In general, with regard to research into complex human behavior, much initial research that addresses such complex, higher-order phenomena begins with the detection of a consistent pattern of interrelations. Initially, a process of pattern detection does not yet fit the orthodox criteria of "prediction and control" (Hayek 1998), a phenomenon important to note.

Both Hayek (1964) and Hanson (1965), coming from different fields of innovative research, point out that critiques of patterns of complex phenomena with a broad scope, such as MacLean's triune (three-in-one) brain, tend to overlook certain important points. Thus, initially the explanatory contribution of a pattern merely delineates a consistent pattern of complex interrelations that do not yet offer a statistical explanation. One indication of pattern validity is not merely accidental but persistent occurrence, although such recurrence may not necessarily include all its details.

Only after a pattern's detection can subsequent phases of research compare and sort it out among related phenomena heuristically useful for later study. If a pattern persistently forms, then it can become predictable despite initially incomplete data: and despite the impossibility of predicting individual instances or all the detailed circumstances under which the pattern recurs. In general patterns of complex phenomena do not allow prediction of particular individual events, as possible with simple phenomena. Recurrence of a pattern of complex order, however, can be defined only within general circumstances, the recurrence of which can be falsifiable, thereby permitting empirical prediction (Hayek 1964).

As Hayek (1964) elaborated, great practical importance hinges on knowing the conditions in which a specific pattern will appear and to know what depends on its preservation. This is applicable to MacLean's concepts of the limbic system and of the triune brain, essentially containing three phylogenetically different parts.

A less abstract clinical application of such principles, guiding the detection of complex patterns, led to the hypothesis of a new subtype of partial seizures, "Limbic Psychotic Trigger Reaction" (LPTR). This presents a further elaboration of MacLean's conceptualizations. LPTR has been consistently found in repeatedly clinical observations of a specific class of partial seizures, in which essential features of the triune brain concept become manifest, observable, and potentially measurable. Of specific relevance in LPTR is the relationship between the evolutionarily young prefrontal lobes and the old limbic system, noted to be reciprocally interrelated (Nauta 1971; Weinberger 1984).

A final noteworthy point, on all levels of pattern detection from the most abstract to the clinical, holds that a theory applies to a kind of classes or situations that give data certain general properties (i.e., that the data belong to the class defined by the scope of the variables). One need not know anything about individual attributes of the data so long as we are satisfied to know merely the sort of pattern that will appear; not its particular manifestation. Nonetheless, pattern detection extends the range of theoretical knowledge, as has been the case with MacLean's triune brain.

Difference between Pattern Detection and Statistics

Hayek (1964) further elaborates that pattern detection provides explanations only of the principle and describes merely the general character of complex, higher-level generalities. Thus, the study of complex pattern addresses relationships (i.e., systematic connections among elements that are organized into structures). By contrast, statistics deal with large numbers, essentially by eliminating complexity. Statistics deal merely with a multiplicity of relations, disregarding the relations among the individual elements with different attributes, as if these elements had no systematic connections. Statistics assume that information on the frequency of the individual elements of a collective suffices for an explanation of the phenomena and of the elements of which they consist. In general, Hayek considers it a futile, naive belief that statistics could discover regularities without an appropriate theory. Further, all theories describe only a range of possibilities. A correct interpretation of a theory excludes other conceivable courses of events outside the range of the theory, and can thus be falsified. In conclusion, Hayek (1964) cites Popper's succinct statement that a theory's empirical content consists of what it forbids.

Clinical Contribution: A New Subtype of Partial Seizure Implicating a Fronto-limbic Imbalance

Emphasizing the integration of basic research findings with reports on human experience, MacLean has focused on the long studied partial seizures of Temporal Lobe Epilepsy (TLE), which occur, however, typically with clouding of consciousness and amnesia.

Inspired by his work with its evolutionary focus, I proposed a new pattern of symptoms and signs, a subtype of partial limbic seizures, called "Limbic Psychotic Trigger Reaction" (LPTR) (Pontius 1981–2002). LPTR's value for the study of experience rests on LPTR patients' ability to report their bizarre experiences because they have no quantitative impairment of consciousness and thus remember their acts and experiences.

LPTR constitutes a working hypothesis, and as Cummings (1983: 879) points out regarding medical syndromes in general, they all can ultimately be verified or disconfirmed by experimentation and observation. Note, however, that for even the major mental syndromes delineated a century ago, such as schizophrenia and manic-depressive illness, none of their various competing neurophysio-pathological hypotheses has been conclusively verified despite great technical advances (Arnold 1997). Difficulties in verification are compounded when the symptomatology is transient, as in seizures that probably involve neurotransmitters, possibly a decrease in serotonin levels in syndromes with aggression, such as in LPTR.

Additional obstacles arise in cases of felonies requiring detention in maximum security facilities, where legal considerations hamper the use of "objective" tests with so far nonportable equipment. Moreover, even abnormal objective test findings, however, can only reveal correlations so far, not causation of behavior, and are therefore still generally excluded from court testimony. Meanwhile, the diagnosis rests mostly on detailed history-taking and careful clinical observations of repeated, consistent patterns, such as these characteristic of partial seizure phenomena.

LIMBIC PSYCHOTIC TRIGGER REACTION (LPTR): A PROPOSED PARTIAL SEIZURE. A CONTRIBUTION TO THE LIMBIC SYSTEM CONCEPT IN THE FORM OF A PROPOSED FRONTO-LIMBIC IMBALANCE

As elaborated and exemplified elsewhere (Pontius 1981–2002), the proposed LPTR symptomatology has been consistently found and replicated in 21 bizarre cases that fit no other known diagnosis. So far, there were 17 homicidal cases (Pontius 1981–2002), 3 fire setters (Pontius 1999), and 1 bank robber (Pontius 2001). All cases met essentially the 16 inclusion and 13 exclusion criteria (see Table 10.1), which may vary by degree, but not in essence.

Table 10.1. Inclusion and Exclusion Criteria for LPTR

Inclusion criteria for LPTR at the time of act.

1. Transient psychosis: hallucinations (of any modality, formed or unformed), and or delusions (frequently of grandeur)—all with new content, in cases of pre-existing psychosis.
2. Transient autonomic hyperactivation (e.g., epigastric sensations, nausea, bladder incontinence, ejaculation, ice cold sensations, or profuse sweating.
3. Seizure-like course: A brief aura-like phase with ("cognitive") puzzlement or perceptual distortions is followed by ictus with brief psychosis, homicidal acts typically wilh.some automatization, and finally by lingering inefficient behavior post-ictally.
4. Flat affect during the acts.
5. No quantitatively significant alteration of conscousness.
6. No amnesia for the essential features of the acts, which are remorsefully recalled.
7. Highly individualized trigger stimuli revive experiences either in concrete or symbolic ways.
   Revived are:
8. Mild to moderate repetitive stressful experiences (based on subjective judgement), ruminated by social loners. Such a pattern of intermittent reexperiencing (e.g., through memory revival) implicates the neurophysiological mechanism of seizure kindling, to which the limbic system (amygdala) is particularly susceptible. Secondary to an implicated limbic seizure, a temporary frontal hypofunctioning is implicated, because both systems are reciprocally interrelated, leading to a transient fronto-limbic imbalance.
9. Motiveless acts.
10. No planning, no premeditation of the acts.
11. Ego-dystonic, out of character acts.
12. No blaming of others or justifying acts, but subjectively assuming full personal responsibility for the acts, linked with serious suicidal acts in some patients.
13. No use of drugs or alcohol, at least not close to the acts at toxic levels..
14. No dementia or mental retardation.
15. In the few cases with primary psychosis, LPTR may be superimposed as a different syndrome of brief duration.
16. Typically no family history of seizure disorders, though individuals may have had various previous seizures.

Exclusion criteria for LPTR in the absence of required inclusion criteria

1. Long-standing psychosis, as in schizophrenia, paranoia. and mania without new atypical symptoms.
2. Long-standing recurrence of autonomic hyperactivation, as in various panic attacks (e.g., with sensations of suffication).
3. Explosive onset, as in intermittent cxplosive/dyscontrol disorders, or in the proposed organic aggressive syndrome: These all lack aura-like warning and recur over time.
4. Strong emotions, as in provoked impulsive acts or in acts of passion.
5. Clouding of consciousness or disorientation during the act, as in temporal lobe epilepsy (TLE).
6. Amnesia for the act, as in TLE.

Table 10.1, continued

7. Typical prior history of recurrently triggered seizures by modality-specific, nonindividualized stimuli as in reflex epilepsy (e.g., as evoked by reading text of any content).
8. History of severe, unusual trauma (e.g., war or natural catastrophies as in post traumatic stress disorder.
9. Motivation for the act.
10 Planning, premeditation.
11. Habitual violence, as in various personality disorders, (e.g., anti-social, impulsive, narcissistic, borderline, and conduct disorders), all persisting over time.
12. Blaming certain traumatic events or others, or justifying behavior. as in "abuse excuses," and/or in the above personality disorders.
13. Drug, or alchohol use or abuse, acute or chronic, or withdrawal syndromes following such abuse.

Note. It is of note that in all 14 cases (and in 2 newly identified ones) the essential criteria were present (Pontius, 1981, 1984, 1987, 1993b, 1994, 1996). As is the case with any syndrome in cases where the essential pattern of LPTR is preserved, not all of the criteria would be required, except for the following essential criteria: Transient psychosis within a pattern that implicates a partial limbic seizure with no significant quantitative alteration of consciousness and without significant amnesia for the unplanned, stimulus-triggered, motiveless acts.

In addition to the 14 (now 16) white homocidal men, LPTR has also been implicated in three male juveniles charged with motiveless unplanned setting of fires (Pontius 1993b) and one man with bizarre bank robbery (Pontius 1994).

It is important to observe that several of the clinical symptoms are objectifiable by reports from frequently present witnesses (because the acts were unplanned) and from police reports (because of the patients' typical confessions).

LPTR consists of the following 13 symptoms and signs, that show indications of being neurophysiologically interrelated, not at all haphazardly assembled as is the case with natural phenomena.

LPTR symptomatology comprises: (1) lack of drive motivation; (2) lack of preplanning of the act and of its concealment; (3) no prior history of (severe) aggression; (4) flat affect around the time of the act; (5) typically a known history of (frequently overlooked) closed head injury or of other insult to the brain, e.g. febrile infantile seizures; (6) specific, individualized trigger stimuli implicated in the evoked out-of-character act. The stimulus constellation acutely revives the memory of intermittently experienced past stresses, each one by itself not severe; (7) typically, some automatized action sequence reminiscent of "auto-piloted" action; culminated in motiveless, purposeless acts—evoked (not emotionally provoked) by the trigger stimulus; (8) typically, an auralike puzzled state ("cognitive mismatch"), lasting about 5 minutes, followed by ictus-like symptomatology (about 20 minutes); (9) transient autonomic, prevailingly parasympathetic arousal (e.g., nausea, vertigo, "ice cold" sensations or profuse sweating, "tingling," urinary incontinence, erection, or ejaculation); (10) transient hallucinations (of any modality, formed or unformed) and/or delusions (frequently of grandeur); all such psychotic symptoms are new ones in those rare cases with prior psychosis; (11) no significant quantitative alteration of consciousness, therefore no essential memory loss, enabling virtually full recall of the acts; (12) indications of transient prefrontal-lobe dysfunctioning around the time of the act, secondary to implicated limbic hyperactivation, and potentially persisting (for some hours) post-ictally; and mostly (13) self-confession of the act, with subjective feelings of responsibility and profound remorse (unless there is underlying schizophrenia with its habitually flat affect).

Noteworthy, is the fact that the symptoms occurred in the three phases that characterize seizures: aura, ictus, post-ictus.

Hypothesized Neurophysiological Mechanism of Seizure Kindling

Importantly perhaps, all 21 cases of LPTR so far occurred in social loners, with a "schizoid/avoidant personality." Loners do not share nor compare their hurts with others but ruminate on them, not laying them to rest. This personality type appears to contribute to the outstanding sequence of events leading to LPTR: The LPTR symptoms appear (within c. 5 minutes) after a chance encounter with an individualized trigger stimulus that revived the memory of past merely mild to moderate hurts, each one in itself seemingly innocuous (Table 10.2).

This sequence of events characterizes seizure kindling (Goddard 1967; Goddard & Mcintyre 1986). Kindled seizures in primates are typified by the nonconvulsive "behavioral" type (Wada 1978): The trigger stimulus, in itself innocuous and subthreshold, resembles the preceding stresses that the trigger revives. Thereby the specific stimulus that resembles past stresses directly or symbolically appears to represent the last one in a series of similar hurts.

A hypothesis alternative to the kindling mechanism (albeit a hypothesis not as fitting to the history and symptoms) might suggest that a spontaneously occurring aura (Fried 1997a: 119–120) of an extended kind may play a primary role in the LPTR symptomatology. Fried likens an experiential aura to a spontaneously appearing memory. Both these phenomena cannot be eradicated at will and cannot be eliminated by local tissue removal, implicating the neuronal network uses parallel distributed processing (Fried 1997a).

Discussion of LPTR as a New Subtype of Partial Seizure

The goal of the presentation and discussion of LPTR entails impetus to further inquiry into the complexity of human action. Whether LPTR should be classified as a simple or a complex partial seizure depends on the classification used. Meldrum (1990) and Gram (1990) used the preservation of consciousness as a criterion for simple seizures, while Trimble (1992: 193) cited Gastaut and Geschwind's criterion for complex partial seizures, namely impaired organized cerebral functioning. This criterion is congruent with Dam's (1992) formulation.

Table 10.2 Specific Interrelation Between Mild to Moderate Stresses, Specific Trigger Stimuli Reviving The Stresses, and Homicidal Acts in LPTR

Case	Mild/Moderate Stresses	Stimuli Triggering Homicidal Acts
1.	Several admissions to mental hospitals by parents "for no reason."	Fatally punching brother's heart after reading library card "Lizzy Borden," who too had been "wrongly" sent to mental hospitals by parents.
2.	Forced to perform fellatio as a child and repeatedly forced to eat spagetti, causing "gagging."	Fatally shooting brother-in-law after he had been forced to dump "dirty pictures" and hearing of hallucinating the term "child molester."
3.	Being called "boob" (idiot) as a child by adoptive mother with big breasts ("boobs").	Stabbing "friend" after hearing him say "boob" while passing by a domed Church with a statue of Christ, whom "friend" seemingly "criticized" when saying "boob."
4.	Boot camp training with sights and sounds of live ammunition, often reexperienced over years by listening to "graduation tapes": "The Sounds of Boot Camp" with sergeant's commands: Kill! Kill!	Shooting blindly at eight policemen after hearing their sirens and crackling sounds in the underbrush and seeing their car lights flashing.
5.	Being taunted and worried about small penis since childhood. Wife, whose faithfulness he did not doubt had dropped hints about the sexual prowess of the restaurant owner.	Fatal shooting of a restaurant owner and missing several other persons after only seeing wife's car near restaurant.
6.	Being repeatedly refused cigarettes by mother	Fist attack on old female stranger whose gait and voice, refusing cigarette, recalled mother's behavior.
7.	Being repeatedly criticized for "erratic" driving	Knife attack on male stranger, driving "erratically" while giving patient a ride.
8.	Being the only one of five male family members who did not fulfill father's wish to become an officer in the Armed Services from which he "flunked."	Fatal stabbing of female stranger while she was talking about her husband and son being officers in the Armed Forces.
9.	Seeing father's photo in family living room in posture with fly rod ever since father had died of a heart attack after an argument with patient who was four years old at the time.	Fatal drowning of male stranger fishing with a fly rod, standing sideways in same position as patient's late father in photo.

Table 10.2, continued

10. Hearing mother crying when hit by father. Patient had helped her by hitting father back. As an adult, patient repeatedly saved his crying and choking infant by whacking her on the back.

Fatal hitting of his crying and choking infant "to save her" a day after patient's mother died.

11. Repeated leg injuries inflicted by stepfather during childhood and later by stepfather-like codefendant, and repeated watching of karate movies with fixed action program, culminating in stabbing the prostrate loser.

Fatal stabbing of prostrate male stranger whom he first heard before he could see his mouth move (as in English-dubed karate movies), while patient also suffered leg pain.

12. Being bitten in finger by brother as a child, later inguinal hernia operation under local anesthesia.

Stabbing friendly male stranger, moving his mouth while eating, which led To patient's belief that he was about to be "cannibalized," while hallucinating that his testicles and entire body were being cut.

13. Tonsilectomy as a child, later recurrent painful throat infections with painful external swellings, relieved through touching his throat.

Fatal strangulation of female stranger. All happened in the context of sexual foreplay, when unwittingly touching the victim's throat in a highly specific manner. A previous potential victim was not attacked, as she had slightly changed her position by chance.

14. Loneliness since an anal rape as a child by a "friendly" man, while having stomach aches and seeing leaves moving. Later, only seeing or hearing the sound of moving leaves and/or stomachaches repeatedly revived extreme feelings of loneliness, threatening annihilation.

Fatal hitting of female lover, who insisted on increased emotional closeness, unbearable to patient in context of revived loneliness during severe stomachaches with unformed visual hallucinations.

15. Girl friend had repeatedly mentioned his painful divorce in context of his ex-wife's name.

Girl friend mentioned again ex-wife's name, and he "knew like the amen in church" that she would continue with painful divorce details, whereupon he strangled her.

16. Being repeatedly jilted by women with "excuses:" "it's not your fault."

Hearing female neighbor talk deceptively to her boy friend while a TV sitcom was on about rejecting women saying 7 times "its not your fault," whereupon he attacked one woman

Table 10.2, continued

	with a frying pan and stabbed a second one with a kitchen knife.
17. Secretive parents repeatedly made unpleasant plans driving him to some unknown destination (e.g., doctors), which made him increasingly suspicious of unrevealed plans about him.	The male survivor of a machete attack had seemed to move secretively behind a screen when another man said without explanation: "I have to make a phone call," he killed him with a kitchen knife.

LPTR would also be consistent with Smythies' (1992: 271) definition of consciousness as "the total of what we can introspect (i.e., our sensory fields . . . inner images, thoughts, emotions as we experience these directly." Such definition would favor a classification of LPTR as a complex partial seizure with special emphasis on impairment of volition and of emotional concomitants of the action.

In general, as Trimble (1992) pointed out, of the two main kinds of seizures, convulsive and nonconvulsive, those with the striking, readily observable symptomatology of convulsions have historically been more readily accepted than the "behavioral" (i.e. nonconvulsive seizures). The latter may go unnoticed, except if "arrest" (i.e. staring is present and observable). Even dramatically out-of-character acts are not readily attributed to seizures because of the ubiquitous belief in "free will." It is therefore imperative to obtain patients' spontaneous (not questionnaire-engendered) accounts of their perplexing experiences during behavioral seizures.

DIFFERENTIAL DIAGNOSES OF LPTR AND ITS OPPOSITE SYNDROME E

Previously, various differential diagnoses of LPTR have been ruled out in detail (Pontius 1981-2002) so that here only a summary of various disorders needs mention. Each other possibility typically persists over lengthy periods of time (e.g., the major psychoses, such as schizophrenia and affective disorders with depression and/or mania). Also distinct from LPTR are the persistent, frequently recurrent, virtually habitual "Impulse Control Disorders," including episodic dyscontrol. Each of these persistent disorders are also linked with strong emotions, and occur typically without psychosis. Among the partial seizures, temporal lobe epilepsy differs from LPTR most strikingly because of TLE's clouded consciousness causes memory consolidation difficulties, that then result in at least partial amnesia.

Other Criminal Acts Not Due to Seizures or Psychoses

Based on three decades as a forensic neuropsychiatrist, I must point out a certain inaccurate generalization by MacLean (1990), that he based on anecdotal accounts of crimes without having the benefit of specific histories and diagnoses (MacLean 1990: 569-570). Such anecdotal accounts give the impression that persons in general act without emotions during homicide or other criminal acts. Absence of emotion in such instances indicates partial seizures or certain cases of a major psychosis, such as schizophrenia.

By contrast, "compulsive social acts" (MacLean 1990), as well as impulsive acts, typically occur with very strong emotions, when honestly reported without trying to gain some legal advantage out of such a denial. Further, often surviving victims of either "compulsive" or "impulsive" acts have reported emotionally aroused verbal outbursts expressed by their attackers.

Even "cold-blooded" psychopaths, who selectively lack empathy, experience emotions related to self-gratification during their crimes, such as triumphant feelings of power and superiority as well as "remorse" for having been caught.

Two Opposite Homicidal Syndromes: "Syndrome E" vs. LPTR

A recently hypothesized Syndrome E (Fried 1997b) possesses special interest because its symptomatology presents virtually a mirror image of LPTR (see Pontius 2000 & Table 10.3 below).

Table 10.3. Comparison Between Two Hypothesized Syndromes: Syndrome E vs. Limbic Psychotic Trigger Reaction (LPTR)

SYNDROME E (I. Fried, *Lancet* 1997, 350: 1845–1848)	LPTR (A. A. Pontius)
1. Long lasting	c. 20 minutes duration
2. None	Suggestive of seizure-like phases (aura, ictus, post-ictus)
3. Obsessive ideation	Rumination
4. Group-shared ideology	Re. individual moderate stresses
5. Selected defenseless victims	Unselected victims, by chance, unwittingly providing trigger stimulus
6. Rapid desensitization	Reverse: deepening, persistent guilt feelings with voluntary surrender to police

Table 10.3, continued

7. Initial "elation" later   Reverse: consistently flat affect
diminished affective reactivity

8. None   Brief psychosis (hallucination and/
or delusions (e.g., of grandeur)

9. Autonomic hyperarousal   Same

10. General environmental dependence   Specific, individualized environmental or internal trigger stimuli

11. Group contagion   Reverse: loners, acting alone

Risk Factors

Male sex, ages 15-50   Social isolation (possibly more
prevalent in caucasians)
(Schzoid/avoidance type)

Early Prevention by Increased Awareness of Syndromes

"Isolation" of males "showing emerging   Providing ruminating social loners
obsessive ideology, hyperarousal,   with companions ("Big Brothers")
diminished affective reactivity, group   to prevent seizure kindling
dependent aggression"

Differential Diagnoses

Individuals acting violently   Other partial seizures and/or
psychoses (e.g., temporal lobe
epilepsy; schizophrenia, respectively); episodic dyscontrol, impulsive
behaviors, and other long-persistent
syndromes

Suggested Pathopsysiology
Deficient Interaction Between Prefrontal Cortices/Amygdala

a)   dorsolateral prefrontal cortex

Relatively unaffected: planning intact,   Reverse: briefly affected: no
problem-solving intact   planning, defective problem-
solving

b)   orbitofrontal cortex

Hyperactive: obsessive ideation   Not affected

Table 10.3, continued

Repetitive acts	Typically single acts

c)   medial prefrontal cortex

Suggested hyperactivity	Reverse: no motive and
Motivation and elation	Consistently flat affect

d)   ventromedial prefrontal cortex

Affected: generating emotions not	Possibly transiently affected
appropriate to the images conjured	
by certain "acts of stimulation/stimuli"	

e)   interaction prefrontal cortex/amygdala

Amygdala tonically inhibited by	Reverse: initially fleeting amygdala
Prefrontal activation	hyperactivation, with transient
	Secondary prefrontal inhibition

Syndrome E applies to ideologically motivated ethnic mass murderers, who act in groups, plan their acts on selected helpless victims, act with "elation" (at least initially), and show no signs of psychosis or seizure-like behavior.

Correspondingly, Syndrome E suggests the opposite neurophysiopathology to that of LPTR. In comparison to LPTR, Syndrome E hypothesizes a reversed sequence of dysfunctioning within the context of a shared fronto-limbic imbalance or "fronto-limbic fracture" (Fried 1997b). Thus, an initial limbic dysfunctioning is hypothesized in LPTR, while "Syndrome E" hypothesizes a certain initial prefrontal dysfunctioning. (Given the reciprocity between the two systems, this leads to a fronto-limbic imbalance in both syndromes.)

A certain difference between LPTR and Syndrome E stems from different limbic/amygdalar subfunctions: Syndrome E emphasizes emotional dysfunction associated with the amygdala, while LPTR focus on aggression implicating either amygdalar and/or hypothalamic dysfunctioning, both of which are inter-related

With regard to any localization hypotheses, Cummings (1992) warns that any putative neuropathology will not be able to pinpoint precise locations in the brain. Specifically, any strict localization is suspect and simplistic in partial seizures from the limbic system and temporal lobes, because the temporal lobes' tracts connect to all areas of the brain (Williamson et al. 1987). Thus, for example, Dam (1992: 122) pointed out that the symptomatology of TLE and related syndromes actually involves frontal lobe seizures in 10% of such cases.

Thus, much research is still obviously needed in LPTR; this is all the more indicated because LPTR patients' preserved consciousness enables their quite unique accounts of pathological experiences. Such experiential accounts may contribute to the study of the "binding problem," of central relevance in neuroscience (Fried 1997a: 120). Aspects of such binding among various behavioral components, resulting in a unified experience and a potential disruption of binding by a seizure, as possibly in LPTR, may benefit greatly from reports by patients with retained memory, as in LPTR.

DISCUSSION: ELABORATION OF MACLEAN'S EPISTEMICS BASED ON TEMPORAL LOBE EPILEPSY BY ADDING LIMBIC PSYCHOTIC TRIGGER REACTION

A. The Sense of Self and Consciousness

This section focuses on the uniquely human experience in relation to the sense of self, including originating acts through free will and being responsible for them. To this point, evaluation of experiences during the partial seizure of Temporal Lobe Epilepsy (TLE) has been hampered by at least partial amnesia associated with the events. Thus, fortuitously, the LPTR new subtype of partial seizures may help because consciousness is quantitatively preserved, as well as the memory for the acts committed during LPTR. The preserved consciousness is probably stems from the absence of temporal neocortical involvement in LPTR in contrast to TLE. Otherwise, both TLE and LPTR implicate archicortical and subcortical limbic structures within the temporal lobe.

Thus, the symptomatology of both TLE and LPTR share certain perplexing features that raise philosophical questions centered about the sense of self. During any seizure, even during the partial (i.e., nonconvulsive, "behavioral" seizures of TLE as well as of LPTR), "free will" is seriously impaired. Thus, without willing them, such patients may perform bizarre, out-of-character, unintended, purposeless acts. To the onlooker such acts seem to be willed acts. As long known in TLE, routine and subroutine behaviors occur during a seizure, that surprisingly seem appropriately executed, as summarized by MacLean (1990: 576). For example, TLE patients may travel around to unintended places, buying bus tickets and performing other appropriate acts for days. But this happens during a state of clouded consciousness because they recall nothing afterwards. Thus, not surprisingly, during the preserved consciousness of LPTR similar unwilled, unintended, auto-piloted but recalled acts can occur.

To rule out malingering, the skillful evaluator must consider various behavioral concomitants (see 16 inclusion and 13 exclusion criteria, Table 10.1) aside from LPTR patients' self-reports. Malingering by LPTR patients is ruled out by their exaggerated sense of responsibility for all their acts. They typically insist on being punished, mostly after having voluntarily reported their crimes. Such not self-serving traits, uncommon in the usual criminal, strongly support the validity of LPTR patients' self-accounts and render them valuable for philosophical conceptualization.

Thus, LPTR patients are able to share their strange involuntary acts and experiences quite fully and as completely, much as another kind of layperson shows cognizance of an event both as an experiencing subject as well as an objective observer. As laypersons, they may overlook certain subtle behavioral changes and thus are more likely to underreport than to over report possible additional symptoms in support of a seizure diagnosis.

All LPTR patients have shared with me their sense of the extreme discrepancy between their unintended and motiveless acts and their strong feeling of being responsible for them without having willed them. Such subjective experiences emerge from the philosophical construct of the sense of self, essentially anchored in the limbic system, as MacLean (1990) proposes, particularly because of the limbic connections with the thalamus. The thalamus mediates all exteroceptive input as well as the input from the viscera, mostly via the great visceral nerve, the vagus. (See Appendix on a new hypothesis about hippocampal irritation through recurrent vagal stimulation possibly through recurrent otorhinopharyngeal infections).

With regard to the sense of self, it is puzzling that all LPTR patients subjectively maintained to have been the actors of their bizarre acts, including homicide, for which they assume full responsibility and suffer tormenting guilt feelings. The LPTR patients could not conceive of having not been responsible even for the most obviously auto-piloted acts, more so as they knew and remembered having committed them. Even those men who appropriately described their acts as having occurred like a reflex felt responsible.

By analogy, a person does not feel guilty if he kicked someone by chance during a knee reflex test. Thus, do people draw a demarcation line with regard to their sense of self and their responsibility by distinguishing between a simple reflex motion compared to a rather complex series of acts occurring during a partial seizure of TLE or LPTR? When increasing the complexity of involuntarily elicited acts to the degree of electrical stimulation of brain (e.g., limbic) structures, at what point does the sense of free will blurr? This remains a basic question of human existence and predicament. Possibly during LPTR, despite preserved consciousness, some splitting of the sense of self might occur which selectively impairs the assessment of one's emotional and volitional involvement in acts.

B. Subjective/Objective Experience

The above discussed paradoxical sense of self during partial seizures, especially during LPTR with preserved consciousness, raises questions about subjective/objective aspects of experience. Such patients retain a sense of subjective responsibility for obviously purposeless, unwilled auto-piloted acts during partial seizures, presenting signs and symptoms that implicate brain events objectively beyond their control. What could be an essential distinction between between subjective and objective experiences?

This age-old question occupied philosophers, who insisted on a clear dichotomy between the subjective and the objective until Kant (1781) redefined this superficially strict dichotomy his last, but often neglected version of the categorical imperative, discussed elsewhere (Pontius 1971). MacLean (1990), with a philosophical background has hinted perceptively at certain innate bases of human experiences that occur within specific constraints, revealing the hallmarks of "hard-wired" determinants. Such a universally shared basis of human experiences that extends beyond subjective ones could therefore be characterized as constituting an objective given shared by all humans beyond their subjective individual modifications.

Although not directly and completely communicable in detail and by subjective elaboration, numerous indications imply that human experiences occur within specific patterns constituting built-in constraints of subjective experience. Such patterns merely vary or modify to some extent by subjective life experiences within the person's sociocultural milieu. Myths and rituals share certain basic themes worldwide, something not surprising, since all humans share the same brain structures, though utilized to different degrees as required for a cultural group's survival needs. Jung (1957) called such recurrent universal patterns of experiences, archetypical patterns of behavior and considered them to be analogous to animals' fixed action patterns known to ethologists, such as Tinbergen and Lorenz, also referred to by MacLean (1990) in such a context.

This theme of built-in objective constraints of subjectively experiencing constitutes yet another area for future exploration of the sense of self, to which, so far, some contributions have been made in the forensic studies of six schizophrenic men who committed bizarre acts. Two dismemberment murderers each tried to create an ancient god-like male-female combination out of his victim (Pontius 1975). Three firesetters attempted to unite extreme opposites by fire (Pontius 1972). One man repeatedly threatened in writing to assassinate three consecutive American presidents. His plans showed essential themes of ancient king-killing rituals, distributing parts of the king's body over the land to fertilize and rejuvenate it by propitiating a divine female creator (Pontius 1974). All these otherwise unexplainable acts had the hallmark of reenacting world-wide ancient myths or rituals, of which these uneducated men had been unaware. Thus, universally shared, archetypically behavior patterns can be expressed not only in dreams, but also in psychotics' action patterns, which would remain incomprehensible without such an assumption.

During the fleeting psychosis associated with LPTR, no such more cognitively determined archetypical themes have been reported so far. In congruence with LPTR's neuroethological context, there emerged primitive animalistic patterns of defensive or predatory killing (Pontius 1981-2002), primitive destructiveness by fire (Pontius 1999), or simplistic acquisitional acts in "bank robbery" (Pontius 2001).

Both the animalistic patterns of LPTR and the "archetypical" patterns in some schizophrenics imply a hard-wired organic basis for species-specific patterns of experience and behavior even in humans, thereby requiring a refined determination of the subjective and the objective aspects of experience and action.

CONCLUSION: NEUROETHOLOGICAL ASPECTS OF PARTIAL SEIZURES IN LIMBIC PSYCHOTIC TRIGGER REACTION (LPTR)

A concluding survey will now follow, underlining the neuroethological aspects of a clinical contribution to MacLean's creative conceptualization, presented as the proposed partial seizures of Limbic Psychotic Trigger Reaction (LPTR) (Pontius 1981–2002). Thereby human experience is added to the ethological background that we share with all mammals.

A) Reciprocal Relation Between the Old Limbic and the New Frontal Lobe Systems:

The validity of the coexistence of evolutionarily old and new parts and functions in humans' "triune brain" becomes most directly manifest in the specific, primarily neuroethological aspects of limbic seizures. Such factors are most apparent in that subtype of partial seizures proposed as Limbic Psychotic Trigger Reaction (LPTR) (Pontius 1981–2002) during which the patients do not lose consciousness, defined in quantitative terms and operationally as responsiveness to simple commands and as the ability to perform willful acts. In all these aspects of consciousness, LPTR patients are not impaired, and they do lay down memories of their acts, which they recall, talking about them with deep distress.

On a more comprehensive level of defining consciousness, however, there is an essential qualitative difference during LPTR as compared with the LPTR patients' usual behavior. Thus, LPTR patients cannot perform activities (except possibly during their aura; see Pontius, in press) that are not only thoughtfully planned, but also willed and with emotional concomitants. Instead, they act with flat affect, unthinking and without volition like automatons, "autopiloted" or "like a reflex," as some patients put it.

Based on such symptomatology characteristic of seizures, it seems reasonable to deduce that a limbic hyperactivation during LPTR seizures temporarily overwhelms the evolutionarily younger prefrontal lobe system, since both systems are reciprocally interrelated (Nauta 1971; Weinberger 1984).

The human prefrontal lobe system essentially mediates and integrates various aspects of socialized behavior. Thus, socially destructive consequences can ensue even if there is a transient disturbance of the normal fronto-limbic balance. Such behavioral consequences can range from socially inappropriate, self-injurious acts (as astutely portrayed by Proust's M. Swann, who proposed marriage to a "despised courtesan" upon hearing a specific piece of music) (Pontius 1993b); to bizarre, unthinking, primitive robbing of a bank by a devout monk with sudden delusions of grandeur (Pontius 2001); to senseless firesetting by three juveniles upon encounter with fire-related stimuli (Pontius 1999). The wide range of such strangely out-of-character acts, all of which also occurred with fleeting autonomic activation and psychosis, also include unplanned, motiveless, reflex-like homicidal acts in 17 social loners (Pontius 1981–2002) reminiscent of animals' defensive or predatory patterns of killing.

B) Suggested Etiological Factors:

1. Chronic Deprivation of Limbically Mediated Basic Needs and Functions Necessary for Mature Socialization.

        a.   Social Bonding: All mammals need social contact. If experimentally isolated, primates show behavioral changes similar to those occurring in socially isolated humans (Kling 1986), as elaborated by Gruter and Masters (1986).

b. Normal Forgetting, Habituation: Douglas & Pribram (1966) observed that hippocampectomized monkeys lost habituation to repetitive stimuli, reacting to them, as if they were new. These authors emphasized that forgetting is part of normal memory.

In human social loners, normal forgetting is hampered by their lack of sharing and comparing their hurts with others. Instead, they perhaps ruminate on their hurts until their minds endow everyday common stresses with exaggerated emotional validation or meaning that may implicate amygdalar involvement. After such intermittently experienced subthreshold stresses, a specific lack of habituation can occur, called reverse habituation. Intermittent exposures (such as by memory rumination) prevents habituation for which continued stimulation is required and thus sets the stage for seizure kindling (Goddard 1967). Of all brain systems, the limbic system is most susceptible to kindling particularly its amygdala and hippocampus (Goddard & McIntyre 1986). In primates, kindling typically elicits behavioral seizures (Wada 1978) in contrast to the convulsive ones kindled in lower mammals. Additionally, some human cases of inadvertent kindling have been reported (Heath et al., 1957; Sramka et al. 1984).

c. Normal Remembering has Context-Relevance vs. Memory Priming by a Cue. In LPTR an individualized trigger stimulus (suddenly reviving such patients' memories of past hurts but without context-relevance) resembles priming by a cue in animals (Eiserer & Hoffman 1983).

2. Disturbance of Normal Balance between Reciprocally Related Brain Systems

a. An imbalance between prefrontal and limbic systems may be indicated by the symptomatology of LPTR, as implied by seizure-related limbic hyperactivation associated with relatively secondarily too weak prefrontal controls.

b. Amygdalar-hippocampal imbalance. Both these limbic structures, hippocampus and amygdala, reciprocally interrelate, as experimentally shown with cats (Adamec 1987: 448–450). Thus, an initial overactivation of either one may elicit a temporary imbalance between them, thereby contributing to a functional fragility of certain limbic functions (possibly facilitating kindling?).

aa) Amygdalar stimulation elicits aggression especially in dominant animals, but has a reverse effect on submissive ones. A human case of electrically elicited amygdala aggression has also been reported (Mark & Ervin 1970). In many respects, LPTR aggression resembles "sham rage" (Kaada 1967) which can be elicited by hypothalamus stimulation. Decorticate cats with sham rage demonstrate posture and certain behavior indistinguishable from emotionally elicited rage, as elaborated elsewhere (Pontius 2001a).

bb) "Experiential Phenomena"—reportable by humans only. A striking analogy exists between amygdalar hyperactivation from memory revival of hurts during the aural phase of LPTR and similar effects elicited by direct electrical amygdalar stimulation of electrode implants in presurgery patients (Gloor et al. 1982). Further, electrical stimulation of amygdalar implants in presurgery patients elicited "experiential phenomena" (Gloor et al. 1982) strikingly similar to those of LPTR (Pontius 1997, Table 14, p.162). Gloor et al.'s reports are congruent with those by Wieser (1983), Fried (1997b), and Palmini & Gloor (1992), all of which elicited "experiential phenomena" through direct electrical stimulation in various brain areas that was similar to auras spontaneously experienced during partial seizures of the temporal lobes. These three reports thereby supported the ability to frequently localize (though not to lateralize) the source of seizures based on the kind of patients' auras.

cc) A possible hippocampal overstimulation might occur through recurrent vagal stimulation in recurrent nasopharyngeal infections (see Appendix).

APPENDIX

Hypothesis about potential limbic irritation by recurrent vagal stimulation in recurrent infections of the oro-nasopharynx (including sinuses).
4 cases of partial seizures (3 with homicide in Limbic Psychotic Trigger Reaction (LPTR) and 1 case with episodic exhibitionism in Temporal Lobe Epilepsy (TLE)

An understanding of potential etiological factors in partial seizures can further benefit from increased specification. In general, space-occupying and/or irritating lesions of limbic structures, particularly in the hippocampus are implicated. Herein a new kind of potential irritative impact on certain limbic structures through vagal stimulation is hypothesized. The proposed testable working hypothesis links vagal limbic (especially hippocampal) stimulation with certain cases of partial seizures based on MRI findings of infections of sinuses (2 cases of LPTR and 1 case of TLE), or of nasal mucosa (1 case of LPTR). In addition, 1 case of LPTR, who did not get a MRI scan, had a history of recurrent severe aphtous stomatitis).

This hypothesis was inspired by Paul MacLean's triune brain (1990: 514) experimentally demonstrating that "only vagal stimuli were effective in eliciting complete excitation of hippocampal units." Furthermore, in testing the thalamus (closely interconnected with limbic structures), he found that 27% of the units tested in the medial dorsal nucleus of the thalamus were responsive to vagal volleys. Other limbic structures, too, respond to vagal stimulustion: In animal experimentation with the awake encéphale isolé preparation (reported by Dell & Olson, 1951 as cited by MacLean, 1990: 468) showed that vagal shock evoked a slow-wave response in the amygdala and within the buried cortex within the anterior rhinal sulcus.

It is of note, that the hippocampus indirectly influences the amygdala, as both structures are interconnected and these two limbic structures are also the most susceptible to seizure kindling of all brain structures tested by Goddard & McIntyre (1986).

Thus, it appears reasonable to speculate that spontaneous recurrent mild vagal stimulation can occur in association with recurrent infections in areas with vagal afferents, such as those of the naso-pharynx areas that happened to appear on brain MRI scans, and that such vagal stimulation may have asserted a certain irritative impact on limbic structures, particularly on the hippocampus (Pontius & LeMay, in press).

Thus, MacLean's experimental findings (1990: 497, 514, 531, 562; 1992 & 25 fig. 24; reinforced by personal communication 7/8/1999) have focused attention on the important role of the hippocampus and its relevance in partial seizures: As he emphasized, due to its position, the hippocampus enables the integration of information from two systems, the exteroceptive one (from all sensory modalities) as well as interoceptive system (especially from the vagus, "the great visceral nerve", afferents of which also subserve the naso-pharynx).

Thus, by way of such integration of the extero- and intero-ceptive systems, the hippocampus plays a central role specifically with respect to those functions known to be impaired in partial seizures: The hippocampus influences neurovegetative, somato-visceral, and emotional functions "in, regard to mechanisms underlying a feeling of individuality, that, in turn, is requisite for certain aspects of memorization," as MacLean (1990: 497–498) put it.

MacLean's conclusion appears to be congruent with the even more comprehensive one offered by Trimble, Mendez & Cummings (1997, p.127 in *The Neuropsychiatry of Limbic and Subcortical Disorders*, S. Salloway, P. Malloy, J. Cummings, Eds.). They stated that "the hippocampus may be a nodal area for delusions given its role in memory, in receiving emotional valencing from the amygdala, and in facilitating, perceptual associations."

In the context of delusional experiences, it may also be of note that recent imaging studies of the brain in presurgery patients by Fried (1997: 118; ibid.book) showed that auras and various psychotic symptoms and experiential phenomena known to occur in partial seizures could also be elicited by direct electrical brain stimulation within the temporal lobe. A comprehensive study by Palmini & Gloor (1992) assigned localizing, though not lateralizing, significance to most types of auras when elicited by careful history taking. With respect to an implicated role of extero- and/or intero-ceptive experiences in partial seizures, their influences can be represented in the phenomenology of aural delusions in TLE (MacLean 1990: 496).

Further, specifically in LPTR, any one of both kinds of extero- or interoceptive experiences (and their typical input into the hippocampus) might also be represented by the phenomenology of the various individualized stimuli. Such stimuli are viewed as triggering seizure kindling, since those stimuli appear to represent and constitute the final stimuli in a preceeding series of a similar kind, and thereby ultimately kindling the limbic seizure of LPTR.

Alternatively, it could be hypothesized that the auras and experiential phenomena in LPTR may already represent ictal events, or at least merge imperceptibly into ictal events whereby a proposed kindling mechanism would not be necessary. Rather, recurrent sinusitis or other nasopharyngeal infections could just constitute a sufficiently irritating hippocampal stimulation to elicit a seizure.

With respect to a more comprehensive role of the ventromedial temporal lobe (which includes hippocampus and amygdala), recent research by Arnold (1997) and van Hoesen (1997: 19–20, 27–28) has implicated this area in a variety of psychiatric disorders (including schizophrenia) and in neurological disorders, particularly those following mechanical injuries to the particularly vulnerable area around the tentorium cerebelli. (Here it may also be of note that the MRI of LPTR case 17 showed that "the subarachnoid spaces in the posterior fossa and supratentorial compartments are dilated").

MRI findings of sinus or nasal infections in 3 cases of LPTR:
It is of note that only for the following six most recent unselected felony cases examined by me on court orders had MRI scans become potentially available. Thus, the following findings appear to be remarkable.

Case #13, homicides during LPTR, age 32, whose family declined to pay for an MRI, had, however, recurrent severe, very painful aphtous stomatitis, requiring bed rest for 4 days at a time with temperature up to F 104.

Case #14, homicides during LPTR, age 43: On MRI the nasal cavity shows mucosal thickening left more than right.

Case #15, age 40, homicide during LPTR. MRI showed mild dilation of the ventricles and prominence of the sulci, more than would be expected for his age. Impression "Mild cortical atrophy and a large retention cyst in both maxillary sinuses." No focal right temporal lobe pathology.

Case #16. age 36, homicide during LPTR: MRI within normal limits.

Case #17, age 28, homicide during LPTR c. 10 minutes after an externally interrupted homicide attempt at another person was aborted by a witness. His MRI showed "atrophy involving the posterior fossa and supratentorial portions of the brain. Note is made of extensive inflammatory changes involving both maxillary and the right ethmoid sinuses."

One differential case of partial seizures turned out not to be LPTR but TLE (of which only this one case of mine had an MRI). This 34-year-old man had episodic exhibitionism without physical contact. His MRI showed "Chiari malformation (extension of the cerebellar tonsils below foramen magnum to the level of bilateral frontal ethmoid of C 1 and left maxillary sinusitis, mucosal thickening and inflammation."

In summary, three out of the four LPTR cases who had MRI scans showed signs of inflammation in the nasal-pharyngeal area (incl. sinus), as did the one TLE patient. In addition, one LPTR case who had no MRI had recurrent severe aphtous stomatitis, leaving only one out of six partial seizure patients without problems in the naso-pharyngeal area. These findings may alert the clinician to a potential link between partial seizures and vagal overstimulation. Such may also occur in other areas of the body. It just happens that MRI scans of the brain also depict the areas here presented.

In addition, the findings on MRI or on other scans need to be supplemented by extensive detailed history taking, as emphasized by Fenwick (1993: 569), who stated that MRI or other "objective tests" being reported as "within normal limits" may be highly significant when combined with clinical and neuropsychometric findings which implicate temperolimbic damage. Thus "normal" findings on "objective tests" do not exclude the possibility of fleeting partial seizures.

REFERENCES

Adamec, R.E. 1987. "Commentary on A. A. Pontius' 'Psychotic trigger reaction': Neuropsychiatric and neurobiological (limbic?) aspects of homicide, reflecting on normal action." *Integrative Psychiatry*, 5, 130–134.

Arnold, S.E. 1997. "The medial temporal lobe in schizophrenia." In S. Salloway, P. Malloy, & J. L. Cummings (eds): *The Neuropsychiatry of Limbic and Subcortical Disorders*, Washington DC: American Psychiatric Press, pp.155–166.

Broca P. 1878. "Anatomie comparee des circonvolutions cerebrales: le grand lobe limbique et la scissure limbique dans la serie des mammifieres." *Revue Anthropologique* Ser 21: 384–498

Cummings, J. L. 1993. "Frontal-subcortical circuits and human behavior." *Archives of Neurology*, 50: 873–880.

Dam, M. 1992. "Localization related to epileptic syndromes. " In M.R. Trimble & T.G. Bolwig (eds.): *The Temporal Lobes and the Limbic System*, Petersfield UK: Wrightson Biomedical Publishing, pp.115–127.

Douglas, R. J. & Pribram, K. H. 1966. "Learning and limbic lesions." *Neuropsychologia,* 4: 197–214.

Eiserer, L. A. & Hoffman, A. A. 1983. "Priming of ducklings' response by presenting an imprinting stimulus*." Journal of. Comparative Physiology*, 82: 345–350.

Fenwick, J. (1993) in *British Journal of Psychiatry*, 163: 565–573)

Fried, I. 1997a. "Auras and experiential responses arising in the temporal lobe." In S. Salloway, P. Malloy, & J. L. Cummings (eds*): The Neuropsychiatry of Limbic and Subcortical Disorders,* Washington DC: Am. Psychiatric Press, pp.113–122 (a).

Fried, I. 1997b. "Syndrome E". *Lancet*, 350: 1845–1848 (b).

Geschwind, N. 1984*. Clinician scientists,* 224: 243.

Gloor, P., Olivier, A., Quesney, L .F., Andermann, F., & Horowitz, S. 1982. "The role of the limbic system in experiential phenomena of temporal lobe epilepsy." *Annals Neurology*, 12: 129–142.

Goddard, C. V. 1967. "Development of epileptic seizures through brain stimulation at low intensity." *Nature,* 214: 1020–1021.

Goddard, C. V. & McIntyre, D. C. 1986. "Some properties of a lasting epileptogenic trace kindled by repeated electrical stimulation of the amygdala in mammals. In B. K. Doane, K. E. Livingston(Eds) *The Limbic System: Functional Organization and Clinical Disorders,* New York: Raven, pp. 95–105.

Gram L. 1990. "Epileptic seizures and syndromes." *Lancet,* 336: 161–163.

Gruter, M., & Masters, R. D, (Eds.) 1986. *Ostracism. A Social and Biological Phenomenon.* NY: Elsevier.

Hanson, N. R. 1965. *Patterns of discovery.* Cambridge: Cambridge University Press.

Hayek, F. A. 1964. "The theory of complex phenomena." In M. Bunge (ed): *The Critical Approach to Science and Philosophy.* London: Free Press of Glencoe, Collier & Macmillan: pp. 332–349

Heath, R. G., Monroe, R. R., & Mickle, W. 1957. "Stimulation of the amygdaloid nucleus in a schizophrenic patient." *American Journal of Psychiatry,* 111: 862–863.

Jung, C. G. 1977. "The psychology of dementia praecox." In C. G. Jung: *Collective Psychiatric Studies.* Princeton: Princeton University Press.

Kaada, B. R. 1972. Brain mechanims related to aggressive behavior. In C. Clements & D. Lindsley (eds.). Aggression and Defense: Neural Mechanisms and Social Patterns. Berkeley, CA: University of California Press.

Kant I. 1771. *Die Metaphysik der Sitten.* Berlin: Akademie Ausgabe.

Koob, G. F. & Nestler, E. J. 1997. "The neurobiology of drug addiction." In S. Salloway, P. Maloy, & J. L. Cummings (eds): *The Neuropsychiatry of Limbic and Subcortical Disorders.* Washington, DC: American Psychiatric Press, pp.179–194.

Kuhn, T.S. 1977. *The Essential Tension; Selected Studies in Scientific Tradition and Change.* Chicago: University of Chicago Press.

MacLean, P. D. 1952. "Some psychiatric implications of physiological studies on the frontotemporal portion of the limbic system (visceral brain*). Electroencephalography, Clinical Neurophysiology,* 4: 407–418.

MacLean, P. D. 1990. *The Triune Brain in Evolution.* NY: Plenum Press.

MacLean, P. D. 1992. "The limbic system concept." In M. R. Trimble & T. G. Bolwig (eds): *The Temporal Lobes and the Limbic System,* Petersfield, UK: Wrightson Biomedical Publishing, 1992, pp. 1–13

Mark, V. H. & Ervin, F. P. 1970. *Violence and the Brain.* NY: Harper & Row.

Mayberg, H. S. 1997. "Limbic-cortical dysregulation: A proposed model of depression." In S. Salloway, P. Malloy, & J. L. Cummings (eds): *The Neuropsychiatry of Limbic & Subcortical Disorders.* Washington DC: American Psychiatric Press, pp.167–178.

Mega, M. S., Cummings, J. L., Salloway, S., & Malloy, P. 1997. "The limbic system: An anatomic, phylogenetic, and clinical perspective." In S. Salloway, P. Malloy, & J.L. Cummings (Eds*): The Neuropsychiatry of Limbic and Subcortical Disorders.* Washington DC: American Psychiatric Press, pp. 3–18.

Meldrum, B. S. 1990. "Anatomy, physiology, and Pathology of epilepsy." *Lancet,* 336: 228–231.

Nauta, W. 1971. "The problem of.the frontal lobes-a reinterpretation*." Journal of Psychiatric Research,* 8: 167–187.

Palmini, A. & Gloor, P. 1992. "The localizing value of auras in partial seizures: a prospective and retrospective study." *Neurology,* 42: 801–808.

Papez, J. W. 1937 "A proposed mechanism of emotion." *Archives Neurology & Psychiatry,* 38: 725–733.

Pontius, A. A. 1971. "The subject-object relationship in concepts by Kant and Jung. *Kant Studien,* 62: 121–125.

Pontius, A.A. 1972. "Play, mediator of opposites - its concretization during arson trans.). *Zeitschrift fuer Analytische Psychologie & Ihre Grenzgebiete,* 3: 219–232.

Pontius, A.A. 1974a. "Threats to assassinate the king-president while propitiating mother: Some aspect of dangerousness." *Journal of Analytical Psychology,* 19: 38–53.

Pontius, A.A. 1974b. "Dismemberment murder as an unconscious ritual (trans.)." *Analytische Psychologje,* 5: 136–148.

Pontius, A.A. 1981. "Stimuli triggering violence in psychosis." *Journal of Forensic Sciences*, 26: 123–128.

Pontius, A.A. 1987. "Psychotic trigger reaction: Neuro-psychiatric and neurobiolobical (limbic?) aspects of homicide, reflecting on normal action." *Integrative Psychiatry*, 5: 116–139.

Pontius, A.A. 1993a. "Neuroethological aspects of certain limbic seizure-like dysfunctions: Exemplified by limbic psychotic trigger reaction (motiveless homicide with intact memory)." *Integrative Psychiatry*, 9: 151–167.

Pontius, A.A. 1993b. "Overwhelming remembrance of things past: Proust portrays limbic kindling by external stimulus-Literary genius can presage neurobiological patterns of puzzling behavior." *Perceptual & Motor Skills*, 73: 613–621.

Pontius, A.A. 1995. "Retroductive reasoning in a proposed subtype of partial seizures, evoked by limbic 'kindling'." *Psychological Reports*, 76: 55–62.

Pontius, A.A. 1996 "Forensic significance of the Limbic Psychotic Trigger Reaction." *Bulletin of the American Academy of Psychiatry and the Law*, 24: 125–134.

Pontius, A.A. 1997. "Homicide linked to moderate repetitive stresses kindling limbic seizures in 14 cases of Limbic Psychotic Trigger Reaction." *Aggression & Violent Behavior*, 2: 125–141.

Pontius, A.A. 1999a. "Motiveless firesetting: Implicating partial limbic seizure kindling by revived memories of fires in 'Limbic Psychotic Trigger Reaction.'" *Perceptual & Motor Skills*, 88: 970–982.

Pontius. A.A. 1999b. "Homicidal acts in Fried's 'Syndrome E' of ethnic mass murderers opposite to those of 'Limbic Psychotic Trigger Reaction': Neurobiological polar extremes suggest level of voluntariness in Impulse Control Disorders." *Talk, Annual Meeting of the American Academy of Psychiatry and the Law*.

Pontius, A.A. 2000. "Comparison between two opposite homicidal syndromes (Syndrome E vs. Limbic Psychotic Trigger Reaction)." *Aggression & Violent Behavior*, 5: 423–427.

Pontius, A.A. 2001. "Two bank robbers with 'antisocial' and 'schizoidavoidant' personality disorders, comorbid with partial seizures: Temporal lobe epilepsy and Limbic Psychotic Trigger Reaction, respectively." *Journal of Developmental & Physical Disabilities*,13: 191–197.

Pontius, A.A. 2002. Neurological aspects of violence, particularly in youths. In R. Corrado & R. Roesch (Eds.) *Proceedings NATO Advanced Workshop "Multi-Problem Violent Youth.* Crakow, Poland.

Pontius, A.A. (in press). A serial murderer learns to regain volition by recognizing the aura of his partial seizures of "Limbic psychotic trigger reaction." *Clinical Case Studies.*

Pontius, A.A. & LeMay, M.J. (in press). Aggression in temporal lobe epilepsy and "limbic psychotic trigger reaction" implicating vagus kindling of hippocampus/ amygdala in sinus problems on MRIs. *Aggression & Violent Behavior.*

Raine A., Meloy, J. R., Bihrle, S. 1998. "Reduced prefrontal and increased subcortical brain functioning assessed using PET in predatory and affective murderers."*Behavioral Sciences & Law*, 16: 319–332.

Reich, D.S., Mechler, F., Victor, J. 2001. Independent and redundant information in nearby cortical neurons. Science, 224. 2566–2568.

Ridley, R.M. & Baker, R.F. 1983. "Is there a relationship between social isolation, cognitive inflexibility, and behavioral stereotype? An analysis of the effects of amphetamine in the marmoset." In K. A. Miczek (ed): *Primate Models of Neuropsychiatric Disorders.* London: Alan R. Liss.

Salloway, S. 1997. "Paroxysmal limbic disorders in neuropsychiatry." In S. Salloway, P. Malloy, J. F. Cummings (Eds): The *Neuropsychiatry of Limbic and Subcortical Disorders.* Washington DC: American Psychiatric Press, pp.95–112.

Smythies, J.R. 1992. "Brain and consciousness." In M.R. Trimble & T.G. Bolwig (eds): *The Temporal Lobes and the Limbic System.* Petersfield UK: Wrightson Biomedical Publishing. pp. 267–276.

Sramka, M., Sedlak, P., & Nadvornik, P. 1984. "Observation of kindling phenomenonin treatment of pain by stimulation in thalamus." In W.H. Sweet, S. Abrador & J. Martin-Rodriguez (Eds): *Neurosurgical Treatment in Psychiatry.* NY: Elsevier, pp. 651–654.

Trimble, J. R. 1992. "The Gastaud-Geschwind syndrome. In M.R. Trimble & T.G. Bolwig (eds.): *The Temporal Lobes and the Limbic System.* Petersfield UK: Wrightson Biomedical Publishing. p.129.

Trimble, M.R. & Bolwig, T.G. 1992. *The Temporal Lobes and the Limbic System.* Petersfield UK: Wrightson Biomedical Publishing.

Trimble, M.R., Mendez, M.F., Cummings, J.L. 1997. "Neuropsychiatric symptoms from the temperolimbic lobes." In S. Salloway, P. Malloy, J.L. Cummings (eds): *The Neuropsychiatry of Limbic and Subcortical Disorders.* Washington DC: American Psychiatric Press, pp. 123–132.

Van Hoesen, G.W. 1997. "Ventromedial temporal lobe anatomy, with comments on Alzheimer's disease and temporal injury." In S. Salloway, P. Malloy, J.L. Cummings (eds): *The Neuropsychiatry of Limbic and Subcortical Disorders.* Washington DC: American Psychiatric Press, pp. 19–30.

Wada, J. A. 1978. "The clinical relevance of kindling: Species, brain sites and seizure susceptibility." In K. E. Livingston & O. Hornykiewicz (eds*): Limbic Mechanisms: Continuing Evolution of the Limbic System Concept.* NY: Plenum, pp. 369–388.

Weinberger, D.R. 1984. "Computed tomography (CT) findings in schizophrenia: Speculation on the meaning of it all." *Journal of Psychiatric Research,* 18: 477–490.

Weiser, H. G. 1983. Depth-recorded limbic seizures and psychopathology. *Neuroscience and Behavior Review.* 7: 427–440.

Williamson, P.D.; Wieser, H.G.; Delgado-Escueta, A.V. 1987. "Clinical characteristics of partial seizures." In J. Engel (ed.) *Surgical Treatment of the Epilepsies,* NY: Raven Press, pp. 101–120.

Yakovlev, P. I. 1948. "Motility, behavior, and the brain." *Journal of Nervous & Mental Disease,* 107: 313–335.

11

NEURAL AND FUNCTIONAL ASPECTS OF PRIDE AND SHAME

Glenn E. Weisfeld

INTRODUCTION

In this chapter an ethological perspective will be applied to the role of the frontal lobes in the emotion of pride and shame. First the neural mediation of emotion in general will be described using fear as an example. Then the mediation of dominance motivation will be traced; many ethologists believe that dominance behavior underlies pride and shame in humans. Next the mediation of complex social behavior by the prefrontal cortex will be addressed. Last, a modification of the emotion-reason dichotomy will be proposed in light of the foregoing discussion.

THE PRIMACY OF EMOTION

The study of comparative neuroanatomy makes clear that motivated behaviors evolved earlier than complex cognitive capacities. The brain stem, basal ganglia, and limbic system antedated expansion of the neocortex, as MacLean (1990) has tirelessly emphasized.

This phylogenetic view is compatible with a functional, ethological perspective. Natural selection acts most directly on behavioral acts. Animals must behave in adaptive ways first and foremost. The earliest protozoan must have exhibited endogenous behavior, a basic property of animals. Action must have evolved first, and only later been guided by sensory stimuli, perception, learning, and cognition. Consistent with the biogenetic law, sensation and especially cognition develop somewhat behind motoric capacities. And basic emotions, such as pride and shame, develop before higher cognitive abilities and therefore do not depend on them (Weisfeld 1997a).

NEURAL MEDIATION OF EMOTION

In the last few years the phylogenetic approach to the study of behavior has been advanced dramatically by Joseph LeDoux and by Jaak Panksepp. These investigators have adopted an ethological approach to the study of the brain. Ethologists investigate the basic behaviors that have evolved in a given species. An ethological approach to neuroanatomy starts with one of these basic, species-wide behaviors and seeks to analyze its neural mediation. This is opposite to the experimental and clinical approach of starting with a particular brain structure and trying to determine its behavioral effects.

One advantage of complementing the experimental and clinical approaches with the ethological approach is that the latter emphasizes a complete, balanced view of the animal's entire set of evolved behaviors, its ethogram. Ethology, with its focus on behavior as it occurs in natural or semi-natural habitats rather than in laboratory or clinical settings, draws attention to the essential adaptive behaviors of the organism. By contrast, the clinical and experimental views of the organism's behavior are liable to be fragmented and artificial, comprising isolated neural mechanisms such as the function of the cranial nerves and the perception of visual stimuli. Ethology focuses on emotions, or motives, because these generally correspond with the behavioral elements of an animal's ethogram—feeding, mating, defensive aggression, flight, and so on.

Taking this functional, ethological approach, LeDoux (1996) traced the neural pathway for the rat's response to fear stimuli.

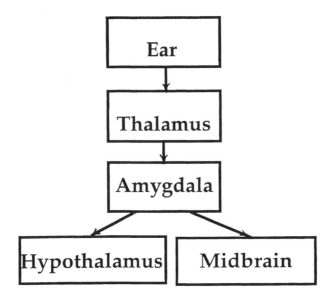

Figure 11.1. Limbic Fear Pathway

In the simplest, most archaic form, a mammal typically responds to species-specific signs of danger, such as a snake, by a defensive act, such as freezing. Neural impulses travel from sensory receptors to the thalamus to the central nucleus of the amygdala and midbrain (Figure 11.1). This same general route mediates a conditioned fear response, say, to a tone that has been repeatedly paired with electric shock.

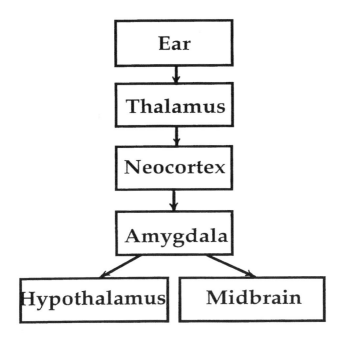

Figure 11.2. Neocortical Fear Pathway

This conditioned fear response occurs even in the absence of the neocortex. The neocortex merely refines responsiveness to stimuli, so that in its absence the rat also freezes in reaction to tones that differ from the warning one (Figure 11.2). In other words, with inadequate specification of the stimulus, the organism errs on the side of caution and freezes. The neocortex merely refines the emotional response, but is not essential for it. Thus these neural mechanisms are consistent with a phylogenetic analysis of the evolution and importance of the limbic system compared with the neocortex. Analogously, the primary somatosensory cortex refines localization of pain stimuli, which are less precisely localized by subcortical structures.

Additional components of the emotion of fear are evoked through the amygdala also. The hypothalamus directs the sympathetic division to orchestrate appropriate adjustments of the viscera, and directs the pituitary to do the same for the endocrine system. The freezing response itself, and associated emotional expressions (or displays), are coordinated by the midbrain, which is a primitive, brain stem structure that mediates various fixed action patterns (Panksepp 1998). The affect of fear seems to register in the amygdala, and possibly also the hypothalamus and limbic midbrain; the pleasure and pain centers of the brain are confined to limbic structures. Contextual cues associated with fear (i.e., the subject's surroundings when traumatized), are remembered by the hippocampus. Thus the characteristic facets of an emotion—eliciting stimuli, affect, overt behavior, emotional expressions, and visceral and hormonal adjustments—are all accounted for by LeDoux's model.

This system seems to be representative of other mammalian emotional pathways too, involving various senses in addition to audition. Emotions in general are elicited by sensory input passing through the thalamus to the amygdala, hippocampus, and other limbic structures and on to the hypothalamus and midbrain.[1] Responsiveness likewise is modified via a neocortical detour between the thalamus and the limbic system. Thus, the limbic system and especially the amygdala seem to have evolved to modify brain stem mechanisms of motivated behaviors. The origins of this system are indicated by the fact that the oldest part of the amygdala, the medial nucleus, receives inputs from the vomeronasal organ, which responds to pheromones bearing social information. The amygdala appears to be especially devoted to social and alimentary emotions. Patients with amygdaloid seizures report anger, guilt, sadness, loneliness, disgust, and (in women only) erotic sensations (Gloor 1997).

ROLE OF THE AMYGDALA IN DOMINANCE BEHAVIOR

It has been proposed by human ethologists such as Freedman (1967), Barkow (1975), Mazur (1983), Savin-Williams (1977), and of course by Darwin (1872) that the emotion of pride and shame in humans evolved from dominance and subordination behavior in other species. This hypothesis is supported by evidence of behavioral, expressional, and hormonal parallels between dominance/submission in simians and pride/shame in humans (reviewed by Weisfeld 1980, 1994, 1997a). Do neuroscience data also support this interpretation? What is known of the neural mediation of dominance/submission behavior in simians and of pride/shame in humans?

Panksepp (1998) reviewed the neural pathways of various mammalian emotions. The route for inter-male, or dominance, aggression passes from sensory receptors to the thalamus to the medial amygdala to the preoptic-anterior hypothalamic area to the periaqueductal grey of the midbrain (Figure 11.3). The neurons in this amygdala-to-limbic midbrain pathway are rich in testosterone receptors, consistent with the strong sex difference in dominance aggression (Ellis 1986). This is the same general route taken by fear, but it constitutes a separate pathway. Likewise, the route for angry aggression (or rage) is parallel to, but distinct from, these other two.

The amygdala seems to direct dominance and submission behavior. Amygdalar stimulation typically enhances aggressive behavior in dominant animals and submissive behavior in subordinates (Huntingford & Turner 1987).

Bilateral amygdalar lesions in lizards, hamsters, dogs, and monkeys often result in a decline in dominance aggression and/or a fall in rank (Kling & Mass 1974; Kling & Brothers 1992). In one representative study, two macaques with amygdalar lesions failed to form a dominance relationship (Kling 1972).

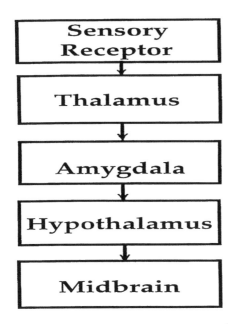

Figure 11.3. Dominance Pathway

The amygdala is also involved in other functions essential for participation in dominance hierarchies. These include *individual recognition*; some amygdalar neurons fire in response to photographs of particular individuals in cats (Kling & Brothers 1992). Maintenance of a dominance hierarchy necessitates keeping track of individuals' ranks.

Another such function is *sending emotional expressions* (e.g., threat and submission displays). Electrical stimulation of the amygdala in monkeys and humans can elicit various vocal and facial expressions, including those of threat (Kling & Brothers 1992). In psychomotor epilepsy, patients sometimes exhibit threat displays such as hissing, spitting, stamping, teeth gritting, and fist clenching (MacLean 1990). Amygdalar lesions can reduce dominance and submission displays in lizards (Kling & Brothers 1992) and simians (Kling & Mass 1974), thus showing the role of this structure as well as of the basal ganglia in these displays (MacLean 1990). Facial displays in primates seem to arise in the amygdala and other limbic structures and to be organized in the midbrain and executed by brain stem nuclei via the cranial nerves (Panksepp 1998).

In addition, the amygdala seems to participate in *receiving facial and vocal expressions*. Lesions can reduce monkeys' (Kling & Mass 1974) perception of threat signals and people's perception of the emotional meaning of tone of voice. Humans whose amygdalas were stimulated would sometimes report experiencing mnemonic fragments of threat displays, accompanied by negative affect (Kling & Brothers 1992).

Lastly, a wide range of *affects* seem to be mediated by the amygdala, especially fear, which is exhibited by subordinate animals particularly (Gloor 1992). Psychomotor epilepsy, which involves the amygdala and other temporal lobe structures, can result in self-reports of various other affects, as mentioned above, including guilt, shame, and "troubled conscience" (MacLean 1990; Gloor 1992). Thus the amygdala, implicated in dominance behavior, appears to be involved in the emotion of pride/shame. This emotion, and feelings of dominance and subordination in other primates, seem to be related to brain serotonin levels; serotonin receptors abound in the amygdala. High serotonin levels characterize competitively successful monkeys and men, and selective serotonin re-uptake inhibitors (e.g., fluoxetine) counteract clinical depression. Serotonin levels rise in male vervet monkeys in response not only to a rise in rank but also to receiving a submission display or to copulation (Masters & McGuire 1994). On the other hand, serotonin levels fall when the male observes another male copulating, as though the subject has been humbled. Similarly, plasma testosterone level, which also acts on amygdalar receptors and is associated with self-reported euphoria, rises in response to a monkey's or man's triumph (Mazur & Booth 1998).

Thus, the amygdala appears to participate in various behavioral and affective functions of direct relevance to dominance behavior.

ROLE OF THE ORBITOFRONTAL CORTEX IN DOMINANCE: BEHAVIOR IN PRIMATES

But the structure that is most specifically associated with dominance behavior is the orbitofrontal cortex (OFC), especially its posterior portion. Consistent with its role in emotion, this is a limbic structure. Its cytoarchitecture, connections, and early ontogenetic development (much earlier than the rest of the prefrontal cortex) confirm its limbic origin (Fuster 1997; Kandel, Schwartz & Jessell 1995). Further, it is affectively sensitive, as revealed by stimulation and self-stimulation studies (Passingham 1983; Rolls 1975; Fuster 1997). Various neurons respond to primary and secondary reinforcers; thus, frontal lobotomy can reduce the agony of painful stimulation (Rolls 1999). Stimulation of the OFC can elicit the emotional expression of smiling as well as pleasure in humans (MacLean 1990). It is the only cortical area that projects directly to the hypothalamus, where the various affects converge and perhaps are compared so that behavior can be prioritized.

If pride and shame evolved from dominance aggression, then we would expect the functions of the amygdala to be similar to those of the OFC and the two structures to be closely connected. Indeed, research has revealed many similarities between them. Like amygdalar lesions, OFC lesions in monkeys often result in reduced aggressiveness and lower rank (Fuster 1997). Both structures receive multimodal sensory input from the thalamus and also direct information from the olfactory bulb. Both respond to a range of primary and secondary reinforcers (Rolls 1999). The OFC sends signals to the amygdala and also directly to the hypothalamus and midbrain (Figure 11.4), thus both projecting to and bypassing the amygdalar pathway for dominance. These frontal lobe projections may contribute to emotional expression (Crosby, Humphrey & Lauer 1962), as do downstream amygdalar outputs. Furthermore, the OFC and amygdala are involved in the recognition of faces and facial expressions (Rolls 1999). Electrical stimulation of the OFC, like the amygdala, can result in autonomic changes (Butter, Snyder & McDonald 1970). And, like the amygdala, the OFC is rich in serotonin receptors (Masters & McGuire 1994). Serotonin receptors are more abundant in dominant vervet monkeys than in subordinates (Damasio 1994).

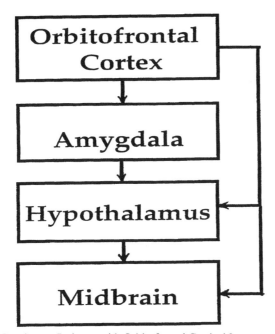

Figure 11.4. Dominance Pathway with Orbitofrontal Cortical Imput

What, then, do these two structures do differently, so that both are necessary? Morgan's canon reminds us that lower neural structures ought to be invoked to explain a given behavior wherever possible; in phylogenetic terms, we might say that even primitive organisms needed to fulfill all the functions necessary for survival and reproduction, so that any capacities that evolved later had to be elaborations of these earlier mechanisms. In general, primitive brain structures are not superseded by later ones, but are modified by them. Nature is basically conservative, and evolution tends to proceed by accretion, not by radical replacement. In the case of the OFC, this structure, which is cephalad to the amygdala and evolved later, appears to modulate the actions of the amygdala (see Panksepp 1998). The OFC does not seem to have eclipsed the amygdala. Indeed, the amygdala expanded in the primate line leading to hominids (Kling & Brothers 1992), perhaps mainly to process inputs from the OFC. Chance (1961) suggested that this burgeoning of the amygdala and associated parts of the prefrontal cortex in hominid evolution relates to the increased complexity of dominance competition in our species, to be discussed below.

One clue to the relation between the OFC and the amygdala may be found in the processing of olfactory stimuli, olfaction being a primitive vertebrate sense that partially bypasses the thalamic sensory relay station (Stuss & Benson 1986). The amygdala receives information directly from the olfactory bulb and vomeronasal organ (Halgren 1992; Gloor 1997). This information might include the odor of a threatening adult male. Thus, the amygdala may respond to direct, unprocessed olfactory releasers (i.e., it may contain more innate releasing mechanisms). By contrast, the OFC is considered the highest-order processor of olfactory information. The anterolateral (neocortical) part of the OFC, especially on the right side, may interpret olfactory and gustatory information and then pass it on to the amygdala for a more refined behavioral response (Gloor 1997). The OFC receives input from all sensory modalities and is the only cortical structure to do so. In sum, these neocortical regions of the OFC may act as other areas of the neocortex do in the conditioning of emotional responses: They may refine emotional responsiveness to stimuli from various sensory modalities. They may provide a less direct but more precise pathways for learned emotional reactions.

The OFC does seem to refine dominance behavior as mediated by the amygdala. As noted above, monkeys with bilateral OFC lesions usually withdraw from dominance encounters and therefore fall in rank (Fuster 1997). In addition, lesions often result in behavior that is inappropriate for the animal's rank. A dominant animal may defer to a subordinate; a subordinate may attack a superior and seem surprised at being attacked in return (Fulton 1951). A low-ranking operate may steal food from under the nose of a dominant one (Brody & Rosvold 1952). Thus, bilateral OFC lesions in a group of monkeys usually destabilize the dominance hierarchy.

Brody and Rosvold (1952) attributed this hierarchical disorganization to the "disappearance or marked diminution of learned avoidance responses in the low-status animals" (p. 415). Lesioned high-status animals might likewise fail to retain attack responses learned previously. Snyder (1970) explained the effects of OFC lesions as resulting from decreased aggression, inappropriate or diminished submission signaling, and inability to perceive threat signals. However, these deficits could be accounted for by ignorance of cagemates' ranks, as proposed by Brody and Rosvold. Recent evidence indicates that the OFC can learn and unlearn associations faster than the amygdala (Rolls 1999), which it generally inhibits (Davidson 2001). Thus, the OFC may mediate learning about other animals' ranks, much as the auditory neocortex helps to identify tones associated with pain. An OFC-lesioned animal generally avoids dominance encounters, but perhaps from an inability to choose appropriate opponents rather than from a disinclination to compete. Sometimes a lesioned animal exhibits heightened aggression, but still falls in rank because of a deficit in appropriate hierarchical behavior (Mass 1972).

Another observation supports the notion of a loss of sensitivity to social ranks with bilateral OFC lesions. A chacma baboon in which both prefrontal areas were removed no longer exhibited jealousy when another monkey was petted (Bianchi 1922). This sort of tripartite social comparison resembles the effect of witnessing another vervet male copulate with a female: a lowering of serotonin levels and hence of self-perceived rank (see preceding section).

ROLE OF THE ORBITOFRONTAL CORTEX IN PRIDE AND SHAME IN HUMANS

The limbic orbitofrontal cortex, then, seems to be involved in dominance behavior in simians. It also plays a major role in pride and shame in humans. Clinical evidence in humans, including studies of various lobotomy surgical procedures, suggests that decreased motivation for social success is a direct effect of OFC lesions. People with bilateral OFC lesions seem unconcerned with their social standing and reputation. They tend to be boorish, impolite, and unrestrained, and may lie, cheat, boast, neglect their appearance, and swear profusely (Fuster 1997). Prefrontal leucotomy patients have reported a decline in feeling or emotion (Partridge 1950). The famous Phineas Gage was described as lacking deference for others (i.e., submissive behavior). Such patients seem not to be affected by the societal values that otherwise guide and constrain human behavior. It is as though they lack dominance motivation, that is, the urge and ability to protect, communicate, and advance one's standing by the multiplicity of values that guide human behavior. Likewise, these patients characteristically neglect their occupations, the highly specialized and culturally variable paths to social standing.[2]

There have been few studies of OFC lesions in children, but one such case suggests that damage early in life appears to be permanent. A 3-year-old boy who sustained a 3-inch incisive wound of the left eye orbit near the midline subsequently exhibited severe and intractable behavioral problems. If reprimanded, he understood that he had broken a rule but showed no signs of shame in demeanor; instead, he often immediately asked for a favor. Asked how he felt when his mother yelled at him, he replied that he did not like it "because her voice goes up real high and I don't like the way it sounds." He used profanity freely, and in a word association test came up with "tit" and "nigger" for words beginning with "t" and "n." Due to his size, aggressiveness, and quick temper, he terrorized his classmates. He had no friends; he antagonized other children by swearing at them, throwing things at them, or knocking them out of his way. Despite his exemplary home background and a well-ordered, superior private school, he did schoolwork only when required to do so before being allowed to go home for the day (from patient's medical record and observations by Carol C. Weisfeld, his teacher).[3]

As these clinical cases indicate, OFC lesions interfere with a multitude of social acts, not just physically aggressive behaviors as in other species. That is, the human OFC mediates the panoply of acts that affect social standing in our species. Unlike other primates, we complete for dominance in multiple, culturally variable ways. Physical traits count, but so do various accomplishments, attributes, altruistic deeds, allies, and acts of propriety (or impropriety). Almost any act has status value (i.e., influences one's social standing). We do not just lunge for a piece of bread; we ask politely. We engage in elaborate strategies to advance our social standing and to avoid losing face.[4]

Where does the social salience of these various deeds and attributes register in the brain? The learned, culture-specific values by which our acts are assessed by others may be represented in the OFC. As discussed earlier, learned dominance cues may register in the OFC of monkeys and humans. Like the amygdala, the OFC may assign emotional valence to previously neutral stimuli, including ranks to other individuals and prestige value to various actions and "status symbols."

The effects of temporary derangement of this system for constraining behavior within socially approved bounds are illustrated by some cases of epileptic automatism. These episodes arise from ictal interference with functioning of the temporal lobe, and may invade adjacent structures, usually bilaterally. The automatism may be restricted to rhythmic chewing or swallowing, or may extend to complex, purposive movements (Gloor 1997):

[The] patient does not respond normally to social signals . . . and may therefore not interact in any socially insightful or appropriate way with persons around him and may in addition engage in socially unacceptable behavior such as undressing in a public place. This probably indicates a combination of defects that are partially perceptual—not at an elementary level, but rather on the level of relating environmental signals to the fund of personal memories and acquired social attitudes that guide our behavior in everyday living. This probably indicates a lack of proper interplay of temporal and frontal association cortex with the hippocampal system and the amygdala (p. 707).

In summary, the OFC seems to modulate dominance behavior by processing multimodal sensory stimuli and acting on the amygdala and other downstream limbic structures. The OFC appears to mediate learned dominance/subordination cues as well as affective processes involved in success and failure. Clinical lesions to the OFC also usually involve the adjacent, dorsolateral area of the prefrontal cortex, and the two areas are interconnected. Therefore the dorsolateral prefrontal cortex will be considered next.

FUNCTIONS OF THE DORSOLATERAL PREFRONTAL CORTEX

The dorsolateral prefrontal cortex is distinct, in its connections and functions, from the limbic OFC (Fuster 1997). In laboratory studies on monkeys, dorsolateral ablations do not seem to affect social rank as do orbital lesions (Kling & Mass 1974). The dorsolateral cortex has been implicated in the ability to carry out a series of actions aimed at a later objective. The dorsolateral cortex (DL) is considered the highest level of organization of the voluntary motor system of the frontal lobe, as will now be reviewed very briefly.

The simplest, most primitive level is the primary motor cortex in the precentral gyrus. Neurons from this area, laid out somatotopically, send output to the motor neurons of the spinal cord via the pyramidal and extrapyramidal tracts. This constitutes the basic wiring diagram for voluntary action; all the motor units are innervated.

The premotor cortex constitutes the next higher level of organization. Here more organized, functionally meaningful movement patterns are represented. The premotor cortex is more directly related to adaptive behaviors than is the primary motor area, through which it operates. The premotor area mediates the execution of functional, rather than robotic, skilled movement patterns, such as driving a car (Crosby, Humphrey & Lauer 1962). These motor skills are presumably built up through practice; we develop skills appropriate for our particular environment and circumstances. The supplementary motor area, dorsal to the premotor cortex, seems to be active when we mentally rehearse a contemplated action, as well as while we carry out the act (Kolb & Whishaw 1990).

The DL seems to supervise and coordinate even more complex functional actions, those protracted over some period of time. It operates through the premotor and primary motor areas. A DL lesion might result in difficulty in carrying out a purposeful series of actions, such as those involved in taking a cigarette and a match from their packages and lighting the cigarette (Crosby et al. 1962), or making a sandwich. A patient with a DL lesion might perform actions out of sequence or perseverate at one step in the process. The DL is also necessary for performing delayed-response tasks, in which the rhesus or human infant must pause for some interval before making the correct response (Levin et al. 1991). Likewise, the DL has been shown to be essential for the Piagetian capacity of object permanence in rhesus and human infants, the ability to remember the existence of objects that have passed from view (Diamond 1985).

The DL is one of the last parts of the cortex to develop and evolve, and is far larger in humans than in the chimpanzee (Girgis 1971). It therefore can be expected to mediate some of our most distinctively human aptitudes, of which the formulation and execution of long-term plans is certainly one. The late ontogeny of the DL is reflected by children's impulsiveness and their difficulty in sustaining attention to a task. The prefrontal cortex grows rapidly between ages 2 and 5 (Petrie 1952); by about age 5, children are generally low enough in impulsiveness to enter school and sustain attention to the teacher or task. Not until adolescence is the area fully myelinated, thus allowing for the full maturity of sustained attention, planning, and logical chains of reasoning by about age 12 (Fuster 1997). Presumably, behavioral maturation in adulthood is largely a matter of developing adaptive plans for practical and social tasks, and continuing to refine these plans in the light of experience. Consistent with the late evolution of this structure, it can be lesioned quite extensively without causing very profound or even noticeable behavioral deficits, let alone death. For example, IQ may remain unchanged (Teuber 1972).

The DL is connected with the lateral thalamus, dorsal caudate, and hippocampus, and with other high-order areas of the neocortex. This would allow it to assemble perceptual information and memories of past events in order to build up a plan of action. A person needs to remember the elements of the plan while constructing and executing it, an aptitude sometimes referred to as working memory and doubtless demanded in delayed response tasks. DL lesions can also disrupt the directing of eye and head movements, which appear to be involved in attention (Fuster 1997). Being able to sustain attention on sources of task-relevant visual input would seem to be essential for planning. Children with attention deficit disorder sometimes show decrements on prefrontal lobe function tests.

What of the role of the adjacent OFC in these planned movement sequences? The OFC seems to aid this capacity by buffering the DL from distraction (Fuster 1997). It insulates the DL from interference by extraneous sensory input, and thus lessens impulsiveness. The observed failure of OFC patients to pursue their occupation, or exhibit "drive" and "motivation," may result partly from interference in the planning function of the DL (Stuss & Benson 1986). By contrast, some patients with obsessive-compulsive disorder show heightened activity of the OFC, as though they are overly fixated on a goal (Malloy 1987; Panksepp 1998).[5] Malloy (1987) suggested that their behavior is opposite to that of sociopaths, who are impulsive and often exhibit diminished OFC activity (Fuster 1997; Pontius 1972; Schore 1994). However, attention deficit disorder may be a more directly opposite condition to obsessive-compulsive disorder, since sociopathy adds the symptom of reduced sensitivity to pride and shame. The impulsivity of sociopaths may stem from reduced sensitivity to social evaluation. The sociopath is freed from the constraints imposed by social evaluation, and therefore can formulate intentions simply and quickly.

EMOTIONAL NATURE OF PREFRONTAL LESION DEFICITS

It seems incomplete to reduce the antisocial behavior of prefrontal lobe patients to impulsiveness and planning deficits alone, however. Again, this is not simply a cognitive deficit, but also an emotional one, at least insofar as the OFC is involved. OFC patients may not have forgotten the rules of politeness, but they are unmoved by them. Sociopaths can engage in long-term planning, often with diabolical consequences, and may feign remorse and empathy, but are largely impervious to pride, shame, and empathy.

Emotional terms such as shame are invoked in most contemporary explanations of OFC pathology (e.g., Fuster 1997; MacLean 1990), whereas previously these effects were often explained as deficits in foreseeing the consequences of one's actions or in the capacity for fear. One of the earliest allusions to an emotional deficit associated with OFC lesions was offered by MacLean (1949), who explicitly mentioned a decrease in guilt. It is only certain consequences that the patient fails to foresee or to care about. I once observed a man who had suffered a stroke around the anterior portion of the circle of Willis. He could very well anticipate the pain of an injection; in fact, he protested vociferously and shamelessly about receiving it. Thus, he foresaw, and feared, pain but he did not anticipate or experience shame. He was boorish and profane, and appeared unconcerned with pursing his career as a professor—with maintaining his social status. In another case, a middle-aged man with a frontal lobe tumor delighted in playing practical jokes such as turning a garden hose on his neighbors (Critchley, O'Leary & Jennett 1972). Obviously, he too foresaw the consequences of his actions, but did not fear the outrage of his victims.

The distinctively emotional nature of OFC function may have been obscured in the earlier literature by (1) the interconnections between and proximity of the OFC and DL, which is involved in planning; (2) a failure to appreciate the limbic nature of the OFC; and (3) the prevalence of behaviorism over ethology in American psychology.

The emotional nature of prefrontal lobe function is suggested by an additional line of argument. Planning any action probably requires anticipating various types of affective consequences, not just pride and shame. Biological goals are emotional; we seek to execute behaviors that make us feel better. We mentally rehearse our possible courses of action by imagining their affective consequences, and then choose the most promising one. We also ruminate over past successes and failures, repeatedly experiencing the affects associated with the events, presumably so that we learn from these reenactments (Nesse 1990). Temporal lobe seizures, probably involving the hippocampus and amygdala, sometimes result in vivid recollections of past experiences, complete with the original affective tone (LeDoux 1996). Then too, when we experience an emotion vicariously, by imagining its occurrence, we tend to undergo some of the visceral changes associated with that emotion, indicating that the anticipatory experience is actually emotional and not just cognitive.[6] If we merely contemplated various possible action sequences, we would have no way of evaluating them. All evaluation is affective (see Pugh 1977).

This evaluation of the affective payoffs of various extended plans seems to involve the prefrontal cortex in humans (Damasio 1994), although other species that lack this structure can foresee future events and formulate simple plans or intentions. Well before Damasio, Nauta (1973) proposed that this interaction between the frontal cortex and the limbico-subcortical axis could be, among other things, an important prerequisite for the normal human ability to compare alternatives of thought and action plans. This suggestion attributes to the limbico-subcortical axis the function of a "sounding board" or "internal test-ground" enabling man to preview the affective consequences in any particular action he might consider (p. 312).

Consistent with this interpretation, the OFC contains neurons that fire only in response to stimuli that have been paired with rewards. Such neurons would be necessary for anticipating the payoff of a given course of action (Panksepp 1998).[7] MacLean (1993) added some insights to this matter of behavioral planning. First, he recognized the emotional nature of planning and the involvement of the frontal lobe. He noted that "the frontal cortex affords an endless number of prospects that at the emotional level can induce concern and anxiety or joyful anticipation" (p. 81). He observed that this ability to anticipate emotional consequences is diminished by prefrontal lobotomy. He invoked the term "envision" for this capacity and related it to the fact that the visual part of the pulvinar nucleus is connected with the prefrontal cortex. We envision the consequences of our actions.

Damasio (1994) suggested that the DL specializes in evaluating impersonal, abstract plans. Social planning seems to include the OFC as well. OFC lesions do not seem to impair the ability to solve hypothetical social problems affecting imaginary people, but only the subject's ability to formulate his own social plans (Bechara, Damasio, Damasio & Anderson 1994). Such a patient may deliberate endlessly, unable to take a simple decision. Much earlier, Teuber (1964) characterized this effect of an OFC lesion as follows: "the patient is not altogether devoid of capacity to anticipate the course of events, but cannot picture himself in relation to those events as a potential agent. Abnormal fixity, or abnormal oscillation of action, other-directedness, and impulsiveness, all could follow from such a change" (p. 440). These two abilities seem to be developmentally distinct as well. Moore (1999) concluded that patients who sustain prefrontal cortical damage in infancy never develop the ability to analyze moral situations involving others, but patients with damage in adulthood may.

In summary, the OFC, acting on the amygdala, seems to motivate us to maintain and enhance our prestige, or social rank, or self-esteem. It contains neurons that respond to stimuli that have been paired with rewards, perhaps including representations of socially valued deeds. The DL seems to participate in evaluation of the anticipated emotional consequences of planned courses of action. Anticipation of the affective consequences, for pride and shame specifi- cally, of our planned actions appears to involve the OFC as well as the DL.

NEURAL MEDIATION OF COMPLEX SOCIAL BEHAVIOR

MacLean (1993) drew attention to another complexity of human social behavior: our allegiance to our families. He implicated the connections between the prefrontal cortex and the adjacent thalamocingulate division in parental behavior. He went on to propose that parental tendencies came to be extended to nonkin as well: "it might be supposed that a sense of parental responsibility generalizes to other members of the species, becoming what we variously qualify as conscience, empathic concern, and altruism" (p. 81). In sociobiolog- ical terms, we first evolved parental tendencies, and later these capacities were recruited in the service of kin altruism and reciprocal altruism. Unlike the maternal behavior of most other mammals, which consists largely of fixed action patterns triggered by releasers and primed by hormones, primate mothering is highly flexible and empathic (Fernald 1992). This capacity for empathy, a vicarious emotional state, may have provided an emotional impetus for flexible altruistic behavior toward nonkin as well as kin (Trivers 1971).

Accordingly, cingulate gyrus lesions in rhesus monkeys resulted in a loss of grooming and of "acts of affection" toward others (Kling & Mass 1974). The operates behaved as if they were inanimate, walking over them or even sitting on them.

The prefrontal cortex may also play a role in parental and altruistic behavior. Animals and people with prefrontal lesions sometimes lose their affection toward their master or family (Levin et al. 1991), perhaps because of a reduction in empathy via connections with the anterior cingulate gyrus. For example, a man and a woman who both had sustained OFC damage in infancy were later insensitive to the welfare of their own infants and were unable to form friendships (Moore 1999). Another factor in animals may be loss of fear of the master resulting from the frontal cortical damage; cf. inappropriate dominance and submission behavior in OFC-lesioned monkeys. Dogs with prefrontal leucotomies showed a loss of fear for superiors and consequently an instability of social ranks (Fox 1965).

The OFC and amygdala seem to be involved in another aspect of reciprocal altruism and dominance hierarchization. Social arrangements such as dominance hierarchies, territories, and the exchanges of reciprocal altruism are enforced by anger (Trivers 1971). Anger prompts "moralistic aggression," which punishes individuals who violate social norms regarding reciprocity, dominance hierarchy prerogatives, territorial boundaries, possession, and so on. (Weisfeld 1980, 1994). For example, animals whose dominance prerogatives are usurped typically react with rage. Prefrontal ablations in apes and monkeys sometimes result in a decrease in anger when the animal is mistreated (Damasio 1994; Levin et al. 1991), and a decline in gratitude (Bianchi 1922). Likewise, human frontal lobe patients often do not sustain their anger (Panksepp 1998). The functionally related amygdala may participate as well. Monkeys and people with bilateral amygdalar lesions tend to be calmer and less readily angered—the tameness part of the Klüver-Bucy syndrome (Aggleton 1992). Thus, the OFC-amygala complex may play a role in the intense aggression that animals and people employ to protect their dominance status in hierarchies and other social contracts.

REASON VS. EMOTION: A FALSE DICHOTOMY

Because of the prevasiveness of pride and shame in human affairs, the human OFC adds a whole new layer of emotionality to our behavior. Pride and shame are constant, unavoidable considerations in our voluntary, motivated behavior. When we perform an altruistic deed or avoid committing an antisocial act, we are driven by a distinct emotion. Under these circumstances, we are not acting purely rationally. The OFC of the limbic system exercises control even over these "civilized" behaviors. Consistent with this idea of fundamental control by the limbic system over the neocortex, there are many more neural fibers going from the limbic system to the neocortex than the reverse (Panksepp 1998).

In fact, there is no such thing as a rational motive; it's an oxymoron. All motivation is emotional, even if it entails long-term and calm deliberation (i.e., rational support). Our motives are the subroutines for adaptive behavior. There would have been no adaptive point in evolving a "motive" not to be emotional, not to strive to fulfill our various biological needs in the most efficient and assiduous fashion possible. Our powers of rationality, of perception and cognition, are the servants of our behavioral imperatives. They can never replace or even suppress our set of motives. If we "control" our impulses long enough to satisfy our needs more diplomatically or effectively, this only demonstrates the power of emotion to guide future action. In short, there is no evolved imperative to guide behavior except for our emotions. Any such force for rationality would have to negotiate with our affects, and so would have to be emotional itself. The affects evolved so that the rest of our brain would know what course of action to pursue, what motive to address next. This requires that the affects be distinguishable from each other, which they are, and that they be quantitatively comparable even though they are qualitatively distinct. Where would "rationality" fit into such a mechanism for comparative measurement? On what authority would it preempt a basic motive such as the need for food or air? There is no higher priority—no other priority—than fulfilling the imperatives of fitness.

Then too, how would one "learn" to control one's emotions, except through operant conditioning, the experience of reward or punishment following a particular act? Again, the role of emotion is inescapable. Perhaps some of this learning occurs through observational learning, but this probably entails vicariously experiencing the emotions of the model. Emotion also guides memory and attention: We preferentially attend to and remember emotionally salient stimuli. So any rational process is "contaminated" by emotional tone (Zajonc 1984).

The misconception that rationality guides human behavior has contributed to neglect of the basic, universal emotion of pride and shame. We need to include this emotion in the human ethogram; it is omitted from most psychologists' lists of the basic emotions (as is sex!). It may not be flattering to us as a species to admit that we are subject to the sin of pride as well as those of gluttony, lust, sloth, and so on. But it is only realistic to acknowledge this, and to recognize the adaptive value for our own species, as well as for others, of a motive to compete with one's rivals.

Despite the fact that we humans retained the dominance motive in evolving from our primate ancestors, this motive became greatly elaborated in our species. The increased complexity of our criteria for dominance was probably related to expansion of the prefrontal cortex and amygdala. We are evaluated for our accomplishments and contributions as well as for our physical prowess and mate value.

The neural connections necessary for utilizing all this sociocultural information in our planning are built up in the prefrontal cortex through various forms of socialization, just as connections accumulate in the secondary sensory and motor cortical areas as we acquire various perceptions and skilled movements. This sociocultural information is garnered through individual experience, exposure to models of successful behavior, formal instruction about proper behavior such as that provided during puberty rites, and even parables and jokes that edify us about social foibles to avoid (Weisfeld 1993). We learn to formulate courses of action that do not result in cognitive dissonance, in the feelings of discomfort that occur when our actions compromise our self-esteem. Psychologists speak of internalization of norms, but this is nothing more than learning societal values about social behavior just as we learn which foods to eat and which dangers to avoid.

Another misleading idea is that of conscience, or the superego. There is no supra-egoistic force that censors our baser instincts, no cultural invention or product of group selection. Rather, there is a full-fledged instinct, or emotion—pride and shame—that we seek to fulfill along with all our other emotions. It is certainly a powerful and pervasive emotion, as argued above. But its adaptive value lies only in its potential to be redeemed for tangible prerogatives of rank sooner or later. Therefore, we sometimes sustain a loss of status in order to reap some ulterior benefit. For example, we may embarrass ourselves in our zeal to aggress against some tormentor, or we may violate a traffic law in our haste to get to a movie. If conscience were superordinate over the other emotions, this sort of result would never occur.

Our kin socialize us to participate in the regulated competition of social hierarchies and reciprocal altruism, because this is generally the best strategy for maximizing individual fitness in human society. But our psychological allegiance to these values, our conscience itself, ought not to obscure the fact that this motive is only one among many. Confusion about the notion of conscience may also arise because we often pursue two emotional goals at a time, and pride/-shame is usually one of these emotions. We try to get water on a hot day without sneaking ahead in the line to the water cooler. We try to steal a nap without attracting the notice of the lecturer. But, again, the way to make sense of these processes is to consider all the human emotions, and only them.

TOWARD AN ETHOLOGICAL PSYCHIATRY

In conclusion, an evolutionary approach to neuroscience suggests keeping in mind the ancestral way of life—adaptive problems—of our species. Naturalistic tests of neurological functioning might be devised that take into account the highly social nature of human behavior and the paramount importance of emotion and motivation. More specifically, it suggests that neurological tests are needed that assess our evolved emotional capacities. This would lead to a new, more ethologically valid set of diagnostic categories, one based on the assumption that behavioral pathology usually arises as an aberration from normal, evolved emotional functioning (see McGuire & Troisi 1998; Nesse & Williams 1994).

Further, an evolutionary perspective fosters a balanced view of the whole organism. All of the basic human emotions, the building blocks of voluntary behavior, are assessed. A model of only some of the emotions, such as those in which expression is prominent, would be as weak as a model of only some of the endocrine glands, some of the essential nutrients, or some of the bones. Behavioral disease may seldom resolve itself into a circumscribed malfunction of a single motive; other neural mechanisms and bodily systems may be affected also, as in other forms of disease. But for an assessment of the patient's condition and hence a direction for therapy, it seems sensible to systematically evaluate the function of each emotion. In particular, the neglected and yet pervasive emotion of pride and shame needs to be expressly included in any assessment of psychological functioning.

NOTES

1. When an emotion arises from interoceptors (e.g., hunger and thirst), the pathway seems to originate in the hypothàlamus. Nevertheless, a high fraction of amygdalar cells in cats and humans respond to visceral information such as blood CO_2, heart rate, and respiration rate (Halgren 1992).

2. A possibly related symptom of frontal lobe pathology is *Witzelsucht*, or facetiousness. Although this affliction strikes all of us on occasion, it seems to be related to right frontal lobe damage (Levin, Eisenberg & Benton 1991). It may be caused by a combination of social insensitivity (reduced capacity for shame) and mania, which often results from right frontal lobe lesions, that is, from greater left than right frontal lobe activity. Clinical series cited by Levin et al. suggest that the right orbital gyrus is typically involved. Likewise, episodes of ictal laughter apparently can result from a stimulating lesion of the left orbital area (Loiseau, Cohadon & Cohadon 1971). Similarly, clinical depression is associated with increased utilization of serotonin in the lower medial prefrontal cortex, primarily on the left side; experimentally induced pleasant thoughts are related to reductions in regional blood flow, especially to the right prefrontal and bilateral tempero-parietal regions (McGuire, Fawzy, Spar & Troisi 2000).

3. It is possible that a lesion sustained before age 3 might not lead to derangement of the pride/shame system because the latter seems to mature between ages 2 and 5. Other brain areas might assume the function of the lesioned ones. At age 2 children typically begin to exhibit concern with personal success and failure, and dominance hierarchies gradually take shape from 2 to 6 (Weisfeld & Wendorf 2000).

4. Clinical cases such as these suggest that the OFC mediates guilt, shame, embarrassment, and feelings of occupational failure alike. Therefore, these different terms may not reflect evolutionarily separate emotions, but merely semantic distinctions. For example, subjects often refer to experiencing "guilt" when privately contemplating their transgression of social norms, and to "shame" when the offense is public (Weisfeld 1997a). The affect is likely to be identical in the two situations since apparently it is mediated by the same neural structure (although Stuss & Benson [1986] suggested that drive and motivation are disturbed most by pathology involving the [neocortical] medial convexity and frontal polar structures, whereas social disinhibition seems to be most pronounced following [limbic] orbital frontal disturbance). Likewise, a multitude of terms are used to refer to competitive behavior in humans, including social comparison, self-esteem, power motivation, rivalry, achievement motivation, and approval motivation. But these terms all involve the affect of pride and shame, whether explicitly referred to or not. Moreover, the characteristic emotional displays of this emotion—direct gaze, relaxed demeanor, and erect posture and their antithetical expressions—are typical primate

dominance displays, suggesting a single, common evolved origin for this emotion (Weisfeld & Linkey 1985). Distinctions among shame, guilt, embarrassment, and the like may be useful therapeutically, but they probably do not reflect fundamentally different motives (Weisfeld 1997a). It is unlikely that more than one of these motives exists in our primate relatives, or that humans evolved any new motives not possessed in rudimentary form in simians (Panksepp 1994).

5. Obsessive-compulsive disorder also seems to involve the basal ganglia. Recognition of this fact provides a nice illustration of the benefits of ethological thinking. The obsessive hand washing of patients is reminiscent of self-cleaning in animals, which involves the basal ganglia. Rapoport (1989) reasoned that pathological hand washing might reflect an abnormality in these structures. Indeed, patients were found to have low levels of serotonin in these areas, and responded therapeutically to serotonin-enhancing drugs (Wise & Rapoport 1988).

6. Nevertheless, visceral feedback is unlikely to play a major role in these vicarious affective experiences, any more than it does in directly experienced emotions. These visceral adjustments to emotional state doubtless evolved to set the body in an appropriate pattern of visceral activation, not to provide the brain with belated feedback about its own output. Additional arguments against the James-Lange theory of the origin of affects were offered by Cannon (1927) and remain valid. For example, quadriplegics are not emotionally impaired by their reduced visceral feedback; they do not show affects that are inappropriate for their situations, for example, they do not feel hungry when they should be angry, as might be the case if affects depended mainly on visceral feedback. For further discussion, see Weisfeld (1997b), Panksepp (1998), and Rolls (1999).

7. A recent study has offered some additional details on this capacity (O'Doherty, Kringelbach, Rolls, Hornak & Andrews 2001). Patients with OFC lesions tend to show deficits on gambling tasks, i.e., being able to make choices based on anticipated gains and losses. An fMRI study of normal patients revealed heightened activity in the lateral OFC when they made a choice that caused them to lose money, and deactivation when they were rewarded. The opposite pattern was observed for activity in the medial OFC. The magnitude of the change in activation was related to the extent of the gain or loss. Thus, lesions in this region may affect ability to gauge the consequences of one's actions.

REFERENCES

Aggleton, JP: The functional effects of amygdala lesions in humans: a comparison with findings from monkeys. In JP Aggleton (Ed.), *The Amygdala: Neurobiological aspects of emotion, memory, and mental dysfunction.* (pp. 485–503). NY: Wiley-Liss, 1992.

Barkow, JH: Social prestige and culture: A biosocial interpretation. *Current Anthropology,* 1975; 16: 553–572.

Bechara, A, Damasio, AR, Damasio, H, Anderson, SW.: Insensitivity to future consequences following damage to human prefrontal cortex. *Cognition,* 1994; 50: 7–15.

Bianchi, L: *The Mechanisms of the Brain and the Function of the Frontal Lobes.* Edinburgh: E & S Livingstone, 1922.

Brody, EB, Rosvold, HE: Influence of prefrontal lobotomy on social interaction in a monkey group. *Psychosomatic Medicine,* 1952; 14: 406–415.

Butter, CM, Snyder, DR & McDonald, JA: Effects of orbital frontal lesions on aversive and aggressive behaviors in rhesus monkey. *Journal of Comparative & Physiological Psychology,* 1970, 72: 132–144.

Cannon, WB: The James-Lange theory of emotions: A critical examination and an alternative theory. *American Journal of Psychology,* 1927, 39: 106–124.

Chance, MRA: The nature and special features of the instinctive social bond of primates. In SL Washburn (Ed.), *Social Life of Early Man* (pp. 17–33). Chicago: Aldine, 1961.

Critchley, M, O'Leary, JL Jennett, B: *Scientific Foundations of Neurology.* Philadelphia: E. A. Davis Co., 1972.

Crosby, EC, Humphrey, T, Lauer, EW: *Correlative Anatomy of the Nervous System.* NY: MacMillan Co., 1962.

Damasio, AR: *Descartes' Error: Emotion, Reason, and the Human Brain.* NY: Grosset/ Putnam, 1994.

Darwin, C: *The Expression of the Emotions in Man and Animals.* London: Murray/ Chicago: University of Chicago Press, 1872/1965.

Davidson, RJ: The neural circuitry of emotion and affective style: prefrontal cortex and amygdala contributions. *Social Science Information,* 2000; 40, 11–37.

Diamond, A: Development of the ability to use recall to guide action, as indicated by infants' performance on AB. *Child Development,* 1985; 56: 868–883.

Ellis, L: Evidence of neuroandrogenic etiology of sex roles from a combined analysis of human, nonhuman primate, and nonprimate mammalian studies. *Personality & Individual Differences,* 1986; 7: 519–551.

Fernald, A: Human maternal vocalizations to infants as biologically relevant signals: An evolutionary perspective. In JH Barkow, L Cosmides & J Tooby (Eds.), *The Adapted Mind: Evolutionary Psychology and the Generation of Culture.* New York: Oxford University Press, 1992.

Fox, MW: *Canine Behavior.* Springfield, Ill.: Charles C. Thomas, 1965.

Freedman, DG: A biological view of man's social behavior. In W. Etkin (Ed.), *Social Behavior from Fish to Man.* Chicago: University of Chicago Press, 1967.

Fulton, JF: *Frontal Lobotomy and Affective Behavior.* NY: W. W. Norton & Co., 1951.

Fuster, JM: *The Prefrontal Cortex: Anatomy, Physiology, and Neuropsychology of the Frontal Lobe.* Philadelphia: Lippincott: Raven, 1997.

Girgis, M: The orbital surface of the frontal lobe of the brain and mental disorders. *Acta Psychiatrica Scandinavica,* 1971, Supplementum 222.

Gloor, P: Role of the amygdala in temporal lobe epilepsy. In JP Aggleton (Ed.), *The Amygdala: Neurobiological Aspects of Emotion, Memory, and Mental Dysfunction.* (pp. 505–538). New York: Wiley-Liss, 1992.

Gloor, P: *The Temporal Lobe and Limbic System.* NY: Oxford University Press, 1997.

Halgren, E: Emotional neurophysiology of the amygdala within the context of human cognition. In JP Aggleton (Ed.), *The Amygdala: Neurobiological Aspects of Emotion, memory, and mental dysfunction.* (pp. 191–228). NY: Wiley-Liss, 1992.

Huntingford, F, Turner, A: *Animal Conflict.* New York: Chapman & Hall, 1987.

Kandel, ER, Schwartz, JH., Jessell, TM (Eds.): *Essentials of Neural Science and Behavior.* Norwalk, CT: Appleton & Lange, 1995.

Kling, A: Effects of amygdalectomy on social-affective behavior in non-human primates. In BE Eleftheriou (Ed.), *The Neurobiology of the Amygdala.* (pp. 511–536). NY: Plenum Press, 1972.

Kling, AS, Brothers, LA: The amygdala and social behavior. In JP Aggleton (Ed.), *The Amygdala: Neurobiological Aspect of Emotion, Memory, and Mental Dysfunction.* (pp. 353–377). NY: Wiley-Liss, 1992.

Kling, A, Mass, R: Alterations of social behavior with neural lesions in nonhuman primates. In RL Holloway (Ed.), *Primate Aggression, Territoriality, and Xeno-phobia.* (pp. 361–386). NY: Academic Press, 1974.

Kolb, B, & Whishaw, IQ: *Fundamentals of Human Neuropsychology.* NY: Freeman, 1990.

LeDoux, J: *The Emotional Brain: The Mysterious Underpinnings of Emotional Life.* NY: Simon & Schuster, 1996.

Levin, HS, Eisenberg, HM, Benton, AL (Eds.): *Frontal Lobe Function and Dysfunction.* NY: Oxford University Press, 1991.

Loiseau, P, Cohadon, F, Cohadon, S: Gelastic epilepsy: A review and report of five cases. *Epilepsia,* 1971; 12: 313–323.

MacLean, PD: Psychosomatic disease and the 'visceral brain.' *Psychosomatic Medicine,* 1949; 11: 338–353.

MacLean, PD: *The Triune Brain in Evolution: Role in Paleocerebral Functions.* N Y: Plenum, 1990.

MacLean, PD: Cerebral evolution of emotion. In M. Lewis & JM Haviland (Eds.), *Handbook of Emotions.* (pp. 67–83). NY: Guilford Press, 1993.

Malloy, P: Frontal lobe dysfunction in obsessive-compulsive disorder. In E Perecman (Ed.), *The Frontal Lobes Revisited.* (pp. 207-233). NY: IRBN Press, 1987.

Mass, R: The effects of dorsolateral frontal ablations on the social behavior of a cagedgroup of eleven stumptail macaques. Doctoral dissertation, Rutgers University, New Brunswick, NJ, 1972.

Masters, RD, McGuire, MT (Eds.): *The Neurotransmitter Revolution: Serotonin, Social Behavior, and the Law.* Carbondale: Southern Illinois University, 1994.

Mazur, A: Hormones, aggression, and dominance in humans. In B Svare (Ed.), *Hormones and Aggressive Behavior.* NY: Plenum, 1983.

Mazur, A, Booth, A: Testosterone and dominance in men. *Behavioral & Brain Sciences,* 1998; 21: 353–397.

McGuire, MT; Fawzy, F; Spar, J & Troisi, A: Dysthymic disorder, regulation-dysregulation theory, CNS blood flow, and CNS metabolism. In L Sloman & P Gilbert (Eds.), *Subordination and Defeat: An evolutionary approach to mood disorders and their therapy* (pp. 71–93). Mahwah, N. J.: Lawrence Erlbaum, 2000.

McGuire, MT, Troisi, A: *Darwinian Psychiatry.* NY: Oxford University Press, 1998.

Moore, P: No plasticity for bad behavior. *BioMed News,* October 28, 1999.

Nauta, WJH: Connections of the frontal lobe with the limbic system. In LV Laitinen & KE Livingston (Eds.), *Surgical Approaches in Psychiatry.* (pp. 303–312). Baltimore: University Park Press, 1973.

Nesse, R: Evolutionary explanations of emotions. *Human Nature,* 1, 261–289, 1990.

Nesse, R, Williams, GC: *Why We Get Sick.* New York: Random House, 1994.

O'Doherty, JO; Kringelbach, ML; Rolls, ET; Hornak, J & Andrews, C: Abstract reward and punishment representations in the human orbitofrontal cortex. *Nature Neuroscience,* 2001; 4, 95–102.

Panksepp, J: Evolution constructed the potential for subjective experience within the neurodynamics of the neomammalian brain. In P Ekman & RJ Davidson (Eds.), *TheNature of Emotion: Fundamental Questions* (pp. 396–399). Oxford: Oxford University Press, 1994.

Panksepp, J: *Affective Neuroscience: The Foundations of Human and Animal Emotions.* NY: Oxford University Press, 1998.

Partridge, M: *Pre-frontal Leucotomy.* Springfield, Mass.: Charles C. Thomas, 1950.

Passingham, R: *The Frontal Lobes and Voluntary Action.* Oxford: Oxford University Press, 1993.

Petrie, A: *Personality and the Frontal Lobes.* NY: Blakiston Co., 1952.

Pontius, AA: Neurological aspects in some types of delinquency especially among juveniles: Toward a neurological model of ethical action. *Adolescence,* 1972; 7: 289–308.

Pugh GE: *The Biological Origin of Human Values.* New York: Basic Books, 1977.

Rapoport, JL: The biology of obsessions and compulsions. *Scientific American,* 1989, 260, 82–89.

Rolls, ET: *The Brain and Reward.* NY: Pergamon Press, 1975.

Rolls, ET: *The Brain and Emotion.* Oxford: Oxford University Press.

Savin-Williams, RC: Dominance in a human adolescent group. *Animal Behaviour,* 1977; 5: 400–406.

Schore, AN: *Affect Regulation and the Origin of the Self: The Neurobiology of Emotional Development.* Hillsdale, NJ: Lawrence Erlbaum, 1994.

Snyder, DR: Fall from social dominance following orbital frontal ablation in monkeys *Proceedings of the 78th Annual Convention, of the APA,* 1970, pp. 235–236.

Stuss, DT, Benson, DF: *The Frontal Lobes.* NY: Raven Press, 1986.

Teuber, HL: The riddle of the frontal lobe function in man. In JM Warren & K Akert (Eds.), *The Frontal Granular Cortex and Behavior.* (pp. 410–444). NY: McGraw-Hill, 1964.

Teuber, HL: Unity and diversity of frontal lobe function. *Acta Neurobiologiae Experimentalis,* 1972; 32: 615–656.

Trivers, RL: The evolution of reciprocal altruism. *Quarterly Review of Biology,* 1971; 46: 35–57.

Weisfeld, GE: Social dominance and human motivation. In DR Omark, FF Strayer &DG Freedman (Eds.), *Dominance Relations: An Ethological View of Human Conflict and Social Interaction.* pp. 273–286. New York: Garland, 1980.

Weisfeld, GE: The adaptive value of humor and laughter. *Ethology & Sociobiology,* 1993; 4: 144–169.

Weisfeld, GE: Aggression and dominance in the social world of boys. In J Archer (Ed.), *Male Violence.* (pp. 42–69). London: Routledge, 1994.

Weisfeld, GE: Discrete emotions theory with specific reference to pride and shame. In NL Segal, GE Weisfeld & CC Weisfeld (Eds.), *Uniting Psychology and Biology: Integrative perspectives on human development.* (pp. 419–443). Washington, DC: American Psychological Association, 1997a.

Weisfeld, GE: Review of Joseph LeDoux, *The Emotional Brain: The Mysterious Underpinnings of Emotional Life. Human Ethology Bulletin,* 1997b; 12: 13–19.

Weisfeld, GE, Linkey, HE: Dominance displays as indicators of a social success motive. In S Ellyson & J Dovidio (Eds.), *Power, Dominance, and Nonverbal Behavior.* (pp. 109–128). New York: Springer-Verlag, 1985.

Weisfeld, GE, Wendorf, CA: The involuntary defeat strategy and discrete emotions theory. In L Sloman & P Gilbert (Eds.), *An Evolutionary Approach to Mood Disorders and Their Therapy* (pp. 121–145). Mahwah, NJ: Lawrence Erlbaum.

Wise, SP, & Rapoport, JL: Obsessive-compulsive disorder: Is it a basal ganglia dysfunction? *Psychopharmacology Bulletin,* 1988, 24: 380–384.

Zajonc, RB: On the primacy of affect. *American Psychologist,* 1984; 39: 117–123.

12

THE TRIUNE BRAIN AND THE FUNCTIONAL ANALYSIS OF ATTENTION

Allan F. Mirsky and Connie C. Duncan

INTRODUCTION

Modern concepts of attention have evolved from earlier notions of attention as a single monolithic function to that of a group of separate functions, each serving a specific, articulated role in the organism's interaction with the environment. Moreover, some theorists have posited that each specific attentional function depends on the integrity of a distinct brain region, with the regions forming an integrated system within the intact brain. We have proposed a heuristic model of the factors involved in human attention.[1] Our model is derived in large part from neuropsychological findings in patients with seizures or other neuropsychiatric disorders. MacLean's concept of the *triune* brain provides a remarkable armature upon which to build a model of the organization and development of attentional functions in the human brain. The concept of the triune brain also provides an explanation for how this organization of attention developed from an evolutionary point of view. In this chapter, we describe our model and relate it to MacLean's concepts of reptilian, neomammalian, and mammalian brains.

THE EVOLUTIONARY PERSPECTIVE

The theoretical context that guides our conceptual view of the neuro-psychology of attention is, broadly speaking, evolutionary-developmental. The basic neural foundation for attention is a brain stem system that has existed for millions of years, and is still present and functioning in the brains of modern reptiles.

The model is based on the concept of the triune brain, as delineated by MacLean.[2, 3] According to this theory, the brain of higher mammals consists of three interconnected tissue complexes, corresponding to major evolutionary developments. The oldest of these is *the reptilian* or R-complex. Overlaid on this is the *paleomammalian* or limbic system complex. The highest developmental complex, manifest in the explosive growth of the forebrain in higher mammals (and especially primates), is the *neomammalian.* These three interconnected tissue complexes are illustrated in Figure 12.1.

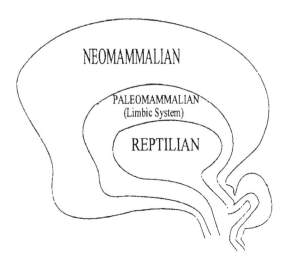

Figure 12.1. The Triune Brain (after MacLean)

The R-complex consists of masses of gray matter at the center of the cerebrum. Included are the basal ganglia (caudate, putamen, globus pallidus) and their connections to the thalamic, tegmental, and pontine regions of the brain stem. As illustrated in Figure 12.1, the R-complex is overlaid by and interconnected with the paleomammalian complex which includes the limbic system (amygdala, hippocampus, cingulate gyrus, and related structures) and the more primitive (paleomammalian) cortex. The neomammalian component, enveloping and extensively interconnected with the earlier structures, comprises primarily the phylogenetically newer neocortex and the thalamic structures.

MacLean[3] has pointed out that the brain of the reptile consists of little more than a brain stem and several ganglia; the paleomammalian and neomammalian "brains" are represented only in rudimentary form in the brain of the reptile. Nevertheless, this reptilian brain supports a complex series of behaviors, including sustained attention or vigilance. From the point of view of evolution, therefore, the capacity for sustained attentive behavior may be present in many species in which there is no more than a rudimentary forebrain or telencephalon. We define "sustained attention" as the *capacity to maintain the focus of sensory receptors on an aspect or aspects of the internal or external environment for an appreciable interval of time, sufficient to accomplish a task or meet a need significant to the organism.*

MacLean's analysis of the R-complex in the human brain leads to the view that this clump of ganglia, which constitutes virtually all of the reptilian brain, can support a variety of behaviors that could be characterized as *vigilant, attentive, and sustained.* The following passage illustrates this point dramatically, in the case of a giant Komodo lizard lying in wait to ambush a deer: "He proceeds to a favored ambush site . . . Well camouflaged by his own colors and the surrounding herbage, he hides himself about 1 m from the trail where he can lunge forward and grip the deer . . . he remains so motionless that one might think that he was asleep or dead . . . Finally the moment arrives! . . . (he) lunges forward, grabbing a large stag by the hind leg." [3 p. 131]

As evolution progressed to other species, the brain developed additional volume and complexity. Augmented capacity for attentive behavior was thus overlaid on the more primitive, although in many aspects adequate, brain stem system of the reptile. Therefore, whereas the system for maintenance of attentive behavior in the human (or higher primate) includes limbic and neocortical components, the brain stem remains a key component and may be the keystone of the entire system. Additional evidence of the essential role of brain stem structures in attention is provided by the capacity of the newborn human for sustained visual attention, which exists well before the neocortex is fully myelinated (see review by Lipsett and Eimas[4]); this capacity would therefore appear to be heavily dependent on subcortical structures in the paleomammalian and reptilian portions of the human brain.

CONTRIBUTIONS FROM THE STUDY OF EPILEPSY: CONVERGING CONCEPTS OF THE REPTILIAN BRAIN AND THE CENTRENCEPHALON

The writings of MacLean have emphasized the critical role of deep subcortical structures in the maintenance and elaboration of numerous behaviors, including, as we have pointed out, vigilance or sustained attention. A similar conclusion could have been reached on the basis of an entirely different line of evidence, namely, the behavioral and electrophysiological signs associated with various types of seizure disorders, particularly as manifest in the clinical phenomenon of petit mal or *absence epilepsy.*

MacLean took considerable advantage of the knowledge to be gained from the experiments in nature that comprise seizure disorders. Particularly memorable is his discussion of how elaborate, articulated behaviors might occur in complex partial epilepsy without any recollection on the part of the patient. MacLean[5] accounted for this by noting that the hippocampus, the master control mechanism for memory, was inoperative throughout such episodes—in a seizure-induced bioelectric storm—and thus memory function was temporarily suspended.

As background, it should be noted that Hughlings Jackson[6] enunciated the principle of three levels of differentiation or integration of functioning of the central nervous system. The first two levels were concerned, respectively, with representation of body parts and coordination of movements or sensations. The highest level of integration was a functional rearrangement of sensory and motor behavioral components that constitute the neural basis of consciousness. Jackson suggested that this highest level might reside in the frontal lobes or, to use MacLean's terminology, the neomammalian brain. In contrast, the neurosurgeon Wilder Penfield and the neurologist Herbert Jasper proposed that the third level was localized deep within the brain stem or "centrencephalon."[7]

The concept of the centrencephalic system was derived from the results of numerous experimental studies of the electrical activity of the brain in animals. The results pointed to a major coordinating role for midline brain stem structures in the functioning of neural activity in the forebrain, which eventually makes conscious activity possible. Penfield and Jasper maintained, further, that petit mal seizures provide an example of a disorder of the centrencephalic system: the primary manifestation of this type of seizure is a brief interruption of consciousness or attention that occurs in conjunction with bilaterally-symmetrical, three-per-second EEG discharges. A petit mal seizure was described in 1954 by Penfield and Jasper[7]:

> There is a loss of consciousness which may be associated with no other outward manifestation than a blank stare, an arrest of what one might call voluntary activity. The return of consciousness may likewise be without sign except for the resumption of his previous train of thought as shown by speech or action. The patient himself may have no knowledge of the gap unless he perceives that his position has changed or his surroundings have altered . . . Thus, the clinician is brought to a consideration of consciousness and unconsciousness, in spite of himself and however insecure he may feel, when forced to pass over so much deep water on the thin ice of his own psychological insight (p. 480).

Figure 12.2 provides an example of the bilaterally symmetrical and synchronous three per-second spike-and-wave EEG seizure discharges that characterize absence epilepsy.[8] These seizures were considered to be "centrencephalic" in origin, emanating from deep, centrally-located structures with widespread connections to both cerebral hemispheres. In Penfield's[9] words:

> Interference with the centrencephalic system of the higher brain stem produces loss of consciousness. In the presence of deep coma due to a small critically placed local lesion in the higher brain stem, the motor mechanism may seem to remain intact. The patient lies in bed and moves occasionally as in deep sleep, like the enchanted "sleeping beauty" of the French nursery tale . . . When epileptic discharge occurs in the gray matter of the centrencephalic system of the higher brain stem, the patient is initially unconscious because the discharge interferes with local ganglionic function . . . The system of nerve fibers and ganglionic centers within the brain stem may be called centrencephalic since, because of its central position, it provides symmetrical connections with the whole brain. Through it, one may suppose that *this part of the cortex, or that part, could be used*

simultaneously or in sequence, depending upon the pattern and the requirements of the existing state of consciousness (italics added). (p. 1444)

The italicized portion of text suggests that different regions of the cortex may be implicated in different attentional functions, according to the requirements of the situation, and relates directly to the theoretical localization of attention functions in cortical areas that we have proposed.[1]

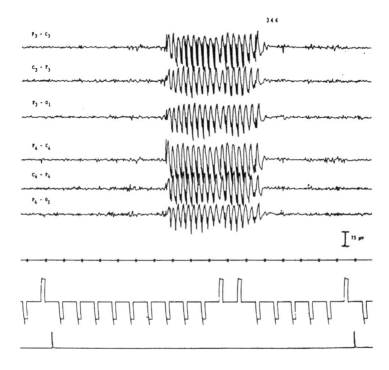

Figure 12.2. Bilateral Symmetrical and Synchronous Three per Second Spike-and-Wave EEG Seizure Discharges (with permission) (see Appendix for more detail).

Penfield and Jasper[7] proposed that the diagnostic label *petit mal* epilepsy be replaced with *centrencephalic* epilepsy. In their theorizing, therefore, consciousness was either localized in, or regulated by, deep brain stem structures. The reasoning is analogous to that used by MacLean in accounting for the memory blackout during a hippocampal seizure. In the case of an absence attack, however, the seizure is in the centrencephalon, or, we may say, the reptilian brain. Thus, attention is temporarily suspended. Figure 12.3 illustrates the centrencephalic system of Penfield and Jasper, the central integrating mechanism for coordinating and regulating the activities of the two cerebral hemispheres.

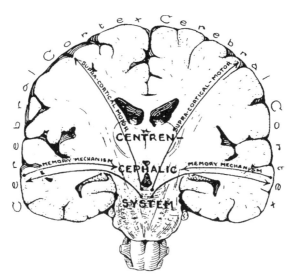

Figure 12.3. The Centrecephalic System of Penfield and Jasper (with permission) (see also Appendix).

CONTRIBUTIONS FROM THE STUDY OF ATTENTION AND CONSCIOUSNESS: CONVERGING CONCEPTS OF THE REPTILIAN BRAIN: THE CENTRENCEPHALON AND THE ASCENDING RETICULAR ACTIVATING SYSTEM

We are struck by the similarity of views represented by MacLean's reptilian brain and Penfield and Jasper's centrencephalon. It is also remarkable that these two approaches converge with that represented by the concept of the "ascending reticular activating system," originating from the reticular core of the brain stem, as enunciated by Lindsley.[10] The ascending reticular activating system is a deep subcortical system with widespread connections to the forebrain that are crucial for the maintenance of alertness and arousal. Figure 12.4 depicts Lindsley's conceptualization of the ascending reticular activating system, with the reticular formation of the brain stem forming its base.

Based on 30 years of neurophysiological research, Lindsley[10] proposed the following definition of the organization of attentional functions:

Wakefulness is maintained by excitation of the reticular formation and the ARAS [ascending reticular activating system] through collaterals from all sensory pathways, by corticifugal impulses originating in various regions of the cortex and by humoral factors which affect particularly the rostral portions of the reticular formation...Attention is closely allied to arousal and wakefulness and, like wakefulness and consciousness, appears to be a graded phenomenon extending from general alerting, as in the orienting reflex, to specific alerting, *as when attention is focused upon a given sense mode and dominates sensory input to the point of exclusion of other sense modes. Still higher or more finely focused attention may be restricted to a limited aspect of a given sense mode* (italics added) (p. 1589)

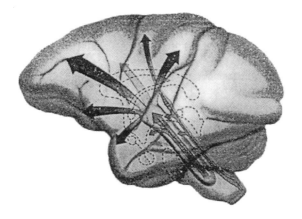

Figure 12.4. Lindsley's Ascending Reticular Activating System (with permission) (see also Appendix).

As in the case of the quotation from Penfield[9] above, the portion in italics presages the theoretical, functional localization of attention functions in cortical areas that we have proposed.[1]

There is thus considerable overlap among the three concepts of reptilian brain, centrencephalon, and reticular activating system. Such overlap is to be expected, as the three concepts all draw from the same repository of data concerning the organization and development of attentional functions within the central nervous system.

LOCALIZATION OF ATTENTION FUNCTIONS IN THE BRAIN: THE BRAIN STEM AND BEYOND

Our thesis is that the system responsible for the regulation of consciousness also supports those aspects of attentive behavior characterized as "sustained." This view is supported by the results of numerous experiments showing that the capacity for sustained attention or vigilance is dependent upon the integrity of the midline brainstem system (reptilian brain, centrencephalon, or reticular core of the brain stem).

Some of this research involved the development of monkey models that permitted direct exploration of brain structures and systems thought to be involved in the maintenance of sustained attention. All of these experiments involved monkeys trained to perform tests of sustained attention. They comprise lesion studies[11] of the effects of electrical stimulation of subcortical brain regions,[12,13] and the recording and identification of "attention" cells in subcortical and cortical areas of the monkey brain.[14, 15] This work is described in detail in the original publications; we excerpt here some of the key results indicating the critical role of brain stem (reptilian brain) structures in the support of sustained attention.

Figure 12.5 presents sagittal sections of the macaque brain, indicating the location of electrical brain stimulation-induced effects on a test of sustained attention, a monkey version of the Continuous Performance Test[16] As shown in Figure 12.5, critical points for inducing lapses of attention (i.e., errors of omission) cluster in the mesencephalic and pontine reticular formations and in the pons.

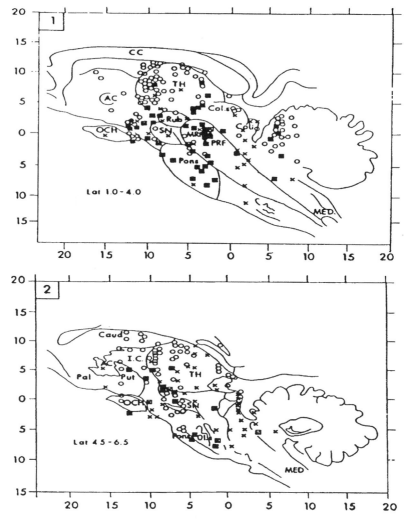

Figure 12.5. Location of Electrical Brain Stimulation-induced Effects. Macaque Brain, Sagittal View (with permission) (see Appendix for more detail).

Figure 12.6 depicts frequency histograms of task-related neuronal activity in single cells in the monkey recorded during performance of a similar test of sustained attention. The animals were trained to respond ("go") to one stimulus, and withhold a motor response ("no go") to another stimulus. In these experiments, cells that fired only on "go" trials were labeled Type I, and were considered motor cells. In contrast, cells that fired for both "go" and "no-go" trials were classified as attention-related cells.[14, 15] The Type II cells, such as those seen in the lower portion of Figure 12.6, were found frequently in the region of the mesencephalic reticular nuclei. The consensus of the results of the various experimental approaches was that a critical area for sustained attention lies in the medial portions of the pontine and mesencephalic reticular formation–the heart of the reptilian brain or centrencephalon.[17]

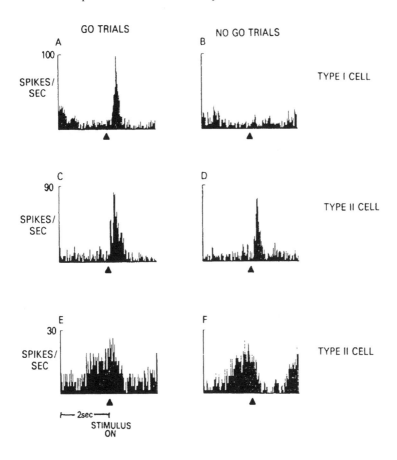

Figure 12.6. Frequency Histograms of Task-related Neuronal Activity in Single Cells in the Monkey (with permission) (see Appendix for more detail).

However, in addition to attention functions dependent upon an intact brain stem, extensive research conducted over the past three decades indicates a major role of limbic and neocortical structures in the support of attention. We believe that the various functions of attention have become differentiated and articulated as the brain has evolved. Our reasoning is similar to MacLean's, in that certain "limbic" attention functions are overlaid on the reptilian or centrencephalic brain, and that still others are neocortical and contained within the neomammalian brain. These, in turn, overlie the paleo-mammalian brain. Moreover, the structures supporting these functions are inter-connected.

Figure 12.7 shows some of these structures, along with their tentative functional roles, as assigned by our model of attentions

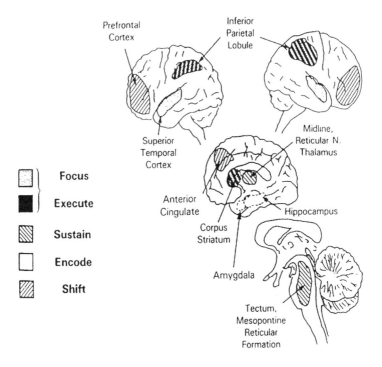

Figure 12.7. Structures of Attention and their Functions (with permission) (see Appendix for more detail).

Our work indicates that it is essential to consider attention as a multi-faceted process or capacity, and MacLean's work has suggested a model of how these attention functions may be organized—from an evolutionary point of view. The figure summarizes our proposal for a beginning taxonomy of attentive functions, stimulated, in part, by MacLean's model of the behavioral capacities that appear in the three strata of the triune brain.

CONSTRUCTS OF THE ATTENTION MODEL

The primary constructs of our model of attention may be summarized as follows:

1. Attention is a complex process or set of processes. It can be subdivided into a number of distinct functions, including *sustain and stabilize, encode, focus, execute,* and *shift.*

2. These functions are supported by different brain regions, which have become specialized for this purpose, but which are nevertheless organized into a system. This system has advanced in complexity over the course of brain evolution.

3. The system organization allows for shared responsibility for attentional functions. This implies that the functional specialization is not absolute and that some structures may substitute for others in the event of injury.

4. *Sustaining* a focus on some aspect of the environment is the major responsibility of the reptilian brain, which comprises rostral midbrain structures, including the mesopontine reticular formation and midline and reticular thalamic nuclei. We believe that the function we have labeled *stabilize,* controlling the regularity of response, may also be dependent upon midline-thalamic and brain stem structures.[18,19] Sustaining a focus of attention is the phylogenetically earliest attention function.

5. *Encoding* of stimuli is dependent upon the hippocampus and amygdala. This function is supported by the limbic or paleomammalian brain.

6. The function of *focusing* on environmental events is shared by superior temporal and inferior parietal cortices, as well as by structures that comprise the corpus striatum.

7. The *execution* of response depends heavily on the integrity of inferior parietal and corpus striatal regions. By MacLean's analysis, *focusing and execution* are dependent upon both the reptilian and neomammalian brains (corpus striatum and temporo-parietal cortex as seen in Figure 12.7), but this requires further study and analysis.

8. The capacity to *shift* focus from one aspect of the environment to another in a flexible, adaptive manner is dependent upon the integrity of the prefrontal cortex, including the anterior cingulate gyrus. This capacity may be a unique function of the neomammalian brain.[20]

9. Damage or dysfunction in one of these brain regions can lead to circumscribed or specific deficits in a particular attention function.

These nine points are the primary tenets of our attention model. Ordinarily, the three brain layers operate together harmoniously, as a system, except when there is a structural or functional lesion. We have written elsewhere on the use of our model in studies of neuropsychiatric disorders, including schizophrenia,[21] infantile autism,[22] absence epilepsy,[1] attention-deficit hyperactivity disorder,[23] malnutrition,[24] and parasite infection;[25] and we believe that it provides a valuable heuristic for both theoretical and practical clinical applications.

APPENDIX
DETAILED EXPLANATION OF FIGURES

Figure 12.1. Schematic diagram of the evolution of the human cerebrum. The brain expands in hierarchic fashion along the lines of three basic patterns that may be characterized as reptilian, paleomammalian, and neomammalian (after MacLean).

Figure 12.2. The relation between a burst of spike-and-wave activity and performance in a patient with petit mal epilepsy. The top six channels in the tracing represent a standard antero-posterior EEG run, with electrode placements determined by the 10–20 system. Note the symmetrical and synchronous three-per-second pattern that characterizes petit mal (absence) seizures. The next channel is a 1–s time mark. Below this are represented the stimuli presented to the patient; those that required a response are seen as upward deflections from the baseline; other stimuli appear as downward deflections. The patient's responses are shown on the lowest channel, indicated as upward deflections. The patient failed to respond to the two stimuli occurring during the spike-and-wave burst, but responded correctly to those before and after the burst. Reproduced from Mirsky and Tecce[8] (with permission).

Figure 12.3. According to Penfield and Jasper, the centrencephalic system is the chief central integrating mechanism for various areas of cortex. It is defined as the neuron system, centering in the higher brain stem, having equal functional relationships with the two cerebral hemispheres. The to-and-fro projection pathways are considered as integral parts of the system. Indicated are the connections involved in making records of past experience available (memory mechanism) and executing voluntary movements (supra-cortical motor). Reproduced from Penfield and Jasper (with permission).[7]

Figure 12.4. The ascending reticular activating system projected schematically on the monkey brain. The reticular formation, consisting of the multineuronal, multisynaptic central core of the region from medulla to hypothalamus, receives collaterals from specific sensory pathways and projects diffusely upon the cortex. Reproduced from Lindsley (with permission).[10]

Figure 12.5. Sagittal sections of macaque brain showing the location of electrical brain stimulation-induced effects on a sustained attention test (CPT) in the monkey. Points which when stimulated caused errors of *omission* on the test (filled squares) are concentrated in the more medial portions (lateral 1.0-4.0, upper figure) of the lower brain stem (i.e., reptilian brain). Points which when stimulated caused errors *of commission* (Xs) are concentrated more in the lateral sections of the brain (lateral 4.5–6.5, lower figure). The open circles indicate no behavioral effect of stimulation. Abbreviations: MRF, mesencephalic reticular formation; PRF, pontine reticular formation; MED, medulla oblongata; Col s, superior colliculus; Col i, inferior colliculus; AC, anterior commissure; OCH, optic chiasm; CC, corpus callosum; TH, thalamus; IC, internal capsule; Rub, red nucleus; SN, substantia nigra; Caud, caudate nucleus; Pal, pallidum; Put, putamen. Reproduced from Bakay Pragay, Mirsky et al. (with permission).[12]

Figure 12.6. Frequency histograms based on the number of spike potentials recorded during go and no-go trials in three task-related cells in the brain of the monkey. Each histogram typically summarizes 15 to 20 trials. The black triangle indicates the onset of the task stimulus; the interval used for summating spikes was 32 ms. The Type I cell (top row of figure) fires during go trials but shows no responses during no-go trials; the Type II cell (middle row of figure) is active only poststimulus; and the Type II Anticipatory cell (bottom row of figure) begins to fire about 1 s prior to stimulus onset. Type II cells, active in both go and no-go trials, are thought to form part of an attention system in the brain, and are found in many locations in the reticular formation (reptilian brain). Reproduced from Mirsky and Duncan (with permission).[17]

Figure 12.7. Semi-schematic representation of the proposed attention system of the human brain. Functional specializations are tentatively attributed to distinct brain regions. The assignment of function is not intended to be absolute or exclusive; moreover, in the case of injury or disease, some functions may be assumed by the remaining, intact portions of the system. Adapted from Mirsky, et al. (with permission).[1]

NOTES

1. Mirsky AF, Anthony BJ, Duncan CC, Ahearn MB, Kellam SG: Analysis of the elements of attention: A neuropsychological approach. *Neuropsychology Review,* 1991; 2: 109–145.

2. MacLean PD: The Brain in Relation to Empathy and Medical Education. *Journal of Nervous and Mental Desease*, 1967; 144: 374–382.

3. MacLean PD: *The Triune Brain in Evolution: Role in Paleocerebral Functions.* NY: Plenum Press, 1990.

4. Lipsett LP, Eimas PD: Developmental psychology. *Annual Review of Psychology,* 1972; 23: 1–50.

5. MacLean PD: A mind of three minds: Educating the triune brain. In Chall J, Mirsky AF (Eds): *Education and the Brain.* Chicago: University of Chicago Press, 1978, pp. 308–342.

6. Jackson JH: Selected writings of John Hughlings Jackson. Taylor J (Ed): *Volume I, On Epilepsy and Epileptiform Convulsions.* London: Hodder and Stoughton, 1931.

7. Penfield W, Jasper HH: *Epilepsy and the Functional Anatomy of the Human Brain.* Boston: Little Brown, 1954.

8. Mirsky AF, Tecce, JJ: The analysis of visual evoked potentials during spike-andwave EEG activity. *Epilepsia,* 1968; 9: 211–220.

9. Penfield W: Neurophysiological basis of the higher functions of the nervous system Introduction. In Field J, Magoun HW, Hall VE (Eds): *Handbook of Physiology, Section 1: Neurophysiology, Volume III.* Washington, DC: American Physiological Society, 1960; pp. 1441–1445.

10. Lindsley DB: Attention, consciousness, sleep and wakefulness. In Field J, Magoun HW, Hall VE (Eds): *Handbook of Physiology, Section 1: Neurophysiology, Volume III.* Washington, DC: American Physiological Society; 1960, pp. 1553–1593.

11. Mirsky, AF, Oshima HI: Effect of subcortical aluminum cream lesions on attentive electroencephalogram in monkeys. *Experimental Neurology,* 1973; 39: 1–18.

12. Bakay Pragay E; Mirsky AF; Fullerton BC; Oshima HI; Arnold SW: Effect of electrical stimulation of the brain on visually controlled (attentive) behavior in the *Macaca mulatta. Experimental Neurology,* 1975; 49: 203–220.

13. Mirsky AF, Bakay Pragay E, Harris S: Evoked potential correlates of stimulation induced impairment of attention in *Macaca mulatta. Experimental Neurology,* 1977; 57: 242–256.

14. Bakay Pragay, E; Mirsky, AF; Ray, CL; Turner, DF & Mirsky, CV Neuronal activity in the brain stem reticular formation during performance of a "go-no go" visual attention task in the monkey. *Experimental Neurology,* 1978; 60: 83–95.

15. Ray C; Mirsky AF; Bakay Pragay E: Functional analysis of attention-related unit activity in the reticular formation of the monkey. *Experimental Neurology,* 1982; 77: 544–562.

16. Rosvold HE, Mirsky AF, Sarason I, Bransome ED Jr, Beck LH: A continuous performance test of brain damage. *Journal of Consulting Psychology,* 1956; 20: 343–350.

17. Mirsky AF, Duncan CC: Behavioral and electrophysiological studies of absence epilepsy. In Avoli N, Gloor P, Kostopoulos G, Naquet R (Eds): *Generalized Epilepsy: Neurobiological Approaches.* New York: Plenum, 1990, pp. 254–269.

18. Tatman JE: *Elements of Attention and Concentration in Normal Aging Adults: Locus of Decline.* Unpublished master's thesis, The American University, Washington, DC, 1992.

19. Mirsky AF: Disorders of attention: A neuropsychological perspective. In Lyon GR, Krasnegor NA (Eds): *Attention, Memory and Executive Function,* Baltimore: Paul H. Brookes, 1995, pp. 71–95.

20. Goldstein K, Scheerer M: Abstract and concrete behavior: An experimental study with special tests. *Psychological Monographs,* 1941; 53: 1–151.

21. Mirsky AF; Yardley SJ; Jones BP; Walsh D; Kendler KS: Analysis of the attention deficit in schizophrenia: A study of patients and their relatives in Ireland. *Journal of Psychiatric Research,* 1995; 29: 23–42.

22. Pascualvaca D; Fantie BF; Papageorgiou M; Mirsky AF: Attention capacities in children with autism: Is there a general deficit in shifting focus? *Journal of Autism and Developmental Disorders,* 1998; 28: 467–478.

23. Mirsky AF; Pascualvaca DM; Duncan CC; French LM: A model of attention and its relation to ADHD. *Mental Retardation and Developmental Disabilities Research Reviews,* 1999; 5: 169–176.

24. Levav M; Mirsky AF; Schantz PM; Castro S; Cruz ME: Parasitic infestation in malnourished school children: Effects on behavior and EEG. *Parasitology,* 1995; 110: 103–111.

25. Levav M; Mirsky AF; Cruz ME; Cruz I: Neurocysticercosis and performance on neuropsychological: A family study in Ecuador. *American Journal of Tropical Medicine and Hygiene,* 1995; 53: 552–557.

PART V

INTERPRETATIONS AND CHALLENGES

13

FROM PHYSICS AND EVOLUTIONARY NEUROSCIENCE TO PSYCHOTHERAPY: PHASE TRANSITIONS AND ADAPTATIONS, DIAGNOSIS AND TREATMENT*

James Brody

INTRODUCTION

This chapter proposes the combining of models from statistical physics with the evolutionary neuroscience of Paul MacLean. "Chaos," "stasis," and "phase transition" apply broadly in statistical physics and offer a platform for our understanding of biological organizations. Darwinian natural and sexual selection, nature's reliance on two sexes, and the dynamic properties of genes, families, culture, and morality suggest striking similarities with the phases and transitions seen in physical systems. There is also a basis through binary and tertiary models for MacLean's triune brain concept. Integrating these ideas from physics, evolution, and neuroscience should provide useful insights and lead to a unified theoretical approach for the diagnosis and treatment of human emotional disorders.

PHYSICS AND THE REQUIREMENTS FOR EVOLUTION TO OCCUR

Introduction: Coherence and Metaphor

According to a review in *Nature,* statistical physics has earned 16 Nobel prizes in physics and chemistry.[1] Further, "statistical physics, and more specifically the theory of transitions between states of matter, more or less

---

*This chapter is based on presentations given in Boston (7/99), Manhattan (11/99) and Amherst, MA (6/00). Thanks to Howard Bloom, Donald Mender, M.D., Ladislav Kovac, Ph.D., for their encouragement.

defines what we know about 'everyday' matter and its transformations . . . (and) . . . is promising to offer insights into phenomena once considered outside the physicist's domain: traffic flow, economics, cell biology and allometric scaling (the relation of biological functions to body mass), to name a few."[1, p. 74]

This chapter attempts to relate a few concepts of statistical physics to the evolutionary neuroscience of Paul MacLean. The first part establishes the necessary concepts borrowed from physics. The second part connects these ideas with MacLean's concepts of the limbic system and the triune brain. Finally, the integrated model is applied to diagnosis and therapy of emotional distress. It will be argued here that (1) some models from statistical physics apply to human groups and individual CNS organization, (2) our developmental paths are necessarily more channeled than we often realize, and (3) there is a coherent physical and evolutionary model for our psychological characteristics, a model that might inform our clinical work. The following sketch, and it is only that, reaches across customary disciplinary gaps. In addition to bridging from physics to biology, the following paragraphs jump several more levels to reconstruct basic aspects of how people weave order in their lives and how we view psychopathology. It's a stretch!

This discussion incurs the risk of our dealing with metaphors, behavior patterns that are similar to each other only through our descriptions and explanations of them. Life grew from simple combinations of molecules to ever more complex ones that even at the bacterial level seem to parallel human organizations.[2, 3, 4, 5] These similarities may be independent metaphors or it may be that they arise from a shared statistical environment that builds and supports only particular kinds of organizations. The similarities discussed in this chapter—like those in statistical physics—occur at many levels of inorganic and biological organization and may be analogous products that were sculpted, independently at times, from different origins in response to similar environmental contingencies.

Evolution Steers between Stasis and Chaos

Kauffman observes: "a *phase boundary* separates networks that exhibit frozen, orderly dynamics from those that exhibit chaotic dynamics. The existence of this boundary leads us to a very general and potentially very important hypothesis: Parallel-processing systems lying in this interface region between order and chaos may be those best able to adapt and evolve. Further, natural selection may be the force which pulls complex adaptive systems into this boundary region." [6, p. 218]

Inorganic and organic molecules are not solitary but take part in decision networks. There are two phases in these networks, static and chaotic.[6, 7, 8, 9] *Chaos* is sometimes synonymous with "indecision." A person (or decision unit, or network of units) participates in several larger networks at the same time but there are conflicting, unresolved demands from each of them. *Phase* refers to a substance's having strikingly different properties in response to just a small change in its temperature or some other environmental variable. For example, water is one phase for groups of the molecule H_2O. Ice and steam are two other phases. Networks are in a static (frozen, ordered, or unchanging) phase if modifying the activity of a few participants has no impact on the larger network. Network responses involve only a small part of the organization and are fast, invariant, and of short latency regardless of the antecedent. They are independent to the extent that there is no cascading of changes throughout the entire system. Reflex arcs are a useful example in which the stretch receptor in the knee triggers leg movement but with no reactions in the neck, arm, or eye. Static nets do not evolve even if reproduced because there is no variability on which natural selection can act.[6]

In contrast, the decision units—transistors, genes, neurons, or people—in a chaotic phase are interconnected in a manner whereby changing the activity of one unit triggers adjustments throughout the entire network.[6, 7] Chaotic networks amplify small changes but in unpredictable ways. They appear to be irreversible, may never repeat themselves, and may never attain a new steady state. The weather, smoke patterns, the turbulence of a flowing stream, and human lives often show chaotic effects wherein a tiny difference in the initial conditions leads to substantially different outcomes that will never be repeated. Chaotic networks also do not evolve because there is no consistency that can be reproduced after natural selection has culled some of the variations.

Evolution occurs between stereotypy (rigidity, stasis) and indecision (chaos). Changing too quickly outruns the niche but changing too slowly entails lost opportunities; either gambit leads to a childless heap of dried fur and stained bones. The trick is to stay in the middle, in a phase transition between rapid stereotypy and indecision, creating and defending linearity and coherence but also allowing some changes with circumstance, using tricks from past experience whether such were learned or evolved, taught by our mother or encoded in our genes.

The Generality of Phase Transitions

Phase boundaries, also called phase transitions, are common. Our most personal sense of one is when we float in a pool of water, too heavy to rise in the air and too light to sink. We also find them in magnetism and conductivity and in fluids and gases. It can be argued that water itself is a phase boundary between steam and ice, one that is essential in order for complex life to evolve. The earth's orbit, our atmosphere, average global temperature range, and present climate all have the property of a phase boundary that separates contrasting and almost limitless extremes in solidity or temperature.

There are phase transitions in the number of hours that we sleep and in physiological variables such as heart rate, blood pressure, and in the partial pressures of oxygen and carbon dioxide in our blood. Neural firing patterns sometimes exhibit a narrow range of increased sensitivity to small changes in input while being generally resistant to changes on either side of that range.[10]

Traffic flow,[11] crowd panic,[12] and even hand clapping in auditoriums move between randomness and coherence.[13] Human life occupies a phase boundary that runs 26,000 miles laterally but from only three miles below to five miles above the surface of the earth, a distribution like that of a water spider. *And most important for this discussion, we show phase transitions when we organize ourselves into groups through our logical and social computations.*[14]

Phase Transitions Bring Symmetry to the Neo-Darwinian Model

Hamilton explained how selfish genes can evolve altruism,[15] but it is also evident that, starting with bacterial communities long ago, altruistic genes evolved selfishness. Species and people can drift to either side of a phase boundary and, like a tacking sailboat running into the wind, must be able to come about. Kauffman remarks: *"tentative evidence supports the hypothesis that parallel-processing systems coevolving to carry out complex tasks . . . do in fact evolve both from the ordered regime and from the chaotic regime."* [6, p. 232] Speciation itself represents a decision, a movement from a larger group into two smaller ones and a simplification, an extinction, through the elimination of intermediate forms.

It is possible to find "simplify" and "complicate" at many levels. For example, we have opposing muscle groups—extensors that push things away from us (simplifiers) and flexors that pull us together (complicators). Miller discusses natural selection and sexual selection as processes for uniformity and variation.[16] Bloom draws a similar model with his concepts of "conformity enforcers" and "diversity generators" in cultures of bacteria and human groups.[2] Stevens and Price discuss "distancing" of individuals; that is, you can have a position within a hierarchy but may also participate to varying degrees in that hierarchy, moving yourself from chaotic to static networks and back again by varying your connectedness.[17]

Thus, we should be able to distinguish processes such as aggression, migration, abortion, helplessness, and the development of social tools or technologies that simplify a life or a social organization from those that help it to become more complex such as bonding, empathy, kin selection, reciprocity, altruism, and moral codes. Individuals as well as groups and species oscillate between degrees of connectedness, and it is another stretch but not a leap to reconsider why moralists sin and sinners periodically hide behind morals.

The Number "3"

Minor shifts in relationships in a phase boundary steer its inhabitants rapidly into chaos or stasis. Kauffman found that *chaotic and static phases are largely a function of the average number of interconnections between members of the network and not the number of participants.*[9] Having an average of fewer than two interconnections in a Boolean net of 100,000 binary units is associated with stasis and fast but invariant outcomes from any input; an average of four or more interconnections produces chaos and decision times of *a billion years or more.* The shift between decision and indecision occurs when the average number of interconnections is between 2.5–3.5. *In this narrow range of connectedness, a "decision" appears in 317 msec even in networks of 100,000 participants—a time consistent with biological events.*[9]

There are some fascinating implications from these effects. They suggest a reason why we have two sexes (plus 1 dependent child for 4 years) instead of three sexes or five. Removing or adding connections and tasks between people will make individual behavior, respectively, more variable or less so. According to Sigmund, 2 competitors will produce oscillations in the population frequency of each of them.[18, p. 56-59] Add a third and the frequencies tend to stabilize for each of them. It is tempting to speculate that any stable biological system will have at least three mutually regulatory components such as an activator, an inhibitor, and a switch. In a variation of this schema, some species have the same relationships observed in the game *Stone-Paper-Scissors.* That is, species A dominates species B and B dominates C, but C dominates A![18] Increasing the number, the diversity, of species usually increases the stability of the entire network.

Triality, MacLean, and Neural Architecture

MacLean's evolutionary triune concept of reptilian (brainstem-striatal), mammalian (limbic), and neomammalian (neo- or isocortex) reflects this triality and may indeed be an expression of decision nets within evolved neural architecture.[19] After all triality is common to other psychological concepts, for example, Freud's id, ego, and superego.[20] And clinical research gives us a tripartite set of responders, possible responders, and nonresponders to nearly any variable. Triage has been with us since the ancient Egyptians and the concept of a triune deity, a Holy Trinity, perhaps as long.[21] Pythagoras talked about triangles, so do modern Bowen family therapists[22] and some ethologists.[23] In addition psychologists create lots of 2x2 and some 3x3 tables but derive correlations in order to understand larger ones. We are apparently no different from primitive peoples, 8-month old human infants, or rhesus monkeys—all of whom keep exact count of 3 or fewer objects but turn to magnitude estimation for quantities larger than 6 unless formal training is given in counting, a step that changes 99 objects into a single one, rank-ordered between the two objects, 98 and 100.[24]

COMPUTATIONAL PROBLEMS AND OUR SENSE OF "MAYBE"

I have mentioned examples from physics that involve liquids, magnetism, or conductivity. parallel phenomenon exists for logical computations, *one that takes us out of physics and into human social behavior.*[14, 25, 26] Consider this example from Hayes[14] of a SAT or "satisfiability" problem: "You are chief of protocol for the embassy ball. The crown prince instructs you either to invite Peru or to exclude Qatar. The queen asks you to invite either Qatar or Romania or both. The king, in a spiteful mood, wants to snub either Romania or Peru or both. Is there a guest list that will satisfy the whims of the entire royal family?"

Hayes's protocol example translates easily into ones that contain hunter and gatherer variables such as past resource availability, profitable search tactics (each member is given assignments that match his or her skills: not everybody gets to throw a spear!), and the presence of competing demands within and between groups. Time of year, health of the participants, stockpiles of equipment, and available technologies are all factors in the computations *which could easily become foundations for selective pressures in human groups.* The anthropologist, Sarah Hrdy, observes: "humans . . . live in families where mothers simultaneously care for multiple young. Closer birth spacing . . . exacerbated dilemmas confronted by mothers who must then decide on how to allocate resources among dependent young with competing needs."[27, p. 203-204] It is easy to imagine that any advantage in negotiating such conflicts would translate into enhanced reproductive success.

According to Hayes, solution time varies linearly with the number of participants but shows a phase transition related to the number of demands that each of them makes.[14] One or two demands (variables) from each participant (clause) can be solved with linear-time algorithms and are trivial. Solution difficulty increases sharply when there are *three* or more variables per clause.[14, 25, 26] Hayes comments, "there is a critical value . . . below which almost all cases are (rapidly) satisfiable and above which they are almost all unsatisfiable (at whatever length investment is made)."[14] The really "difficult" problems for computational scientists or for mothers of three children are in the phase boundary between possible and impossible, the ones that will take persistence and cleverness to unravel. Because of conflicting social demands, we cannot solve them easily but we can not simply walk away from them. *Such problems are the essence of the word "maybe."*

Humans Occupy Decision Networks

Langton remarked once that life evolves to the edge of chaos.[7] People and species are similarly guided. In good times and in moments of speculation we take on more tasks, but dump the excess in bad. Unlike Kauffman's transistors, *humans move themselves into greater or lesser degrees of involvement with other humans,* serving their own self interest by either maneuver. This steering is accomplished by genes, receptors, channel capacity, hormones, social learning, sudden changes in status, and our executive functions. (Further, blocking these personal maneuvers elicits substantial affective distress!)

Mercenaries, bounty hunters, and outlaws are guided primarily by their immediate self interest. At the opposite extreme, Hamlet was immobilized, split between his own ambition and loyalties to other people. He became a western icon for chaotic indecision. He has his equals in the anonymous many of us who dare not act without first consulting every relative and every neighbor or who are paralyzed by the conflicts between our self-interest and our duties to an abusive partner. Mothers who do not allow hierarchies between their young children and women who go directly from child care to attending their ailing parents also lose themselves in a steel web of conflicting duties and incompatible agendas.

Disconnecting allows an independent decision to do or don't do, one that occurs without disrupting the rest of an orderly network; chaos and indecision, however, are characterized by the words "reactive," "convulsive," "unpredictable," or "endless." A bias toward indecision is reflected in words such as "cooperative," "mutualistic," "rule-bound," "traditional," "other-directed," and "enabler." Sensitive people sometimes immerse themselves in chaotic networks but feel "ambivalent", "confused," "guilt-ridden," or "helpless." Once people are wrapped in a network, more extreme conditions of unpredictability elicits panic and words like "trapped," "overwhelmed," or "paralyzed."

Tracking Our Individual Phase Transitions

Ball remarks, "The point is that phase transitions are global and abrupt—they show matter behaving at its most nonlinear, with effects quite out of proportion to cause."[1] Given the power of phase transitions, it is small wonder that we pay so much attention to adjusting our task loads and personal ties, that we generate so much affect in connection with those adjustments, and that we have such ambivalence about them and argue forever about free will *vs.* determinism, selfishness *vs.* sharing, and men *vs.* women.

Events on complexity's scale, like water to a fish, surround us so much that we must balance our lives within it. Therefore, we have tactics—conscious and unconscious, volitional and not—that help us to navigate between confinement and isolation. Such tactics are emergent in our self-talk, our language that explains to our self what we did. The words "simplify" and "complicate" merely head the index of a long list of words that describe variations in our connectedness.

Slack time? Most of us validate the expression "Work expands to fill the time available" with hobbies, new relationships, and incomplete obsessions. On the other hand, if we are overwhelmed or short of resources, then our emotions and our executive functions rearrange priorities, make lists, shunt work off to other people, or discontinue tasks. Even an essayist straddles a phase boundary between monotony and circumstantiality when she manages the number of ideas —probably an average of 2.5—on the page at any one time. If we don't use our executive functions for these decisions, we feel "overwhelmed" or want time for ourselves. Anger or depression, guilt, or denial will then automatically adjust our task list on the basis of immediate self-interest instead of more long term outcomes.

Isolation increases personal instability. In human lives, impulsiveness and stereotypy are associated with developmental immaturity, illness and its residuals, drug or alcohol abuse, senescence, injury, depression, being alone, having no further resources at risk, being rushed for time or selfish and overconfident. It is also noteworthy that suicidality accompanies all these factors. It may be that suicide is best understood both as a form of migration and as the ultimate simplifier.

Many of these phenomena may reflect an erosion of cross-talk between the various decision units of a human mind. Eibl-Eibesfeldt gives fascinating examples of these effects, taken from Ertel's study of dogmatism in German politics during the Nazi era and in Nietzsche's writing during alternating health and syphilitic crises.[28, pp. 46-50] Along these lines, solitary confinement in prison is associated with higher risks of psychotic episodes and suicidal attempts.[29] Jamison records many examples of poets, novelists, painters, and composers who were unstable to the extent of suicide although it is unclear how much social isolation was a cause or a result of their instability.[30] (Indeed, each factor may feed the other.) Sensory deprivation research in universities was halted because of its destabilizing effects on randomly selected college students, effects comparable to those of prisoners in solitary confinement.[29] McGuire and Troisi also show the frequency of bizarre behavior by a mental patient, displayed as a function of the number of observers.[29, p. 76] There is, consistent with Kauffman, a sharp drop between two and three observers! "Independent scholars" demonstrate some of these effects and social isolation is sometimes associated with their creativity. Along similar lines, Kuhn observed that paradigm shifts come from either younger scientists or from older ones who are new to a field.[31]

Making a Phase Transition: Our Favorite Tools

Temperature, water availability, and atmospheric gases all vary both randomly and systematically in relation to their contexts. So do competitors and predators whether viral or furred and because of high rates of mutation, drift, migration, and environmental stress, so do genes. This variability must be managed for the daily pursuit of our self-interests as well as our long-term survival. Further, survival and evolution require that we seek variety and new opportunities. Thus, our rudders oscillate between novelty and familiarity and consist of some evolutionary processes (natural and sexual selection) and some of their products (alliances and hierarchies; genes, receptors, learning, and mental executive functions). I suggest that *natural and sexual selection operate at a species level and across generations whereas alliances and hierarchies achieve for an individual what natural and sexual selection do for a species.*

Natural and Sexual Selection: Steering Left or Right Across Generations

Natural selection corrects for mismatch between niches and individual traits. Therefore, in a stable niche it eventually reduces differences between individuals. Small differences in traits for obtaining food or avoiding predators lead to cumulatively greater numbers of offspring who carry the more advantageous characteristics.

On the other hand, sexual selection increases variation and operates in a different niche, one that consists of the receptors of possible mates. Receptor systems are sensitive to small differences between individuals of the same sex. Small gradations are magnified as only one participant successfully mates out of 10 or a hundred contenders in each generation.[32]

Receptors alert predators as well as mates and predation helps ensure that costumes (size, brightness and contrast, symmetry), activity level, and resources are correlated with both survival and with healthier children.[16] If you draw attention to yourself and are clumsy, you will probably die sooner. It is, therefore, no surprise that displays interact with niche abundance and with predators. Safer, richer environments and high population turnover lead to both fancier costumes and greater behavioral variability that explores settings to their limits. Bad times erode the advertising budget and we all slink when in dangerous neighborhoods.

Alliances and Hierarchies Manage Individual Differences within a Generation

The structural variability of the brain does not usually affect gross anatomical features that are characteristic for the animal species. But the size and position of cortical areas, the distribution of neurotransmitters, and peptides, the thickness of fiber tracts, the number of neurons constituting a nucleus, the recruitment of muscles during stereotyped behaviors such as locomotion, and particularly the microanatomy of neurons and neuronal circuits vary significantly from individual to individual in virtually all animal species. [33, p 10]

One part of the brain, the anterior commissure...varies seven-fold in area between one person and the next . . . the massa intermedia . . . is not found at all in one in four people. The primary visual cortex can vary three-fold in area . . . our amygdala . . . can vary two-fold in volume—as can our hippocampus . . . Most surprising, our cerebral cortex varies in non-learning impaired people nearly two-fold in volume. [34, p 143]

It appears likely for many reasons that a "universal human nature"[35] is an assembly of traits that does not exist in an individual human or perhaps even within groups of them. Alliances and hierarchies manage differences between people *within* each generation; they make corrections that correspond to those made *between* generations by natural and sexual selection.

One explanation for hierarchies is that they minimize spilled blood within a group; dominance and priority are decided by ritualistic displays.[36] Hierarchies also, like sexual selection, magnify differences in the consequences experienced by each participant. Small disparities in ability have large effects on differential reproductive success because dominant members inhibit reproduction by subordinates. However, a third explanation can be offered.

We are genetically and psychologically different from each other and, like bacteria who swap packets of DNA when distressed, we help each other. Differences between people lead to economic and social exchanges. As Krebs and others have pointed out, we offer things that are easy for us to make in return for goods and services that are difficult.[37, 38, 39]

While alliances allow mutual aid, they also slow things down. As in Kauffman's simulations, organizational slowing will occur as soon as 2 parties begin to work as equals for a common goal. Further, decision times will accelerate indefinitely as you include a 3rd, 4th, or more members, each with conflicting demands. (The same temporal changes are also seen in SAT problems.) *Humans make hierarchies within a few moments after a social contact is made and prevent an explosion in the latencies of decisions made by a group.* Seven individuals take the lead from one or two. Debate shortens in primate troops, human regiments, academic committees, and families. Amy tells her little brothers what to do and life continues with less interruption for her mother.

Weaving Self-interest and Morals at the Edge of Chaos

Ed Wilson commented to Bob Wright, "I've always wanted to transform messy subjects into scientifically orderly subjects."[40, p. 138] It is perhaps no coincidence that Ed has been fascinated with weaver ants for much of his life. Like Ed and his ants, we each weave our own structures by exploring, collecting, and modifying the things around us in a process of active Darwinism, [41, 42] one that also glimmers in the phrase "free will." Even singletons and hermits walk this same course, filling their worlds with pets, collections, and dreams when other people do not fit in.

Stasis and chaos are managed by cooperative or selfish gambits in searches for a balance of variation and linearity. Genes and receptor systems are one foundation of that search. However, some new toys—learning, our mental executive functions, culture, and morals—allow humans and chimps to speed their experiments, conduct them more systematically *and* retract bad ideas without fatalities. Our sense of maybe is one result, science is another. While female ducks might grow iridescent feathers through sexual selection over a hundred generations, some hominid women can change lipstick twice in 3 minutes for the same reasons. The ducks may go extinct in order to shed their markers, women usually do not.

Genes

Genes are an accumulation of receptors and strategies that worked in our past and that may be needed again in our futures. They stabilize us across niches and generations and narrow the range of our likely responses so that we are less random and more apt to use behaviors that have worked for us in the past. Genes are functional parallels to a weaver, taking nucleotide fibers and aligning them into a single experience that can be acted upon by other experiences. Because of genes our future behavior is less chaotic and more orderly than might be expected otherwise.

Linearity is observed in physical development as well in the behavior of identical twins, but it is true that different outcomes can be elicited by varied environments from a common set of genes.[43] Skomer voles will be aggressive or tame as a function of their rearing and some grasshoppers will be fat and wingless or lean and winged as a function of their diet.[10] It is as if the same genes can work either side of a phase transition. However, genes have a range of normal variability that is often small or that leads to very predictable bifurcations, not purees, in response to variations in niche conditions. As Darlington observed, genes will give you a stomach in one place and a liver in another but never produce "stiver" in between.[44]

Receptors

There is some evidence that receptor characteristics—whether for serotonin or for sparkles of light—are more stable than effector sequences. C.U.M. Smith describes approximately 14 types of serotonergic receptor and dates them back 700 million years and their precursors back perhaps 2.5 *billion* years.[45] The receptor characteristics of our ancestors, mates, and predators shaped and shape us three times—once through long intervals of phylogeny, again through the 9 months after our personal conception, and again every day between our birth and death.

Receptors, whether for glucose levels, a suitable mate, or an insect automatically make priorities for us, anchoring us to tasks and locations through neurochemistry and conditioning. Satisfying our receptors often "feels good" and guides us on searches in a manner that underlies active Darwinism. Given the conservatism of receptor systems and the variability seen in genetically based response sequences, *careful study of receptor mechanisms may be a more reliable cue to our phylogeny than any schema founded on either bones or behavior "modules."*

Executive Functions

Executive functions are the most newly evolved, most variable between individuals, and most newly analyzed tool that we have for pursuit of our long term self-interests. Working memory, word retrieval, a sense of time, task prioritization, regulation of affect, and our ability to sit under a tree while we analyze situations and synthesize novel solutions—all are thought to be aspects of human executive functions.[46, 47] We make a stack of tasks to be done, arrange them in temporal priority, and return to our stack if we are interrupted. An infinite array of stimuli are filtered and organized and reactions are delayed or implemented in a process of continuous negotiation between self interest and external demands.

Abrupt, go/no-go decisions are inhibited as a wider array of inputs is considered. We discover "maybe" as we accumulate memories, experiences and consequences, form alliances and with all of these aids, look at more options before making an irretrievable commitment. On the other side, we do not spend so long pondering all likely outcomes that we fail to make any response at all. Thus, we steer along the phase boundary of maybe but from two directions, whether we are with no obligations or mired in the affective slop and goo of primate reciprocities.

Strategic Bias: Men Scatter, Women Gather?

Although there is overlap between human males and females in every behavior including lactation,[48] there are also differences in the average performances shown by each group,[49] perhaps hedging our species' bets by exploring "maybe" along parallel tracks. One explanation for two sexes is that they follow opposite boundaries of a phase transition while collecting resources and scattering gametes but with complementary tactics, sharing their respective gains. The partnerships between men and women, however contentious, could mean that whenever one sex is successful, the other benefits. (And so does our species.)

Axons: Males and tools—jokes to slogans. Allman points out that neurons reduce information: many influences are carried into the dendritic tree and condensed into a do or don't-do by a uniform pulse down the axon.[50] We can expect that any single neuron will simplify a decision network just like, as Allman points out, a bacterium or a stock broker.[50] This same process is reflected in the aggregate behavior of males and females!

Males are usually more active and independent than females all through school and their reproductive years. Males hold an order of magnitude more records in literature, music, the arts, and athletics from mutual competition.[51] It could be said that males are biased towards impulsiveness and motor output rather than towards motor inhibition. Some of this outflow is verbal. Younger males interrupt in class and older males tend to dominate politics and religion, transforming the jokes of youth into slogans that may achieve goals of dominance and popularity, the same goals originally met by the jokes. *Males often interrupt and emit more words but females are usually superior in both receptive and expressive abilities.*[49] The interesting possibility exists that males make announcements to other males that neither the sender nor the receiver comprehends fully and women listen not for content but for thought order, word flow, and hints of sincerity and kindness.

"Making a mark" means exerting leadership in the arenas of religion, politics, the arts, or law. It is plausible that much of our legal edifice, tax codes, political traditions, scientific, and religious beliefs are a byproduct of guys showing off against each other. There are also significant implications not only for creativity and invention but also for the opposite phenomenon of organizational incompetence in which males exaggerate personal assets but minimize those of their competition,[51] a strategy that closely parallels the lies that we tell in courtship, politics, and sometimes before armed conflicts.

Dendrites?: Females—rules and networks. Females appear to have a bias towards monitoring environmental details, reflected in their superior incidental memory and recognition for subtle cues from other people.[52] Their sense of smell is keener than that of a male and they are usually better at recognizing discord in the facial expressions of other women.[53] Females are usually more compliant than males and better able to sit at desks and follow teachers' directions through school. While human females take in a wider spectrum of influences before acting, both verbal rules and social networks limit chaotic outcomes for them. This "bias towards chaos" is honored in recognition of feminine sensitivity but ridiculed with talk about their shopping, driving, and changing their minds.

Learning, Family, and Culture

Learning tracks the environment more immediately and specifically than if we relied solely on genes or hormones. The memory from a half second ago guides our next response as we search for linearity, whether in a fight or a banquet.

Family and peers are sometimes considered to be in opposition to one another[47] but both confer stability either across generations or within a group of the same chronological age. Parents and peers do complementary things; they can also substitute for each other but with more static or chaotic outcomes, respectively, and encourage the chances of survival should either one be missing.

The tools and rules of culture are functionally the same as genes, family, and peers but work over intermediate amounts of time. All guide us to use first the solutions that appear to have worked in our pasts. All stabilize the behavior of individuals and groups of individuals across time and niche changes.

Morality

Chaos and stasis helped structure our genome and became unrecognized pillars for our conduct and how we view it. Moral codes are a spun web that sanctions both initiative and restrictions on it. In human relationships and cultures the fences around personal action include tradition, rules, memories, and fears about pain, sickness, or confinement. They also include spite, guilt, shame, and worry about what might happen to our children.

People who are surrounded by reactive networks but ignore them see themselves as independent or self-actualizing but may be punished as "impulsive," "unilateral," "inconsiderate," "egoistic," "narcissistic," "selfish," or "uncooperative" by the other members. On the other hand, that same individual will appear average in a disconnected network where he bothers very few people at any one time. There can also be an overly cooperative individual in a static, disconnected network, distressed by the lack of reciprocity but working excessively to create and maintain it by complicating everyone else's lives!

Constrained actions and actors generally receive greater social approval in such words as "responsible," "dependable," "cooperative," "thoughtful," and "mature." We each find exactly these sentiments in our personal Greek chorus that prompts, praises, and scolds us. There is also a tendency for the dissipation of human and natural resources to be judged as bad except in displays such as weddings and holidays.

KAUFFMAN'S PHYSICS AND MACLEAN'S EVOLUTIONARY NEUROSCIENCE: TOWARD DIAGNOSIS AND THERAPY

The power of Kauffman's analysis lies in the generality of the phenomena that it describes, whether in computer simulations or in personal dilemmas. Thus, we can have unstable networks in human groups or within a human mind; the rules should be the same in either world. The model also combines nicely with a sketch of MacLean's model of the phylogenetic changes in the ways species solve adaptive problems. When extended to humans, a coherent "DSM V" [54] may result!

Diagnosis and a Foundation for DSM V?

Modularity—the concept that we have specialized routines for accomplishing survival tasks such as hunting, mate selection, managing plants, rearing children, and other chores—will some day lead to an appreciation that every human has a unique mosaic of traits. We not only look different, we act different. Such an appreciation will enrich both our labels and the assistance that we given to each client. However, I ignore the intricacies of "modules" in order to simplify the description as presented in Table 13.1. The 3 columns in the table correspond to (1) immobility, (2) stereotypy, and (3) the transition between them. The rows attempt to arrange our miseries in a plausible phylogenetic order and to the right or left side of the center column as a function of relative impulsiveness or constraint. (Please note the order is approximate and applies within mammals).

TABLE 13.1: A Phase Transition and Phylogeny

Chaos	Phase Transition	Stasis
Paralysis from indecision. Rapidly shifting incomplete strategies, excessive response inhibition after minor inputs	WNL re adaptive challenges	Unilateral, stereotyped, short latency behavior
Hypochondria, free-floating anxiety, helplessness, illness/waiting. "Depression" secondary to illness	Self-maintenance: Cleaning, movement feeding/hunting, self-defense. Variable activity level	Specific phobias: Poison, animals, insects, excess heat, cold, fire, water. Escape. Hyperactivity in novel or richer settings, mania. OCD?
Withdrawal, submission. Expectations of task failure. Social phobia. Depression from territory or mating defeats	**R-complex?** Self Defense, territory, dominance, submission, short term mating, escape, migration Agonic hierarchies	Assault Excess displays (dominance & mating). Territories exceed ability. Migration/suicide
Excess Guilt. Dependent PD, avoidant PD, "enabler," excessive humility. Depression (social failure, anticipated resource loss)	**Limbic?** Peer & family bonding, long-term mating. Alliances/hedonic hierarchies. Delayed reciprocity, raise-the-stakes. Child investment, Economic swaps Team hunting & gathering	Antisocial PD, borderline PD, OCPD, narcissistic PD. Grandiosity, spite, selfishness, rejection sensitivity. Depression, suicide
Inconsistent use of routine behavior, highly "other-directed" "To be or not to be," an endless question	**Neocortical/Orbital** Executive functions refine paleo tasks via language. Delayed gratification, task sequencing, affect regulation, planning. Social exchange of information	Excess reliance on a few adaptations Narcissistic PD OCD Task specific, rigid inhibitions. Residuals of infection Senescence

Column on the Left: Creatures of "Us"

Anxiety and social confinement are associated with fretting, worry, and generalized inhibition of coherent behavior. We can be indecisive or we can revert to more primitive thinking, becoming even more helpless and forgetful and failing to make subtle distinctions or to engage in problem solving. We look for allies to protect us, to arrange our lives, or to pick up our load. Constrained behavior—anxiety disorders, many depressions, and some of the personality disorders—nest with the "internalizing" ones.

Column on the Right: Creatures of "Me" and of the Moment

Impulsive behaviors—defined not on the basis of speed but of inaccuracy and a failure to consider other people and delayed consequences—include mania, dysthymia, some of the personality disorders, and some aspects of ADHD. They generally overlap with "externalizing" disorders. Injury, immaturity, aging, infections and their aftermath, developmental arrest, depression, grandiosity, and genomic imbalances are plausible foundations for impulsive, ratcheted behavior. Small children and childish adults (some of the personality disorders, some criminals, and people in a manic state) tend to sever reciprocal ties, exerting unilateral initiative while minimizing concern for other people or the environment.

Some drugs simplify the user's life, either by eroding worry, guilt, and spite (alcohol and cannabis, the benzodiazepines, the antidepressants and mood stabilizers) or by increasing initiative and improving sustained attention (the stimulants, mood stabilizers, and one of the atypical "neuroleptics," risperidone). The more primitive expressions of this bias may be reflected in our experience of traumatic avoidance learning, food poisoning, PTSD, OCD (safety, hoarding, and cleansing rituals), or escape (migration and suicide).

Alternating from Center to Left or Right and Back Again

Miller discusses "protean behavior," nearly random sequences of behavior that are useful for escaping predators, developing novel solutions, or for exploring new settings.[55] Creative brainstorming, daydreams, and moments of hypervigilance and racing thoughts are momentary trips further into chaos; utility depends on aligning their content with practical requirements. Doing so can produce new art forms or advertising campaigns or the invention of polymerase chain reactions.[56]

The Rows: A Phylogenetic Sketch; Behavior We Share with Bacteria

We are still tubes that follow our mouths. Even before we were worms, however, we were viruses and bacteria. We were active or waiting, advancing or retreating. We signaled success and replicated or after a failure, waited for better times or explored another niche. We also formed organizational nets with impressive capacity for parallel information processing and collective problem solving.[2] Thus, activity level, initiative, sleep and appetite, and avoiding the stench of death are all recursive elaborations of very old mechanisms. The same holds true for our reactions to allergens, poisons or to a glut of food. Depression may well have started as being poisoned, hungry or thirsty, too hot or too cold or too alone. Imagine salmonella discovering thawed hamburger after a period of starvation. Would they have a manic episode? Probably. And lithium would probably calm them down.

Structure and Variation in Mammals

MacLean defined a triune brain in which the brain stem and striatum, the limbic system, and the neocortex are seen as three stages in the evolution of the human brain.[19] It seems reasonable to expect different behaviors from each of them. Erratic sleep cycles, helplessness, deep pain, nausea, and physical harm disturb insects, lizards, mice and men. It is tempting within mammals to extend this analysis to reproduction, mother-infant attachment, grooming, social alliances, and economic swaps. However, pioneering analyses such as MacLean's have some dangers.

First, our common sense will mislead us about physical and behavioral relationships. For example, the geneticists have found that whales and hippos are siblings! This kind of surprise is also seen in clinical research. An array of behavioral problems from depression to guilt to grandiosity to OCD to weight and sleep regulation all respond to changes in serotonin. A family of discomforts has been defined by their responses to a single medicine and we, after listening to Prozac[57] now have the concept of serotonin spectrum disorders that provide a single umbrella for our emotional whales and hippos. This is not a unique tale. For millennia we considered illness to be an outcome of damnation rather than of germs and contaminated water. As with Prozac and depression, a new tool—the microscope—ended a superstition and a stack of books, written by the authorities who practiced it, moved to the history section in the library.

Second, evolution is disorderly. It is noted for redirecting an existing structure rather than designing something from scratch for a new purpose. Further, we are just beginning to unravel the extent to which retroviruses and reverse mutations scribbled freely in genomes. This latter phenomenon makes it possible for a physical trait to appear, then disappear back to an earlier form, and then reappear. Thus, tracing a reflex through time and arranging a phylogenetic order for it becomes very difficult since those traits are usually more labile than sensory or physical ones.[58]

Third, overlaying and highly interconnected evolutionary elaborations such as the striatum, limbic system, and neocortex are not surprising when evolution refines basic interrelated components that have been there for a long time. Capping the entire striatum with a cortex could have resulted from a change in a homeobox regulator gene, one that operates early in ontogeny and affects many cell types and physical structures but now operates one more time, one step further removed from the brain stem. It is possible that such a genetic change would be relatively simple, one that does not instruct the creation of entirely new systems. Epigenetic instructions might need merely to state "do it again one more time" after elaboration of the limbic areas. In another section of the ectoderm, our fingers, hand, wrist, and forearms can be seen as the repeated splitting of an upper arm bone—a process mirrored in our legs, ankles, feet, and toes.[59] Our cortical layers may allow an increase in resolution similar to what we observe in our fingers because the cortex is a step or two after the decisions that first sculpted a brain stem. *Did we get fingers at about the same time that we got a cortex?*

One result is that we can expect highly similar modules at all levels of the CNS; any new ones may come from doing old things in a more elaborate way, possibly the product of genetic instructions that add a layer to old neural structures and, via local decisions between the layers, connect them in a more complex way, almost inevitably slowing decisions while enhancing the emergent qualities of thoughtfulness, cooperation, and a sense of maybe. At the same time, global diagnoses for one disorder or another will fragment into more modular, more specific ones. The refinements that we see in learning disabilities will also be discovered in characteristics, and possible adaptations, such as mating, spatial orientation, child care, plant awareness, and so on.

MacLean's R (protoreptilian) Complex

The R-complex, which designates the forebrain striatum as integrated with the neural chasis (midbrain, hindbrain, and spinal cord), may govern much of our ancestral behavioral repertiore. Our sensitivity to personal helplessness, the rustles and scent of a predator or of a lover, the salty velvet liquor of blood, the distressed look of an infant—all possibly started about the same time that we gained fur and feathers. We might expect such old stimuli to elicit fear sequences that condition quickly, extinguish slowly, and are not particularly open to verbal interventions. Pavlov's results with interoceptive conditioning had many of these characteristics. So do the traits associated with post traumatic stress disorder.

Biologic motion,[60] sensory filters,[61] and fragmented Jungian evolutionary research findings[62] all suggest that innate stimuli exist for humans, stimuli also powerful in other creatures and that, after a single reinforced trial, may elicit disproportionate waves of fear, immobilization, anxiety, disgust, or anger in one direction; elation, silliness, curiosity, pride, and arrogance in another. Some of us exclaim "gross" or "I'm going to throw up" at the thought of a news item about water leaking from coffins that were removed from an old cemetery. If we consider that we share receptor mechanisms, there is less surprise that most of us will nurture a helpless chick or baby squirrel or that one species may protect the young of another.

It is a step from sensory guides to the motor and communication sequences that satisfy them. Our daily posturing, our advances and retreats, and many of the large motor sequences that we display when making a sale or standing in line for a cup of coffee are recognizable by our dog or cat and possibly by a lizard. Reptiles may share our foundations for assertion, claiming territory, courtship, and submission, finding a home, establishing and defending territory, ritualistic displays for dominance, defense or surrender, triumph, hoarding, greeting, social groups, flocking, and migration.[19] (Any temptation to include lizards in our lineage is often panned. However, mice—a close genetic relative to humans— have homeobox regulator genes that are similar to *drosophila* and to humans![63, 64] If we share these fundamentals with *drosophila* and other bilaterally symmetrical species, we may as well include Komodo Dragons in our family!)

Despite the wired characteristics of the brain stem, it is open to definition by outer experiences. Because of this feature, we can travel a life course of either impulsiveness or stability as a function of early events. And more immediately from moment to moment, we repeat whatever it was that we were thinking or doing when we got a reinforcement. Outside consequences turn neuromotor randomness into routines; each of us solves a problem with whatever systems were active when it was first solved. Thus, it becomes certain that with increased neural complexity and increased environmental variability, no two creatures will ever use identical neurological structures in order to solve the same external problem. Individual differences in brain structure[34] are consistent with this speculation; so is the analysis presented in a recent book by Edelman and Tononi.[65]

The Limbic System or MacLean's Paleomammalian Complex

The limbic system, a designation given this tissue complex by MacLean in 1952 and also included in his paleomammalian complex, introduced a new level of persistence to striatal routines as emotion led to increased duration and amplitude of overt behaviors. Limbic intensity and persistence formed enduring pair bonds and allowed differential investments in their young on the basis of size, liveliness, emotionality, and impulsiveness. Between adults or children, within or between generations, emotions amplify selfishness and feuds or protect reciprocity, bonding, and investment. Disruptions in nursing, infant care, peer relationships, or the loss of a close ally or a lover might shift whole theaters of behavior for long intervals. (Or might not. See Cohen[66] and Harris[67] for a review of findings that children can have great resilience to parental aberrations.)

The Neocortex or MacLean's Neomammalian Complex

The neocortex, included in MacLean's neomammalian complex because of its conspicuous development in the higher mammals, is the most newly refined section of our brain and depends on extensive interconnections with as well as the integrity of many older systems. Thus, we can expect it to be less predictable (more chaotic) in comparison with either the limbic system or brain stem (reptilian complex).

Indeed, there is such extensive connectivity within the brain that it would appear to be an exception to Kauffman's findings that large arrays of units can work quickly—again, 100K units can have a coherent output within 300 msec— *if they are sparsely connected.*[9] It may be that each neuron participates in thousands of different networks in the CNS but is directly influenced by only a few other neurons in any particular decision. Thus, you can get many decisions per unit of time and by large arrays but by a different array from instant to instant. Learning, when it involves increased speed and lessened response variability, may involve simplification in neural networks as much as it may involve making new connections and maturation may involve the pruning of inactive cells by a similar process. While we acquire some capacities as we mature, we appear to lose the potential for many, many others.

The chaos in neural organization, however, becomes a strength when it allows equivalencies between formerly arbitrary stimuli and the creation of distinctions between cues that are physically very similar. It also allows the loose, sometimes misleading, attachment of language as both an excuser and an instructor for behavior.[68] Language and negotiation are essential components of socialization and have enormous advantages for the cohesion of highly variable individuals who then make up for each other's deficits. Because of their evolutionary complexity and late maturation, we can expect greater variability in language and planning functions than in our other abilities.[69] And because of cultural demands on us—i.e., SAT computations and our dependence on communication skills—there will not only be more deficits in these areas but their impact will be more severe. It follows that problems in socialization can be more of a personal handicap than is a missing limb. *In addition to expecting greater variability in linguistic and executive functions, we will have to listen carefully to our clients both to understand their unique ways of analyzing and solving problems and to adapt our suggestions to their particular skills.* Special education teachers have attempted this chore for a decade; therapists may soon emulate them.

Refinement of our psychological adaptations, reciprocity computations, and social networks seems to have accompanied the elaboration of our executive functions. The prefrontal area appears essential for our executive functions that let us make agendas, stack our priorities, segment time, swap plans, and use our imaginations to solve problems.[47, 69] These capacities depend upon the integration of data from many other cortical and subcortical layers.

THERAPY

First, because of genes and early developmental tuning, resilience blesses some of us and curses others. A client with a productive history will recover quickly from a crisis almost regardless of what a therapist does to him but a history of systematic deterioration is less often consistent with recovery. Thus, it may be that, like major universities, successful practitioners recruit successful clients.

Second, the abruptness of switching between chaos and stasis, immobility and stereotypy, can be modulated as when an ordinary electric switch becomes a dimmer switch and complicates a circuit. Increasing the number of interconnections in parts of a human network—through experience, alliances, or maturation—will slow the action. Decrease those connections by injury, intoxication, or social isolation and decisions speed up, becoming both more staccato and more stereotyped. Thus, clients with intact executive functions (or a recent history of such) will be more deliberate, needing us less and discovering their own solutions. Such clients will better share plans and integrate the information from talk therapy. On the other hand, clients who have difficulty with planning, constructive imagination, self-observation, and systematic problem solving are often less able to apply methods recommended in therapy and more reactive to environmental changes in their job, sleep pattern, family status, friends, and seasonal activities. Such people will need our help to discover effective changes and help from other allies to maintain them.

Constraint, Impulse

We need to "keep our act together" at the same time that we want to have fun and most of us negotiate this conflict from moment to moment with our children, peers, spouses, and employers. We also negotiate with our pet, our lawn, automobile, and the wiring in our basement that consistently blows out a fuse when we most need to use our computer. Our clients often represent one of two kinds of negotiator, internalizers and externalizers, and treatment consists of moving either strategist towards the middle. We seek more freedom for the internalizers who are frightened and trapped but some limits, boundaries, and complications for the externalizers, whom we call impulsive, selfish and thoughtless. (Successful treatment will also produce freedom for the wives, parents, teachers, and parole officers who originally sent them our way!)

Simplifiers can be interchangeable and include allies who do things for you, lessened guilt (including tools such cognitive therapy or fluoxetine), forming lines and hierarchies, making lists, delegating tasks, breaking chores into smaller segments, putting things off, and old memories of being safe and in control. Chain saws and bulldozers, assertion training and visualization, Prozac and alcohol, cannibis, or cocaine are simplifiers just as are fungi, bacteria, and neuronal apoptosis. *Complicators can also be interchangeable*, and include allies who force you to stay out of trouble, bosses, mates, teachers, parents, contracts, ministers, legal authorities, moral codes, deadlines, rules, and lawyers who are working for someone else. Cement, fences, signs, and walls are complicators and so are pets, school, and television shows.

Tuning

Age, reproductive standing, access to resources, seasons of the year, and significant niche changes (divorce, empty nest, job changes, moving) will have enduring effects on the client perhaps by altering the particular set of genes that are active! Explanations can reduce anxiety that the client may have about "losing their mind" as they become a different "person." Therapy can provide information about tactics in a current relationship or job. However, it can encourage changes in activities, perhaps the client's returning to arenas of earlier success or to those wherein family members were successful. Study the client's victories and repeat them; avoid battles entirely or engage them in an order in which they can be won.

Active Darwinism

We seek and build niches that give us more choices. The label *Active Darwinism* describes this process by which organisms select and modify their environments.[41, 42, 70, 71] Furthermore, we apply a Darwinian consequence to our worlds when we choose homes, toys and tools, plants and pets that suit us and duplicate them with saws and hammers or with selective breeding of other creatures. To the extent that humans are selective factors, environments compete for human approval; environments and creatures in them that meet human demands are kept and multiplied.

Despite structural order from phase transitions and from phylogeny, development makes no two brains identical in neuroanatomical detail [33, 34] or in their tricks that acquire food, partners, or possessions. While evolution specifies reinforcement systems and environment offers choices, we differ in the strategies and neuroanatomy that we use to achieve those rewards, in our selecting and arranging environments, and in our explanations for what we do.[72] Thus:

1. No single template defines our clients. Their assets and liabilities, freckles, smiles, and PET scans will be unique for every one of them.
2. Whatever other natures our clients may have, the moment-to-moment effort to regulate complexity will be a part of their every struggle and their every satisfaction.
3. Each client is on a quest for experiences that meet her particular allotment of psychological adaptations; each therapist also has her own quest. Therapists and clients recruit each other for their own purposes. It follows that in therapy as in marketing, practitioners who carefully respect their client's individual nature will be more popular and possibly

more effective than those who do not. (Some of this respect for the client's individual nature will entail breaking current practices and recognizing the sometimes identities of traits and circumstances between that client and members of his immediate biological family.)

4. Clients will always pick among the therapist's offerings whether or not that is the therapist's intent. The richer the menu offered, the greater the chance for client satisfaction and clients will reinforce therapists for developing suitable menu options.

5. There will be some conflict of interests to the extent that client and therapist characteristics do not match. However, greater similarity between client and therapist might predict stronger alliances between them. "This one REALLY understands me!" *Active Darwinism will be reflected in our picking friends who agree with us but listening to contrary advice may be a violation of our instincts. Seeking conflicting opinions may be newly evolved, easily impaired, and an important diagnostic marker of its own.*

6. While there will be substantial uniformity of automatic thoughts— perhaps because, as MacLean approach suggests, we all started with the same "lizard"—there will also be substantial variability between people. The array of automatic thoughts available to the client will vary with his or her age, reproductive standing, access to resources, seasons of the year, and significant changes in his or her niche.

7. To the extent that language reflects evolved sensory and motor conflicts with regard to chaos and stasis, stereotyped client verbal patterns will sometimes reflect conflicts between genes.[73]

CLOSING

This brings to a close my efforts to indicate how combining elements of statistical physics with the evolutionary perspective of Paul MacLean can throw light upon aspects of evolutionary theory and phenotypic development. For clinical applications, I have suggested that such insights can lead in the direction of a more coherent diagnostics and therapy and a model that is uniform for physical systems as well as for human dilemmas. It will take time, opportunity, talent, and effort to pull this structure together.

Ball cautions, "Despite the proven value to cell biology of some concepts from the study of phase transitions . . . there remains much scepticism as to whether any biological phenomena can arise from the sort of collective, emergent behavior of statistical, interacting ensembles rather than the closely controlled protein relays to which cell biologists are accustomed."[1] But, I look at a crouching cat and a modern sports car, note the similarities in their proportions and their suspensions, and "know" that the same physical and statistical rules guided the evolution of each. The role of phase transitions in human conduct has a similar quality of obvious truth for anyone favorably disposed to the concepts. However, there is a second group of analysts—often composed of scientists and engineers in stasis—who will insist on knowing the formulae for attraction and repulsion and the variables that participate in each one. (Perhaps of necessity, there's also a *third* group, one chaotic in circumstances and ideas, who doesn't believe numbers and graphs!)

A similar skepticism will exist for applying phase models to such evolutionary human behavioral features as ambivalence, impulsiveness, and guilt—until some tools for prediction and manipulation are created. T-mazes and operant chambers, stop watches and microswitches, lab assistants, and electromechanical programming gadgets made it possible for nearly anyone to observe similar functional relations in the behavior of a wide array of birds and mammals. Likewise, data from population biology and math from Haldane, Pearson, and Sewall Wright revived Darwinism.[74] Systematic awareness of phase transitions in human conduct awaits a tinker and mathematician as well as a rat and pigeon to uncover them.

Some theoretical issues for research to explore include: (1) our emotional reactions to inter- and intrapersonal chaos, order, and phase transitions, (2) the role of natural and sexual selection and of alliances and hierarchies in life's oscillation between chaos and stasis, and (3) the possibility of sexual roles allowing a species to pursue risk and constraint at the same time. More clinically, and as sketched in Table 13.1, I would (4) rearrange how we view pathologies and (5) incorporate the formal recognition of various constraints and simplifiers that we offer to our clients and the complementary roles of such. We might also formalize (6) the idea that more primitive threats and rewards will override newer ones, and (7) the probability that response competition, through reciprocal inhibition, will occur in a hierarchic manner between our varied psychological adaptations.[75, 76, 77, 78] Finally, we can begin to align clinical views with those of common sense, that the striking behavioral similarities found in twins reared apart will also be found between generations in a family and that such patterns can more deliberately inform the choices that each of us makes.

Karl Pribram asked, "How is it that I can sense so much and do so little?"[79] As Pribram himself taught us, one of the important decisions for life is that of go/no-go, the cueing of action or inhibition.[20, 46, 47, 50, 80] Along these lines, Allman[50] reminds us that an *E. coli* merges the influences from a dozen receptors but its motor, its flagellum, turns either clockwise or counterclockwise. Neurons take in a wide array of information but generate relatively few outputs. A floor trader in the stock market considers a lot of factors but compresses them into "buy" or "wait" while he adjusts his course from moment to moment.[50] His decisions are an adaptive walk between chaos and stasis, taken in the same manner as a bacterium, a neuron, a bird, a species, a diagnostician, or a scientist like Karl Pribram or Paul MacLean.

NOTES

1. Ball P: Transitions still to be made. *Nature*, 1999; 402: 73–76.

2. Bloom H: *Global Brain: The Evolution of Mass Mind from the Big Bang to the 21st Century.* NY: Wiley, 2000.

3. Smith CUM: *Elements of Molecular Biology.* (2nd Ed.). NY: Wiley, 1996.

4. Haig D: The Social Gene. In J R Krebs & N Davies (Eds.) *Behavioral Ecology: An Evolutionary Approach.* London: Blackwell Science, 1997, pp. 284–306.

5. Wright R: *Nonzero: The Logic of Human Destiny.* NY: Pantheon, 2000.

6. Kauffman S: *Origins of Order: Self-Organization and Selection in Evolution.* NY: Oxford, 1993.

7. Langton C; Taylor C; Farmer J D; & Rasmussen S: (Eds.) *Artificial Life II : Proceedings of the Workshop on Artificial Life.* Held February, 1990 in Santa Fe, New Mexico (Santa Fe Institute Studies in the Sciences of Complexity). vol. 10. Redwood City, CA: Addison Wesley, 1992.

8. Waldrop M: *Complexity: The Emerging Science at the Edge of Order and Chaos.* NY: Touchstone, 1992.

9 Kauffman S: *At Home in the Universe: The Search for the Laws of Self Organization and Complexity.* NY: Oxford, 1995.

10. Fentress J: Personal communication.

11. Casti J: *Complexification.* New York: Harper Collins, 1994.

12. Glausiusz J: Joining hands. *Discover*, July, 2000; 32–34.

13. Helbing D, Farkas I, & Vicsek T: Simulating dynamical features of escape panic. *Nature*, 2000; 407: 487–490.

14. Hayes B: Can't get no satisfaction. *American Scientist*, 1997; 85: 108–112.

15. Hamilton W: The evolution of altruistic behavior. *American Naturalist*, 1963; 97: 354–356. Reprinted in Hamilton, WD *Narrow Roads of Geneland: The Collected Papers of WD Hamilton, Vol 1, Evolution of Social Behavior.* NY: Freeman, 1996; pp. 6–8.

16. Miller G: How mate choice shaped human nature: A review of sexual selection and human evolution. In Crawford C & Krebs D (Eds) *Handbook of Evolutionary Psychology.* Mahwah, NJ: Erlbaum, 1998; pp. 87–130.

17. Stevens A & Price J: *Evolutionary Psychiatry: A New Beginning.* (2nd Ed.) NY: Routledge, 2000.

18. Sigmund K: *Games of Life: Explorations in Ecology, Evolution, and Behaviour.* NY: Oxford, 1993.

19. MacLean P: *The Triune Brain in Evolution: Role in Paleocerebral Functions.* NY: Plenum, 1990.

20. Freud S: *The Psychopathology of Everyday Life.* NY: Macmillan, 1901.

21. Finger S: *Minds Behind the Brain: A History of the Pioneers and Their Discoveries.* NY: Oxford, 2000.

22. Kerr M: Chronic anxiety and defining a self: An introduction to Murray Bowen's theory of human emotional functioning. *The Atlantic,* September, 1988; 35–58.

23. Smuts B: Triangles in baboons. Presentation at The Relationship System and Individual Variation in functioning, Georgetown Family Center, Georgetown, Washington, D.C., April 16, 2000.

24. Hauser M: Why humans are the wrong species in which to study the evolution of human intelligence. Presentation at Human Behavior and Evolution Society Annual Meeting, Amherst, MA, June 9, 2000.

25. Monassin R; Zecchina R; Kirkpatrick S; Selman B; & Troyansky L: Determining computational complexity from characteristic 'phase transitions.' *Nature*, 1999; 400: 133–137.

26. Anderson P: Computing: Solving problems in finite time. *Nature,* 1999; 400: 115–116.

27. Hrdy S: *Mother Nature: A History of Mothers, Infants, and Natural Selection.* NY: Pantheon, 2000.

28. Eibl-Eibesfeldt I: *Human Ethology.* NY: Aldine de Gruyter, 1989.

29. McGuire M & Troisi A: *Darwinian Psychiatry.* NY: Oxford, 1998.

30. Jamison K: *Touched by Fire: Manic Depressive Illness and the Artistic Temperament.* NY: Free Press, 1993.

31. Kuhn T: *The Structure of Scientific Revolutions* (3rd Ed), Chicago: Univ. of Chicago Press, 1992.

32. Bateman A: Intrasexual selection in *drosophila. Heredity,* 1948; 2: 349–368.

33. Sporns O: Selectionist and instructionist ideas in neurobiology. In O Sporns & G Tononi (Eds) *Selectionism and the Brain: International Review of Neurobiology.* NY: Academic, 1994; 37: 4–26.

34. Skoyles J: In Bloom, H. (2000) *Global Brain: The Evolution of Mass Mind from the Big Bang to the 21st Century.* NY: Wiley, 2000, p. 143.

35. Tooby J & Cosmides L: The psychological foundations of culture. In Barkow J, Cosmides L, & Tooby J (Eds): *The Adapted Mind: Evolutionary Psychology and the Generation of Culture.* NY: Oxford, 1992.

36. Lorenz K: *On Aggression.* NY: Harcourt, 1966.

37. Krebs D: Evolution of moral dispositions in the human species. Presentation at the Hunter School of Social Work, Manhattan, NY, May 5, 1999.

38. Dunbar R: *Grooming, Gossip, and the Evolution of Language.* Cambridge, MA: Harvard University Press, 1996.

39. Ridley M: *Origins of Virtue.* NY: Penguin, 1996.

40. Wright R: *Three Scientists and Their Gods: Looking for Meaning in a Age of Information.* NY: Times Books, 1988.

41. Popper K: *In Search of a Better World. Lectures & Essays from Thirty Years.* London: Routledge, 1995.

42. Brody J: Active Darwinism offsets mismatch. Presentation at Human Behavior and Evolution Society, Amherst, MA, June 8, 2000.

43. Bouchard T; Lykken D; McGue M; Segal N; & Tellegen A: Sources of human psychological differences: The Minnesota study of twins reared apart. *Science,* 1990; 250: 223–228.

44. Darlington C: Introduction. In Galton, F. *Hereditary Genius.* Gloucester, MA: Peter Smith, 1972.

45. Smith CUM: Deep time and the brain: Message of the molecules. Paul MacLean Symposium, Boston, July 16, 1999.

46. Bronowski J: *A Sense of the Future.* Cambridge, MA: MIT Press, 1977.

47. Barkley R: *ADHD and the Nature of Self Control.* NY: Guilford, 1997.

48. Diamond J: *Why is Sex fun?: The Evolution of human sexuality.* NY: Basic, 1997.

49. Kimura D: *Sex and Cognition.* Cambridge, MA: MIT Press, 1999.

50. Allman JM: *Evolving Brains.* NY: Scientific American Library, 1999.

51. Miller G: Human Language and Intelligence as Sexually Selected Fitness Indicators. Given at the Hunter School of Social Work, April 14, 1999.

52. Buss D: The psychology of human mate selection: Exploring the complexity of the strategic repertoire. In Crawford C & Krebs D (Eds.) *Handbook of Evolutionary Psychology.* Mahwah, NJ: Erlbaum, 1998, pp. 405–430.

53. Goos LM & Silverman I: *Sex Related Factors in the Perception Of Threatening Facial Expressions.* Manuscript submitted for publication, 2000.

54. American Psychiatric Association *Diagnostic and Statistical Manual of Mental Disorders.* 4th Ed., Washington, D.C., 1994.

55. Miller, G. *The Mating Mind: How Sexual Choice Shaped the Evolution of Human Nature.* NY: Doubleday, 2000.

56. Mullis K: *Dancing Naked in the Mind Field.* NY: Vintage, 2000.

57. Kramer P: *Listening to Prozac.* NY: Viking, 1993.

58. Hess E: Ethology: An approach to the complete analysis of behavior. In Newcomb, T (Ed) *New Directions in Psychology.* NY: Holt Rinehart, & Winston, 1962.

59. Goodwin B: *How the Leopard Changed Its Spots: The Evolution of Complexity.* NY: Simon & Schuster, 1994.

60. Neri P; Morrone C; & Burr D: Seeing biological motion. *Nature,* 1998; 395 (6705): pp. 894–896.

61. Lettvin J; Maturana H; McCulloch W; & Pitts W: What the frog's eye tells the frog's brain. *Proceedings Institute of Radio Engineering* 1959; 47: pp. 1940–1951.

62. Maloney A, Sickler C & Cortez D: Archetypes and evolutionary psychology: An empirical inquiry. Presentation at Human Behavior and Evolution Society, Davis, CA, July 11, 1998.

63. Maynard Smith J: *Shaping Life: Genes, Embryos and Evolution.* New Haven: Yale University Press, 1999.

64. Ridley M: *Genome: The Autobiography of a Species in 23 Chapters.* NY: Harper Collins, 2000.

65. Edelman G & Tononi G: *A Universe of Consciousness: How Matter Becomes Imagination.* NY: Basic Books, 2000.

66. Cohen D: *Stranger in the Nest: Do Parents Really Shape Their Child's Personality, Intelligence, or Character?* NY: Wiley, 1999.

67. Harris J: *The Nurture Assumption.* NY: Free Press, 1998.

68. Gazzaniga M: *Nature's Mind.* NY: Basic Books, 1992.

69. Pennington B: *Diagnosing Learning Disorders: A Neuropsychological Framework.* NY: Guilford, 1991.

70. Plomin R: *Genetics and Experience: The Interplay between Nature and Nurture.* Thousand Oaks, CA: Sage, 1994.

71. Bouchard T; Lykken D; McGue M; Segal N; & Tellegen, A: Sources of human psychological differences: The Minnesota study of twins reared apart. *Science,* 1990; 250: 223–228.

72. Belew R & Mitchell M: (Eds.) *Adaptive Individuals in Evolving Populations: Models & Algorithms.* Reading, MA: Addison Wesley, 1996.

73. Haig D: Asymmetric relations: Internal conflicts and the horror of incest. *Evolution and Human Behavior,* 1999; 20: 83–98.

74. Maynard Smith J: *Evolution and the Theory of Games.* NY: Cambridge, 1982.

75. Sherrington C: *The Integrative Action of the Nervous System.* New Haven, CT: Yale University Press, 1906/1961.

76. Wolpe J: *Psychotherapy by Reciprocal Inhibition.* Stanford, CA: Stanford University Press, 1958.

77. Brody J: Competing psychological adaptations. Behavior OnLine, <http://www.behavior.net/ forums/evolutionary> April 10, 1997.

78. Buss D: The evolution of happiness. *American Psychologist,* 2000; 55(1): 15–23.

79. Pribram K: MacLean's Work and the Informational Sciences. Paul MacLean symposium, Boston, July 17, 1999.

80. Miller G; Pribram K; & Galanter E: *Plans and the Structure of Behavior.* NY: Adams, Bannister, Cox, 1986.

14

EVOLUTIONARY AND PHILOSOPHICAL ISSUES IN TRIARCHIC THEORY[1]

Seymour W. Itzkoff

INTRODUCTION

MacLean is a pioneer in his endeavor to show that human behavior is substrated by neurological structures inherited from our ancient reptilian and mammalian ancestors. He must be seen as a trailblazer in attempting to link human behavior with the varying levels of phylogenetic structures that are part of our evolutionary inheritance. In this chapter I argue, that contrary to MacLean, the selective power of humans considered from the evolutionary standpoint does not lie in the various R-complex and limbic system heritages of behavior, even though they constantly erupt from the depths of our neurological past to dominate individual and social actions. Rather the selective power of humans is rooted in the isocortex which hosts our ability to think, reason, and to create laws and principles to guide the future of our society as well as prevail over all other living species.

CONCEPTUAL PERSPECTIVE AND ITS LIMITATIONS

"The focus of the present book will be on protoreptilian and paleo-mammalian formations and their role in nonverbal aspects of mentation and behavior."[2] MacLean thereby endeavors to show that human behavior is composed of neurological structures inherited from our ancient reptilian and mammalian ancestors. In this he is close to contemporary sociobiological thinking. He must be seen as a trailblazer in attempting to link human behavior with the varying levels of phylogenetic structures that are part of our evolutionary inheritance. In this neuroarchitectural endeavor he is even more of a pioneer. His research reveals the actual morphologies and patterns of structural interactions inherited from this reptilian and mammalian base. Naturally he is concerned to connect the past with the neo-pallium and modern human isocortical structures and behaviors.

Even given MacLean's recognition of the crucial role of causal thinking in the powerfully selective rise of humans to dominance, his acceptance of the role of language in coordinating the higher integrative conceptual powers of modern humans, the paleoneurological substrate nevertheless interests him most as he explores the morphological and neurological heritages that underlie all human behavior:

the phenomenology of psychomotor epilepsy suggests that without a co-functioning limbic system, the neo-cortex lacks not only the requisite neural substrate for a sense of self, of reality, and the memory of ongoing experience, but also a feeling of conviction as to what is true or false. This presents a problem of crucial epistemological significance because there is no evidence that the limbic structures of the temporal lobe are capable of comprehending speech, nor is there any basis for inferring a capacity to communicate in verbal terms. Hence, it would appear that the manufacture of belief in the reality, importance, and truth or falsity of what is conceived depends on a mentality incapable of verbal comprehension and communication . . . it is one thing to have a primitive, illiterate mind for judging the authenticity of food or a mate, but where must we stand if we must depend on that same mind for belief in our ideas, concepts, and theories?[3]

He should be puzzled, for here his empirical research and theoretical conclusions are less developed. But he brought about a phenomenal achievement: the revealing of our phylogenetic morphological and psychological heritage structurally embedded in the R-complex and then in the limbic system, then as these interact with the recently developed brain structures. Throughout his writings MacLean shows an intimate knowledge of evolutionary research, using it often to guide his own technical analyses of the various dimensions of brain organization. As such, in viewing the sigificance of what he has learned, and what he is about to embark on in pursuing this research, the evolutionary perspective is both an enhancement and a limitation of his and others' research to come. Because, without the most accurate interpretations describing the significance and placement of these structures in light of the evolutionary facts, his interpretations will be both limited and inhibitory. His states his perspective clearly in the following passage:

In its evolution the human forebrain expands along the lines of three basic formations that anatomically and biochemically reflect an ancient relationship, respectively to reptiles, early mammals, and late mammals. The three formations are labeled at the level of the forebrain that constitutes the cerebral hemispheres comprised of the telencephalon and diencephalon.[4]

MACLEAN'S EVOLUTIONARY FULCRUM

A critical evolutionary issue could affect our understanding of the significance of MacLean's research as it concerns the internal paleoarchitectural relationship of the three phylogenetic layers of brain function. This lies in the role of the cortex in the shaping of the structures, and the cortex's evolutionary role in the positive selection of the vertebrate tetrapods. Throughout MacLean's work he continuously refers to the ostensible adaptive functioning of these structures, thus their role in natural selection. If these assumptions are not accurate, or if they need significant modification, we will see the human brain and its ostensible sociobiological imperatives in a wholly new light. MacLean committed himself to the task of showing a line of continuity between the development of each new tetrapod neuromorphological structure as it evolves concomitantly with the Darwinian behavioral enhancements reflective of this shift. Yet in the end it is this continuity, even dominance, of the past over the present that holds the central role in MacLean's evolutionary drama.

In summary, except for their derivation from the original stock (the stem reptiles), all extant reptiles have a lineage entirely separate from the therapsids. For comparative neurobehavioral studies on reptiles I chose to focus on lizards because as will be explained, they suggest a closer resemblance to early mammal-like reptiles than other existing forms . . . it is requisite to characterize the structures of the basal forebrain that represent a common denominator in reptiles, birds, and mammals, and finally to comment on the long-standing, enigma regarding their functions. In regard to the question of correspondence of structures in the three classes of animals, the evidence rests on phylogenetic, embryological, neuroanatomical, and neurrochemical data.[5]

The basic thrust of MacLean's evolutionary interpretation therefore places human functioning at the causal beck and call of the prior established brain and neurological structures. The evolutionist is enjoined to view the behavioral power of the R- (striatal) complex and the limbic system as central to the adaptive and selective destiny of the line leading to humans. The dimensions of inductive thought, prediction, anticipation, organization and assimilation of perception through memory, epitomized in cortical functioning, for him fade in evolutionary significance when compared to the evidence of the modern reification of more ancient brain and neurologically-rooted behavioral patterns.

For example, MacLean takes up the so-called challenge displays in various animal lines, including humans, to show this continuity, the carry-over from animals to humans. MacLean sees Diane Fossey's research on silverback gorillas as close to the display of lizards. Jane Lawick-Goodall's description of the chimpanzee "bipedal swagger," also reminds MacLean of reptile behavior.

As in the case of lizards, the stilted, staccato steps of the displays of the great apes seem to carry the message of a series of exclamation marks. The *Schragstellung* gait of the Komodo dragon . . . calls to mind the goose step of a military parade. The question naturally arises as to whether the striking similarity between the challenge displays of animals as diverse as lizards and gorillas represent "convergent" or "parallel" evolution. Among different species the sideways presentation and the stilted, staccato steps have such an uncanny resemblance that it would almost seem that the challenge display had been genetically packaged and handed up the phylogenetic tree of mammals.[6]

To argue that R-complex and limbic system functions are subordinate in an evolutionary sense to the basic function of cognitive and intellective assimilation would give an entirely differing cast to MacLean's research. Perhaps the enormously complex reptilian and mammalian brain and neurological functions in fact accompany the true, the core selective dynamic in the evolution of the vertebrates. Such a central evolutionary process involves cognitive brain function. The R-complex and limbic system structures and functions in reality constitute ancillary adaptive elements varying in their expression among a wide variety of vertebrate forms, on land, in the seas, and in the air.[7]

The evolutionary question thus remains: which of the three systems was the crucial selective element driving the succession of land tetrapods? How did these elements become morphologically and physiologically assimilable, behaviorally adaptively coordinated with the decisive selective factor? How do we evaluate each of these structural and behavioral elements in their furtherance of the general homeostatic success of the line? Finally, where should we look to discover the more progressive and decisive selective dimension, that which took us from the waters to the air and land, finally to the sweeping vertebrate dominance of Homo sapiens sapiens (*Hss*)?[8]

Differing answers to this question result in differing perspectives on contemporary human behavior, altruistic or aggressive patterns, hierarchy, dominance/submission, obsessional behavior, magic and superstition, even the variety of language functions, song, poetry, declamation, and narrative.

A critique of MacLean's evolutionary perspective stems from Hss' paradigmatic intellective behavior. It focuses, by contrast, on a triarchic theory centering on the brain's increasing cortical discriminations, first in the vertebrates, then in the land-roaming tetrapods, integrating information, expanding the time zone of prediction and survival. Rather, in the contemporary culmination of this one-billion year evolutionary romance glows a neglected "nova," the iso- or neo-cortex. This brain structure can both regulate and dominate the functions and behaviors of the R-complex and limbic system. To understand human behavior—whether "primitive," pathological, or civilizational, we must look to the evolutionary meaning of the brain and intelligence. And we must examine how both the reptilian and mammalian systems have been systemically reincorporated as buttresses for the adaptive and selective survival of the line.

WHAT EVOLUTION TELLS US ABOUT TRIARCHIC THEORY

Taxonomy establishes vertebrates within the over two dozen animal phyla. The subkingdom of animals now compares to the subkingdoms of plants, fungi, and various protozoa subkingdoms, fellow participants in the eukaryote kingdom of complex sexually reproducing unicellular and multicellular life forms. Finally, taxonomy includes the so-called prokaryote kingdoms, the eubacterial and archaebacterial worlds, from which the eukaryotes separated unknown billions of years ago.[9] The distinctions are clear. Our line consists of life forms with characteristics that include motility, heterotrophy (herbivores and carnivores), that become environmental and ecological chance takers in highly variable spatial and time frames. We are movers and opportunists, feeding on sessile, embedded opters for the status quo of momentary spatio/temporal success.

A 4-billion-year time scale, allows for much Darwinian innovation. At each point in the evolutionary progression, those who have peeled off for the good life have by and large distinguished themselves evolutionary-wise from the unstable by their high rates of extinction. Evolutionary instability, animal lines ever at the edge of annihilation, takers of chances with change, became the theme of the successful from the standpoint of our own evolutionary destiny.[10] In this time-deep zone of adaptation, biochemical and temperature parameters remained conducive to multicellular eukaryote heterotrophic life and thereby provided a selective groove of ever-increasing positive value given to creatures able to negotiate dangerous and variable ecologies requiring movement and change.[11] These circumstances produced an internal guidance system selected for its adaptation to instability through phenotypic, behavioral means, a slow genetic pathway strewn with intergenerational boulders. Environmental, ecological, and organic change often happened quickly and radically. The brain furnished the adaptive means for momentary avoidance and survival, in contradistinction to a gradualism selectively culling existing genetic diversity.[11]

The basic eukaryote cell is a highly complex energy machine with an internal homeostatic structure that enables it to traverse diverse environments and to feed upon victims randomly encountered, and then enveloped by the never-ending explorations of their cilia and undulipoda.[12] The chordates and, later, true vertebrate fish continued that mainline adaptive tack. Concomitantly, vast numbers of conservative stay-at-home-lancelets and tunicates, armored bottom-dwelling Agnathans were either eliminated or permanently consigned to the periphery as "things" changed.

The brain so became the preeminent adaptive and selective dimension instrumental in the flowering, diversification, and maintenance of the vertebrates in the front ranks of animal phyla. Jerison views brain size in relation to body size as the desideratum of intelligence in the vertebrates. He maintains that no real advance in intelligence emerged even when the proto-amphibians came onto the land surfaces some 370mya and quickly radiated and evolved into the stem reptiles.[13] Certain visual specialization in the advanced Dipnoi seemed to produce an expanded cerebellum beyond that of most other fish families. The sharks and skates, ancient and only partially evolved vertebrate forms, possess relatively large brains in comparison with the vast panorama of the sea denizens. This argues for the relative indifference of the oceans, seas, and lakes to body structure/brain-intelligence relationships, once a basic adaptive surge of its original inhabitants had occurred.[14]

Of course the land surfaces then uninhabited by animals could provide a barrier to intelligent behavior. But the brain rapidly opened the door to a dominant highly visual reptile brain outfitted with a number of ancillary neuro/morphological and behavioral functions. The striatal or R-complex of brain-behavior structures inherited from an ancient vertebrate body plan underwent a long perfecting in the seas, but then showed evidence of existing on land and in the air, from c.500–200mya. The R-complex fixed connections among phenomena-temporal-momentary, conformity or nonconformity with precedent conditions, ritualistic displays and changes in behavior, hunting, homing, mating, selecting homesites, establishing territory, engaging in various types of display, breeding, imprinting, forming social hierarchies, and selecting leaders.

MacLean, of course, recognized that the transition from reptile to mammal did not represent a mere superimposition of mammalian accretions onto preexisting reptilian structures. Existent reptilian morphologies reorganized and expanded. MacLean based his analysis of the shift between reptile and mammal neurologies on the evolutionary transition between still reptilian therapsid cynodonts and the earliest mammal, "Morganucodon," c.220–200mya. In all likelihood this transition took place gradually, for, several cynodonts, dog-like or larger in size, lived into the Jurassic alongside the now mouse-sized early mammals. More orthodox Darwinian branchings could have the proto-animals already separating from the therapsid/cynodont line during the mass extinctions of the Permian (250–245mya), both groups the remnants of a once-luxuriant synapsid/therapsid reptile clade. The latter were to be supplanted by the visually vigorous archosaurs, parallel in the time to the first mammal appearance, c. 220-200mya.[15]

MacLean's evolutionary interpretation centers on the formation of the limbic system, and not on the selective impact of cortical expansion. According to Jerison, the earliest mammals already had a brain-body ratio 5–10 times what existed in the classic fish/amphibian/reptile brain. The lower multiple might also be applied to the therapsid cynodonts. MacLean: "the widening of the brain seen in the therapsid-mammalian transition might be interpreted as a reflection of the development of limbic parahippocampal cingulate, and entorhinal cortex, rather than of the neocortex."[16] Clearly this represents an important and controversial issue.

MacLean included in the limbic system the olfactory bulb, septum, fornix, hippocampus, amygdala, and cingulate gyrus. Indeed, he superceded in his analysis the neocortex, represented in all vertebrates, by emphasizing the unique expansion and reorganization of the limbic system of the mammalian line.[17] What MacLean interprets as an evolutionary advance provided by the limbic system has to be seen in the context of a proliferating extroverted reptilian evolutionary thrust, as compared with a clearly defensive mammalian posture. The question concerns the evolutionary context during which the limbic system began to be shaped away from traditional reptilian morphological patterns. In the competitive contexts of the late Triassic, c.220–190mya, the developing mammalian suite of limbic system adaptations was generally homeostatic and defensive rather than exemplifying an expansive adaptive and thus demographic trend.

It is difficult not to factor in as part of the expansion of the mammal brain the basic neocortical values that instrumentally reorganized these innovative mammalian limbic structures. During the c.150my of mammalian evolution under the shadow of the dinosaurs, intensive selective dynamics were taking place. However, once the mammalian suite of adaptations had carved out its life space, it is doubtful that this evolutionary trend was in large part shaped by the pressures of the reptilian hordes. The original Permian climatic and ecological crisis (250–45mya) more than likely shaped the mammalian body plan. Miniaturization was probably a defensive preadaptation along with internal homeothermy, nocturnal vision, and exploration. Useful, too, for some mammals, was the ancient placental pattern of internal gestation.

Besides the archosaurs/dinosaurs, mammals likely needed to defend against other cynodonts. So opportunity arose for these then-tiny creatures. c. 200mya, when the visually adapted and energetically mobile archosaurs pressed the therapsid cynodonts into extinction. Jerison, but not Quiroga, for example, believed that the therapsid/cynodont brain was more reptile than mammal-like, therefore implicitly arguing, as I do here, for a longer period of separated if parallel evolution of the two lines. "Although there may have been some expansion of the cerebellum . . . (T)he mammal like reptiles, in short were reptilian and not mammalian with respect to the evolution of their brains."[18] I find it persuasive that intraspecific adaptive and selective dynamics pushed much of mammalian evolution c. 215–65mya. This early 5–10 times expansion in brain/body ratios may have resulted from this earlier post-Permian (245–15mya) evolutionary dynamic. Not the limbic system so much as the expanding cortex perhaps comprised the locus of their powerful adaptive and selective thrust into dominance.[19]

It is often thought that the suzerainty of the placental mammals over a wide variety of other mammal lines, marsupials, multituberculates, and monotremes stemmed from a new reproductive innovation late into mammalian history, c. 100–65mya. Yet placental reproduction can be traced back to sharks and skates living in the seas some 400mya.[20] Today there are many forms of fish that reproduce in the viviparous and oviparous manner, as any aquarium lover can testify. The advantages of viviparity cannot be assigned merely to reproductive efficiency. Ultimately, placental reproduction gave increased opportunity for the extension of fetal brain growth within the womb as compared with brain truncated fetal birth in marsupial young. Many evolutionists see the reproductive patterns of the marsupials as an insignificant advance beyond other vertebrate oviparous reproductive patterns. Note, in addition to the monotreme's ancient reproductive structures, they possess comparative cortical impotency at maturity.[21] The final phase of brain-body ratio growth, 10–30X the classic reptile brain, led to the dominance of the placental mammals by the KT boundary in the Paleocene, c. 65mya. The power of the mammals cannot be argued to lie within R-complex/limbic system functionalities. Rather the dominating feature stemmed from neocortical capacity linked to the reconstituted 150my-heritage of existing mammalian morphologies and behaviors.

Isaacson phrases the evolutionary implications of the accretative mammalian defensive morphological suite as follows:

Another way to conceptualize the limbic system may be to see it as a regulator of the R complex. On the basis of behavioral analysis, this regulation seems to be inhibitory in nature. Stimulation of the limbic system often produces a suppression of ongoing behavior, and lesions made within it often seem to "release" various activities . . . The r complex is necessary for ritualistic displays and the averbal communication associated with them. At the human level, MacLean believes that certain behavioral tendencies are due to an inheritance of dispositions mediated by this same, primal brain region. These include certain violent reactions, the preference for routine or 'ritualistic' actions, and some form of displacement activities.[22]

In the evolutionary tradition that spans the period from the eukaryote impact on the evolutionary flux of life to the vertebrate land living tetrapods, mammals and primates inherited the line of succession of this time-deep adaptive tradition. From about the period of presumed placental diversification, evidence, molecular as well as fossil/geological, c.100–90mya, the primates exemplify this adaptive trend: motility, adaptability to variable environments, omnivorous food habits, defensiveness, nonspecialized behavior, higher-than-average body-brain ratios, and high intelligence.

The particular specialized adaptive niche occupied by the primates took a long time to be grooved into the genetic morphological and behavioral memory bank. Much contemporary controversy concerns the place of *Homo* and its immediate antecedents. To be fair with the history of these controversies over human evolution, we ought to place the various positions on these issues into the *hypothetical.* On the basis of modern Darwinism, the roots of the hominids will likely be found on an outer branch, as with the mammals and their most ancient aqueous progenitors, the Osteolepiforms.[23]

It thus took c.150my, from c.365–215mya, for the power of higher intelligence to make its first land-adaptive impact, meaning the survival of the remnant products of the reptile, synapsid, therapsid, cynodont line. The survivors probably represent a long deviant proto-mammal branch. Then, another 125my allowed the higher brain-to-body ratio of the placentals to demonstrate its adaptive and selective power. The primates were a not hidden peripheral spiral of this ancient defensive, intelligent, outlander tradition. But they did not make their ultimate taxonomic success until the coming of *Hss,* with that creature's devastating selective power over almost all of animal and plant life. The primates needed some 75–80my to effect this most recent impact of intelligence and adaptability over other distant taxa. The hominids themselves needed 35-30my from the time of their most probable separation from the various anthropoid branches in the Oligocene to establish the power of their enveloping isocortex.

THE SOCIOBIOLOGY OF THE LIMBIC SYSTEM

Paul MacLean discusses the impact of the neopallium on human behavior. He is an especially clear and honest scientist when he demurs from the possibility of exploring the full role of Homo's new brain in its interaction with the older levels. His continuing focus on the supposedly dominating role of the older structures, however, raises questions both of balance and realism. Are we humans truly in the thrall of the striatal complex and the limbic system in cultural behavior, given that our uniqueness as mammals is characterized by the vast expansion of the new brain, the isocortex? I quote again from MacLean:

Recalling that in this chapter (#28 "Special Role of Prefrontal NeoCortex") our primary concern is with paleopsychic processes, we focus in this final discussion on human evolution as it pertains to (1) shedding of tears with crying; (2) the role of play in acculturation and creativity; and (3) the "memory of the future" All of these topics reflect in some degree the concurrent evolution of a sense of empathy and altruism. Since they are conditions that appear to depend particularly on the linkage of the frontal neocortex with the thalamocingulate division in the limbic system, it is relevant as background to summarize what is known about the time course of the evolution of the present-day human cranium with its distinctive elevation of the brow overlying the prefrontal region of the brain.[24]

MacLean's discourse involves a highly technical analysis of the morphologies of the human brain as they impact on the above typically sociobiological, limbic system behaviors: laughing, yawning, courtship, submissive behavior, territoriality, challenge displays, deceptive behavior, routinizing behavior, reenactment behavior, perseverative behavior, epilepsy, dejection, fear, desire, anger, gratulant (gratifying, triumphal, successful, ecstatic) exhultation, affection, searching behavior, protective, aggressive or caressive behavior; handedness, sound communication and speech, weapon and child carrying, the evolution of tearing, play, and laughter.

At core, MacLean's argument places the locus of certain basic and untutored responses in the limbic system. The human limbic system becomes the regulator that prevents or shapes those earlier rigid, stereotyped, and autonomous drives centered in the reptilian complex: amygdaloid area-aggressive behavior; septal area sexual function. MacLean notes that sexual behavior in the paleomammals originated in rhinencephalon and the olfactory structures.[25]

In an important interpretation of the implications of MacLean's theory, two scholars at the University of Palermo, M. Ernandes and S. Giammanco, probe the powers of the R-complex and the limbic system in order to clarify human hierarchical institutions, both religious and political. In concordance with MacLean, the R-complex fixes connections among phenomena-temporal-momentary; conformity or nonconformity, with precedent conditions, ritualistic changes in behavior. The limbic system adds an emotional element, producing relaxation when activities are completed, anxiety when they are brusquely interrupted or changed. The neocortex possesses "induction" capacity from particular phenomena with causal connections felt in all perceptual experience. In humans, R-complex factors lead to obsessional and magical behavior and compulsions. In humans a language factor adds to these R-complex elements.[26]

Underneath these behaviors certain brain structures provide a level of biological causation. In the R-complex, neurons form masses, nuclei or ganglia. The limbic system includes pallial or cortical structures in addition to nuclei. These include: (a) paleopallium-piriform cortex; (b) medial pallium, (i.e., hippocampus-archipallium); and (c) dorsal pallium-neopallium. The isocortex possesses 6 layers. Biochemically, all three brain types exhibit acetylcholine and dopamine typical of R-complex, and serotonin.[27] Ernandes and Giammanco write: "Following MacLean's model, in the serotenergic system we can distinguish a reptilian part (i.e., of the R-omplex) and a mammalian part (i.e., of the limbic system), the latter being formed in particular by raphes obscurus and dorsal raphes nuclei. Ascending fibres extend from the pontine nuclei (MRN and DRN) to several telencephalic regions, among which are basal ganglia."[28]

Reduction in serotenergic action leads to (a) increase of intraspecific competition; (b) increase of magical thought; (c) temporal epilepsy. Reduction in serotenergic function weakens the limbic system's ability to resist hierarchy-making structures, as well as obsessive-compulsive disorders.[29]

Although inhibited by the limbic system, the human brain's R-complex preserved and still preserves the structures and hierarchy-forming functions that give rise to submission to leaders. MacLean sees "the immensely powerful being" as created by the action of the R-complex on the neocortex. Ernandes and Giammanco see the weakening over the span of human evolution of the inhibitory influence of the limbic system on the R-complex's influence over the neocortex.[30]

The question is, why did this happen, why the weakening? They answer that the brain makes causal connections between temporally variable inputs of perceptual information in a rationally verifiable and experientially adaptable manner, if the cortex can find the cause. In the case of magical thought, when inputs cannot be organized cortically in rational verifiable behavior, the result is nonfunctional illogical responses, that is, faith. Magical thought thus stems from its unconscious origins in the R-complex. The neocortex makes this conscious and tries to give it an appearance of rationality by embedding these emotions (limbic system) in a nexus of associated symbolism.[31]

Such symbolic systems lead to the acceptance of powerful human gods, as well as supernatural forces and gods. "Initiatory rites occur at critical ages of individual development with emotional involvement. They mainly operate on the limbic system and the r-complex. The limbic system provides the ingredients for the strong affective feeling of conviction attached to beliefs, while the r-complex is the seat of 'imprinting,' until religious beliefs as to the existence of a supernatural Powerful Being become strong and well established."[32]

From Desmond Morris: "in a behavioral sense, religious activities consist of the coming together of large groups of people to perform repeated and prolonged submissive displays to appease a dominant individual. The dominant individual takes many forms in different cultures, but always has a common factor of immense power."[33]

EVOLUTIONARY CRITIQUE

Because MacLean always followed the mainline evolutionary perspectives of the Darwinians, the direction of his highly technical and specialized morpho-neurological research on the brain adhered closely to the accepted evolutionary perspective. He colored his evolutionary interpretation, however, with the comparative functions of the so-called striatum or R-complex and the more recently evolved limbic structures. Even more MacLean saw the behavioral impacts of these latter systems on human life, considering but not emphasizing the impact of Homo's cortical accretions. So, too, in turning to the evolutionary record, he tended to view mammal evolution as adaptively and selectively defined by the behavioral impact of limbic system structures. To MacLean, they provide definition, in contrast with the underlying reptilian R-complex, and thus have been decisive in the selective sense.

We have here the traditional chicken-or-egg argument. Which element, traditional limbic structures or cortical causal and evaluative factors, tilted the selective equation? The debate transitions into the evolution of the hominids. Here the isocortical growth explosion unanimously seems the reason for hominid and *Hss* success. MacLean understandably pointed to the ongoing impact on behavior of these phylogenetically ancient structures. Compared to the base primates, they possess inordinate prominence in Homo's brain. Still, the isocortex maintains its roles as the decisive selective element in human evolution. The isocortex seeks out causes, relationships, and ventures predictions of the future. In its hyper-corticality linked with the ancient mammalian structures, this brain structure discovered the keys to mastering the physical and biological world.

MacLean, as we have noted above, viewed the innovative mammalian physical and brain structures—lactation, the protective nursing mother, the audio-vocal cries of protection and defense, play—as crucial adaptive factors that allowed for the positive selection of this class of animals. These led to their eventual domination over the other tetrapods, reptiles, and amphibians. The more contextual evolutionary perspective would place a much greater emphasis on the larger cortex of the mammalian brain, as compared with the reptiles, because it fostered the adaptive efficacy of these animals. Indeed, as MacLean notes, a number of these adaptations may already have been part of the therapsid/cynodont suite of adaptations (homeothermy, internal gestation) before the evidentiary extrusion of the mammals 215–200mya.

Most have conceded that, compared with the extroverted visual and energetically dynamic reptile adaptive patterns, the mammalian suite of brain/behaviors originally had defensive functions. But without the suzerainty of a larger cortex to coordinate such defenses behaviors, their selective impact on the evolutionary destiny of the mammals would have been marginal, as evident in a number of marsupial and monotreme lines. These lines, without the competitive pressures exerted by placentals would have held their own against existing reptile forms, and, indeed, with a limbic brain, did proliferate. Emotional control epitomized in the limbic areas without the coordinating powers of the neocortex, however, would have never won the selective battle for the placentals.

And, of course, the primate line, once an intelligent, defensive, side branch of the placentals, made its living by "staying out of the way" through protective brain-power. Eventually, use of that brainpower linked to a powerful and energetically dynamic limbic system, destroyed innumerable long prospering species that existed to that point. MacLean admits the closely linked morphological and behavioral connections in the human brain between the various parts of the limbic system and the isocortex. So much so, it is difficult to see where one function ends and the other kicks in. Still, the following quotation reflects the deep impression of the power of the limbic system on human behavior.

[T]he complete lack of memory for what happened during automatisms (psychomotor epilepsy) is primarily owing to a disturbance of limbic function and a resulting failure of the integration of internally and externally derived experience, upon which a sense of reality of the self depends. Without an integrated sense of self, there is, so to speak, no place to deposit a memory of ongoing experience . . . [T]he limbic cortex receives more extensive input from interoceptive systems than the neocortex and, also of crucial importance, receives input from the various exteroceptive systems. It should be recalled at this point that psychomotor epilepsy provides evidence that the limbic system is involved in self-realization, as evident by such experiences during the aura as feelings of enhanced feelings of reality. increased awareness, or self-duplication ('mental diplopia')... the phenomenology of psychomotor epilepsy reveals that even the least obtrusive feelings generated by limbic activity are tinged with some degree of affect...the saying that 'something does not exist until you give it a name': Something does not exist unless it is imbued with an *affective* feeling, no matter how slight.[34]

An intimacy between feeling and thought in human interpersonal and cultural behavior has long been commented upon. A seeming axiom holds each issue from a differing dimension of the human psyche. Yet emotions cannot be individually suppressed in our living actions without human suffering. The artist, scientist, musician, even the philosopher, needs the juices of affect to undergird, to give spirit to, his mentation. This completely concords with MacLean's views. At the same time, the raw feelings of "blood," of nationalism, of power, of love and sex, religious or ethnic zealotry without the rigor and restraints of thought or reason, become inchoate and animalistic. Eventually, without cognitive discipline, they turn any human activity into "blind obedience to powerful beings."

The selective power of humans considered from the evolutionary standpoint does not lie in the various R-complex and limbic system heritages of behavior, even though they constantly erupt from the depths of our neurological past to dominate individual and social actions. True human power is rooted in the isocortex, our ability to think, reason, analyze, abstract from momentary perception, and create laws and principles whose impact on other humans and the world beyond may not be evident for weeks, months, years.

Sociobiological fascination, clearly influential in MacLean's metainterpretations, derives from a need to search for a unity of derivation in our biological nature. But such reductionist views miss the great biological story in the "super-primate" revolution heralded in the isocortex of *Homo.* The missed "story!" can be found in the evolutionary processes that created this unprecedented brain. Such conceptual myopia is exemplified in the quickness of reputable scientists to swallow "humans-as-third-chimpanzee" science fiction.

The hegira leading to *Hss* has been long in coming. The hominids in all likelihood expelled and pushed the African anthropoids into extinction, except for the peripheral and now highly specialized chimpanzees and gorillas. Indeed, it is likely that much of African ape evolution since the Miocene, 20mya, has been selectively influenced by the increasingly successful australopithecines and then their supplanters, *Homo*. Only recently has the weight of evidence replaced the lineal view of the fossil record with a new awareness of the long-in-process branching nature of hominid evolution.

Scientific opinion has now solidified the awareness that the first truly modern humans were the Cro-Magnons, *Hss*, of Europe and West Asia. The power of their ballooning cortex is revealed in the spontaneous symbolic effusions of their technology, art, and social discipline. In the richness of their cultural productions, we can envision the workings of the paleoneurological structures. But they are filtered through and disciplined by the isocortex. There had been, before this bursting of traditional hominid boundaries c.45,000 B.P. many forms of *Homo*. It is difficult to know what their cultural potential could have been were they to have lived within the protective bosom of the Cro-Magnons. The Neanderthals, a primitive progressive erectine type with a large brain, are increasingly viewed as having lived side by side with the Cro-Magnons in Europe and West Asia, and for at least 10,000 years. Perhaps they were even protected by the moderns. Certainly, much interbreeding took place. Skulls as far back as 90,000 B P—Qafzeh, Skuhl. in the Near East, later, Predmost and Mladec in Moravia, 35,000 B.P—reveal such a relationship. Most recently discovered is an apparently post-Neanderthal hybrid child, at about 23,000 B.P.

In addition, large populations of humans lived away from the center of this final evolutionary thrust that received, though only gradually and variably, the genetic biochemistry that produced the modern cortex. Our contemporary inheritance, then, is mixed in terms of the cortical and cultural assimilation of these evolutionary dynamics. But, the ancient paleoneurology exists in all humans, an inheritance dated in the tens and hundreds of millions of years. And it shows itself in the variety of human interpersonal behaviors, as well as cultural and civilizational life-styles. Some of us can fall under the thrall of R-complex and limbic passions of allegiance to human tyrants, religions that demand the debasement of human reason to myth, magic and superstition. Weak cognitive profiles are victimized by the devotional totems emanating from Hollywood or Yankee Stadium. Highly intelligent and educated peoples, such as the Germans or Japanese, can surrender their rationality to "the myth of the state."[35] The Cro-Magnons, at 30,000 B.P, evidence in their art, monuments, and technology little mythology or violence. The classical Greeks and the early modern Europeans were intellectually moved to draft written constitutions in which democratic practices acted to nullify the sway of the ancient neurological regime. This represents strong evidence for the latent powers of the neocortex in human sociobiological affairs.

PHILOSOPHICAL INJUNCTIONS FOR RESEARCH AND POLICY

The 20th century witnessed a powerful resurgence in the glorification of "paleocerebral functioning." From the throwing off of Victorian behavioral modalities for the freedoms of sexual as well as cultural expression, cinema, literature, and so on, the frontal brain areas of restraint and discipline ceded their suzerainty to the "let-it-all-hang-out" expressivity of the older behavioral regime. In addition, the susceptibility of the masses, ceding their rationality to the unlimited god-like powers of tyrannical leaders such as Hitler and Stalin, the toleration for the massive genocides unleashed by these human animals, allows us to witness at first-hand the paradoxical character of the human brain.

Paul MacLean sees opportunities for a higher form of animal behavior through the union of limbic and cortical functioning in the human animal:

The possibility is suggested that through the neofrontal connections with the thalamo-cingulate division, a parental concern for the young generalizes to other members of the species, a psychological development that amounts to an evolution from a sense of responsibility to what we call conscience.[36]

What is substantially new in the known history of biology is that this concern extends not only to the human family, but to all living things—an evolutionary turnabout that could affect a turnabout in what has heretofore seemed a vicious life-death struggle long recognized as the struggle between good and evil.[37]

It is well and good to identify the source of so-called human altruism in the nurturing concern of parents for their young. This sense of responsibility, however, is not strictly rooted in the genetics of neofrontal/ thalamocingulate maternity. Nurturing is now a freely chosen behavior, and, equally, discarded in neglect and cruelty. We human beings can extend our sense of "responsibility" and "conscience" toward the young of others. In similar cognitive acquiescence, we can act to destroy the children of strangers. The puzzling voluntarism of human intraspecific violence finds a parallel in the mystery of mental dysfunction. We human animals uniquely display this. Some would place a sociobiological tonality onto these malfunctionings as heralding defeat and biological ostracism. Yet the behaviors seem to have persisted over long spans of time. The biochemistry that we now see as complicit, at least in part, has not been expelled from the genome. In fact, many individuals afflicted with bipolar syndrome are socially successful and creative persons.

Hans Eysenck hypothesized a close relationship between schizophrenia and genius; they seem to occupy different sides of a sometimes permeable brain behavioral membrane. The genius sees in the given symbolic structure possibilities inherent in the fluid malleability of factual reality. The schizophrenic envisions possibilities that are beyond the facticity of the given. The sense of possibility in one grows out of a sense that the real is never permanently embedded. In the other there is no public facticity from which to envision real possibilities.[38] Who can say where in triune brain structure this fluidity of thought is made possible?

MacLean often points to epileptic seizures as revealing the interdependence of the new brain on the older morphologies. So, too, we can view the charismatic demagogue transformed into the tyrant as an exemplar of the "demonic" power pathologies inherent in the ancient structures when allied with humans in crafty and unscrupulous intelligence.

What we see in the historical working out of an extremely variable, yet radically new set of brain structures in this interbreeding super-species, *Homo sapiens,* is the slow, variable, and inexorable march toward domination of the dictates of cortical intelligence in human behavior. We cannot depend on inchoate instinctive mammalian motivations to direct us into the future. The neocortex must not suppress, but rather discipline those paleoneurological juices, our evolutionary vertebrate heritage. Intelligence and rationality need to consolidate, if not establish their suzerainty in our thinking and behaving. It is to be hoped that this process will define the internationalization of the larger human community.

NOTES

1. Triarchic rather Triune because the former reflects the semi-independent variability of the three morphological structures in terms of their behavioral correlates. Triune implies as with the "Trinity" a merging of three factors in a unity of expression.

2. MacLean, P. D. 1990. *The Triune Brain in Evolution,* NY: Plenum, p. 10.

3. MacLean, 1990. pp. 578–579.

4. MacLean, P. D. 1968 "Alternative neural pathways to violence," in *Alternatives to Violence,* L, Ng., ed., New York: Time-Life Books, pp. 24–34.

5. MacLean, 1990, pp. 33-35.

6. MacLean, 1990, pp. 232–233. See also Gadjusek, D. C. 1970. "Physiological and psychological characteristics of Stone Age Man," in *Symposium on Biological Bases of Human Behavior, Eng. Sc.,* 33: 58–59.

7. Janvier, P. 1984. "The relationship of the Osteostraci and the Galeaspida," *Journal of Vertebrate Paleontology,* 4: 344–358; Long, J. 1995 *The Rise of the Fishes,* Baltimore: Johns Hopkins University Press, pp. 30, 32, 34.

8. Radinsky, L. 1987. *The Evolution of Vertebrate Design,* Chicago: University of Chicago Press. pp. 50–52.

9. Woese, C. R., Kandler, O., and Wheelis, M. L. 1990. "Towards a Natural System of Organism: Proposal for the Domains Archae, Bacteria, Eucarya," *Proceedings. National Academy of Science,* 87: 4576–4579; Kandler, O. 1993. *Progressive Botany,* 54: 1-24; de Duve, C. 1995. *Vital Dust,* NY: Basic Books; Sogin, M. 1991. "Early Evolution and the origin of the Eucaryotes," *Current Opinion Genetic Development,* 1: 457–463.

10. Henderson, L. 1913 *The Fitness of the Environment,* NY: Macmillan.

11. Nisbet, E. G. 1991 *Living Earth,* New York: Harper Collins, p.111; Dawkins, R. 1995. *River Out of Eden.* NY: Basic Books.

12. Margulis, L. 1992. *Simbiosis and Cell Evolution, 2nd* edition. San Francisco: W. H. Freeman; Wilford, J. N. 1996. "First Branch in Life's Tree Was 2 Billion Years Old," *The New York Times* reported in *Science,* 1/30/96.

13. Jerison, H. 1973. *Evolution of the Brain and Intelligence,* NY: Academic Press.

14. Smith, H. 1961. *From Fish To Philosopher,* New York: Anchor-Doubleday, pp. 120–121; Long, J. 1995. *The Rise of the Fishes,* Baltimore: Johns Hopkins Press, pp. 201, 209; Jerison, H., 1973, *op. cit.,* p, 28.

15. MacLean, 1990, pp. 95–97.

16. MacLean, 1990, p. 257; Jerison, H. 1973.op. cit.

17. Radinsky, 1987, The Evolution of Vertebrate Design, op. cit.

18. Jerison, H. 1973. Op. Cit., p 154; Quiroga, J.C. 1979. "The brain of two marnmal-like reptiles (Cynodontia-Therapsida)," *Jnl. Hirnforsch,* 20: 341–350; Quiroga, J. C. 1980. "The brain of a mammal-like reptile *Probaingnathus jenseni (*Therapsida, Cynodontia). A correlative paleo-neurological approach to the isocortex at the reptile-mammal transition," *Jnl. Hirnforsch,* 21: 299–336.

19. Jerison, H. 1982. "The Evolution of Biological Intelligence," in R. J. Sternberg, ed., *Handbook of Human Intelligence,* Cambridge, Eng.: Cambridge University Press, pp. 723–791; Jerison, H. 1977. "The Theory of Encephalization," *Annals of the N Y Acad. of Sciences:* 299: 146–160.

20. Bone, Q., Marshall, N., Blaxter, J. 1995. *Biology of Fishes,* London: Blackie Academic and Professional, pp.178, 180–182.

21. MacLean, 1990, p. 92; Gadow, H. F. 1911. "Reptiles-Anatomy" *in Encyclopaedia Britannica,* 11th ed., New York: Cambridge University Press, v. 23, p. 170.

22. Isaacson R. L. 1982. *The Limbic System,* 2nd ed., NY: Plenum Press, p. 246.

23. Ahlberg, P. E., and Johanson, Z. 1998. "Osteolepiforms and the ancestry of tetrapods." *Nature,* Vol. 395, 10/22/98, 792–794.

24. MacLean, 1990, p. 552.

25. Ernandes, M. and Giammanco, S. 1998. "MacLean's Triune Brain and the Origin of the 'Immense Power of Being' Idea," *Mankind Quarterly,* Winter 1998, Vol. 39: 2, 173–201 (184).

26. Ernandes, M. and Giammanco, S., 1998, p. 184.

27. Ernandes, M. and Giammanco, S., 1998, p. 180; see, Voogd, J. R., et. al. 1998. in Niewenhuys, R., et al., eds., *The Central Nervous System of the Vertebrates,* Berlin-Springer-Verlag, pp. 1636–2097 (p. 1872).

28. Ernandes, M. and Giammanco, S., 1998, p. 191.

29. Ernandes, M. and Giammanco, S. 1998, p. 192; Rapoport, J. L. 1989. "The Biology of Obsessions and Compulsions," *Scientific American,* 260:3: 62–69.

30. Ernandes, M. and Giammanco, S. 1998, p. 187.

31. Ibid, p. 184.

32. Ibid, p. 188.

33. Morris, D. 1994. *The Naked Ape,* London: Vintage/ Random House, p. 121.

34. MacLean, 1990. p. 578.

35. Cassirer, E. 1945. *The Myth of the State,* New Haven: Yale University Press.

36. MacLean, 1990. p. 562; MacLean, P. D. 1985a. "Brain evolution relating to family, play, and the separation call," *Archives General Psychiatry,* 42: 405–417.

37. MacLean, 1990. p. 562.

38. Eysenck, H. 1995. *Genius: The Natural History of Creativity,* Cambridge: Cambridge University Press.

15

MACLEAN'S EVOLUTIONARY NEUROETHOLOGY: ENVIRONMENTAL POLLUTION, BRAIN CHEMISTRY, AND VIOLENT CRIME

*Roger D. Masters**

INTRODUCTION

The evolutionary perspective in the study of the brain and social behavior is the hallmark of Paul MacLean's science. His limbic system and triune brain concepts have been among the most influential in neuroscience over the most recent decades. The full significance of the evolutionary neuroethology which he so tirelessly championed, however, has yet to be felt within the social sciences and even less yet in areas of social policy where it potentially illuminates some important, even urgent areas of concern. This chapter reports the results of findings in environmental pollution, specifically the effects of heavy metals upon violent social behavior, and emphasizes the necessity for bringing the perspective of evolutionary neuroscience into our social sciences and our social policy-making.

ENVIRONMENTAL POLLUTION, NEUROCHEMISTRY, AND BEHAVIOR

Building upon the work of such pioneering figures as Ramon y Cajal, Hughlings Jackson, C. Judson Herrick, Karl Pribram, Paul MacLean and others, evolutionary neuroscience continues to transform our understanding of human behavior. It has revealed not only the evolutionary history of our neural architecture but also anatomic structures and chemical mechanisms underlying emotion, cognition, and motor coordination (e.g. MacLean 1990; Purves et al.

* The research on silicofluoride toxity reported here was suggested by and conducted in collaboration with Myron J. Coplan (PE, Intelliquity consulting, Natick, MA), whose expertise and precision have been invaluable.

1997; Gazzaniga, Ivry & Mangun 1998; McGuire & Troisi 1998). However, for most social scientists, following Locke and the behaviorist tradition in psychology, the brain remains a black box responding to environmental stimuli. This outdated view of the brain as a *tabula rasa* still resonates in the widespread assertions of the "social construction" of human cultural and political behavior.

Although many traditional assumptions about the human brain are clearly false, the social sciences remain dominated by a generation totally unaware of neuroscientific research. As a result, it is commonplace to "explain" learning deficits, substance abuse, and antisocial behavior solely by such factors as poverty, socioeconomic status, and racial or sexual prejudice. Of course, these conditions greatly influence all of us. But their effects are mediated by each individual's central nervous system, a product of millions of years of species evolution, that processes similar information in varying ways due to differential genetic propensities, fetal and neonatal development, diet, maternal and paternal bonding, early learning and social experience—along with myriad other inputs to the human brain. To understand how such complex factors contribute to violent behavior, an understanding of the revolutionary advances in neuro-science becomes both invaluable and indispensable (Raine 1993; Wilson & Petersilia 1995; Niehof 1999). We begin this discussion by considering the effects of environmental elements that are toxic to the proper functioning of our evolved neural architecture.

Neurotoxins and Their Effects

Neurotoxins are among the factors that can change brain function and thus alter behavior (on the following, in addition to Aschner & Kimelberg 1996; Purvis et al. 1997; and Gazzaniga, Ivry and Mangun 1998; see esp., Lippard & Berg 1994). The central nervous system (CNS) is perhaps the subtlest and most sensitive chemical system in the human body—as most of us learned the first time we drank too much alcohol.

Mere environmental exposure to toxic chemicals is, however, not the whole story. Evolution has also built in a degree of protection for the nervous system. Given the complexity of neurochemistry, it should hardly be a surprise that natural selection has to some extent buffered the central nervous system against potentially harmful chemicals in the environment.

If a toxin is swallowed, its effects depend on whether it crosses the gut-blood barrier. Once in the bloodstream (whether from ingestion or wounds), toxins must also cross the blood-brain barrier before they can influence brain function and behavior. However, because the selective passage of many toxic chemicals through cell membranes is determined by a variety of physicochemical variables including size, charge, hydrophilicity, lipophilicity, etc., toxicologists have focused on toxin-induced health risks such as cancer and birth defects rather than on social behavior.

Despite its buffering effect against certain elements, the blood-brain barrier does, however, possess channels that function to allow the passage of essential elements that play a regulatory role in cellular function. These elements are sometimes positively charged ions ("cations") and sometimes negatively charged ones ("anions"). Many essential elements, including calcium, iron, and zinc, are called divalent cations because they have an electrical charge of 2+. Individuals deficient in these elements are more likely to absorb toxic heavy metals that are also cations, including lead (Pb^{2+}), manganese (Mn^{2+}, Mn^{3+}, Mn^{4+}), cadmium (Cd^{2+}), or aluminum (Al^{3+}). These toxic elements can cross the acetylcholine channel, that allows only positively charged ions to pass into cells with little discrimination between cations (Lippard & Berg 1994: 159). Inhalation of toxins provides a more direct and more dangerous route, because some molecules can move through the nasal cavity to the brain directly, bypassing the blood-brain barrier altogether.

Within the brain, another mechanism of detoxification can sometimes fail, leading to unwanted behavioral effects. Glial cells function to absorb the products of chemical reactions in the brain and release them to the bloodstream (Aschner & Kimelberg 1996). But this process is subject to a number of biochemical constraints that sometimes do not effectively remove toxins. For example, the cellular surface of neurons normally maintains a net electrochemical balance between positive and negative charges—the so-called Donnen Equilibrium. If this balance is disturbed with a resulting net negative charge, uptake of positive cations increases without regard to the toxicity of the elements involved. As a result, the combination of an imbalance in normal chemical elements plus exposure to such toxic metals as lead, manganese, cadmium, or aluminum can easily result in brain uptake (Lippard & Berg 1994: ch. 6).

Based on these considerations, we hypothesize that such heavy metals more likely influence *behavior* than do many industrial neurotoxins. To be sure, endocrine disruptors (Coburn, Dumanoski and Myers 1997) can also have important effects on behavior, as is suggested by recent findings linking them with a preference for same-gender sexual partners (Crews et al. 2000). Despite these facts, traditional studies of the toxicity of many elements including cadmium (Ashner & Kimelberg 1996: Ch. 11) and fluoride (e.g., Dunipace et al. 1989, 1996; Jackson et al. 1997), have continued to focus almost entirely on cancer and similar diseases.

One difficulty in studying the effects of heavy metals on behavior is that exposure does not alone account for dysfunctional outcomes. Neuronal uptake of heavy metals largely depends on other factors such as dietary deficits, stress, or exposure to substance abuse, which damage the brain's normal mechanisms of defense against toxins (Bryce-Smith 1983, 1986; Ashner & Kimelberg 1996). Hence the poor, with diets lacking sufficient calcium, iron, or zinc, are at higher risk for the negative effects of heavy metals. Likewise affected are those persons with hypolactasia or other genetic conditions that predispose toward diets low in calcium and other essential minerals.

Of the heavy metals harmful to normal learning and behavior, lead is the best known (Needleman, ed. 1991; Needleman 1998). Its effects were noted long ago by Benjamin Franklin, who wrote a friend: "the Opinion of this mischievous Effect from Lead is at least above Sixty Years old; and you will observe with

Concern how long, a useful Truth may be known and exist, before it is generally receiv'd and practic'd on." (Masters, Hone and Doshi 1998:13). Manganese and cadmium have also been associated with increased aggressiveness or hyperactive behavior and learning, deficits. In addition, long-term exposure to manganese or to organophosphates has been implicated in a form of Parkinsonism (Dicalzi et al. 2000; Pryadarshi et al. 2000; Weiss 2000). Some researchers believe aluminum is a risk factor in Alzheimer's Disease although evidence is lacking.

Environmental exposure leading to uptake of heavy metals can therefore contribute as a co-factor to many behavior deficits and social dysfunctions. Among the conditions that have been studied are learning disabilities (Bryce-Smith 1983, 1986), low IQ (Needleman, ed. 1991), attention deficit disorder (ADD) as well as hyperactivity (ADHD) (Tuthill 1996; Manuzza 1989, 1998), teenage pregnancy, alcoholism, drug abuse, and crime (Masters, Hone and Doshi 1998). In each case, neurochemical imbalances that interfere with normal information processing and impulse control number among the risk-factors associated with dysfunctional or anti-social behaviors.

Specific mechanisms underlying these findings have been studied at the neuroanatomical level. For instance, attentional focusing, and behavioral inhibition represent functions regulated by circuits in the basal ganglia (structures deep in what MacLean called the R-complex). Two inhibitory circuits in this structure, regulated by the neurotransmitters dopamine and GABA (gamma-amino butyric acid), facilitate continued information search and optimize responses to environmental stimuli (Purvis et al. 1997: 348–349; Gazzaniga, Ivry and Mangun 1998: 412–420). By reducing the levels of these neurotransmitters, lead or manganese can produce defects in inhibition (Masters, Hone and Doshi 1998). Not surprisingly, therefore, recent studies have shown substantial numbers of hyperactive (ADHD) children with elevated levels of lead (Tuthill 1996) or manganese in head hair. Masters, Hone and Doshi. have compiled data revealing that head hair has been used as a marker of heavy metal uptake over the preceding 2–3 months (1998: 13–48).

Other factors that contribute to observed correlations include vulnerability of neuroanatomical structures to heavy metal toxicity. One important structure for learning, whose functions are only now being understood by neuroscientists is the hippocampus. There CA1 and CA3 neurons establish lasting connections between synaptic firing patterns through longterm potentiation (LTP), that increases responses when paired stimuli are perceived, as well as long term depression (LTD), which reduces associative responses as part of habit formation. These basic mechanisms for learning and habituation depend on calcium, magnesium, and the neurotransmitter glutamate (Purvis et al. 1997: 440–451; Gazzaniga, Ivry and Mangun 1998: 285–287). Lead can both lower levels of glutamate and replace calcium, thereby disrupting the normal regulatory functions of ion channels. Such neurotoxic effects may explain why lead uptake so widely correlates with lower IQ and other learning disabilities (Bryce-Smith 1983; 1986; Needleman, ed. 1991; Needleman 1998).

EMPIRICAL EVIDENCE LINKING NEUROTOXIC METALS AND BEHAVIORAL DYSFUNCTION

No single risk-factor explains everything in human antisocial behavior. Poor impulse control and low IQ can be traced to factors other than toxic metals, ranging from genes to sociocultural backgrounds (Masters and Coplan 1999b). However, the contribution of heavy metals can be disentangled from these factors by three types of findings. First, body levels of lead, manganese, or cadmium can be measured among persons with specific behavioral dysfunctions—ranging from hyperactivity to violent criminal records—and compared to comparable individuals who do not exhibit the behavior in question (e.g., Walker 1998). Second, geographic levels of the same behavioral dysfunctions can be compared in communities that do and do not have sources of environmental pollution with heavy metals (e.g., Masters, Hone and Doshi 1998). Third, time-series data can be examined to assess whether changes in levels of pollution influence rates of learning disabilities and antisocial behavior (e.g., Masters 2001). At all three levels, evidence shows heavy metal neurotoxicity to be a significant risk-factor contributing to problems of learning and self control.

Heavy Metals as a Risk Factor to Individuals

As noted, studies over the last decade in the U.S. and Europe repeatedly found a linear inverse relationship between individual lead levels (as measured in blood or head hair) and IQ (Bryce-Smith 1983, 1986). Some critics have gone to extreme lengths to challenge these findings—for example by claiming that because impulsive children eat lead paint that, in turn, causes low IQ, impulsivity rather than lead toxicity represents the root cause (Juberg 1977: 9). In a series of carefully controlled studies, Herbert Needleman and his colleagues (Needleman, ed. 1991; Needleman et al. 1996) have demonstrated the error of this hypothesis. Most recently, this research team has compared infants at birth, showing that there were no early differences in the response patterns of children subsequently found to have higher lead uptake and attention deficit disorder (Needleman 1999).

Poor impulse control apparently contributes to the learning deficits associated with heavy metal toxicity. This finding is plausible on neuro-ethological grounds. For example, ritalin, the most widely used medication for hyperactivity, increases dopamine—a neurotransmitter with inhibitory functions whose levels are reduced among individuals who absorb too much lead. Indeed Walker (1998) has reported that removing lead is an effective therapy for hyperactivity and notes that, since cocaine and ritalin have similar effects on dopamine, drugging ADHD children to make life easier for parents and teachers is both medically unwise and ethically unsound.

Given an association between poor impulse control during childhood and subsequent violent behavior (Manuzza et al. 1989, 1998), others focused on levels of lead and manganese in the head hair of criminals. Seven different groups of violent offenders were compared to those in the same prison convicted of property crime. This provided a valuable test. Robbery and theft are more likely to be preceded by planning than barroom brawls. Hence these studies provide an assessment of impulsiveness that takes into consideration other factors leading to criminal behavior. In all seven samples, the violent offenders had significantly higher levels of either lead and cadmium or manganese (Masters, Hone and Doshi 1998).

Two prospective studies confirmed these findings by showing that children with early evidence of high lead uptake more likely exhibit later behavioral dysfunction (Denno 1993; Needleman 1996). The larger of these samples, based on data from the Philadelphia Biosocial Study, revealed that blood lead levels at age 7 significantly predicted juvenile and adult crime (Denno 1994).

Environmental Pollution with Heavy Metals: a Geographic Risk Factor

A second approach analyzes the extent that heavy metal pollution associates with geographical areas at risk for higher rates of behavior dysfunction. Although anecdotal data are risky, it may be worth noting that a numberof the major school shootings in the United States over the last two years have occurred in communities that are Superfund sites. Only in Springfield, Oregon— where Kip Kinkle acted alone—is there no evidence of industrial releases of heavy metals. Springfield is about 40 miles from the nearest Superfund pollution site. In all other cases—most notably Littleton, Colorado, where the Superfund site was ignored by all the journalists—there is striking evidence of toxic pollution with heavy metals and other toxins (Rymer and Alpert 1999).

The Environmental Protection Agency's Toxic Release Inventory for lead and manganese, two of the principal heavy metals implicated in poor impulse control, provided more convincing statistical data for these heavy metals. Comparing all counties in the United States on over twenty socio-economic and demographic measures, including income levels, population density and size, racial composition, and education, industrial releases of heavy metal pollution were a statistically significant risk factor for higher rates of violent crime (Table 15.1). Lead or manganese pollution *interact* with each other and with above average rates of alcoholism. Communities with any two or all three of these risk-factors have signficantly higher rates of violent crime than those with only one (Masters, Hone & Doshi 1998).

Pollution with neurotoxins like lead can, moreover, last for many years (Bailey et al. 1994). Indeed, although forest areas may be able to recycle toxic metals quickly, some estimates suggest that in an urban soil, lead toxicity may last for up to fifty years. Because children play in the dirt and lick their fingers—a behavior increased by the sweet taste of lead—neighborhoods adjoining heavily used urban highways represent areas of risk. Within a number of American urban communities, including cities as different as Milwaukee and New Orleans, careful studies by Howard Mielke and associates found that areas along highways that were heavily traveled when automobiles used leaded gasoline have higher levels of lead in the soil around housing units (Mielke 1998).

Table 15.1. Factors Associated with U.S. Crime Rates, 1985–1991

All U.S. Counties Reporting Data from 14 Independent Variables

	Violent Crime - 1985			Violent Crime - 1991			Increase 1985 to 1991		
	Stan. Coeff.	t-value	Probability	Stan. Coeff.	t-value	Probability	Stan. Coeff.	t-value	Probabil
Demographic Variables									
Population	0.178	4.047	0.0001	0.199	4.528	0.0001	0.121	2.161	0.0306
Population Density	0.171	8.433	0.0001	0.150	7.441	0.0001	0.046	1.811	0.0730
%Black	0.230	13.1	0.0001	0.298	17.21	0.0001	0.237	10.785	0.0001
%Hispanic	0.141	8.818	0.0001	0.144	9.045	0.0001	0.092	4.516	0.0001
Socio-Economic Variables									
Per Capita Income	n.s.	n.s.	n.s.	n.s.	n.s..	n.s.	n.s.	n.s.	n.s.
Black Poverty	0.399	9.851	0.0001	0.425	10.51	0.0001	0.219	4.26	0.0001
Hispanic Poverty	-0.056	1.645	0.1001	n.s.	n.s..	n.s.	n.s.	n.s.	n.s.
Median Grade Completed	0.054	2.913	0.0036	0.082	4.473	0.0001	0.070	3.032	0.0025
Public Policies									
Welfare Per Capita	-0.316	5.717	0.0001	-0.396	7.184	0.0001	-0.260	3.711	0.0002
Police/Capita	0.145	8.267	0.0001	0.089	5.077	0.0001	n.s.	n.s.	n.s.
Public Water/Capita	0.091	5.515	0.0001	0.089	5.427	0.0001	0.059	2.807	0.0050
Toxic Metals									
Lead Toxic Release	0.043	2.633	0.0085	0.038	2.275	0.0230	n.s.	n.s.	n.s.
Manganese Toxic Release	0.047	2.901	0.0037	0.078	4.792	0.0001	0.077	3.741	0.0002
%Pre-1939 Houses	-0.143	8.460	0.0001	-0.158	9.509	0.0001	-0.091	4.298	0.0001
number of counties	2881			2754			2659		
Adjusted r-squared	0.418			0.445			0.146		
F-test	148.979			159.468			32.405		
probability	0.0001			0.0001			0.0001		

Note: Compiled from EPA and FBI data.

Temporal Effects of Pollution from Leaded Gasoline

As Mielke's work suggests, environmental pollution can continue to influence behavior long after the original release of the toxins. In addition to prolonged exposure, toxins can produce delayed effects because exposure of the fetus or infant often produces lasting damage to normal brain structure and chemistry (Wong et al. 1992; Aschengau, Ziegler and Cohen 1993; Levitt 1999). In humans, delayed behavioral dysfunctions due to low-level exposure to lead and other heavy metals show as subtle effects (Mendlesohn et al. 1998) and may not become readily apparent until manifested in anti-social behavior in teenage years (Needleman, ed. 1991, esp. Ch. 11-12; Denno 1993; Needleman 1996).

The national phase-out of leaded gasoline provided an interesting way to study such a proposed delayed effect of lead on behavioral dysfunction for two reasons. First, longitudinal studies have shown striking declines in lead levels in children since the ban on sales of leaded gas, indicating that in this case public policy significantly reduced exposure and uptake of a dangerous neurotoxin. Second, since humans absorb 40 to 50% of inhaled lead as compared to only 5 to 15% of ingested lead (Needleman ed. 1991: 81), effects of nasal exposure to leaded gasoline likely have been especially great. Whereas uptake of ingested toxins is thought to be dependent on dietary deficits, fumes of tetraethyl lead from gasoline pumps could even harm pregnant women and their fetuses as well as infants with diets not deficient in calcium and other essential minerals. If so, one can hypothesize that the long-term effects of exhaust from lead gasoline on fetal and infant development could have been responsible for behavioral problems when those affected reached teen-age and early adulthood.

The recent decline in violent crime rates in the United States provides a way of testing this hypothesis. While correlation does not prove causation, it can suggest possible risk-factors that deserve further analysis. The continuous fall in rates of murders and other violent crimes since 1991 has elicited many explanations from social scientists and criminologists (Wilson and Petersilia 1995), but only one seems to have looked at leaded gasoline sales (Nevin 2000). This should not be surprising, since the contemporary sales of leaded gas are negatively related to rates of crime. From the perspective of brain development, however, attention should focus instead on prenatal and neonatal neuronal damage that is only manifest years later. It appears conceivable that the harmful effects of leaded gasoline were temporarily delayed until those exposed before the age of 2 grew up.

Time-series data for all violent crime and for the sales of leaded gasoline 17 years earlier show roughly parallel down-turns in the early 1990s (Warren, Silverman and Sonnenborn 1999). A similar analysis of homicide and lagged rates of leaded gas sales is more useful, however, because it permits an assessment of effects that differ due to the age of the offender. Lagged gasoline sales not only track murder rates during their rise for 15 years prior to the 1977 ban, but in the five subsequent years for which we have data. But while gasoline consumption peaked at 1.7 times the baseline level, the homicide rate by 14-17 year olds peaked at over 3 times the baseline. The peak rate for the 18-24 age group was clearly not as high, suggesting greater impulsiveness among the younger cohort. That this difference might stem from the combined effects of pre-natal and neonatal exposure to particulate lead in gasoline exhaust is reinforced by the more precipitous decline in crime among younger offenders once rates began to fall in 1993 (see tables and figures in Masters 2001 for detail).

These findings add weight to the hypothesis that the strongest long-term effects of exposure to residues of tetraethyl lead were due to prenatal and neonatal development, reflecting the importance of long-term body stores of lead in current neurotoxicity (Gulson et al. 1995). To be sure, many factors contribute to crime (Wilson and Petersilia 1995). But because most socioeconomic and cultural variables usually invoked to explain crime either did not change in a manner that could explain the data or are themselves in need of explanation, the ban on leaded gas seems to have played an unexpected role in the sudden drop in criminal violence 17 years later (Nevin 2000).

It might be objected that the number of years chosen for the lagged variable, while based on the lag needed to track prenatal exposure of those 14 to 17 at the time of FBI crime reports, is arbitrary. Alternative explanations, however, are not entirely satisfactory. For example, some experts have claimed that the decline in violent crime since 1991 is due to the falling demand for crack cocaine. But this merely displaces the problem, since one has to ask why the demand for crack declined. This is particularly important because lead down-regulates dopamine whereas cocaine up-regulates dopamine—in that respect cocaine acts on dopamine the way Prozac acts on serotonin (cf. Martin 1983; Dewey 1986; Cook et al. 1995). Moreover one factor associated with enhanced lead uptake (silicofluoride usage in public water supplies, discussed in detail below) is correlated with increased levels of cocaine use at the time of arrest in an NIJ study of over 30,000 criminals in 24 cities. Because this effect was predicted by our research (Masters, Coplan & Hone 1999b) whereas it does not follow from traditional socioeconomic or racial models of substance abuse and crime, changes in cocaine usage cannot be invoked as a cause that is unrelated to absorption of lead from the environment.

Given linkages between lead and deficits in impulse control based on the neurochemical mechanisms outlined above, the hypothesis of a lagged positive effect from removing lead gasoline could be further tested by looking at additional measures that reflect impulsive behavior (Nevin 2000). One report suggests, for example, that sales of leaded gas highly correlate with the consumption of alcohol (DelRosso et al. 1999). Another tentative study suggests that rates of teen-age pregnancy were weakly correlated with leaded gasoline sales, albeit with a lag time of 14 years (Lauer et al. 1999). While both drinking and sexual promiscuity seem at first connected to impulsiveness, alcohol consumption provides an especially interesting test because the genetics and biochemistry of alcoholism gained wide study over the last decade.

Whereas the effects of lead neurotoxicity described above concern behaviors associated with dopamine, the consensus of recent scholarship points to crucial deficits in another neurotransmitter, serotonin (Masters & McGuire 1994: Ch. 6). Little evidence links lead toxicity to abnormal serotonergic function, whereas manganese clearly down-regulates serotonin levels (Ashner & Kimelberg 1996). In addition, data on crime indicate that rates of alcoholism influence behavior independently of industrial releases of either lead or manganese, reinforcing the belief of many researchers that alcoholism is strongly influenced by genetic factors. It follows from this as well as the diverse socioeconomic and cultural factors influencing alcohol consumption that the pattern of correlation between leaded gas sales and alcohol consumption should differ from that observed for homicides by young males.

The data confirm this hunch, pointing to puzzling associations that might further implicate lead neurotoxicity in social behavior. The correlation between leaded gasoline sales in the 1960s and 1970s and alcohol consumption 17 years later is negative ($r = -.307$). Nor do leaded gasoline sales strongly associate with the same year's alcohol consumption ($r = .228$). Oddly enough, however, if statistics are matched with a lag of 5 years, there is a stronger association ($r =$

.689). This suggests that recent lead exposure may influence some aspect of alcoholic consumption, since a lag of 5 years means that when leaded gasoline sales ended, the principal effect probably concerned children between the ages of 8 and 13 (the average age when teenages first start drinking [Masters and Coplan 1999a]).

Because alcoholism is primarily associated with serotonin, a neurotransmitter that is not a primary target of lead toxicity, these data suggest that the influence of lead on drinking behavior might concern the impulsivity with which people consume alcohol rather than the fact of consumption itself. If so, we might expect differences in the *kinds* of alcohol consumed to be more susceptible to lead toxicity than the overall consumption patterns.

When alcohol sales are broken down into beer, wine, and spirits (hard liquor), this is precisely what we find. If each year's sales of leaded gas are correlated with *contemporary* sales of each type of beverage, it becomes obvious that leaded gasoline was associated with a shift from beer and wine to distilled spirits as the drink of choice. The correlation between sales of spirits in years between 1949 and 1993 and sales of leaded gasoline during, the same year is .811 (p = .000), whereas both beer and wine sales are negatively and weakly correlated with leaded gas.

Unlike crime, the effect of exposure to leaded gasoline on alcohol seems to be a breakdown of aversion to the effects of rapid inebriation, at most triggered by lowering inhibition in late childhood. The correlation implies that the effect may have been strong, but many other cultural factors could also have contributed to the growing market for beer and wine. However that may be, since the brain dysfunction associated with alcohol consumption differs from that underlying homicide, it is not surprising that the precise pattern of association with exposure to fumes from leaded gasoline is also different.

These temporal relationships need further study. Although it is necessary to control for diverse social and geographic factors, the differences noted above are consistent with other data showing the behavioral effects of lead intake. If confirmed, such complex findings as the lagged effects of banning leaded gasoline on homicide and a markedly different pattern of influence on drinking patterns would constitute additional evidence for the neurotoxicity hypothesis (Masters 2001).

INDIRECT FACTORS ENHANCING LEAD UPTAKE

In some respects, the most intriguing and important analyses concern factors that enhance the uptake of lead. While pollution in the form of leaded gasoline fumes that are inhaled by pregnant mothers and infants would directly impact the developing brain, uptake of other sources of heavy metals may be enhanced by additional risk-cofactors in the environment.

Research with Myron Coplan and Brian Hone focused on one such factor, the use of silicofluorides in the fluoridation of public water supplies. Virtually all testing of fluoridation chemistry (with the exception of several early studies) has focused on the efficacy of sodium fluoride (NaF) in preventing caries. More recently, a few studies have considered the health effects of NaF—but none consider fluosilicic acid (H_2SiF_6) and sodium silicofluoride (Na_2SiF_6) and compare them to sodium fluoride (Coplan, Hone & Masters 1999a). EPA officials admit that they have no data on health or behavior effects of these chemicals (Fox 1999). Because the silicofluorides are used in the water treatment for over 90% of Americans receiving fluoridated water, this failure to study them is all the more surprising (Coplan, Masters & Hone 1999).

These chemicals deserve study because, in a sample of 250,000 children in Massachusetts, those living in communities using silicofluorides had significantly higher average blood lead levels than those in communities that do not fluoridate at all or that use sodium fluoride (Masters & Coplan 1999). Multivariate analyses shows that lead uptake from known environmental sources of pollution, such as average lead levels in 90th percentile first draw water and percent of housing built before 1940, was significantly higher in communities that also use SiF in water treatment (see Figure 15.1).

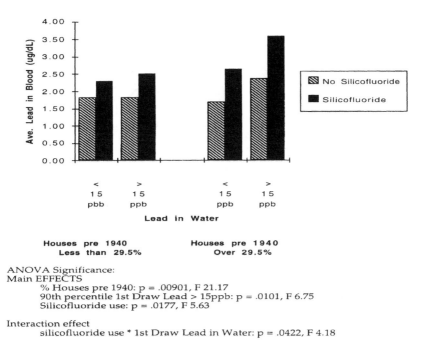

ANOVA Significance:
Main EFFECTS
    % Houses pre 1940: p = .00901, F 21.17
    90th percentile 1st Draw Lead > 15ppb: p = .0101, F 6.75
    Silicofluoride use: p = .0177, F 5.63

Interaction effect
    silicofluoride use * 1st Draw Lead in Water: p = .0422, F 4.18

Note: Derived from EPA and state data.

Figure 15.1. Factors Associated with Childrens' Blood Levels. Massachusetts.

Moreover, using a matched set of towns that do and do not fluoridate with these chemicals, SiF is associated with higher rates of crime and higher educational expenditures.

These associations between SiF and higher percentages of children with lead in excess of 10mcg/dL have been confirmed in studies of rural counties in Georgia and Wisconsin as well as in the 35 urban counties sampled in the National Health and Nutrition Evaluation Survey or NHANES III (Masters, Coplan & Hone 1999b). While these national data from NHANES III do not include counties with populations under 500,000, they show graphically that the greater vulnerability of racial minorities to higher lead uptake—long noted in studies of lead toxicity—is enhanced in communities using silicofluoride in their water (see Figures 15.2a and 15.2b).

Fluoridation and Race as Factors In Blood Lead of Children 3-5, NHANES III

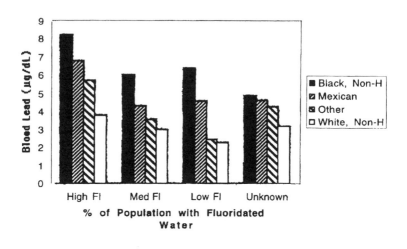

Source	DF	Sum of Squares	Mean Squares	F Value	Pr > F
Model	15	4113.841	274.2581	15.7	0.0001
Error	1811	31628.18	17.46448		
Corrected Total	1826	35742.02			

Source	DF	Type III SS	Mean Square	F Value	Pr > F
FL_GROUP	3	769.5048	256.5016	14.69	0.0001
RACE	3	1215.789	405.2629	23.2	0.0001
FL_GROUP*RACE	9	427.3706	47.48563	2.72	0.0038

Source: NHANES (National Health and Nutrition Evaluation Survey (NIH).

Figure 15.2a. Fluoridation and Race as Factors in Blood Level of Children 3–5

Fluoridation and Race as Factors in Blood Lead of Children 5-17, NHANES III

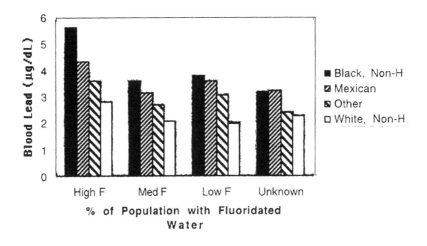

Source: NHANES (National Health and Nutrition Evaluation Survey (NIH).

Source	DF	Sum of Squares	Mean Squares	F Value	Pr > F
Model	15	5672.469	378.1646	44.58	0.0001
Error	6106	51799.4	8.483361		
Corrected Total	6121	57471.87			

Source	DF	Type III SS	Mean Square	F Value	Pr > F
FL_GROUP	3	982.8809	327.627	38.62	0.0001
RACE	3	1385.593	461.8644	54.44	0.0001
FL_GROUP*RACE	9	673.1287	74.79207	8.82	0.0001

Figure 15.2b. Fluoridation and Race as Factors in Blood Level of Children 5–17

These findings have been further confirmed by comparable statistical analyses of venous blood lead levels in a sample of over 150,000 children in New York state communities of 15, 000 to 75,000 population (Masters, Coplan, Hone & Dykes 2000). Once again, ethnic minorities were a substantially higher risk if exposed to SiF treated water, especially if other environmental sources of lead (such as old housing) were also prevalent in the community. All told, therefore, data in these three studies confirm the effects of silicofluoride in tests of blood lead for over 400,000 children.

In addition, we found behavioral correlations between SiF usage and antisocial behaviors otherwise associated with lead neurotoxicity, not only in county-level data for 1985 and 1991 (Tables 2a,b; Figures 3a,b), but in the alcoholism and cocaine consumption of over 30,000 criminals tested for drug use by the NIJ in 24 large cities (Masters, Coplan & Hone 1999a). The effect of SiF on cocaine usage—noted above in passing—was predicted as a behavioral correlate of lead neurotoxicity because cocaine, unlike the other drugs tested (which did not show higher usage in SiF communities) is a nonselective dopamine reuptake inhibitor (see Tables 15.2a, b; Figures 15.3a, b).

Table 15.2a. Multiple Regression-Causal Factors Associated with Rates of Violent Crime in All U.S. Counties, 1985

Variable:	Coefficient:	Std. Err.:	Std. Coeff.:	t-Value:	Probability:
INTERCEPT	-0.005056				
**%SiF	0.000368	0.000133	0.044933	2.779132	0.0055
UNEMPLOYMEN...	0.000076	0.000013	0.106014	5.988623	0.0001
PC INCOME BL...	-9.92E-09	5.69E-09	-0.028883	1.742151	0.0816
PC INCOME	9.53E-08	1.91E-08	0.115025	4.989345	0.0001
MEDIAN GRADE...	0.000205	0.000069	0.081833	2.971707	0.003
MEDIAN YEAR ...	0.000003	0.000004	0.01226	0.719065	0.4722
% BLACK	0.00005	0.000003	0.313211	17.565442	0.0001
% GRADUATE ...	-0.000022	0.000007	-0.096468	2.965084	0.0031
% RURAL	-0.000027	0.000001	-0.349944	18.728391	0.0001

CONFIDENCE INTERVALS Variable:	95% Lower:	95% Upper:	90% Lower:	90% Upper:	Partial F:
INTERCEPT					
**%SiF	0.000108	0.000628	0.00015	0.000587	7.723575
UNEMPLOYMEN...	0.000051	0.000101	0.000055	0.000097	35.863607
PC INCOME BL...	-2.11E-08	1.25E-09	-1.93E-08	-5.50E-10	3.035091
PC INCOME	5.78E-08	1.33E-07	6.39E-08	1.27E-07	24.893561
MEDIAN GRADE...	0.00007	0.00034	0.000091	0.000318	8.831041
MEDIAN YEAR ...	-0.000005	0.000011	-0.000004	0.00001	0.517055
% BLACK	0.000044	0.000056	0.000045	0.000055	308.544769
% GRADUATE ...	-0.000036	-0.000007	-0.000034	-0.00001	8.791723
% RURAL	-0.00003	-0.000024	-0.000029	-0.000024	350.752619

Note: Again, presence or absence of silicofluorides is a significant predictor of violent crime. Interestingly, in this group of nine predictive variables, only the median year of house construction is NOT significant. Compiled from EPA and FBI data.

Table 15.2b. Multiple Regression-Causal Factors Associated with Rates of Violent Crime in All U.S. Counties, 1991

Variable:	Coefficient:	Std. Err.:	Std. Coeff.:	t-Value:	Probability:
INTERCEPT	-0.026874				
**%SiF	0.000922	0.00019	0.076136	4.847215	0.0001
UNEMPLOYMEN...	0.000064	0.000017	0.062928	3.693542	0.0002
PC INCOME BL...	-3.96E-09	8.09E-09	-0.007926	0.489639	0.6244
PC INCOME	1.28E-07	2.63E-08	0.108872	4.869223	0.0001
MEDIAN GRADE...	0.000504	0.000095	0.140963	5.304905	0.0001
MEDIAN YEAR ...	0.000014	0.000006	0.039495	2.411564	0.0159
% GRADUATE ...	-0.000058	0.00001	-0.178521	5.719072	0.0001
% RURAL	-0.000041	0.000002	-0.376415	20.749842	0.0001
% BLACK	0.00008	0.000004	0.351002	20.358866	0.0001

CONFIDENCE INTERVALS

Variable:	95% Lower:	95% Upper:	90% Lower:	90% Upper:	Partial F:
INTERCEPT					
**%SiF	0.000549	0.001295	0.000609	0.001235	23.495494
UNEMPLOYMEN...	0.00003	0.000098	0.000035	0.000092	13.642253
PC INCOME BL...	-1.98E-08	1.19E-08	-1.73E-08	9.36E-09	0.239747
PC INCOME	7.65E-08	1.80E-07	8.48E-08	1.71E-07	23.70933
MEDIAN GRADE...	0.000317	0.00069	0.000347	0.00066	28.142022
MEDIAN YEAR ...	0.000003	0.000026	0.000004	0.000024	5.81564
Variable:	95% Lower:	95% Upper:	90% Lower:	90% Upper:	Partial F:
% GRADUATE ...	-0.000078	-0.000038	-0.000075	-0.000041	32.70778
% RURAL	-0.000045	-0.000037	-0.000044	-0.000038	430.555948
% BLACK	0.000072	0.000088	0.000074	0.000087	414.483444

Note: In 1991, silicofluorides are again a significant predictor of violent crime controlling for eight other variables. Unlike 1986, in 1991 age of housing is a significant predictor whereas per capita income among blacks is no longer significantly associated with rates of violent crime in the U.S. Compiled from EPA and FBI data.

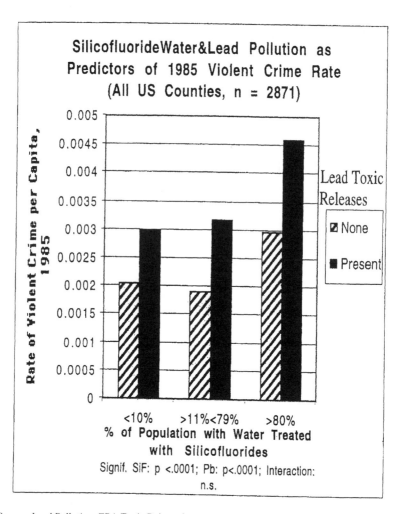

Source: Lead Pollution: EPA Toxic Release Inventory

Figure 15.3a. Silicofluoride Water and Lead Pollution of Predictors of 1985 Violent Crime Rate

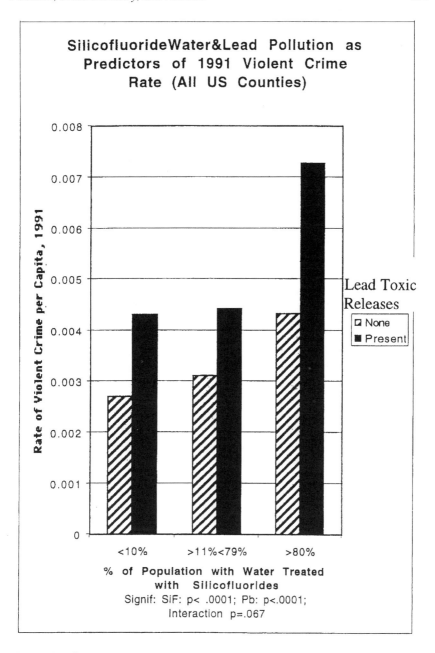

Note: Derived from EPA and FBI data.

Figure 15.3b. Silicofluoride Water and Lead Pollution as Predictors of 1991 Violent Crime Rate

The time-series data showing the lagged effects of leaded gasoline sales suggest another manifestation of SiF enhancement of anti-social behavior due to lead neurotoxicity. Leaded gas sales were virtually the same in 1960 and in 1980, three years after the peak sales in 1977. But 17 years after the second of these dates, the 14–17 and 18–24 homicide rates had only fallen from their peak values to 1.5 times their earlier base rates. Although other factors contribute to rates of violent behavior, the impact of socioeconomic or demographic causes of homicidal behavior seems to have been strengthened at the same time due to increasing SiF usage. Combined with other evidence presented here, this suggests that violent crime rates peaked around 1992–94 and subsequently declined in part due to the changing sales of leaded gasoline, with effects modified by other likely environmental influences such as SiF usage as well as more conventional socio-economic or cultural factors.

Finally, since lead neurotoxicity has also been implicated in ADHD and other learning disabilities (Tuthill 1996; Needleman 1999), we have also begun to explore the possibility that rates of these learning problems are higher in communities that treat water supplies with silicofluorides. A first test, using an informal survey in a set of small New York cities with populations between 40,000 and 70,000 with and without SiF treated water, showed risk ratios of about 1.38 both for high school students coded with a learning disability and for students receiving medication for ADD/ADHD.

These findings are congruent with data linking environmental pollution, alcoholism, and substance abuse to crime (see Wilson and Petersilia 1995, Ch. 13). Diverse research perspectives are thus consistent with neurotoxin-induced dysfunctions that increase alcohol and drug usage as a crude form of self-medication. Because substance abuse can in turn exacerbate learning deficits and antisocial behavior, this perspective suggests that neurotoxicity may be one of the triggering factors in a multifactorial system leading to increased risks of anti-social behavior (Masters, Coplan & Hone 1999b).

TOWARD THE SOCIAL SCIENCE OF THE FUTURE

Paul MacLean's evolutionary neuroscience and its applications illuminate a deep flaw in conventional social science: the attempt to study human social behavior in abstraction from the way the brain evolved and how it actually works in contemporary environments. Our industrial and technological civilization adds elements into the environment that the brain did not confront and to which it did not adapt in its long process of evolution. Significant among these elements is industrial pollution of the environment with heavy metals. The analysis of this heavy metal pollution as a risk co-factor in learning disabilities, substance abuse, and crime shows that linkages go far beyond merely insightful historical footnotes. Indeed, this approach touches the very heart of many vital public policy debates.

It should be obvious that examining the possible behavior effects of lead and other toxic elements is far from a "reductionist" approach to human behavior. Many other factors, including genes, diet, socioeconomic status, demography, and technology come into play. While the ban on the sale of leaded gasoline was based on a general notion of the dangers of lead toxicity, political dialogue, prudent judgment, and effective decision-making—not some automatic effect of heavy metals themselves—were the basis of this public policy. Indeed, the toxicity of leaded gasoline was well known to those who introduced it, and the original approval of its use rested on economic and political interests rather than science.

Integrating environmental factors such as pollution with evolutionary neuroscience in the study of behavior adds something of great importance to our knowledge. The data presented above, for example, suggest that the public policy decision to ban leaded gasoline may have been far more effective than even its most fervent supporters have imagined.

These effects also cast new light on the political bias that surrounds many environmental issues. On the left, social ills are often blamed on economic or cultural factors that have been described as "socially constructed." On the right, the costs of environmental legislation have often been said to exceed its benefits by far. If our data are valid and predictive, neither side has even begun to understand the true dimensions of our social problems and the gains from dealing with them in a scientifically effective manner.

Whether we are assessing the consequences of established policies or proposing new initiatives, it is increasingly necessary to follow Paul MacLean's footsteps into the challenging, complex, and utterly fascinating terrain that links disciplines that have too long been ignored by conventional social scientists. In the long run, such interdisciplinary perspectives must transform the insularity of academia if our civilization is to survive the technological changes that will continue to assault us in the 21st century.

REFERENCES

Alexander, Richard. 1992 (1983). "Biology and the Moral Paradoxes," in Margaret Gruter and Paul Bohannan, eds., *Law, Biology and Culture.* (2nd ed., NY: Primis - McGraw Hill, pp. 109–118.

Aschengau, A., Ziegler, S., and Cohen. A. 1993. "Quality of Community Drinking Water and the Occurrence of Late Adverse Pregnancy Outcomes," *Archives of Environmental Health.* 48: 105–113.

Aschner, M. and Kimelberg, M. 1996. *The Role of Glia in Neurotoxicity.* Boca Raton,FL, CRC Press.

Bailey, A.J., Sargent, J.D., Goodman, D.C., Freeman, J., and Brown, M.J. 1994. "Poisoned Landscapes: The Epidemiology of Environmental Lead Exposure in Massachusetts Children 1990–1991," *Social Science Medicine.* 39: 757–776.

Boehm, Christopher. 1992 (1983). "The Evolutionary Development of Morality as an Effect of Dominance Behavior and Conflict Interference," in Margaret Gruter and Paul Bohannan, eds., *Law, Biology and Culture.* 2nd ed., NY: Primis-McGraw Hill, pp. 141–153.

Bohannan, Paul. 1992 (1983). "Some Bases of Aggression and Their Relation to Law," in Margaret Gruter and Paul Bohannan, eds., *Law, Biology and Culture.* (2nd ed.), New York: Primis - McGraw Hill, pp. 154–164.

Bryce-Smith, Derek. 1983. "Lead Induced Disorder of Mentation in Children." *Nutrition and Health.* 1: 179–194

Bryce-Smith, Derek. 1986. "Environmental Chemical Influences on Behaviour and Mentation," *Chemical Society Review.* 15, 93–123.

Campbell, Donald. 1992 (1983). "Legal and Primary-Group Social Controls," in Margaret Gruter and Paul Bohannan, eds., *Law, Biology and Culture.* (2nd ed., New York: Primis-McGraw Hill, pp. 165–176.

Coburn, Theo; Dumanoski, Dianne; and Myers, John Peterson. 1997. *Our Stolen Future.* New York: Plume.

Cook, E.H.; Jr., Stein, M.A.; Krasowski, M.D.; Cox, N J.; Olkon, D.M.; Kieffer, J.E.; and Leventhal, B.L. (1995) "Association of attention-deficit disorder and the dopa-mine transporter gene." *American Journal of Human Genetics.* 56, 993–998.

Crews, D; Willingham, E; and Skipper, J.C. 2000. Endocrine disruptors: present issues, future directions. *Quarterly Review of Biology.* 75: 243–260.

DelRosso, Matt; Dreisbach, Chris; Evans, Andrew; and Phinney, John. 1999. "Anxamination of the Biochemistry of Alcoholism." Unpublished Research Report, Department of Government, Dartmouth College, Hanover, NH.

Dewey, W. L. 1986. "Cannabinoid Pharmacology," *Pharmacology Review.* 38: 125-178.

Denno, Deborah. 1994. "Gender, Crime and the Criminal Law Defense," *Journal Of Criminal Law and Criminology.* 85: 80–180.

Dicalzi, Gianluigim; Pira; Enrico; Herrero Hernandez, Elena; Valentini, Consuelo; Turbiglio, Marco; and Meliga, Fabrizio. 2000. "Occupational Mn Parkinsonism: Magnetic Resonance Imaging and Clinical Patterns Following CaNa2EDTA Chelation," *NeuroToxicology.* 21: 863–866.

Dunipace, A. J.; Zhang, W.; Noblitt, T. W.; Li, Y.; and Stookey, G. K. 1989. "Genotoxic Evaluaton of Chronic Fluoride Exposure: Micronucleus and Sperm Morphology Studies," *Journal of Dental Research.* 68: 1525–1528.

Dunipace, A. J.; Wilson, C. A.; Wilson, M. E.; Zhang, W.; Kaftawy, A. H.; Brizendine, E. J.; Miller, L.; Katz, B. P.; Warrick, J. M.; and Stookey, G. K. 1996. "Absence of Detrimental Effects of Fluoride Exposure in Diabetic Rats," *Archives of Oral Biology.* 41: 191–203.

Fukuyama, Francis. 1999. "The Great Disruption: Human Nature and the Reconstitution of Human Order," *Atlantic.* vol. 283, #5 (May 1999), pp. 55–80.

Gazzaniga, M., Ivry, R.B., and Mangun, G. R., 1998. *Cognitive Neuroscience.* N.Y.: W. W. Norton.

Gulson, B.L.; Mahaffey, K.R.; Mizon, K. J.; Korsch, M. J.; Cameron, M.A.; and Vimpani, G. 1995. "Contribution of Tissue Lead to Blood Lead in Adult Female Subjects Based on Stable Lead Isotope Methods," *Journal of Laboratory and Clinical Medicine,* 125: 705–712.

Hoebel, Bartley. 1992 (1983). "The Neural and Chemical Basis of Reward," in Margaret Gruter and Paul Bohannan, eds., *Law, Biology and Culture.* 2nd ed., New York: Primis-McGraw Hill, pp. 119–135.

Jackson, Richard D.; Kelly, Sue A.; Noblin, Timothy W.; Zhang, Wu; Milson, Marie E.; Dunipace, Ann J.; Li, Yinrriing; Katz, Barry P.; Rizendine, Edward J.; and Stookey, George K. 1997. "Lack of Effect of Long-Term Fluoride Ingestion on Blood Chemistry and Frequency of Sister Chromatid Exchange in Human Lymphocytes," *Environmental and Molecular Mutagenesis.* 29: 266–271.

Juberg, D.R. 1997. *Lead and Human Health.* New York: American Council on Science and Health.

Lauer, Josephine A.; McConnel, Erin P.; Sutton, Robert D.; Keller, Jennifer L.; Huntington, Ayn C.; Russell, Kate C.; and Middleton, W. Robert. 1999. "ADD/ADHD and Lead Toxicity: An in-depth study on the implications of the disorder related to lead," Unpublished research report, Department of Government, Dartmouth College, Hanover, NH.

Lejoyeux, M. 1996. "Use of serotonin (5-hydroxytryptamine) reuptake inhibitors in the treatment of alcoholism," *Alcohol Alcohol Supplement.* 1: 69–75.

Levitt, Miriam. 1999. "Toxic Metals, Preconception, and Early Childhood Development," *Social Science Information.* 38: 179–201.

Lippard, S. and Berg, J. 1994. *Principles of Bioinorganic Chemistry.* Mill Valley, CA: University Science Books.

MacLean, Paul D. 1990. *The Triune Brain in Evolution: Role in Paleocerebral Functions.* New York: Plenum.

MacLean, Paul D. 1992 (1983). "A Triangular Brief on the Evolution of Brain and Law," in Margaret Gruter and Paul Bohannan, eds., *Law, Biology and Culture.* (2nd ed., New York: Primis - McGraw Hill), pp. 83–97.

Manuzza, S., et al. 1989. "Hyperactive Boys Almost Grown Up," *Archives of General Psychiatry.* 46: 1073–1079.

Manuzza, S., et al., 1998. "Adult Psychiatric Status of Hyperactive Boys Grown Up," *American Journal Of Psychiatry.* 155: 493–498.

Martin. W. R. 1983. "Pharmacology of Opioids", *Pharmacology Review*, 35: 283–323.

Masters, Roger D. 1992 (1983). "Evolutionary Biology, Political Theory and the State," in Margaret Gruter and Paul Bohannan, eds., *Law, Biology and Culture.* 2nd ed., New York: Prirnis-McGraw Hill, pp. 177–194.

Masters, Roger D. 2001. "Biology and Politics: Linking Nature and Nurture," *Annual Review of Political Science.* 4: 345–369.

Masters, Roger D.; Hone, Brian; and Doshi, Anil. 1998. "Environmental Pollution, Neurotoxicity, and Criminal Violence," in J. Rose, ed., *Environmental Toxicology.* London: Gordon and Breach, pp. 13–48.

Masters, Roger D. and McGuire, Michael T. 1994. *The Neurotransmitter Revolution.* Carbondale, IL: Southern Illinois University Press.

Masters, Roger D. and Coplan, Myron J. 1999a. "Water Treatment with Silicofluorides and Lead Toxicity," *International Journal of Environmental Studies.* 56: 435–499.

Masters, Roger D. and Coplan, Myron J. 1999b. "A Dynamic, Multifactorial Model of Alcohol, Drug Use, and Crime: Linking Neuroscience and Behavior to Toxicology," *Social Science Information.* 38: 591–634.

Masters, Roger D.; Coplan, Myron J.; and Hone, Brian T. 1999. "Silicofluoride Usage, Tooth Decay, and Children's Blood Lead," Poster Presentation, Environmental Influences on Children: Brain, Development, and Behavior, Conference at New York Academy of Medicine, New York, NY, May 24–25, 1999.

Masters, Roger D.; Coplan, Myron J.; Hone, Brian T.; and Dykes, James. 2000. "Association of Silicofluoride Treated Water with Elevated Blood Lead," *NeuroToxicology.* 21: 1091–1100.

McGuire, M. T., and Troisi, A., 1998. *Darwinian Psychiatry*. N.Y.: Oxford University Press.

Mendelsohn, Alan L.; Dreyer, Benard P.; Fierman, Arthur H.; Rosen, Carolyn M.; Legano, Lori A.; Kruger, Hillary A.; Limb, Sylvia W.; and Courtlandt, Cheryl D. 1998. "Low-Level Lead Exposure and Behavior in Early Childhood," *Pediatrics*. 101 No. 3 March 1998, p. 10.

Mielke, H. 1998. "Lead in the Inner Cities," *American Scientist*. 87: 62-73.

Needleman, Herbert L., ed. 1991. *Human Lead Exposure*. Boca Raton, FL: CRC Press.

Needleman, Herbert L., et al., 1996. "Bone Lead Levels and Delinquent Behavior," *JAMA*. 275: 363–369.

Needleman, Herbert L. 1999. "Environmental Neurotoxins and Attention Deficit Disorder, " Presentation at Conference on Environmental Neurotoxins and Developmental Disability, N. Y. Academy of Medicine, New York (May 24-25, 1999).

Nevin, Rick. 2000. "How Lead Exposure Relates to Temporal Changes in IQ, Violent Crime, and Unwed Pregnancy," *Environmental Research*. Section A 83: 1–22.

Pryadarshi, Anumeet; Khuder, Sadik A.; Schaub, Eric A.; and Shrivastava, Snigdha. "A Meta-Analysis of Parkinson's Disease and Exposure to Pesticides," *NeuroToxicology*. 21: 435–440.

Purves, D. et al., 1997. *Neuroscience*. Sunderland, MA: Sinauer.

Raine, A. 1993. *The Psychopathology of Crime*. San Diego. Academic Press.

Tuthill, R. W. 1996. "Head Lead Levels Related to Children's Classrooom Attention Deficit Behavior," *Archives of Environmental Health*. 51: 214–220.

Walker, Dr. Sydney. 1998. *The Hyperactivity Hoax: How to Stop Drugging Your Child and Find Real Medical Help*. NY: St. Martin's Press.

Warren, Joshua, Silverman, Chad, and Sonnenbom, Andrew. 1999 "An Analysis of Leaded Gasoline and its Relationship to Violent Crime." Unpublished research report, Department of Government, Dartmouth College, Hanover, NH.

Weiss, Bernard, 2000. "Vulnerability to Pesticide Neurotoxicity is a Lifetime issue," *NeuroToxicology*. 21: 67–74.

Wilson, J. Q. and Petersilia, J., eds. 1995. *Crime*. San Francisco, Institute for Contemporary Studies.

PART VI

SOCIAL PSYCHOLOGY AND SOCIAL THEORY

16

REIFICATION AND HEGEMONY: THE HUMAN BRAIN AS THE LINKAGE BETWEEN MACRO AND MICRO LEVEL POLITICAL PHENOMENA

Steven A. Peterson

INTRODUCTION

One of the most interesting of human phenomena is the tendency of people to give their beliefs superordinate status over those ideas' creators. This is often termed reification (sometimes hypostatization) when those ideas are taken as "givens" and as being external to the individuals who created those ideas. This chapter explores the psychobiological bases of human reification. It also discusses how the individuals' tendency to reify can produce social stability. To use Antonio Gramsci's (1957) terms, if individuals within a society have similar reifications and accept these, then a society wide hegemony can develop. One important contributor to the development of this project has been Paul MacLean. His research and theoretical work both inform much of the argument developed below. While one may disagree with aspects of MacLean's thought, his body of research provides valuable insight into a psychobiology of reifying.

In this chapter, we consider the following: A. The nature and underlying psychobiology of reification; B. The nature of hegemony and how the tendency to reify can support the development of hegemony; C. The extent to which people can come to be less subservient to their own creations and live in, for want of a better term, a more "authenticated" world; D. The value of the work of Paul MacLean in illuminating various aspects of this project.

REIFICATION DEFINED

A common human phenomenon is holding fiercely to a deeply held view, value, concept, or idea and, perhaps, accepting this as "outside" ourselves and a guide to our behavior. In the process, one comes to perceive this as a "given" or as "in the nature of things." Philosophers have referred to this as reification or, perhaps more accurately, hypostatizing, attributing "a separate or higher reality to something, thus abstracting it from its relationship of dependence on other things." (Clark 1976: 6). Reification is a process by which values, beliefs, and other human "creations" become transmuted into "things-in-themselves," and are considered apart from the human activity that actually created them. Berger and Luckmann define reification in much the same terms, when they note that this is "the apprehension of human phenomena as if they were things, that is, in non-human or possibly suprahuman terms . . . [R]eification is the apprehension of the products of human activity as if they were something else than human products—such as facts of nature, results of economic laws, or manifestations of divine will." (1966: 89).

The irony of the human ability to create a conceptual world is that its products may be accorded superordinate status over their creators—perhaps as the delusions of schizophrenics become seen as "outside" them (for more complete discussion of this analogy, see Peterson with Sicherman 1995) It seems very easy for people to come to accept living in a world of abstractions, which they consider as guides to their behavior.

Only when there is questioning of the dominant, reified values guiding the people are there likely to be significant prospects for change.[1] One must no longer view the totality of reigning values, products of human relations, as things-in-themselves, as eternal verities, as superordinate guides to behavior. One must discern that these things are actually creations of human activity, not separate from that activity, and, therefore, changeable or endable.[2]

NEUROPHYSIOLOGICAL BASES OF REIFICATION

Reification is a complex phenomenon; few such behaviors are going to be localized in a single area within the brain. Uttal has summarized the implication nicely when he states that (1978: 342): "almost all complex behaviors can be affected by almost any part of the brain and that the sort of localization that occurs must be interpreted more in the form of a system of interconnecting nuclei than in terms of any theory of sharply demarcated functions of single centers." The psychobiological roots of reification are important to consider, since their very existence indicates that part of the human condition is an ease of creating abstractions which then escape our control, being transmuted into things-in-themselves, and which ultimately lead us to accept the transcendence of our own creations. That is, it is easy for us to overconceptualize the world and create and accept grand explanations. It is as if we are designed to search for a faith, for concepts to subordinate ourselves to (on the evolutionary advantage of this, see Peterson 1981. On pathologies associated with this, see Peterson with Sicherman 1995).

ORGANIZING CONCEPT: THE SCHEMA

Arbib, Erdi, and Szentagothai (1998) have argued that the concept of the schema is central to linking brain function with brain structure. A schema is the brain's internal representation of "reality" "out there." These structures help make sense of a complex world, a world producing a wide array of stimuli which impinge upon the individual. Morton Hunt notes (1982: 173):

> Our method of making categories has a simple and obvious biological rationale: it is the mind's way of representing reality in the most cognitively economical form. In the real world . . . traits occur in 'correlational structures'; observable characteristics tend to go together in bunches . . . We may not have innate ideas . . . but our minds filter and compile incoming data in such ways that we tend to form prototypes and categories without help or instruction.

The basic idea of schema theory is that much of what people see and comprehend about the world is more closely tied to the internal schema than to the external stimulus itself. As a theory of comprehension, schema theory states that we often understand only those events that are consistent with our schemata, and that we either ignore or misunderstand those events that are not. As an orientation toward memory, schema theory states that enduring memory does not typically occur independent of schemata. If our comprehension of things is guided and organized by schemata, so is our memory.

Arbib et al. claim that their (1998: 35) "contribution has been to provide a schema theory that can bridge from the external characterization of function to the interactions of brain regions and the inner workings of neural circuitry." They consider two categories of schema—a perceptual schema and the motor schema. In the process, they attempt to, then, link perception and action. In the final analysis, they note that through the schema (Arbib et al. 1998: 344), "The brain 'models' the world so that when we recognize something, we 'see' in it things that will guide our interaction with it." Ulric Neisser, a leading cognitive psychologist, speaks generally of the psychobiological roots of schemata (the plural form of the term schema) (1976: 54):

> From the biological point of view, a schema is part of the nervous system. It is some active array of physiological structures and processes: not a center in the brain, but an entire system that includes receptors and afferents and feed-forward units and efferents. Within the brain itself there must be entities whose activities account for the modifiability and organization of the schema: assemblages of neurons, functional hierarchies, fluctuating electrical potentials, and other things still unguessed.

G. J. Dalenoort (1982) has suggested that cell assemblies underlie schemata. Representations are stored in dispersed cell assemblies in humans' long term memory (LTM). Reifications are one subspecies of schemata. They are internal representations of ideas that people transmute into reality "out there." Thus, one part of a psychobiology of reification is to explore the neurological roots of schemata.

THE NEUROPHYSIOLOGY OF REIFICATION

In the following paragraphs, we consider the following brain areas: the basal ganglia, the thalamus, the hypothalamus, the limbic system, the neocortex (is there hope for creating a more authentic world here?), and an internal reward system based upon either (both) endogenous opiates or (and) dopamine. (For a detailed atlas of the human brain, see Mai, Assheuer, and Paxino 1997.)

To help guide the discussion of a neuropsychology of reification, Figure 16.1 outlines a circuit diagram suggesting the substrates for reifying; text elaborating upon this model is presented below (the author freely notes that experts advance somewhat different sets of afferents and efferents to each of the brain structures in the circuit diagram; thus, the diagram in Figure 16.1 is something like a "consensus" version).

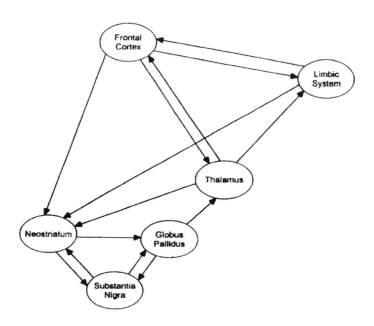

Figure 16.1. Circuit Diagram for Reification

Basal Ganglia

Key structures in the basal ganglia include the substantia nigra (very important for producing a key neurotransmitter, dopamine), the neostriatum (composed of the putamen and caudate nucleus), and the globus pallidus.

The basal ganglia have traditionally been looked at as central to motor control (e.g. Arbib et al.1998; Cote & Crutcher 1991; Denny-Brown 1962; Beatty 1995; Rolls & Williams 1987). However, studies suggest that these centers can have a measurable impact on aggression (Senault 1979), arousal (Hornykiewicz 1966), learning and memory processes (e.g., Crosson 1990, 1997; Gambarian, 1979; Gambarian et al. 1979; Middleton & Strick 1994; Kolb & Whishaw 1996), species-typical (or, in more common terms, "instinctive") behavior (Murphy et al. 1981), neglect (Heilman, Watson, & Valenstein 1997) language (Crosson 1990), and some cognitive functions (Beatty 1995; Cools & van den Bercken 1977; Middleton & Strick 1994; Oberg & Divac 1979). Among the very young, the basal ganglia may even substitute somewhat for damaged or not yet developed functions of the neocortex (Teuber 1976; Buchwald et al. 1975).

What of reification or hypostatization? Paul MacLean argues, based upon his experimentation across a range of animal species, that:

The reptilian brain [neostriatum and pallidum] seems to be hidebound by precedent. Behaviorally, this is illustrated by the reptile's tendency to follow roundabout, but proven, pathways, or operating according to some rigid schedule. Customs of this kind appear to have some survival value and raise the question to what extent the reptilian counterpart of man's brain may determine his obeisance to precedent in ceremonial rituals, religious convictions, legal actions, and political persuasions (1973: 10).

Repetitiveness appears to be one behavior associated with this (MacLean 1990: 150, 236–238). That is, abstract ideas as guides to behavior may be elemental products of the operation of the basal ganglia. People can, as a result, come to cling jealously and zealously to tradition and habit and this might be generalized to ideas, beliefs, and values (and see MacLean 1990; Keyes 1992). In another essay, MacLean elaborates (1972: 146–147):

Is it possible that through these neural elaborations nature has revamped the striatal complex so that it serves as a playback mechanism not only for ancestral behavior, but also currently learned performance? We close with one more thought. It is traditional to belittle the role of instincts in human behavior. But how should we categorize those actions that seem to stem from a predisposition to ritualistic, compulsive, or imitative behavior . . . or to a propensity to seek and bow to precedent?

The extension to hypostatizing is obvious. Afferents (incoming nerve fibers to a particular brain structure) to the neostriatum (NS) come from all areas of the cerebral cortex, from various nuclei in the thalamus, and from the substantia nigra (e.g., Cowan & Powell 1966; Peele 1977). Efferents from the NS (fibers leaving a brain center) project to both the substantia nigra and the pallidum (Carpenter 1991; Beatty 1995). The pallidum receives projections from the cerebral cortex, the thalamus, and the substantia nigra (Peele 1977). In turn, it projects nerve fibers to several nuclei in the thalamus, in particular, the lateral ventral, anterior ventral, and centrum medianum nuclei (Kemp & Powell 1971; Peele 1977).

Thalamus

The thalamus receives afferents (incoming nerve signals) from the pallidum and substantia nigra in three of its nuclei—the lateral ventral, anterior ventral, and centrum medianum. Additional relevant afferents for these nuclei include the neocortex and other thalamic nuclei, making them uniquely situated to correlate and integrate input from a wide variety of brain centers. The lateral ventral and anterior ventral nuclei project to both motor and sensory areas of the neocortex (Peele 1977). The centrum medianum projects to the neostriatum (NS), completing a neostriatum –> pallidum –> thalamus –> neostsiatum loop. It also projects to other thalamic areas, such as the dorsomedial nucleus which, in turn, has nerve connection to the hypothalamus and amygdala, the latter a key center in the limbic system (Peele 1977: 291–294). Peele has suggested that (1977: 293) "the dorsomedial nucleus would appear to be involved in mechanisms underlying emotional expression" and that this nucleus projects to both the neostriatum and the pallidum. This series of connections may provide the link between "affect" (centered to a large extent in the limbic system, the seat of emotions) and "rigidification" (centered to some extent in the basal ganglia).

Functions of the thalamus vary across nuclei, as implied in the previous paragraph. The dorsal tier nuclei seem associated to some extent with the "mobilization of mental energy," speech, and memory (Fuster 1973; Bennett 1977: 202–205). Some studies have indicated that lesions in the anterior nuclei are related to diminished emotional reactivity in some animal species. The dorsomedial nucleus appears to have both inhibitory and initiating centers for emotional behavior (Bennett 1977: 143–144). The latter nucleus, once more, projects nerve fibers to both NS and pallidum, linking the basal ganglia to the thalamus.

The thalamus is apt to be a part of the system involved in organizing the propensity to take part in reifying or hypostatizing because of its role as a relay station to the neocortex. It is centrally located so that it can collate information from a variety of areas that send data to the neocortex through thalamic nuclei (Clark 1975; Kelly 1991; Kelly & Dodd 1991; Lezak 1995).

Limbic System

Some experts argue that the limbic system is a basic center for species-specific behavior. Schmidt, for instance, has claimed that for humans this would translate into "'emotions,' 'affective behavior,' 'feelings'. . . In this sense one function of the limbic system would be to control the expression of the emotions"(1978: 266). Thus, the limbic system—and especially the amygdala and septum—is key to understanding emotion (Beatty 1995; Lezak 1995).

MacLean has applied this general perspective to the expression of affect toward values and beliefs. He notes (1977: 319):

It is of special epistemological interest that at the beginning of a limbic discharge, a patient may have an intense free-floating feeling of what is real, true, and important or experience eureka-type feelings such as occur in mystical revelation or under the influence of psychedelic drugs. Ironically, it seems that the ancient limbic system has the capacity to generate strong affective feelings of conviction that we attach to our beliefs, regardless of whether they are true or false!

Elsewhere, MacLean has noted that sensations associated with epileptic seizures—associated with limbic discharges—include (1990: 48) "the feeling that what is happening or what one is thinking at the moment is all important; feelings of certainty and conviction; and feelings of revelations of the truth." If he is correct, this would seem to link the limbic system with affective coloration of reified values or concepts; that is, the limbic system adds emotion to reified values and beliefs (and see Isaacson, 1982; on questions about the limbic system concept, see LeBar & LeDoux 1997).

Neocortex

People view the neocortex as the seat of higher cognitive and intellectual functions. This view, as we have already seen, is oversimplified, since other brain centers are also involved in such functions. Nonetheless, as Gardner has put it: "Human behavior is correlated to a large extent with the relatively massive size of the forebrain. Here reside most of the mechanisms governing learning, memory, intelligence, language, emotion, and behavior" (1975: 374–375).

Different areas of the neocortex have extensive connections with many of the structures thus far noted. Efferents from all parts of the neocortex project to the basal ganglia, the thalamus, the limbic system, and—indirectly—the hypothalamus. In turn, the neocortex receives nerve messages directly from the limbic system and thalamus and indirectly from the basal ganglia and hypothalamus (Gardner 1975; Peele 1977). This set of connections raises the possibility that there can be a cortical overriding of holding fiercely to ideas. Schmidt, for instance, has noted that (1978: 306) "one of the roles of the frontal lobes is related to the *learned control of innate behavior pattern*."

The neocortex has an important role in emotional processes. The limbic system does not work alone to produce affect. Connections between the neocortex and the limbic system suggest that (Schmidt 1978: 266) "it is in the neocortex that environmental events receive their affective coloration and thus their 'meaning' to the organism." In short, the limbic system produces primitive emotions and the neocortex interprets these. Extensive reciprocal connections between the frontal lobes of the neocortex and the limbic system indicate that this neocortical area has as one role the learned control of species-specific behavior patterns and emotions (Schmidt 1978: 305–306). Clinical findings, indeed, show that frontal lobe problems are associated with difficulty in controlling behaviors and emotions (e.g., Beatty 1995).

Randall Sengel (1979) has linked memories with emotion in his delineation of a neurological basis for cooperative behavior (For political applications, see Davies 1976). His central hypothesis is that (1979: 49) "during human evolution, the emotional states associated with defense, competition, and hunting could reinforce successful cooperative behavior through the influence of the limbic system and/or emotionality for social behavior." The author notes that the limbic system links affect with memory and learning. Sengel asserts that (1979: 50): "It is assumed that any perceptual experience which acquires an emotional connotation during memory storage will, upon recall and comparison, endow current experience with emotional and motivational significance." In like fashion, learning of ideas or concepts can, through limbic system connections, cloak these abstractions with affect. (For an argument which relies on holological theory and comes to similar conclusions, see G. Schubert 1983.)

Sengel's argument is a good base upon which to elaborate some of the cognitive functions of the CNS. Incoming information is processed and may be stored in long-term memory. Preexisting schemata help to shape how memories are stored. Information may be either assimilated (fit into an existing schema) or lead to accommodation (in which a schema changes somewhat to take into account new information). Assimilation is likely to take place under normal circumstances, as we tend to be conservative with our schemata. That is, we tend to assimilate information to fit with our existing schemata. And, to complete the argument with respect to hypostatizing, a reification is simply a schema, a mental representation of a concept, value, or belief.

Returning once more to Sengel's argument, these reifications would be linked with the lirnbic system and, hence, affect. It is also easy to see how these reified notions could be linked to the neostriatum where "rigidification" takes place.

BIOCHEMISTRY OF REIFICATION (THE INTERNAL REWARD SYSTEM)

The actual motivation to reify ideas and beliefs may be a product of what James Danielli (1980) once referred to as the "internal reward system." Danielli asserts that his overall argument becomes more plausible in light of recent work on CNS opiate peptides-enkephalins and endorphins, substances which have both analgesic (pain-reducing) and euphoric effects. Studies suggest that such substances could underlie this reward system. Others have suggested that dopamine, another significant product of the basal ganglia (especially the substantia nigra), could be associated with reward (Depue & Collins 1999). The naturally occurring opiates are concentrated in the pallidum, caudate nucleus, hypothalamus, thalamus, and amygdala and affect the firing of neurons in other areas of the brain such as the hippocampus and neocortex (e.g., Guillemin 1978; Pert 1978).

Solomon Snyder has said of the opiates' functions: "The dorsal medial thalamus is strongly associated with frontal and limbic cortical areas involved in emotional regulation and so may relate to the euphoria produced by opiates." (1978: 307). His contention suggests a tie-in between orchestration of affect by interacting brain centers and enkephalin neurons in the thalamus. Very specifically, Stein and Belluzzi say that endorphins may serve as transmitters in neural systems for the mediation of pleasure and reward (1979: 375). Their work indicates that the endogenous opiates serve as reinforcers. Significantly, though, we also find that dopamine may serve some of the same functions (e.g., see Lippa et al. 1973; Rolls et al. 1974).

Danielli has speculated that analogous processes underlie small-group and large-group social activities. In both instances, release of the opioid peptides would subserve motivation to carry out specific behaviors related to small groups (e.g., play or social grooming) and large groups (e.g., religious rituals or spectator participation at football games and other "mob activities").

It is logical to extend Danielli's argument into the realm of ideas and beliefs. Danielli has asserted, in short, that humans do certain things because it feels good to do so. The mechanism for this could be the opioid peptide-rooted reward system or a dopamine-based one. Just so, such a system could also encourage people to think certain things because it would feel good to do so. Therefore, the hypostatizations which people learn (rigidified through the basal ganglia and charged with affect through the limbic system) may upon their exercise activate the internal reward system and reinforce, by the "pleasure" thus induced, their continued acceptance by the individual and behavior consistent with these.

SUMMARY

Reifying and the brain may thus be wed. Social conditioning brought on through a concurrence of messages transmitted and reinforced by influential agencies of socialization (e.g., religion, the family, the media, schools, and so on) leads to an increased probability of individuals learning appropriate sets of values and beliefs. Mechanisms underlying learning and memory would process these and then store them in long-term memory. Coupling these values with the internal reward system would provide a motivation for adherence to these values and behavior consistent with them. The euphoria associated with deeply held values would lend these great potency (through the release of endogenous opiates or dopaminergic reinforcement). Corticostriatal connections, in turn, would rigidify these values, possibly through dopaminergic (e.g., Broekkamp et al. 1977) and/or endorphinergic reinforcement. Extensive reciprocal cortico-limbic and indirect pallido-limbic links through the thalamus would provide the means whereby values stored in long-term memory and rigidified by neostriatal processing would be clothed in affect, once more, through the reinforcing effects of dopamine and/or endorphins.

Finally, cortico-striatal, cortico-thalamic, and cortico-limbic pathways would allow for the conscious override of hypostatized values and beliefs and their effects. How easy or difficult the override would be is a function of the extent to which the values have been conditioned and reinforced in the first place.

Nonetheless, cortical efferents from integrative centers provide a theoretical basis for positing this override potential. Thus, there is a place for human will within this model.

THE CONCEPT OF HEGEMONY: ITS POLITICAL SIGNIFICANCE

The Italian Marxist Antonio Gramsci elaborated the idea of hegemony in the early part of the twentieth century; his views represent the starting point for analysis. Gramsci's hegemony emphasizes how values supportive of dominant interests in society get passed on to the masses and thereby, once accepted by the multitudes, come to reinforce the domination of the existing elite. Dawson, Prewitt, and Dawson state that (1977: 26):

> Hegemonic theory starts with the assumption that government would not be possible unless the strains and tensions associated with the unequal allocation of values in society were somehow muted . . . Unless the losers come to see that the way things are is 'natural' or 'appropriate' or 'legitimate,' social disruptions are likely. Socialization is viewed as the learning that leads the losers to accept the way things are, even to think that the way things are is in their best interests.

Normally, citizens come to accept things the way that they are—as benign, useful, legitimate, and "right." As Gramsci puts it, "humans are (1957: 59) conformist to some conformity." This supports the continuation of the status quo—and, by definition, those who benefit from the current state of affairs maintain their sway with this sort of mindset. Those who are powerful and wealthy will stay that way, in part, because the bulk of the people accept this situation. How do the mass of people come to accept values that lead to their continuing status as losers in the struggle for life and reward? Williams, summarizing Gramsci, states that hegemony is: "an order in which a certain way of life and thought is dominant, in which one concept of reality is diffused throughout society in all its institutional and private manifestations, informing with its spirit all taste, morality, customs, religious and political principles, and all social relations, particularly in their intellectual and moral connotations" (1960: 587).

The basic premise is that those in power who control the economic and political structures also control the transmission of messages, the views of reality, to the masses. In a capitalist society, those who are not wealthy are continually told that (a) if they work really hard, they can make it and get rich—so do not rock the boat and jeopardize your chances of joining the elite; (b) if the elite get wealthier, then this will trickle down and benefit those who are not in the ranks of the well-to-do. By being told this over and over, the mass of people come to accept their status in society and allow the powerful to stay powerful, the wealthy to stay wealthy.

Hegemony, according to Gramsci, is the result of a bloc of interests united behind a common set of values and norms, which—upon being transmitted to the mass of people through the many institutions of society—reinforce the power of that bloc. Although a hegemony tends to be stable, change can take place, perhaps through the emergence of a politically conscious working class.

The power of hegemony is illustrated by what did *not* happen during the 1930s. Think about this for a moment. At the depth of the Great Depression, nearly one quarter of the American work force was unemployed. That rate was still in the upper teens later in the 1930s. Should one not have expected a growing and radicalized American working class demanding major changes in the system? Obviously, a working class movement demanding major changes did not develop.

Hegemony may help to explain this. Polls from the late 1930s asked a sample of Americans the extent to which they supported the free enterprise system. A clear majority of every social group examined supported capitalism—even among the unemployed working class. More telling, only a minority of unemployed working class people had anything like "class consciousness," a sense of themselves as workers having an interest in opposition to a capitalist class.

Why did a working class consciousness and support for radical change not emerge among the unemployed working class? Poll data show, simply, that the working class—including those who were unemployed—accepted individualist and liberal ideals. In short, those workers most likely, one would think, to challenge the legitimacy of the system accepted the key tenets of liberalism; as a result, they did not develop a class consciousness. Liberal hegemony dampened the chances of a major working class movement to challenge the system (Verba & Schlozman 1977).

SOCIOBIOLOGY OF REIFICATION: THE LINK TO HEGEMONY

One argument advanced in this chapter is that the individual's tendency to reify may be linked to the society wide hegemony that can develop. What mechanism is available to explain this link between the micro and the macro levels? Sociobiology appears to provide an explanation.

One requirement for reproductive success in social species is group stability and social order. Alexander states that humans accept limitations (in the form of justice, ethics, and morals—all reified notions) on absolute freedom. He suggests (1975: 96) that "individual humans tolerate such restrictions because it has for millions of years been less profitable reproductively to go it alone." Edward O. Wilson elaborates in his discussion of religious beliefs:

The extreme plasticity of human social behavior, Bergson notes, is both a great strength and a danger. If each family worked out its own rules of behavior, the society as a whole would disintegrate into chaos. To counteract selfish behavior and the dissolving power of high intelligence and idiosyncrasy, each society must codify itself. Within broad limits any set of conventions works better than none at all. Because arbitrary codes work, organizations tend to be inefficient and marred by unnecessary inequities . . . .

But the arbitrariness of sanctification engenders criticism, and within the more liberal and self-conscious systems visionaries and revolutionaries set out to change the system. Their ultimate purpose is to elevate codes of their own devising. Reform meets repression, because to the extent that the reigning code has been sanctified and mythologized, the majority of people regard it as beyond question, and disagreement is defined as blasphemy (1978: 185–186).

Here, Wilson is working at the society wide level of analysis. The important point is that even arbitrary codes may be sanctified. When these systems of sanctification exist and are accepted pretty much as given by the mass of people, then the odds of social order are much increased providing, in the final analysis, an environment more conducive for individuals' reproductive success. Conformity to sanctifications (which are, to use our terminology, reified values) confers, then, reproductive advantage to individuals. Wilson further states:

The ability of individuals to conform [recall Gramsci's phrase: "conformist to some conformity"] permits them to enjoy the benefits of membership with a minimum of energy expenditure and risk, and their behavior is sustained over long periods of time as the norm. Although the rivals of the conformists in the society may gain momentary advantage through selfishness and irreverence, it is lost in the long run through ostracism and repression (1978: 187).

The key point is that when individuals accept certain values within a society as given—as they reify these values—this influences social stability which, in turn, affects individuals! reproductive success. Thus, through inclusive fitness doctrine, we can hypothesize that there is a selection advantage for people to see the world populated with reifications standing apart as "ideas become real."

DISCUSSION

Is it possible to live in a world without the dominating presence of reifications as guides to human behavior? Martin Heidegger warns against over-theorizing and overconceptualizing. For Heidegger, the study of phenomenology "expresses a maxim which can be formulated as 'To the things themselves.' It is opposed to all free-floating constructions and accidental findings" (Heidegger 1967: 295). For humans to understand what it is that is "out there," we should try to prevent our preconceptions and problematic methodologies from obscuring the nature of the things themselves that we are observing. As Calvin Schrag puts it, "The data are always prior to man's logical and epistemological theories concerning them." (1967: 279).

Following Heidegger, one might argue that we need to prevent overtheorizing and overconceptualization and to get back to "the real," to the things of life themselves. Of course, this is too easy, since it is pretty clear that humans' preconceived notions inevitably shape their interpretation of the world around them. Human cognition and the human brain probably make this so (Peterson 1981). However, human "will" can play a role in at least reducing the unthinking tendency to act almost delusionally in accepting reified values and beliefs without much question (on the analogy between accepting reifications and schizophrenia, see Peterson with Sicherman 1995).

Recall the argument that the neocortex is in a position to override unthinking adherence to reifications. "Normal" people are in a position that schizophrenics are not—in a position to will themselves back to "reality" and out of the dream world of reifications.

To live in a de-reified (or, perhaps, more positively stated—an "authentic" world) world would be difficult to achieve and even more so to sustain. Berger and Pullberg (1965) argue that while something like widespread de-reification might take place, new sets of rigidified values would normally rather quickly spring up to take their place. Anthropologist Vernon Reynolds has said:

It is because the norms of social life are taken by people as *givens* that they react to them, whether by conformity or deviance, in such powerful ways. Once their arbitrariness is grasped they lose their power, and the individual is 'free.' Once the 'implicit' becomes 'explicit' we see it for what it is—an idea, a construct in the minds of those around us that earlier we shared.

But, in de Musset's words, *'qui s'eleve, si'sole.'* The price for standing apart, for observing, for ceasing to be *engage* is the very price of freedom—a falling apart of the security structures of the mind, a frightening took into the unknown . . . (1976: 206, 209):

What sociologists have called "reification" of social norms and situations, i.e., the process by which the individual comes to believe in the reality and fixity of social forms, can be seen as a sanity-promoting process. Reynolds, it follows, concludes that de-reification would be most difficult to sustain.

What would an "authenticated" world look like? A Hobbesian war of each against all, without commonly held values to maintain social order? A world in which people would learn to appreciate the myriad different understandings of different people with differing experiences? Or is the question absurd, given that humans are likely programmed to view the world in a reified manner? These are the key, larger issues that future discussion ought to focus upon.

NOTES

1. Of course, as Donald Keyes reminds us (personal communication), there may be benign hypostatizations (or reifications which actually serve useful social purposes. He suggests a project of differentiating benign from non-benign reification. Indeed, this distinction probably calls for elaboration, but that is beyond the scope of this paper.

2. There is an interesting analogy between hypostatizing and certain schizophrenic symptoms (For full argument, see Peterson and Sicherman 1995) Believing that the products of human activity are outside of human control and are "given" to us, is on its face, delusional—just as DSM suggests for religious and other cultural groups with strongly held beliefs. In such cases, people's sense of identity gets lost and overwhelmed by the values that they have adopted—they become playthings of a higher or external force (witness David Koresh's acolytes, willing to burn to death to follow him in their delusion that he was the Messiah come back). This is, in form, little different than the

delusions and hallucinations that can drive the behavior of schizophrenics. The question is: who's normal and who's crazy?(see Rosenhan 1973). Individuals will become guided by higher values or beliefs, and one continues to behave, perhaps appropriately, when there are abundant data that one is following the wrong course of action. Obviously, when one meets a schizophrenic in the acute stage of the problem, one knows that a schizophrenic is not a normal person. But is it so very different in kind (albeit it is in degree) to see a true believer in action, ignoring facts from the surrounding world in order to promulgate and continue supporting his or her religious values? Or political views? Or personal philosophy? This is a question worthy of serious refection.

REFERENCES

Alexander, Richard D. 1975. The Search for a General Theory of Behavior. *Behavioral Science* 20: 77–100.

Arbib, Michael A., Peter Erdi, and Janos Szentagothai. 1998. *Neural Organization: Structure, Function, and Dynamics.* Cambridge, MA: MIT Press.

Beatty, J. 1995. *Principles of Behavioral Neuroscience.* Dubuque, IO: William C. Brown.

Bennett, Thomas L. 1977. *Brain and Behavior.* Monterey: Brooks/Cole.

Berger, Peter and Stanley Pullberg 1965. Reification and the Sociological Critique of Consciousness. *History and Theory.* 3: 196–211.

Berger, Peter and Thomas Luckmann. 1966. *The Social Construction of Reality.* NY: Anchor Books.

Broekkamp, C.L.E. et al. 1977. Neostriatal Involvement in Reinforcement and Motivation. In A. R. Cools et al. (eds.), *Psychobiology of the Neostriatum.* Amsterdam: North-Holland Publishing Co.

Buchwald, N- A., C. D. Hull, M. S. Levine, and J. Villablanca. 1975. The Basal Ganglia and the Regulation of Response and Cognitive Sets. In M. A. Brazier (ed.), *Growth and Development of the Brain.* NY: Raven Press.

Carpenter, Malcolm. 1991. *Core Text of Neuroanatomy.* Baltimore: Williams and Elkins, 4th edition.

Clark, John P. 1976. *Max Stirner's Egoism.* London: Freedom Press.

Clark, Ronald G. 1975. *Manter and Gatz's Essentials of Clinical Neuroanatomy and Neuropsychology.* Philadelphia: F. A. Davis.

Cools, A. R. and J. H. L. van den Bercken. 1977. Cerebral Organization of Behavior and the Neostriatal Function. In A.R. Cools et al (eds.), *Psychobiology of the Neostriatum.* Amsterdam: North-Holland Publishing.

Cote, Lucien and M.D. Crutcher. 1991. The Basal Ganglia. In Eric Kandel, James Schwartz, and Thomas M. Jessell (eds.), *Principles of Neural Science.* N Y: Elsevier, 3d edition.

Cowan, W.H, and T.P.S. Powell. 1966. Strio-pallidal Projection in the Monkey. *Journal of Neurology, Neurosurgery, and Psychiatry,* 29: 426–439.

Crosson, Bruce. 1992. *Subcortical Functions in Language and Memory.* NY: The Guilford Press.

Crosson, Bruce. 1997. Syndromes Due to Acquired Basal Ganglia Damage. In Todd E. Feinberg and Martha J. Farah (eds.), *Behavioral Neurology and Neuropsychology.* New York: McGraw-Hill.

Dalenoort, G. J. 1982. In Search of the Conditions for the Genesis of Cell Assemblies. *Journal of Social and Biological Structures,* 5: 161–187.

Danielli, James F. 1980. Altruism and the Internal Reward System or the Opiate of the People. *Journal of Social and Biological Structures,* 3: 87–94.

Davies, James C. 1976. Ions of Emotion and Political Behavior. In Albert Somit (ed.), *Biology and Politics.* Paris: Mouton.

Dawson, Richard, Kenneth Prewitt, and Karen Dawson. 1977. *Political Socialization.* Boston: Little Brown, 2nd edition.

Denny-Brown, D. 1962. *The Basal Ganglia and Their Relation to Disorders of Movement.* London: Oxford University Press.

Depue, Richard A. and Paul F. Collins. 1999. Neurobiology of the Structure of Personality. *Behavioral and Brain Sciences.* 22: 491–517.

Fuster, Joaquin. 1973. Transient Memory of Neuronal Activity in the Thalamus. In Karl H. Pribram and Aleksandr R. Luria (eds.), *Psychobiology of the Frontal Lobes.* NY: Academic Press.

Gambarian, L.S. 1979. The Hippocampus, Behavioral Organization, and Working Memory.*Behavioral and Brain Sciences,* 2: 329–330.

Gambarian, L., Z. Sarkisyan, and V. Bayandurov. 1979. The Role of the Globus Pallidus in the Achievement of Delayed Response in Cats. *Biological Abstracts,* 67: 3222.

Gardner, Ernest. 1975. *Fundamentals of Neurology.* Philadelphia: W. B. Saunders.

Gramsci, Antonio. 1957. *The Modern Prince & Other Writings.* NY: International Publishers (trans. Louis Marks).

Guillemin, Roger. 1978. Peptides in the Brain. *Science,* 202: 390–402.

Heidegger, Martin. 1967. Phenomenology and Fundamental Ontology. In Joseph J. Kockelmans (ed.), *Phenomenology.* Garden City: Anchor Books.

Heilman, Kenneth M., Robert T. Watson, and Edward Valenstein. 1997. Neglect: Clinical and Anatomic Aspects. In T.E. Feinberg and M.J. Farah (eds.), *Behavioral Neurology and Neuropsychology.* N Y: McGraw-Hill.

Hollandsworth, James G., Jr. 1990. *The Physiology of Psychological Disorders.* New York: Plenum.

Hornykiewicz, Oleh. 1966. Dopamine and Brain Function. *Pharmacological Review,* 18: 925–964.

Hunt, Morton. 1982. *The Universe Within.* NY: Simon and Schuster.

Isaacson, Robert L. 1982. *The Limbic System.* NY: Plenum Press, 2nd edition.

Kelly, James P. 1991. The Neural Basis of Perception and Movement. In E. R.Kandel, J. H. Schwartz, and T. M. Jessell (eds.), *Principles of Neural Science.* NY: Elsevier, 3rd edition.

Kelly, James P. and Jane Dodd. 1991. Anatomical Organization of the Nervous System. In E. R. Kandel, J. H. Schwartz, and T. M. Jessell (eds.), *Principles of Neural Science.* NY: Elsevier, 3rd edition.

Kemp, Janet M. and T. P. S. Powell. 1971. The Connexions of the Striatum and Globus Pallidus: Synthesis and Speculation, *Philosophical Transactions of the Royal Society of London,* Series B, Biological Sciences, 262: 441–457.

Keyes, C. Don. 1992. Ethical Judgment and Brain Function: An Interpretation of Paul MacLean's Hypothesis. *Journal of Social and Evolutionary Systems,* 15: 387–398.

Kolb, Bryan and Ian Q. Whishaw. 1996. *Human Neuropsychology.* NY: W. H. Freeman, 4th edition.

LeBar, Kevin S. and Joseph E. LeDoux. 1997. Emotion and the Brain: An Overview. In T. Feinberg and M. J. Farah (eds.), *Behavioral Neurology and Neuropsychology.* NY: McGraw-Hill.

Lezak, Muriel Deutsch. 1995. *Neuropsychological Assessment.* NY: Oxford University Press, 3rd edition.

Lippa, Arnold S., S. M. Antelman, A. E. Fisher, and D. R.Canfield. 1973. Neurochemical Mediation of Reward: A Significant Role for Dopamine? *Pharmacology, Biochemistry and Behavior* 1: 23–28.

MacLean, Paul D. 1972. Cerebral Evolution and Emotional Processes. *Annals of The New York Academy of Sciences,* 193: 137–149.

MacLean, Paul D. 1973. Man's Limbic and Reptilian Inheritance. In T. J. Boag and D. Campbell (eds.), *A Triune Concept of Brain and Behavior.* Toronto: University of Toronto.

MacLean, Paul D. 1977. On the Evolution of Three Mentalities. In Silvano Arieti and Gerard Chrzanowski (eds.), *Psychiatry: A World View,* Volume II. N Y: John Wiley.

MacLean, Paul D. 1990. *The Triune Brain in Evolution: Role in Paleocerebral Functions.* NY: Plenum.

Mai, Jurgen K., Joseph Assheuer, and George Paxinos. 1997. *Atlas of the Human Brain.* San Diego, CA: Academic Press.

Middleton, Frank A. and Peter L. Strick. 1994. Anatomical Evidence for Cerebellar and Basal Ganglia involvement in Higher Cognitive Function. *Science,* 266: 458–461.

Murphy, Michael R., Paul D. MacLean, and Sue C. Hamilton. 1981. Species-Typical Behavior of Hamsters Deprived from Birth of the Neocortex. *Science,* 213: 459–461.

Neisser, Ulric. 1976. *Cognition and Reality.* San Francisco: W. H. Freeman.

Oberg, R., and I. Divac. 1979. Cognitive Functions of the Neostriatum. In I. Divac and R. Oberg (eds.), *The Neostriatum.* Oxford: Pergamon Press.

Peele, Talmage L. 1977. *The Neuroanatomic Basis for Clinical Neurology.* NY: McGraw-Hill.

Pert, Agu. 1978. The Effects of Opiates on Nigrostriatal Dopaminergic Activity. In Jan M. van Ree and Lars Terenius (eds.), *Characteristics and Functions of Opioids.* NY: Elsevier/North-Holland Publishing Co.

Peterson, Steven A. 1981. Sociobiology and Ideas-Become-Real. *Journal of Social and Biological Structures,* 4: 125–143.

Peterson, Steven A. with Jessica Sicherman. 1995. Schizophrenia and Reification: Who's (Really) Crazy? *Journal of Social and Evolutionary Systems* 18: 33–53.

Reynolds, Vernon. 1976. *The Biology of Human Action.* San Francisco: W. H. Freeman.

Rolls, E. T., P. H. Kelly, and S. G. Shaw. 1974. Noradrenaline, Dopamine, and Brain-stimulation Reward. *Pharmacology, Biochemistry, and Behavior,* 2: 735–740.

Rolls, E. T. and G. V. Williams. 1987. Sensory and Movement Related Neuronal Activity in Different Regions of the Primate Striatum. In J. S. Schneider and T. I. Kidsky (eds.), *Basal Ganglia and Behavior.* NY: Hans Huber.

Schmidt, Robert F. (ed.). 1978. *Fundamentals of Neurology.* NY: Springer-Verlag, 2nd edition.

Schrag, C. 0. 1967. Phenomenology, Ontology, and History in the Philosophy of Heidegger. In J. Kockelmans (ed.), *Phenomenology.* Garden City: Anchor Books.

Schubert, Glendon. 1983. Psychobiological Politics. *Canadian Journal of Political Science,* 16: 535–576.

Senault, B. 1979. Tentative Analysis of Apomorphine-Induced Intra-Specific Aggressive Behavior in the Rat According to Adams' Classification. *Behavioral and Brain Sciences,* 2: 226–227.

Sengel, Randal A. 1979. Cooperative Behavior: A Neurosocial Hypothesis. *Man-Environment Systems,* 9: 48–54.

Snyder, Solomon. H. 1978. Opiate Receptors and Morphine-Like Peptides. *Harvey Lectures* 73: 291–314.

Stein, Larry and James D. Belluzzi. 1979. Brain Endorphins. In Earl Usdin, William E. Bunney, Jr., and Nathan S. Kline (eds.), *Endorphins in Mental Health Research.* NY: Oxford University Press.

Teuber, Hans-Lukas. 1976. Complex Functions of Basal Ganglia. In M. D. Yahr (ed.), *The Basal Ganglia.* NY: Raven Press.

Uttal, William R. 1978. *The Psychobiology of Mind.* Hillsdale, NJ: Lawrence Erlbaum Associates.

Verba, Sidney and Kay Lehman Schlozman. (1977). "Unemployment, Class Consciousness, and Radical Politics: What Didn't Happen in the Thirties." *Journal of Politics,* 39: 291–323.

Williams, Gwyn A. (1960). Gramsci's concept of *egemonia. Journal of the History of Ideas,* 21: 586–599.

Wilson, Edward 0. 1978. *On Human Nature.* Cambridge, MA: Harvard University Press.

17

UPSHIFTING AND DOWNSHIFTING THE TRIUNE BRAIN: ROLES IN INDIVIDUAL AND SOCIAL PATHOLOGY

*Kent Bailey**

INTRODUCTION

This chapter represents the most current application of phylogenetic regression-progression theory. I introduced my approach to phylogenetic regression over 20 years ago (Bailey 1978) and subsequently addressed it in several publications (Bailey 1985, 1987a, 1988, 1991). The regression-progression approach has, from the outset, drawn heavily from MacLean's triune brain formulation (Bailey 1987b). This chapter refines and extends my general theory and details how the vagaries of human experience may be construed in terms of dynamic patterns of regression and progression. Finally, the theory is applied in a brief analysis of the Columbine killings in April 1999 where two young men—Eric Harris and Dylan Klebold—killed 12 classmates, a teacher, and themselves in an "inexplicable" act of violence.

HIERARCHIES OF MODULES AND ADAPTATIONS

Modern evolutionary psychology views the human brain as a collection of highly specialized neuromodular coordinations that evolved to solve specific fitness problems in the environments of evolutionary adaptation (EEAs) of human evolution. Various deep-structure modules subserve fundamental processes of memory, sensation/perception, spatial orientation, nonverbal and verbal communication, behavioral coordination and output, intuitive processes,

---

* I wish to thank Valerius Geist for his personal support and for his clear delineation of "classic regression." Thanks also to the many people who provided helpful feedback including Patrict Callahan, Paul Gilbert, and Bill Tillier.

and cognition (Matlin & Foley 1992); these co-integrate in numerous ways to form complex motivational/emotive/behavioral/conceptual adaptations of the human mind (Kendrick, Sadalla & Keefe 1998). The Swiss Knife metaphor (Cosmides 1994) is frequently used to characterize the specificity/functionality of module-based adaptations such as male jealousy, kin recognition, space preference and territoriality, sexual orientation and mate preference, strategies governing reciprocity (Cosmides & Tooby 1992), balanced social relations (Bailey 2000), and so on (see Pinker 1994). Unfortunately, we do not have a reasonably complete neurohistological, neurochemical, or neurofunctional understanding of any single module, and integrated adaptations are even more elusive. We are even more in the dark regarding how various modules/ adaptations excite, inhibit, complement, or otherwise interact with each other.

The implicit *hierarchical arrangement* of the various modules and adaptations adds another important level of complexity. Clearly, modular processes/ adaptations differ in ancestral history and complexity ranging from the wood tick's reaction to a single molecule of bombykol (see Bailey 1987b), to the specialized bug detector units in frog's brains (Lettvin et al. 1959), to the highly integrated hormonal and neural mechanisms underlying maternal behavior in rats (Fahrbach & Pfaff 1982), to the neurologically circumscribed lateral hypothalamic stalk and attack patterns in cats (Moyer 1976), and, finally, on to the neocortically mediated conceptual modules of human beings. The brain and its functions have been viewed hierarchically over most of the history of neuroscience (Smith 1992), and it is important to focus on how ancestrally older and newer motivational/behavioral/cognitive systems operate in the vertical dimension.

Neuroscientists are making steady progress in mapping complex functional relationships across vertical levels of the brain. For example, Le Doux's (1996) model of fear and aversive conditioning features hierarchical co-integration of phylogenetically older and newer brain systems that govern processes of learning and extinction, escape responses, memory of past fear experiences, and, in humans, various subjective meanings associated with threatening and dangerous events. At the simplest level of Le Doux's model, the amygdala identifies and processes potentially dangerous stimuli quickly, reactively, and nonconsciously in a strict stimulus-response or releaser-action pattern. The amygdala represents a kind of "triggering device for the execution of survival functions" (Le Doux 1996: 224), and, under circumstances of extreme threat or when higher functions (e.g., the hippocampus or prefrontal circuits) are disabled, the amydala can operate essentially on its own. In humans, emotional reactivity and response to threat typically operate within a complex, hierarchical feedback system involving the amygdala, the hippocampus, and the prefrontal neocortex where the latter two systems exert modulatory control over the automatic and quick-reacting amygdala. Given that connections "down" from the higher two centers are weaker than connections "up" from the amygdala (Le Doux 1996), fairly frequent neurological regression or shortcircuiting of the more advanced amygdala-hippocampus-prefrontal neocortex would be expected: "This may explain why it is so easy for emotional information to invade our conscious thoughts, but so hard for us to gain conscious control over our emotions" (Le Doux 1996: 265).

THE BRAIN AS AN ORGAN OF INHIBITION

The human brain operates primarily as an organ of inhibition (see Smith 1992). With the brain's 100 billion or so neurons and the possibility that any one neuron can have synaptic connections with perhaps ten thousand others (Wilson 1999), the possibilities for neural outputs far outnumbers the particles in the universe (Restak 1984). Moreover, Restak (1984) states that the brain's potential for creating and transmitting information is vastly greater than that of the entire genotype (approximately 10^5 for genetic possibilities and 10^{15} for neuronal possibilities). Without a rigid and extensive system of internal inhibition governing these synaptic possibilities, the brain would degenerate into chaos and disorder. The schizophrenic's "word salad" is viewed as a major departure from the norm, but idiosyncratic word sequences are trivial compared to the brain's potential for disorder. The integrity of organs, organ systems, and behavior all are premised on small streams of excitation amid oceans of inhibition within the brain, and failures of inhibition go to the heart of matters of normality and abnormality from the individual cell to the individual self to society at large.

Neuropsychology and psychology in general basically study the dynamics of *inhibition* and *release* in the brain. Aside from the ongoing activation of vital metabolic systems that maintain life, the stream of human behavior is a function of the selective activation of a few single or several interactive modular systems and the simultaneous widespread inhibition of all other competing modular systems. Paul MacLean and many others in the history of neuroscience have emphasized both the *hierarchical* and the *inhibitory* natures of the brain in producing orderly and functional behavior. These concepts underpinned the studies of the great English neuroscientist John Hughlings Jackson on epilepsy and the mind in general (Taylor 1932).

In *Human Paleopsychology* (1987b), I suggested that pathological releases of function in epileptic and epileptoid conditions could serve as a model for many forms of individual and social pathology above and beyond epilepsy per se. That is, many forms of pathology reflect the *release* of unwanted and socially inappropriate material into consciousness, feelings, fantasy, and/or overt behavior, and often this release is of *evolutionarily older systems* that fit poorly with or interfere with the situation at hand. MacLean's triune brain theory fit perfectly with this line of reasoning, and it seemed intuitively appealing to me to speak of progressing up (upshifting) and regressing down (downshifting) the triune brain system that begins with the most ancient R-complex and proceeds up through the newer paleomammalian level, and, finally, on up to the newest level of functioning in the neocortex.

THE PROCESS OF REGRESSION (DOWNSHIFTING)

The phylogenetic progression-regression theme is widespread in the literature on human paleopsychology, evolutionary psychopathology, and related areas, but is seldom addressed directly. Indeed, most evolution-based models implicitly revolve around the fundamental assumption that all human behavior constantly fluctuates between evolutionarily older and newer levels of functioning where the "primitive" gains ascendance one moment, the phylogenetically "advanced" at another, or the two levels blend or intermix in some way. Unfortunately, little attention has been paid to the specifics of this process, and my phylogenetic progression-regression model represents one attempt to address the dynamics of movement and inhibition/release between the older (primitive) and newer (advanced) poles of human response. Most simply, any discernible movement toward the lower pole would constitute *phylogenetic regression*, whereas analogous movement toward the higher pole would constitute *phylogenetic progression*. Table 17.1 summarizes several direct and indirect attempts to define phylogenetic regression, and it is clear that "regression down the triune brain" is an especially meaningful variation on the theme.

Table 17. 1. Variations on the Phylogenetic Regression Theme

The main point here is that in a matter of seconds, a culturally refined, controlled individual can regress to the emotionality characteristic of his evolutionary forebears, and at that moment he is little different from them . . . under severe stress, threat, provocation, or loss of "control" through alcohol ingestion, drugs, and so forth, we temporarily lose our humanity, our culture, our rationality (Bailey 1978: 22).

Although a variety of ecological pressures may move a culture away from its ancestral form, the existence of innate biases with respect to human behavior will produce a tendency for us to return to ancestral ways of behaving. This process is called *ancestralization* (Crawford 1998: 292; emphasis in original).

At heart we are still a primitive people. We evolve far more slowly than our culture . . . Culture may dress up the appearance of people, but it seems to be too shallow to affect their nature deeply. In crises our natures reverts (Edey & Johanson 1990: 389).

Some of the pathologies of sexual behavior observed can be explained as phylogenetic regressions to an archaic agonistic sexuality . . . we can state that sexuality without love and affiliation is a pathological regression to an archaic reptile stage level of sexuality (Eibl-Eibesfeldt 1989: 259).

[Circumstances] . . . which could, ideally, lead to nurturance and growth, leads instead to conflictual, agonic interactions. We are thrown back in time, as a kind of

Table 17.1, continued

phylogenetic regression, where the attachment and hedonic modes were yet to evolve (Gilbert 1989: 196).

Thus we have the phenomenon . . . that I have called "downshifting." When the individual detects *threat . . . full use of the great new cerebral brain is suspended, and faster-acting, simpler brain resources take larger roles* (Hart 1983: 108; emphasis in original).

We overcome this [xenophobia and aversion to outsiders] to some extent through cultural learning . . . *But put stress on the system, and the age-old dispositions are dominant* (Holloway 1974: 8; emphasis added).

[In regression] both the phylogenetic and ontogenetic clocks are turned back (Meerlo 1962: 79) . . . regressive behavior is so much more seductive and contaminating than civilized, restrained behavior (p. 78).

Most of us today seem to have a latent emotional affinity with members of our groups . . . our own kind collectively; such feelings show up in times of crisis, or in evocative situations (Mellen 1981: 273).

In mammals, the autonomic nervous system response to challenge follows a phylogenetic hierarchy, starting with the newest structures and, when all else fails, reverting to the most primitive structural system (Porges 1997: 66).

Indeed, *grand mal* epilepsy can . . . be described as a disease in which the cognitive drivers are all turned off because a kind of electrical storm in the brain, and the victim is left momentarily with nothing operative but his neural chassis. This is a profound impairment, *temporarily regressing the individual back several hundreds of millions of years* (Sagan 1977 57–58; emphasis added).

In man, the neocortical mantle is thought to be the seat of logical and mathematical reasoning, knowledge and understanding, analytical and synthetic processes, invention and fantasy, philosophy and religion, meditation and intuition. However . . . some behaviors and aspects of mental disease suggest a regression of brain functioning to a predominantly paleomammalian (limbic) or reptilian level. In this last instance . . . *the breakdown of social, familial, parental behavior, and personal care is often accompanied by the emergence of asocial, hostile, and aggressive behaviors, and "reptilian" man emerges* (Valzelli 1981: 38; emphasis added).

Each of the quotes in Table 17.1 proceeds from a basic "return to animality" metaphor, but from there each approach develops its own distinctive emphasis: Bailey emphasizes loss of control over emotionality, Meerlo the "seductive" nature of regression, Eibl-Eibesfeldt the re-activation of older agonic and sexual mechanisms, Eibl-Eibesfeldt and Gilbert the de-activation of affectional systems, Edney and Johanson the thin veneer of culture, Crawford a return to earlier ancestral patterns, and most imply some form of neurological regression from higher to lower centers (especially Bailey, Hart, Sagan, and most notably

Valzelli). Note the number of quotes that emphasize *danger, stress, or privation* as the primary elicitors of the regressive process (Bailey, Hart, Holloway, Mellen; see also Geist 1978). The proposed stress-regression linkage will be discussed further in the next section.

In a recent personal communication subsequently excerpted in the *ASCAP Newsletter* (January 2000a), Valerius Geist described the "classic" form of phylogenetic regression whereby a member of a particular species occasionally—when under stress—will activate patterns of behavior distinctive to closely related ancestral species:

> I will illustrate a classical regression I witnessed in the Munich zoo in Siberian elk [wapiti] . . . Red deer males advertise via vocalizations, attracting females and then trying to keep them close by . . . To keep his harem together, the rutting stag herds his harem using threats, even violence. He also has the problem, of course, of approaching females in order to breed. So his courtship posture and behaviour is the antithesis of his herding postures and behaviour . . . The female when the male approaches in courtship posture, lowers her head, while opening and closing her mouth rapidly. That stops the bull, he turns, and roars or bugles away from the female. That is, he lets her know that he obeyed her cut-off signal.
>
> In a pen was a deantlered Siberian elk bull, a female and a calf. The bull had just killed female No. 4, whereupon the staff, belatedly, sawed off his antlers. He had [previously] controlled a harem of five cows. The bull, seeing only *one* cow assumed the herding posture towards her and continually followed, even rushed her, wanting her back in the "harem." This went on unendingly so the female by this time was haggard, skin and bones, not able to escape the bull. By the time I saw her, she no longer used the species-specific "cut-off signal," rather, she squatted trying to urinate while opening her mouth as if vocalizing—except no sound emerged. She was trying, therefore, exactly what [primitive] Old World Deer females do upon courtship of the male: they squat to urinate, and head lowered, they vocalize. A perfect, most meaningful regression (Geist 2000a: 6–7).

DEFINING ASPECTS OF REGRESSION IN HUMANS

Several core assumptions follow from the phylogenetic progression-regression model (see Bailey 1978, 1985, 1987b). First, *it is far easier and simpler to regress than to progress phylogenetically*—regression merely requires reactivation or passive release of previously evolved motivational, emotional, and behavioral coordinations, whereas progression requires years of cultural programming to effect context-appropriate outputs.

Second, phylogenetically older coordinations stored lower in the triune brain are more quickly and efficiently activated (e.g., the fast-acting amygdala previously discussed by Le Doux) than are more phylogenetically recent, neocortically mediated outputs involving large amounts of cultural content. Gilbert (1989) discussed how quickly lower psychoneural functions can be brought into action, and Bailey, Tipton, and Taylor (1977) provided empirical support for the hypothesis that "instinctual stimuli" such as a threatening stare are processed more quickly in profoundly retarded subjects than in presumably more cognitively oriented mildly retarded subjects.

Third, reactivation of previously evolved coordinations, patterns, and systems is inherently *pleasurable* in many instances (Bailey 1987b; Hernnstein 1977), whereas activation of "higher" neural coordinations, patterns, and systems subserving progression are more often hedonically neutral, unpleasurable, or even aversive. Bailey, Burns and Bazan (1982) found that college students reported considerably more subjective pleasure for visceral experiences such as eating, drinking, having sex, receiving a back rub, and so forth, than for neocortically mediated activities such as studying, writing a computer program, attending a lecture, or writing a term paper. The pleasure/regression link is not a hard and fast rule, however, for a number of ancient adaptations are clearly *unpleasurable* when activated (e.g., anger, rage, fear, jealousy, envy, submissiveness, and the like Gilbert 1999). Thus, when species-typical *approach* kinds of adaptations are regressively activated the rule seems to hold, but it breaks down where *avoidance, loss, and pain-related* systems are involved.

Fourth, individual differences are systematically *reduced* in regression but may be either reduced (conformity) or augmented in progression (individualism; "free will"). Generally, individual differences (and "free will") are smoothly and progressively reduced with regression down the triune hierarchy, but *gender differences* represent a special case. Whereas males and females show typical patterns of reduced inter individual differences for regression *within* their respective genders, patterns are more complex *between* the genders. Human gender differences tend to be *augmented* in regression to lower mammalian levels of the MacLean hierarchy but such differences tend to disappear at the lowest levels of the reptilian brain. For example, men and women tend to easily fall into their ancestral gender patterns when under stress, high sexual arousal, or in producing and parenting offspring (Bailey 1987b). But gender differences may be negligible or absent in reptilian rage reactions or screams of anguish during serious injury. Obversely, human gender differences tend to be recovered as a function of the reptilian-to-paleomammalian *progression*, but such differences may be either *neutralized, reduced,* or *augmented* in progression to higher levels of the neocortex where cultural mandates require certain gender styles or where "free will" allows a range of choices in gender style.

Fifth, any stimulus condition that compromises or nullifies neocortical control over lower systems may incite regression, but *stress—especially stress related to survival of self or kin—*is fundamental to the process. In my model, the *stress* ⟶ *regression* intercoordination is viewed as an evolved adaptation that assures that ancestrally proven coping mechanisms are readily accessible when needed (as in Geist's classic regression above). Geist (1978) suggests that stress in the form of high arousal and/or extreme privation (i.e., hunger and starvation) may actually reduce blood flow to the neocortex and thus leave the lower centers to their own "older" devices. Natural selection is both efficient and economical, and it makes sense that frequent reactivation of species-typical adaptations and even prehuman adaptive patterns would be generally preferable to the creation of novel solutions for each challenge encountered.

Sixth, phylogenetic regressions may be either *passive* or *active*. Passive regression "refers to an uncontrolled or dyscontrolled loss of neocortical ability to inhibit archaic impulses and imperatives. Here one effortlessly slips back, often unconsciously, into species . . . patterns of behavior" (Bailey 1987b: p. 99). This is the most common form of phylogenetic regression and may be set into motion by any internal condition or external circumstance that weakens, compromises, or immobilizes rational, conscious, culturally targeted, and neocortically mediated controls over the far more ancient, powerful, and fitness-targeted reptilian and paleomam-malian systems. Internal eliciting conditions for regression include brain damage/ dysfunction, physical disease and illness, alcohol, and other drugs, fatigue, activation of internal stress mechanisms and so forth; certain of these internal conditions appear to encourage regression to the lower centers by occupying neocortical resources that would be otherwise used for inhibition (e.g., coping with serious disease), others directly interfere with or compromise neocortical inhibitory processes (e.g., brain damage or alcohol intake), and in some cases the ancient systems of response just simply overwhelm the neocortex as in a powerful stress response that forces phylogenetically newer responses into the background.

External primers and elicitors of regression are even more numerous than internal ones, and reflect any and all stimuli and situations that lead to regression through the weakening of neocortical inhibitions, the activation and amplification of lower systems, or, most probably, some concurrent combination of neocortical inhibition and reptilian/paleomammalian activation (Bailey 1987b). Examples of the latter combinatorial type include being provoked into an angry fight even when one is a "pacifist" neocortically. We shall see later that the "inexplicable" behavior of Eric Harris and Dylan Klebold in the Columbine tragedy conforms to this model quite well. On the fateful morning of their attack, there was a mighty release of primitive emotion from the lower levels of the brain, on the one hand, and a complete renunciation of morality, culture, rationality, and higher things, on the other.

Whereas passive regression represents a kind of yielding or surrender to lower and more powerful systems of the brain, there are times when consciousness, rationality, culture, and self-perceived morality *side with ancient imperatives and even aggravate and amplify them*. In *active regression*, the culturally programmed neocortex fans the flames of regression by providing dissonance-reducing rationalizations and justifications for primitive eruptions and outpourings of ancient adaptations and coordinations. The more pernicious forms include ideology-based warfare, terrorism, ethnocentrism, racial prejudice, political jingoism, religious cultism, and fear and hatred of any and all things different. However, mild and even neutral forms may be seen in advertising, the media, entertainment, education, and even science when neocortical propaganda and high-sounding self-delusion serve to amplify and mask "true" underlying concerns with sex, dominance, rank, and general selfishness regarding the individual and his or her inclusive fitness system. Indeed, the history of science is rife with dramatic stories of warfare, spite, revenge, and even physical violence between scientists over matters of priority, rank, recognition, money, and sometimes minute differences in theory or ideology. A quick read of Roger Lewin's (1988) wonderful *Bones of Contention* will leave little doubt on this point.

THE REGRESSION-PROGRESSION CONTINUUM-
THE SPECIES CONTINUUM

All behavior in a species population may be seen as falling somewhere on a theoretical *species continuum* proceeding from the most phylogenetically primitive to the most phylogenetically advanced patterns of response for the species in question (Bailey 1987b). Phylogenetically ancient and simple species such as bacteria, trilobites, or the wood tick have little or no neural tissue; this is reflected in their truncated species continua. Such organisms are at the mercy of their few, simple, invariant, and species-specific patterns of survival and reproduction, and they fit the deterministic "selfish gene" model very well (Dawkins 1976). Such patterns are subserved by very simple modular processes composed of highly specific neurostructural, neurophysiological, and behavioral components, or what Gardner (1988, 1996) calls *basic plans*; motivational, emotional, and cognitive components will be added in later and more complex species. In essence, these simple organisms carry out the fundamental adaptational thema of their species and do little or nothing else.

By contrast, phylogenetically more recent and complex species such as reptiles, early mammals, early primates, and modern humans have extended continua that reflect both the total *number of adaptations* available, the *levels of complexity of available adaptations,* and the degree of *plasticity* or *malleability* of available adaptations in response to environmental inputs (e.g., see Geist 1978 on alternative responses to differing ecological pressures). Simple organisms (e.g., bacteria) are characterized by few adaptations of low complexity, whereas complex organisms such as apes and human beings are characterized by numerous in-built and highly complex hardware and software programs that dramatically widen respective species continua at the upper end.

As the species continuum widens, behavioral possibilities widen accordingly—including *enhanced individual differences* in pursuing survival and reproductive fitness, occasional moments of *detachment* from strict biological imperatives, and complex and highly integrated adaptations may sometimes be *deconstructed* into their separate behavioral, motivational, emotional, and cognitive components. Thus, with wider species continua, the response outputs of particular species members may deviate somewhat from those of other members, and brief periods of "individual freedom" may be interspersed among the more fixed, automatic, and species-specific patterns of adaptation to environmental demands.

Given that natural selection operates primarily by building onto and extending pre-existing systems or *primitive characters*, the extended continua of more recent and complex species reflect *derived characters* (Martin 1992) or accretions *primarily at the upper or progressive end of the scale.* Thus, the lower segments (and perhaps mid-segments) of closely related species continua (e.g., chimpanzees versus humans) tend to overlap greatly due to shared ancestry going back to a common ancestor. Indeed, given the logic of the species continuum, it follows that the wider continua of more phylogenetically recent and complex species in a genus or family (e.g., apes and humans) are determined mainly by newly evolved neurostructures and associated physiological and componential functions (viz., behavior, motivation, emotion, and thought) that provide some adaptive advantage in progressively complex and demanding environments. In those instances where natural selection more or less substitutes one adaptation for another at essentially the same point on the species continuum, some degree of evolution has occurred but the continuum itself has not been extended appreciably. Moreover, when a new but lower level reptilian or paleomammalian adaptation evolves into the system, the organism may be accorded more physiological or behavioral options, but again, little in the way of continuum extension. In sum, continuum extension occurs mainly by virtue of accretions at the uppermost end of the scale where significantly modified preexisting adaptations (i.e., derived characters) or new adaptations extend the system.

THE HUMAN SPECIES CONTINUUM

For human beings, the species continuum forms, in theory, from n number of subcontinua representing motivational, emotional, behavioral, and fantasy components operating at a given moment in time. Such subprocesses are few in simple animals and are highly integrated and firmly directed toward fitness goals, but dissonances between subprocesses may be seen in conflict situations (Hinde 1970), displacement activities (Eibl-Eibesfeldt 1989), or deceptive behavior (Eibl-Eibesfeldt 1989). Deception is especially widespread in birds and mammals and Geist (1978; 2000) discusses many rich examples including mountain sheep "lying" about their intent to clash to catch the opponent unawares; young male mountain sheep faking estrus to gain acceptance of older males; the broken wing display of plovers and other birds to lure predators away from young; sham feeding by ungulates as a means of catching predators off guard; and so on.

With more complex and highly evolved mammals and primates, some control over the interaction of subprocesses is possible, and human beings are masters of the capacity to feel one way and act another or to wish for one thing yet pursue another. Nevertheless, most human behavior is species-congruent, orderly and goal-directed, and significant decomposition of complex adaptations is the exception rather than the rule. Ultimately, however, humans are blessed and burdened with the freedom to not only temporarily de-couple from the evolutionary process, but to manipulate the subprocesses underlying response output as well. Thus, one might be smiling at a person while simultaneously harboring hatred and perhaps imagining harm coming to the person; essentially, several regressive and progressive subprocesses may be simultaneously active with momentary placement on the continuum roughly reflecting the algebraic average of the subprocesses at any one point in time. Practically, however, it is probably best to assume that the overall progression-regression continuum reflects more or less congruent subprocesses under normal conditions, but careful analysis of continuum dynamics requires close attention to possible dissonant and conflicting processes, especially where pathological reactions are concerned.

Whereas the normal person exerts considerable control over activation/deactivation of component processes, the mentally ill person often fluctuates between extreme eruptions of "pure" regressive and context-inappropriate material (e.g., strangers may be seen as prey, predators, tribal enemies, close kin, inviting sex objects, territorial interlopers, etc.), or, contrariwise, day-to-day adaptations (especially social ones such as a brief conversation on today's news with a family member or friend) may decompose into internally dissonant hodgepodges of feelings, perceptions, behaviors, verbalizations, and fantasies. Hallucinations, delusions, confusional and obsessional states, phobic and anxiety states, bizarre and inappropriate behavior, and numerous other pathological manifestations may be seen as problems of phylogenetic progression-regression and disintegration of subcomponential processes.

Judith Rapoport is chief of child psychiatry at NIMH, and her biological model of obsessions and compulsions is remarkably similar in form to my more general formulation (Rapaport 1989). A key feature of her model is the idea that certain behavioral subroutines such as grooming and territoriality have been programmed into the human brain over the course of evolution, but they typically remain suppressed in everyday affairs. Put pressure on the system, however, and these ancient modular processes re-activate or "release" with a vengeance and may be replayed repeatedly much like a tape in a broken VCR. The patient is at the mercy of her circumscribed, irrational, and commanding obsessions (dirt, germs, toxins, bodily wastes, etc.) or compulsions (excessive bathing and grooming, contaminant avoidance/removal, checking, hoarding, etc.), that emanate primarily from the basal ganglia (basic structures in MacLean's reptilian brain). Whether released by stress or brain malfunction, these remarkably uniform "fixed action patterns" spring into action when higher brain centers fail in their modulatory and suppressive functions. Rapoport suggests that many other psychiatric problems ranging from nail biting and phobias to a variety of impulse disorders may fit the model as well.

THE PRIMITIVE POLE ON THE HUMAN CONTINUUM

In theory, the overall human species continuum is anchored by the least cognitive, least consciously self-controlled, least culturally conditioned, most blindly motivated and most psychoneurally ancient response ever experienced/emitted by a member of the species (Bailey 1987b). In the MacLeanian sense, the lower pole would be anchored by the most reptilian response ever experienced by any member of species *Homo sapiens*. In modern humans, the most primitive response of a Ted Bundy (e. g., vicious biting of a victim's buttocks as she was being killed), Jeffrey Dahmer (numerous brutal murders and body mutilations, storage of body parts, and cannibalism) or Gary Heidnik (even more cannibalism than Dahmer) would seem to plumb depths of prehuman animality, but we can only surmise what the "most primitive" of all humans responses might be in the abstract. Practically, however, the idea that atavistic *predatory tendencies* lie in the deep recesses of the reptilian brain which can erupt into overt patterns of stalking, brutal killing, and cannibalism serves as a meaningful baseline for "deepest levels of primitiveness" in this chapter.

When in the hypothetically deepest of regressive states, primitive emotions and drives of the subcortical centers are in full control (see Bailey 1987b; Buck 1999; Geist 1978; Le Doux 1996); psychological functions are dominated by unconscious (Le Doux 1996), narcissistic, selfish (Buck 1999), and opportunistic themes; finer linguistic outputs, future projections, self-control, and abstract problem-solving are muted or lost; and the motive apparatus is dominated by the "selfish gene," kin-selective processes, and current and/or ancestral fitness-targeted imperatives. At such times, the person truly is not himself or herself but is rather a temporary creation of past evolutionary processes. Once the state passes, the person may feel shocked and dismayed by his or her loss of humanity.

THE ADVANCED POLE ON THE HUMAN CONTINUUM

By contrast, the mirror-image advanced pole on the human species continuum is anchored theoretically by the least animalistic, least evolutionarily programmed, least motivational-emotional, most coolly rational, and most cognitively complex response ever emitted by any human being in the modern era. The most phylogenetically advanced level is reached when motivation/emotion processes are minimal and rational thought is maximized to the fullest (see Bailey 1987b; Bailey Burns, & Bazan 1982). "Distance-from-the-genes" (see Scheller & Axelrod 1984; Symonds 1979) is maximal and the person is essentially distanced from the resources of his or her primitive self. Thought can occur for thought's sake with minimal interference from the lower centers and some freedom of choice enters the picture. To quote Dabrowski (1972), "By higher level of psychic development we mean a behaviour which is more complex, more conscious and having greater freedom of choice, hence greater opportunity for self-determination" (p. 70).

As with the primitive pole, it is not possible to identify any single "most advanced response," but the great physicist and cosmologist Stephen Hawking illustrates our general points very nicely. He was unremarkable as a student and only began to have his momentous insights about the universe after suffering the crippling and deadly disease amyotrophic lateral sclerosis (Boslough 1984). Although confined to a wheelchair and dependent on others for his daily needs, Hawking's mind seemed to stretch to greater heights as the disease, for all practical purposes, nullified the body and much of the motivational and emotional processes (Bailey, 1987b). He has been described as the nearly perfect "cerebral being" (Boslough 1984), who may spend more time at the highest and most creative levels of human cognitive functioning of any person on earth. Indeed, as Einstein's heir apparent, he may be the first theoretical physicist to reconcile the twin pillars of modern physics—Einstein's theory of general relativity and modern quantum-mechanics theory (Boslough 1984). At his best, Stephen Hawking would certainly be near the apex of human abstraction and complexity of thought, and at those times the farthest from his animal nature.

Psychological health and happiness, however, requires much more than pure cerebrality. Indeed, personal spontaneity, emotional warmth, sexiness, assertiveness, and being "real" require some degree of regressive access to our paleomammalian selves. Much of the practice of psychotherapy (Bailey, Wood & Nava 1992) is salubriously regressive in this respect. From the standpoint of mental health, the goal would be to avoid disruptive and regressive psychopathology on the one hand (excess responsivity toward the primitive pole) while simultaneously avoiding constricting and suprarational fixation at the advanced pole. Normal, healthy, and happy human behavior is typically found somewhere well within the polar extremes—that is, within the human species *modal range of response.*

THE SPECIES MODAL RANGE

Each species continuum has its hypothetical modal range of response, or a preferred zone of species-specific or species-typical response output. In extremely ancient and simple organisms, the species modal range of response is essentially the same as the overall species continuum. In more phylogenetically advanced species, the modal range of response is considerably narrower than the overall species continuum, with a relatively large submodal residue at the lower end of the continuum (the zone of regression) and a relatively small supramodal residue (zone of progression) at the upper end. Of course, the more advanced the species (e.g., human beings), the greater the width of the supramodal zone of accretion and the greater the potential to phylogenetically progress beyond the modal zone when opportunities arise.

The species modal range represents a kind of species comfort zone or ecological niche wherein the organism experiences its greatest degrees of physiological homeostasis, reproductive viability, and fidelity to its species mandates. When a species or species member stays appropriately within its "normal" zone of response, biological and reproductive fitness are maximized, but when organisms stray too far below (regression), or above (progression), their modal zones, individual and inclusive fitnesses may be diminished accordingly. Thus, movement out of the species modal zone is, by definition, not typical or frequently sought, but it does allow additional options for dealing with unusual or rare challenges and demands. For modern humans in advanced societies, one such demand is to "progress at all costs" in the domains of self-control, good citizenship, education, and occupation in order to successfully compete in a world far different from ancestral ones.

The species modal zone is not to be confused with the so-called EEA or environment of evolutionary adaptation, first suggested by John Bowlby. Indeed, they are quite different. The species modal zone is the medium within which *previously evolved adaptations* are "proximally" activated in the pursuit of *survival,* whereas the EEA is a special species-deviant medium within which special ecological pressures lead to *new adaptations* that will "ultimately" lead to higher survival rates in new species variations or entirely new species. For example, Geist's (1978) privation- stressed *maintenance phenotype* is subjected to significant evolutionary pressures and is, thus, a variation of the EEA concept, as is his *dispersal phenotype,* which is subjected to the ecological "pressures" of superabundance "that are normally found during the colonization of vacant habitats"(Geist 2000b). By contrast, the prosaic species modal zone is particularly well defined in stable populations characterized by evolutionary stasis, phylogenetic inertia, and the constant repetition of previously proven behaviors. Once new and different ecological pressures are brought to bear on stable modal zones, they will then resemble or become EEAs or zones of evolutionary change. Nature resists change, however, and it is doubtful that most members of most species are significantly involved in the evolutionary process— that only occurs over vast expanses of time to a relatively few mutant individuals. Indeed, the great masses of living beings inhabit their species modal or comfort zones and not zones of evolutionary change.

Although complex animals have the option to move out of the species zone, *they seldom do so.* Herrnstein (1977; see also Bailey 1987b) argues that individual deviations from species norms is experienced as aversive in higher animals, whereas conformity to species mandates is experienced as subjectively pleasurable. These dynamics of pleasure and displeasure appear to be nature's way of keeping species members within their appropriate species ranges of response.

Some degree of continuum movement occurs *within* a given species modal range, but the more interesting forms are those from the species modal zone to lower and more ancient forms of response (regression) or to newer and higher forms of response (progression). Thus, the species modal zone serves as a kind of broad baseline from which deviations down or up constitute regression or progression respectively. Further, this logic leads to what might be called the *hegemony of regression*; that is, given that all animals (including humans) have far wider submodal than supramodal ranges of response, it follows that when deviations from species norms do occur, they are far more likely to occur in the regressive direction. This makes sense evolutionarily, for an animal under stress or environmental challenge has far more to gain in fitness by recovering tried and proven old adaptations than by gambling on new accretions with little record of success (see Geist 1978).

THE INDIVIDUAL CONTINUUM

Each member of a particular species has its own *individual continuum* and *individual modal range of response.* This is where behavior of living beings occurs. The actual individual continuum is embedded within its hypothetical species continuum and, by definition, cannot be wider than that continuum. In simple animals, the individual and species continua overlap greatly, the individual modal range of response and the species ranges of response overlap greatly, and there is relatively little variation in adaptational processes either within or between members of the species. The effects of what Wilson (1975) calls *phylogenetic inertia* is especially evident in simpler species; that is, simple organisms seldom stray from their evolved genetic programming that is, ultimately, targeted toward species-defined fitness imperatives.

As more complex organisms evolved, both *within-individual* and *between-individual* sources of variation entered the picture. Rather than all members of an ancient species carrying out species mandates in virtually the same way, where individual and species continua and their respective modal ranges were virtually identical, many new possibilities entered the equation. For example, human beings vary greatly in the respective widths of their personal continua (e.g., a regressed schizophrenic versus Stephen Hawking), in the dynamics of movement on their individual continua (patterns of progression-regression), in the width and placement of their modal ranges of response on their individual continua, and in the congruence between personal modal ranges and the hypothetical species modal range of response. All of this potential for variation does not imply limitless personal freedom or even the probability that most human beings will deviate all that much from species mandates to survive and reproduce; indeed, even though people have the potential for vast amounts of variation due to high intelligence, accumulated knowledge, cultural programming, and various environmental pressures, phylogenetic inertia and the pleasure of acting "normally" as a species member keeps most individual zones of response near the species one.

CONTINUUM DYNAMICS AND MISMATCH THEORY

In 1995, I outlined the basic principles of mismatch theory in a symposium chaired by Charles Crawford at the Human Behavior and Evolution Society meeting at Santa Barbara. Mismatch theory is based on the following fundamental assumptions: (1) human morphology and behavior evolved in zones of time called EEAs; (2) the human species ceased to evolve, in any great degree, beyond late *Homo sapiens* some 40,000 years ago; (3) massive cultural and environmental changes have occurred since that time; (4) current human beings often find their naturally evolved selves *mismatched* or at odds with current physical, social, and cultural environments; and (5) the frequency and magnitude of such mismatches for a given person are positively correlated with both physical disease and psychopathology. Essentially, many modern human beings in highly technological societies are much like "fishes out of water" ecologically (Ahern & Bailey 1997), and their bodies and minds yearn unconsciously for enough phylogenetically regressive "matches" and "rematches" to make life fulfilling, pleasurable, and secure (Bailey 1996 ASCAP series).

Although the term mismatch is not always used, this line of reasoning has been productively applied to the genesis and treatment of physical disease

(Eaton, Shostak, & Konner 1998; Lappe' 1994; Nesse & Williams 1995; Williams & Nesse 1991) including reproductive cancer in women (Coe & Steadman 1995; Eaton et al. 1994), the problem of drug addiction (Nesse & Berridge 1997), the practice of psychotherapy (Bailey 2000; Glantz & Pearce 1989), modern angst and despair (Wright 1995), problems in the classroom (Bernhard 1988) and the workplace (Bernhard & Glantz 1991), and the problems of modern life in general (Tooby & Cosmides 1990). The strengths and weaknesses of mismatch theory have been discussed at length by Crawford (1998; see also Geist 1978), and he calls for both more rigorous theory and more rigorous research paradigms for assessing EEA-current environment differences.

Continuum theory construes mismatch as a condition in which the personal modal range of response sufficiently differs from the hypothetical species modal range so as to induce dishomeostasis physically and internal tension and subjective discomfort psychologically. In theory, the species modal range in current humans overlaps greatly with that of *Homo sapiens* 40,000 years ago, for only so much disparity can be tolerated at the population level; thus, most human beings of the world are expected to "match" species requirements well enough to avoid pathological effects. Individual modal ranges, however, can be all over the place, and many individuals—especially those who have progressed highly in modern technocracies—find themselves estranged and distanced from nature (Bailey 1996 ASCAP series; Wright 1995). Many of the various "diseases of civilization" (Eaton, Shostak, & Konner 1988; Nesse & Williams 1995), including cancer, heart disease, and many other medical conditions, crime and drug addiction, anxiety and depression, anorexia and bulimia, and so on, reflect major disparities in the species and personal modal ranges. Treatment and therapy for such conditions—whether they are primarily medical or psychological—often feature various back-to-nature themes that implicitly encourage increased congruence between the species and individual modal ranges of response.

SPECIES CONTINUA IN EARLIER VS. MODERN *HOMO SAPIENS*

A brief comparison of the species continua and modal ranges for *Homo sapiens* (just following the "great cultural leap forward" [Diamond 1989] around 40,000 years ago) and modern human beings will help to illustrate continuum dynamics and the regression-progression model. Prior to the great leap, our hunting and gathering ancestors were essentially the same as moderns in the genetic, neurolog-ical, and behavioral *potential* for speech and language, complex kinship and social relations, tools and technology, and culture in general, but the Rubicon had not yet been crossed. No one knows exactly why, but relatively conservative and stagnant cultural patterns suddenly gave way in the Late Paleolithic to the creation and storage of new ideas that were the seeds of modern civilization. In Valerius Geist's (1978) terminology, the privation-stressed, static, and survival-obsessed *mainten-ance phenotype* of early *Homo* was more or less permanently supplanted by the growth, future-oriented, and resource maximalization policies of the *dispersal phenotype.* During the last 20–35 thousand years new tools of bone, antler and ivory appeared, and other innovations included spear throwers, needles and sewing, more elaborate personal adornments and decorations, endowed burials (e.g., various materials were interred with the deceased), complex art forms, and progressively more elaborate habitation sites (Shick & Toth 1993). Kinship patterns were leading to stronger, more well-defined sexual contracts, a firmer sense of family that included a greater proportion of fictive kin and in-laws as well as genetic relatives, more complex coalition-building made possible by marriage across previously isolated or antagonistic groups, and the burgeoning of trade and reciprocal relations among unfamiliars and people from distant locales (see Shreeve 1995 for an excellent discussion).

Once the great leap forward had occurred, both the species continuum and the species modal range were extended considerably over those of *Homo erectus* (see Walker & Shipman 1996) and the earlier versions of *Homo sapiens.* With little in the way of new phylogenetic adaptations, *Homo* now surged forward by virtue of exaptation (viz., the exploitation of old adaptations for new purposes, see Gould & Vrba 1982; see also Fernald 1992) and processes of cultural evolution subserved by fast-paced positive feedback mechanisms that contrasted with the vastly slower, negative feedback processes of organic evolution. Once cultural material could be stored permanently in the form of cave art, stone and metal tools and artifacts, and later writing, culture could feed on itself and grow at a geometric rate. It is these forms of social, technological, and cultural growth that have produced the modern human society with its staggering advances in knowledge, technology, and control over Mother Nature. Aside from these mighty cultural advances, the human being of today is little different emotionally or motivationally from the earliest *Homo* or even from other animals for that matter: otherwise "why do we continue to do the things other animals do?" (MacLean 1978). In sum, the wider *species continuum* and the wider *modal range* in modern humans reflect a small number of phylogenetic accretions at the progressive-cognitive of the scale that allow for seemingly limitless generation, storage, and application of complex cultural information.

Figure 17.1 compares earlier *Homo sapiens* with modern human beings in terms of continuum dynamics and MacLeanian processes of progression and regression. The species continua and modal ranges are estimated but hopefully provide reasonable approximations of those that characterize early and modern human beings. Note first that both the species continuum and modal range of response is appreciably wider in modern humans, as are both the submodal zone of regression and the supramodal zone of progression. In sum, modern human beings have far more options for response outputs both within and out of the species modal range of response, and the options are particularly rich at the neocortically-mediated progressive end of the scale.

Although the theoretical options for response available to moderns are vast, their modal range of response is only marginally wider than that of earlier *Homo.* However, the modern modal range has shifted *in toto* toward the progressive pole by virtue of presses to master a highly complex culture and compete in highly aggressive economic and informational meritocracies.

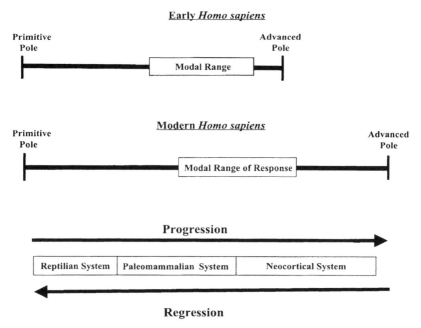

Figure 17.1. Species Continua and Modal Zones for Homo Sapiens

In advanced societies, the daily life of people is dominated by *preparation* (e.g., formal education) for such competition in the early years and pressure to *produce* culturally, materially, and intellectually in young adulthood, mid-life, and increasingly in the later years. When given the chance, however, most people prefer to "regress" toward the low end of the modal range for dinner with friends, relaxation and recreation, sexual activity, or a walk in the mountains, and at those times—aside from the trappings of culture—they are not very different motivationally and emotionally from earlier *Homo.* As Figure 17.1 shows, such benign regressions "matches" today's person very closely with the middle area of earlier *Homo's* modal zone of response. Theoretically, that should be the area on the modern species continuum that produces the greatest subjective pleasure, sense of security, and salubrious effects. Indeed, that is basically the area on the continuum that *we evolved to occupy.* It should be no surprise then that when the smoke and fire of the workday subsides, we long for the archetypal "hunting and gathering" experience of our ancestors.

OVERVIEW OF THE MODEL:
MOVEMENT ON THE CONTINUUM

In phylogenetic progression-regression theory, a given individual is characterized by the *range* of his/her primitive⇔advanced response continuum, by the *modal region* of response (e.g., whether typical behavior is generally nearer the lower or higher pole), and by the frequency and amplitude of *movement* on the continuum. Most normal persons in modern technological cultures have wide primitive-advanced continua due to educationally and culturally extended upper poles, and, given numerous social presses for appropriate culturally "advanced" behavior, they tend to operate publicly well above their species modal range mid-points. However, lower points would be expected on respective continua for private behavior, private feelings, and private fantasies, where cultural pressures to conform are diminished or nullified. Of all expressions, fantasies would seem to most freely reflect the inner world of feelings, motives, and fleeting images that have been carried over in the evolutionary process (Bailey, Burns & Bazan 1982). Public behavior, by contrast, is typically least connected to the older systems, and is more likely to follow the immediate mandates of group process, social etiquette, and rule of law.

Clearly, issues of normality/abnormality, social propriety, conformity/nonconformity, hypocrisy, deception, and realness as a person revolve around the dynamics of progression-regression and the congruence and noncongruence of component subsystems operating at any one time. Our selfish, inherently amoral and potentially brutal natural selves must always be tidied up for culture, and much of this involves hiding, repressing, rationalizing, and sublimating the socially unacceptable *outward* aspects of our ancient adaptations. That is, one set of continuum dynamics may characterize presentable behavior while an entirely different and even contradictory set may characterize the inner world of self, motives, and feelings. For example, sociopaths who have the benefits of reasonably high intelligence and a charming social presentation are often able to manipulate and victimize others through guile, deception, and subtle forms of intimidation (Cleckley 1976; Mealey 1995; Meloy 1988; Tillier 2000). By misrepresenting his true motivations of selfishness, greed, and predation, the skillful sociopath is able to play his ancient regressive games with impunity.

The complexity of continuum dynamics is evident in the truncated or *phylogenetically fixated* behavior and reliance on subneocortical mechanisms seen in the mentally retarded (Bailey, Tipton & Taylor 1977; Hereford, Cleland, & Fellner 1973; MacAndrew & Edgerton 1964), the highly variable regression-progression patterns of the schizophrenic, the inwardly regressive yet outwardly progressive behavior of the manipulative sociopath (Meloy 1988), the regressive limbic disturbances in severe depressives (problems in eating, sleeping, pleasure-unpleasure, sexuality, aggression, and sociality in general) in conjunction with progressive neocortical inputs such as guilt and self-recrimination, the sudden regressive, epileptoid discharges of aggression in otherwise normal persons (Bailey 1987b), and so forth. As we will see, the epileptoid, fundamentally predatory, and apparently pleasurable actions of Eric Harris and Dylan Klebold at the Colombine High School rampage on April 20, 1999, are explicable from the progression-regression standpoint as well.

BRIEF ANALYSIS OF THE COLUMBINE KILLINGS:
THE FATEFUL TUESDAY MORNING

On Tuesday morning, April 20, 1999, Eric Harris and Dylan Klebold, unloaded two black duffel bags filled with guns and bombs and began to shoot their classmates at Columbine High School in Littleton, Colorado. Four hours later, twelve students and a teacher had been killed and Harris and Klebold were found in the school library dead from self-inflicted gunshot wounds.

Eric Harris

The parents, older brother and Eric lived in an upper-middle class subdivision on the outskirts of Littleton, Colorado. The father was a highly decorated Air Force officer, the mother was well-liked in the neighborhood, and the older brother was a successful athlete. Overall, the family appeared normal to neighbors and friends. Eric was extremely shy but bright and capable in school. He had a talent for computers, loved violent video games, and assumed a leadership role among his small circle of friends. He seldom had a girl friend and was often lonely and depressed. He sought sanctuary in the Trenchcoat Mafia from the taunts and abuse from the "jocks" at school.

Although Eric was probably clinically depressed, extremely angry, and socially alienated, no one would have deduced beforehand that he or Dylan Klebold were capable of their vicious killing spree. However, there were a number of aggravating circumstances in Eric's background that probably contributed to—but did not directly cause—his "inexplicable" behavior. Included among these were frustration and anger due to his role as "social outcast"; being bullied and humiliated by athletes at school; frustration, anger, and thoughts of revenge toward various "enemies"; violent fantasies and racist ideology expressed on a personal website; fascination with guns, killing, military violence, and Adolph Hitler; fascination with violent video games such as Doom and Duke Nukem; use of alcohol, prescription drugs, and the serotonergic antidepressant Luvox; concerns over his sick dog; rejection from the Marine Corps five days before killings; and the recent breakup of close friendship with male neighbor Brooks Brown.

Dylan Klebold

Dylan Klebold was loved and doted upon by his liberal and affluent parents. They feared problems with older brother Byron but never with the quiet, shy, and accommodating Dylan. The mother came from a wealthy and prominent Jewish family and the father was a successful geophysicist before going into real estate. The Klebolds looked like the perfect family to neighbors and friends. Dylan was a tall, extremely bright, and quiet kid with a knack for math and computers. He towered over others physically, but tended to lack motivation and direction. He was lonely and insecure and would often hand out cookies to classmates to make a good impression. Dylan seemed like a basically normal person whose most fateful personality trait was his willingness to follow others, *especially Eric Harris.*

Whereas Eric Harris suffered from depression, chronic rage, and possible pharmacological complications, Dylan Klebold was essentially a normal young man. However, he appeared to identify with and model after Eric's anger, violent and paranoid obsessions, and, subsequently, *phylogenetically downshifted right along with him* to the point of killing his classmates. Indeed, while in the regressive state during the killings, Klebold appeared every bit as vicious and inhuman as the instigator Eric Harris. Dylan Klebold personifies what Joost Meerlo (1962) calls the "seductive" and "contaminating" nature of such regression. Not only is phylogenetic regression easy to elicit, inherently pleasurable, and responsive to stress, it is also extremely easy to effect through processes of identification and modeling. Psychological research has shown that modeling disinhibition is far easier than modeling inhibition (Bandura 1969), and passive phylogenetic regression is a form of disinhibition involving loss of neocortical control over the reptilian and paleomammalian centers (Bailey 1987b). The Columbine killings show that even a normal person such as Dylan Klebold can do the most horrific things while under the influence the "modeling" influence of someone in a deeply regressive state of mind.

THEORETICAL OVERVIEW

The Columbine killings illustrate a number of major theoretical points discussed in this chapter. First, the human triune brain is composed of extremely ancient, primitive, selfish (Buck 1999) and nonrational reptilian neurostructures at the first level (e.g., "self-preservational programming," Cory 1999), moderately ancient, primitive, and often irrational paleomammalian neurostructures at the second level (e.g., motivation, emotion, concrete empathy and "affectional programming," Cory 1999), and, finally, relatively new, sometimes rational neocortical capacities for language communication, abstract empathy and otherness, foresight, self-reflection, personal choice, and unprecedented technological achievements (e.g., "executive programming" in Cory's 1999 system). For better or worse, human beings can downshift or upshift within the triune system, and the Columbine killings were extreme examples of downshifting or phylogenetic regression.

Second, the human brain is composed of supernumerous modular processes and various coordinations of modular processes that generally work in a smooth and integrated way. In the EEAs of human evolution, these processes were targeted toward individual and inclusive fitness, but that is not always the case today (Tooby & Cosmides 1990). Orderly behavior and adaptive outputs of the brain are determined by exceptionally complex processes of *inhibition* and *release* that operate within the overall triune system. Epilepsy (see Sagan 1977), epileptoid dyscontrolled behavior (Monroe 1978), and sudden forms of phylogenetically regressive behavior reflect a temporary breakdown of inhibitory processes where older, often ego-dystonic motivational/behavior/cognitive intercoordinations are "released" from their neocortical bondage.

The evening and early morning before the Columbine attack, the behavior of Eric Harris and Dylan Klebold was unremarkable, but as the attack began their actions resembled the epileptoid dyscontrol syndrome of violent criminals (see Monroe 1978) and the arousal, stalk, and kill predatory behavior of animals (see Bailey 1987b; Fox 2001; Meloy 1997; Miller 2000)—with astonishing rapidity, ancient "reptilian" and predatory coordinations essentially co-opted and over-whelmed the thinking part of the brain as the attack progressed over a two-hour period. Eric Harris and Dylan Klebold were, indeed, "not themselves" during the attack, for their actions came more from ancient predatory reptilian and mammalian tendencies programmed into the triune brain than from their own personalities, temperaments, environmental backgrounds, or moral training. Had they lived, they would have been as puzzled as anyone as to why they performed such vile misdeeds (as was the case with Ted Bundy, see Michaud & Aynesworth 1983).

Third, the Columbine attack showed the *ease* with which ancient and culturally repulsive processes can be suddenly re-activated, especially in young males of the species. Moreover, the young killers gave every evidence of *enjoying* the killing spree, and the event was a kind of killing festival for them. This disturbing fact cannot be explained by any existing sociocultural theory, and the "pleasure" aspect of the killings forces us to acknowledge the *predatory nature of the attack* (see Fox 2001; Meloy 1997; Miller 2000). Indeed, predatory aggression is the only form of aggression that appears *pleasurable* in animals (Moyer 1976), and we recall Washburn and Hamburg's (1972) admonition that "man has been a predator for a long time and his nature is such that he easily learns to enjoy killing other animals . . . (and) . . . man easily learns to enjoy torturing and killing other human beings" (p. 294).

Fourth, almost all mass and serial murderers are men, and Eric Harris and Dylan Klebold regressed not only to predatory violence but to "phylogenetic maleness" as well. I have argued (Bailey 1987b) that phylogenetic maleness often plays a part in most forms of human violence, crime, and mayhem, including rape, murder, sexual deviations, and even vandalism (Bailey 1988, 1991). More recently, Wrangham and Peterson (1996) have discussed the "demonic male" from the evolutionary standpoint, and they describe the twin pillars of predatory maleness, *male bonding* and the *lethal raid.* Certainly, male bonding played a central role in the "lethal raid" of Eric Harris and Dylan Klebold, as well as a more general "dark side" of male violence goes far back into human ancestry (Ghiglieri 1999). As Ghiglieri (1999) says, "We live in a world in which cheaters, robbers, rapists, murderers, and war-mongers lurk in every human landscape" (p. 246). Many males—such as Harris and Klebold—seem ready to downshift to such predatory or demonic maleness with astonishing ease and rapidity.

Fifth, a long-term accumulation of stresses, hassles, frustrations, and humilia-tions can set the stage for a sudden regressive release of sometimes murderous and deadly predatory violence. In my paleoanalysis of the serial murderer Ted Bundy, I outlined the numerous conditions that helped to "prime" and "elicit" his stalking and killing behavior (see Bailey 1987b, Table 9.2). These included an illegitimate birth, ambivalence toward the mother, rejection by his foster father, confused self-identity, rejection by women, fascination with pornography, use of alcohol and marijuana, fantasies about killing, and a host of other variables. In my view, however, these conditions could never lead to murderous sexual aggression *without the existence of sexual and predatory centers deep in the brain that are accessible via phylogenetic regression.* The killing sprees of Ted Bundy or Eric Harris and Dylan Klebold are not directly caused by stress or an accumulation of stressors, although they no doubt help to set off the reaction. It is the readiness of the reptilian and paleomammalian systems in the brains of human males to be "set off" that more accurately captures the asocial behavior of the Bundys, Harrises and Klebolds.

Sixth, there was a significant element of *active or neocortically augmented regression* in the months leading up to and during the Columbine killings. Racist philosophy, hatred of enemies, thoughts of revenge against the jocks, and a sense of self-as-victim made it that much easier for Harris and Klebold to dehumanize their enemies and turn them into prey to be brutalized and killed in the most cold-blooded fashion. This form of regression lies behind the most demonic and depraved aspects of the human condition, including racism, genocide, war, and hatred of all things different from one's self and kin.

Seventh, lethal regressions of the Harris and Klebold type involve a *deactivation* of higher affectional, empathic (MacLean 1977), prosocial, moral and prefrontal processing of future consequences (see Buck 1999) simultaneous with the *activation* of subcortical predatory, rage, and violence areas of the brain (Valzelli 1981). As Harris and Klebold gleefully and brutally killed their school-mates, the warmth, love, and kinship areas of the brain were completely shut down, and people became mere objects or "prey." MacLean's (1982) more phylogenet-ically advanced third or thalamocingulate division of the limbic system governing "family-related behavior" was clearly deactivated, as was any indication of attachment or love (Buck 1999), friendship, caring or altruism, or even the barest traces of kinship (see Bailey 2000). Adding fuel to the fire was the deactivation of fear, aversion, and punishment processes that typically inhibit aggression and violence (and psychopathy, see Mealey 1995); this probably involved selective de-activation of the amygdala/hippocampus/prefrontal fear axis (see Le Doux 1996) where fear functions were more or less shut off and defensive functions were subdued (Harris and Kelbold were not subjected to counterattack by their victims), but predatory attack and generalized aggression functions of the amygdala were left unconstrained (see Bailey 1987b: 365–372).

Lastly, Eric Harris and Dylan Klebold were essentially normal but somewhat evolutionarily "mismatched" members of species *Homo sapiens* whose individual species continua were extended due to education and privilege, whose modal ranges of response were similarly extended, and whose supramodal or progressive ranges were extended quite above the norm. They were highly educated and intelli-gent young men whose frustration and anger set them on a path of regression that ultimately nullified all of their cultural achievements and led to the deaths of 15 people, including themselves.

REFERENCES

Ahern S, Bailey, KG: *Families-By-Choice: Finding Family in a World of Strangers.* Minneapolis, MN: Fairview Press.

Bailey KG: The concept of phylogenetic regression. *Journal of the American Academy of Psychoanalysis* 1978; 6; 5–35.

Bailey, KG: Psychobiological regression and aggression. Invited address in symposium in tribute of Paul D. MacLean held at the Chicago Academy of Sciences, May 1983.

Bailey KG: Phylogenetic regression and the problem of extreme aggression. *Journal of Social and Biological Structures* 1985; 8, 207–244.

Bailey KG: Human paleopsychology: Roots of pathological aggression. In Neuman GG (Ed.), *Origins of human aggression: Dynamics and etiology.* NY: Human Sciences Press, 1987a.

Bailey KG: *Human Paleopsychology: Applications to Aggression and Pathological Processes.* Hillsdale, NJ: Erlbaum, 1987b.

Bailey KG: Phylogenetic regression-progression and the problem of rape motivation. *New Trends in Experimental and Clinical Psychiatry* 1988; IV: 235–251.

Bailey KG: Human paleopsychopathology: Implications for the paraphilias. *New Trends in Experimental and Clinical Psychiatry* 1991;VII; 5–16.

Bailey KG: Mismatch Theory and Psychopathology. In Crawford CB (Chair), *Human Behavior and Evolution Society Conference.* Santa Barbara, CA, 1995.

Bailey, KG: Series of Articles on Mismatch Theory. *ASCAP Newsletter* February, March, April, December, 1996.

Bailey KG: Evolution, kinship, and psychotherapy: Promoting psychological health through human relationships. In Gilbert, P, Bailey, KG (Eds), *Genes on the Couch: Explorations in Evolutionary Psychotherapy.* London: Routledge, 2000.

Bailey KG, Burns DS, Bazan LC: A method for measuring "primitive" and "advanced" elements in pleasures and aversions. *Journal of Personality Assessment* 1982; 46; 639–646.

Bailey KG, Tipton RM, Taylor PF: The threatening stare: Differential response latencies in mild and profoundly retarded adults. *American Journal of Mental Defiency* 1977; 31; 599–602.

Bailey KG, Wood HE; Nava GR: What Do Clients Want? Role of Psychological Kinship in Professional Helping. *Journal of Psychotherapy Integration* 1992; 2; 125–147.

Bandura, A: *Principles of Behavioral Modification.* New York: Holt, Rinehart & Winston, 1969.

Bernhard JG: *Primates in the Classroom: An Evolutionary Perspective in Children's Education.* Amherst: University of Massachusetts Press, 1988.

Bernhard JG, Glantz K: Management theory. In Maxwell M (Ed.), *The Sociobiological Imagination.* NY: State University of New York Press, 1991.

Boslough J: Inside the Mind of a Genius. *Reader's Digest* 1984; Febuary; 118–124.

Buck R: The biological affects: A typology. *Psychological Review* 1999; 106;301–336.

Cleckley H: *The Mask of Sanity.* St. Louis: Mosby, 1976.

Coe K, Steadman L: The human breast and ancestral reproductive cycle: A preliminary inquiry into breast cancer etiology. *Human Nature* 1995; 6; 197–220.

Cory GA: *The Reciprocal Modular Brain in Economics and Politics.* NY Kluwer Academic/ Plenum Publishers, 1999.

Cosmides L: *Emergence of evolutionary psychology.* Distinguished early career address, American Psychological Association, Los Angeles, CA, 1992.

Cosmides L, Tooby J: Cognitive adaptations for social exchange. In Barkow, JH, Cosmides L, Tooby J: *The Adapted Mind.* NY: Oxford University Press, 1992.

Crawford C: Environments and adaptations: Then and now. In Crawford C & Krebs DL (Eds.), *Handbook of Evolutionary Psychology: Ideas, Issues, Applications.* Mahwah, NJ: Erlbaum, 1998.

Dabrowski, K: *Psychoneurosis is not an illness.* London: GRYF Publications, Ltd., 1972.

Dawkins R: *The Selfish Gene.* New York, NY: Oxford University Press, 1976.

Diamond, J: The great leap forward. *Discover* 1989; May; 50–60.

Eaton, SB, Shostak, M, Konner, M: *The Paleolithic Prescription.* NY: Harper & Row, 1988.

Edey MA, Johanson DC: *Blueprints: Solving the Mystery of Evolution.* Boston: Little, Brown and Company, 1989.

Eibl-Eibesfeldt I: *Human Ethology.* New York: Aldine de Gruyter, 1989.

Fahrbach SA, Pfaff DW: Hormonal and neural mechanisms underlying maternal behavior in the rat. In Pfaff DW (Ed), *The Physiological Mechanisms of Motivation.* NY: Springer-Verlag, 1982.

Fernald A: Human maternal vocalizations to infants as biologically relevant signals: An evolutionary perspective. In Barkow JH, Cosmides L, Tooby J (Eds.), *The Adapted Mind: Evolutionary Biology and the Generation of Culture.* NY: Oxford University Press, 1992.

Fox, R: *The Human Nature of Violence.* Official Publication of the Social Issues Research Centre, Oxford UK 2001.

Gardner R Jr.: Psychiatric Syndromes as Infrastructure for Intra-specific Communication. In Chance, MRA (Ed.), *Social Fabrics of the Mind.* London: Erlbaum, 1988.

Gardner R Jr.: Renaissance times for evolutionary and sociophysiological medicine. *ASCAP Newsletter* 1996; 9; 20–24.

Geist V: *Life Strategies: Human Evolution, Environmental Design.* NY: Springer-Verlag, 1978.

Geist V. Personal communication on "classic regression": excerpted in *ASCAP Newsletter;* January, 2000a; 6–7.

Geist V. Personal Communication; June, 2000b.

Ghiglieri MP: *The Dark Side of Man: Tracing the Origins of Male Violence* Reading, MA: Perseus Books, 1999.

Gilbert P: *Human Nature and Suffering.* Hillsdale NJ: Erlbaum, 1989.

Gilbert P: The Evolved Basis and Adaptive Functions of Cognitive Distortions. *British Journal of Medical Psychology.* 1998; 71; 447–464.

Gilbert P: Personal communication, December 1999.

Glantz K, Pearce JK: *Exiles from Eden.* NY: Norton, 1989.

Gould SJ, Vbra ES: Exaptation: a missing term in the science of form. *Paleobiology* 1982; 8; 4–15.

Hart L: *Human Brain and Human Learning.* NY: Longman, 1983.

Hereford, S, Cleland CC, Fellner M: Territoriality and scent-marking: A study of profoundly retarded enuretics and encopretics. *American Journal of Mental Deficiency* 1973; 77; 426–430.

Herrnstein RJ: Doing what comes naturally. *American Psychologist* 1977; 32; 1013–1016, 1977.

Hinde, RA: *Animal Behaviour: A Synthesis of Ethology and Comparative Psychology.* New York: MCGraw-Hill, 1970.

Holloway RL (Ed.): *Primate Aggression, Territoriality, and Xenophobia: A Comparative Perspective.* NY: Academic Press, 1974.

Kendrick, DT, Sadalla, EK, Keefe, RC: Evolutionary cognitive psychology: The missing heart of modern cognitive science. In Crawford, C, & Krebs, DL: *Handbook of Evolutionary Psychology.* Mahwah, NJ: Erlbaum, 1998.

Lappé M: *Evolutionary Medicine: Rethinking the Origins of Disease.* San Francisco, CA: Sierra Club Books, 1994.

Le Doux J: *The Emotional Brain.* NY: Touchstone, 1996.

Lettvin JY, Maturana HR, McCullough WS, Pitts WH: What the frog's eye tells the frog's brain. *Proceedings of the Institute of Radio Engineers* 1959; 47; 1940–1951.

Lewin R: *Bones of Contention.* NY: Simon & Schuster, 1988.

MacAndrew C, Edgerton R: The everyday life of institutionalized idiots. *Human Organization* 1964; 23; 312–318.

MacLean, PD: On the evolution of three mentalities. In S. Arieti & G. Chrzanowski (Eds.), *New Dimensions in Psychiatry: A World View.* NY: Wiley, 1977.

MacLean PD: A mind of three minds: Educating the triune brain. In the *Seventy-seventh Yearbook of the National Society for the Study of Education.* Chicago: University of Chicago Press, 1978.

MacLean PD: A triangular brief on the evolution of brain and law. *Journal of Social and Biological Structures* 1982; 5; 368–379.

MacLean PD: *The Triune Brain in Evolution.* NY: Plenum Press, 1990.

Martin R: Classification and evolutionary relationships. In S Jones, R Martin & D Pilbeam (Eds), *The Cambridge Encylopedia of Human Evolution.* NY: Cambridge University Press, 1994.

Matlin, MM, Foley, HJ: *Sensation and Perception.* (3rd ed.). Boston: Allyn & Bacon, 1992.

Mealey, L: The sociobiology of sociopathy: An integrated evolutionary model. *Behavioral and Brain Sciences* 1995; 18; 523–599.

Meerlo, JAM: The dual meaning of human regression. *Psychoanalytic Review* 1962; 49; 77–86.

Mellen SLW: *The Evolution of Love.* San Francisco CA: Freeman, 1981.

Meloy, JR: *The Psychopathic Mind: Origins, Dynamics, and Treatment.* Northvale, NJ: Jason Aronson, 1988.

Meloy, JR. Predatory violence during mass murder. *Journal of Forensic Science* 1997; 42; 326–329.

Michaud SG, Aynesworth H: *The Only Living Witness.* NY: Linden Press/Simon & Schuster, 1983.

Miller, L: The predator's brain: Neuropsychodynamics of serial killers. In LB Schlesinger (ed.) *Serial offender: Current Thought, Recent Findings.* Boca Raton: CRC Press, 2000.

Mithen S: *The Prehistory of the Mind.* London: Thames and Hudson, 1996.

Monroe, RR: *Brain Dysfunction in Aggressive Criminals.* Lexington, MA: Lexington Books, 1978.

Moyer, KE: *The Psychobiology of Aggression.* New York: Harper & Row, 1976.

Nesse RM, Berridge KC: Psychoactive drug use in evolutionary perspective. *Science* 278; 1997, 63–66.

Nesse R, Williams G: *Why We Get Sick*: Random House, 1995.

Pinker S: *The Language Instinct.* New York: William Morrow, 1994.

Porges SW: Emotion: An Evolutionary By-Product of Neural Regulation of the Autonomic Nervous System. In CS Carter, I Lederhendler & B Kirkpatrick (Eds), *The Integrative Neurobiology of Affiliation.* NY: Academy of Sciences, 1997.

Rapoport JL: The Biology of Obsessions and Compulsions. *Scientific American* 1989; 260; 82–89.

Restak R: *The Brain.* New York: Bantam, 1984.

Sagan C: *The Dragons of Eden.* New York: Ballentine Books, 1977.

Scheller RH, Axelrod R: How genes control an innate behavior. *Scientific American* 1984; 250; 54–62.

Schick KD, Toth N: *Making Silent Stones Speak.* NY: Simon & Schuster, 1993.

Shreeve, J: *The Neanderthal Enigma.* New York: Avon. 1995.

Smith R: *Inhibition: History and Meaning in the Sciences of Mind and Brain.* Berkeley, CA: University of California Press, 1992.

Symonds D: *The Evolution of Human Sexuality.* NY: Oxford University Press, 1979.

Taylor J (Ed): *Selected Writings of John Hughlings Jackson,* Vol. 1 London: Hodder & Stoughton, 1932.

Tillier B: Personal communication, March 2000.

Tooby J, Cosmides L: The past explains the present: Emotional adaptations and the structure of ancestral environments. *Ethology and Sociobiology* 1990; 11; 375–421.

Valzelli, L: *Psychobiology of Aggression and Violence.* NY: Raven Press, 1981.

Walker A, Shipman, P: *The Wisdom of the Bones: In Search of Human Origins.* NY: Alfred A. Knopf, 1996.

Washburn SL, Hamburg DA: Aggressive behavior in old world monkeys and apes. In Dolinhow PC (Ed.), *Primate Patterns.* NY: Holt, Rinehart & Winston, 1972.

Williams GC, Nesse RM: The Dawn of Darwinian Medicine. *The Quarterly Review of Biology* 1991; 66; 1–22.

Wilson DR: *Manic-Depression: Triune Neuroethology, Evolutionary Epidemiology and Hawk-Dove Analysis.* Paper presented at the MacLean symposium in Boston, Mass., July 1999.

Wilson, EO: *Sociobiology: The Modern Synthesis.* Cambridge, MA: Harvard University Press, 1975.

Wrangham R, Peterson D: *Demonic Males.* Boston: Houghton Mifflin, 1996.

Wright R: The evolution of despair. *Time* 1995; 146 (Aug); 50–57.

18

ALGORITHMS OF NEURAL ARCHITECTURE, HAMILTON'S RULE, AND THE INVISIBLE HAND OF ECONOMICS

Gerald A. Cory, Jr.

INTRODUCTION

This chapter builds upon the triune modular brain concept of Paul MacLean to create a new model of our neural architecture called the conflict systems neurobehavioral (CSN) model. It develops reciprocal algorithms of behavior, involving the tug and pull between ego and empathy, neocortical representations of phylogenetically established self-preservation and affectional brain structures. These algorithms are applied to the ubiquitous phenomenon of social reciprocity. The same fundamental algorithms are further shown to be the underlying dynamic of social exchange as well as the transactional market governed by the so-called laws of supply and demand. The reciprocal algorithms are offered as the evolved mechanism complement to Hamilton's rule of inclusive fitness. The linkage of their mathematical expressions is demonstrated. The neural algorithms are also expressed in the invisible hand concept of Adam Smith, which, as a basic economic concept, has been the source of much theoretical speculation in microeconomic theory. The linkage of Hamilton's rule with the reciprocal neural algorithms combined with the sourcing of economic and social exchange in the neural dynamic allows a theoretical basis for the integration of evolutionary psychology with evolutionary neuroscience as a foundation for economics and the social sciences.

To proceed with developing the conflict systems neurobehavioral (CNS) model, I begin with the work of Paul D. MacLean. MacLean, who was founder and longtime chief of the Laboratory of Brain Evolution and Behavior of the National Institutes of Health, is our leading evolutionary neuroscientist. MacLean's triune brain concept has been one of the most influential ideas in brain science since World War II (e.g., see Durant in Harrington 1992: 268). Nevertheless, it has also been criticized in some quarters of neuroscience.[1]

Although much of this criticism has recently been shown to be inaccurate and based upon misinterpretations of MacLean's position,[2] the presentation in this chapter is adjusted to accommodate those criticisms where clarification is indicated. In his encyclopedic summary of the last fifty years of brain research, MacLean (1990) documents the human brain as an evolved three-level interconnected, modular structure (see Figure 18.1). This structure comprises a self-preservational, maintenance component inherited from the stem reptiles of the Permian and Triassic periods (between 225–250 mya), called the protoreptilian complex, a later modified and evolved mammalian affectional complex, and a most recently modified and elaborated higher cortex.

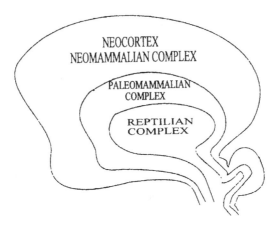

Figure 18.1. A Simplified, Modified Sketch of the Interconnected Modular Triune Brain Structure. After MacLean. As represented here the three brain divisions do not constitute distinct additions but rather modifications and elaborations of probable preexisting homologues reflecting phylogenetic continuity.

As brain evolution progressed in the branching vertebrate line ancestral to humans, simple protoreptilian brain structure was not replaced, but provided the substructure and homologues for subsequent brain development while largely retaining its basic character and function. Accordingly, the brain structure of early ancestral vertebrate life forms (i.e., early fishes, amniotic anapsid reptiles) became the substructure and provided the homologues for the mammalian modifications and neocortical elaborations that followed and which have reached the greatest development in the brain of humankind. Appreciating the qualitative differences of the three levels is important to understanding the dynamics of human subjective experience and behavior.

The protoreptilian brain tissues in humans are proposed, as they did in the stem vertebrates, to govern the fundamentals, or the daily master routines, of our life-support operations: blood circulation, heartbeat, respiration, basic food-getting, reproduction, and defensive behaviors, which were functions and behaviors also found in the ancient stem reptiles. Located by MacLean in what are usually called the hindbrain and the midbrain (i.e., the brain stem) as well as in certain structures at the base of the forebrain (i.e., the basal ganglia), this primal and innermost core of the human brain made up almost the entire brain in ancestral fishes, amphibians, and amniotes (although not necessarily their modern representatives).

The next developmental stage of our brain, which comes from rudimentary mammalian life and which MacLean called the paleo- or "old" mammalian brain, is identified with the structures designated collectively as our limbic system. Developing from homologues preexisting in the protoreptilian brain, these newly elaborated limbic tissue clusters included such physiological structures as the amygdala, the hypothalamus, the hippocampus, the thalamus, and the limbic cingulate cortex. Behavioral contributions to life from these modified and elaborated paleo-mammalian structures, or limbic system, included, among other things, the mammalian features (absent in the stem vertebrates) of warm-bloodedness, nursing, infant care, and extended social bonding. These new characteristics were then neurally integrated with the life-support functional and behavioral circuitry of the protoreptilian brain tissues to create the more complex life form of mammals.

The neocortex, which MacLean called the neo- or "new" mammalian brain, is the most recent stage of brain modification and elaboration. This great mass of hemispherical brain matter that dominates the skull case of higher primates and man, by elaborating the preexisting homologues present in the brains of early vertebrates, overgrew and encased the earlier ("paleo") mammalian and protoreptilian neural tissues, but essentially did not replace them. As a consequence of this neocortical evolution and growth, those older brain parts evolved greater complexity in support of these new tissue structures and in response to the behavioral adaptations necessary to life's increasingly sophisticated circumstances.

TOWARD A NEW BEHAVIORAL MODEL

The unique features of the human brain evolved over a period of several million years in a primarily kinship based foraging society where sharing or reciprocity was essential to survival and which reinforced the adaptive evolution of the mammalian characteristics of self-preservation and affection.[3] Ego and empathy, self-interest and other-interest, are key features of our personal and social behavior. To relate these to MacLean's concept we need a subjective/behavioral rather than a neurophysiological vocabulary—one that will express what the presence of our protoreptilian and paleomammalian brain structures mean with regard to our day-to-day, subjectively experienced, behavioral initiatives and responses to one another and the world we live in. In computer-related vocabulary, familiar to us all through cognitive psychology and artificial intelligence, I use the software designer's vocabulary of programs and programming. I will speak of our three developmental brain levels as behavioral programs or sets of programs that subjectively drive and generate specific, and objectively observable, behaviors.[4]

From the predominantly survival-centered promptings of the ancestral proto-reptilian tissues, as elaborated in the human brain, arise the motivational source for egoistic, surviving, self-interested subjective experience and behaviors. Here are the cold-blooded, seemingly passionless, single-minded behaviors that we have generally associated with the present-day lizard, the snake, and that most maligned of fishes, the shark.[5]

Here is a world revolving almost exclusively around matters of self-preservation. The protoreptilian brain structures, then, will be referred to as our self-preservation programming.

From the infant nursing, care-giving, and social bonding initiatives and responses of the mammalian modifications and elaborations arise the motivational source for nurturing, empathetic, other-interested experiences and behaviors. Here are the warm-blooded, passionate, body-contacting, bonding behaviors that we've come to identify with the lion, the wolf, the primates.[6]

Here is a world in which nearly single-minded self-preservation is simultaneously complemented and counterpoised by the conflicting demands of affection. The early mammalian modifications, then will be referred to as our affectional programming.[7]

Before I go on to discuss the neo-mammalian neocortical structures in behavioral terms, I wish to pause to consider how these first two sets of programs function together.

Our Evolved Brain and the Sources of Subjective/Behavioral Conflict

These core behavioral program modules, composed of (or served by) sets or subsystems of modules, of our brain structure serve as dynamic factors of our behavior. They are energy-driven by our cellular as well as overall bodily processes of metabolism as mediated by *hormonal, neurotransmitter, and neural architecture.* Each is an inextricable part of our makeup, because each is "wired into" our brain structure by the process of evolution. The degree of genome control seems, however, to vary with the mechanism. Older brain parts like the hindbrain and parts of the limbic system, phylogenetically old and necessary for survival, seem to be more closely under genetic control. Other more recent tissues in the neocortex depend also on development and environmental experience. Damasio (1999, 1994) uses the terms *preset* and *preorganized*, apparently (and appropriately, I think) to avoid the implication of an overly deterministic prewiring in some brain regions. Behavioral conflict exists, then, simply by virtue of the presence of these two large-scale energy-driven modular program sets in our lives—up and running even prior to birth. Their mere physiological presence sets us up for a life of inner and outer struggle, as we are driven by and respond to their contending demands.[8] Conflict is more than an externalized, objective ethical, moral, or decision-making dilemma, however. *Subjectively, feelings of satisfaction* occur when we can express our felt motives, while *feelings of frustration* occur when either our self-preservational or affectional impulses cannot be expressed in the behavioral initiatives and responses we wish to make.

Behavioral tension then arises. Experienced as subjectively defined variants such as frustration, anxiety, or anger, behavioral tension occurs whenever one of our two fundamental behavioral programs—self-preservation or affection—is activated but meets with some resistance or difficulty that prevents its satisfactory expression. This subjective tension becomes most paralyzing when both programs are activated and seek contending or incompatible responses *within a single situation*. Caught between "I want to" and "I can't"—for example, "I want to help him/her, but I can't surrender my needs"—we agonize. Whether this tension arises through the thwarted expression of a single impulse or the simultaneous but mutually exclusive urgings of two contending impulses, whenever it remains unresolved or unmanaged it leads to the worsening condition of behavioral stress.

The Blessing of Tension and Stress

The evolutionary process by which the two opposite promptings of self-preservation and affection were combined in us enhanced our ability to survive by binding us in social interaction and providing us with the widest range of behavioral responses to our environment.[9] Our inherently conflicting programs are a curse, then, only to the degree that we fail to recognize them as a blessing. Our self-preservation and affection programs allow us a highly advanced sensitivity to our environment, keeping our interactive social behaviors within survival limits as well as enabling us to perceive and appreciate the survival requirements of others. Ironically, the accompanying behavioral tension—*even the stress!*—is an integral part of this useful function, for it allows us to more immediately evaluate (a subjective function) our behavior and the effect it is having on ourselves and others.[10]

Behavioral tension serves as an internal emotional compass that we can use to guide ourselves through the often complicated and treacherous pathways of interpersonal relations.

Behavioral stress tells us that we are exceeding safe limits for ourselves and others, and for our larger social, economic, and political structures.

Behavioral tension and stress are, at this point perhaps needless to say, inherently and necessarily subjective. But of course all of this requires a certain level of consciousness, perhaps best designated self-aware consciousness, coupled with the ability to generalize our internally experienced motives. If all we possessed were the conflicting programs of self-preservation and affection, we would, be among the life forms whose behaviors are governed by instinct. We would be driven by the urgings of fight, or flight, or bondedness; and every so often—like the legendary mule who, thirsty and hungry, looked back and forth between water and hay, unable to move—we would be caught in the indecision of those urgings.

But whether or not other mammals with paleomammalian brain structures, with self-preservation and affection programming, experience conscious conflict from these two behavioral priorities, we certainly do. We can reflect and genera- lize not only upon our choices, but upon the meanings they have for our personal as well as our species' existence and significance. And it is in that capacity to reflect, to self-consciously experience, generalize, and decide upon the tug-and-pull of our conflicting urgings, that we come to the third stage of brain development in MacLean's model: the neomammalian or "new" mammal- ian brain structures—what I have designated the executive programming.

THE CONFLICT SYSTEMS NEUROBEHAVIORAL (CSN) MODEL

The neural substrate of consciousness is still a matter of considerable specul- ation and debate (e.g., see Edelman & Tononi 2000; Damasio 1999, 1994; Cory 2000a; Searle 1997; Smith 1996). Although the emerging mechanisms are still somewhat unclear, I follow the position here that there is no homunculus (little person) or other Cartesian dualistic process involved. Nevertheless, it seems that our expanded and elaborated neocortex (or isocortex), anchored in and interconnected with our earlier mammalian and protoreptilian brain systems, is part of the "dynamic core" (Edelman & Tononi 2000; cf. Dennett 1998) neces- sary to our *self-aware* or *self-reflective* consciousness. As well, our elaborated neocortex provides us with the evolutionarily unique and powerful ability to use verbal and symbolic language to create concepts and ideas by which to interpret our consciousness, to describe the feelings, motives, and behaviors that arise within us and in response to our social and environmental experiences.[11] It is with this so-called executive programming that we acquire the ability to name, to comment upon, to *generalize*[12] and to *choose* between our contending sets of behavioral impulses: self-preservation, commonly called, at a high level of cognitive generalization, "egoistic" or "self-interested" behavior, and affection, which we call, at an equally high level of cognitive generalization, "empathetic" or "other-interested" behavior. *Empathy allows us the critical social capacity to enter into or respond emotionally to another's self-interest as well as other emotional states.*[13]

Although the positioning of ego and empathy in Figure 18.2 (facing the reader) is primarily for illustrative purposes only and is not intended to suggest a definitive lateralization, there is some evidence to suggest that the right hemisphere is favored for emotion and the left for more analytical self- preserving behaviors (e.g., see Damasio 1994; Tucker, Luu, & Pribram 1995; Brownell & Martino 1998). However, Heller et al. (1998), after noting that it is well established that particular regions of the right hemisphere are specialized to interpret and express emotional information, argue that the total experience of emotion is not lateralized but involves dynamic interactions between forward and posterior regions of both hemispheres as well as subcortical (limbic) structures. Such complex, highly generalized capacities as ego and empathy should more safely be thought of as engaging the interaction of both hemi- spheres. Davidson (1995), for example, hypothesizes that the left and right anterior regions of the brain are key components of an affective regulatory system for approach and avoidance behaviors.

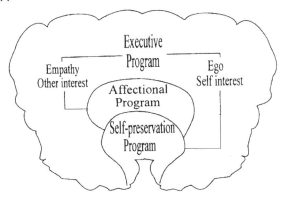

Figure 18.2. The Conflict Systems Neurobehavioral Model. A simplified cutaway representation of the brain showing the behavioral programs and the derivation of Ego/self-interested and Empathy/other-interested motives and behaviors. I should note that earlier models, e.g., Freud (id, ego, and superego) postulated three-part conflictual models. Freud, however, was unable to tie his model to brain circuitry and it remained ungrounded in neural science because brain research had simply not advanced to that point.

In other words, our executive programming, especially our frontal cortex,[14] has the capability and the responsibility for cognitively representing these limbic and protoreptilian brain connections and inputs and making what may be thought of as our moral as well as rational choices among our conflicting, impulsive, and irrational or nonrational motivations. This self conscious, generalizing, choosing capacity accompanied, of course, with language, is what differentiates us from even closely related primate species and makes findings in primate behavior, although highly interesting and unquestionably important, insufficient in themselves to fully understand and account for human behavior.

EXECUTIVE PROGRAMMING AND NEURAL NETWORKS

According to Joaquin Fuster, of the Neuropsychiatric Institute, UCLA, the frontal cortex constitutes the highest level of a hierarchy of neural structures (reaching down to the motoneurons and anterior roots of the spinal cord), that represents and executes the actions of the organism. Because of its topmost position in this neural hierarchy, the frontal cortex has been named the "executive of the brain and the organ of creativity." (1999: 187; see also Goldberg 2001).

Fuster, thus, designates the frontal neocortex as the neural substrate for executive functioning (cf. Pribram 1973, 1994). There are, however, a number of competing models for executive functioning, some tied to neural substrate, some not. Bernard Baars and colleagues of the Wright Institute have proposed a

Neural Global Workspace Model (GW), which combines the concepts of attention, working memory, and executive function into a theater metaphor. Baars and colleagues (Newman et al. 1997; cf. Harth 1997) review other neuroscience and neural network models that deal with attention, binding, resource allocation, and gating that share significant features with their own GW model for conscious attention (for an alternative model based on an evolutionary and clinical approaches and which draws upon MacLean's triune concept, see Mirsky 1996).[15] The authors acknowledge that the models they present implement only partial aspects of their GW theory. Notably neglected are the influences of memory and affective systems upon the stream of consciousness (1997: 1205). The CSN model presented in this paper attempts to incorporate the affective (generalized into empathy) neural substrate necessary to initiate and maintain sociality.

It is noteworthy that distributed artificial intelligence (DIA) models more closely approximate interpersonal behavior in that they seem to reflect an effort at intelligent balance between the competitive self-interest and cooperation which is necessary to the operation of complex social organizations (Newman et al. 1997: 1196; Durfee 1993).

Underpinning the CSN model, the neural substrate for self-survival (generalized as ego) mechanisms may proceed from circuits in the basal ganglia and brain stem (protoreptilian complex) through connections with the amygdala, other limbic structures (early mammalian complex), and probable cortical representations which add emotion or passion (see Kandel et al. 1995: 595–612), ultimately to be gated into the frontal cortex by thalamocortical circuitry (e.g., see LaBerge 1995; Crick 1994; Baars 1997, 1988; Sherman & Guillery 2001).

Likewise, the mammalian nurturing (affectional) substrate and its associated motivation, a fundamental component underlying empathy, may originate in the septal and medial preoptic limbic (see Fleming et al. 1996; Numan 1994, Numan & Sheehan 1997) areas, proceed through hippocampal and amygdaloid circuitry (Brothers 1989; Bachevalier 2000) as well as other limbic structures, and in turn, be gated into the orbital and frontal cortex by neuromodulating thalamocortical circuits (to include the cingulate cortex), where the conflict with egoistic imputs is resolved in the executive or Global Workspace of conscious self-awareness. The neuromodulating and gating of *affect* as well as cognition by the thalamocortical circuitry is supported by neurologists Devinsky and Luciano (1993), who report that the limbic cingulate cortex, a cortical structure closely associated with the limbic thalamus, can be seen as both an *amplifier* and a filter, which joins *affect* and *intellect* interconnecting the *emotional and cognitive components of the mind* (1993: 549).

Tucker, Luu, and Pribram (1995) speculate that the network architecture of the frontal lobes reflects dual limbic origins of the frontal cortex. Specifically, the authors speculate that two limbic-cortical pathways apply different motivational biases to direct the frontal lobe representation of working memory. They suggest that the dorsal limbic mechanisms projecting through the cingulate gyrus may be influenced by hedonic evaluations, *social attachments*, initiating a mode of motor control that is holistic and impulsive. On the other hand, they suggest that the ventral limbic pathway from the amygdala to the orbital frontal cortex may implement a more restricted mode of motor control reflecting the adaptive constraints of *self-preservation* (1995: 233–234). The orbital frontal cortex via its connections to the anterior cingulate gyrus, amygdala and other limbic structures seems especially important to the interaction of ego and empathy (Damasio 1994; Schnider & Gutbrod 1999; Fuster 1999; see also Weisfeld, this volume). Such findings are consistent with the CSN model in which ego and empathy represent conflicting subcortical inputs into the cortical executive. Several researchers have posited the dynamic of conflicting modules, vying for ascendency in behavior and consciousness (e.g., Edelman & Tononi 2000; Edelman 1992; Dennett 1998; Pinker 1997).

Although it is beyond the scope of this chapter to attempt to deal with the as yet partially understood detailed electrochemical physiology of such egoistic/empathetic conflict, it is appropriate to acknowledge that such behavior is made possible in part by the complex electro-chemical excitatory and inhibitory interactions among groups of interconnected neurons (e.g., see the discussions in Koch 1999; Cowan et al. 1997; Fuster 1997: 102–149; Gutnick & Mody 1995).

The role of hormones and neurotransmitters must also be acknowledged in any complete analysis. For instance, from the egoistic perspective, testosterone is associated with competitiveness and power urges. Serotonin levels in humans seem related to confidence and self-esteem. On the empathetic side, oxytocin, arginine vasopressin, and prolactin are important to pair bonding and maternal as well as paternal caring behavior. Opioids (endorphins and enkaphalins) seem important to positive social relationships. For readers interested in more detail, two recent and wide-ranging volumes update the research focusing specifically on affiliation and affection: Carter et al. (1997), *The Integrative Neurobiology of Affiliation*, and Panksepp (1998), *Affective Neuroscience*. Panksepp especially speculates on the contrast between testosterone-driven power urges and oxytocin and opioid mediated affectional behavior (1998: 250–259; see also Toates 2001). Damasio reminds us, however, that there is a popular tendency to overemphasize the efficacy of hormones by themselves. Their action depends upon neural architecture and their effects may vary in different brain regions (1994: 77–78).

THE MAJOR RANGES OF RECIPROCAL BEHAVIOR

The two master, inclusive and modular programs of self-preservation and affection that have been wired into our brain structure operate dynamically according to a set of *subjectively experienced* and *objectively expressed* behavioral rules, procedures, or algorithms. Understanding the workings and applications of these algorithms is the key to grasping the role of dialectical conflict, tension, and stress in our personal and interactive lives.

The major ranges of the conflict systems neurobehavioral behavioral model (Figure 18.3) illustrate the features of this ego-empathy dynamic. In the display, subjectively experienced internal as well as interpersonal behavior is divided from right to left into three main ranges called the egoistic range, the dynamic balance range, and the empathetic range. Each range represents a varying mix of egoistically and empathetically motivated behaviors. The solid line stands for ego and pivots on the word "ego" in the executive program of the brain diagram. The broken line stands for empathy and pivots on the word "empathy" in the diagram.

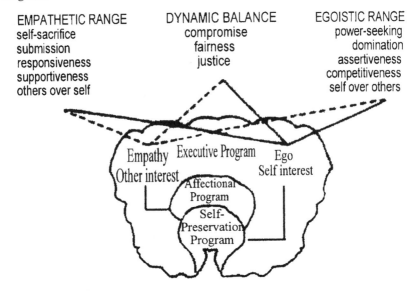

Figure 18.3. The Major Ranges/Modes of Behavior. To simplify the graph, the three points are intended to mark the center points of each range, with varying mixes of ego and empathy on either side of each point. The graph thus intends to communicate, not a zero-sum, either/or set of behavioral options or expressions, but a spectrum of the increasing or decreasing (depending on direction of movement) proportions of ego and empathy in behavior (see note 16). The graph represents only what may be thought of as central tendencies of interactive behavior and is far too simple to represent all the shadings of emotion and motivation.

The Egoistic Range

The egoistic range indicates behavior dominated by self-preservation programming. Since the two behavioral programs are locked in inseparable unity, empathy is present here, but to a lesser degree. Behavior in this range is self-centered or self-interested and may tend, for example, to be dominating, power-seeking, or even attacking, where empathy is less. When empathy is increased, ego behavior will become less harsh and may be described more moderately as controlling, competitive, or assertive. As empathy is gradually increased the intersection of the two lines of the diagram will move toward the range of dynamic balance. Ego behavior will be softened as empathy is added. But the defining characteristic of the egoistic, self-interested range is *self-over-others*. Whether we are blatantly power-seeking or more moderately assertive, in this range we are putting ourselves, our own priorities, objectives, and feelings, ahead of others.

The Empathetic Range

The empathetic range represents behavior weighted in favor of empathy. Ego is present, but is taking a back seat. When ego is present to a minimal degree, empathetic behavior may tend to extremes of self-sacrifice and submission. When ego is increased, empathetic behaviors become moderated and may be described as supportive, responsive, or any of a variety of "others first" behaviors. As the influence of ego is gradually added, empathetic behavior will approach the range of dynamic balance. In the empathetic range, the key phrase to remember is *others-over-self* or others first. Whether we are at the extreme of self-sacrifice or more moderately responsive, we are putting the priorities of others ahead of our own.

The Dynamic Balance Range

The range of dynamic balance represents a working balance between ego and empathy. At this point our behavioral programs are operating in roughly equal measure. I speak of "working," "rough," or "dynamic" balance because the tug-and-pull between the two programs continues ceaselessly. The dynamic nature of the programming means that "perfect" balance may be a theoretical point, unattainable in practice. Our more balanced behavior tends to be characterized by equality, justice, sharing, and other behaviors that show respect for ourselves and others. In fact, respect for self and others is the keynote of the range of dynamic balance.[16]

Energy or Activity Level

The extent to which the programs of self-preservation and affection, ego and empathy, are out of balance, or pulling against each other, is a measure of behavioral tension. We experience this behavioral tension both internally and between ourselves and others, in any relationship or interaction. Unmanaged or excessive tension becomes, of course, behavioral stress. But that is not all. Important also is the degree of energy we give to the interaction or the relationship. The amount of energy we put into any activity depends mostly upon how important we think it is or how enthusiastic we feel about it. In competitive sports or contests, qualitative differences in energy are easily observed. In intellectual contests, like chess, the energy invested may be intense, but much less obvious.

THE PROPOSED ALGORITHMS OF INTERPERSONAL BEHAVIOR

From the dynamic interplay of ego, empathy, and activity level come the following algorithmic rule statements which may be considered a research program to be tested empirically.

1. Self-interested, egoistic behavior, because it lacks empathy to some degree, creates tension within ourselves and between our selves and others. The tension increases from low to high activity levels. And it increases as we move toward the extremes of ego.

Within ourselves, the tension created by the tug of neglected empathy is experienced as a feeling of obligation to others or an expectation that they might wish to "even the score" with us.

Within others, the tension created by our self-interested behavior is experienced as a feeling of imposition or hurt, accompanied by an urge to "even the score."

Children often reveal the dynamic of such behavior in a clear, unsophisticated form. Imagine two children playing on the living-room floor. One hits the other. The second child hits back, responding in kind. Or the children may not hit each other at all. One might instead call the other a bad name. The second child reciprocates, kicking off a round of escalating name-calling. One child may eventually feel unable to even the score and will complain to a parent to intervene. Most of us have experienced such give-and-take as children and have seen it countless times in our own children and grandchildren. Similar behavior is embarrassingly observable among adults. It can be seen in husband- and-wife arguments, bar fights, hockey games, political campaigns, even in sophisticated lawsuits. The rule operates not only in such highly visible conflict situations, but also in very subtle interactions—in the small behavioral exchanges, the ongoing give-and-take of all interpersonal relations.

Expressive of the underlying conflictual excitatory/inhibitory dynamic of the neural architecture, we can say that

The reactions that build in ourselves and others do so potentially in proportion to the behavioral tension created by egoistic, self-interested behavior.

That is, the harder I hit you, the harder you hit me in return. Or the fouler a name you call me, the fouler a name I call you in return. Or perhaps with more sophistication, I resolve the tension in me by an act of visible "superiority." I ignore you—although I *could* call you an even fouler name, if I chose.

Behavior on the other side of the scale is described in the second rule statement:

2. Empathetic behavior, because it denies ego or self-interest to some degree, also creates tension within ourselves and others. This tension, likewise, increases as activity levels increase and as we move toward extremes of empathy.

Within ourselves, the tension created by the tug of the neglected self-interest (ego) is experienced as a feeling that "others owe us one" and a growing need to "collect our due." This tension, especially if it continues over time, may be experienced as resentment at being exploited, taken for granted, not appreciated, or victimized by others.

Within others, the tension created is experienced as a sense of obligation toward us.

The reactions that build in ourselves and others, again, are in proportion to the behavioral tension created. And again, the unmanaged, or excessive tension is experienced as behavioral stress.

When we do things for others—give them things, make personal sacrifices for them—it can make us feel righteous, affectionate, loving. But we *do* want a payback. That's the tug of self-interest. It can be very slight, hardly noticeable at first. But let the giving, the self-sacrifice, go on for a while, unacknowledged or unappreciated (that is, without payback to the ego), and see how we begin to feel. The tension, the stress, starts to show. We complain that others are taking advantage of us, taking us for granted, victimizing us. Self-interest cannot be long short-changed without demanding its due. We may eventually relieve the stress by blowing up at those we have been serving—accusing them of ingratitude, withdrawing our favors, or kicking them out of the house. Or we may sandbag the stress, letting it eat away at our dispositions, our bodies.

On the other hand, when we do things for others, they often feel obliged to return the favor in some form to avoid being left with an uneasy sense of debt. Gift-giving notoriously stimulates the receiver to feel the need to reciprocate. Think of the times when you have received a holiday gift from someone for whom you had failed to buy a gift. Sometimes the sense of obligation prompted by the empathetic acts of others can become a nuisance.

The third rule statement describes the relative balance between the contending motives:

3. Behavior in the range of dynamic balance expresses the approximate balance of ego and empathy. It is the position of least behavioral tension. Within ourselves and others, it creates feelings of mutuality and shared respect.[17]

For most of us it is an especially satisfying experience to interact with others in equality, with no sense of obligation, superiority or inferiority. To work together in common humanity, in common cause, is to experience behavioral dynamic balance. Of course, there are many versions of the experience of dynamic balance: the shared pride of parents in helping their child achieve, the joy of athletes in playing well as a team, the satisfaction of coworkers in working together successfully on an important project.[17]

RECIPROCITY THROUGH CONFLICT

These algorithms of behavior operate in the smallest interactions, the vignettes, of everyday personal life. The dynamic of behavioral tension provides that for every interpersonal act, there is a balancing reciprocal. A self-interested act requires an empathetic reciprocal for balance. An empathetic act, likewise, requires a balancing self-interested reciprocal. This reciprocity goes back and forth many times even in a short conversation. Without the reciprocal, tension builds, stress accumulates, and either confrontation or withdrawal results. If not, and the relationship continues, it becomes a tense and stressful one of inequality or domination/ submission, waiting and pressing for the opportunity for adjustment.

These, then, are the proposed basic interpersonal algorithms of our three-level brain. These algorithms show how we get to reciprocity through conflict. I propose that they shape the conflict and reciprocity, the give-and-take, at all levels of our interactive, social lives.

Overemphasis on either self-interest or empathy, exercise of one program to the exclusion of the other, creates tension and stress in any social configuration—from simple dyadic person-to-person encounters up to and including interactions among members of the workplace, society at large, social groups, and entire economic and political systems.

THE QUESTION OF SCIENCE: PHYSICS VS. SOCIAL

The algorithmic rules of reciprocal behavior proposed here, as central tendencies of behavior, operate *very imperfectly*. I suspect that this will be true of any behavioral algorithms or principles proposed at this level of generalization (cf. Maynard Smith 2002). The proposed algorithms, then, can only approximate, but not fully achieve, the precision of the laws of classical physics or even quantum mechanics. This is in part because they are achieved through the process of organic evolution (which involves some random processes and natural selection) and therefore cannot operate as immutable universal physical laws but as generalized algorithms with degrees of variation.

The idealized, or rather statistically generalized, tug and pull of ego and empathy presented here may be further probabilized in actuality by genetic, gender and developmental, individual experience and learning, and other environmental shaping and reinforcing factors. In other words, *genetically speaking*, given the individual differences in genetic inheritance that we see in such obvious things as in hair, skin, or eye color, some individuals *behaviorally* may be more or less as strongly wired or preorganized for self-preservation and affection as others. But granting *gender* and *developmental* differences, every human being is, nevertheless, similarly wired or preorganized with the fundamental brain architecture unless he/she has very serious genetic defects indeed. Influential developmental psychologists like Jean Piaget (1965) of Switzerland and Lawrence Kohlberg (1984) of Harvard, operating from a behavioral perspective, have constructed and tested theories of childhood moral development. In the theories of both men moral stages of development emerge much the same in all cultures when the child experiences anything approaching a normal family life. Such generalized moral stages could not be found across cultures if they were not genetically based on the species-wide brain structure and its associated behavioral potentialities.

From the standpoint of *individual learning, socialization,* and other *environmental* factors, modifications in biological structures and potentialities occur in early development and throughout life. As writers such as G. H. Mead (1934) have assured us long before the emergence of evolutionary neuroscience, life or the brain develops in an interactive social context. *Individual* life experiences may facilitate, suppress, strengthen, or otherwise modify the expression of these inherited biological programs. Environmental factors, to include physical constraints as well as our socially and scientifically accepted institutions and paradigms, may also shape and reinforce the expression of the evolved algorithmic dynamic. Individual learning experience or environmental factors of the individual life *cannot,* however, *eliminate* the genetic structure and programming of the brain; that is, not without radical injury, surgical, or genetic intervention. And the behavioral tension will be there to both resist the changes and to shape the experience, even shape the environment itself, in a dynamic manner.

Because of these factors, the behavioral algorithms are *statistical*—much in the same way as are the second law of thermodynamics and quantum theory of physics. That is, they do *not* allow *precise* prediction of specific behavior at the basic unit of analysis—the individual, molecular, or subatomic level respectively—but only on the aggregated basis of statistical probability. The proposed algorithmic rules of reciprocal behavior, as here presented, may nevertheless very well prove to be *equally* as valid and useful to social science as the laws of physics are to physical science. They do not and cannot, however, have the immutable quality of physical laws such as gravity. As products of organic evolution and developmental processes, they inevitably involve *more probabilities* because of individual differences, genetic and learned, in the evolved basic units.

An admittedly loose, but perhaps interesting, analogy can be made between the inclusive spectrum of possible behaviors of the conflict systems neurobehavioral model and the particle wave function of quantum physics. As the wave function of a particle is defined to include all the possible values of a particle according to probability, the "wave" function of behavior can be thought to include all possible internal and interpersonal behavioral probabilities (mixes of ego and empathy) extending across the egoistic, empathetic, and dynamic balance ranges. Externally, observed behavior is predictable from the model, as is quantum behavior, only on a probability basis specified by the metaphorical wave function. The behavioral "wave" function, like that of particle physics, collapses or reduces to one behavior in a decision, action, or observation. If it doesn't collapse, we see frustration, tension, and indecisiveness—ambiguous behavior stalled in uncollapsed waveform.

Upon observation by an *external* observer, the wave function of behavior can be considered to collapse to a specifically observable behavior on the part of the individual and that is the end of it. But this would be an overly simplistic "objective" perception somewhat more characteristic of the now largely superceded radical behavioristic perspective. *Internally*, subjectively, we experience a much more complex process because we have conscious access to the dynamic. We know in our conscious awareness the tension, the difficulty, the struggle we go through in important issues of ego and empathy conflict. Even yet, in the surely much simpler processes of quantum physics we still do not fully understand what set of dynamics leads to the wave function collapse.[18] In behavior, the dynamic lies in the complexities of subjective preconsciousness and/or self-aware consciousness.

THE UNIVERSAL NORM OF RECIPROCITY

The norm of reciprocity has long been a major theme in anthropology and sociology (e.g., see Gouldner 1960; van Baal 1975; Bowles & Gintis 1998: esp. Ch. 17) and more recently in economics (e.g., Fehr & Gachter 2000). This universally observed norm, found in all societies, primitive and modern, has been accounted for, or shown to be possible, in evolutionary theory by such concepts as kin selection, inclusive fitness (Hamilton 1964), reciprocal altruism (Trivers 1971, 1981; Alexander 1987), and game theory (Maynard Smith 1982; Axelrod & Hamilton 1981). These efforts draw upon gene-centered perspectives, which see such reciprocity as basically selfish. More recently, extensive reciprocity seen as based not upon selfishness, but empathy, has reportedly been observed in the behavior of rhesus monkeys (de Waal 1996). F. de Waal's approach is a welcome departure that tries to escape the selfishness of gene-centered approaches and looks to the implied motivational mechanisms. All these approaches, however, to include that of de Waal's, have been based on the external observation of behavior. They have not attempted to identify or even speculate upon the neural mechanisms within the organism that must necessarily have been selected for by the evolutionary process to accomplish the functions of motivating, maintaining, and rewarding such observed reciprocal behavior.

I suggest it is time now to consider fully what the newer findings of neuroscience add to the discussions from the gene-centered and ethological perspectives. I think that at this time in our evolutionary thinking, it has been established beyond any reasonable doubt, by the work of Hamilton, Trivers, Alexander, Maynard Smith, et al., that even from the most hard-core selfish gene perspective, the basis for the closely related behaviors of reciprocity, cooperation, and altruism has, from the Darwinian or the Neo-Darwinian perspective, been established in the human genome (e.g., see the summary in Corning 1996). The presence of these behaviors has further been confirmed by quantities of observational data in primates, even in studies of early protohuman hominids (Isaac 1978), and by extensive anthropological and sociological observation.

In other words, we now know that we must have, wired into our brain and nervous system, the neural mechanisms that make such behaviors possible. It is time, therefore, with the full emergence of neuroscience, to make every effort to identify and specify these brain mechanisms and extrapolate the implications of their presence and functioning for our personal and social lives. Although it has failed to adequately incorporate the literature of evolutionary neuroscience, this is, in fact, the thrust of the emergent subdiscipline of evolutionary psychology (Cosmides & Tooby 1989; Tooby & Cosmides 1989; Barkow, Cosmides, & Tooby 1992; Crawford & Krebs 1998; Buss 1999).

THE EVOLUTION OF THE MARKET

To understand the behavior of the modern day free enterprise market as it is shaped by our inherited brain structure and behavior, it is helpful to go back to early times—to reconstruct as best we can the days before the market appeared.

The Family or Group Bond

In those times, when people consumed what they produced, the excess that they shared with, gave to, or provided for the needs or demands of the family or community was in the nature of natural affection or empathy. The reward for the empathetic, supplying act was emotional—there was not a specific, but a diffuse value assigned to it. It also had social effects—the givers, providers gaining status in the group. The emotional and the social effects were both directly governed by the reciprocal algorithms of behavior.

Let us look more closely. The provider, say the warrior brought meat from the hunt or the wife brought berries and fruits from the field, tanned skins, and so on, to give to the family or group (cf. Willhoite 1981: 242). The act of providing, giving, created behavioral tension in the giver, who acting empathetically denied ego to some degree and required a response of acknowledgment, gratitude, respect, affection, or some other reaffirmation of ego. This providing or giving also created behavioral tension in the receivers. It was a service to their ego, their needs or demands—to their own preservation—which created tension requiring an offsetting empathetic response, a thank-you, an expression of appreciation or respect. In any family or close group, even now, this dynamic flows constantly, even in the smallest activities. In the small group the rewards, the reciprocations, are largely not quantified, but are diffuse. They become obligations—bonds—that hold the group together for protection or mutual survival. Nevertheless, they must achieve some approximation of balance or the unresolved tension will build within the group and become disruptive. Expressions for *thank you* and *you're welcome*, found in all known human languages, reflect this reciprocity.

The Gift

From these early, primitive behavioral exchanges, emerged the gift: an empathetic act of providing or serving that followed the same algorithmic behavioral rules that governed provision for survival. It created tension in the giver—an expectation of reciprocity—and tension in the receiver, who was bound to reciprocate. The rewards associated with the gift were diffuse, unspecified, unquantified—except by some subjective measure of feeling, emotion, or behavioral tension. A gift to a warrior or chief might vaguely obligate his protection. A gift to a prospective mate might vaguely obligate his or her attentions.

From Gift to Transaction

From the gift evolved the transaction—namely the gift with the reciprocal specified or quantified. The transaction is the beginning of the contract, perhaps of the market itself. The transaction operates, however, by the same algorithms of behavior as the gift—except that it attempts to head off the residual, unresolved behavioral tension that creates a condition of obligation or bonding. After all, in the market, we may be dealing with strangers not to be seen again. Nevertheless, it retains its essential mammalian characteristics as an act of empathy, of nurturing, which requires a balancing reciprocal act in payment to ego.

When we encounter its equivalent in the impersonalized market economy of today, how often do we feel the subjective experience of the transaction? We take our sick child to the doctor, who empathetically and carefully applies the knowledge it took 10 years and a fortune to gain. We pay the bill—that is, we make a return gift with money that represents a portion of our accumulated education and labor. The scenario is repeated in transactions with the plumber, the carpenter, the computer maker. The behavioral algorithms still apply, but the feeling, the subjective experience has to a large degree been lost.

Behavioral Tension Yet Drives the Transaction

But wait! Let the transaction go wrong, the expected reciprocals not be forthcoming and the behavioral tension becomes immediately and personally felt. The reality of the transaction—the market—reveals itself with clarity and intensity. No one likes to be cheated or short-changed. And most will be motivated to take some action to correct the imbalance in expected reciprocity or harbor the behavioral tension indefinitely to be acted upon in the future.

The evolution of the transactional market (demand and supply) as shaped by neural architecture can be summarized in Figure 18.4.

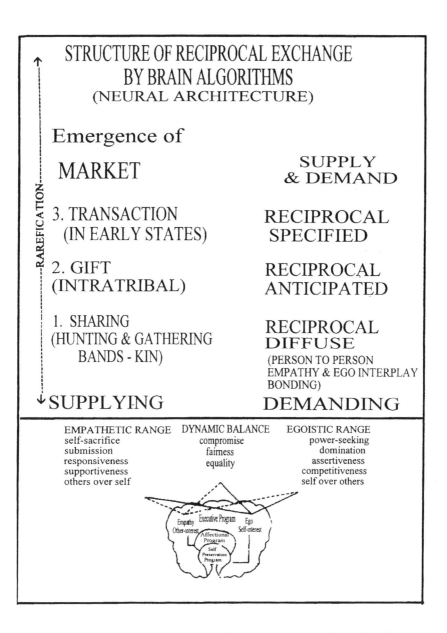

Figure 18.4. Evolution of Market Exchange Based on Dynamics of Neural Architecture

METAECONOMICS AND MULTIPLE-UTILITY

From the transactional perspective, the CSN model also provides under-pinning for what is called metaeconomics and the question of multiple utilities (Lynne 1999, 2000; Lutz 1993; Etzioni 1986). The CSN model shows that the tug and pull between ego and empathy goes on constantly within us and between us as we interact socially. To the extent that our economic transactions or choices are social, and they inevitably are, they will involve the tug-and-pull of ego and empathy to some degree. The very nature of social or market exchange is transactional or interpersonal. The idea that we make independent choices separate from interpersonal or social concerns is largely illusional. The transac-tional atom when opened up is shown to be composed of ego and empathy in a state of negotiated tension (Cory 1999: 77–78). There is therefore some degree of behavioral tension from the tug and pull of ego and empathy, an implicit, if not actual, dual or multiple motive or perhaps utility on both sides in every social or market choice or transaction. The degree of tug and pull or behavioral tension will depend upon the triviality or significance of the transaction—something neoclassical theory does not discriminate.

The confounding of *self-reference* with *self-interest* is a fundamental fallacy of the neoclassical approach that allows the subsuming of all motives under the rubric of self-interest and obscures the roughly equal role of empathy. Taking the individual as the starting point, microeconomic theory mistakenly *transforms* this individual or self-referential *perspective* into an all-inclusive *motive* of self-interest. From this logically unwarranted transformation any other motive is seen as proceeding from self. Therefore empathy (and its derivatives of cooper-ation and altruism, even love) can be trivialized as tastes or preferences indis-tinguishable in significance from coffee, tea, or milk. But the hidden duality of ego and empathy is seen in every demand curve and supply curve, especially when both are combined to show price equilibrium. The dual roles are always present implicitly if not explicitly. The supplier performs the empathetic role; the demander performs the egoistic role. (See Appendix 18.1 for examples of the hidden duality of ego and empathy within the customary self-referential neo-classical perspective.)

In terms of physics, the neural network architecture of ego and empathy may be seen as interlocked, often conflictual motive forces, each with its own moti-vated vector, which in their interactional dynamic produce a resultant vector that determines choice. But the organic, neural dynamic is more complex than the representation as forces of physics suggests. The choice does not necessarily mark the once and for all release or resolution of behavioral tension, as assumed in the mathematical representations of classical economics. Owing to the neural capacity for memory combined with emotion, important choices may carry a residual of behavioral tension that may be cumulative in its social effects. And the organic social algorithm is, further, homeostatic in its function—like other algorithmic physiological regulatory processes of the body (e.g., blood sugar, body temperature) that serve to adjust function and behavior to keep us, for the most part, within survival limits.

THE INVISIBLE HAND IN THE STRUCTURE AND BEHAVIOR OF THE MARKETPLACE

To understand the function of the invisible hand in the socio-economic market, it helps to maintain a clear distinction between structure and behavior.

Structure

The invisible hand as the tug and pull of ego and empathy is expressed in the market structure as *demand* and *supply*. The reciprocal dynamic tends to work despite the unidimensional overemphasis on self-interest in classical economics by the fallacy of self-reference. This is because the *very structure* itself of the market is the institutionalized product of the ego/empathy dynamic of our evolved neural architecture. Our self-survival ego *demand*s are rooted ultimately in our ancestral protoreptilian or vertebrate neural complexes. Contrastingly, the act of *providing* or *supplying*, is fundamentally an act of mammalian nurturing. The market exchange system originated from this dynamic. The market could never have evolved or been maintained on the basis of ego or self-interest alone. Without empathy we would not know how or what to do to respond to the needs of others.

Behavior

Behavior, in individual choices and transactions within the above institutionalized structure, may vary considerably in the mix of ego and empathy motives on both the demand and supply sides. Nevertheless, even in the most ego-skewed (or self-interested) market behavior, the overall *tendency* of the market will be toward a balance of ego and empathy. Individual and collective actors, whether seemingly motivated primarily by self-interest or not, will be compelled by the very evolved and institutionalized market structure itself—to survive in the market—to perform the structural equivalent of empathy. That is, they will be required to provide (supply) a proper service or product to fill the needs (demand) of others.

To the degree, however, that empathy is a *consciously* included and recognized *behavioral* motivational component within the *market structure*, the product or service provided may be enhanced in quality and the emergence of trust in market relationships will be facilitated. Conversely, the overemphasis on self-interest in the neoclassical paradigm tends to vitiate the development of quality and the emergence of trust in the market. Aside from the scientifically inaccurate concept of the market in neoclassical economics, this vitiation of quality and trust is one of its greatest drawbacks, in practice.

Reciprocity through conflict is achieved in the range of dynamic balance where behavioral tension operating freely *tends* to pull us. In dynamic balance, ego and empathy provide for the emergence of *cooperation and fairness, trust and morality,* in interpersonal, social, and economic exchange activities. Taking the dynamic balance range to be approaching or approximating the equilibrium of ego and empathy as driven by behavioral tension, we can derive the formula:

BT (behavioral tension) = Ego/Empathy[19] = ±1 (as dynamic equilibrium or
unity, dynamic balance)

or

$$BT = \frac{Ego}{Emp} = \pm 1 \text{ (approx. equilibrium or unity)}$$
dynamic balance

The above formula (with either ego or empathy as the numerator or denominator to avoid the inconvenience of fractions) gives basic mathematical expression to interaction of ego (demand) and empathy (supply). As the two motives intersect freely in the marketplace, we *tend* to have equitable exchange—or in the case of specific products and services, we *tend* toward equilibrium price, or fair price. (See Appendix 18.2 for the clarifying effect of the above formula on the standard treatment in calculus for demand and supply.) Since the evolved algorithmic dynamic works imperfectly, I use the word *tend*.

The formula or equation proceeding out of our evolved neural network architecture thus provides the unifying linkage between neuroscience and economics or social exchange theory. The behavioral tension driving toward the proximate dynamic balance between demand and supply in the marketplace accounts for the motive force for the venerable Invisible Hand—that illusive dynamic previously accounted for variously by the hand of Deity, Newtonian mechanics, or other inappropriate physical processes (see Cory 1999: 92–95; Ingrao & Israel 1990).

The marketplace is thus clearly a product of the dynamic of our evolved neurological architecture. The same dynamic formula can be shown to underlie not only market and social exchange but also power relationships, social stratification, relations of inequality, and even cost-benefit analysis. Kept free (by appropriate institutions) of the skewing effects of excessive wealth accumulation and the pressure of powerful special interests, both a democratic free enterprise system and a democratic political system will, in accord with the neural architecture, tend toward a dynamic equilibrium which minimizes economic and political inequalities.

On the other hand, the behavioral tension or inequality within a market system or a political system may be indexed by the same dynamic formula to the extent that it departs from dynamic equilibrium and the ratio begins to diverge increasingly.

THE SOCIAL BRAIN, INCLUSIVE FITNESS, HAMILTON'S RULE, AND THE EQUATION OF OUR NEURAL ARCHITECTURE

I suggest that the equation developed from our neural architecture expresses the central tendency of the social brain proposed by the Group for the

Advancement of Psychiatry (GAP) (Gardner, this volume) as well as representing the motivating mechanism anticipated by the concept of inclusive fitness so central to evolutionary psychology. W. D. Hamilton (1964), in his kin selection model, formalized the issue of how genes for cooperation and altruism could evolve in his kin selection model. The core of this inclusive fitness model is that it weighs the effect of genes not only on the individual that carries them but also on kin individuals who share the same genes. According to what has come to be called Hamilton's rule, genes coding for cooperation, reciprocity or altruism could evolve if the costs of cooperative behavior to the individual were outweighed by the benefits to related individuals carrying the same genes. Hamilton's rule is expressed varyingly as

$$rb - c > 0 \quad \text{or} \quad c < rb$$

In this formula r is the coefficient or degree of relatedness or kin, b is the benefit of the cooperative or altruistic behavior to the kin, and c is the cost of the behavior to the individual. The equation predicts that as r increases, benefits will exceed costs and cooperation, reciprocity, or altruism would be favored by natural selection. Hamilton's rule gives the basic formula for inclusive fitness from the external gene's eye view. Hamilton did not speculate on the actual mechanisms created by the genes to motivate and/or sustain such behavior. The formula of our social neural architecture derived from the CSN model expresses this motivating mechanism and establishes linkage with Hamilton's formula. In other words the equation deriving from the CSN model expresses the function of the neural architecture which the genes actually *did* produce under the terms of Hamilton's rule. The proposed social brain formula can, in fact, be expressed in the same cost/benefit terms that Hamilton uses. Empathy can be considered the cost to the behaving individual, ego can be benefit to the survival requirements of the recipient. Substituting cost and benefit into the formula, we get the gene-based operational mechanism for Hamilton's rule (see Cory 1999: 97–100).

$$BT = \frac{\text{Benefit}}{\text{Cost}} = \pm 1$$

According to the algorithms of our social neural architecture, *any* empathetic, cooperative, or altruistic behavior will serve to improve the odds of survival of self *plus* others inclusively over purely egoistic or self-interested behavior. This is compatible with Hamilton's rule which says that as long as the benefit to related individuals exceeds the cost to the behaving individual, the genes supporting such behavior can be favored by natural selection. Of course, once the neural mechanism, the social architecture, is in place, as it has been for thousands of years, the empathetic or altruistic behavior may be extended to nonkin—even the universe itself—by appropriate education and socialization through the medium of language that draws upon, modifies, and elaborates the existing neural substrate (e.g., see Buss 1999: 228; cf. MacLean 1990: 562).

CONCLUSION

In conclusion the neural algorithms of our social brain function as competing or conflicting neural networks, both excitatory and mutually inhibitory, interacting with each other within homeostatically prescribed limits (see Levine & Jani this work for a neural network model of the ego/empathy dynamic; cf. Leven 1994). They represent the gene-produced operational mechanism predicted by Hamilton's external gene's eye rule of inclusive fitness. Their interactive dynamic can be mapped on to mathematical operations or formulas identifiable with social stratification and inequality as well as the invisible hand of economic supply and demand. As the ratio diverges from approximation to plus or minus 1 or unity, it serves to index the behavioral tension and stresses among ourselves and within our social and political structures. The equations expressing their dynamic interactions approaching equilibrium or unity as reflected in exchange and political economy are as follows:

Neuroscience:

$$\text{BEHAVIORAL TENSION} = \frac{\text{EGO}}{\text{EMPATHY}} = \pm 1 \text{ (approx. equilibrium or unity)}$$
$$\text{dynamic balance}$$

Social Psychology:

$$\text{INTERPERSONAL TENSION} = \frac{\text{EGO}}{\text{EMP}} = \pm 1 \text{ (approx. equilibrium or unity)}$$
$$\text{dynamic balance}$$

Economics:

$$\text{EQUILIBRIUM PRICE} = \frac{\text{DEMAND}}{\text{SUPPLY}} = \pm 1 \text{ (approx. equilibrium or unity)}$$
$$\text{dynamic balance}$$

Political Economy:

$$\text{POLITICAL TENSION} = \frac{\text{DOMINATION}}{\text{SUBORDINATION}} = \pm 1 \text{ (approx. equilibrium or unity)}$$
$$\text{dynamic balance}$$

Invisible Hand
 Of economics:
 Of politics:

$$\text{BT} = \frac{\text{EGO}}{\text{EMP}} = \pm 1 \text{ (approx. equilibrium or unity)}$$
$$\text{dynamic balance}$$

The CSN model, emerging from evolved neural architecture, not only offers a mathematically represented mechanism for the social brain of psychiatry, it permits the unifying of evolutionary neuroscience with the central inclusive fitness concept of evolutionary psychology. Further, it anchors market theory firmly in neuroscience and supports the introduction of the moral component of empathy into the rational calculus of economics and other social sciences. The model supports on-going efforts in economics and sociology to introduce cooperation and fairness, trust and morality into the neoclassical calculus and definitively counters the long-prevailing, inaccurate, and troubling self-interested bias of received microeconomic theory. The CSN model provides the basis for a new research program to develop and test the hypotheses proceeding therefrom and to explore the potential implications for rethinking aspects of contemporary economic and political policy.

APPENDIX 18.1
NEURAL ARCHITECTURE AND THE DUALITY OF THE MARKET

The Demand, Supply, and Equilibrium curves that follow are presented in very simplified form. They, nevertheless, illustrate the essential features of all such curves.

I. The Demand Curve

Price	Quantity
$50	1 unit
$30	3 units
$10	5 units

The demand curve slopes downward because as price increases on the y-axis, the quantity people are willing and able to buy generally decreases (x-axis). Even the single actor perspective of the demand curve shows the duality of exchange expressive of our neural architecture: Price = give = empathy; Quantity = take = ego. In other words, price is what we give, quantity is what we take. The demand curve, therefore, illustrates the reciprocal, give-and-take, empathy-ego social exchange relationship.

II. The Supply Curve

Price	Quantity
$50	5 units
$30	3 units
$10	1 unit

Price per unit

The supply curve slopes upward because as price increases (y-axis) suppliers are willing and able to provide more units. The supply curve, like the demand curve, shows the duality of exchange expressive of our neural architecture. From this perspective: Quantity provided = give = empathy; Price = take = ego. Again, the supply curve illustrates a reciprocal, give-and-take, empathy-ego social exchange relationship.

III. Equilibrium in the Market

Price	Quantity Supply	Demand
$50	5 units	1 unit
$30	3 units	3 units
$10	1 unit	5 units

Price per unit

The duality of exchange expressive of our neural architecture is most clearly seen in the graph of demand and supply curves combined to show their equilibrium point. The supplier performs the empathetic structural or institutional role; the demander performs the egoistic structural or institutional role. In standard economics the demand and supply curves are related only at the point of equilibrium.

The formula derived from our neural architecture provides a significant insight:

$$BT = EP \text{ (equilibrium price)} = \frac{\text{Demand}}{\text{Supply}} = \pm 1 \text{ (approx equilibrium or unity)}$$
dynamic balance

In economics price is treated as exogenous. That is, demand and supply curves are related only at the equilibrium price. Price as an exogenous variable draws them together but remains essentially unexplained. The formula from neural architecture demonstrates the continuing relationship between demand and supply and the source of motivation for change that brings demand and supply into equilibrium—behavioral tension that motivates buyers and sellers to change their behavior. Thus, all points on the demand and supply curves that do not match the equilibrium point are indicators of behavioral tension. This effectively unifies the dynamics of neural architecture with economics.

The Problems with Empathy as a Preference or Taste

Currently economics proceeding from the self-reference perspective treats self-interest as the only primary motive. Empathy is treated as a taste or preference. The problems with such treatment are:

1. Empathy becomes optional. You may have such a taste or preference or not. This is distorting because empathy is not optional but a fundamental motive of our neural architecture roughly equal with self-interest or ego.
2. It trivializes empathy. Empathy as a preference or taste is indistinguishable from a taste or preference for Fords or Mercedes or for tennis shoes or sandals.
3. It distortingly forces a rational self-interested perspective.
4. It misconstrues the real nature of the market.
5. It obscures the dynamic shaping effect of the ego/empathy interplay in all social exchange.
6. It is not consilient with evolutionary neuroscience—a more fundamental science.

APPENDIX 18.2: CALCULUS IN PRICE THEORY

As represented in standard texts (e.g., see Landsburg 1992) on price theory, demand and supply are functions that convert prices to quantities.

$$D(P) = \text{Quantity demanded at price P}$$

$$S(P) = \text{Quantity supplied at price P}$$

Derivatives are expressed as follows:

The fact that the demand curve slopes downward is expressed by the inequality

$$D'(P) < 0 \quad \text{OR} \quad \frac{dQd}{dP} < 0$$

The fact that the supply curve slopes upward is expressed by the inequality

$$S'(P) > 0 \quad \text{OR} \quad \frac{dQs}{dP} > 0$$

Equilibrium price is the price at which

$$D(P) = S(P)$$

Equilibrium quantity is the common value.

Again, in this case as well as in the illustrations of the demand, supply, and equilibrium curves, when treated in the standard manner demand and supply are related *only* at the point of equilibrium—the equilibrium price. Price, again, is an exogenous variable that brings them together but remains essentially unexplained. Demand and supply are treated separately prior to the equilibrium point. The calculus model used in economics as reflected above does not represent the relationship of behavioral tension that *exists at all other points*. The formula from neural architecture does this:

$$BT = EP = \frac{DEMAND}{SUPPLY} = \pm 1 \text{ (unity, approx. equil.)} \quad \text{dynamic balance}$$

This reinforces or confirms the previous insight that all other points (prices) on the demand and supply curves are indicators of behavioral tension. Behavioral tension in equilibrium, then, equals price in equilibrium, and price or behavioral tension not in equilibrium is what motivates demanders and suppliers to alter prices or respond to them. Such is the essence of any negotiating process in the market, no matter how formalized. It is seen clearly in domestic flea markets and in many similar institutions (e.g., bazaars) around the world. Price, thus, becomes an endogenous variable; that is, one that we can explain or account for (Cory 2001a, b).

NOTES

1. See Reiner (1990) and Campbell (1992). A great deal of unreflective and inaccurate criticism of MacLean's position by Reiner and Campbell is obviated by a close reading of MacLean's recent work.

2. Cory (1998, 1999) documents in detail the inaccuracies and misrepresentations of MacLean's work in the reviews by Reiner (1990) and Campbell (1992), which have been relied on by other scholars. Cory concludes that the triune brain concept, when properly represented, is soundly grounded in evolutionary neuroscience, and with some clarifications, is the most useful concept for linking neuroscience with the more highly integrated concepts of the social sciences. Although the concept may lack the desired

precision for some neurophysiological researchers, as modified in this paper it is totally adequate and useful for the behavioral propositions put forth here.

3. For example, see Humphrey (1976), Isaac (1978), Erdal and Whiten (1996), Cummins (1998), and Tooby and DeVore (1987). Cosmides and Tooby surmise that cognitive development in humans allowed a widening and diversification of items of social exchange (1989: 59).

4. For earlier versions of the behavioral model developed here see Cory (1974, 1992, 1996). Also compare the model of human communication by Dingwall (1980) based in reflexive(striatal or reptilian) affective (limbic or paleo mammalian), and cognitive (neocortical or neomammalian). Dingwall draws upon Lamendella (1977). See also Leven (1994).

5. Experimental work in animals as diverse as lizards and monkeys shows the reptilian complex is involved in displays of agonistic and defensive social communication. Also it is noteworthy that partial destruction of the reptilian complex eliminates the aggressive, territorial display (MacLean 1993: 108).

6. The division of function between the protoreptilian complex and the limbic system is not clear cut, but rather entangled. The lower structures of the limbic node have been shown to augment the self-preservational behavior of feeding, fighting, and self-protection (MacLean 1990, 1993: 109), adding passion or emotion to them (Kandel, et. al. 1995: 595–612). The newer structures in the upper half of the limbic node, especially the septal, including the medial preoptic area, and thalamocingulate division, are involved in the affectional, family-related behavior (Panksepp 1998; Numan & Sheehan 1997; Fleming et. al. 1996; MacLean 1993: 109).

7. Positing the affectional programming draws not only upon current neuroscience but also the extensive literature on the concepts of social bonding and attachment, especially the work done on higher primates and man. For fundamental work on lower animals see the pioneering work of the Austrian ethologist and Nobel prize winner Konrad Lorenz (1970 & 1971). Particularly relevant here would be the work of psychologist, Harry F. Harlow on the nature of love and attachment in rhesus/macaque monkeys (1965, 1986). Harlow described five affectional systems in monkeys—maternal, mother-infant, age-mate, heterosexual, and paternal (1986). In this chapter I have proposed one all-inclusive affectional program. It is personally interesting to me that Crews (1997) argues that affiliative behaviors evolved from reproductive behaviors. This is a position that I took in 1974 in the first version of the conflict systems neurobehavioral model (Cory 1974) presented in this chapter. There has been a recent resurgence of interest in the evolutionary biological basis of affection and empathy, especially in primates (e.g., Goodall 1986; de Waal 1996). In the case of humans, the work of Spitz (1965) and British psychiatrist John Bowlby (1969, 1988) is of special interest. All the foregoing reflect field observations, experimental behavioral observations and clinical work. None of them penetrate the brain itself. More recent work in computer modeling of neural processes has focused primarily on cognition and avoided dealing with the more complex issues of affiliation and emotion. For example, Churchland and Sejnowski in their extensive and well known work on the computational brain acknowledge the neglect of these critical areas (1992: 413). From the standpoint of neuroscience, it is also notable that Kandel, Schwartz, and Jessell, authors of the most widely used text on introductory neuroscience also show this neglect (1995). See also Damasio 1999. Extensive research has been done on the role of the amygdala in emotion, but such research has generally focused on the emotion of fear (LeDoux 1997). The neglect is not difficult to explain. Research on such complex pathways within the brain, in spite of great progress in recent years, is still in its very early stages. The unknowns are still very vast. Currently the best summary of research in neuroscience on the nurturing, caring, family-related behavior are contained

in Panksepp (1998); Numan and Sheehan (1997); Fleming et al. (1996); MacLean (1990: 380–410; 520–562). For a popular treatment see Taylor (2002)

8. In cognitive neuroscience brain modules are commonly seen as competing and also cooperating (e.g., see Crick 1994, Baars 1997). The idea of competing or conflicting modules contriving behavioral tension is also acknowledged by Pinker (1997: 58, 65).

9. The evolution of the neocortex, our big brain, was in all probability greatly enhanced by the tug and pull of our conflicting programs. Humphrey (1976) sees the function of the intellect providing the ability to cope with problems of interpersonal relationships. See also the discussion in Masters (1989: 16–26) and Erdal and Whiten (1996). Cummins (1998) argues that interpersonal relationships, competing and cooperating with conspecifics for limited resources, is the chief problem confronting social mammals. Cummins concentrates on dominance hierarchies which she sees as dynamic rather than static.

10. Damasio's "somatic marker" hypothesis by which emotions become connected by learning to certain behavioral scenarios is an example of a functional mechanism for producing behavioral tension/stress (1994: 165–201). Also see the comment on chronic mental stress (1994: 119–120). Tension and stress are mediated by hormones and neurotransmitters acting within neural architecture, rather than through the so-called hydraulic pressure model of earlier psychodynamic models.

11. A language module did not, of course, pop out of nowhere and appear in the neocortex. The capacity for spoken language involved modifications of supporting anatomical structures including the laryngeal tract, tongue, velum (which can seal the nose from the mouth) and the neural connections that tied in with motor areas necessary for the production of speech. These all evolved relatively concommitantly from the hominid ancestral line and, combined with the elaboration of the neocortical structures of thought and syntax, made language possible. This example of the complexity of language development provides a caveat to avoid overly simplistic one for one specialized module for specific behavioral or functional adaptation positions. The work of Philip Lieberman, a linguistic psychologist at Brown University, is especially relevant for the understanding of this very complex language capability. See the up-to-date treatment of these issues in Lieberman (1998, 2000).

12. The ability to self-consciously generalize is apparently a unique gift of the neocortex with it billions of neurons interconnected into hierarchical networks. The level of generalization issue in all our disciplines likely springs from this. That is, we can move from parts to wholes in generalizing and from wholes to parts in analyzing freely up and down throughout our neural networks. Generalizing (and implicitly analyzing) been recognized by scholars in many disciplines as perhaps the defining characteristic of the human brain (e.g., Hofstader 1995: 75; Einstein 1954: 293). This generalizing capacity loosens up the tight wiring of routines and characteristics of earlier brain structures and allows us to manage and, to some degree, overcome the mechanisms that we inherited in common with kindred species (e.g., see Panksepp 1998: 301). In other words, the generalizing, analyzing capacities of the neocortex change the rules of the game for us humans by freeing us up from the blind tyranny of primitive mechanisms. This capacity must always be weighed when trying to apply findings in, for example, even primate ethology to humans. One of the reasons our feelings and motives are so difficult to verbalize and communicate to others is probably because the earlier evolved brain (reptilian and limbic) systems are nonverbal. Their input enters the neocortex through neural pathways as inarticulate urgings, feelings. It falls to the neocortex with its verbal and generalizing ability to develop words and concepts to attempt to understand, represent, and convey these inarticulate urgings. MacLean (1992: 58) states that the

triune brain structure provides us with the inheritance of three mentalities, two of which lack the capacity for verbal communication.

13. My use of the term empathy here includes the affectional feelings of sympathy which are dependent upon empathy, plus cognitive aspects (Hoffman 1981, 2000). Losco has noted that empathy, amplified by cognitive processes, could serve as an evolved mediator of pro-social behavior (1986: 125). Empathy and sympathy are frequently used inclusively, especially in more recent writing (Eisenberg 1994; Batson 1991). For this reason, in order to suggest the inclusion of sympathy, I have chosen to use the term empathetic rather than the more usual empathic. The positing of the ego and empathy dynamic goes back to the historical juxtaposition of self-interest or egoism and sympathy or fellow feeling of in the thought of David Hume, Adam Smith, and Schopenhauer (Wispe 1991). The present articulation goes back to my doctoral thesis done at Stanford University (1974). The conflict systems neurobehavioral model was applied in several programs which I authored for corporate management training through the education and consulting corporation United States Education Systems during the period 1976–85. Recently Roger Masters (1989) has also noted the possible innate roots of contradictory impulses to include selfishness and cooperative or altruistic behavior in human nature.Trudi Miller (1993) has also drawn our attention to this historical duality and suggested its applicability for today. Neither Hume, Smith, Schopenhauer, Wispe, Masters nor Miller, however, attempted to articulate a model of behavior based upon this duality, or as MacLean calls it "triality", acknowledging the role of the neocortex in articulating the otherwise nonverbal urgings (1993).

14. The frontal neocortex especially has long been recognized to be involved in executive functions. See the excellent summary and discussion of findings in Miller and Cummings (1999), Fuster (1997: 150–84). See also Pribram (1973; 1994). Although executive function is frequently equated with frontal cortex function Eslinger (1996) reminds us that the neural substrate of executive functions is better conceptualized as a neural network which includes the synchronized activity of multiple regions, cortical and subcortical (1996: 392). Eslinger also notes the usual neglect of critically important affectively based empathy and social and interpersonal behaviors in neuropsychological, information-processing, and behavioral approaches (390–391).

15. Levine (1986) has also considered MacLean's triune modular concept as a useful tool in network modeling.

16. The dynamic of the model, the tug and pull of ego and empathy, self- and other-interest allows the expression of the mix of motive and behavior as a range or spectrum. The usual dichotomizing of self-interest and altruism is seen only at the extremes of ranges. All or most of behavior is a mix of varying proportions. Jencks (1990: 53–54) also notes that every motive or act falls somewhere on a spectrum or range between the extremes of selfishness and unselfishness. Teske (1997) sees a blend of self-and other-interest in his identity construction concept.

17. See Eckel and Grossman (1997). Without making any connection with brain science or the reciprocal algorithms of behavior, the authors use a typology of fairness (for me, for you, for us) which expresses the conflict systems model and the reciprocal algorithms of behavior.

18. That is, in physics it is not known exactly why and how wave function collapses or reduction occurs and how eigenstates are determined (e.g., see Hameroff & Penrose 1996: 311). The standard Copenhagen Interpretation sees collapse as occurring at randomly measured values when the quantum system interacted with its environment, was otherwise measured, or consciously observed; (e.g., see Stapp's 1972 well-known article on the Copenhagen Interpretation). Penrose (1994) and Hameroff and Penrose (1996) introduce a new physical ingredient they call objective reduction (OR), which

become guided and tuned into orchestrated OR, in which quantum systems can self-collapse by reaching a threshold related to quantum gravity. Harth notes, in summarizing his sketchpad model, that "the transformation from the extended activities in the association areas and working memory to specific mental images may be likened to the collapse of a wave function in quantum mechanics." He does not, however, imply any quantum effect (1997: 1250).

19. Since the formula represents a reciprocal tug and pull dynamic of neural architecture in which the deviation from equilibrium indexes behavioral tension, either ego or empathy may be expressed as numerator or dominator for convenience sake to keep the quotient a whole number and not a fraction (see Cory 1999: 97–100).

REFERENCES

Alexander, Richard D. 1987. *The Biology of Moral Systems.* Hawthorne, NY: Aldine de Gruyter.

Axelrod, R. and Hamilton, W. 1981. "The Evolution of Cooperation." Pp. 1390 in *Science,* V. 211.

Baal, J. van 1975. *Reciprocity and the Position of Women.* Amsterdam: Van Gorcum, Assen.

Baars, Bernard J. 1997. *In the Theatre of Consciousness: The Workspace of the Mind.* Oxford: Oxford University Press.

Baars, Bernard J. 1988. *A Cognitive Theory of Consciousness.* Cambridge: Cambridge University Press.

Bachevalier, J. 2000. "The Amygdala, Social Cognition, and Autism." Pp. 509–543 in *The Amygdala: A Functional Analysis.* ed. by J. P. Aggleton Oxford: Oxford University Press.

Barkow, J., Cosmides, L. and Tooby, J. (Eds.), 1992. *The Adapted Mind: Evolutionary. Psychology and the Generation of Culture.* NY: Oxford University Press.

Batson, C. Daniel. 1991. *The Altruism Question: Toward a Social-Psychological Answer.* Hillsdale, NJ: Lawrence Erlbaum Associates.

Bowlby, John. 1988. *A Secure Base. Parent-Child Attachment and Healthy Human Development.* NY: Basic Books.

Bowlby, John. 1969. *Attachment.* Vol. 1. NY: Basic Books.

Bowles, S. and Gintis, H. 1998. *Recasting Egalitarianism.* London: Verso.

Brothers, L. 1989. " A Biological Perspective on Empathy." *American Journal of Psychiatry,* 146, 10–19.

Brownell, H. and Martino, G. 1998. "Deficits in Inference and Social Cognition: The Effects of Right Hemisphere Brain Damage on Discourse." Pp. 309–328 in *Right Hemisphere Language Comprehension: Perspectives from Cognitive Neuroscience.* Ed. by M. Beeman and C. Chiarello. Mahwah, NJ: Lawrence Erlbaum Associates.

Buss, David M. 1999. *Evolutionary Psychology.* Boston: Allyn and Bacon.

Campbell, C.B.G. 1992. "Book Review (MacLean: The Triune Brain in Evolution)." Pp. 497–498 in *American Scientist,* V. 80 (Sept-Oct 19 1992).

Carter, C. Sue, Lederhendler, I., and Kirkpatrick, B. (Eds.). 1997. *The Integrative Neurobiology of Affiliation.* NY: New York Academy of Sciences, Vol. 807.

Churchland, P. and Sejnowski, T. 1992. *The Computational Brain.* Cambridge, MA: MIT Press.

Corning, Peter A. 1996. "The Cooperative Gene: On the Role of Synergy in Evolution." Pp. 183–207 in *Evolutionary Theory.* V. 11.

Cory, Gerald A., Jr. 2001a. "Neural Network Theory and Neuroscience: Applications to Socio-Economic Theory." *Paper presented at the 13th Annual Meeting on Socio-Economics,* University of Amsterdam, June 28-July 1, 2001.

Cory, Gerald A., Jr. 2001b. "Transaction Costs, the Firm and Evolved Neural Architecture." *Paper presented at the 76th Annual Conference of the Western Economic Association International,* San Francisco, July 4-8.

Cory, Gerald A., Jr. 2000a. "From MacLean's Triune Brain Concept to the Conflict Systems Neurobehavioral Model: "The Subjective Basis of Moral and Spiritual Consciousness." *Zygon: Journal of Religion & Science,* Vol 35. No.2, pp. 385–414.

Cory, Gerald A., Jr. 2000b. *Toward Consilience: The Bioneurological Basis of Thought, Behavior, Language, and Experience.*NY: Kluwer Academic/Plenum.

Cory, Gerald A., Jr. 1999. *The Reciprocal Modular Brain in Economics and Politics: Shaping the Rational and Moral Basis of Organization, Exchange, and Choice.* NY: Plenum Press.

Cory, Gerald A., Jr. 1998. "MacLean's Triune Brain Concept: in Praise and Appraisal." Pp. 6–19, 22–24. *Across-Species Comparisons and Psychopathology Society (ASCAP) Newsletter,* V. 11. No. 07.

Cory, Gerald A., Jr. 1996. *Algorithms, Illusions, and Reality.* Vanc., WA: Ctr for Behavioral Ecology.

Cory, Gerald. A., Jr. 1992. *Rescuing Capitalist Free Enterprise for the Twenty First Century.* Vanc. WA: Ctr for Behavioral Ecology.

Cory, Gerald A., Jr. 1974. *The Biopsychological Basis of Political Socialization and Political Culture.* Ph.D. Dissertation, Stanford University.

Cosmides, Leda and Tooby, John. 1989. "Evolutionary Psychology and the Generation of Culture, Part II." Pp. 51–97 in *Ethology and Sociobiology,* V. 10.

Cowan, W., Jessell, T, and Lipursky, S. (Eds.). 1997. *Molecular and Cellular Approaches to Neural Development.* NY: Oxford University Press.

Crawford, C. and Krebs, D. (Eds.). 1998. *The Handbook of Evolutionary Psychology.* Mahwah, NJ. Lawrence Erlbaum.

Crews, D. 1997. "Species Diversity and the Evolution of Behavioral Controlling Mechanisms." In *The Integrative Neurobiology of Affiliation,* ed. by C. Carter, I. Lederhendler, and B. Kirkpatrick, 1–21. NY: Annals of the New York Academy of Sciences, vol. 809.

Crick, Francis. 1994. *The Astonishing Hypothesis: The Scientific Search for the Soul.* NY: Charles Scribner's Sons.

Cummins, Denise D. 1998. "Social Norms and Other Minds: The Evolutionary Roots of Higher Cognition." Pp. 30–50 in *The Evolution of Mind.* Ed. by D. Cummins, D. and C. Allen. Oxford: Oxford University Press.

Damasio, Antonio. 1999. *The Feeling of What Happens.* NY: Harcourt.

Damasio, Antonio. 1994. *Descartes Error: Emotion, Reason, and the Human Brain.* NY: Grosset/Putnam.

Davidson, R. J. 1995. "Cerebral Asymmetry, Emotion, and Affective style." Pp. 361-387 in *Brain Asymmetry.* Ed. by R. J. Davidson and K. Hugdahl. Cambridge, MA: MIT Press.

Dennett, Daniel C. 1998. "Reflections on Language and Mind." Pp. 284–293 in *Language and Thought.* Ed. by P. Carruthers and J. Boucher. Cambridge, MA: Cambridge University Press.

de Waal, Frans de. 1996. *Good Natured: The Origins of Right and Wrong in Humans and Other Animals.* Cambridge, MA: Harvard University Press.

Devinsky, Orrin and Luciano, Daniel. 1993. "The Contributions of Cingulate Cortex to Human Behavior." Pp. 5275–56 in *Neurobiology of Cingulate Cortex and Limbic Thalamus: A Comprehensive Handbook.* Ed. by B. Vogt, and M. Gabriel. Boston: Birhauser.

Dingwall, J. 1980. "Human Communicative Behavior: A Biological Model." Pp. 1–86 in *The Signifying Animal.* Ed. by I. Rauch and G. Carr. Bloomington, IN: Indiana University Press.

Durfee, E. H. 1993. "Cooperative Distributed Problem-Solving Between (and within) Intelligent Agents." Pp. 84–98 in *Neuroscience: From Neural Networks to Artificial Intelligence.* Ed. by P. Rudomin et al. Heidelberg: Springer-Verlag.

Eckel, Catherine C. and Grossman, Philip. 1997. "Equity and Fairness in Economic Decisions: Evidence from Bargaining Experiments." Pp. 281–301 in *Advances in Economic Psychology.* Ed. by G. Antonides and W. F. van Raaij. NY: John Wiley.

Edelman, G. 1992. *Bright Air, Brilliant Fire.* NY: Basic Books.

Edelman, G. and Tononi, G. 2000. *A Universe of Consciousness.* NY: Basic Books.

Einstein, A. 1954. "Physics and Reality." Pp. 290–323 in *Ideas and Opinions.*NY: Crown.

Eisenberg, Nancy. 1994. "Empathy." Pp. 247–253 in *Encylopedia of Human Behavior.* Ed. by V. S. Ramachandran. NY: Academic Press.

Erdal, David and Whiten, Andrew. 1996. "Egalitarianism and Machiavellian Intelligence in Human Evolution." Pp. 139–150 in *Modelling the Early Human Mind.* Ed. by P. Mellars and K. Gibson. Cambridge: The McDonald Institute.

Eslinger, Paul. J. 1996. "Conceptualizing, Describing, and Measuring Components of Executive Function." Pp. 367–395 in *Attention, Memory, and Executive Function.* Ed. by G. Lyon and N. Krasnegor. Baltimore: Paul H. Brookes Publishing Co.

Etzioni, A. 1988. *The Moral Dimension: Toward a New Economics.* NY: MacMillan.

Etzioni, A. 1986. "The Case for a Multiple-Utility Conception." *Economics and Philosophy*, 2: 159–183.

Fehr, Ernst and Simon Gachter. 2000. "Fairness and Retaliation: The Economics of Reciprocity." *Journal of Economic Perspectives.* V. 14, N. 3: 159–181.

Fleming, Alison S., Morgan, H. and Walsh, C. 1996. "Experiential Factors in Postpartum Regulation of Maternal Care." Pp. 295-332 in *Parental Care: Evolution, Mechanisms, and Adaptive Intelligence.* Ed. by J. Rosenblatt and C. Snowden. NY: Academic Press.

Fuster, J. M 1999. "Cognitive Functions of the Frontal Lobes." Pp. 187–195 in *The Human Frontal Lobes.* Ed. by B. Miller and J. Cummings. NY: The Guilford Press.

Fuster, J. M. 1997. *The Prefrontal Cortex: Anatomy, Physiology, and Neuro-psychology of the Frontal Lobe.* Third Edition. NY: Lippincott-Raven.

Gazzaniga, M. S. 1985. *The Social Brain: Discovering the Networks of the Mind.* NY: Basic Books.

Goldberg, Elkhonon. 2001. *The Executive Brain: Frontal Lobes and the Civilized Mind.* NY: Oxford University Press.

Goodall, Jane. 1986. *The Chimpanzees of Gombe: Patterns of Behavior.* Cambridge, MA: Harvard University Press.

Gouldner, Alvin. 1960. "The Norm of Reciprocity; A Preliminary Statement." *American Sociological Review*, 25: 161–178.

Grossman, J., Carter, A., Volkmar, F. 1997. "Social Behavior in Autism." Pp. 440–454 in *The Integrative Neurobiology of Affiliation.* Ed. by C. S. Carter, I. Lederhendler and B. Kirkpatrick. NY: Annals of the NY Academy of Sciences (Vol. 809).

Gutnick, M. J. and Mody, I. (Eds.). 1995. *The Cortical Neuron.* Oxford: Oxford University Press.

Hameroff, S. and Penrose, R. 1996. "Orchestrated Reduction of Quantum Coherence in Brain Microtubules: A Model for Consciousness." Pp. 507–39 in *Toward a Science of Consciousness: The First Tuscon Discussions and Debates.* Ed. by S. Hameroff, A. Kaszniak, and A. Scott. Cambridge, MA: The MIT Press.

Hamilton, W. D. 1964. "The Genetical Evolution of Social Behavior, I & II." Pp. 1–16, & 17–52 in *Journal of Theoretical Biology*, V. 7.

Harlow, Harry. F. 1986. *From Learning to Love: The Selected Papers of H. F. Harlow.* Ed. by C. Harlow. NY: Praeger.

Harlow, Harry F and Harlow, M. K. 1965. "The Affectional Systems." Pp. 386–334 in *Behavior of Non-Human Primates.* Ed. by A. M. Schrier, H. F. Harlow, and F. Stollnitz. NY: Academic Press.

Harrington, Anne (Ed). 1992. *So Human a Brain.* Boston: Birkhauser.

Harth, Erich. 1997. "From Brains to Neural Nets." Pp. 1241–1255 in *Neural Networks,* V. 10. N. 7.

Heller, Wendy; Nitschke, J. and Miller, G. 1998. "Lateralization in Emotion and Emotional Disorders." Pp. 26–32 in *Current Directions in Psychological Science,* Vol. 7. N.1.

Hoffman, M. 2000. *Empathy and Moral Development.* Cambridge: Cambridge University Press.

Hoffman, M. 1981. "Is Altruism Part of Human Nature?" Pp. 121–137 in *Journal of Personality and Social Psychology,* 40.

Hofstader, Douglas. 1995. *Fluid Concepts and Creative Analogies.* NY: Basic Books.

Humphrey, N. K. 1976. "The Function of the Intellect." Pp. 303–317 in *Growing Points in Ethology.* Ed. by P.P.G. Bateson and R. H. Hinde. Cambridge: Cambridge University Press.

Ingrao, Bruna and Israel, G. 1990. *The Invisible Hand: Economic Equilibrium in the History of Science.* Trans. by I. McGilvray. Cambridge: Cambridge University Press.

Isaac, Glynn. 1978. "The Food-sharing Behavior of Protohuman Hominids." Pp. 90–108 in *Scientific American,*. V. 238.

Jencks, Christopher. 1990. "Varieties of Altruism." Pp. 53–67 in *Beyond Self-Interest.* Ed. by Jane J. Mansbridge. Chicago: University of Chicago Press.

Kandel, E. R., Schwartz, J.and Jessell, T. 1995. *Essentials of Neural Science and Behavior.* Norwalk, CT: Appleton & Lange.

Koch, Christof. 1999. *Biophysics of Computation: Information Processing in Single Neurons.* NY: Oxford University Press.

Kohlberg, Lawrence. 1984. *The Psychology of Moral Development.* V. 2. San Francisco: Harper & Row.

LaBerge, D. L. 1995. *Attentional Processing: The Brain's Art of Mindfulness.* Cambridge, MA: Harvard University Press.

Lamendella, J. 1977. "The Limbic System in Human Communication." Pp. 157–222 in *Studies in Neurolinguistics.* Vol. 3. Ed. by H. Whitaker and H. A. Whitaker. NY: Academic Press.

Landsburg, S. E. 1992. *Price Theory and Applications.* NY: The Dryden Press.

LeDoux, Joseph E. 1997. *The Emotional Brain.* NY: Simon & Schuster.

Leven, Samuel J. 1994. "Semiotics, Meaning, and Discursive Neural Networks." Pp. in 65–82 in *Neural Networks for Knowledge Representation and Inference.* Ed. by D. Levine, and M. Aparicio. Hillsdale, NJ: Lawrence Erlbaum Associates.

Levine, Daniel S. 1986. "A Neural Network Theory of Frontal Lobe Function." Pp, 716–727 in *Proceedings of the Eighth Annual Conference of the Cognitive Science Society.* Hillsdale, NJ: Lawrence Erlbaum Associates.

Lieberman, Philip. 2000. *Human Language and Our Reptilian Brain*. Cambridge, MA: Harvard University Press.

Lieberman, Philip. 1998. *Eve Spoke*. New York: Norton.

Lorenz, Konrad. 1970 & 1971. *Studies in Animal and Human Behavior*. Vol. 1 & 2. Trans. by R. Martin. Cambridge, MA: Harvard University Press.

Losco, Joseph. 1986. "Biology, Moral Conduct, and Policy Science." Pp. 117-144 in *Biology and Bureaucracy*. Ed. by E. White and J. Losco. Lanham, MD: University Press of America.

Lutz, Mark A. 1993. "The Utility of Multiple Utility: A Comment on Brennan. "*Economics and Philosophy*, 9: 145–154.

Lynne, Gary. 2000. "A Metaeconomics Look at the Case for a Multiple-Utility Conception." Prepared for *Roundtable at 12th Annual Meeting Society for the Advancement of Socio-Economics*, London School of Economics, July 7–11, 2000.

Lynne, Gary. 1999. "Divided Self Models of the Socioeconomic Person: The Meta-economics Approach." *Journal of Socio-Economics* 28: 267–288.

MacLean, Paul D. 1993. "Human Nature: Duality or Triality." Pp. 107–112 in *Politics and the Life Sciences*. V. 12. N. 2.

MacLean, Paul .D. 1992. "Obtaining Knowledge of the Subjective Brain." Pp. 57–70 in *So Human a Brain*. Ed. by Anne Harrington. Boston: Birkhauser.

MacLean, Paul D. 1990. *The Triune Brain in Evolution: Role in Paleocerebral Functions*. NY: Plenum.

Masters, R D. 1989. *The Nature of Politics*. New Haven, CT: Yale University Press.

Mauss, Marcel. 1954. *The Gift*. Trans. by I. Cunnison. NY: Norton.

Maynard Smith, J. 2002. "Equations of Life." Pp. 193–211 in *It Must be Beautiful: Great Equations of Modern Science*. Ed. by G. Farmelo. London: Granta Books.

Maynard Smith, J. 1982. "The Evolution of Social Behavior–a Classification of Models." Pp. 28–44 in *Current Problems in Sociobiology*. Ed. by King's College Sociobiology Group. Cambridge: Cambridge University Press.

Mead, G. H. 1934. *Mind, Self, and Society*. Chicago: University of Chicago Press.

Meaney, M. 2001. "Maternal Care, Gene Expression, and the Transmission of Individual Differences in Stress Reactivity Across Generations." *Annual Review of Neuro-science*, 24: 1161–1192.

Miller, Bruce L. and Jeffrey L. Cummings,.J. L. (Eds.). 1999. *The Human Frontal Lobes*. NY: The Guilford Press.

Miller, T. C. 1993."The Duality of Human Nature." Pp. 221–41 in *Politics and the Life Sciences*. V. 12.N. 2.

Minsky, M. 1979. "The Social Theory." Pp. 423–450 in *Artificial Intelligence: An MIT Perspective*. Vol. 1. Ed. by P. Winston and R. Brown. Cambridge, MA: MIT Press.

Mirsky, Allan F. 1996. "Disorders of Attention: A Neuropsychological Perspective." Pp. 71–95 in *Attention, Memory, and Executive Function*. Ed by G. Lyon and N. Krasnegor. Baltimore: Paul H. Brookes Publishing Co.

Newman, James, Baars, B J., and Sung-Bae, Cho. 1997. "A Neural Global Workspace Model for Conscious Attention." Pp. 1195–1206 in *Neural Networks*, Vol 10, N. 7.

Numan, M. 1994. "Maternal Behavior." Pp. 221–302 in *Physiology of Reproduction*. 2nd edition. Vol. 2. Ed. by E. Knobil and J. Neill. NY: Raven Press.

Numan, M. and Sheehan, T. 1997. "Neuroanatomical Circuitry for Mammalian Maternal Behavior." Pp. 101–125 in *The Integrative Neurobiology of Affiliation*. Ed. by C. S. Carter, I. Lederhendler, and B. Kirkpatrick. NY: New York Academy of Sciences, Vol. 807.

Panksepp, Jaak. 1998. *Affective Neuroscience*. NY: Oxford University Press.

Penrose, Roger. 1994. *Shadows of the Mind*. London: Oxford University Press.

Piaget, Jean. 1977. *The Development of Thought.* Trans. by A. Rosen. NY: Viking Press.

Piaget, Jean. [1932] 1965. *The Moral Judgement of the Child.* NY: Free Press.

Pinker, Steven. 1997. *How the Mind Works.* NY: Norton.

Pribram, Karl H. 1994. "Brain and the Structure of Narrative." Pp. 375–415 in *Neural Networks for Knowledge Representation and Inference.* Ed. by D. Levine and M. Aparicio. Hillsdale, NJ: Lawrence Erlbaum Associates.

Pribram, Karl H. 1973. "The Primate Frontal Cortex–Executive of the Brain." Pp. 293–314 in *Psychophysiology of the Frontal Lobes.* Ed. by K. Pribram and A. Luria. NY: Academic Press.

Reiner, Anton. 1990. "An Explanation of Behavior" (review of MacLean's *The Triune Brain in Evolution*). Pp. 303–305 in *Science,* V. 250 (Oct 12, 1990).

Schnider, A. and Gutbrod, K. 1999. "Traumatic Brain Injury." Pp. 487–505 in *The Human Frontal Lobes.* Ed. by B. Miller and J. Cummings. NY: The Guilford Press.

Searle, J. R. 1997. *The Mystery of Consciousness.* NY: The NY Review of Books.

Sherman, S. and Guillery, R. 2001. *Exploring the Thalamus.* NY: Academic Press.

Smith, Adam. 1911[1789]. *The Theory of Moral Sentiments.* New Edition. London: G. Bell.

Smith, C.U.M. 1996. *Elements of Molecular Neurobiology* (2nd edition), Chichester: Wiley.

Spitz, Rene A. 1965. *The First Year of Life.* NY: International Universities Press.

Stapp, Henry P. 1972. "The Copenhagen Interpretation." Pp. 1098–1116 in *American Journal of Physics,* 40(8).

Taylor, S. E. 2002. *The Tending Instinct.* NY: Henry Holt.

Taylor, S. E., Klein, L. C., Lewis, B. P., Gruenewald, T. L., Gurung, R. A. R., & Updegraff, J. A. 2000. "Biobehavioral responses to stress in females: Tend-and-befriend, not fight-or-flight." *Psychological Review,* 107: 411–429.

Teske, Nathan. 1997. "Beyond Altruism: Identity-Construction as Moral Motive in Political Explanation."Pp.71–91 in *Political Psychology,* V. 18, N. 1.

Toates, Frederick. 2001. *Biological Psychology.* NY: Prentice-Hall.

Tooby, John and Cosmides, Leda. 1989. "Evolutionary Psychology and the Generation of Culture, Part I." Pp. 29–49 in *Ethology and Sociobiology,* V. 10.

Tooby, John and DeVore, I. 1987 "The Reconstruction of Hominid Behavioral Evolution through Strategic Modeling." In *Primate Primate Models for the Origin of Human Behavior.* Ed. by W. G. Kinsey. NY: SUNY Press.

Trivers, R. L. 1981. "Sociobiology and Politics." Pp. 1–44 in *Sociobiology and Human Politics.* Ed. by E. White. Lexington , MA: D.C. Heath & Company.

Trivers, R.L. 1971. "The Evolution of Reciprocal Altruism." Pp. 35–57 in *The Quarterly Review of Biology,* 46.

Tucker, Don M., Luu, Phan, and Pribram, Karl H. 1995. "Social and Emotional Self-Regulation." Pp. 213–239 in *Annals of the New York Academy of Sciences,* V. 769.

Willhoite, F. 1981. "Rank and Recipocity: Speculations on Human Emotions and Political Life." Pp. 239–258 in *Sociobiology and Human Politics.* Ed. by E. White. Lexington, MA: D. C. Heath.

Wispe, Lauren. 991. *The Psychology of Sympathy.* NY: Plenum Press.

19

TOWARD A NEURAL NETWORK THEORY OF THE TRIUNE BRAIN

Daniel S. Levine and Nilendu G. Jani

INTRODUCTION

From the viewpoint of the computational modeler and systems theorist, Paul MacLean's major contribution to behavioral and cognitive neuroscience is not so much his evolutionary perspective. In fact, his great work entails a view of human nature that includes motivations other than mere survival.[1,2,3] Rather, his modular approach commands attention. The functional division of the brain into a part related to habits and instinctive behavior, a part related to emotional and social behavior, and a part related to higher cognitive and semantic processing provides a useful basis for modeling, even if the assignment of brain areas to these parts turns out to differ somewhat from what MacLean has exactly proposed.[4] Many neural network modelers, including the authors of this chapter, have devoted much of their careers to trying to understand what MacLean called the "man, horse, and crocodile" within us[5] and the brain systems that subserve communication between these three "animals." This chapter reports on these efforts.

AN INTELLECTUAL MOVEMENT ABOUT EMOTION

Like many other scientific pioneers, MacLean anticipated an intellectual movement not prominent until years after his major work was published. Emotions are now in vogue, not just in psychology and neuroscience but also in neural network theory and even in artificial intelligence. Many engineers and computer scientists as well as biologists now realize that human and animal emotions represent, among other things, a source of positive and negative values. Such a value source, rather than interfering with rational decision-making, actually facilitates decision-making, as Antonio Damasio[6] showed with his studies of patients whose valuation is blunted through damage to the orbitofrontal cortex.

Before Damasio's book and a few others appeared, emotion often seemed a "dirty word in science,"[7] regarded as inferior to reason, and indeed as a "lower animal" heritage interfering with higher cognition. Yet MacLean is numbered in a relatively small group of behavioral neuroscientists who forthrightly spoke of emotion as an integral part of all decision making. Another, Walle Nauta, anticipated Damasio's "somatic marker" hypothesis as he noted that frequently a plan we decide on rationally does not get implemented if thinking about it makes us feel sick.[8] Still another was Karl Pribram, who did a long series of studies relating arousal and various midbrain and limbic system functions to attentional processing.[9]

While neural networks and artificial intelligence in the early years tended toward the primacy of rationality, several important modelers as early as the 1970s also insisted on the importance of emotional (and instinctive) processes in any theory of biological intelligence. These included Stephen Grossberg, Harry Klopf, Paul Werbos, and Gershom-Zvl Rosenstein.

WHAT NEURAL NETWORKS ARE AND ARE NOT

Neural networks, now a fad, exude a mystique. Yet their study is really nothing more than the quantitative theory of how neural and cognitive systems are organized.[10] (While neural networks are used for engineering purposes as well as biological modeling, the biologically relevant sort are essentially indistinguishable from the large system aspect of computational neuroscience. The distinction between those two terms is more sociological than it is scientific.)

Many people upon hearing the term "neural network" think of a very specific three-layer structure, variously called back propagation networks or multilayer perceptrons, developed by Paul Werbos[11] and popularized by David Rumelhart and James McClelland.[12] This is in fact the type of neural network that has had the widest engineering applications so far because it has some intriguing mathematical properties that enable it to solve a wide class of input-output mapping problems. Yet this is only one of many types of neural networks in the current literature, and not generally regarded as the type closest to the actual architecture of the brain.

So neural networks are not a particular narrow class of structures. Yet, what are they? No definition has gained universal agreement. The closest is probably one developed in 1988 by a team of experts commissioned by the United States Department of Defense:

a neural network is a system composed of many simple processing elements operating in parallel whose function is determined by network structure, connection strengths, and the processing performed at computing elements or nodes . . . Neural network architectures are inspired by the architecture of biological nervous systems, which use many simple processing elements operating in parallel.[13]

The specific type of structures used in neural network models depend on the class of cognitive and behavioral functions they are trying to reproduce. For example, it has been argued that sensory pattern categorization and motor control require fundamentally different types of neural network architectures.[14]

EARLY NEURAL NETWORK MODELS
OF EMOTION, DRIVE, AND REINFORCEMENT

Several early neural network models derived from first principles included drive or motivational representations, particularly models of classical (Pavlovian) conditioning. Grossberg, building on his own previous network models of pattern learning, asked how a network exposed to two or more patterns can learn both patterns without confusing them or learning a meaningless mixture of them.[15] For example, animals can learn that one stimulus predicts food reinforcement and another stimulus predicts sexual reinforcement. Grossberg found that this type of learning was facilitated by having nodes in the network that represent drives such as the hunger and sex drives, in addition to the sensory and motor representations that were included in earlier versions of his network. He postulated these drive sources as analogous to hypothalamus or limbic system areas. Further extensions of this network included both positive and negative drive loci, and opponent processing of changes in affective value of events.[16]

Motivation also played a prime role in the model of Klopf,[2,17] who for a short time worked in the same laboratory as MacLean at Poolesville, Maryland. Klopf regarded the seeking of pleasure and avoidance of pain as the force driving every organism's behavior, and indeed regarded survival (or homeostasis) as a subgoal of net pleasure maximization (for which he coined the term *heterostasis).* This type of "hedonism," Klopf believed, also occurs at the level of single neurons, which "try" to maximize depolarization from other neurons and minimize hyperpolarization. The theory integrated aspects of the triune brain, in that each of the three parts of the brain tries separately to maximize its own positive stimulation. The reticular formation, part of the reptilian brain, is the final arbiter of decisions, and the limbic and neocortical systems have specific functions in implementing those decisions. As with Grossberg's work, this theory evolved into a computational model of the time course of Pavlovian conditioning.[18]

Similar ideas for quantitative representation of emotional variables developed independently in Russia, largely in isolation from Western scientists. There Pavlov's tradition dominated in science, and was encouraged as socially useful by a repressive government interested in emotional control of its people. In this framework Rosenstein developed an abstract neural network model based, as was Klopf's, on the notion that organisms seek to optimize the level of a certain variable.[19,20] By analogy to economics, where such optimization models have always been popular, Rosenstein called this variable *Income.* He related Income to dopamine level, and explained schizophrenic systems in terms of a tendency to seek Income not available from other sources.

The connections with economics are also prevalent in the work of Werbos, whose back propagation network was motivated in part by efforts to develop better and more brain-related predictors of economic time series than were then available.[11,21,22] The basic back propagation model was but one of a series of network architectures Werbos developed, architectures that were designed to maximize (positive) reinforcement. This was done through learning, and an essential feature was to monitor which connection strengths should be changed at any time to most efficiently increase reinforcement. His work and others' led to principles that are known both in biology and in engineering as *reinforcement learning* or *adaptive critic* design.

TRIUNITY IN MODELS OF COGNITIVE TASKS

The last section shows that biologically motivated neural network principles have a longer history than generally believed. Yet another 10 to 20 years would transpire before networks had evolved to the point of modeling anything close to the "triune brain" at a system level. This scientific evolutionary process is still underway.

A first example includes the model by Daniel Levine and his colleagues of the effects of frontal lobe damage on the Wisconsin Card Sorting Test.[24,25] On this test, the subjects have to figure out the criteria for classifying cards based on the experimenter saying "right" or "wrong" without saying why. At various points the experimenter changes the classification criterion (which could be color, shape, or number of the designs of the card faces) without warning. Errors made by people with dorsolateral prefrontal damage on this test are mainly of a perseverative nature; that is, they classify cards by criteria that were formerly, but are no longer, correct.

The card-sorting model of Levine and his co-workers is not neuro-anatomically correct but includes subnetworks conceived as analogous to the triune brain. The network includes two layers coding features (color, shape, or number) and card categories, considered analogous to parts of the "neomam-malian" visual neocortex. The interactions between feature and category layers are modulated by signals representing attentional biases toward one or another of the three feature classes. These biases are in turn influenced by two sets of signals, one connoting positive or negative valuation (from the experimenter), the other connoting cognitive habit based on previous responses. Prefrontal damage is mimicked by weakening of the influence of the "paleomammalian" valuation signals (based on the strong connectivity between prefrontal cortex and various limbic and hypothalamic areas). In the absence of strong effects of negative feedback, a positive feedback loop develops between the categori-zations, the attentional biases, and the "reptilian" habit signals. Mortimer

Mishkin and his co-workers confirmed this in a study of the dissociable influences of motor habits, mediated by the "reptilian" basal ganglia, and memory of rewards, mediated by the "paleomammalian" limbic system.[26]

The interactions among rewards, penalties, habits, and biases have been extended to models of other prefrontal-related cognitive tasks, such as verbal fluency[27] and sequence learning and classification.[28,29] Also, several more recent models of the Wisconsin Card Sorting Test have incorporated more detailed anatomy and physiology of the prefrontal cortex and its interactions with the basal ganglia and limbic system. The most detailed of these models so far is that of Oury Monchi and John Taylor,[30] which is based on the structure of loops between the frontal (both motor and prefrontal) cortex, basal ganglia, and thalamus.[31] Lateral inhibition between different cell populations in the basal ganglia mediates competition between different attracting states of the network that represent choices (in this case, categorization criteria). These choices are in turn influenced by reward and penalty via signals to the prefrontal cortex from the amygdala via the anterior cingulate gyrus (a part of the Papez circuit for representing emotions). Another variant of the Monchi-Taylor network has been utilized to model recency discrimination, and there are extensions in progress to a model of delayed matching to sample.

Jose Contreras-Vidal and Wolfram Schultz included all three parts of the triune brain in a model of how dopamine influences the acquisition of conditioned responses.[32] Their model, like that of Monchi and Taylor,[30] depends on interactive loops between cortex, basal ganglia, and thalamus, with different parts of the basal ganglia (and associated areas of prefrontal cortex) responsive to the timing of the reward and to its occurrence or nonoccurrence.

MODELING RECIPROCITY

The models discussed in the last section are steps toward unified, biologically realistic models of interactions among the three parts of MacLean's triune brain. They are not so much the separate biological computers MacLean described[5] as they are functional modules in an overall dynamical system for making flexible responses to a nonstationary environment. Each of the models so far includes only parts of the overall picture. Other parts of the picture have so far been modeled only at the macro or cognitive level, and not yet mapped in detail to brain areas.

For example, the two authors are currently developing a neural network model based on the social and economic theory of the reciprocal modular brain propounded by Gerald Cory.[33] Cory argued, and we agree, that current economic theories have tended to overemphasize the self-interested side of economic behavior. In fact, he went on, people are equally motivated by the need to help and empathize with others, in part because social systems are based on reciprocity and people need to give benefits to others in order to receive benefits in return. Hence his socioeconomic model is based on a tug-of-war between the claims of self-interest, mediated roughly by MacLean's reptilian brain, and of empathy and social bonding, mediated by MacLean's old mammalian brain. If a person denies either selfish or empathic claims for too long, she or he experiences discomfort and attempts to reestablish some degree of balance between the two.

We modeled this tug-of-war using a neural network in which nonlinear dynamics represented competitive interactions between neuron populations (represented as network nodes) each coding different criteria or feature classes, and variable attentional biases toward one or another of these criteria. This was part of the foundation of the Wisconsin Card Sorting model of Leven and Levine.[24] It was also studied mathematically by Grossberg and Levine in a general setting with an arbitrary number of nodes.[34] Grossberg and Levine showed that if the attentional biases remained the same over time, the system always reached a steady state, and the numerical variables in the steady state represented which features were retained in short-term memory. However, we asked, what happens if the two nodes represent "selfishness"and "empathy," and the attentional biases between them vary over time? Is it possible to oscillate between one or another of those criteria being more dominant, in either a periodic or chaotic fashion? If the network does reach a steady state, under what conditions can the steady state be one of balance between selfishness and empathy, rather than one of them dominating the other over time?

Figures 19.1and 19.2 show examples of the behavior of our network. In all neural networks, there are variables called *node activities.* These activities are abstract but if the nodes represent brain areas they correspond roughly to electrical activity in the area. If the nodes represent psychological entities such as concepts, percepts, or emotions, the activities correspond roughly to the amount that the concept is actively thought about, the percept is perceived, or the emotion is felt. The graphs represent activities of the "selfishness" and "empathy" nodes in our network.

Both figures represent cases where the mathematical parameters representing attentional biases toward selfishness and toward empathy are time-varying. In Figure 19.1, there are two sets of biases, one in favor of selfishness and one in favor of empathy. The biases between the two regimes reverse when either variable (selfishness or empathy) gets below a fixed threshold. Periodic oscillations are obtained between the two variables. We have also simulated the case, not shown here, whereby the biases are changed at fixed time intervals. In that case while there is an overall dominance of selfishness (due to the way other network parameters were set), the activity of the empathy node becomes larger than that of the selfishness node whenever the biases are shifted. The waves in the two variables do not, however, repeat themselves; hence the changes between the two variables could be described as chaotic rather than periodic. In either case, an effective and lasting balance between selfishness and empathy has not been achieved.

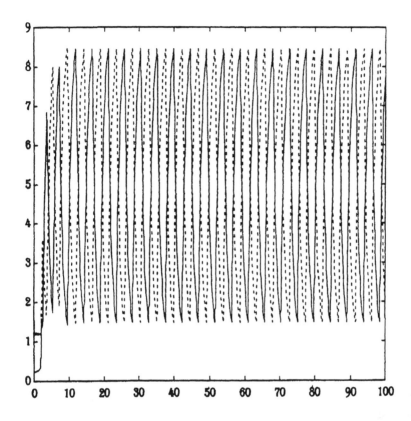

Figure 19.1. Oscillatory Interaction between "Selfishness" and "Empathy" Node Activities when Biases in Network Shift at Regular Time Intervals

This type of balance between the selfishness and empathy systems was obtained in Figure 19.2 by adding to the network a third node representing an idealized "frontal lobe executive." As Cory suggested, the frontal lobes exert a kind of higher-order mediating function that makes sure that neither the self-interest nor the empathic claims are neglected.[33] The influence of the frontal mediation parameter causes biases in favor of empathy or selfishness to shift when either variable is too low, but to shift in a gradual rather than a sudden manner.

We add the caveat that this network is primitive compared with both the anatomical interconnections of the brain and the interacting behaviors it seeks to represent. None of the actual connectivity between the prefrontal cortex and either the basal ganglia, midbrain transmitter systems, or limbic system has yet been incorporated here.

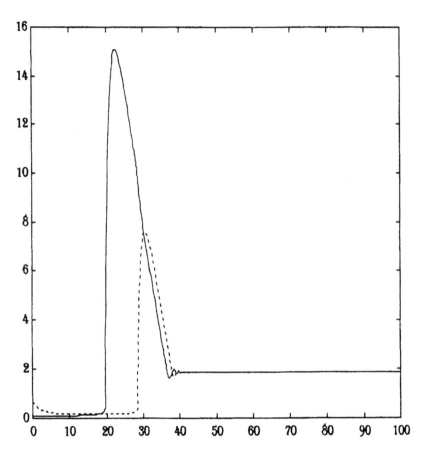

Figure 19.2. Graph of "Selfishness" and "Empathy" Activities with Addition of Frontal Executive" Node

Yet these simulations show that an abstract system of reciprocity between conflicting claims might have some of the basic properties of a socioeconomic system based on interactions of the triune brain. Our model also mimics some properties of the prefrontal executive in mediating between claims of different parts of the triune brain. The oscillations obtained in the network with an absent or weak frontal executive reinforces the suggestion made elsewhere[35] that the perseverative behaviors of prefrontally damaged patients are exaggerations of perseverative, "stuck" behavior common in humans whose frontal lobes are physically intact (but may at times be stuck in "Park"!). Indeed, this is what MacLean suggested much earlier with his powerful metaphor of our disassociated three brains as "a man, a horse, and a crocodile in the same room."[5]

CONCLUSIONS

One of the authors (D.S.L.) got his start in behavioral neuroscience in the late 1960s when he arrived with a mathematics background at the National Institutes of Health. Paul MacLean, one of his mentors, challenged him to develop a mathematics of emotions, where "positives" and "negatives" prevailed but no "zero." On the abstract level, this has already been accomplished by the dynamical systems approach to neural networks. What has not been done yet is the development of a good model for *specific* emotions (anger, fear, joy, and so forth) and their interrelationship. Models have not yet captured the intricate connections between the limbic system, hypothalamus, and what Pribram called the "four Fs": feeding, fleeing, fighting, and sex.[36]

Yet as computational modeling becomes more and more a part of neuro-physiology and neuropsychology, the current methods and architectures are likely to reach that point in the next several years. In this process of theoretical understanding, the triune brain, as a source both of functional constructs and of metaphors, will remain useful.

Some of the details of MacLean's earlier formulation of triune concepts have been modified by the development of science. MacLean incorporates much of this modification in his updated and encyclopedic *The Triune Brain in Evolution* published in 1990. For example, the mapping between specific brain areas and roles is fully acknowledged to be more complex than the rather neat parcellation of his earlier articles (e.g., see Pribram [37] for other ideas about the limbic system, and Houk, Davis & Beiser[38] for newer hypothesis about the basal ganglia). Also, the idea from these earlier articles about three separate biological computers with different information processing styles has gradually yielded to a more integrated dynamical systems approach in which all three brains play constructive roles. The paranoid streak that MacLean discussed and related to limbic system and R-complex information-processing[39,40] actually has a neocortical component as well, because paranoia *directed at a particular group* requires the neocortical facility of categorization. Similarly, information processing of a caring and cooperative nature requires parts of all three brains.

Yet it is not in the minutiae but in the overarching concepts that triunity remains scientifically useful. MacLean was one of several scientists promoting the ideas that emotion is coequal with reason in decision-making and that instinct or habit is dissociable from emotion. Both of these are seminal ideas in behavioral neuroscience, and modern computational theories increasingly assume them as basic truths.

The triune brain can also be a source of valuable metaphors for explaining processes in a number of disciplines. Sam Leven reviews the literature about different processes in a wide range of social science areas including organizational management, decision theory, developmental psychology and many others.[41] He finds analogues of the instinctive/emotional/rational "triunity" in all of them. For example, he cites work in managerial psychology[42] describing three styles of people at work: implementing (an "instinctive" process); pathfinding (an "emotional" process); and problem solving (a "rational" process). Leven applied this same set of distinctions to different theories of learned helplessness, one relying mainly on physiological responses, one on feelings, and one on cognitions, and integrated all three theories into a qualitative neurochemical network model.[43] Are all these processes subcases of a broad principle of brain organization? It has been suggested elsewhere that the three styles Leven discusses might all be attracting states of the same mathematical dynamical system in our brains.[44] Years of exciting work lie ahead. But it is clear that theoretical neuropsychology as a partner with experiment is here to stay, and that the triune brain remains one of the key concepts in the elaboration of this partnership.

NOTES

1. Klopf AH: *The Hedonistic Neuron: a Theory of Memory, Learning, and Intelligence.* Washington:Hemisphere, 1982.

2. Levine DS: Steps toward a neural theory of self-actualization. *World Congress on Neural Networks, San Diego* (Vol. I, pp. 215–220). Hillsdale, NJ: Lawrence Erlbaum Associates, 1994.

3. Maslow AH: *Toward a Psychology of Being.* NY: Van Nostrand, 1968.

4. MacLean PD: *The Triune Brain in Evolution: Role in Paleocerebral Functions.* NY: Plenum, 1990.

5. MacLean PD: New findings relevant to the evolution of psychosexual functions of the brain. *Journal of Nervous and Mental Disease,* 1962; 135, 289–301. (Quotation is on p. 289.)

6. Damasio A: *Descartes' Error: Emotion, Reason, and the Human Brain.* NY: Grosset/Putnam, 1994.

7. Levine DS, Leven SJ (Eds.): *Motivation, Emotion, and Goal Direction in Neural Networks.* Hillsdale, NJ: Lawrence Erlbaum Associates, 1992, p. vii.

8. Nauta WJH: Personal communication, March 1971.

9. Pribram KH, McGuinness D: Arousal, activation, and effort in the control of attention. *Psychological Review,* 1975; 82, 116–149.

10. Levine DS: *Introduction to Neural and Cognitive Modeling.* Mahwah, NJ: Lawrence Erlbaum Associates, 2000.

11. Werbos PJ: Beyond regression: New tools for prediction and analysis in the behavioral sciences. Unpublished doctoral dissertation, Harvard University, 1974. Reprinted as *The Roots of Backpropagation: From Ordered Derivatives to Neural Networks and Political Forecasting.* NY: Wiley, 1993.

12. Rumelhart DE, McClelland JL (Eds.): *Parallel Distributed Processing: Explorations in the Microstructure of Cognition.* Vol 1 and 2, Cambridge, MA: MIT Press, 1986.

13. *DARPA Neural Network Study.* Alexandria, VA: AFCEA International Press, 1988, p. 60.

14. Gaudiano P, Grossberg S: Vector associative maps: Unsupervised real time error-based learning and control of movement trajectories. *Neural Networks,* 1991; 4, 147–183. (Reference is on pp. 180–181.)

15. Grossberg S: On the dynamics of operant conditioning. *Journal of Theoretical Biology,* 1971; 33, 225–255.

16. Grossberg S, Schmajuk NA: Neural dynamics of attentionally-modulated Pavlovian conditioning: conditioned reinforcement, inhibition, and opponent processing. *Psychobiology,* 1987; 15, 195–240.

17. Klopf AH: Brain function and adaptive systems: a heterostatic theory. Air Force Cambridge Research Laboratories Research Report AFCRL-72-0164, Bedford, MA, 1972.

18. Klopf AH: A neuronal model of classical conditioning. *Psychobiology,* 1988; 16, 85–125.

19. Rosenstein GS: Income and choice in biological control systems. *Reports of the Sixth Symposium in Cybernetics (Part 4). Decision Making in Biological Systems of Control* (pp. 107–110). Tbilisi: Mezniereba, 1972. (Russian.).

20. Rosenstein G-Z: *Income and Choice in Biological Control Systems.* Hillsdale, NJ: Lawrence Erlbaum Associates, 1991.

21. Werbos, PJ: Generalization of backpropagation with application to a recurrent gas model. *Neural Networks,* 1988; 1, 339–356.

22. Werbos PJ: *The Roots of Backpropagation: From Ordered Derivatives to Neural Networks and Political Forecasting.* NY: Wiley, 1993.

23. Barto AG: Connectionist learning for control: an overview. In T Miller, RS Sutton & PJ Werbos (Eds.), *Neural Networks for Control.* (pp. 5–58). Cambridge, MA: MIT Press, 1990.

24. Leven SJ, Levine DS: Effects of reinforcement on knowledge retrieval and evaluation. IEEE *First International Conference on Neural Networks.* (Vol.II, pp. 269–279). San Diego: IEEE/ICNN, 1987.

25. Levine DS, Prueitt PS: Modeling some effects of frontal lobe damage: novelty and perseveration. *Neural Networks,* 1989; 2, 103–116.

26. Mishkin M, Malamut B, Bachevalier, J: Memories and habits: two interacting systems. In G Lynch, JL McGaugh, & NM Weinberger (Eds.): *Neurobiology of Learning and Memory.* (pp. 65–77). New York, London: Guilford, 1984.

27. Parks RW, Levine DS: Neural network modeling of Wisconsin Card Sorting and verbal fluency tests: Applications with frontal lobe-damaged and Alzheimer's disease patients. In RW Parks, DS Levine & DL Long (Eds.): *Fundamentals of Neural Network Modeling: Neuropsychology and Cognitive Neuroscience* (pp. 357–380). Cambridge, MA: MIT Press, 1998.

28. Bapi RS, Levine DS: Modeling the role of the frontal lobes in performing sequential tasks. I. Basic structure and primacy effects. *Neural Networks,* 1994; 7, 1167–1180.

29. Bapi RS, Levine, DS: Modeling the role of the frontal lobes in sequential task performance. II. Classification of sequences. *Neural Network World,* 1997; 1/97, 3–28.

30. Monchi O, Taylor JG: A hard wired model of coupled frontal working memories for various tasks. *Information Sciences Journal,* 1998; 113, 221–243.

31. Alexander GE, DeLong MR, Strick PL: Parallel organization of functionally segregated circuits linking basal ganglia and cortex. *Annual Review of Neuroscience,* 1986; 9, 357–381.

32. Contreras-Vidal JL, Schultz W: A predictive reinforcement model of dopamine neurons for learning of approach behavior. *Journal of Computational Neuroscience,* 1999; 6, 191–214.

33. Cory GA Jr: *The Reciprocal Modular Brain in Economics and Politics: Shaping the Rational and Moral Basis of Organization, Exchange, and Choice.* NY: Plenum Press, 1999.

34. Grossberg S, Levine DS: Some developmental and attentional biases in the contrast enhancement and short-term memory of recurrent neural networks. *Journal of Theoretical Biology,* 1975; 53, 341–380.

35. Levine DS: Don't just stand there, optimize something! In DS Levine & W Elsberry (Eds.): *Optimality in Biological and Artificial Networks?* (pp. 3–18). Mahwah, NJ: Lawrence Erlbaum Associates, 1997.

36. Pribram KH: The intrinsic systems of the forebrain. In J Field, HW Magoun, VE Hall (Eds.), *Handbook of Physiology, Neurophysiology II.* (pp. 1323–1344). Washington, DC: American Physiological Society, 1960.

37. Pribram KH: Emotion: a neurobehavioral analysis. In KR Scherer & P Ekman (Eds.), *Approaches to Emotion* (pp. 13–38). Hillsdale, NJ: Lawrence Erlbaum Associates, 1984.

38. Houk JC., Davis JL, Beiser DG (Eds.): *Models of Information Processing in the Basal Ganglia.* Cambridge, MA: MIT Press, 1995.

39. MacLean PD: The paranoid streak in man. In A Koestler & J Smythies (Eds.): *Beyond Reductionism.* (pp. 1–21). London: Hutchinson and Company Limited, 1969.

40. MacLean PD: Triune brain. In G. Adelman (Ed.): *Encyclopedia of Neuroscience* (vol. II, pp. 1235–1237). Boston: Birkhauser, 1987.

41. Leven SJ: *Choice and Neural Process.* Unpublished doctoral dissertation, University of Texas at Arlington, 1987.

42. Leavitt H: *Corporate Pathfinders.* Homewood, IL: Dow Jones-Irwin, 1986.

43. Leven SJ: Learned helplessness, memory, and the dynamics of hope. In DS Levine & SJ Leven (Eds.): *Motivation, Emotion, and Goal Direction in Neural Networks.* (pp. 259–299). Hillsdale, NJ: Lawrence Erlbaum Associates, 1992.

44. Levine, DS: Do we know what we want? *World Congress on Neural Networks, Washington, DC* (Vol. 2, pp. 955–962). Mahwah, NJ: Lawrence Erlbaum Associates, 1995.

20

CONCLUSION:
CONVERGENCES AND FRONTIERS

Gerald A. Cory, Jr. and Russell Gardner, Jr.

As shown in the varied articles that comprise this volume, MacLean's influence spans many disciplines. Although this single volume cannot capture the full range of MacLean's influence, it does delineate some major thrusts that draw substantially upon his contributions. In this chapter we attempt to sum up the main features of the various chapters and identify some convergences and frontiers deriving from the emerging literature, which spans multiple disciplines and perspectives.

CONVERGENCES

Pribram's chapter assisted us in identifying some of the divergent aspects of neuroscience that have shaped directions in research for the decades since the 1950s. As Pribram also noted some of these divergent paths have now tended to move toward convergence. Three major thrusts of divergence can be identified. They are the issues or perspectives of (1) reduction vs. integration; (2) evolutionary phylogenetic vs. comparative structural functional; and (3) cognitive and objective vs. emotions and subjectivity. The third chapter by Cory illustrated how legitimate differences in scientific perspective can become distorted by academic isolation, partisanship, and careless scholarship. Although the pursuit of these divergent paths in specific research programs is legitimate, even necessary, for sharp focus in many research programs, the emerging convergences are equally necessary and productive.

Our leading sociobiologist, Edward O. Wilson of Harvard, catches the essence of the reductive/integrative process when he writes that much of the history of biological science may be seen dynamically as a tension between unit and aggregate, reduction and holism. Considering an equilibrium in this tension as neither desirable nor possible, he concludes that: "As large patterns emerge,

ambitious hard-science reductionists set out to dissolve them with nonconforming new data. Conversely, whenever empirical researchers discover enough
new nonconforming phenomena to create chaos, synthesizers move in to restore
order. In tandem the two kinds of endeavors nudge the discipline forward"
(Wilson 1993: 243).

Reduction and phylogenetic perspectives are not mutually exclusive. The
chapter by Smith on the implications of the relatively new discipline of
molecular biology for understanding the evolution of brains and social
communication made this clear. Nothing could be more reductionist from the
larger organism or human perspective than the study of molecules that make up
the trillions of cells of our bodies. The very process of moving up the scale of
integration from molecules to the human organism as a whole illustrates
dramatically the interdependence of the reductionist/integrationist perspectives
in science. Nowhere is the convergence of the two perspectives more conspicuous or more necessary to the understanding of science. The discovery of HOX
genes common to species from worms to the highest vertebrates graphically
makes the case for homology, defined as phylogenetic relatedness or similarity
based on informational continuity. And homology only makes sense in an
evolutionary perspective. The remarkable conservation of homologous structure
and function from the molecules and body plans of early life certainly converges
with the evolutionary perspective of MacLean, whose triune brain concept
emphasizes the conservation of ancient mechanisms from which subsequent
variation and development proceed. A standard comparative approach to
anatomical structure and function must converge to a fully evolutionary
perspective for an adequate explanation of such research-revealed phenomena.
As Smith notes, "the hallmark of Paul MacLean's neuroscience is its evolutionary perspective" as well as its emphasis on conservation of ancient
protocols.

In the chapter by Greenberg we saw the validation of the position by
MacLean (1990) that research should be continued to clear up the question of
whether the basal ganglia are limited to motor circuitry as traditionally held or
whether they also contribute to species-typical behavior patterns and have a role
in higher cognitive processes. This was listed as a point of questionable speculation on MacLean's part in the *Science* review of October 1990. Greenberg
reported on the extensive new findings that show these basic forebrain nuclei to
be involved not only in many species-typical behaviors, but also in the
sequencing of complex cognitive responses up to and including language.
Cognitive neuroscientist and linguist Philip Lieberman, in his recent *Human
Language and Our Reptilian Brain* (2000), explores in detail the extensive role
of these early forebrain nuclei in the evolution and production of language as
well as the sequencing of higher level cognitive behavioral repertoires.

The chapters in Part III illustrated the well-documented influence of
MacLean's evolutionary thought on what has in recent years come to be called
evolutionary psychiatry. Gardner discussed how MacLean's focus on social
behaviors stemming from adaptations originating in deep time, supported by
data from the genome project as well as other genetic and brain research,

combined to respond to psychiatry's need to connect brain actions with normal human communicative behavior. Gardner reported that, based on these new findings and data, during its Spring 2000 meeting, the research committee of the Group for the Advancement of Psychiatry (GAP), a specialty think-tank, issued a written recommendation that psychiatry's basic science should be designated sociophysiology or the social brain. The utility of the social brain concept was further supported by Price, Sloman, and Wilson, who related the pathological syndromes of depression and mania to phylogenetic roots in the triune brain structure. The convergences from the various perspectives are notable and the symptomatology becomes explicable when viewed from the evolutionary perspective. Price commented on the clarifying effect of triune brain theory upon ideas of depression and mania. From the phylogenetic perspective, depression can be seen as neocortical malfunction or interference with de-escalation and escalation adaptive social strategies wired into our earlier reptilian and mammalian brain structures. Sloman described an involuntary defeat strategy (IDS) as an adaptive de-escalation of agonistic behavior of probable reptilian origin which made possible social hierarchies the attachment aspects of which find themselves in the later evolved mechanisms of the early mammalian accretions. An ineffective IDS is described as leading to psycho-pathological symptoms. In his discussion of primarily manic pathology, Wilson perceived that the converging evidence on brain research confirms that the brain evolved quite in keeping with MacLean's synthesis. Brain evolution was seen to be characterized by phylogenetic accretion of successively higher and more pluralistic mechanisms for executive action, without, however, obviating the capacity of the earlier reptilian and mammalian mechanisms to override executive control in times of urgency and/or pathology.

The varied chapters in Part IV illustrated further the converging insights from MacLean's evolutionary formulations. Harris argued that the all-important human highly generalized capacity for empathy relies on integration of phylogenetically older and newer structures of the brain. He saw the deficits of the perplexing syndrome of autism as resulting from the failure of this integration in the ontogenetic developmental processes. Empathy, the capacity to enter into the emotional states of others, depends upon cognitive represent-ation and integration of our earlier self-maintaining reptilian mechanisms and the later emerging kinship-bonding mechanism of our paleomammalian structures. Harris cited the new observations of empathic behavior in primate species, especially in macaque monkeys and bonobo chimpanzees. The chapter by Pontius, on the other hand, focused on a very specific syndrome which she has identified as the Limbic Psychotic Trigger Reaction (LPTR). In a very detailed and thorough analysis, Pontius described LPTR as a disconnect reaction between the higher control centers of the brain and the emotional limbic centers, which results in the otherwise inexplicable cases of motiveless homicide. As a longtime forensic psychiatrist troubled by the etiology of this unusual syndrome, Pontius found that MacLean's triune brain concept provided a convergent explanatory framework and perspective for this otherwise baffling syndrome.

Weisfeld returned to a higher level of integration in his examination of the neural and functional aspects of pride and shame. At the outset he reminded us that the study of comparative neuroanatomy makes clear that motivated behaviors evolved earlier than complex cognitive capacities. As MacLean emphasized repeatedly in his writings: The brain stem, basal ganglia, and limbic system antedated the expansion of the neocortex. Weisfeld followed MacLean's lead in his emphasis upon the primacy of emotions and the conservation of primitive brain structures, reminding us in phylogenetic terms that even primitive organisms needed to fulfill all the functions necessary for survival so that any capacities that evolved later had to be elaborations of the earlier mechanisms. Although care must be taken in overgeneralizing this principle, especially in passing across the various phyla, converging evidence from evolutionary genetics in the form of ancient neuropeptides, proteins, and HOX genes supports this principle of conservation.

The chapter by Mirsky and Duncan proceeded from an evolutionary perspective, drawing upon the concept of the triune brain to build a model of the organization and development of attentional functions in the human brain. The basic neural foundation for attention is the brain stem system that has existed for millions of years and is still present and functioning in the brains of modern reptiles and in earlier vertebrates. Mirsky and Duncan pointed out convergence of MacLean's reptilian brain with the centrencephalon concept of neuroanatomists Penfield and Jasper, and also with Lindsley's concept of the ascending reticular activation system. Added to these significant convergences from varying research perspectives of the foundational vertebrate attentional system, are the subsequent limbic and neocortical components of the paleo- and neomammalian brain structures. The capacity to shift focus from one aspect of the environment to another in a flexible, adaptive manner is dependent upon the integrity of the prefrontal cortex, including the anterior cingulate gyrus, and may be a unique function of the neomammalian brain. Mirsky and Duncan concluded that while ordinarily the three brain regions operate together harmoniously, damage or dysfunction in any one of these brain regions, brain stem, limbic, and neocortical, can lead to circumscribed or specific deficits in a particular attention function.

The chapters in Part V represented a change in focus. Brody presented a provocative attempt to argue for convergences in physics and triune theory. Drawing principally upon the work of physicist Stuart Kauffman, Brody saw evolution as constrained by the fluctuations of the triarchic pattern of stasis, chaos, and the integrative, phase transition. Brody argued that these concepts from statistical physics suggested a platform in biology for Darwinian natural selection as well as a basis in neural architecture for the pursuit of binary and tertiary models such as MacLean's triune brain concept. He presented the implications for theory as well as diagnosis and therapy of such a convergent perspective.

The chapter by Itzkoff, proceeding from an evolutionary perspective, argued for a reversal of the usual emphasis on the precedence of primitive mechanisms in discussions of evolved brain structure. Building upon the work of Jerison and others, Itzkoff saw the neo- or isocortex as leading the Darwinian evolutionary selection path from early vertebrate neural architecture to the brain of *Homo sapiens*. Although we end up with a largely chicken-or-egg question in our current state of knowledge, Itzkoff's chapter reminds us that in evolution, like adaptive behavior, feedback and general recursiveness in interaction among the many variables prohibits a simplistic linear account of brain evolution. For example, Gilsofi and Mora (2000) recently argued uniquely for the previously neglected role of temperature regulation in the progressive encephalization that characterized mammalian evolution. Once again we are reminded that science progresses in a seemingly dialectical manner by successive divergences and convergences, by successive reductions and integrations.

The chapter by Masters proceeded from the perspective of evolutionary neuroscience to examine the effects of environmental pollution upon abnormal social behavior. Masters presented provocative and disturbing evidence that the introduction of heavy metals (e.g., lead, cadmium, aluminum, and others) into the environment through industry and technology has produced defects in the functioning of our evolved neural architecture contributing to violent behavior and learning deficits. These heavy elements were not present at modern levels in our environment of evolutionary adaptation and therefore our nervous system did not evolve adequate protection against them. When uptaken into the brain and nervous system, these elements interfere with the normal neurological functioning and information processing. Social science has previously attempted to explain the resulting deviancy by purely social factors. Masters argued that a complete understanding—even prevention and mitigation—of such deviant behaviors must include a full grasp of the new findings proceeding from evolutionary neuroscience. Based upon a clearly demonstrated need for such cross-disciplinary exchange, Masters concluded with an appeal for an end to academic insularity and convergence to a unified scientific approach to confront the challenges of our industrial and technological civilization.

The chapters in Part VI carried forward the challenge by Masters for a convergence with the social sciences necessitated by the advances in evolutionary biology and neuroscience. Proceeding from a different level of integration toward the same objective of convergence, they comprised a bridging effort between the concepts of evolutionary neuroethology and those of social psychology and socio-economic theory. Peterson drew upon MacLean's thought to discuss the human tendency to give created beliefs superordinate status. This tendency to reification becomes understandable when seen as rooted in the species-typical ritualizing behaviors of the neostriatum, MacLean's protoreptilian brain. Peterson argued that although reification and the related concept of hegemony have stabilizing effects on society, they also contributed to the sanctifying of domination and social inequality.

Bailey presented his model of paleopsychology, which builds upon and extends MacLean's research and concepts, to develop new clinical insights as well as a bridge from individual into social psychology. Bailey saw the human brain as capable of upshifting to control by the higher and more recently evolved neocortical centers as well as downshifting to control by the more primitive paleomammalian and reptilian centers. From his research among students, Bailey concluded that the rewards of primal functioning (i.e., eating, drinking, sex, etc.); were (with some notable exceptions) inherently more pleasurable and satisfying than the higher cortical ones of planning and studying. Under conditions of stress (or damage, dysfunction) and given the right environmental cues, individual behavior might downshift to more ancient reptilian patterns of behavior that are inappropriate, undesirable, and even destructive in modern social situations. In illustration of this downshifting capacity Bailey analyzed insightfully the behaviors of serial killer Ted Bundy, and two normal youths who precipitated the Columbine school massacres.

Cory's chapter was complementary to Bailey's in certain aspects. Whereas Bailey emphasized the downshifting (as well as upshifting) between neocortical control and evolutionarily older brain systems, Cory—remaining essentially at the neocortical level—saw the dynamic of social life based in the largely conflictual dynamic between the older self-preservational programming of the reptilian or early vertebrate brain tissues and the later evolved affectional mechanisms of the early mammalian brain regions as they were represented in the neocortex as ego and empathy, respectively. In Bailey's terms, then, Cory emphasized the upshifted neocortical spectrum of representation.

Moving further into socio-economic theory and drawing upon a wide range of multidisciplinary research, Cory derived reciprocal algorithms of behavior from this neocortically represented ego/empathy conflictual dynamic to account for the ubiquitous reciprocity of behavior found in all human societies. These algorithms were offered as the evolved functional complement in neural architecture to Hamilton's cost/benefit equation of inclusive fitness and can be expressed in essentially the same cost/benefit terms. This linkage of Hamilton's rule with the evolved algorithms of neural architecture establishes a needed bridging linkage between the disciplines of evolutionary psychology and evolutionary neuroscience. The reciprocal algorithms were further expressed as mathematical operations comparable to the dynamics of social stratification as well as the laws of supply and demand of economic theory. The tying of reciprocal algorithms of evolved neural architecture to the fundamental shaping dynamics of human social and economic exchange activities indicates a possible path for theoretical unification of evolutionary neuroscience and evolutionary psychology with the social sciences. Additionally, the perspectives of Bailey and Cory may well converge to provide a useful multidimensional model of individual and social behavior applicable to numerous areas of social psychology and social theory.

Further supporting this thrust into social psychology and social theory, the chapter by Levine and Jani reported their ongoing efforts to model a neural network architecture representing the triune dynamic. Preliminary results showed that the model developed had features that could match the socio-economic exchange dynamic postulated by Cory.

FRONTIERS

The foregoing paragraphs have shown the various convergences from several disciplinary perspectives, some of which also indicate frontiers for future research. In this remaining section we will point out further the frontiers of research and integration that challenge us from the evolutionary perspective.

The frontiers of research extend in both directions from evolutionary neuroscience—up the scale of integration and down—in both reductive and holistic directions. The emergent disciplines of biophysics and molecular biology are moving us in a reductive direction that is throwing almost dazzling new light on the nature of life itself and the evolutionary process. New detail and new concepts will emerge as the linkages between ancient DNA, RNA, neuropeptide and protein configurations, and body plans merge with our still-developing grasp of brain evolution.

In the opposite direction, moving up the scale of integration, new research and developments are taking us up the standard hierarchy of academic disciplines, giving us new insights into our psychological, even social and economic functioning. For instance, the pleasure-pain principle has been a mainstay of psychoanalytical as well as behavioral psychology since Freud's popularization of it in his writings. This was complemented more recently by the agonic/hedonic systems structure so effectively presented and developed by Michael R. A. Chance and others (see Chance, 1988, 1984; also Montagner et al. 1970; Hold 1976; Pearce and Newton 1969). Both perspectives have led to useful insights and interpretations. MacLean's formulation further provides the foundation in neuroscience for the emergence of another perspective on the structure of behavior—the dynamic interplay of self-preservation and affectional circuitry, neocortically represented in the concepts of ego and empathy as set out by Cory (1999; also this volume). Neither perspective is exclusive of the others but each allows insightful and useful discriminations and interpretations that vary from their particular viewpoints. The evolutionary perspective based on MacLean's triarchic concept presents a frontier for research that has yet to be fully explored in its implications for social theory.

Also at the immediate frontier of research is the necessity to integrate with evolutionary neuroscience the findings of the research programs progressing under the general academic rubric of evolutionary psychology. In their article "The Seven Sins of Evolutionary Psychology" Panksepp and Pankepp (2000) have detailed convincingly the case for integration. As noted in the introductory chapter, current mainstream evolutionary psychology fails to even acknowledge the seminal early work of evolutionary neuroscience. Cory's proposed linkage of Hamilton's rule and the reciprocal algorithms of our evolved neural architecture may represent a helpful step in that direction. We should correct this isolation first in such closely related fields so that we are avoiding needless duplication of effort—reinvention of the wheel. In our departmented university system of disciplines, such isolation persists in many areas of modern science. A full integration of evolutionary neuroscience with evolutionary psychology is in the interest of good science and will avoid the repetition of awkward omissions and interpretations such as noted above and as seen so conspicuously in Pinker's unfortunate, and likely inadvertent, misrepresentation of MacLean's position (Pinker 1997: 370, 580).

We are not the first to make this call for the breakdown of isolation and the improvement of communication among the scientific disciplines. Numerous scholars have made this appeal. Among them, biologist Lynn Margulis made an eloquent appeal some years ago (1997, 1998). And E. O. Wilson has issued his call for consilience—the unification of the natural with the social sciences (1998). Wilson, primarily an entomologist and population biologist, nevertheless recognizes that neuroscience is the key to consilience. Responding to the call for consilience, Paul Lawrence and Nitin Nohria (2002) of the Harvard Business School, proceeding from a business management perspective, have presented a welcome and thought-provoking effort at linking evolved brain structure with the dynamics of management.

The evolutionary perspective promoted by MacLean in neuroscience, and as argued for in this volume, is increasingly being recognized as a necessary perspective (Panksepp 1998; Damasio 1999; Lieberman 2000; Cory 1999, 2000; Gilsofi & Mora 2000). We hope that the convergences indicated in the varied chapters of this volume will contribute to the achievement of this worthy challenge that confronts the scientific community in this new millennium.

REFERENCES

Chance, Michael R. A. 1984. "Biological Systems Synthesis of Mentality and the Nature of the Two Modes of Mental Operation: Hedonic and Agonic." *Man-Environment Systems*, 14 (2), 143–157.

Chance, Michael R. A. (Ed.). 1988. *Social Fabrics of the Mind*. Hillsdale, NJ: Lawrence Erlbaum Associates.

Cory, Gerald A., Jr. 1999. *The Reciprocal Modular Brain in Economics and Politics*. NY: Kluwer Academic/Plenum Publishers.

Cory, Gerald A., Jr. 2000. *Toward Consilience: The Bioneurological Basis of Behavior, Thought, Experience, and Language*. NY: Kluwer Academic/Plenum Publishers.

Damasio, A. R. 1999. *The Feeling of What Happens*. NY: Harcourt Brace.

Gilsofi, Carl V. and Francisco Mora. 2000. *The Hot Brain: Survival, Temperature, and the Human Body*. Cambridge, MA: The MIT Press.

Hold, B.C.L. 1976. "Attention structure and rank specific behaviour in pre-school children." In M.R.A. Chance and R.R. Larsen (eds.) *The Social Structure of Attention*. NY: John Wiley.

Lawrence, Paul R. and Nohria, Nitin. 2002. *Driven: How Human Nature Shapes Our Choices*. San Francisco: Jossey-Bass.

Lieberman, Philip. 2000. *Human Language and Our Reptilian Brain*. Cambridge, MA: Harvard University Press.

Margulis, Lynn. 1998. *Symbiotic Planet: A New Look at Evolution*. NY: Basic Books.

Margulis, Lynn and Sagan, Dorion. 1997. *Slanted Truths: Essays on Gaia, Symbiosis and Evolution*. NY: Copernicus Books.

Montagner. H.; Henry, J.; Lombardst, M.; Restoin, A.; Benedini, M.; Godard, F.; Boillot, F., Pretot, M.; Bolzoni, D.; Burnod, J.; & Nicolas, R. 1970. "Behavioral: Profile and Corticosteriod Excretion Rhythms in Young Children from 1–6 years." In V. Reynolds and N.G. Burton-Jones (eds.). *Human Behavior and Adaptation*. London: Taylor and Francis.

Panksepp, Jaak. 1998. *Affective Neuroscience*. NY: Oxford University Press.

Panksepp, Jaak and Jules B. Panksepp. 2000. "The Seven Sins of Evolutionary Psychology." Pp 108–131 in *Evolution and Cognition*, Vol 6, No 2.

Pearce. J. and S. Newton. 1969 *The Conditions of Human Growth*. NY: Citadel.

Pinker, Steven. 1997. *How the Mind Works*. NY: Norton.

Wilson, Edward O. 1998 *Consilience: The Unity of Knowledge*. NY: Alfred A. Knopf.

Wilson, Edward O. 1993. "Analyzing the Superorganism: The Legacy of Whitman and Wheeler." Pp. 243–255 in *The Biological Century*. Ed. by R. B. Barlow, Jr., J. E. Dowling, and G. Weissmann. Cambridge, MA: Harvard University Press.

Name Index

SUBJECT INDEX

ABOUT THE CONTRIBUTORS AND EDITORS

Kent Bailey, Professor Emeritus of Psychology, Virginia Commonwealth University, Richmond, VA

James Brody, Clinical Psychologist, 1262 West Bridge St., Spring City, PA

Gerald A. Cory, Jr., Director, The Center for Behavioral Ecology and San Jose State University, San Jose, CA

Connie C. Duncan, Research Associate Professor of Psychiatry, Uniformed Services University of the Health Sciences, Bethesda, MD

Russell Gardner, Jr., Clinical Professor of Psychiatry, Medical College of Wisconsin, Madison, WI

Neil Greenberg, Professor, Department of Ecology and Evolutionary Biology, University of Tennessee, Knoxville, TN

James C. Harris, Professor of Psychiatry and Behavioral Sciences and Pediatrics, Johns Hopkins University School of Medicine, Baltimore, MD

Seymour W. Itzkoff, Professor, Smith College, Northhampton, MA

Nilendu G. Jani, Iconoci, Inc. Bedford, TX

Daniel S. Levine, Professor of Psychology, University of Texas at Arlington, Arlington, TX

Roger D. Masters, Professor, Department of Government, Dartmouth College and Foundation for Neuroscience and Society, Hanover, NH

Allan F. Mirsky, Chief, Section on Clinical and Experimental Neuropsychology, National Institute of Mental Health, Bethesda, MD

Jaak Panksepp, Chicago Institute for Neurosurgery and Neuroresearch, Chicago, IL

Steven A. Peterson, Professor, School of Public Affairs, Penn State Harrisburg Middletown, PA

Anneliese A. Pontius, Associate Clinical Professor of Psychiatry (retired), Harvard Medical School, Boston, MA

Karl H. Pribram, Professor Emeritus, Stanford University, Distinguished Professor and Eminent Scholar, Radford University, Distinguished Research Professor, Georgetown University

John S. Price, Retired: Former Consultant Psychiatrist, UK National Health Service, Odintune Place, Plumpton, E. Sussex, UK

Leon Sloman, Associate Professor, Department of Psychiatry, Honorary Consultant in Psychiatry, Center for Addiction and Mental Health, University of Toronto, Ontario, Canada

C.U.M. (Chris) Smith, Honorary Visiting Fellow, Vision Sciences, Aston University, Birmingham, UK

Glenn E. Weisfeld, Professor of Psychology, Wayne State University, Detroit, MI

Daniel R. Wilson, Professor & Chairman of Psychiatry, School of Medicine, Creighton University, Omaha, NE